C0-CDU-976

ATLA BIBLIOGRAPHY SERIES

edited by Dr. Kenneth E. Rowe

1. *A Guide to the Study of the Holiness Movement,* by Charles Edwin Jones. 1974.
2. *Thomas Merton: A Bibliography,* by Marquita E. Breit. 1974.
3. *The Sermon on the Mount: A History of Interpretation and Bibliography,* by Warren S. Kissinger. 1975.
4. *The Parables of Jesus: A History of Interpretation and Bibliography,* by Warren S. Kissinger. 1979.
5. *Homosexuality and the Judeo-Christian Tradition: An Annotated Bibliography,* by Thom Horner. 1981.
6. *A Guide to the Study of the Pentecostal Movement,* by Charles Edwin Jones. 1983.
7. *The Genesis of Modern Process Thought: A Historical Outline with Bibliography,* by George R. Lucas, Jr. 1983.
8. *A Presbyterian Bibliography,* by Harold B. Prince. 1983.
9. *Paul Tillich: A Comprehensive Bibliography . . .,* by Richard C. Crossman. 1983.
10. *A Bibliography of the Samaritans,* by Alan David Crown. 1984.
11. *An Annotated and Classified Bibliography of English Literature Pertaining to the Ethiopian Orthodox Church,* by Jon Bonk. 1984.
12. *International Meditation Bibliography, 1950 to 1982,* by Howard R. Jarrell. 1984.
13. *Rabindranath Tagore: A Bibliography,* by Katherine Henn. 1985.
14. *Research in Ritual Studies: A Programmatic Essay and Bibliography,* by Ronald L. Grimes, 1985.
15. *Protestant Theological Education in America,* by Heather F. Day. 1985.
16. *Unconscious: A Guide to Sources,* by Natalino Caputi. 1985.
17. *The New Testament Apocrypha and Pseudepigrapha,* by James H. Charlesworth. 1987.
18. *Black Holiness,* by Charles Edwin Jones. 1987.
19. *A Bibliography on Ancient Ephesus,* by Richard Oster. 1987.
20. *Jerusalem, the Holy City: A Bibliography,* by James D. Purvis. 1988.
21. *An Index to English Periodical Literature on the Old Testament and Ancient Near Eastern Studies,* Volume I, by William G. Hupper. 1987.

JERUSALEM, THE HOLY CITY

A Bibliography

by

JAMES D. PURVIS

ATLA Bibliography Series, No. 20

The American Theological Library Association

and

The Scarecrow Press, Inc.

Metuchen, N.J., & London

1988

Library of Congress Cataloging-in-Publication Data

Purvis, James D.
Jerusalem, the Holy city.

(ATLA bibliography series ; no. 20)
Includes indexes.
1. Jerusalem--Bibliography. I. Title. II. Series.
Z3478.J4P87 1988 [DS109.9] 016.95694'4 87-4758
ISBN 0-8108-1999-6

Manufactured in the United States of America

To my sons, James Jr., Jeffrey, and Gregory, and to my grandson, James Michael, who have brought me much joy.

JERUSALEM, THE HOLY CITY: A BIBLIOGRAPHY

Editor's Foreword ix

Preface xi

PART ONE: GENERAL STUDIES ON JERUSALEM

1. GENERAL STUDIES AND HISTORICAL OVERVIEWS 1

2. GEOGRAPHICAL / TOPOGRAPHICAL STUDIES 7

3. ARCHAEOLOGICAL EXCAVATIONS AND STUDIES 25

4. THE WATER SYSTEM 43

5. CITY WALLS AND GATES

A. BIBLICAL PERIOD 52

B. SECOND TEMPLE PERIOD 57

C. MEDIEVAL 64

6. TOMBS AND RELATED MATERIALS 67

PART TWO: JERUSALEM DURING THE BIBLICAL PERIOD, TO 587 B C.

7. JERUSALEM BEFORE DAVID 88

8. JERUSALEM DURING THE BIBLICAL PERIOD 93

9. THEOLOGY/MYTHOLOGY OF THE CITY AND THE SANCTUARY 99

10. THE KINGSHIP OF YHWH AND THE THRONE OF DAVID 111

11. YHWH'S SANCTUARY: TRADITIONS OF THE PRE-SOLOMONIC CULTUS / TENT, ARK, AND CHERUBIM 122

12. YHWH'S SANCTUARY: SOLOMON'S TEMPLE 131

13. YHWH'S SANCTUARY: CULTIC FUNCTIONARIES AND CULTIC ACTIVITIES 143

14. THE CITY AND TEMPLE OF EZEKIEL'S VISION 156

15. THE BABYLONIAN DESTRUCTION OF JERUSALEM 160

PART THREE: JERUSALEM DURING THE SECOND TEMPLE PERIOD

16. JERUSALEM DURING THE SECOND TEMPLE PERIOD / THE CITY AND SANCTUARY IN JEWISH THOUGHT 163

17. ZERUBBABEL'S TEMPLE 174

18. HEROD'S TEMPLE 178

19. THE ESSENES AND JERUSALEM 193

20. THE JEWISH REVOLT AGAINST ROME AND THE DESTRUCTION OF JERUSALEM, A. D. 70 200

PART FOUR: ROMAN JERUSALEM

21. ROMAN JERUSALEM FROM A. D. 70 TO CONSTANTINE / THE BAR KOKHBA REVOLT 210

PART FIVE: JERUSALEM IN JUDAISM

22. JEWISH PRESENCE IN JERUSALEM FROM JULIAN II TO MODERN TIMES / JERUSALEM IN JEWISH THOUGHT 219

PART SIX: CHRISTIAN JERUSALEM

23. JERUSALEM IN THE NEW TESTAMENT

A. GENERAL 240

B. TOPOGRAPHY OF THE GOSPELS AND ACTS 243

C. THEOLOGICAL JUDGMENTS ON THE CITY AND SANCTUARY 246

D. THE HEAVENLY CITY AND SANCTUARY 254

E. THE CHURCH AS TEMPLE 258

24. JERUSALEM IN CHRISTIAN THOUGHT, ART, AND SENTIMENTALITY 261

25. BYZANTINE JERUSALEM 267

26. CRUSADER JERUSALEM 282

27. JERUSALEM AS GOAL OF CHRISTIAN PILGRIMAGE 293

28. CHRISTIAN CHURCHES AND COMMUNITIES OF JERUSALEM 303

29. THE CHURCH OF THE HOLY SEPULCHRE 320

30. RIVAL SITES FOR GOLGOTHA AND THE TOMB OF JESUS 335

31. THE CHURCHES OF MT. SION 340

32. THE CHURCHES OF GETHSEMANE, THE MOUNT OF OLIVES, AND BETHANY

A. GETHSEMANE 345

B. THE MOUNT OF OLIVES 349

C. BETHANY 354

33. THE POOL OF BETHESDA AND THE CHURCH OF ST. ANNE 355

34. THE PRAETORIUM AND THE WAY OF THE CROSS 359

35. THE CHURCH OF ST. STEPHEN 365

PART SEVEN: JERUSALEM AS A MUSLIM CITY

36. JERUSALEM AS A MUSLIM CITY / THE CITY UNDER THE ADMINISTRATION OF MUSLIM AUTHORITIES 368

PART EIGHT: JERUSALEM IN MODERN TIMES

37. JERUSALEM IN THE NINETEENTH AND EARLY TWENTIETH CENTURIES 388

38. JERUSALEM UNDER BRITISH ADMINISTRATION 406

39. THE DIVIDED CITY, 1948-1967 411

40. JERUSALEM FROM 1967 TO THE PRESENT 415

Indexes

Index of Authors 432

Index of Subjects 481

Editor's Foreword

The American Theological Library Association Bibliography Series is designed to stimulate and encourage the preparation of reliable bibliographies and guides to the literature of religious studies in all of its scope and variety. Compilers are free to define their field, make their own selections, and work out internal organization as the unique demands of the subject indicate. We are pleased to publish this bibliography of Jerusalem by James Purvis as number twenty in our series.

James D. Purvis took his undergraduate studies in history and his theological studies at Drake University. He pursued doctoral studies in Old Testament at Harvard University. His teaching career began at Connecticut College and since 1966 he has been Professor of Religion in the College of Liberal Arts at Boston University. In 1986 he received his university's Metcalf Award for Excellence in Teaching. He is the author of THE SAMARITAN PENTATEUCH (1968), plus many journal articles, and has contributed to several important symposia and dictionaries in biblical, archaeological, and Jewish studies.

Kenneth E. Rowe
Series Editor

Drew University Library
Madison, New Jersey 07940

Preface

This bibliography has developed from reading-lists prepared originally for students in an undergraduate course at Boston University, "The Holy City: Jerusalem in Time, Space, and Imagination." The course is concerned primarily with Jerusalem as a holy city, but deals with all aspects of Jerusalem and its history, from ancient to modern times. The discrete units or chapters of this bibliography reflect the organization and presentation of materials in this classroom experience.

I have been encouraged by colleagues to make this bibliography available to a wider audience. It has been expanded but it remains a bibliography for students, for graduate and theological students as well as undergraduates. It may be said to be comprehensive in the subject matter it treats but it does not purport to be exhaustive. In certain cases (for example, archaeological studies on monuments and holy sites), I have attempted to locate as many titles as possible. In other areas I have been selective. But, overall, I have tried to include works which are representative of the history of modern scholarship (from the19th century to the present) in the areas I have delineated.

Most of the entries are in English, many are in French, German, and Italian, and a few in Spanish and other western languages. I have not included titles in western languages in non-Latin scripts, such as Russian, modern Greek, Armenian, and Georgian. Articles and some books in modern Hebrew have been included (under English translations of titles) where these have been judged to be accessible in North American libraries. Many of these include summaries in western languages (usually English) and some have been published also in translation. A few of the works cited contain editions of Arabic texts, but the bibliography does not include titles published in Arabic-- again, because of the problem of accessibility.

Thanks are due to my students, with whom I have been pleased to have been a student of Jerusalem and her history, and especially to Laurie Braaten, David Ball, Ron Lahti, and Susan Kornblum, who assisted in bibliographical research. Gratitude is also expressed to the staff of the libraries of the Boston Theological Institute, especially to William Zimpfer, Elizabeth Swayne, Stephen Pentek, and Loumona Petroff of the library of the Boston University School of Theology. My thanks also to the Custody of the Holy Land and the Studium Biblicum Franciscanum, Jerusalem, for the use of their libraries and other courtesies, and to the staff of the libraries of the Hebrew University, Jerusalem. A special word of thanks is extended to the office staff of the Department of Religion, Boston University, to Lisa Mankita Fay, Sarah Lown, and Justine Covault, and also to Julie Koniuto. Thanks also to Dean Geoffrey Bannister and Associate Deans Michael Mendillo and Ernest Blaustein of the College of Liberal Arts / Graduate School, Boston University, for their encouragement and for a grant to assist in manuscript preparation. I am grateful to my colleagues at Boston Universty for their support, especially to Chairman Alan Olson of the Department of Religion and Merlin Swartz, who advised me on Islamic matters. My thanks also to faculty colleagues in Biblical Studies in the Boston Theological Institute who encouraged and helped me, especially to Fr. Carney Gavin of the Harvard Semitic Museum, Professor John Townsend of the Episcopal Divinity School, Fr. Philip King of Boston College, and Professor emeritus H. Neil Richardson of the Boston University School of Theology.

Finally, I wish to express my gratitude and thanks to my wife Kathryn, for her constant encouragement, support, patience, and love.

James D. Purvis
Boston University

One

General Studies and Historical Overviews

Albertson, Erik W. [1] Jerusalem. Stockholm: Askild, 1971, 248 pp.

Amit, Izhak [2] Jerusalem, Earth and Heaven. Tel-Aviv: Sifriyat Ma'ariv, 1977, 114 pp.

Avi-Yonah, Michael. [3] Jerusalem. New York: Orion Books, 1960. 200 pp.

Avi-Yonah, Michael. [4] Jerusalem the Holy: A Short History. New York: Schocken, 1976, 24 pp, 130 pls. [Primarily photographs.]

Aviram, J. (ed.) [5] Jerusalem through the Ages. Jerusalem: Israel Exploration Society, 1968, xi + 68 + 264 pp. [18 articles in Hebrew with English summaries; 4 in English; 1 in French; 1 in Italian.]

Bahat, Dan. [6] Carta's Historical Atlas of Jerusalem: An Illustrated Survey. Jerusalem: Carta, 1983, 96 pp.

Bauer, Johannes B. and Marböck, Johannes (eds.). [7] Memoria Jerusalem: Freundesgabe Franz Sauer zum 70 Geburtstag, Graz: Akademische Druck-u Verlagsanstalt, 1977, 238 pp.

Baedeker's Jerusalem. [8] Norwich, United Kingdom: Jarrold and Sons, 1983, 180 pp.

Ben-Chorin, S. [9] Ich Lebe in Jerusalem. Aktuelles Taschenbuch. Gerlingen: Bleicher, 1979, 263 pp.

Benvenisti, David. [10] Tours in Jerusalem. Jerusalem: Kiryat Sefer, 1985, 400 pp.

Berneim, A. See Maraini, Fosco. [57]

Bishko, Herbert. [11] This is Jerusalem. Tel-Aviv: Heritage Publishers, 1972, 2nd edn., 1972, 84 pp.

Bocker, Uli. See Rabinovich, Abraham. [66A]

Bonnetain, Nicole. See Catarivas, Daniel; Bonnetain, Nicole; and Moatti, Jacqueline. [16]

Borrmans, Maurizio. [12] Gerusalemme. Atti dellla xxvi Settimane Biblica, Associazione Biblica Italiana. Brescia: Paideia, 1982, 300 pp.

Boudet, Jacques. [13] Jerusalem, a History. New York: Putnam's, 1967, 294 pp.

1/General Studies and Historical Overviews

Braun, Werner. See Rozenthal, Gabriella. [69]

Braun, Werner. [14] Jerusalem: The Living City. Jerusalem: Armon, 1967, photographs, no pagination.

Capa, Cornell. [15] Jerusalem, City of Mankind. Introduction by T. Kollek with J. R. Moskin. New York: Grossman Publishers, 1974, 127 pp.

Catarivas, Daniel; Bonnetain, Nicole; and Moatti, Jacqueline (eds.). [16] Histoire de Jérusalem, d' Abraham à nos jours. Paris: Pont Royal, 1965, 294 pp.

Chouraqui, André. [17] Jérusalem, une métropole spirituelle. Collection Voir l' Histoire. Paris: Bordas, 1981, 125 pp.

Chouraqui, André. [18] Vivre pour Jérusalem. Paris: Desclée de Brouwer, 1973, 306 pp.

Comay, Joan. [19] The Jerusalem I Love. Photographer, David Harris; general editor, Mordecai Raanan. Tel-Aviv: Leon Amiel Publishers, 1976, 158 pp. [Primarily photographs.]

Conder, Claude R. [20] The City of Jerusalem. London: John Murray, 1909, 334 pp.

Cust, L. G. A. [21] Jerusalem, a Historical Sketch. New York: Macmillan, 1924, 222 pp.

De Munter, L. See De Swaef, A. and De Munter, L. [22]

De Swaef, A. and De Munter, L. [22] Jerusalem, de Heilige Stad. Gent: Commissariaat van het Heilige Land, 1969, 206 pp. + 102 photographs.

Dressaire, Léopold. [23] Jérusalem à travers les siècles: Histoire-archéologie-sanctuaires. Paris: Maison de la Bonne Presse, 1931, 544 pp.

Foster, Dave. [24] Jerusalem: The Christian Herald Photoguide. Chappaqua, NY: Christian Herald, 1980, 127 pp.

Foucherand, L. See Leconte, R. [53]

de Foy, Guy Philppart. See Hureau, Jean and de Foy, Guy Philppart. [36]

Gafni, Shlomo. [25] The Glory of Jerusalem: An Explorers Guide. Jerusalem: Jerusalem Publishing House, 1978.

Gafni, Shlomo and Van der Heyden, A. [26] The Glory of Jerusalem. Cambridge: Cambridge University Press, 1982, 127 pp.

Gibbon, David. [27] Return to Jerusalem. New Malden, England: Colour Library International, 1977, 62 pp. [Primarily photographs.]

Gilbert, Martin. [28] Jerusalem History Atlas. New York: Macmillan, 1977, 136 pp.

Gray, John. [29] A History of Jerusalem. New York: Frederich & Praeger, 1969, 336 pp.

Grindea, Miron (ed.). [30] Jerusalem: The Holy City in Literature. London: Kahn and Averill, 2nd edn., 1981, 244 pp. [Originally published as Jerusalem: A Literary Chronicle of 3,000 Years. Rochester, NY: University of Rochester, 1968.]

Guérin, V. [31] Jérusalem, son histoire, sa description, ses établissements religieux. Paris: Plon, 1889, 496 pp.

Har-El, Menashe. [32] This is Jerusalem. Jerusalem: Canaan Publishing House, 1977, 350 pp.

Harris, David. See Comay, Joan. [19]

Hertzberg and Steurnagel. [33] "Jerusalem," in Die Religion in Geschichte und Gegenwart, 3. Tübingen: Mohr (Siebeck), 1929, 84-92.

"History," [34] in Israel Pocket Library: Jerusalem. Jerusalem: Keter, 1973, 3-214.

Huigens, Petrus. [35] Jeruzalem, Stad der Waarheid. Baarn: Bosch and Keuning, 1964, 167 pp.

Hureau, Jean and de Foy, Guy Philppart. [36] Jérusalem aujourd' hui. Paris: Editions J. A., 1982, 239 pp. + 70 pls. [Primarily photographs.]

Hurley, Frank. [37] The Holy City: A Camera Study of the Holy City and its Borderlands. Sydney / London: Angus and Robertson, 1949, no pagination.

Israel Pocket Library: Jerusalem. [38] Jerusalem: Keter, 1973, 370 pp. [Compiled from materials originally published in Encyclopaedia Judaica.]

Jacoby, Hilla and Jacoby, Max. [39] Hallelujah Jerusalem. Hamburg: Hoffmann und Campe, 1980, 206 pp. [Primarily photographs.]

Jacoby, Max. See Jacoby, Hilla and Jacoby, Max. [39]

Jagodnik, Franklin. See Stein, Henia and Jagodnik, Franklin. [74]

"Jerusalem," [40] in Encyclopaedia Britannica, 12. Chicago: Encyclopaedia Britannica, Inc., 1969, 1006-1009, 1009A-1009J, 1010.

"Jerusalem," [41] in Encyclopaedia Judaica, 9. Jerusalem: Macmillan, 1971, 1378-1591.

Jerusalem: Past and Present. [42] Introduction by R. J. Z. Werblowsky; photographs by G. Naladian. Tel Aviv: Friedman, 1969, 259 pp.

Join-Lambert, Michel. [43] Jerusalem. Trans. by C. Haldane. London: Elek / New York: Putnam's, 1958, 223 pp.

Join-Lambert, Michel. [44] Jérusalem: Israélite, chrétienne, musulmane. Paris: Guillot, 1957, 173 pp.

Kaminker, Sarah F. [45] Footloose in Jerusalem: Eight Guided Walking Tours Illustrated with Maps and Nineteenth Century Engravings. New York: Crown Publishers, 1981, 166 pp.

Klein, H. Arthur. See Klein, Mina C. and H. Arthur. [46]

Klein, Mina C. and H. Arthur. [46] Temple beyond Time: The Story of the Site of Solomon's Temple at Jerusalem. New York: Van Nostrand, 1970, 191 pp.

Kollek, Teddy. See Capa, Cornell. [15]

Kollek, Teddy and Pearlman, Moshe. [47] Jerusalem-- Sacred City of Mankind: A History of Forty Centuries. New York: Random House / London: Weidenfeld & Nicolson, 1968, 287 pp.

Kotker, Norman. [48] The Earthly Jerusalem. New York: Scribner's, 1969, 307 pp.

Landay, Jerry M. [49] Dome of the Rock: Three Faiths of Jerusalem. New York: Newsweek, 1972, 172 pp.

Lande-Nash, Irene. [50] 3000 Jahre Jerusalem: Eine Geschichte der Stadt von den Anfängen bis zur Eroberung durch die Kreuzfahrer. Tübingen: Wasmuth, 1964, 243 pp.

La Sor, William S. [51] "Jerusalem," in G. W. Bromiley (ed.), International Standard Bible Encyclopedia, 2. Grand Rapids, MI: Eerdmans, 1982, 998-1032.

Laubscher, F. [52] Jerusalem, Widerspruch und Verheissung: Geschichte einer Stadt. Konstanz: Bahn, 1979, 338 pp.

Leconte, R. [53] Jérusalem et les Lieux Saints. Album des Guides Bleus. Paris: Hachette, 1954, 128 pp. [Mostly photographs; photographer, L. Foucherand.]

Lieber, Alfred. [54] "An Economic History of Jerusalem," in J, M. Oesterreicher and A. Sinai (eds.), Jerusalem. New York: John Day, 1974, 31-52.

Madaule, Jacques. [55] Jerusalem, die heilige Stadt dreir Religionen. Die Welt der Religionen, 5. Freiburg: Herder, 1982, 138 pp.

Maisel, J. See Thubron, Colin. [75]

Mann, Sylvia (ed.). [56] Tour Jerusalem. Jerusalem: Evyatar Publishing House, 1972, 166 pp.

Maraini, Fosco. [57] Jerusalem, Rock of Ages. Photographs by A. Berneim and R. Schwerin. London: H. Hamilton, 1969, 122 pp.

Marböck, Johannes. See Bauer, Johannes and Marböck, Johannes. [7]

Médam. Alain. [58] La cité des noms. Paris: Galilée, 1980, 323 pp.

Moatti, Jacqueline. See Catarivas, Daniel; Bonnetain, Nicole; and Moatti, Jacqueline. [16]

Moskin, J. R. See Capa, Cornell. [15]

Naladian, G. See Jerusalem: Past and Present. [42]

Nantet, Jacques. [59] Les mille et une Jérusalem. Paris: Lattès, 1977, 195 pp.

Oesterreicher, John M. and Sinai, Anne (eds.). [60] Jerusalem. Prepared under the auspices of the American Academy for Peace in the Middle East. New York: John Day, 1974, 302 pp.

Otto, Eckart. [61] Jerusalem-- die Geschichte der heiligen Stadt: Von den Anfängen bis zur Kreuzfahrerzeit. Stuttgart: Kohlhammer, 1980, 236 pp.

Papas, William. [62] People of Old Jerusalem. New York: Holt, Rinehart and Winston, 1980, no pagination.

Parkes, James. [63] The Story of Jerusalem. London: Cresset, 2nd rev. edn., 1950, 40 pp.

Pearlman, Moshe. See Kollek, Teddy and Pearlman, Moshe. [47]

Perowne, Stewart H. [64] Jerusalem and Bethlehem. London: Phoenix House, 1965, 78 pp.

Peters, F. E. [65] Jerusalem: The Holy City in the Eyes of Chroniclers, Visitors, Pilgrims, and Prophets from the Days of Abraham to the Beginnings of Modern Times. Princeton: Princton University Press, 1985, 656 pp.

Pfeiffer, Charles F. [66] Jerusalem through the Ages. Grand Rapids, MI: Baker, 1967, 94 pp.

Rabinovich, Abraham. [66A] Jerusalem, the Measure of the Year. Photographs by Uli Bocker. Jerusalem: Carta, 1985, 160 pp.

Raanan, Mordecai. See Joan Comay. [19]

Rohde, Peter P. [67] Jerusalem. Copenhagen: Carit Andersen, 1972, 202 pp.

Rosovsky, Nitza. [68] Jerusalemwalks. New York: Holt, Rinehart and Winston, 1982, 289 pp.

Rozenthal, Gabriella. [69] Jerusalem, with 40 Color Plates by Werner Braun. Garden City, NY: Doubleday, 1968, 104 pp.

Schmerer, Constance. [70] Off the Beaten Track in Jerusalem. Los Angeles: Nas Publishers, 1972, 116 pp.

Schwerin, R. See Maraini, Fosco. [57]

Shalem, Diane. See Shamis, Giora and Shalem, Diane. [71]

Shamis, Giora and Shalem, Diane. [71] The Jerusalem Guide. Jerusalem: Abraham Marcus, 1973, 170 pp.

Shore, Michael M. J. [72] Jerusalem Breezes: A Human Panorama and a Hope for Peace. New York: Shengold, 1981, 123 pp.

Sinai, Anne. See Oesterreicher, John M. and Sinai, Anne (eds.). [60]

Stein, Henia and Jagodnik, Franklin. [73] Jerusalem, Most Fair of Cities: Essays, Poems, Legends, and Biblical Quotations. Jerusalem: Armon, 1977, 120 pp.

Steurnagel. See Hertzberg and Steurnagel. [33]

Thubron, Colin. [74] Jerusalem. London: Heineman / Boston: Little, Brown, 1969, 256 pp.

Thubron, Colin. [75] The Great Cities: Jerusalem. Photographs by J. Maisel. Amsterdam: Time-Life Books, 1976, 200 pp.

Uris, Jill and Uris, Leon. [76] Jerusalem: Song of Songs. Garden City, NY: Doubleday, 1981, 318 pp.

Uris, Leon. See Uris, Jill and Uris, Leon. [76]

Van der Heyden, A. See Gafni, Shlomo and Van der Heyden, A. [26]

Watson, Charles M. [77] The Story of Jerusalem. New York: Dutton, 1912, 330 pp. Reprinted, Lendeln, Liechtenstein: Kraus, 1971.

Werblowsky, R. J. Z. See Jerusalem: Past and Present. [42]

Two

Geographical / Topographical Studies

Aharoni, Yohanan. [78] The Land of the Bible: A Historical Geography. Translated and edited by A. F. Rainey. Philadelphia: Westminster, 1979, 481 pp.

Aharoni, Yohanan and Avi-Yonah, Michael. [79] The Macmillan Bible Atlas. New York: Macmillan, 1968; rev. edn., 1977, 184 pp.

Alhassid, Naomi. See Ben-Arieh, Yehoshua and Alhassid, Naomi. [106]

Alt, Albrecht. [80] "Jerusalem Aufstieg," Zeitschrift der deutschen Morgenländischen Gesellschaft, 79 (1925), 1-19. Also in Kleine Schriften zur Geschichte des Volkes Israel, 3. Munich: Beck'sche Verlagsbuchhandlung, 1959, 243-257.

von Alten, Baron. [81] "Die Davidsstadt, der Salomoteich und die Graber der Könige in Jerusalem," Zeitschrift des deutschen Palästina-Vereins, 3 (1880), 116-176.

von Alten, Baron. [82] "Die der Stadt zugewandte Umgebung des Tempelberges als die Unterstadt des Josephus nachgewiessen," Zeitschrift des deutschen Palästina-Vereins, 2 (1879), 189-200.

von Alten, Baron. [83] "Zion," Zeitschrift des deutschen Palästina-Vereins, 2 (1879), 18-48.

Amiran, David H. K. [84] "The Cartographic Survey of Jerusalem, 1940: A Contribution to the Methodology of Mapping in Urban Geography," in Eretz-Israel: Archaeological, Historical and Geographical Studies, 17. Jerusalem: Israel Exploration Society, 1984, 97-100 (Hebrew), 5* (English summary).

Amiran, David H. K.; Shachar, Arie; and Kimhi, Israel (eds.). [85] Atlas of Jerusalem, with companion volume, Building History from the Earliest Times to the Nineteenth Century: Urban Geography of Jerusalem. Jerusalem: Israel Academy of Sciences and Humanities, Hebrew University, Israel Exploration Society, Massada Press / Berlin: de Gruyter, 1973, 53 maps, 173 pp.

Ashbel, Dov. [86] The Climate of Jerusalem: A Century of Meteorological Observations, 1846-1952, 3 vols. Jerusalem: Hebrew University Meteorological Dept., 1953-1959.

Ashbel, Dov. [87] "The Climate of Jerusalem throughout the Ages," in Judah and Jerusalem: The Twelfth Archaeological Convention. Jerusalem: Israel Exploration Society, 1957, 157-165 (Hebrew), viii (English summary).

Avi-Yonah, Michael. Aharoni, Yohanan and Avi-Yonah, Michael. [79]

2/Geographical / Topographical Studies

Avi-Yonah, Michael. [88] "Building History from the Earliest Times to the Nineteenth Century," in D. H. K. Amiran, A. Shachar, and I. Kimhi (eds.), Urban Geography of Jerusalem: A Companion Volume to the Atlas of Jerusalem. Jerusalem: Israel Academy of Sciences and Humanities, Hebrew University, Israel Exploration Society, Massada Press / Berlin: de Gruyter, 1973, 13-19.

Avnimelech, M. [89] "Influence of Geological Conditions on the Development of Jerusalem," Bulletin of the American Schools of Oriental Research, 181 (1966), 24-31.

Avnimelech, M. [90] "The Influence of the Geology of Jerusalem on its Development," in Judah and Jerusalem: The Twelfth Archaeological Convention. Jerusalem: Israel Exploration Society, 1957, 129-136 (Hebrew), vii (English summary).

Bahat, Dan. See Wilson, Charles W. [332]

Bahat, Dan. [91] Carta's Historical Atlas of Jerusalem: An Illustrated Survey. Jerusalem: Carta, 1983, 96 pp.

Baldi, Donato. See Lemaire, Paulin and Baldi, Donato. [235]

Barclay, James T. [92] The City of the Great King, or Jerusalem as It Was, as It Is, and as It Is To Be. Philadelphia: James Challen, 1857. Reprinted, New York: Arno, 1977, 627 pp.

Barrois, Georges Augustin. [93] "David, City of," in Interpreter's Dictionary of the Bible, 1. New York: Abingdon, 1962, 782.

Barrois, Georges Augustin. [94] "Hinnom, Valley of the Sons of," in Interpreter's Dictionary of the Bible, 2. New York: Abingdon, 1962, 606.

Barrois, Georges Augustin. [95] "Jehoshaphat, Valley of," in Interpreter's Dictionary of the Bible, 2. New York: Abingdon, 1962, 816.

Barrois, Georges Augustin. [96] "Kidron, Brook," in Interpreter's Dictionary of the Bible, 3. New York: Abingdon, 1962, 10-11.

Barrois, Georges Augustin. [97] "Moriah," in Interpreter's Dictionary of the Bible, 3. New York: Abingdon, 1962, 438-439.

Barrois, Georges Augustin. [98] "Olives, Mount of," in Interpreter's Dictionary of the Bible, 3. New York: Abingdon, 1962, 596-599.

Barrois, Georges Augustin. [99] "Ophel," in Interpreter's Dictionary of the Bible, 3. New York: Abingdon, 1962, 605.

Barrois, Georges Augustin. [100] "Zion," in Interpreter's Dictionary of the Bible, 4. New York: Abingdon, 1962, 959-960.

Becker, F. See Dalman, Gustaf and Becker, F. [164]

2/Geographical / Topographical Studies

Ben-Arieh, Yehoshua. [101] "The First Surveyed Maps of Jerusalem,' in Eretz-Israel: Archaeological, Historical and Geographical Studies, 11. Jerusalem: Israel Exploration Society, 1973, 64-74 (Hebrew), 24* (English summary).

Ben-Arieh, Yehoshua. [102] "Frederick Catherwood Map of Jerusalem, 1833," Quarterly Journal of the Library of Congress, 31 (1974), 150-160.

Ben-Arieh, Yehoshua. [103] "The Geographical Exploration of the Holy Land," Palestine Exploration Quarterly, (1972), 81-92.

Ben-Arieh, Yehoshua. [104] "The Old City: Its Appearance, Sources of Livelihood, Water Supply and Sanitation," in Jerusalem in the 19th Century: The Old City. Jerusalem: Yad Izhaq Ben-Zvi / New York: St. Martin's Press, 1984, 14-37.

Ben-Arieh, Yehoshua. [105] The Rediscovery of the Holy Land in the Nineteenth Century. Jerusalem: Magnes / Detroit: Wayne State University, 1979, 266 pp.

Ben-Arieh, Yehoshua and Alhassid, Naomi. [106] "Some Notes on the Maps of Jerusalem, 1470-1600," in A. Cohen (ed.), Jerusalem in the Early Ottoman Period. Jerusalem: Yad Izhaq Ben-Zvi, 1979, 112-151 (Hebrew), x-xi (English summary).

Benzinger, Immanuel. See Schick, Conrad and Benzinger, Immanuel. [284-285]

Bergheim, Samuel. [107] "The Identification of the City of David-- Zion and Millo," Palestine Exploration Fund, Quarterly Statement, (1895), 120-123.

Beswick, S. [108] "The Place Called Bethso," Palestine Exploration Fund, Quarterly Statement, (1880), 108-109.

Beswick, S. [109] "Valley of Hinnom," Palestine Exploration Fund, Quarterly Statement, (1881), 102-104.

Birch, W. F. [110] "Acra South of the Temple," Palestine Exploration Fund, Quarterly Statement, (1886), 26-31, 151-154; (1888), 108.

Birch, W. F. [111] "Ancient Jerusalem-- Zion and Acra, South of the Temple," Palestine Exploration Fund, Quarterly Statement, (1894), 282-284.

Birch, W. F. [112] "Ancient Jerusalem: Zion or Acra, South, Not North, of the Temple," Palestine Exploration Fund, Quarterly Statement, (1893), 70-76.

Birch, W. F. [113] "The Approximate Position of the Castle of Zion," Palestine Exploration Fund, Quarterly Statement, (1886), 33-34.

Birch, W. F. [114] "The City and Tomb of David," Palestine Exploration Fund, Quarterly Statement, (1881), 94-97.

Birch, W. F. [115] "The City and Tomb of David on Acra, Commonly Called Ophel," Palestine Exploration Fund, Quarterly Statement, (1884), 196-198.

Birch, W. F. [116] "The City and Tomb of David on Ophel," Palestine Exploration Fund, Quarterly Statement, (1911), 187-189.

Birch, W. F. [117] "The City of David," Palestine Exploration Fund, Quarterly Statement, (1885), 100-108, 208-212; (1888), 44-46.

Birch, W. F. [118] "The City of David: Zion Not at Goliath's Castle," Palestine Exploration Fund, Quarterly Statement, (1895), 263-264.

Birch, W. F. [119] "The City of David and Josephus," Palestine Exploration Fund, Quarterly Statement, (1884), 77-82; (1885), 61-65, 100-108, 208-212; (1888), 44-46.

Birch, W. F. [120] "Notes: 1. Acra South of the Temple; 2. Professor Socin's Criticisms; 3. Captain Conder's Note on Jerusalem; 4. The Approximate Position of the Castle of Zion," Palestine Exploration Fund, Quarterly Statement, (1886), 26-34.

Birch, W. F. [121] "Notes and Queries, 1: Acra," Palestine Exploration Fund, Quarterly Statement, (1906), 157.

Birch, W. F. [122] "Notes on Prae-Exilic Jerusalem," Palestine Exploration Fund, Quarterly Statement, (1884), 70-75.

Birch, W. F. [123] "Reply to Captain Conder's Notes on Zion," Palestine Exploration Fund, Quarterly Statement, (1888), 42-44.

Birch, W. F. [124] "The Site of the Acra," Palestine Exploration Fund, Quarterly Statement, (1908), 79-82.

Birch, W. F. [125] "Topheth and the King's Garden," Palestine Exploration Fund, Quarterly Statement, (1897), 72-75.

Birch, W. F. [126] "The Valley of Hinnom," Palestine Exploration Fund, Quarterly Statement, (1899), 65-67; (1909), 229-230.

Birch, W. F. [127] "The Valley of Hinnom and Zion," Palestine Exploration Fund, Quarterly Statement, (1882), 55-59.

Birch, W. F. [128] "Zion (or Acra), Gihon, and Millo (All South of the Temple)," Palestine Exploration Fund, Quarterly Statement, (1893), 324-330.

Birch, W. F. [129] "Zion, the City of David (2 Sam. 5)," Palestine Exploration Fund, Quarterly Statement, (1879), 104; (1885), 61-65.

Birch, W. F. [130] "Zion, the City of David, or Acra, South of the Temple," Palestine Exploration Fund, Quarterly Statement, (1886), 151-154.

Birch, W. F. [131] "Zion, the City of David: Where was it? How did Joab make his way into it? And who helped him?" Palestine Exploration Fund, Quarterly Statement, (1878), 129-132, 178-189.

Bitan-Buttenwieser, A. [132] "A Comparison of Sixty Years' Rainfall between Jerusalem and Tel Aviv," Israel Exploration Journal, 13 (1963), 242-246.

Broshi, Magen. [133] "Estimating the Population of Ancient Jerusalem," Biblical Archeology Review, 4/2 (1978), 10-15.

Broshi, Magen. [134] "La population de l' ancienne Jérusalem," Revue biblique, 82 (1975), 5-14.

Broshi, Magen. [135] "The Population of Western Palestine in the Roman-Byzantine Period," Bulletin of the American Schools of Oriental Research, 236 (1979), 1-10.

Buchan, Alexander and Chaplin, Thomas. [136] "Remarks on the Climate of Jerusalem," Palestine Exploration Fund, Quarterly Statement, (1872), 19-29; (1873), 39.

Buhl, Frants. [137] "Jerusalem," in Geographie des alten Palästina. Freiburg, i. b. / Leipzig: Mohr (Siebeck), 1896, 132-140.

Burney, C. F. [138] "The Meaning of the Name 'the Ophel,'" Palestine Exploration Fund, Quarterly Statement, (1911), 51-56.

Burrows, Millar. [139] "Jerusalem: Names, Situation and General Topography," in Interpreter's Dictionary of the Bible, 2. New York: Abingdon, 1962, 843-846.

Byatt, Anthony. [140] "Josephus and Population Numbers in First Century Palestine," Palestine Exploration Quarterly, (1973), 51-60.

Caspari, Wilhelm. [141] "Der Millo in Jerusalem," Zeitschrift des deutschen Palästina-Vereins, 35 (1912), 28-37.

Chaplin, Thomas. See Buchan, Alexander and Chaplin, Thomas. [136]

Chaplin, Thomas. [142] "Das Klima von Jerusalem," Zeitschrift des deutschen Palästina-Vereins, 14 (1891), 93-112, 12 tables.

Chaplin, Thomas. [143] "Observations on the Climate of Jerusalem," Palestine Exploration Fund, Quarterly Statement, (1883), 8-40.

Cheyne, T. K. and Cook, Stanly A. [144] "Hinnom, Valley of," in T. K. Cheyne and J. S. Black (eds.), Encyclopedia Biblica, 2. New York: Macmillan, 1901, 2070-2072.

Clermont-Ganneau, Charles. [145] "Résultats topographiques et archéologiques des fouilles entreprises à Jérusalem par le Palestine Exploration Fund," Journal asiatique, 6th ser., 20 (1872), 145-156.

Clermont-Ganneau, Charles. [146] "The Stone of Zoheleth (I Kings 1,9)," in C. Warren and C. R. Conder, The Survey of Western Palestine, 5. Jerusalem. London: Palestine Exploration Fund, 1884, 293-294

Clermont-Ganneau, Charles. [147] "The Stone of Zoheleth, en Rogel, and the King's Gardens," Palestine Exploration Fund, Quarterly Statement, (1869/1870), 251-253.

Close, Charles F. [148] "The New Maps of Jerusalem," Palestine Exploration Fund, Quarterly Statement, (1925), 217-219.

Cohn, Erich W. [149] "The Appendix of Antonia Rock in Jerusalem," Palestine Exploration Quarterly, (1979), 41-52.

Conder, Claude R. See Smith, George Adam; Smith, W. Robertson; and Conder, Claude R. [292]

Conder, Claude R. [150] "Architectural History of Jerusalem," in C. Warren and C. R. Conder, The Survey of Western Palestine, 5. Jerusalem. London: Palestine Exploration Fund, 1884, 5-85.

Conder, Claude R. [151] "City of David," Palestine Exploration Fund, Quarterly Statement, (1883), 194-195.

Conder, Claude R. [152] "Jerusalem: Names, Natural Site, . . . Topography," in J. Hastings (ed.), Dictionary of the Bible, 2. New York: Scribner's, 1898, 584-586, 591-596.

Conder, Claude R. [153] "Jerusalem of the Kings," Palestine Exploration Fund, Quarterly Statement, (1884), 20-29.

Conder, Claude R. [154] "Jerusalem Topography," Palestine Exploration Fund, Quarterly Statement, (1873), 151-154.

Conder, Claude R. [155] "On the Identification of Scopus," Palestine Exploration Fund, Quarterly Statement, (1874), 111-114.

Conder, Claude R. [156] "Register of Rock Levels, Jerusalem," Palestine Exploration Fund, Quarterly Statement, (1880), 82-91.

Conder, Claude R. [157] "The Tyropoeon Valley," Palestine Exploration Fund, Quarterly Statement, (1880), 77-81.

Conder, Claude R. [158] "The Zion Scarp," Palestine Exploration Fund, Quarterly Statement, (1875), 7-10, 81-89.

Cook, Stanly A. See Cheyne, T. K. and Cook, Stanly A. [144]

Crawley-Boevey, A. W. [159] "Map and Description of Jerusalem by Christian Van Adrichem (1533-1585),"Palestine Exploration Fund, Quarterly Statement, (1909), 64-68.

Dalman, Gustaf. [160] Jerusalem und sein Gelände: Mit einer Einführung von Karl Heinrich Rengstorf und mit Nachträgen auf Grund des Handexemplars des Verfassers von Peter Freimark. Gütersloh: Bertelsmann, 1930. Reprinted, Hildesheim: Georg Olms, 1972, 390 pp.

Dalman, Gustaf. [161] Neue Petra-Forschungen und der Heilige Felsen von Jerusalem. Palästinische Forschungen zur Archäologie und Topographie, 2. Leipzig: Hinrichs, 1912, 172 pp.

Dalman, Gustaf. [162] "Die Nordstrasse Jerusalems," Palästinajahrbuch, 21 (1925), 58-59.

Dalman, Gustaf. [163] "Zion, die Burg Jerusalems," Palästinajahrbuch, 11 (1915), 39-84.

Dalman, Gustaf and Becker, F. [164] "Die Exkursionkarte von Jerusalem und Mitteljudäa," Zeitschrift des deutschen Palästina-Vereins, 37 (1914), 348-370.

Drory, Joseph. [165] "A Map of Mamluk Jerusalem," in B. Z. Kedar (ed.), Jerusalem in the Middle Ages, Selected Papers. Jerusalem: Yad Izhaq Ben-Zvi, 1979, 178-184 (Hebrew).

Duncan, J. Garrow. [166] "Millo and the City of David," Zeitschrift für die alttestamentliche Wissenschaft, 42 (1924), 22-244.

Edelstein, Gershon. See Gibson, Shimon and Edelstein, Gershon. [196]

Edelstein, Gershon; Gat, Y.; and Gibson, Shimon. [167] "Food Production and Water Storage in the Region of Jerusalem," Qadmoniot, 16 (1983), 16-23 (Hebrew). [English summary in Old Testament Abstracts, 7 (1984), 13.]

Edelstein, Gershon and Gibson, Shimon. [168] "Ancient Jerusalem's Rural Food Basket," Biblical Archaeology Review, 8/4 (July/Aug., 1982), 46-54.

Edelstein, Gershon and Kislev, Mordechai. [169] "Mevasseret Yerushalayim: Ancient Terrace Farming," Biblical Archaeologist, 44 (1981), 53-56.

Elster, J. and Kadmon, N. [170] "Cartography: Bernhard von Breitenbach's Map," in Atlas of Israel. Jerusalem: Survey of Israel, Ministry of Labour / Amsterdam: Elsevier, 1970, I/Z.

Erfat, Elisha. [171] "Jerusalem: Geography," in Encyclopaedia Judaica, 9. Jerusalem: Macmillan, 1971, 1513-1516. Also in Israel Pocket Library: Jerusalem. Jerusalem: Keter, 1973, 216-220.

Evans, Geoffrey. [172] "'Gates' and 'Streets:' Urban Institutions in Old Testament Times," Journal of Religious History, 2 (1962), 1-12.

Feigin, Samuel. [173] "The Meaning of Ariel," Journal of BiblicalLiterature, 39 (1920), 131-137.

Fernández, Andrés. [174] "Problemas de Topografia Jerusalén," Estudios Eclesiásticos, 13 (1934), 6-72.

Filson, Floyd V. See Wright, G. Ernest and Filson, Floyd V. [333]

Forbes, S. R. [175] The Holy City Jerusalem, its Topography, Walls and Temple: New Light on an Ancient Subject. Chelmsford: Durrant, 1892, 80 pp.

Fraenkel, Meir. [176] "Zur Deutung von biblischen Flur- und Ortsnamen: J[e]rushalajim," Biblische Zeitschrift, 5 (1961), 83-84.

Fransen, Paul-Irénée. [177] "La vallée de la Gehenne," Bible et Terre Sainte, 158 (1974), 10-17.

Freimark, Peter. See Dalman, Gustaf. [160]

Frick, Frank S. [178] The City in Ancient Israel. Missoula, MT: Scholars Press, 1977, 283 pp.

Gabriel, K. R. and Kesten, H. [179] "Statistical Analysis of Annual Rainfall in Jerusalem, 1860-1960," in Bulletin of the Research Council of Israel, 11 (1963), geological section, 142-145.

Galling, Kurt. [180] "Die Baugeschichte Jerusalems," Zeitschrift des deutschen Palästina-Vereins, 54 (1931), 85-90.

Galling, Kurt. [181] "Die Halle des Schreibers: Ein Beitrag zur Topographie der Akropolis von Jerusalem," Palästinajahrbuch, 27 (1931), 51-57.

Gat, Y. See Edelstein, Gershon; Gat, Y.; and Gibson, Shimon. [167]

Gatt, Georg. [182] "Zur Akrafrage," Theologische Quartelschrift, 71 (1889), 77-125.

Gatt, Georg. [183] "Der Berg Zion," Das Heilige Land, 25 (1881), 126-129, 159-166.

Gatt, Georg. [184] "Die Beschreibung Jerusalems bei Josephus," Das Heilige Land, 26 (1882), 176-181.

Gatt, Georg. [185] "Erklärung der Beschreibung Jerusalems bei Josephus," Das Heilige Land, 38 (1894), 11-15.

Gatt, Georg. [186] "Hatte Jerusalem eine oder mehrere Akra genannte Burgen?" Zeitschrift des deutschen Palästina-Vereins, 10 (1887), 182-187.

Gatt, Georg. [187] Die Hügel von Jerusalem: Neue Erklärung der Beschreibung Jerusalems bei Josephus, Bell. jud. v. 4, 1 und 2. Freiburg: Herder, 1897, 66 pp.

Gatt, Georg. [188] "Jebus, Sion, Stadt Davids," Das Heilige Land, 38 (1894), 15-19.

Gatt, Georg. [189] Sion in Jerusalem, was er war, und wo es lag. Brixen: Commissionsverlag der Buchhandlung des Kath.-polit. Pressvereins, 1900, 141 pp.

Gatt, Georg. [190] "Zur Topographie Jerusalems," Zeitschrift des deutschen Palästina-Vereins, 25 (1902), 178-194.

Gatt, Georg. [191] "Zion und Akra," Das Heilige Land, 25 (1881), 143-201; 26 (1882), 7-11.

Gatt, Georg. [192] "Zur Zion-Akra Frage," Theologische Quartalschrift, 66 (1884), 34-84.

Germer-Durand, Joseph. [193] Topographie de l' Ancienne Jérusalem des origines à Titus. Paris: Feron-Vrau, 1925, 15 pp.

de Geus, C. H. J. [194] "The Importance of Archaeological Research into the Palestinian Agricultural Terraces with an Excursus on the Hebrew word gbi," Palestine Exploration Quarterly, (1975), 65-74.

Gibson, Shimon. See Edelstein, Gershon; Gat, Y.; and Gibson, Shimon. [167]

Gibson, Shimon. See Edelstein, Gershon and Gibson, Shimon. [168]

Gibson, Shimon. [195] "Ancient Jerusalem's Rural Landscape," Bulletin of the Anglo-Israel Archeological Society, (1983/1984), 30-35.

Gibson, Shimon and Edelstein, Gershon. [196] "Investigating Jerusalem's Rural Landscape, Levant, 17 (1985), 139-155.

Glaisher, James. [197] "On the Fall of Rain at Jerusalem in the 32 Years from 1861 to 1892," Palestine Exploration Fund, Quarterly Statement, (1894), 39-44.

Gray, John. [198] "The Situation and Development of the City," in A History of Jerusalem. New York: Praeger, 1969, 15-64.

Grill, Julius. [199] "Beitrage zur hebräischen Wort- und Names erklärung: l. Über Enstehung und Bedeutung des Namens Jerusalem," Zeitschrift für die alttestamentliche Wissenschaft, 4 (1884), 134-148.

Grimme, Hubert. [200] "Der Name Jerusalem," Orientalistische Literaturzeitung, 16 (1913), 152-157.

Guillemot, J.-B. [201] "Étude sur la topographie sacrée de la Cité de Dieu (Jérusalem)," Terra Santa, 11 (1894), 257-260, 273-275; 13 (1896), 58-60, 74-76, 93-95, 103-105, 114-117.

Hamilton, R. W. [202] "Street Levels in the Tyropoean Valley," Quarterly of the Department of Antiquities of Palestine, 1 (1931/1932), 105-110; 2 (1933), 34-40.

Hamme, Liévin. [203] Étude topographique: Fortresse de Sion, Sion (haute ville), Acra (basse ville). Jerusalem: Franciscan Printing Press, 1891, 16 pp.

Hänsler, H. [204] "Streislichter in die Topographie des alten Jerusalem," Das Heilige Land, 57 (1913), 202-210; 58 (1914), 1-13, 99-106, 130-142; 60 (1916), 25-42.

Har-El, Menashe. [205] "Jerusalem, the City that is Compact Together, / 'Walk about Zion and Go Round about Her,'" in This is Jerusalem. Jerusalem: Canaan, l977, 17-77, 111-189.

Har-El, Menashe. [206] "Jerusalem and Judea: Roads and Fortifications," Biblical Archaeologist, 44 (1981), 8-20.

Hitzig, Ferdinand. [207] "Zur Topographie des alten Jerusalem," Zeitschrift der deutschen Morgenländischen Gesellschaft, 21 (1867), 277-279, 495-498.

Hopkins, Ian W J. [208] "The Four Quarters of Jerusalem," Palestine Exploration Quarterly, (1971), 68-84.

Hopkins, Ian W J. [209] Jerusalem: A Study in Urban Geography. Grand Rapids: Baker, 1970, 160 pp.

Hubbard, R. Pearce S. [210] "The Topography of Ancient Jerusalem," Palestine Exploration Quarterly, (1966), 130-154.

Hunsberger, David R. [211] "A Walk through the Hinnom Valley," The Bible Today, 75 (1973), 1267-1271.

Hupfeld, Hermann. [212] "Die topographische Streitfrage über Jerusalem, namentlich die Akra und den Lauf der zweiten Mauer des Josephus," Zeitschrift der deutschen Morgenländischen Gesellschaft, 15 (1861), 185-232.

James, Henry. See Wilson, Charles W. [332]

Jeremias, Joachim. [213] "Die Einwohnerzahl Jerusalems zur Zeit Jesu," Zeitschrift des deutschen Palästina-Vereins, 66 (1943), 24-31.

Kadmon, N. See Elster, J. and Kadmon, N. [170]

Karmon, Yehuda. [214] "The Mountains round about Jerusalem," in J. Aviram (ed.), Jerusalem through the Ages. Jerusalem: Israel Exploration Society, 1968, 96-108 (Hebrew), 62 (English summary).

Karmon, Yehuda. [215] "Topographical Influences on the Judean Roads," in Judah and Jerusalem: The Twelfth Archaeological Convention. Jerusalem: Israel Exploration Society, 1957, 144-150 (Hebrew), viii (English summary).

Kennedy, J. H. [216] "Kidron, The Brook," in J. Hastings (ed.), Dictionary of the Bible, 2. New York: Scribner's, 1898, 837-839.

Kenyon, Kathleen M. [217] "The Site of Jerusalem," in Royal Cities of the Old Testament. London: Barrie and Jenkins, 1971, 13-24.

Kenyon, Kathleen M. [218] "The Topography of Jerusalem and its Problems," in Digging Up Jerusalem. New York: Praeger, 1974, 36-54.

Kesten, H. See Gabriel, K. R. and Kesten, H. [179]

Kimhi, Israel. See Amiran, David H. K.; Shachar, Arie; and Kimhi, Israel (eds.). [85]

Kimhi, Israel. [219] "Aspects of the Human Ecology of Jerusalem," in D. H. K. Amiran, A. Shachar, and I. Kimhi (eds.), Urban Geography of Jerusalem: A Companion Volume to the Atlas of Jerusalem. Jerusalem: Israel Academy of Sciences and Humanities, Hebrew University, Israel Exploration Society, Massada Press / Berlin: de Gruyter, 1973, 109-122.

Kislev, Mordechai. See Edelstein, Gershon and Kislev, Mordechai. [169]

von Klaiber, K. [220] "Noch einmal Zion, Davidstadt und Akra," Zeitschrift des deutschen Palästina-Vereins, 11 (1888), 1-37.

von Klaiber, K. [221] "Zion, Davidstadt und die Akra innerhalb des alten Jerusalem," Zeitschrift des deutschen Palästina-Vereins, 3 (1880), 189-213; 4 (1881), 18-56.

Köhler, Ludwig. [222] "Tagesdauer in Jerusalem," Zeitschrift des deutschen Palästina-Vereins, 50 (1927), 297-298.

Krafft, W. [223] Die Topographie Jerusalem's. Bonn: König, 1846, 273 pp.

Kraus, Hans-Joachim. [224] "Archäologische und topographische Probleme Jerusalems im Lichte der Psalmenexegese," Zeitschrift des deutschen Palästina-Vereins, 75 (1959), 125-140.

Krauss, Samuel. [225] "Zion and Jerusalem, a Linguistic Study," Palestine Exploration Quarterly, (1945), 15-33.

Kümmel, August. [226] Materialien zur Topographie des alten Jerusalem. Halle: Verlag des deutschen Vereins zur Erforschung Palästinas, 1906, 198 pp.

Lagrange, Marie-Joseph. [227] "Topographie de Jérusalem," Revue biblique, 1 (1892), 17-38.

Laperrousaz, Ernest-Marie. [228] "L' interprétation du Cantiques des Cant. et la topographie de Jérusalem," Revue des études juives, 133 (1974), 5-10.

La Sor, William S. [229] "Jerusalem: Names, Physical Features, Topography," in G. W. Bromiley (ed.), International Standard Bible Encyclopedia, 2. Grand Rapids: Eerdmans, 1982, 999-1004.

La Sor, William S. [230] "Kidron, Brook / Kidron, Valley," in G. W. Bromiley (ed.), International Standard Bible Encyclopedia, 3. Grand Rapids: Eerdmans, 1986, 13-15.

La Sor, William S. [231] "Olives, Mount of," in G. W. Bromiley (ed.), International Standard Bible Encyclopedia, 3. Grand Rapids: Eerdmans, 1986, 589-591.

Lee, George A. [232] "King's Valley, / Valley of Shaveh," in G. W. Bromiley (ed.), International Standard Bible Encyclopedia, 3. Grand Rapids: Eerdmans, 1986, 40.

Legendre, A. [233] "Jérusalem: Noms, topographie, . . . topographie ancienne," in F. Vigouroux (ed.), Dictionnaire de la Bible, 3. Paris: Letouzey et Ané, 1926, 1317-1332, 1350-1377.

Lehman, M. [234] "A New Interpretation of Sh^{e}ramôt," Vetus Testamentum, 3 (1953), 361-371. [The topography of Jeremiah 31: 40.]

Lemaire, Paulin and Baldi, Donato. [235] "Jérusalem," in Atlas biblique: Histoire et geographie de la Bible. Louvain: Editions du Mont César, 1960, 269-277.

Le Strange, Guy. [236] "Palestine According to the Arab Geographers and Travellers," Palestine Exploration Fund, Quarterly Statement, (1888), 23-30.

Le Strange, Guy. [237] Palestine under the Moslems from A. D. 650 to 1500. Translated from the Works of the Medieval Arab Geographers. London: Watt, 1890, 604 pp., esp 3-57, 138-223. Reprinted, Beirut: Khayats, 1965. [An abridgment exists entitled History of Jerusalem under the Moslems, 344 pp., with no ascription of place or date (probably Jerusalem, circa 1980).]

McGrigor, A. B. [238] Contributions towards an Index of Passages Bearing upon the Topography of Jerusalem from Writings prior to the Eleventh Century. Glasgow: Maclehose, 1876, 90 pp.

Mallon, Alexis. [239] "Cité de David," in H. Cazelles and A. Feuillet (eds.), Supplément au Dictionnaire de la Bible, 2. Paris: Letouzey et Ané, 1934, 330-341.

Mankin, J. H. [240] "Survey of the Old City of Jerusalem, 1865 and 1935," Palestine Exploration Quarterly, (1969), 37-39.

Marmardjii, A.-S. [241] Textes géographiques arabes sur la Palestine. Paris: Gabalda, 1951, 267 pp.

Masterman, Ernest W. Gurney. [242] "Jerusalem: Name, Natural Site, Climate and Diseases," in J. Hastings (ed.), Dictionary of Christ and the Gospels, 1. New York: Scribner's, 1906, 849-851.

Masterman, Ernest W. Gurney. [243] "On the History of the Ophel Hill," Palestine Exploration Fund, Quarterly Statement, (1929), 138-149.

Masterman, Ernest W. Gurney. [244] "The Ophel Hill," Palestine Exploration Fund, Quarterly Statement, (1923), 37-45.

Mazar, Benjamin. [245] "City of David and Mount Zion," in J. Aviram (ed.), Jerusalem through the Ages. Jerusalem: Israel Exploration Society, 1968, 1-11 (Hebrew), 58 (English summary).

Meistermann, Barnabé. [246] La ville David. Paris: Picard, 1905, 248 pp.

Meyer, Hermann M. Z. [247] "Jerusalem / Cartography," in Encyclopaedia Judaica, 9. Jerusalem: Macmillan, 1971, 1542-1549. Also in Israel Pocket Library: Jerusalem. Jerusalem: Keter, 1973, 262-270.

Milik, J. T. [248] "L' ostracon de l' ophel et la topographie de Jérusalem," Revue biblique, 66 (1959), 550-553.

Milik, J. T. [249] "Le rouleau de cuivre de Qumran (3Q15): Traduction et commentaire topographique," Revue biblique, 66 (1959), 321-357.

Miquel, André. [250] "Jérusalem arabe: Notes de topographie historique," Bulletin d' études orientales, 16 (1958/1960), 7-13.

Mommert, Carl. [251] Topographie des alten Jerusalem, 4 vols. Leipzig: Haberland, 1902-1907.

Mühlau, Ferdinand. [252] "Beitrage zur Palästinaliteratur im Anschluss an Röhricht's Bibliotheca geographica palaestinae," Zeitschrift des deutschen Palästina-Vereins, 16 (1893), 209-234.

Nebenzahl, Kenneth. [252A] Maps of the Holy Land: Images of Terra Sancta through Two Millennia. New York: Abbeville Press, 1986, 164 pp. [Crusader Maps, 11, 32; Madeba Mosaic, 24-25; Marino Sanuto and Petrus Vesconte's Map; Bernard von Breitenbach's Map, 63-68; Buenting's Cloverleaf, 88-89; Christian von Adrichom's Map, 90-91.]

Neumann, W. A. [253] "Beitrage zur Kenntnis der Palästina-Literatur: Anschluss an Röhricht's Bibliotheca geographica palaestinae," Zeitschrift des deutschen Palästina-Vereins, 14 (1893), 113-134.

Nevin, J. C. [254] "Notes on the Topography of Jerusalem: 1. The Site of Acra; 2. General Questions," Palestine Exploration Fund, Quarterly Statement, (1906), 206-213, 278-286.

Olshausen, Justus. [255] Zur Topographie des alten Jerusalem. Kiel: Schwers Wittwe, 1833, 76 pp.

Pace, Giuseppe. [256] "Il colle della città di Davide," Bibbia e Oriente, 25 (1983), 171-182.

Pace, Giuseppe. [257] "Gebus sul monte (Sion) e Shalem sul colle (Ofel, distinto ancora da Moria)." Bibbia e Oriente, 20, (1978), 213-224.

Pfeiffer, Charles F. [258] "The City of Jerusalem," in Baker's Bible Atlas. Grand Rapids: Baker, 1961, 149-154.

Pierotti, Ermete. [259] Topographie ancienne et moderne de Jérusalem. Lausanne: Howard and Delisle, 1869, 178 pp.

Pitcairn, D. Lee. [260] "The Identification of the City of David," Palestine Exploration Fund, Quarterly Statement, (1895), 342-345.

Pope, H. [261] "Recent Light on Jerusalem Topography," Dublin Review, 151 (1912), 277-298.

Rengstorf, Karl Heinrich. See Dalman, Gustaf. [160]

Ritter, Carl. [262] The Comparative Geography of Palestine and the Sinaitic Peninsula, 4. Trans. by W. L. Gage. New York: Appleton, 1866, 1-212.

Robinson, Edward and Smith, Eli. [263] "Jerusalem: Topography and Antiquities," in Biblical Researches in Palestine and the Adjacent Regions: Journal of Travels in the Year 1838, 1. Boston: Crocker and Brewster / London: John Murray, 2nd edn., 1860, 251-364.

Robinson, Edward and Smith, Eli. [264] "Jerusalem-- Topography and Antiquities," in Later Biblical Researches in Palestine and the Adjacent Regions: A Journal of Travels in the Year 1852. Boston: Crocker and Brewster / London: John Murray, 2nd. edn., 1857, 203-263.

Röhricht, Reinhold. See Mühlau, Ferdinand. [252]

Röhricht, Reinhold. See Neumann, W. A. [253]

Röhricht, Reinhold. [265] Bibliotheca geographica palaestinae. Chronologisches Verzeichniss der auf die Geographie des heiligen Landes bezüglichen Literatur von 333 bis 1878 und Versuch einer Cartographie. Berlin: Reuther, 1890, 744 pp; reprinted with corrections, additions, and forward by D. H. K. Amiran, Jerusalem: Universitas, 1963, 816 pp.

Röhricht, Reinhold. [266] "Karten und Pläne zur Palästinakunde aus dem 7 bis 16 Jahrhundert," Zeitschrift des deutschen Palästina-Vereins, 14 (1891), 8-11, 87-92, 137-141; 15 (1892),34-39; 18 (1895), 173-182.

Röhricht, Reinhold. [267] "Marino Sando sen. als Kartograph Palästinas," Zeitschrift des deutschen Palästina-Vereins, 21 (1898), 84-126.

Röhricht, Reinhold. [268] "Die Palästinakarte Bernard von Breitenbach's," Zeitschrift des deutschen Palästina-Vereins, 24 (1901), 129-135.

Röhricht, Reinhold. [269] "Zur Bibliotheca Palaestinae," Zeitschrift des deutschen Palästina-Vereins, 16 (1893), 269-296.

Ron, Zvi. [270] "Agricultural Terraces in the Judaean Mountains," Israel Exploration Journal, 16 (1966), 111-122.

Rosen, Georg. [271] Das Haram von Jerusalem und der Tempelplatz des Moria: Eine Untersuchung über die Identität beider Stätten. Gotha: Besser, 1866, 65 pp.

Rosen, Georg. [272] "Topographisches aus Jerusalem," Zeitschrift der deutschen Morgenländischen Gesellschaft, 14 (1860), 606-621.

Rust, H. [273] "Warum Jeruschalajim?" Theologische Literaturzeitung, 74 (1949), 627-629. [Dual form of name reflects earthly and heavenly cities.]

St. Clair, George. [274] "Jerusalem Topography," Palestine Exploration Fund, Quarterly Statement, (1894), 150-151.

St. Clair, George. [275] "Millo, House of Millo, and Silla," Palestine Exploration Fund, Quarterly Statement, (1891), 187-189.

de Saulcy, L. Félicien J. C. [276] Jérusalem. Paris: Morel, 1882, 336 pp.

Sayce, Archibald. H. [277] "Prae-Exilic Jerusalem," Palestine Exploration Fund, Quarterly Statement, (1884), 171-175.

Sayce, Archibald. H. [278] "The Site of Zion," Palestine Exploration Fund, Quarterly Statement, (1884), 248-250.

Sayce, Archibald. H. [279] "The Topography of Prae-Exilic Jerusalem," Palestine Exploration Fund, Quarterly Statement, (1883), 215-223.

Schattner, Isaac. [280] "The Morphology of the Jerusalem Hills," in Judah and Jerusalem: The Twelfth Archaeological Convention. Jerusalem: Israel Exploration Society, 1957, 137-143 (Hebrew), vii (English summary).

Schick, Conrad. [281] "Die Baugeschichte der Stadt Jerusalem in kurzen Umrissen von den ältesten Zeiten bis auf die Gegenwart dargestellt," Zeitschrift des deutschen Palästina-Vereins, 16 (1893), 237-246; 17 (1894), 1-24, 75-88, 165-179, 251-276.

Schick, Conrad. [282] "Rock Levels in Jerusalem," Palestine Exploration Fund, Quarterly Statement, (1890), 20-21.

Schick, Conrad. [283] "Studien über die Einwohnerzahl des alten Jerusalem," Zeitschrift des deutschen Palästina-Vereins, 4 (1881), 211-221.

Schick, Conrad and Benzinger, Immanuel. [284] "Namenliste und Erläuterungen zu Baurath C. Schick's Karte der näheren Umgebung von Jerusalem," Zeitschrift des deutschen Palästina-Vereins, 18 (1895), 149-172.

Schick, Conrad and Benzinger, Immanuel. [285] "Namenliste und Erläuterungen zu Baurath Dr. C. Schick's Karte der weiteren Umgebung von Jerusalem," Zeitschrift des deutschen Palästina-Vereins,, 19 (1896), 145-220.

Schiller, Ely. [286] Jerusalem and the Holy Land in Old Engravings and Illustrations (1483-1800). Jerusalem: Ariel, 1981, 200 pp. [Numerous early maps.]

Schmelz, Uziel O. [287] "The Evolution of Jerusalem's Population," in D. H. K. Amiran, A. Shachar, and I. Kimhi (eds.), Urban Geography of Jerusalem: A Companion Volume to the Atlas of Jerusalem. Jerusalem: Israel Academy of Sciences and Humanities, Hebrew University, Israel Exploration Society, Massada Press / Berlin: de Gruyter, 1973, 53-75.

Shachar, Arie. See Amiran, David H. K.; Shachar, Arie; and Kimhi, Israel (eds.). [85]

Shachar, Arie. [288] "The Functional Structure of Jerusalem," in D. H. K. Amiran, A. Shachar, and I. Kimhi (eds.), Urban Geography of Jerusalem: A Companion Volume to the Atlas of Jerusalem. Jerusalem: Israel Academy of Sciences and Humanities, Hebrew University, Israel Exploration Society, Massada Press / Berlin: de Gruyter, 1973, 76-90.

Simons, Jan. [289] "The City of Josephus and the City of David, / The South-Eastern Hill," in Jerusalem in the Old Testament: Researches and Theories. Studia Francisci Scholten Memoriae Dicata, 1. Leiden: Brill, 1952, 34-225.

Simons, Jan. [290] "Jerusalem in the Old Testament," in The Geographical and Topographical Texts of the Old Testament. Studia Francisci Scholten Memoriae Dicata, 2. Leiden: Brill, 1959, 530-534. [An index of passages cited in various parts of the book.]

Smith, Eli. See Robinson, Edward and Smith, Eli. [263-264]

Smith, George Adam. [291] Jerusalem: The Topography, Economics, and History from the Earliest Times to A. D. 70, 2 vols. New York: Armstrong / London:

Hodder and Stoughton, 1907-1908, 498 + 631 pp. Reprinted with prolegomenon by S. Yeivin, New York: KTAV, 2 vols in 1, 1972. Reprinted in two vols: 1. Topography, Economics and Historical Geography; 2. History from the Earliest Times to A. D. 70. Jerusalem: Ariel / Warminster, England: Aris and Phillips, 1979, 498 + 631 pp.

Smith, George Adam; Smith, W. Robertson; and Conder, Claude. R. [292] "Jerusalem," in T. K. Cheyne and J. S. Black (eds.), Encyclopaedia Biblica, 2. New York: Macmillan, 1901, 2407-2432.

Smith, W. Robertson. See Smith, George Adam; Smith, W. Robertson; and Conder, C. R. [292]

Spiess, F. [293] Das Jerusalems des Josephus: Beitrag zur Topographie der heiligen Stadt. Berlin: Habel, 1881, 112 pp.

Steinschneider, M. [294] "Zur Geschichte und Topographie Jerusalems," Zeitschrift der deutschen Morgenländischen Gesellschaft, 5 (1851), 380-383.

Steve, M.-A. See Vincent, Louis-Hugues and Steve, M.-A. [313]

Student Map Manual: [295] Historical Geography of the Bible Lands. Jerusalem: Pictorial Archive, 1979, section 14.

Stuhlmueller, Carroll. [296] "The Population of Ancient Jerusalem," The Bible Today, 97 (1978), 1697-1701.

Tenz, J. M. [297] "The Akra of the Greeks," Palestine Exploration Fund, Quarterly Statement, (1907), 290-293.

Tenz, J. M. [298] "Millo and the City of David," Palestine Exploration Fund, Quarterly Statement, (1905), 165-167.

Tenz, J. M. [299] "Notes and Queries, 2: Two Places Called Akra," Palestine Exploration Fund, Quarterly Statement, (1906), 158.

Tenz, J. M. [300] "Zion and Ophel," Palestine Exploration Fund, Quarterly Statement, (1885), 121-123.

Thrupp, Joseph F. [301] Ancient Jerusalem: A New Investigation into the History, Topography, and the Plan of the City. Cambridge: Macmillan, 1855, 416 pp.

Tobler, Titus. [302] Bibliographia geographica palaestinae: Kritische Übersicht, Gedruckter und Ungedruckter Beschreibungen der Reisen in Heilige Land. Leipzig: S. Hirzel, 1867; reprinted, Amsterdam: Meridian, 1964, 265 pp.

Tobler, Titus. [303] "Die neuesten Leistungen in der Planographie von Jerusalem," Zeitschrift der deutschen Morgenländischen Gesellschaft, 7 (1853), 223-228.

Tobler, Titus. [304] Zwei Bücher Topographie von Jerusalem und seiner Umgebungen, 1: Die Heilige Stadt, mit artistischen Beilagen. Berlin: Reimer, 1853, 677 pp.

Tristram, H. B. [305] "Jerusalem," in The Topography of the Holy Land. London: SPCK, 1871, 123-167.

Tushingham, A. Douglas. [306] "Jerusalem," in D. Baily and A. D. Tushingham, Atlas of the Biblical World. New York: World, 1971, 155-166.

Tushingham, A. Douglas. [307] "Yerushalayim," in R. Moorey and P. Parr (eds.), Archaeology in the Levant: Essays for Kathleen Kenyon. Warminster: Aris and Phillips, 1978, 183-193. [Dual form of name reflects upper and lower cities.]

Van Selms, A. [308] "The Origin of the Name Tyropoeon in Jerusalem," Zeitschrift für die alttestamentliche Wissenschaft, 91 (1979), 170-176.

Vilnay, Zev. [309] "Jerusalem and Surroundings," in The Holy Land in Old Prints and Maps. Trans. by E. Vilnay and M. Nurock. Jerusalem: Rubin Mass, 2nd edn., 1965, 41-127.

Vincent, Louis-Hugues. [310] "Acra," Revue biblique, 43 (1934), 205-236.

Vincent, Louis-Hugues. [311] "Les noms de Jérusalem," Memnon, 6 (1913), 87-124.

Vincent, Louis-Hugues. [312] "The P. E. F. Map of Ophel," Palestine Exploration Fund, Quarterly Statement, (1926), 160-162.

Vincent, Louis-Hugues and Steve, M.-A. [313] "Site général de la ville antique; description de Josèphe," in Jérusalem de l' Ancient Testament, l. Paris: Gabalda, 1954, 1-26.

de Vogüé, Melchior. [314] Le temple de Jérusalem: Monographie du haram ech-cherif suivi d' un essai sur la topographie de la Ville Sainte. Paris: Noblet et Baudry, 1864, 142 pp.

Vogt, Ernst. [315] "Das Wachstum des alten Stadtgebietes von Jerusalem," Biblica, 48 (1967), 337-358.

H. B. S. W. [316] "City of David," Palestine Exploration Fund, Quarterly Statement, (1881), 327-328.

H. B. S. W. [317] "The 'City of David' Not the Same as the 'City (Jerusalem) of David's Time,'" Palestine Exploration Fund, Quarterly Statement, (1887), 250-252.

H. B. S. W. [318] "The 'City of David' only a Part of Jerusalem," Palestine Exploration Fund, Quarterly Statement, (1885), 57-58.

H. B. S. W. [319] "The Size of the 'City of David,'" Palestine Exploration Fund, Quarterly Statement, (1887), 55-57.

Walther, J. [320] Étude historique de la topographie de Jérusalem pendant les temps bibliques. Genève: Beroud, 1880, 38 pp.

Warren, Charles. [321] "The Comparative Holiness of Mounts Zion and Moriah," Palestine Exploration Fund, Quarterly Statement, (1869/1870), 76-88.

Warren, Charles. [322] "Hinnom, Valley of," in J. Hastings (ed.), Dictionary of the Bible, 2. New York: Scribner's, 1898, 385-388.

Warren, Charles. [323] "Jehoshaphat, Valley of," in J. Hastings (ed.), Dictionary of the Bible, 2. New York: Scribner's, 1898, 561-562.

Wasserstein, D. [324] "False Bearings in the Topography of Jerusalem," Notes and Queries, 30 (1983), 299-300.

Watson, Charles M. [325] "The Acra," Palestine Exploration Fund, Quarterly Statement, (1906), 50-54.

Watson, Charles M. [326] "The Site of the Acra," Palestine Exploration Fund, Quarterly Statement, (1907), 204-214.

Weill, Raymond. [327] "The P. E. F. Map of Ophel," Palestine Exploration Fund, Quarterly Statement, (1926), 171-175.

Weitz, J. [328] "The Roads in the Hills of Jerusalem," in J. Aviram (ed.), Jerusalem through the Ages. Jerusalem: Israel Exploration Society, 1968, 235-237 (Hebrew), 66 (English summary).

Wieland, David J. [329] "Hinnom, Valley of," in G. W. Bromiley (ed.), The International Standard Bible Encyclopedia, 2. Grand Rapids: Eerdmans, 1982, 717-718.

Wilkinson, John. [330] "The Streets of Jerusalem," Levant, 7 (1975), 118-136.

Wilson, Charles W. [331] "Ancient Jerusalem: Acra North Not South of the Temple," Palestine Exploration Fund, Quarterly Statement, (1893), 164-166.

Wilson, Charles W. [332] Ordnance Survey of Jerusalem, Made with the Sanction of Earl de Grey and Ripon, in 3 parts. Preface by Henry James. London: Lord's Commissioners of Her Majesty's Treasury, 1865, 90 + 26 pp., 39 pl., 5 maps; facsimile reproduction with introduction by Dan Bahat, Jerusalem: Ariel, 1980, 2 vols.

Wright, G. Ernest and Filson, Floyd V. [333] "The History of Jerusalem," in The Westminster Historical Atlas to the Bible. Philadelphia: Westminster, rev. edn., 1956, 105-109.

Yeivin, Samuel. See Smith, George Adam. [291]

Zimmermann, C. [334] Karten und Plan zur Topographie des alten Jerusalem. Basel: Spittler, 1876, 40 pp.

Three

Archaeological Excavations and Studies

Aarons, Leroy and Feinsilver, Goldie. [335] "Jerusalem Couple Excavates under Newly Built Home in Search of their Roots," Biblical Archaeology Review, 8/2 (1982), 44-49

Abel, Félix-M. See Vincent, Louis-Hugues and Abel, Félix-M. [569]

Adler, Cyrus. [336] "The Cotton Grotto, an Ancient Quarry in Jerusalem," Jewish Quarterly Review, 8 (1896), 384-391.

Adler, Cyrus. [337] "The Cotton Grotto, an Ancient Quarry in Jerusalem, with a Note on the Ancient Methods of Quarrying," in G. A. Kohut (ed.), Semitic Studies (Memorial Volume to A. Kohut). Berlin: Calvary, 1897, 73-82.

Amiran, Ruth. [338] "The Tumuli West of Jerusalem: Survey and Excavation," Israel Exploration Journal, 8 (1958), 205-227.

Amiran, Ruth and Eitan, Avraham. [339] "Excavations in the Courtyard of the Citadel, Jerusalem, 1968-1969," Israel Exploration Journal, 20 (1970), 9-17.

Amiran, Ruth and Eitan, Avraham. [340] "Excavations in the Jerusalem Citadel," Qadmoniot, 3 (1970), 64-66 (Hebrew).

Amiran, Ruth and Eitan, Avraham. [341] "Excavations in the Jerusalem Citadel," in Y. Yadin (ed.), Jerusalem Revealed: Archaeology in the Holy City, 1968-1974. New Haven and London: Yale University Press and the Israel Exploration Society, 1976, 52-54.

Amiran, Ruth and Eitan, Avraham. [342] "Herod's Palace," Israel Exploration Journal, 22 (1972), 50-51.

Amiran, Ruth and Eitan, Avraham. [343] "Jérusalem: Cour de la Citadelle," Revue biblique, 77 (1970), 564-570.

Ap-Thomas, D. R. [344] "Excavations in Jerusalem (Jordan), 1962," Zeitschrift für die alttestamentliche Wissenschaft, 74 (1962), 321-322.

Ap-Thomas, D. R. [345] "Jerusalem," in D. W. Thomas (ed.), Archaeology and Old Testement Studies: Jubilee Volume of the Society for Old Testament Studies, 1917-1967. Oxford: Clarendon, 1967, 277-295.

Avi-Yonah, Michael. See Mayer, Leo A. and Avi-Yonah, Michael. [483]

Avi-Yonah, Michael. [346] "Excavations in Jerusalem, Review and Evaluation," in Y. Yadin (ed.), Jerusalem Revealed: Archaeology in the Holy City, 1968-1974.

New Haven and London: Yale University Press and the Israel Exploration Society, 1976, 21-24

Avi-Yonah, Michael. [347] "Jerusalem," in Israel Pocket Library: Archaeology. Jerusalem: Keter, 1974, 121-141.

Avi-Yonah, Michael. [348] "Jerusalem in Archaeology and History," in J. M. Oestrreicher and A. Sinai (eds.), Jerusalem. New York: John Day, 1974, 3-18.

Avigad, Nahman. [349] Archaeological Discoveries in the Jewish Quarter of Jerusalem, Second Temple Period. Israel Museum Catalogue, 144. Jerusalem: Israel Museum, 1976, 26 pp. (English), + 23 pp. (Hebrew).

Avigad, Nahman. [350] Discovering Jerusalem. Nashville: Thomas Nelson, 1983, 270 pp.

Avigad, Nahman. [351] "Excavations in the Jewish Quarter of the Old City," Qadmoniot, 5 (1972), 91-101 (Hebrew).

Avigad, Nahman. [352] "Excavations in the Jewish Quarter of the Old City, Jerusalem," Israel Exploration Journal, 20 (1970), 1-8, 129-140; 22 (1972), 193-200; 25 (1975), 260-261; 27 (1977), 55-57, 145-151; 28 (1978), 200-201; 29 (1979), 123-124; 32 (1982), 158-159.

Avigad, Nahman. [353] "Jerusalem-- "The City Full of People," in H. Shanks and B. Mazar (eds.), Recent Archaeology in the Land of Israel. Washington, DC: Biblical Archaeology Society / Jerusalem: Israel Exploration Society, 1985, 129-140.

Avigad, Nahman. [354] "Jérusalem: Quartier juif," Revue biblique, 77 (1970), 570-572; 80 (1973), 573-579; 84 (1977), 416-418.

Bagatti, Bellarmino. [355] "Nuovi elementi di scavo alla 'torre' del Sion (1895, 1902-1903 e 1969)," Studii Biblici Franciscani, Liber Annuus, 20 (1970), 224-246.

Bahat, Dan. [356] "Jérusalem: Jardin arménien," Revue biblique, 78 (1971), 598-599.

Bahat, Dan. [357] Selected Plans of Historical Sites and Monumental Buildings. Jerusalem: Ariel, 1980, 126 pp.

Bahat, Dan and Broshi, Magen. [358] "Excavations in the Armenian Garden," Qadmoniot, 5 (1972), 102-103 (Hebrew).

Bahat, Dan and Broshi, Magen. [359] "Excavations in the Armenian Garden," in Y. Yadin (ed.), Jerusalem Revealed: Archaeology in the Holy City, 1968-1974. New Haven and London: Yale University Press and the Israel Exploration Society, 1976, 55-56.

Baumann, Emile. [360] "Die Ophelfunde von 1909-11 (auf Grund von H. Vincents Bericht)," Zeitschrift des deutschen Palästina-Vereins, 36 (1913), 1-27.

3/Archaeological Excavations and Studies

Be'er, Haim. [361] "Stones in Jerusalem," in E. Shaltiel (ed.), Jerusalem in the Modern Period: Yaacov Herzog Memorial Volume. Jerusalem: Yad Izhaq Ben-Zvi and Ministry of Defence, 1981, 455-472 (Hebrew), xvi (English summary).

Bellows, John. [362] "Chisel-Drafted Stones at Jerusalem," Palestine Exploration Fund, Quarterly Statement, (1896), 219-223.

Ben-Dov, Meir. [363] "Archaeological Excavation Near the Temple Mount," Christian News from Israel, 22 (1972), 135-142.

Ben-Dov, Meir. [364] "Fragment of a Hebrew Inscription from the First Temple Period on the Ophel," Qadmoniot, 17 (1984), 109-111 (Hebrew). [English summary in Old Testament Abstracts, 8 (1985), 236.]

Ben-Dov, Meir. [365] In the Shadow of the Temple: The Discovery of Ancient Jerusalem. Trans. by Ina Friedman. Jerusalem: Keter / New York: Harper and Row, 1982, 380 pp.

Benzinger, Immanuel. [366] "Researches in Palestine: Jerusalem," in H. V. Hilprecht (ed.), Explorations in Bible Lands during the 19th Century. Philadelphia: Holman, 1903, 596-606.

Besant, Walter. See Committee of the Palestine Exploration Fund [Besant, Walter]: [394-5]

Besant, Walter. [368] "The Excavations at Jerusalem," in Palestine Exploration Fund. Twenty-One Year's Work in the Holy Land: A Record and a Summary, June 22, 1865-June 22, 1886. London: Richard Bentley, 1886, 48-63.

Besant, Walter. [369] "The Excavations at Jerusalem," in Palestine Exploration Fund. Thirty Year's Work in the Holy Land: A Record and a Summary, 1865-1895. London: Watt, 1895, 52-67.

Bliss, Frederick J. See Conder, Claude R. [398]

Bliss, Frederick J. See Tufnell, Olga. [545]

Bliss, Frederick J. See Vincent, Louis-Hugues. [555]

Bliss, Frederick J. [370] "Excavations at Jerusalem," Palestine Exploration Fund, Quarterly Statement, (1894), 169-175.

Bliss, Frederick J. [371] "Second Report on the Excavations at Jerusalem," Palestine Exploration Fund, Quarterly Statement, (1894), 243-257.

Bliss, Frederick J. [372] "Third Report on the Excavations at Jerusalem," Palestine Exploration Fund, Quarterly Statement, (1895), 9-25.

Bliss, Frederick J. [373] "Fourth Report on the Excavations at Jerusalem," Palestine Exploration Fund, Quarterly Statement, (1895), 97-108. The fifth report in this series was published by Dickie, Archibald C. [413].

Bliss, Frederick J. [374] "Sixth Report on the Excavations at Jerusalem," Palestine Exploration Fund, Quarterly Statement, (1895), 305-320.

Bliss, Frederick J. [375] "Seventh Report on the Excavations at Jerusalem," Palestine Exploration Fund, Quarterly Statement, (1896), 9-22.

Bliss, Frederick J. [376] "Eighth Report of the Excavations at Jerusalem," Palestine Exploration Fund, Quarterly Statement, (1896), 109-122.

Bliss, Frederick J. [377] "Ninth Report of the Excavations at Jerusalem," Palestine Exploration Fund, Quarterly Statement, (1896), 208-213.

Bliss, Frederick J. [378] "Tenth Report of the Excavations at Jerusalem," Palestine Exploration Fund, Quarterly Statement, (1896), 298-305.

Bliss, Frederick J. [379] "Eleventh Report of the Excavations at Jerusalem," Palestine Exploration Fund, Quarterly Statement, (1897), 11-26.

Bliss, Frederick J. [380] "Twelfth Report of the Excavations at Jerusalem," Palestine Exploration Fund, Quarterly Statement, (1897), 91-102.

Bliss, Frederick J. [381] "Thirteenth Report of the Excavations at Jerusalem," Palestine Exploration Fund, Quarterly Statement, (1897), 173-181.

Bliss, Frederick J. [382] "Fourteenth Report of the Excavations at Jerusalem," Palestine Exploration Fund, Quarterly Statement, (1897), 260-268.

Bliss, Frederick J. [383] "The Palestine Exploration Fund," in The Development of Palestine Exploration. The Ely Lectures for 1903. New York: Scribner's, 1906, 255-287.

Bliss, Frederick J. and Dickie, Archibald C. [384] Excavations at Jerusalem, 1894-1897. London: Palestine Exploration Fund, 1898, 374 pp.

Brandenburg, E. [385] Die Felsarchitektur bei Jerusalem. Kirchhain, N.-L.: Schmersow / Jerusalem: Jewish Palestine Exploration Society, 1926, 303 pp.

Broshi, Magen. See Bahat, Dan and Broshi, Magen. [358-359]

Broshi, Magen. [386] "'Digging Up Jerusalem,'-- a Critique," Biblical Archaeology Review, 1/3 (September, 1975), 18-21.

Broshi, Magen. [387] "Excavations in the House of Caiaphas," Qadmoniot, 5 (1972), 104-107 (Hebrew).

Broshi, Magen. [388] "Excavations in the House of Caiaphas," in Y. Yadin (ed.), Jerusalem Revealed: Archaeology in the Holy City, 1968-1974. New Haven and London: Yale University Press and the Israel Exploration Society, 1976, 57-60.

Broshi, Magen. [389] "Excavations on Mt. Zion, 1971-1972," Israel Exploration Journal, 26 (1976), 81-88.

Broshi, Magen. [390] "Mount Zion," Israel Exploration Journal, 24 (1974), 285.

Broshi, Magen. [391] "Jérusalem: Quartier arménien," Revue biblique, 79 (1972), 578-581.

Callaway, Joseph. [392] "Jerusalem," in C. F. Pfeiffer (ed.), The Biblical World: A Dictionary of Biblical Archaeology. Grand Rapids: Baker, 1972, 309-323.

Clermont-Ganneau, Charles. [393] Archaeological Researches in Palestine during the Years 1873-1874, 1. Translated by Aubrey Stewart. London: Palestine Exploration Fund, 1896, 528 pp.

Committee of the Palestine Exploration Fund [Besant, Walter]: [394] Our Work in Palestine: Being an Account of the Different Expeditions Sent Out to the Holy Land by the Committee of the Palestine Exploration Fund since the Establishment of the Fund in 1865. New York: Scribner's, Welford, and Armstrong, 1873, 343 pp.

Committee of the Palestine Exploration Fund [Besant, Walter]: [395] Palestine Exploration Fund. Thirty Years' Work in the Holy Land: A Record and a Summary, 1865-1895. London: Watt, 1895, 256 pp.

Conder, Claude R. See St. Clair, George. [504]

Conder, Claude R. See Warren, Charles and Conder, Claude R. [578]

Conder, Claude R. [396] "Explorations in Jerusalem," Palestine Exploration Fund, Quarterly Statement, (1873), 13-22.

Conder, Claude R. [397] "Jerusalem," in J. Hastings (ed.), Dictionary of the Bible, 2. New York: Scribner's, 1898, 584-601.

Conder, Claude R. [398] "Notes on Dr. Bliss's Discoveries," Palestine Exploration Fund, Quarterly Statement, (1895), 330-331.

Conder, Claude R. [399] "Remarks on Masonry," Palestine Exploration Fund, Quarterly Statement, (1897), 145-147.

Conder, Claude R. [400] "Rock Indications at Jerusalem," Palestine Exploration Fund, Quarterly Statement, (1872), 165-173.

Cornfeld, Gaalyah. See Mazar, Benjamin. [493] Assisted by Gaalyah Cornfeld; David N. Freedman, consultant.

Couroyer, B. [401] "Menues trouvailles à Jérusalem," Revue biblique, 77 (1970), 248-252. [Seals, several periods.]

Crowfoot, John W. [402] "First Report of the New Excavations on Ophel," Palestine Exploration Fund, Quarterly Statement, (1927), 143-147.

Crowfoot, John W. [403] "Second Report of the Excavations in the Tyropoean Valley," Palestine Exploration Fund, Quarterly Statement, (1927), 178-183.

Crowfoot, John W. [404] "Excavations in the Tyropoean Valley," Palestine Exploration Fund, Quarterly Statement, (1928), 9-27. See also, Fitzgerald, Gerald M. [424]

Crowfoot, John W. [405] "Excavations on Ophel, 1928: Preliminary Report to December 8," Palestine Exploration Fund, Quarterly Statement, (1929), 9-16.

Crowfoot, John W. [406] "Excavations on Ophel, 1928: Preliminary Report," Palestine Exploration Fund, Quarterly Statement, (1929), 150-166

Crowfoot, John W. [407] "Ophel, 1928: Sixth Progress Report, Covering the Period from December 3 to 22, 1928," Palestine Exploration Fund, Quarterly Statement, (1929), 75-77.

Crowfoot, John W. [408] "Ophel Again," Palestine Exploration Quarterly, (1945), 66-104.

Crowfoot, John W. and Fitzgerald, Gerald M. [409] Excavations in the Tyropoean Valley, Jerusalem, 1927. Palestine Exploration Fund Annual, 5. London: Palestine Exploration Fund, 1929, 135 pp.

Dahlberg, Bruce T. [410] "Archaeological News from Jordan: Jerusalem," Biblical Archaeologist, 28 (1965), 22-26.

Dalman, Gustaf. [411] "The Search for the Temple Treasure at Jerusalem," Palestine Exploration Fund, Quarterly Statement, (1912), 35-39. [The Parker expedition.]

Department of Antiquities of Jordan: [412] "Jérusalem et environs," Revue biblique, 70 (1963), 420-421.

Dickie, Archibald C. See Bliss Frederick J. and Dickie, Archibald C. [384]

Dickie, Archibald C. [413] "Fifth Report on the Excavations at Jerusalem," Palestine Exploration Fund, Quarterly Statement, (1895), 235-248.

Dickie, Archibald C. [414] "Stone Dressing of Jerusalem, Past and Present," Palestine Exploration Fund, Quarterly Statement, (1897), 61-67.

Duncan, J. Garrow. See Macalister, R. A. Stewart and Duncan, J. Garrow. [474]

Duncan, J. Garrow. [415] "Inscribed Hebrew Objects from Ophel," Palestine Exploration Fund, Quarterly Statement, (1924), 180-186.

Duncan, J. Garrow. [416] "New Rock Chambers and Gallaries on Ophel," Palestine Exploration Fund, Quarterly Statement, (1926), 7-14.

Duncan, J. Garrow. [417] "Third Quarterly Report on the Excavation of the Eastern Hill of Jerusalem," Palestine Exploration Fund, Quarterly Statement, (1924), 124-136. For the first and second reports in this series, see Macalister, R. A. Stewart. [469-470].

Duncan, J. Garrow. [418] "Fourth Quarterly Report on the Excavation of the Eastern Hill of Jerusalem," Palestine Exploration Fund, Quarterly Statement, (1924), 163-180.

Duncan, J. Garrow. [419] "Fifth Quarterly Report on the Excavation of the Eastern Hill of Jerusalem," Palestine Exploration Fund, Quarterly Statement, (1925), 8-24.

Duncan, J. Garrow. [420] "Sixth Quarterly Report on the Excavation of the Eastern Hill of Jerusalem," Palestine Exploration Fund, Quarterly Statement, (1925), 134-139.

Dunkel, P. and Hanauer, James Edward. [421] "Excavations at Jerusalem," Palestine Exploration Fund, Quarterly Statement, (1902), 403-405.

Eitan, Avraham. See Amiran, Ruth and Eitan, Avraham. [339-343]

Ellis, Frank T. [422] "Mosaics on Mt. Zion," Palestine Exploration Fund, Quarterly Statement, (1891), 309-310.

Feinsilver, Goldie. See Aarons, Leroy and Feinsilver, Goldie. [335]

Fisher, D. See Snijders, C. and Fisher, D. [542]

Fitzgerald, Gerald M. See Crowfoot, J. W. and Fitzgerald, Gerald M. [409]

Fitzgerald, Gerald M. [423] "The City of David and the Excavations of 1913-1914," Palestine Exploration Fund, Quarterly Statement, (1922), 8-22.

Fitzgerald, Gerald M. [424] "Excavations in the Tyropoean Valley," Palestine Exploration Fund, Quarterly Statement, (1928), 122-125.

Flinders-Petrie, William M. [425] "Notes on the Chisel Marks on Rock Described by Herr Schick," Palestine Exploration Fund, Quarterly Statement, (1892), 26-27.

Freedman, David N. See Mazar, Benjamin. [493] Assisted by Gaalyah Cornfeld; David N. Freedman, consultant.

Friendly, A. [426] "Recent Excavations in Jerusalem," Expedition, 15/3 (Spring, 1973), 15-24.

Galling, Kurt. [427] "Archäologischer Jahresbericht: Jerusalem," Zeitschrift des deutschen Palästina-Vereins, 54 (1931), 80-92.

Gelzer, H. [428] "Inschrift vom Muristan," Zeitschrift des deutschen Palästina-Vereins, 17 (1894), 183-184.

Geva, Hillel. [429] "Excavations in the Citadel of Jerusalem, 1979-1980: Preliminary Report," Israel Exploration Journal, 33 (1983), 55-71.

Geva, Hillel. [430] "Excavations in the Jerusalem Citadel, 1979-1982," Qadmoniot, 15 (1982), 69-74 (Hebrew). [English summaries in Old Testament Abstracts, 6 (1983), 118; New Testament Abstracts, 27 (1983), 302.]

Gibson, Shimon. [431] "Jerusalem (North-east), Archaeological Survey," Israel Exploration Journal, 32 (1982), 156-157.

3/Archaeological Excavations and Studies

Gibson, Shimon. [432] "Lime Kilns in North-East Jerusalem," Palestine Exploration Quarterly, (1984), 94-102.

Gilbert, Martin. [433] "Archaeological Explorations, 1863-1914," in Jerusalem History Atlas. New York: Macmillan, 1977, 48-49.

Gilbert, Martin. [434] "Archaeological Explorations since 1914," in Jerusalem History Atlas. New York: Macmillan, 118-119.

Gonen, Rivka. [435] "Keeping Jerusalem's Past Alive," Biblical Archaeology Review, 7/4 (1981), 16-23. [On restoration projects.]

Guthe, Hermann. [436] "Ausgrabungen bei Jerusalem im Auftrage des deutschen Palästina-Vereins ausgeführt und beschreiben," Zeitschrift des deutschen Palästina-Vereins, 5 (1882), 7-204, 271-378.

Guthe, Hermann. [437] "Ausgrabungen in Jerusalem," Zeitschrift des deutschen Palästina-Vereins, 4 (1881), 115-119.

Guthe, Hermann. [438] "Greichische Inschriften aus Jerusalem," Zeitschrift des deutschen Palästina-Vereins, 233-234.

Hamilton, R. W. [439] "Note on Excavations at Bishop Gobat School, 1933," Palestine Exploration Fund, Quarterly Statement, (1935), 141-143.

Hanauer, James Edward. See Dunkel, P. and Hanauer, James Edward. [421]

Hanauer, James Edward. [440] "Sculptured Figures from the Muristan and Other Notes," Palestine Exploration Fund, Quarterly Statement, (1903), 77-86.

Israel, Felice. [441] "Le iscrizioni ebraico-antiche da Gerusalemme," in M. Borrmans, et al. (eds.), Gerusalemme. Brescia: Paideia, 1982, 163-180.

Israel Exploration Society: [442] Judah and Jerusalem: The Twelfth Archaeological Convention. Jerusalem: Israel Exploration Society, 1957, 208 pp. (Hebrew; English summary on pp. iv-viii.)

Israeli, Yael. [443] Jerusalem in History and Vision. Jerusalem: Israel Museum, 1968, 60 pp. [Exhibition; maps and photographs of artifacts and sites.]

James, Frances. [444] "The Revelation of Jerusalem: A Review of Archaeological Research," Expedition, 22/1 (1979), 33-43.

Jerusalem City Museum: [445] Finds from the Archaeological Excavations near the Temple Mount. Jerusalem: Israel Exploration Society, n. d, 60 pp.

Johns, C. N. [446] "The Citadel, Jerusalem: A Summary of Work since 1934," Quarterly of the Department of Antiquities in Palestine, 14 (1950), 121-189.

Johns, C. N. [447] "Recent Excavations at the Citadel," Palestine Exploration Quarterly, (1940), 36-58.

Kaplan, Mendel. See Shiloh, Yigal and Kaplan, Mendel. [534]

Kenyon, Kathleen M. [448] "Ancient Jerusalem," *Scientific American*, 213/1 (January, 1965), 84-91.

Kenyon, Kathleen M. [449] "Biblical Jerusalem," *Expedition*, 5/1 (Fall, 1962), 32-35.

Kenyon, Kathleen M. [450] *Digging Up Jerusalem*. New York: Praeger / London and Tonbridge: Benn, 1974, 288 pp.

Kenyon, Kathleen M. [451] "Excavations at Jerusalem, 1961," *Antiquity*, 36 (June, 1962), 93-96.

Kenyon, Kathleen M. [452] "Excavations in Jerusalem, 1961-1963," *Biblical Archaeologist*, 27 (1964), 34-52.

Kenyon, Kathleen M. [453] "Excavations in Jerusalem, 1961-1967," *Palestine Exploration Quarterly*, (1962), 72-89; (1963), 7-21; (1964), 7-18; (1965), 9-20; (1966), 73-88; (1967), 65-71; (1968), 97-109.

Kenyon, Kathleen M. [454] "Jerusalem," in *Archaeology in the Holy Land*. London and Tonbridge: Benn / New York: Norton, 4th edn., 1979, 332-335.

Kenyon, Kathleen M. [455] "Jerusalem," in J. Hastings (ed.), *Dictionary of the Bible*, revised edn. by F. C. Grant and H. H. Rowley. New York: Scribner's, 1963, 471-476.

Kenyon, Kathleen M. [456] "Jerusalem," *Israel Exploration Journal*, 17 (1967), 275-277.

Kenyon, Kathleen M. [457] "Jérusalem," *Revue biblique*, 69 (1962), 98-100; 70 (1963), 416-419; 71 (1964), 253-258; 72 (1965), 272-274; 73 (1966), 569-573; 75 (1968), 422-424.

Kenyon, Kathleen M. [458] *Jerusalem: Excavating 3000 Years of History*. New York: McGraw-Hill / London: Thames and Hudson, 1967, 211 pp.

Kenyon, Kathleen M. [459] "Jerusalem: History of the Excavations," in M. Avi-Yonah (ed.), *Encyclopedia of Archaeological Excavations in the Holy Land*, 2. Englewood Cliffs, NJ: Prentice-Hall, 1976, 591-597.

Knight, Nicholas. [460] "Notes and Queries: 1. Specimen of Rock from Solomon's Quarries; 2. Specimen of the 'Hard Jewish' Rock from Solomon's Quarries," *Palestine Exploration Fund, Quarterly Statement*, (1915), 50-51.

Landay, Jerry M. [461] "Jerusalem the Golden," in *Silent Cities, Sacred Stones: Archaeological Discovery in the Holy Land*. London: Weidenfeld and Nicolson, 1971, 217-233.

Laperrousaz, Ernest-Marie. [462] "Quelques apercus sur les dernières découvertes archéologiques faites à Jérusalem et aux alentours de la Ville Sainte," *Revue des études juives*, 131 (1972), 249-267.

Laperrousaz, Ernest-Marie. [463] "Quelques résultats récents des fouilles archéologiques conduites à Jérusalem at aux alentours de la Ville Sainte," Revue des études juives, 129 (1970), 145-159.

Lemaire, André. [464] "Les ostraca paleo-hebreaux des fouilles de l' Opel," Levant, 10 (1978), 156-161.

Lévy, Isaac. [465] "Jérusalem: Quartier nord," Revue biblique, 80 (19730, 579-581.

Livio, Jean-Bernard. [466] "Dix ans de fouilles à Jérusalem," Bible et Terre Sainte, 173 (1975), 4-17.

Macalster, R. A. Stewart. [467] "Address at the Annual General Meeting of the Palestine Exploration Fund," Palestine Exploration Fund, Quarterly Statement, (1924), 108-121.

Macalster, R. A. Stewart. [468] "Excavation and Topography," in A Century of Excavation in Palestine. London: Religious Tract Society, 1925, 76-142.

Macalister, R. A. Stewart. [469] "First Quarterly Report on the Excavation of the Eastern Hill of Jerusalem," Palestine Exploration Fund, Quarterly Statement, (1924), 9-23.

Macalister, R. A. Stewart. [470] "Second Quarterly Report on the Excavation of the Eastern Hill of Jerusalem," Palestine Exploration Fund, Quarterly Statement, (1924), 57-68. For the third-sixth reports in this series, see Duncan, J. Garrow. [417-418].

Macalister, R. A. Stewart. [471] "A Mosaic Newly Discovered at Jerusalem," Palestine Exploration Fund, Quarterly Statement, (1907), 293-295.

Macalister, R. A. Stewart. [472] "On a Remarkable Group of Cult-Objects from the Ophel Excavation," Palestine Exploration Fund, Quarterly Statement, (1924), 137-142.

Macalister, R. A. Stewart. [473] "A Rock-Cut Press near Jerusalem," Palestine Exploration Fund, Quarterly Statement, (1902), 398-403.

Macalister, R. A. Stewart and Duncan, J. G. [474] Excavations on the Hill of Ophel, Jerusalem, 1923-1925. Palestine Exploration Fund Annual, 4. London: Palestine Exploration Fund, 1926, 216 pp.

McCown, Chester C. [475] "Jerusalem," in The Ladder of Progress in Palestine: A Story of Archaeological Adventure. New York: Harper, 1943, 227-243.

Mallon, Alexis. [476] "Fouilles anglaises à l' Ophel," Biblica, 8 (1927), 489-492.

Mallon, Alexis. [477] Le fouilles anglaises à Jérusalem ancienne," Biblica, 6 (1925), 117-122.

Mallon, Alexis. [478] "Fouilles à la 'Cité de David,' au 'tombeau d' Absalom,'" Biblica, 5 (1924), 225-228.

Mallon, Alexis. [479] "Les fouilles de l' Ophel," Biblica, 2 (1921), 394-398.

Mare, W. Harold. [480] The Archaeology of the Jerusalem Area. Grand Rapids: Baker, 1987, 323 pp.

Margovsky, Y. [481] "Jérusalem: Bordj Kabrit et environs," Revue biblique, 78 (1971), 597-598.

Masterman, Ernest W. Gurney. [482] "On the History of the Ophel Hill," Palestine Exploration Fund, Quarterly Statement, (1929), 138-149.

Mayer, Leo A. and Avi-Yonah, Michael. [483] "Concise Bibliography of Excavations in Palestine: Jerusalem," Quarterly of the Department of Antiquities in Palestine, 1 (1932), 163-188.

Mazar, Benjamin. [484] "The Archaeological Excavations near the Temple Mount," in Y. Yadin (ed.), Jerusalem Revealed: Archaeology in the Holy City, 1968-1974. New Haven and London: Yale University Press and the Israel Exploration Society, 1976, 25-40.

Mazar, Benjamin. [485] "The Archaeological Excavations near the Temple Mount," in Israel Yearbook, 1977. Tel Aviv: Israrel Yearbook Publications, 1977, 97-101.

Mazar, Benjamin. [486] "Découverts archéologiques près des murs du Temple," La Terre Sainte, 8-9 (1973), 222-232.

Mazar, Benjamin. [487] The Excavations in the Old City of Jerusalem: Preliminary Report of the First Season, 1968. Jerusalem: Israel Exploration Society, 1969, 24 pp, 15 pls.

Mazar, Benjamin. [488] The Excavations in the Old City of Jerusalem near the Temple Mount: Preliminary Report of the Second and Third Seasons, 1969-1970. Jerusalem: Israel Exploration Society, 1971, 44 pp, 32 pls.

Mazar, Benjamin. [489] "Excavations near the Temple Mount," Qadmoniot, 5 (1972), 74-90 (Hebrew).

Mazar, Benjamin. [490] "The Excavations South and West of the Temple Mount in Jerusalem: The Herodian Period," Biblical Archaeologist, 33 (1970), 47-60.

Mazar, Benjamin. [491] "Herodian Jerusalem in the Light of the Excavations South and Southwest of the Temple Mount," Israel Exploration Journal, 28 (1978), 230-237.

Mazar, Benjamin. [492] "Le mur du Temple," Bible et Terre Sainte, 122 (1970), 8-15.

Mazar, Benjamin. [493] Assisted by Gaalyah Cornfeld; David N. Freedman, consultant. The Mountain of the Lord. Garden City, NY: Doubleday, 1975, 304 pp.

Merrill, Selah. [494] Ancient Jerusalem. New York: Fleming H. Revell, 1908; reprinted, New York: Arno, 1977, 419 pp.

Merrill, Selah. [495] "New Discoveries in Jerusalem," Palestine Exploration Fund, Quarterly Statement, (1885), 222-228; (1886), 21-24.

Murphy-O'Conner, Jerome. [496] "The City of Jerusalem," in The Holy Land: An Archaeological Guide from Earliest Times to 1700. Oxford: Oxford University Press, 1980, 11-111.

Naveh, Joseph. [497] "A Fragment of an Ancient Hebrew Inscription from the Ophel," Israel Exploration Journal, 32 (1982), 195-198.

Negbi, Ora and Oran, Eliézer. [498] "Jérusalem: Colline française," Revue biblique, 77 (1970), 572-573.

Negev, Avraham (ed.). [499] "Jerusalem," in Archaeological Encyclopedia of the Holy Land. London and Jerusalem: Weidenfeld and Nicolson, 1972, 166-172.

Oran, Eliézer. See Negbi, Ora and Oran, Eliézer. [498]

Oran, Eliézer. [500] "Jérusalem: Colline française," Revue biblique, 78 (1971), 429-430.

Rahmani, L. Y. [501] "Environs de Jérusalem," Revue biblique, 72 (1965), 573-574.

Rahmani, L. Y. [502] "Jérusalem," Revue biblique, 70 (1963), 586.

Rolla, Armando. [503] "Scavi archeologici a Gerusalemme nell' ultimo ventennio (1958-1978)," in M. Borrmans, et al. (eds.), Gerusalemme. Brescia: Paideia, 1982, 131-142.

St. Clair, George. [504] The Buried City of Jerusalem and General Exploration of Palestine: A Popular Exposition of Recent Discoveries Made by Colonel Sir Charles Wilson, Colonel Charles Warren, Captain Conder, and Others. London: Palestine Exploration Fund, 1887, 77 pp.

Schick, Conrad. See Flinders-Petrie, William M. [425]

Schick, Conrad. See Warren, Charles. [573]

Schick, Conrad. [505] "Chisel-Marks in the Cotton Grotto at Jerusalem," Palestine Exploration Fund, Quarterly Statement, (1892), 24-25.

Schick, Conrad. [506] "Discoveries North of the Damascus Gate," Palestine Exploration Fund, Quarterly Statement, (1890), 9-11.

Schick, Conrad. [507] "Jerusalem," Palestine Exploration Fund, Quarterly Statement, (1888), 20-22.

Schick, Conrad. [508] "A Jerusalem Chronicle," Palestine Exploration Fund, Quarterly Statement, (1887), 158-160.

Schick, Conrad. [509] "Muristan," Palestine Exploration Fund, Quarterly Statement, (1889), 113-114; (1895), 29, 108-109, 248-249.

Schick, Conrad. [510] "Neu entdecktes Columbarium am Berge des bösen Rathes bei Jerusalem," Zeitschrift des deutschen Palästina-Vereins, 8 (1885), 46-49.

Schick, Conrad. [511] "Neue Funde im Norden von Jerusalem," Zeitschrift des deutschen Palästina-Vereins, 2 (1879), 102-105.

Schick, Conrad. [512] "Notes from Jerusalem," Palestine Exploration Fund, Quarterly Statement, (1887), 151-158.

Schick, Conrad. [513] "The Quarter Bab Hytta, Jerusalem," Palestine Exploration Fund, Quarterly Statement, (1896), 128-131.

Schick, Conrad. [514] "Recent Excavations at Jerusalem," Palestine Exploration Fund, Quarterly Statement, (1877), 9-10.

Schick, Conrad. [515] "The Stones of Jerusalem," Palestine Exploration Fund, Quarterly Statement, (1887), 50-51.

Séjourné, Paul-M. [516] "Les fouilles de Jérusalem," Revue biblique, 6 (1897), 299-306, 464-466.

Shanks, Hershel. [517] "The City of David after Five Years of Digging: Yigal Shiloh Releases Preliminary Report on Excavations in Oldest Area of Jerusalem," Biblical Archaeology Review, 11/6 (Nov./Dec., 1985), 22-38.

Shanks, Hershel. [518] "New York Times Misrepresents Major Jerusalem Discovery: Unique Monumental Structure Inside Israelite Jerusalem Defies Explanation," Biblical Archaeology Review, 7/4 (July/Aug., 1981), 40-43.

Shanks, Hershel. [519] "Politics at the City of David," Biblical Archaeology Review, 7/6 (1981), 40-44.

Shanks, Hershel. [520] "Report from Jerusalem," Biblical Archaeology Review, 3/4 (1977), 14-25.

Shiloh, Yigal. See Shanks, Hershel. [517]

Shiloh, Yigal. [521] "The City of David: Excavation 1978," Biblical Archaeologist, 42 (1979), 165-171.

Shiloh, Yigal. [522] "The City of David Archaeological Project: The Third Season, 1980," Biblical Archaeologist, 44 (1981), 161-170.

Shiloh, Yigal. [523] "Excavating Jerusalem: The City of David," Archaeology, 33/6 (1980), 8-17.

Shiloh, Yigal. [524] Excavations at the City of David, 1. Qedem: Monographs of the Institute of Archaeology, Hebrew University, 19. Jerusalem: Hebrew University,1984, 31+ 34 + 41.

Shiloh, Yigal. [525] "A Hoard of Hebrew Bullae from the City of David," in Eretz-Israel: Archaeological, Historical, and Geographical Studies, 18. Jerusalem: Israel Exploration Society, 1985, 73-87 (Hebrew), 68* (English summary).

Shiloh, Yigal. [526] "Jerusalem: The City of David," Israel Exploration Journal, 28 (1978), 274-276; 29 (1979), 244-246; 30 (1980), 220-221; 32 (1982), 157-158; 33 (1983), 129-131; 34 (1984), 57-58; 35 (1985), 65-67, 301-303.

Shiloh, Yigal. [527] "Jérusalem (Ville de David), 1978," Revue biblique, 86 (1979), 126-130.

Shiloh, Yigal. [528] "New Excavations in the City of David," Qadmoniot, 12 (1979), 12-19 (Hebrew). [English summary in Old Testament Abstracts, 3 (1980), 18.]

Shiloh, Yigal. [529] "New Finds from the City of David Excavations (1981-1983)," Bulletin of the Anglo-Israel Archeological Society, (1983/1984), 26-29.

Shiloh, Yigal. [530] "Past and Present in Archaeological Research on the City of David," in H. Shanks and B. Mazar (eds.), Recent Archaeology in the Land of Israel. Washington, DC: Biblical Archaeology Society / Jerusalem: Israel Exploration Society, 1985, 149-157.

Shiloh, Yigal. [531] "A Table of the Major Excavations in Jerusalem," Qadmoniot, 1 (1968), 71-78 (Hebrew).

Shiloh, Yigal. [532] "Tables of Major Archaeological Activities in Jerusalem since 1863," in M. Avi-Yonah (ed.), Encyclopedia of Archaeological Excavations in the Holy Land, 2. Englewood Cliffs, NJ: Prentice-Hall, 642-647.

Shiloh, Yigal. [533] "Tables of Major Archaeological Activities in Jerusalem since 1863," in Y. Yadin (ed.), Jerusalem Revealed: Archaeology in the Holy City, 1968-1974. New Haven and London: Yale University Press and the Israel Exploration Society, 1976, 131-135

Shiloh, Yigal and Kaplan, Mendel. [534] "Digging in the City of David," Biblical Archaeology Review, 5/4 (July/August, 1979), 37-48.

Silberman, Neil Asher. [535] Digging for God and Country: Exporation, Archeology, and the Secret Struggle for the Holy Land, 1799-1917. New York: Knopf, 1982, 228 pp.

Silberman, Neil Asher. [536] "In Search of Solomon's Lost Treasures," Biblical Archaeology Review, 6/4 (July/August, 1980), 30-41. [The Parker expedition.]

Simons, Jan. [537] "Excavations on the South-Eastern Hill," in Jerusalem in the Old Testament: Researches and Theories. Leiden: Brill, 1952, 68-131.

Simons, Jan. [538] Jerusalem in the Old Testament: Researches and Theories. Studia Francisci Scholten Memoriae Dicta, 1. Leiden: Brill, 1952, 517 pp.

Simons, Jan. [539] "Jerusalem: Exploration, Past and Future," Oudtestamentische Studiën, 8 (1950), 66-84.

Simpson, William. [540] "The Royal Caverns or Quarries, Jerusalem," Palestine Exploration Fund, Quarterly Statement, (1869/1870), 373-379.

Sivan, R. and Solar, Giora. [541] "Discoveries in the Jerusalem Citadel, 1980-1984," Qadmoniot, 17 (1984), 111-117 (Hebrew). [English summary in Old Testament Abstracts, 8 (1985), 211.]

Snijders, C. and Fisher, D. [542] "Gli scavi archeologici a Gerusalemme," L' Architettura, 23 (1977), 110-122.

Solar, Giora. See Sivan, R. and Solar, Giora. [541]

Stager, Lawrence. [543] "The Archaeology of the East Slope of Jerusalem and the Terraces of the Kidron," Journal of Near Eastern Studies, 41 (1982), 111-121.

Steve, M.-A. See Vincent, Louis-Hugues and Steve, M.-A. [570]

Student Map Manual: [544] "Archaeology of Jerusalem: First Temple, Second Temple, and Byzantine Periods." in Historical Geography of the Bible Lands. Jerusalem: Pictorial Archive, 1979, section 14.

Tufnell, Olga. [545] "Excavators Progress: The Letters of F. J. Bliss, 1889-1900," Palestine Exploration Quarterly, (1965), 112-127.

Tushingham, A. Douglas. [546] "The Armenian Garden," Palestine Exploration Quarterly, (1967), 71-73; (1968), 109-111.

Tzaferis, Vassilios. [547] "Chronique archéologique: Jérusalem-- Giv'at Shaul," Revue biblique, 75 (1968), 405.

Tzaferis, Vassilios. [548] "A Hashmonean Fort in Jerusalem," Qadmoniot, 3 (1970), 95-97 (Hebrew).

Tzaferis, Vassilios. [549] "Tower and Fortress near Jerusalem," Israel Exploration Journal, 24 (1974), 84-94.

de Vaux, Roland. [550] "Jérusalem (Ophel)," Revue biblique, 69 (1962), 98-100; 70 (1963), 416-419; 71 (1964), 253-258.

Vincent, Louis-Hugues. See Baumann, Emile. [360]

Vincent, Louis-Hugues. [551] "Aux cavernes royales," Revue biblique, 34 (1925), 587-588.

Vincent, Louis-Hugues. [552] "A travers Jérusalem, notes archéologiques," Revue biblique, 17 (1908), 267-279.

Vincent, Louis-Hugues. [553] "La Cité de David d' apres les fouilles de 1913-1914," Revue biblique, 30 (1921), 410-433, 541-569.

Vincent, Louis-Hugues. [554] "Fouille à l' angle N.-E. de Jérusalem," Revue biblique, 22 (1913), 101-103.

Vincent, Louis-Hugues. [555] "Les fouilles de Jérusalem d' apres M. Bliss," Revue biblique, 5 (1896), 241-247.

Vincent, Louis-Hugues. [556] "Les fouilles de la Cité de David," Revue biblique, 35 (1926), 123-124.

Vincent, Louis-Hugues. [557] "Les fouilles prés du Cénacle," Revue biblique, 11 (1902), 274-275.

Vincent, Louis-Hugues. [558] "Exploration de la Cité de David," Revue biblique, 33 (1924), 429-431.

Vincent, Louis-Hugues. [559] "Jérusalem," in André Robert (ed.), Supplément au Dictionnaire de la Bible, 4. Paris: Letouzey et Ané, 1949, 897-966.

Vincent, Louis-Hugues. [560] "Jérusalem: Canalisation byzantine et arabe au nord de la ville," Revue biblique, 23 (1914), 426-429.

Vincent, Louis-Hugues. [561] "Jérusalem: Au quartier juif," Revue biblique, 34 (1925), 585-586.

Vincent, Louis-Hugues. [562] Jérusalem: Glanures archéologiques," Revue biblique, 33 (1924), 431-437.

Vincent, Louis-Hugues. [563] Jérusalem: Recherches de topographie, d' archéologie et d' histoire, 1: Jérusalem antique. Paris: Gabalda, 1912, 196 pp, 19 pls.

Vincent, Louis-Hugues. [564] Jérusalem sous terre: Les récentes fouilles d' Ophel. London: Horace Cox, 1911, 45 pp, 34 pls.

Vincent, Louis-Hugues. [565] "Recent Excavations on the Hill of Ophel: A Reply to General Sir Charles Warren," Palestine Exploration Fund, Quarterly Statement, (1912), 131-134.

Vincent, Louis-Hugues. [566] "Les récentes fouilles d' Ophel," Revue biblique, 20 (1911), 566-591; 21 (1912), 86-111, 424-453, 544-574.

Vincent, Louis-Hugues. [567] Underground Jerusalem. London: Horace Cox, 1911, 42 pp, 34 pls. English edition of [564.]

Vincent, Louis-Hugues. [568] "Vestiges antiques dans hâret el-Moghârbeh," Revue biblique, 23 (1914), 429-436.

Vincent, Louis-Hugues and Abel, Félix-M. [569] Jérusalem: Recherches de topographie, d' archéologie et d' histoire, 2: Jérusalem nouvelle, 3 parts. Paris: Gabalda, 1914-1926, 1035 pp, 90 pls.

Vincent, Louis-Hugues and Steve, M.-A. [570] Jérusalem de l' Ancien Testament: Recherches d' archéologie et d' histoire, 1-3. Paris: Gabalda, 1954-1956, 809 pp.

Warren, Charles. See St. Clair, George. [504]

Warren, Charles. See Vincent, Louis-Hugues. [565]

Warren, Charles. See Wilson, Charles W. and Warren Charles. [586]

Warren, Charles. [571] "The Diamond Jubilee of the Palestine Exploration Fund," Palestine Exploration Fund, Quarterly Statement, (1925), 61-65.

Warren, Charles. [572] Plans, Elevations, etc. Showing the Results of the Excavations at Jerusalem, 1867-70, Excavated for the Committee of the Palestine Exploration Fund. London: Palestine Exploration Fund, 1884, 50 pls.

Warren, Charles. [573] "Recent Excavations at Jerusalem by Herr C. Schick, K. K. Baurath," Palestine Exploration Fund, Quarterly Statement, (1877), 9-10.

Warren, Charles. [574] "Recent Excavations on the Hill of Ophel, Observations," Palestine Exploration Fund, Quarterly Statement, (1912), 134-135.

Warren, Charles. [575] "Reports on Progress of Works at Jerusalem and Elsewhere in the Holy Land," Palestine Exploration Fund, Quarterly Statement, (1869/1870), 81-148.

Warren, Charles. [576] "The Results of the Excavations on the Hill of Ophel (Jérusalem sous terre), 1909-1911," Palestine Exploration Fund, Quarterly Statement, (1912), 68-74.

Warren, Charles. [577] Underground Jerusalem: An Account of Some of the Principal Difficulties Encountered in its Exploration and the Results Obtained. London: Bentley, 1876, 559 pp.

Warren, Charles and Conder, Claude R. [578] The Survey of Western Palestine, 5: Jerusalem. Palestine Exploration Fund, 1884, 542 pp.

Watson, Charles M. [579] "The Explorations at Jerusalem, 1867-70 / 1894-7," in Palestine Exploration Fund, Fifty Year's Work in the Holy Land: A Record and a Summary,1865-1915. London: Committee of the Palestine Exploration Fund, 1915, 41-52, 107-116.

Weill, Raymond. [580] "La Cité de David. Compte rendue des fouilles exécutées à Jérusalem, sur le site de la ville primitive. Campagne de 1913-1914," Revue des études juives, 69 (1919), 1-85; 70 (1920), 1-36, 149-179; 71 (1920), 1-45.

Weill, Raymond. [581] La Cité de David. Compte rendu des fouilles exécutées à Jérusalem, sur le site de la ville primitive. Campagne de 1913-1914. Paris: Geuthner, 1920, 209 pp, 26 pls.

Weill, Raymond. [582] La Cité de David. Compte rendu des fouilles exécutées à Jérusalem, sur le site de la ville primitive. Campagne de 1923-1925, 2 vols. Paris: Geuthner, 1947, 132 pp, plates.

Weill, Raymond. [583] "La pointe sud de la Cité de David et les fouilles de 1923-1924," Revue des études juives, 82 (1926), 103-117.

Wilson, Charles W. See See St. Clair, George. [504]

Wilson, Charles W. [584] "Ancient Jerusalem," in Palestine Exploration Fund. The City and the Land: A Course of Seven Lectures on the Work of the Society. London: Macmillan, 1892, 3-26.

Wilson, Charles W. [585] "Recent Discoveries at Jerusalem," Palestine Exploration Fund. Quarterly Statement, (1872), 47-51.

Wilson, Charles W. and Warren, Charles. [586] The Recovery of Jerusalem: A Narrative of Exploration and Discovery in the City and the Holy Land. London: Bentley, 1871, part 1, 334 pp.

Yadin, Yigael (ed.). [587] Jerusalem Revealed: Archaeology in the Holy City, 1968-1974. New Haven and London: Yale University Press and the Israel Exploration Society, 1976, 139 pp.

Four

The Water System

Abel, Félix-M. [588] "Inscription grecque de l' aqueduc de Jérusalem avec la figure du pied byzantin," Revue biblique, 35, (1926), 284-288.

Adan, David. [589] "The 'Fountain of Siloam' and 'Solomon's Pool' in the First Century C. E.," Israel Exploration Journal, 29 (1979), 92-100.

Albright, William F. [590] "The Siloam Inscription," in J. B. Pritchard (ed.), Ancient Near Eastern Texts Relating to the Old Testament. Princeton: Princeton University Press, 1954, 321.

Albright, William F. [591] "The Sinnôr in the Story of David's Capture of Jerusalem," Journal of the Palestine Oriental Society, 2 (1922), 286-290.

Amiran, Ruth. [592] "The Water Supply of Jerusalem," Qadmoniot, 1 (1968), 13-18 (Hebrew).

Amiran, Ruth. [593] "The Water Supply of Israelite Jerusalem," in Y. Yadin (ed.), Jerusalem Revealed: Archaeology in the Holy City, 1968-1974. New Haven and London: Yale University Press and the Israel Exploration Society, 1976, 75-78.

Avi-Yonah, Michael and Mazar, Amihay. [594] "Jerusalem: Water Supply," in Encyclopaedia Judaica, 9. Jerusalem: Macmillan, 1971, 1537-1542. Also in Israel Pocket Library: Jerusalem. Jerusalem: Keter, 1973, 253-261.

Baldensperger, Philip J. [595] "The Dragon Well," Palestine Exploration Fund, Quarterly Statement, (1889), 44.

Barrois, A.-G. (= Georges Augustin). [596] "Installations hydrauliques," in Manuel d' archéologie biblique, 1. Paris: Picard, 1939, 213-243.

Barrois, Georges Augustin. [597] "Siloam," in Interpreter's Dictionary of the Bible, 4. New York: Abingdon, 1962, 352-355.

Ben-Arieh, Yehoshua. [598] "Water Supply: Springs, Pools, Cisterns and the Aqueduct," in Jerusalem in the 19th Century: The Old City. Jerusalem: Yad Izhaq Ben-Zvi / New York: St. Martin's Press, 1984, 59-89.

Beswick, S. [599] "The Siloam Inscription," Palestine Exploration Fund, Quarterly Statement, (1884), 255-257.

Beswick, S. [600] "The Siloam Tunnel," Palestine Exploration Fund, Quarterly Statement, (1882), 178-183.

4/ Water System

Birch, W. F. [601] "Defence of the Gutter," Palestine Exploration Fund, Quarterly Statement, (1890), 200-204.

Birch, W. F. [602] "En-Rogel and the Brook that Overflowed," Palestine Exploration Fund, Quarterly Statement, (1889), 45-52.

Birch, W. F. [603] "The Gutter (Tsinnor)," Palestine Exploration Fund, Quarterly Statement, (1890), 330-331.

Birch, W. F. [604] "The Gutter Not Near the Fuller's Field," Palestine Exploration Fund, Quarterly Statement, (1891), 254-256.

Birch, W. F. [605] "Note on the Two Pools," Palestine Exploration Fund, Quarterly Statement, (1879), 179-180.

Birch, W. F. [606] "The Pool that was Made," Palestine Exploration Fund, Quarterly Statement, (1890), 204-208.

Birch, W. F. [607] "Siloam and the Pools," Palestine Exploration Fund, Quarterly Statement, (1883), 105-107.

Birch, W. F. [608] "The Siloam Inscription," Palestine Exploration Fund, Quarterly Statement, (1890), 208-210.

Birch, W. F. [609] "The Valleys and Waters of Jerusalem," Palestine Exploration Fund, Quarterly Statement, (1889), 38-44.

Birch, W. F. [610] "The Waters of Shiloah," Palestine Exploration Fund, Quarterly Statement, (1885), 60.

Birch, W. F. [611] "The Waters of Shiloah (or the Aqueduct) That Go Softly," Palestine Exploration Fund, Quarterly Statement, (1884), 75-77.

Birch, W. F. [612] "The Waters of Shiloah That Go Softly," Palestine Exploration Fund, Quarterly Statement, (1889), 35-38.

Bishop, Eric F. F. [613] "Is Pontius Pilate's Aqueduct Referred to in the Qur'an?" Muslim World, 52 (1962), 189-193.

Braslavi, Joseph. [614] "En-Tanin (Neh. 2: 13)," in Eretz-Israel: Archaeological, Historical, and Geographical Studies, 10. Jerusalem: Israel Exploration Society, 1971, 90-93 (Hebrew), xi (English summary). [The Serpent's Pool = Siloam spring, not En-Rogel.]

Bressan, Gino. [615] "L' espugnazione di Sion in 2 Sam. 5, 6-8 / 1 Chron. 11, 4-6 e il problema del 'Sinnor,'" Biblica, 25 (1944), 346-381.

Bressan, Gino. [616] "El Sinnor (2 Sam 5, 6-8)," Biblica, 35 (1954), 217-224.

Briend, Jacques. [617] "Rogel," in H. Cazelles and A. Robert (eds.), Supplément au Dictionnaire de la Bible, 10. Paris: Letouzey et Ané, 1982, 691-695.

4/ Water System

Brunet, Gilbert. [618] "Les aveugles et boiteux jébusites," in J. A. Emerton (ed.), Studies in the Historical Books of the Old Testament. Vetus Testamentum, Supplement, 30. Leiden: Brill, 1979, 65-72.

Brunet, Gilbert. [619] "David et le sinnôr," in J. A. Emerton (ed.), Studies in the Historical Books of the Old Testament. Vetus Testamentum, Supplement, 30. Leiden: Brill, 1979, 73-86.

Brunot, Amédée. [620] "L' eau à Jérusalem," Bible et Terre Sainte, 101 (1968), 6-15.

Burrows, Millar. [621] "The Conduit of the Upper Pool," Zeitschrift für die alttestamentliche Wissenschaft, 70 (1958), 221-227.

Canaan, Taufik. [622] "Water and 'The Water of Life' in Palestinian Superstition," Journal of the Palestine Oriental Society, 9 (1929), 57-69.

Chaplin, Thomas. [623] "Gihon," Palestine Exploration Fund, Quarterly Statement, (1890), 124-125.

Clermont-Ganneau, Charles. [624] "Notes on Certain Discoveries at Jerusalem: Pool of Strouthion," Palestine Exploration Fund, Quarterly Statement, (1871), 106.

Clermont-Ganneau, Charles. [625] "The Pool of Strouthion," in C. Warren and C. R. Conder, The Survey of Western Palestine, 5: Jerusalem. London: Palestine Exploration Fund, 1884, 295.

Clermont-Ganneau, Charles. [626] "Roman Inscriptions on a Jerusalem Aqueduct," Palestine Exploration Fund, Quarterly Statement, (1901), 118-122.

Clermont-Ganneau, Charles. [627] Les tombeaux de David et des rois de Juda et le tunnel-aqueduc de Siloé. Paris: Imprimerie Nationale, 1897, 48 pp. Also in Recueil d' archéologie orientale, 2. Paris: Leroux, 1898, 254-294.

Cohn, Erich W. [628] "The Appendix of Antonia Rock in Jerusalem," Palestine Exploration Quarterly, (1979), 41-52.

Cole, Dan. [629] "How Water Tunnels Worked," Biblical Archaeology Review, 6/2 (March/April, 1980), 9-10.

Conder, Claude R. [630] "'Ain Silwân / 'Ain Umm ed Deraj / Bir Eyûb / Birket Mamilla / Birket es Sultan," in C. Warren and C. R. Conder, The Survey of Western Palestine, 5: Jerusalem. London: Palestine Exploration Fund, 1884, 345-377.

Conder, Claude R. [631] "En Rogel," Palestine Exploration Fund, Quarterly Statement, (1885), 20.

Conder, Claude R. [632] "The Siloam Tunnel," Palestine Exploration Fund, Quarterly Statement, (1882), 122-131.

Conder, Claude R. [633] "The Tsinnor," Palestine Exploration Fund, Quarterly Statement, (1890), 39-40.

4/ Water System

Dalman, Gustaf. [634] "Die Wasserversorgung des ältesten Jerusalem," Palästinajahrbuch, 14 (1918), 47-72.

Dalton, G. [635] "The Exploration of En-Rogel, or Job's Well," Palestine Exploration Fund, Quarterly Statement, (1923), 165-173.

Dever, William G. See Paul, Shalom M. and Dever, William G. [674]

Driver, Godfrey. [636] "Water in the Mountains," Palestine Exploration Quarterly, (1970), 83-91.

Finn, Elisabeth Anne. [637] "The Tsinnor," Palestine Exploration Fund, Quarterly Statement, (1890), 195-198.

Fischer, J. [638] "Die Quellen und Teiche des biblischen Jerusalem," Das Heilige Land, 77 (1933), 41-55, 89-101; 78 (1934), 15-26, 70-75.

Gilbert, Martin. [639] "Jerusalem's Water Supply and Transport, 1918-1920," in Jerusalem History Atlas. New York: Macmillan, 1977, 70-71.

Gilbert, Martin. [640] "Jerusalem's Water Supply since 1926," in Jerusalem History Atlas. New York: Macmillan, 1977, 120-121.

Görg, Manfred. [641] "Ein problematisches Wort der Siloah-Inschrift," Biblische Notizen: Beiträge zur exegetischen Diskussion, 11 (1980), 21-22.

Gregg, Andrew J. [642] "The Upper Watercourse of Gihon," Palestine Exploration Fund, Quarterly Statement, (1899), 64.

Guthe, Hermann. [643] "Das Schicksal der Siloah-Inschrift," Zeitschrift des deutschen Palästina-Vereins, 13 (1890), 286-288.

Guthe, Hermann. [644] "Die Siloahinschrift," Zeitschrift der deutschen Morgenländischen Gesellschaft, 36 (1882), 725-750.

Guthe, Hermann. [645] Über die Siloahinschrift" Zeitschrift des deutschen Palästina-Vereins, 4 (1881), 250-259.

Hamilton, R. W. [646] "Water Works," in Interpreter's Dictionary of the Bible, 4. New York: Abingdon, 1962, 811-816.

Hanauer, James Edward. [647] "Rock-Hewn Vats near Bîr Eyûb," Palestine Exploration Fund, Quarterly Statement, (1900), 361-365.

Har-El, Menashe. [648] "Water in Jerusalem," in This is Jerusalem. Jerusalem: Canaan, 1977, 151-182.

Hoberman, M. [649] "A Note on the Siloam Tunnel," Levant, 9 (1977), 174-175.

Issar, Arie. [650] "The Evolution of the Ancient Water System in the Region of Jerusalem," Israel Exploration Journal, 26 (1976), 130-136.

"Jerusalem's Water Problem," [651] Near East and India, 40 (1931), 464.

Kautzsch, Emil. [652] "Die Siloahinschrift," Zeitschrift des deutschen Palästina-Vereins, 4 (1881), 102-114, 260-272; 5 (1882), 205-218.

Legendre, A. [653] "Jérusalem: Régime des eaux," in F. Vigouroux (ed.), Dictionnaire de la Bible, 3. Paris: Letouzey et Ané, 1926, 1346-1350.

Levi Della Vida, Giorgie. [654] "The Shiloah Inscription Reconsidered," in M. Black and G. Fohrer (eds.), In Memorium Paul Kahle. Berlin: Töpelmann, 1968, 162-166.

Loffreda, Stanislao. [655] "Ancora sul sinnôr di 2 Sam 5,8," Studii Biblici Franciscani, Liber Annuus, 32 (1982), 59-72.

Luria, Ben-Zion. [656] "And a Fountain Shall Come Forth from the House of the Lord," Dor le Dor, 10 (1981), 48-58.

Luria, Ben-Zion. [657] "The Pool of Israel," Beth Miqra, 57 (1974), 123-135 (Hebrew with English summary).

McCarter, P. Kyle. [658] "Siloam Inscription," in Harper's Bible Dictionary. San Francisco: Harper and Row, 1985, 951-953.

Macgregor, R. [659] "The Spring En-Rogel," Palestine Exploration Quarterly, (1938), 257-258.

Mackowski, Richard M. [660] "The Waters of Jerusalem," in Jerusalem, City of Jesus: An Exploration of the Traditions, Writings, and Remains of the Holy City from the Time of Christ. Grand Rapids: Eerdmans, 1980, 71-87.

Mallon, Alexis. [661] "Travaux hydrauliques à Jérusalem," Biblica, 3 (1922), 396-398.

Massey, W. T. [662] "The Jerusalem Water Supply," Palestine Exploration Fund, Quarterly Statement, (1918), 172-175.

Masterman, Ernest W. Gurney. [663] "Jerusalem: Water Supply," in J. Hastings (ed.), Dictionary of Christ and the Gospels, 1. New York: Scribner's, 1906, 851-853.

Masterman, Ernest W. Gurney. [664] "The Recently Discovered Aqueduct from the Virgin's Fountain," Palestine Exploration Fund, Quarterly Statement, (1902), 35-38.

Maurer, Christian. [665] "Der Struthionteich und der Burg Antonia," Zeitschrift des deutschen Palästina-Vereins, 80 (1964), 137-149.

Mazar, Amihay. See Avi-Yonah, Michael and Mazar, Amihay. [594]

Mazar, Amihay. See Shanks, Hershel. [698]

Mazar, Amihay. [666] "The Ancient Aqueducts of Jerusalem," Qadmoniot, 5 (1972), 120-124 (Hebrew).

Mazar, Amihay. [667] "The Aqueducts of Jerusalem," in Y. Yadin (ed.), Jerusalem Revealed: Archaeology in the Holy City, 1968-1974. New Haven and London: Yale University Press and the Israel Exploration Society, 1976, 79-84..

Merrill, Selah. [668] "An Ancient Sewer at Jerusalem," Palestine Exploration Fund, Quarterly Statement, (1904), 392-394.

Merrill, Selah. [669] "A Bit of the Ancient Upper Gihon Aqueduct," Palestine Exploration Fund, Quarterly Statement, (1903), 157-158.

Michaud, Henri. [670] "Un passage difficile dans l' inscription de Siloé," Vetus Testamentum, 8 (1958), 297-302.

Mommert, Carl. [671] Siloah: Brunnen, Teich, Kanal zu Jerusalem. Leipzig: Haberland, 1908, 96 pp.

Patrich, Joseph. [672] "The Aqueduct from Eitam to the Temple and a Sadducean Halakhah," Cathedra: For the History of Eretz-Israel and its Yishuv, 17 (1980), 11-23 (Hebrew.)

Patrich, Joseph. [673] "A Sadducean Halakha and the Jerusalem Aqueduct," in L. I. Levine (ed.), Jerusalem Cathedra, 2. Jerusalem: Yad Izhaq Ben-Zvi Institute / Detroit: Wayne State University Press, 1982, 25-39.

Paul, Shalom M. and Dever, William G. [674] "Gihon and Warren's Shaft, / The Waters of Shiloah, / Hezekiah's Tunnel," in Biblical Archaeology. New York: Quadrangle, 1974, 130-135.

St. Clair, George. [675] "The Fuller's Field," Palestine Exploration Fund, Quarterly Statement, (1891), 189-190.

Sasson, Victor. [676] "The Siloam Tunnel Inscription," Palestine Exploration Quarterly, (1982), 111-117.

Sayce, Archibald H. [677] "The Ancient Hebrew Inscription Discovered at the Pool of Siloam in Jerusalem," Palestine Exploration Fund, Quarterly Statement, (1881), 141-153, 282-285.

Sayce, Archibald H. [678] "The Siloam Inscription," Palestine Exploration Fund, Quarterly Statement, (1882), 62-63; (1883), 210-215.

Schick, Conrad. [679] "Ancient Bath and Cistern near Bethany," Palestine Exploration Fund, Quarterly Statement, (1891), 9-11.

Schick, Conrad. [680] "The Aqueducts at Siloam," Palestine Exploration Fund, Quarterly Statement, (1886), 88-91.

Schick, Conrad. [681] "Bericht über meine Arbeiten am Siloakanal," Zeitschrift des deutschen Palästina-Vereins, , 5 (1882), 1-6.

Schick, Conrad. [682] "Birket es Sultan, Jerusalem," Palestine Exploration Fund, Quarterly Statement, (1898), 224-229.

Schick, Conrad. [683] "The Dragon Well," Palestine Exploration Fund, Quarterly Statement, (1898), 230-232.

Schick, Conrad. [684] "The Height of the Shiloah Aqueduct," Palestine Exploration Fund, Quarterly Statement, (1891), 18-19.

Schick, Conrad. [685] "Neu aufgedeckte Felscisternen und Felsgemächer in Jerusalem," Zeitschrift des deutschen Palästina-Vereins, 8 (1885), 42-45.

Schick, Conrad. [686] "Old Pool in Upper Kedron Valley, or 'Wady el Jôz,'" Palestine Exploration Fund, Quarterly Statement, (1892), 9-13.

Schick, Conrad. [687] "An Old Pool West of the City," Palestine Exploration Fund, Quarterly Statement, (1895), 109-110.

Schick, Conrad. [688] "Recent Excavations at Shiloah: 1. Searching for a Second Aqueduct," Palestine Exploration Fund, Quarterly Statement, (1890), 257-258.

Schick, Conrad. [689] "Second Aqueduct to the Pool of Siloam," Palestine Exploration Fund, Quarterly Statement, (1886), 197-200.

Schick, Conrad. [690] "The 'Second' Shiloah Aqueduct," Palestine Exploration Fund, Quarterly Statement, (1891), 13-18.

Schick, Conrad. [691] "Shiloah Spring," Palestine Exploration Fund, Quarterly Statement, (1897), 122.

Schick, Conrad. [692] "The Virgin's Fount," Palestine Exploration Fund, Quarterly Statement, (1902), 29-35.

Schick, Conrad. [693] "Die Wasserversorgung der Stadt Jerusalem in geschichtlicher und topographischer Darstellung mit Originalkarten und Plänen," Zeitschrift des deutschen Palästina-Vereins, 1 (1878), 132-176.

Schick, Conrad. [694] "Watercourses Providing the Ancient City with Water from the North-West," Palestine Exploration Fund, Quarterly Statement, (1891), 278-280.

Schick, Conrad. [695] "The West Wall of the Pool of Hezekiah," Palestine Exploration Fund, Quarterly Statement, (1897), 107-109.

Shaheen, Naseeb. [696] "The Siloam End of Hezekiah's Tunnel," Palestine Exploration Quarterly, (1977), 107-112.

Shaheen, Naseeb. [697] "The Sinuous Shape of Hezekiah's Tunnel," Palestine Exploration Quarterly, (1979), 103-108.

Shanks, Hershel. [698] "A New Generation of Israeli Archaeologists Comes of Age: BAR Interviews Amihai Mazar," Biblical Archaeology Review, 10/3 (May/June, 1984), 46-61. [On the aqueducts of Jerusalem.]

Shiloh, Yigal. [699] "The Rediscovery of the Ancient Water System Known as 'Warren's Shaft,'" Qadmoniot, 14 (1981), 89-95 (Hebrew). [English summary in Old Testament Abstracts, 5 (1982), 216.]

Shiloh, Yigal. [700] "The Rediscovery of Warren's Shaft: Jerusalem's Water Supply during Siege," Biblical Archaeology Review, 7/4 (July/August, 1981), 24-39.

Simons, Jan. [701] "The Waterworks of the City of David," in Jerusalem in the Old Testament: Researches and Theories. Leiden: Brill, 1952, 157-194.

Simpson, William. [702] "The Conduit near the Pool of Bethesda," Palestine Exploration Fund, Quarterly Statement, (1888), 259-260.

Snaith, Norman H. [703] "The Siloam Inscription," D. W. Thomas (ed.), Documents from Old Testament Times. London: Nelson, 1958, 209-211.

Stephen, F. W. [704] "Notes on Jerusalem Water Supply," Palestine Exploration Fund, Quarterly Statement, (1919), 15-27.

Steve, M. A. See Vincent, Louis-Hugues. and Steve, M. A. [714]

Stoebe, Hans-Joachim. [705] "Die Einnahme Jerusalems und der Sinnor," Zeitschrift des deutschen Palästina-Vereins, 73 (1957), 73-99.

Sulley, Henry. [706] "On Hezekiah's Tunnel," Palestine Exploration Fund, Quarterly Statement, (1929), 124.

Thomas, John. [707] "Note on the 'Dragon Well,'" Palestine Exploration Fund, Quarterly Statement, (1899), 57-58.

Ussishkin, David. [708] "The Original Length of the Siloam Tunnel in Jerusalem," Levant, 8 (1975), 82-95.

Vetrali, L. [709] "Le iscrizioni dell' acquedotto romano presso Betlemme," Studii Biblici Franciscani, Liber Annuus, 17 (1967), 149-161.

Vincent, Louis-Hugues. [710] Jérusalem sous terre: Les récentes fouilles d' Ophel. London: Horace Cox, 1911, 45 pp. + 34 pl.

Vincent, Louis-Hugues. [711] "Les récentes fouilles d' Opel," Revue biblique, 20 (1911), 566-591; 21 (1912), 86-111, 424-453, 544-574.

Vincent, Louis-Hugues. [712] "Le sinnôr dans la prise de Jérusalem," Revue biblique, 33 (1924), 357-370.

Vincent, Louis-Hugues. [713] Underground Jerusalem. London: Horace Cox, 1911, 45 pp. + 34 pl.

Vincent, Louis-Hugues and Steve, M. A. [714] "Les installations hydrauliques," in Jérusalem de l' Ancien Testament, 1. Paris: Gabalda, 1954, 260-312.

Warner, H. J. [715] "A Simple Solution of Nehemiah iv. 23 (Hebrew verse 17)," Expository Times, 63 (1951/1952), 321-322.

Wenning, R. and Zenger, E. [716] "Die verschiedenen Systeme der Wassernutzung im südlichen Jerusalem und die Bezugnahme darauf in biblischen Texte," Ugarit-Forschungen, 14. Internationales Jahrbuch für die Altertumskunde

Syrien-Palästinas. Neukirchen-Vluyn: Neukirchener Verlag / Kevelaer: Butzon and Bercker, 1982, 279-294.

Whitty, John Irvine. [717] "The Water Supply of Jerusalem-- Ancient and Modern," Journal of Sacred Literature and Biblical Research, 9 (1864), 133-157.

Wilkinson, John. [718] "Ancient Jerusalem: Its Water Supply and Population," Palestine Exploration Quarterly, (1974), 33-51.

Wilkinson, John. [719] "The Pool of Siloam," Levant, 10 (1978), 116-125.

Wilson, Charles W. [720] "Centurial Inscriptions on the Syphon of the High-Level Aqueduct at Jerusalem," Palestine Exploration Fund, Quarterly Statement, (1905), 75-77.

Wilson, Charles W. [721] "Siloam," in J. Hastings (ed.), Dictionary of the Bible, 4. New York: Scribner's, 1898, 515-516.

Wilson, Charles W. [722] "Water Supply of Jerusalem," in Ordnance Survey of Jerusalem. London: Lord's Commissioners of Her Majesty's Treasury, 1865, 77-88.

Wordsworth, W. A. [723] "The Siloam Inscription," Palestine Exploration Quarterly, (1939), 41-43.

Zenger, E. See Wenning R. and Zenger, E. [716]

Five

City Walls and Gates

A. City Walls and Gates: Biblical Period

Alt, Albrecht. [724] "Das Taltor von Jerusalem," Palästinajahrbuch, 24 (1928), 74-98. Also in Kleine Schriften zur Geschichte des Volkes Israel, 3. Munich: Beck'sch Verlagsbuchhandlung, 1959, 326-347.

Avi-Yonah, Michael. [725] "The Newly Found Wall of Jerusalem and its Topographical Significance," Israel Exploration Journal, 21 (1971), 168-169. Reprinted in H. Orlinsky (ed.), Israel Exploration Journal Reader, 1. New York: KTAV, 1981, 876-877.

Avi-Yonah, Michael. [726] "The Walls of Jerusalem," in J. Aviram (ed.), Jerusalem through the Ages. Jerusalem: Israel Exploration Society, 1968, 62-71 (Hebrew), 60 (English summary).

Avi-Yonah, Michael. [727] "The Walls of Nehemiah-- a Minimalist View," Israel Exploration Journal, 4 (1954), 239-248. Reprinted in H. Orlinsky (ed.), Israel Exploration Journal Reader, 2. New York: KTAV, 1981, 860-869.

Avigad, Nahman. See Laperrousaz, Ernest-Marie. [753]

Avigad, Nahman. [728] "The Fortification of the City of David," Israel Exploration Journal, 2 (1952), 230-236. Reprinted in H. Orlinsky (ed.), Israel Exploration Journal Reader, 2. New York: KTAV, 1981, 853-859.

Avigad, Nahman. [729] "The Period of the First Temple," in Discovering Jerusalem. Nashville: Thomas Nelso, 1983, 23-60.

Bahat, Dan. [730] "The Wall of Manasseh in Jerusalem," Israel Exploration Journal, 31 (1981), 235-236.

Birch, W. F. [731] "Nehemiah's Wall," Palestine Exploration Fund, Quarterly Statement, (1889), 206-209; (1890), 126-130.

Birch, W. F. [732] "Nehemiah's Wall and David's Tomb," Palestine Exploration Fund, Quarterly Statement, (1879), 176-179.

Birch, W. F. [733] "The Valley Gate," Palestine Exploration Fund, Quarterly Statement, (1898), 168-169.

Broshi, Magen. [734] "The Expansion of Jerusalem in the Reigns of Hezekiah and Manasseh," Israel Exploration Journal, 24 (1974), 21-26.

5A/City Walls and Gates: Biblical Period

Burrows, Millar. [735] "Nehemiah 3:1-28 as a Source for the Topography of Ancient Jerusalem," Annual of the American Schools of Oriental Research, 14 (1934), 115-140.

Burrows, Millar. [736] "Nehemiah's Tour of Inspection," Bulletin of the American Schools of Oriental Research, 64 (1936), 11-21.

Burrows, Millar. [737] "The Topography of Nehemiah 12: 31-43," Journal of Biblical Literature, 54 (1935), 29-39.

Conder, Claude R. [738] "The South Wall of Jerusalem," Palestine Exploration Fund, Quarterly Statement, (1889), 145-146.

da Deliceto, Gerardo. [739] "Un vano tentativo di reconstruzioni della mura di Gerusalemme (Esd. 4, 12 e Ne. 1, 3b)," in S. Gozzo (ed.), La distruzione di Gerusalemme del 70: nei suoi riflessi storico-letterari. Assisi: Studio Teologico "Porziuncolo," 1971, 181-191.

Fischer, J. [740] "Die Mauern und Tore des biblischen Jerusalem," Theologische Quartalschrift, 113 (1932), 221-188; 114 (1933), 73-85.

Fullerton, Kemper. [741] "The Procession of Nehemiah, Neh. 12: 31-39," Journal of Biblical Literature, 37 (1919), 171-179.

Geva, Hillel. [742] "The Western Boundary of Jerusalem at the End of the Monarchy," Israel Exploration Journal, 29 (1979), 84-91.

Grafman, R. [743] "Nehemiah's 'Broad Wall,'" Israel Exploration Journal, 24 (1974), 50-51.

Gur, M. [744] "At the Gates of Jerusalem," in J. Aviram (ed.), Jerusalem through the Ages. Jerusalem: Israel Exploration Society, 1968, 238-264 (Hebrew), 66 (English summary).

Haag, Herbert. [745] "Jerusalem" in Bibel-Lexikon. Zürich/Köln: Benziger Verlag Einsieder, 1956, 791-799 (section on walls and gates, 792-795).

Haupt, Paul. [746] "The Tophet Gate," Journal of Biblical Literature, 37 (1918), 232-233.

"Jerusalem (Gates of)," [747] in J. Hastings (ed.), Dictionary of the Bible, revised edn. by F. C. Grant and H. H. Rowley. New York: Scribner's, 1963, 476.

Kirmis, F. [748] Die Lage der alten Davidsstadt und die Mauern des alten Jerusalem: Eine exegetisch-topographische Studie. Breslau: Goerlich, 1919, 224 pp.

Laperrousaz, Ernest-Marie. [749] "A propos du 'Premier mur' et du 'Deuxième mur' de Jérusalem ainsi que du rempart de Jérusalem à l' époque de Néhémie," Reuve des études juives, 138 (1979), 1-16.

Laperrousaz, Ernest-Marie. [750] "L' extension préexilique de Jérusalem sur la colline occidentalle," Revue des études juives, 134 (1975), 3-30.

Laperrousaz, Ernest-Marie. [751] "Nouveaux aspects de la Jérusalem biblique," Revue de l' Histoire des Religions, 193 (1978), 144-149.

Laperrousaz, Ernest-Marie. [752] "Le probléme du 'Premier Mur' et du "Deuxième Mur' de Jérusalem après la réfutation décisive de la 'Minamalist View,'" in G. Nahon and Ch. Touati (eds.), Homage a`Georges Vajda. Louvain, 1980, 13-35.

Laperrousaz, Ernest-Marie. [753] "Remarques sur l' origine du 'gros mur' découvert par le Professeur Avigad dans le 'quartier juifs' de Jérusalem," Revue des études juives, 132 (1973), 465-474.

Laperrousaz, Ernest-Marie. [754] "Quelques apercus sur les dernières découvertes archéologiques faites à Jérusalem et aux alentours de la Ville Sainte," Revue des études juives, 131 (1972), 249-267.

Laperrousaz, Ernest-Marie. [755] "Quelques remarques sur le rempart de Jérusalem à époque de Néhémie," in Studia Biblica (Memorial to Alexius Klawek). Folia Orientalia, 21. Kraków: Polska Akademia Nauk, 1980, 179-185.

Laperrousaz, Ernest-Marie. [756] "Quelques résultats récents des fouilles archéologiques conduites à Jérusalem at aux alentours de la Ville Sainte," Revue des études juives, 129 (1970), 145-159.

La Sor, William S. [757] "Nehemiah's Jerusalem" in G. W. Bromiley (ed.), International Standard Bible Encyclopedia, 2. Grand Rapids, MI: Eerdmans, 1982, 1017-1021.

Mitchell, Hinckley G. [758] "The Wall of Jerusalem according to the Book of Nehemiah," Journal of Biblical Literature, 22 (1903), 85-163.

Paton, Lewis B. [759] "The Meaning of the Expression 'Between the Two Walls,'" Journal of Biblical Literature, 25 (1906), 1-13.

Riessler, Paul. [760] "Die Tore und Mauern Jerusalem unter Nehemias," Biblische Zeitschrift, (1906), 347-356.

St. Clair, George. [761] "The 'Broad Wall' at Jerusalem," Palestine Exploration Fund, Quarterly Statement, (1889), 99.

St. Clair, George. [762] "Nehemiah's Night Ride," Palestine Exploration Fund, Quarterly Statement, (1888), 46-48

St. Clair, George. [763] "Nehemiah's South Wall and the Locality of the Royal Sepulchres," Palestine Exploration Fund, Quarterly Statement, (1889), 90-98.

St. Clair, George. [764] "Nehemiah's Wall," Palestine Exploration Fund, Quarterly Statement, (1890), 47-50, 212.

St. Clair, George. [765] "Nehemiah's Wall and the Royal Sepulchres," Palestine Exploration Fund, Quarterly Statement, (1888), 288-289.

St. Clair, George. [766] "The Valley Gate and the Dung Gate," Palestine Exploration Fund, Quarterly Statement, (1897), 69-70.

Schick, Conrad. [767] "Contribution to the Study of the Ancient City Walls of Jerusalem," Palestine Exploration Fund, Quarterly Statement, (1899), 215-217.

Schick, Conrad. [768] "Der Davidsthurm in Jerusalem: Neu untersucht, gemessen und gezeichnet," Zeitschrift des deutschen Palästina-Vereins, 1 (1878), 226-237.

Schick, Conrad. [769] "Nehemia's Mauerbau in Jerusalem," Zeitschrift des deutschen Palästina-Vereins, 14 (1891), 41-62.

Schick, Conrad. [770] "Recent Excavations at Shiloah, 2: Searching for the Gate of the City of David," Palestine Exploration Fund, Quarterly Statement, (1890), 258-259.

Schick, Conrad. [771] "Remains of the Old City Wall," Palestine Exploration Fund, Quarterly Statement, (1890), 21.

Schick, Conrad. [772] "Remains of Ancient City Wall," Palestine Exploration Fund, Quarterly Statement, (1898), 82.

Schick, Conrad. [773] "Das Thalthor im alten Jerusalem," Zeitschrift des deutschen Palästina-Vereins, 13 (1890), 31-36.

Shaheen, Naseeb. [774] "The Siloam End of Hezekiah's Tunnel," Palestine Exploration Quarterly, (1977), 107-112. [Was the pool outside the wall?]

Simons, Jan. [775] "The City of Nehemiah," in Jerusalem in the Old Testament: Researches and Theories. Leiden: Brill, 1952, 437-458.

Simons, Jan. [776] "The Wall of Manasseh and the 'Mishneh' of Jerusalem," in P. A. H. de Boer (ed.), Oudtestamentische Studien, 7. Leiden: Brill, 1950, 179-200.

Steve, M.-A. See Vincent, Louis-Hugues and Steve, M.-A. [781]

Tuland, C. G. [777] " 'zb in Nehemiah 3: 8: A Reconsideration of Maximalist and Minimalist Views," Andrews University Seminary Studies, 5 (1967), 158-180.

Tushingham, A. Douglas. [778] "The Western Hill under the Monarchy," Zeitschrift des deutschen Palästina-Vereins, 95 (1979), 39-55.

Vincent, Louis-Hugues. [779] "Les murs de Jérusalem d' apres Néhémie: Notes de critique textuelle," Revue biblique, 13 (1904), 56-74.

Vincent, Louis-Hugues. [780] "La tour méa (Néhém. iii, 1; xii, 39)," Revue biblique, 8 (1899), 582-589.

Vincent, Louis-Hugues and Steve, M.-A. [781] "Les murs de Jérusalem d' apres Néhémie," in Jérusalem de l' Ancien Testament, 1. Paris: Gabalda, 1954, 237-259.

Wilson, Charles W. [782] "The Walls of Jerusalem," Palestine Exploration Fund, Quarterly Statement, (1905), 231.

Williamson, H. G. M. [783] "Nehemiah's Walls Revisited," Palestine Exploration Quarterly, (1984), 81-88.

Wright, Theodore F. [784] "Nehemiah's Night Ride (Neh. ii, 12-15)," Journal of Biblical Literature, 15 (1896), 129-134.

Wright, Theodore F. [785] "Nehemiah's Night Ride (ii, 12-15)," Palestine Exploration Fund, Quarterly Statement, (1896), 172-173.

Wright, Theodore F. [786] "The Stairs of the City of David (at the Going Up of the Wall), Neh. iii, 15; xii, 37," Journal of Biblical Literature, 16 (1897), 171-174.

Wright, Theodore F. [787] "The Valley Gate and the Dung Gate," Palestine Exploration Fund, Quarterly Statement, (1896), 342.

5. B. City Walls and Gates: Second Temple Period

Albright, William F. [788] "New Light on the Walls of Jerusalem in the New Testament Age," Bulletin of the American Schools of Oriental Research, 81 (1941), 6-10.

Albright, William F. [789] "The Third Wall of Jerusalem," Bulletin of the American Schools of Oriental Research, 19 (1925), 19-21.

Amiran, Ruth. [790] "The First and Second Walls of Jerusalem Reconsidered in the Light of the New Wall," Israel Exploration Journal, 21 (1971), 166-167. Reprinted in H. Orlinsky (ed.), Israel Exploration Journal Reader, 2. New York: KTAV, 1981, 874-875.

Avi-Yonah, Michael. [791] "The Third and Second Walls of Jerusalem," Israel Exploration Journal, 18 (1968), 98-125.

Ben-Arieh, Sara. [792] "Excavations along the Third Wall in Jerusalem," Qadmoniot, 6 (1973), 111-113.

Ben-Arieh, Sara. [793] "The 'Third Wall' of Jerusalem," in Y. Yadin (ed.), Jerusalem Revealed: Archaeology in the Holy City, 1968-1974. New Haven and London: Yale University Press and the Israel Exploration Society, 1976, 60-62.

Ben-Arieh, Sara and Netzer, Ehud. [794] "Excavations along the 'Third Wall' of Jerusalem, 1972-74," Israel Exploration Journal, 24 (1974), 97-107. Reprinted in H. Orlinsky (ed.), Israel Exploration Journal Reader, 2. New York: KTAV, 1981, 888-900.

Ben-Arieh, Sara and Netzer, Ehud. [795] "Where is the Third Wall of Agrippa I?" Biblical Archaeologist, 42 (1979), 140-141.

Ben-Dov, Meir. [796] "Has the 'First Wall' Been Discovered on the Eastern Slope of the City of David?" Qadmoniot, 12 (1979), 93 (Hebrew). [English summary in Old Testament Abstracts, 3 (1980), 94.]

Benoit, Pierre. [797] "Où en est la question du 'troisième mur?'" in E. Testa, I. Mancini, and M. Piccirillo (eds.), Studia hierosolymitana in onore del P. Bellarmino Bagatti, 1: Studia archeologici. Studium Biblicum Franciscanum, Collectio Major, 22. Jerusalem: Franciscan Printing Press, Jerusalem: Fransiscan Printing Press, 1976, 11-126.

Benoit, Pierre. [798] "Les remparts de Jérusalem," Le Monde de la Bible, 1 (1977), 21-35. Reprinted in Exégèse et theologie, 4. Paris: Cerf, 1982, 293-310.

Broshi, Magen. [799] "Along Jerusalem's Walls," Biblical Archaeologist, 40 (1977), 11-17.

5B/City Walls and Gates: Second Temple Period

Broshi. Magen. [800] "Recent Excavations along the Walls of Jerusalem," Qadmoniot, 9 (1976), 75-78 (Hebrew).

Cerny, E. A. [801] "North Wall of Jerusalem," Catholic Biblical Quarterly, 3 (1941), 266-267.

Clarke, N. P. [802] "The Four North Walls of Jerusalem," Palestine Exploration Quarterly, (1944), 199-212.

Clarke, N. P. [803] "Helena's Pyramids," Palestine Exploration Quarterly, (1938), 84-104.

Conder, Claude R. [804] "On the Exploration of Jerusalem-- the Second Wall," Palestine Exploration Fund, Quarterly Statement, (1872), 157-160.

Crowfoot, J. W. [805] "The Four North Walls of Jerusalem," Palestine Exploration Quarterly, (1943), 58-60.

Duncan, J. Garrow; Hanauer, James Edward; and Masterman, Ernest W. Gurney. [806] "The Excavation of the Foundations of the Supposed Third Wall of Jerusalem," Palestine Exploration Fund, Quarterly Statement, (1925), 172-182.

Finegan, Jack. [807] "Ancient Wall in the Russian Alexander Hospice, / Ancient Wall and Arch beside the Damascus Gate, / South Face of a Wall North of Jerusalem," in Archeology of the New Testament: The Life of Jesus and the Beginnings of the Early Church. Princeton: Princeton University Press, 1969, 135-141.

Finn, Elisabeth Anne. [808] "The Second Wall of Jerusalem," Palestine Exploration Fund, Quarterly Statement, (1886), 206-207.

Fisher, C. S. [809] "The Third Wall of Jerusalem," Bulletin of the American Schools of Oriental Research, 83 (1941), 4-7.

Geva, Hillel. [810] "The 'First Wall' of Jerusalem during the Second Temple Period: An Archaeological-Chronological Note," in Eretz-Israel: Archaeological, Historical, and Geographical Studies, 18. Jerusalem: Israel Exploration Society, 1985, 21-39 (Hebrew), 65* (English summary).

Guthe, Hermann and Schick, Conrad. [811] "Die zweite Mauer Jerusalems und die Bauten Constantins am heiligen Grabe," Zeitschrift des deutschen Palästina-Vereins, 8 (1885), 245-287.

Hamilton, R. W. [812] "Excavations against the North Wall of Jerusalem, 1937-38," Quarterly of the Department of Antiquities in Palestine, 10 (1942/1943), 1-53.

Hamilton, R. W. [813] "Note on Recent Discoveries outside St. Stephen's Gate, Jerusalem," Quarterly of the Department of Antiquities in Palestine, 6 (1938),153-156.

Hamrick, Emmet W. [814] "The Fourth North Wall of Jerusalem: A 'Barrier Wall' of the First Century A. D.," Levant, 13 (1981), 262-266.

5B/City Walls and Gates: Second Temple Period

Hamrick, Emmet W. [815] "Further Notes on the 'Third Wall,'" Bulletin of the American Schools of Oriental Research, 192 (1968), 21-25.

Hamrick, Emmet W. [816] "New Excavations at Sukenik's 'Third Wall,'" Bulletin of the American Schools of Oriental Research, 183 (1966), 19-26.

Hamrick, Emmet W. [817] "The Third Wall of Agrippa I," Biblical Archaeologist, 40 (1977), 18-23.

Hanauer, James Edward. See Duncan, J. Garrow; Hanauer, James Edward; and Masterman, Ernest W. Gurney. [806]

Hennessy, J. B. [818] "Jérusalem (Porte de Damas)," Revue biblique, 75 (1968), 250-253.

Hennessy, J. B. [819] "Preliminary Report on the Excavations at the Damascus Gate, Jerusalem, 1964-66," Levant, 2 (1970), v-vi, 22-27.

Hupfeld, Hermann. [820] "Die topographische Streitfrage über Jerusalem, namentlich die Akra und den Lauf der zweiten Mauer des Josephus," Zeitschrift der deutschen Morgenländischen Gesellschaft, 15 (1861), 185-232.

Jacobi, Paul J. [821] "Remnants of Jerusalem's Walls beneath the Lutheran Hostel," Beth Miqra, 56 (1973), 3-7 (Hebrew with English summary).

Jaros, Karl. [822] "Grabungen unter der Erlöserkirche in Jerusalem: Aus der Arbeit des deutschen Institutes für Altertumswissenschaft des Heiligen Landes in Jerusalem," in J. B. Bauer and J. Marböck (eds.), Memoria Jerusalem (Festschrift Franz Sauer). Graz: Akademische Druck-u Verlagsanstalt, 1977, 167-183.

Kenyon, Kathleen M. [823] "Excavations in Jerusalem, 1965," Palestine Exploration Quarterly, (1966), 73-88.

Luria, Ben-Zion. [824] "The Hasmonean Wall of Jerusalem," Beth Miqra, 28 (1983), 180-184 (Hebrew). [English summary in New Testament Abstracts, 28 (1984), 57.]

Luria, Ben-Zion. [825] "The Walls of Jerusalem at the End of the Second Temple Period," in Eretz-Israel: Archaeological, Historical, and Geographical Studies, 10. Jerusalem: Israel Exploration Society, 1971, 160-168 (Hebrew), xiv (English Summary).

Lux, Ute. [826] "Jerusalem, Old City, Church of the Redeemer," Israel Exploration Journal, 22 (1972), 171.

Lux, Ute. [827] "Jérusalem: Quartier du Muristan," Revue biblique, 79 (1972), 577-578.

Lux, Ute. [828] "Vorläufiger Bericht über die Ausgrabung unter der Erlösserkirche im Muristan in der Altstadt von Jerusalem in den Jahren 1970 und 1971," Zeitschrift des deutschen Palästina-Vereins, 88 (1972), 185-201.

Macalister, R. A. Stewart. [829] "The Supposed Fragment of the First Wall of Jerusalem," Palestine Exploration Fund, Quarterly Statement, (1906), 298-301.

Mackowski, Richard M. [830] "The Walls of the Holy City, / The Gates of Jerusalem," in Jerusalem, City of Jesus: An Exploration of the Traditions, Writings, and Remains of the Holy City from the Time of Christ. Grand Rapids: Eerdmans, 39-69.

McNulty, Ilene B. [831] "The North Wall outside Jerusalem," Biblical Archaeologist, 42 (1979), 141-144.

Mallon, Alexis. [832] "Le mur d' Agrippa," Biblica, 6 (1925), 359-360; 8 (1927), 123-128.

Masterman, Ernest W. Gurney. See Duncan, J. Garrow; Hanauer, James Edward; and Masterman, Ernest W. Gurney. [806]

Masterman, Ernest W. Gurney. [833] "Jerusalem: Topography of the City in the Time of Christ-- the City Walls," in J. Hastings (ed.), Dictionary of Christ and the Gospels, 1. New York: Scribner's, 1906, 853-856.

Mayer, Leo A. See Sukenik, Eleazar L. and Mayer, Leo A. [864]

Merrill, Selah. [834] "Recent Discoveries at Jerusalem," Palestine Exploration Fund, Quarterly Statement, (1886), 21-24.

Merrill, Selah. [835] Palestine Exploration Fund, Quarterly Statement, (1888), 63-65. Untitled reply to Schick, Conrad. [844]

Merrill, Selah. [836] "A Section of Agrippa's Wall," Palestine Exploration Fund, Quarterly Statement, (1903), 158-159.

Murphy, Richard T. A. [837] "Arma virumque cano," Catholic Biblical Quarterly, 17 (1955), 233-247. [On L.-H. Vincent and the third wall.]

Netzer, Ehud. See Ben-Arieh, Sara and Netzer, Ehud. [794-795]

Norris, C. T. [838] "New Reasoning Concerning the Fortifications of Jerusalem in the First Century, A.D.," Palestine Exploration Quarterly, (1946), 19-37.

North, Robert. [839] "The Walls of Jerusalem according to Recent Researches," in Judah and Jerusalem: The Twelfth Archaeological Convention. Jerusalem: Israel Exploration Society, 1957, 59-64 (Hebrew), iv-v (English summary).

Paton, Lewis B. [840] "The Third Wall of Jerusalem and Some Excavations on its Supposed Line," Journal of Biblical Literature, 24 (1905), 197-211.

Ross, William. [841] "The Four North Walls of Jerusalem," Palestine Exploration Quarterly, (1942), 69-81.

Schein, Bruce E. [842] "The Second Wall of Jerusalem," Biblical Archaeologist, 44 (1981), 21-26.

Schick, Conrad. See Guthe, Hermann and Schick, Conrad. [811]

Schick, Conrad. See Merrill, Selah. [835]

Schick, Conrad. [843] "The Gate Gennath," Palestine Exploration Fund, Quarterly Statement, (1892), 186-187.

Schick, Conrad. [844] "Line of Second Wall," Palestine Exploration Fund, Quarterly Statement, (1888), 62-63. (With reply by Selah Merrill, 63-65.)

Schick, Conrad. [845] "The New Road North of the City," Palestine Exploration Fund, Quarterly Statement, (1890), 246-247.

Schick, Conrad. [846] "Note on the New German Church in the Muristan, and the Discovery of an Ancient Wall," Palestine Exploration Fund, Quarterly Statement, (1895), 146-147.

Schick, Conrad. [847] "Notes from Jerusalem," Palestine Exploration Fund, Quarterly Statement, (1887), 154-157.

Schick, Conrad. [848] "The Second Wall," Palestine Exploration Fund, Quarterly Statement, (1887), 218-221.

Schick, Conrad. [849] "The Second Wall of Ancient Jerusalem," Palestine Exploration Fund, Quarterly Statement, (1893), 191-193.

Schick, Conrad. [850] "Tombs, or Remainder of Third Wall?" Palestine Exploration Fund, Quarterly Statement, (1895), 30-32.

Schmitt, Götz. [851] "Die dritte Mauer Jerusalems," Zeitschrift des deutschen Palästina-Vereins, 97 (1981), 153-170.

Scott, R. B. Y. [852] "A Further Trace of the Sukenik-Mayer 'Third Wall?'" Bulletin of the American Schools of Oriental Research, 169 (1963), 61-62.

Shiloh, Yigal. [853] "The 'First Wall' in the City of David-- A City Wall from Second Temple Times," Qadmoniot, 13 (1980), 57-58 (Hebrew). [English summary in Old Testament Abstracts, 4 (1981), 102.]

Simons, Jan. [854] "The 'Second Wall' and the Problem of the Holy Sepulchre," in Jerusalem in the Old Testament: Researches and Theories. Leiden: Brill, 1952, 282-343.

Simons, Jan. [855] "The 'Third Wall' or the Wall of Herod Agrippa," in Jerusalem in the Old Testament: Researches and Theories. Leiden: Brill, 1952, 459-503.

Smallwood, E. Mary. [856] "The North Walls of Jerusalem before A.D. 70," in The Jews under Roman Rule. Leiden: Brill, 561-564.

Solomiac, M. [857] "The Northwest Line of the Third Wall of Jerusalem," Bulletin of the American Schools of Oriental Research, 89 (1943), 18-21.

Solomiac, M. [858] Les tours royales de Josèphe Flavius. Jerusalem, 1936, 95 pp.

Solomiac, M. [859] "The Towers and Cisterns of the Third Wall of Jerusalem," Bulletin of the American Schools of Oriental Research, 84 (1941), 5-7.

Spiess, F. [860] "Die neueste Construction der zweiten Mauer Jerusalems und Josephus," Zeitschrift des deutschen Palästina-Vereins, 11 (1888), 46-59..

Staehlin, Wilhelm. [861] "Jerusalem hat Mauern und Tore," in E. Schlink and A. Peters (eds.), Zur Auferbauung des Leibes Christi (Festschrift Peter Brunner). Kassel: Johannes Stauda, 1965, 76-83.

Steve, M.-A. See Vincent, Louis-Hugues and Steve, M.-A. [874]

Strobel, August. [862] "Die Südmauer Jerusalems zur Zeit Jesu (Jos Bell 5, 142ff. Neue Grabungsergebnisse kritisch betrachtet)," in O. Betz, K. Haacker, and M. Hengel (eds.), Josephus-Studien: Untersuchungen zu Josephus, dem antiken Judentum und den Neuen Testament (Festschrift Otto Michel). Göttingen: Vandenhoeck and Ruprecht, 1974, 344-361.

Sukenik, Eleazar L. [863] "Note on the North Wall of Jerusalem," Bulletin of the American Schools of Oriental Research, 26 (1927), 8-9.

Sukenik, Eleazar L. and Mayer, Leo A. [864] "A New Section of the Third Wall, Jerusalem," Palestine Exploration Quarterly, (1944), 145-151.

Sukenik, Eleazar L. and Mayer, Leo A. [865] The Third Wall of Jerusalem: An Account of Excavations. Jerusalem: Hebrew University Press / London: Oxford University Press, 1930, 72 pp. + 10 plans.

Tushingham, A. Douglas. [866] "Yerushalayim," in R. Moorey and P. Parr (eds.), Archaeology in the Levant: Essays for Kathleen Kenyon. Warminster: Aris and Phillips, 1978, 183-193.

Vincent, Louis-Hugues. See Murphy, Richard T. A. [837]

Vincent, Louis-Hugues. [867] "Autour du rempart d' Agrippa," Revue biblique, 34 (1925), 588-592.

Vincent, Louis-Hugues. [868] "La deuxième enceinte de Jérusalem," Revue biblique, 11 (1902), 31-57.

Vincent, Louis-Hugues. [869] "Encore la troisième enceinte de Jérusalem," Revue biblique, , 54 (1947), 90-126.

Vincent, Louis-Hugues. [870] "Fouilles aux abords de la tour Pséphina," Revue biblique, 22 (1913), 88-96.

Vincent, Louis-Hugues. [871] "Fouille à l' angle N.-O de Jérusalem," Revue biblique, 22 (1913), 101-103.

Vincent, Louis-Hugues. [872] "La troisième enceinte de Jérusalem," Revue biblique, 17 (1908), 182-204, 367-381.

Vincent, Louis-Hugues. [873] "La troisième enceinte de Jérusalem," Revue biblique, 36 (1927), 516-548; 37 (1928), 80-100, 321-339.

Vincent, Louis-Hugues and Steve, M.-A. [874] "Les remparts: La première enceinte; la seconde enceinte; la troisième enceinte; autour d' un rempart mouvant," in Jérusalem de l' Ancien Testament, 1. Paris: Gabalda, 1954, 51-174.

Vriezen, K. J. H. [875] "Jérusalem: Quartier du Muristan," Revue biblique, 84 (1977), 275-278.

Vriezen, K. J. H. [876] "Zweiter vorläufiger Bericht über der Erlösserkirche im Muristan in der Altstadt von Jerusalem (1972-1974), " Zeitschrift des deutschen Palästina-Vereins, 94 (1978), 76-81.

5. C. City Walls and Gates: Medieval

Avigad, Nahman. [877] "In the Middle Ages: Muslim and Crusader Remains," in Discovering Jerusalem. Nashville: Thoams Nelson, 1983, 247-255.

Bahat, Dan. [878] "The Church of Mary Magdalene and its Quarter," in Eretz-Israel: Archaeological, Historical, and Geographical Studies, 18. Jerusalem: Israel Exploration Society, 1985, 5-7 (Hebrew), 65* (English summary). [On postern of St. Mary Magdalene.]

Bahat, Dan and Ben-Ari, M. [879] "Excavations at Tancred's Tower," in Y. Yadin (ed.), Jerusalem Revealed: Archaeology in the Holy City, 1968-1974. New Haven and London: Yale University Press and the Israel Exploration Society, 1976, 109-110.

Barton, George A. [880] "Researches of the American School in Palestine, 2: Investigations near the Damascus Gate, Jerusalem," Journal of Biblical Literature, 22 (1903), 176-182.

Beaumont, E. F. See Crace, J. D. and Beaumont, E. F. [888]

Beaumont, E. F. and Watson, Charles M. [881] "Recent Discoveries at Jerusalem," Palestine Exploration Fund, Quarterly Statement, (1914), 165-169.

Ben-Ari, M. See Bahat, Dan and Ben-Ari, M. [879]

Ben-Arieh, Yehoshua. [882] "The City Wall and 'The Citadel of David,' / The City Gates, / The Locking of the Gates," in Jerusalem in the 19th Century: The Old City. Jerusalem: Yad Izhaq Ben-Zvi / New York: St. Martin's, 1984, 15-23.

Bishop, Eric F. F. [883] "Damascus Gate or the Gate of the Pillar in Jerusalem," Catholic Biblical Quarterly, 17 (1955), 553-558.

Broshi, Magen. [884] "Along Jerusalem's Walls," Biblical Archaeologist, 40 (1977), 11-17.

Broshi, Magen and Tsafrir, Yoram. [885] "Excavations at the Zion Gate, Jerusalem, 1974," Israel Exploration Journal, 27 (1977), 28-37.

Büchler, Adolpf. [886] "The Hebrew Graffito in the Golden Gate," Palestine Exploration Fund, Quarterly Statement, (1908), 261.

Cohen, Amnon. [887] "Were the Walls of Jerusalem Built (1536-6) by Abraham Castro?" Zion, 47 (1982), 407-418 (Hebrew), xxi-xxii (English summary).

Crace, J. D. and Beaumont, E. F. [888] "The Damascus Gate, Jerusalem," Palestine Exploration Fund, Quarterly Statement, (1914), 29-33.

Crawley-Boevey, A. W. [889] "The Damascus Gate, or Bab el-Amud," Palestine Exploration Fund, Quarterly Statement, (1912), 196-202.

5C/City Walls and Gates: Medieval

Dalton, J. N. [890] "Note on the 'First Wall' of Ancient Jerusalem and the Present Excavations," Palestine Exploration Fund, Quarterly Statement, (1895), 26-29.

Finn, Elisabeth Anne. [891] "Note on 'The Remains of Old Wall outside the Present North Wall of Jerusalem,'" Palestine Exploration Fund, Quarterly Statement, (1889), 205. The "Note" is to Schick, Conrad. [905]

Gafni, Shlomo S. and Van der Heyden, A. [892] "The City Wall and Its Gates," in The Glory of Jerusalem. Cambridge: Cambridge University Press, 1982, 14-25.

Hanauer, James Edward. [893] "The Maladrerie," Palestine Exploration Fund, Quarterly Statement, (1893), 142.

Har-El, Menashe. [894] "The Gates and Walls of Jerusalem in Our Time," in This is Jerusalem. Jerusalem: Canaan, 1977, 211-274.

Macalister, R. A. Stewart. [895] "The Hebrew Graffito in the Golden Gate," Palestine Exploration Fund, Quarterly Statement, (1908), 164-165.

Magen, M. [896] "Excavations at the Damascus Gate," Qadmoniot, 17 (1984), 17-20 (Hebrew). [English summary in Old Testament Abstracts, 8 (1985), 227.]

Mantell, A. M. [897] "Jerusalem: Newly Opened Gate in the East Wall of the Haram," Palestine Exploration Fund, Quarterly Statement, (1882), 169-170.

Merrill, Selah. [898] "An Excavation North of the City Wall," Palestine Exploration Fund, Quarterly Statement, (1903), 155-157.

Mitchell, Hinckley G. [899] "The Modern Wall of Jerusalem," in Annual of the American School of Oriental Research in Jerusalem, 1. New Haven: Tuttle, Morehouse, and Taylor, 1920, 28-50, 71 pls.

National Parks Authority: [900] The Gates of Jerusalem: A Program of Restoration and Development of the Entrances to the Old City of Jerusalem. A Joint Project of the National Parks Authority and the Municipality of Jerusalem. Tel Aviv: National Parks Authority, 1969, 44 pp.

Nebenzahl, Kenneth. [900A] "Jerusalem, from the Nuremberg Chronicle (1493)," in Maps of the Holy Land: Images of Terra Sancta through Two Millennia. New York: Abbeville Press, 1986, 63, fig. 13. [Cartouche of the medieval city with names for the gates.]

Schick, Conrad. [901] "Excavations inside the New Gate," Palestine Exploration Fund, Quarterly Statement, (1895), 109.

Schick, Conrad. [902] "Old Remains outside Jaffa Gate," Palestine Exploration Fund, Quarterly Statement, (1887), 213-214.

Schick, Conrad. [903] "Remains of Old Wall inside City," Palestine Exploration Fund, Quarterly Statement, (1891), 277-278.

5C/City Walls and Gates: Medieval

Schick, Conrad. [904] "Remains of Old Wall near the North-East Corner of the City," Palestine Exploration Fund, Quarterly Statement, (1889), 65-67; (1890), 21.

Schick, Conrad. [905] "Remains of Old Wall outside the Present Northern Wall of the City," Palestine Exploration Fund, Quarterly Statement, (1889), 63-64.

Schick, Conrad. [906] "A Stair and Postern in the Old Wall," Palestine Exploration Fund, Quarterly Statement, (1895), 30.

Schur, Nathan. [907] "City Walls and Gates," in Jerusalem in Pilgrims and Travellers' Accounts: A Thematic Bibliography of Western Christian Itineraries, 1300-1917. Jerusalem: Ariel, 1980, 15-18.

Séjourné, Paul-M. [908] "Une inscription grecque sur les murs de Jérusalem," Revue biblique, 3 (1894), 260-262.

Séjourné, Paul-M. [909] "Les murs de Jérusalem," Revue biblique, 4 (1895), 37-47.

Sharon, M. [910] "The Ayyubid Walls of Jerusalem, A New Inscription from the Time of al-Mu'azzam 'Isa,'" in M. Rosen-Ayalon (ed.), Studies in Memory of Gaston Wiet. Jerusalem: Hebrew University, Institute of Asian and African Studies, 1977, 179-193.

Steve, M.-A. See Vincent, Louis-Hugues and Steve, M. A. [914]

Steckoll, Solomon. [911] The Gates of Jerusalem. New York: Praeger, 1968, 53 pp.

Tsafrir, Yoram. See Broshi, Magen and Tsafrir, Yoram. [885]

Tsafrir, Yoram. [912] "The Gates of Jerusalem in the Account of Muqaddasi-- New Identifications on the Basis of Byzantine Sources," Cathedra: For the History of Eretz-Israel and its Yishuv, 8 (1979), 147-155 (Hebrew).

Tsafrir, Yoram. [913] "Muqaddasi's Gates of Jerusalem-- a New Identification Based on Byzantine Sources," Israel Exploration Journal, 27 (1977), 152-161.

Van der Heyden, A. See Gafni, Shlomo S. and Van der Heyden, A. [892]

Vincent, Louis-Hugues and Steve, M.-A. [914] "Extension de la ville antique; le rempart actuel, iii: L' enceinte actuelle," in Jérusalem de l' Ancient Testament, 1. Paris: Gabalda, 1954, 39-50.

Watson, Charles M. See Beaumont, E. F. and Watson, Charles M. [881]

Six

Tombs and Related Materials

Abel, Félix-M. [915] "Jérusalem: Tombeau à Batn el-Hawa," Revue biblique, 32 (1923), 108-111.

Abel, Félix-M. [916] "Tombeau et ossuaires juifs récemment découvertes," Revue biblique, 22 (1913), 262-277.

Abel, Félix-M. [917] "Le tombeau d' Isäie," Journal of the Palestine Oriental Society, 2 (1921), 25-33.

Abel, Félix-M. [918] "Le 'Tombeau des rois' à Jérusalem," in Miscellanea Biblica B. Ubach. Scripta et Documenta, 1. Montserrat, 1953, 439-448.

Abercrombie, John R. [919] "A Short Note on a Siloam Tomb Inscription," Bulletin of the American Schools of Oriental Research, 254 (1984), 61-62.

Allegretti, S. [920] "Una tomba del primo periodo romano sul Monte Oliveto," Studii Biblici Franciscani, Liber Annuus, 32 (1982), 335-354.

Amiran, Ruth. [921] "The Necropolis of Jerusalem in the Time of the Monarchy," in Judah and Jerusalem: The Twelfth Archaeological Convention. Jerusalem: Israel Exploration Society, 1957, 65-72 (Hebrew), v (English summary).

Amiran, Ruth. [922] "A Late Bronze Age II Pottery Group from a Tomb in Jerusalem," in Eretz-Israel: Archaeological, Historical, and Geographical Studies, 6. Jerusalem: Israel Exploration Society, 1960, 25-37 (Hebrew), 27* (English summary).

Arensburg, B. and Rak, Y. [923] "Jewish Skeletal Remains from the Period of the Kings of Judaea," Palestine Exploration Quarterly, (1985), 30-34.

Arensburg, B. and Rak, Y. [924] "Skeletal Remains of an Ancient Jewish Population from French Hill, Jerusalem," Bulletin of the American Schools of Oriental Research, 219 (1975), 69-71.

Avigad, Nahman. See Rahmani, L. Y.; Avigad, Nahman; and Benoit, Pierre. [1126]

Avigad, Nahman. [925] "Aramaic Inscriptions in the Tomb of Jason," Israel Exploration Journal, 17 (1967), 101-111.

Avigad, Nahman. [926] "Architectural Observations on Some Rock-Cut Tombs," Palestine Exploration Quarterly, (1947), 112-122.

Avigad, Nahman. [927] "The Burial-Vault of a Nazirite Family from the Second Temple Period on Mount Scopus," in Eretz-Israel: Archaeological, Historical, and Geographical Studies, 10. Jerusalem: Israel Exploration Society, 1971, 41-49 (Hebrew), ix (English summary).

Avigad, Nahman. [928] "The Burial-Vault of a Nazirite Family on Mt. Scopus," Israel Exploration Journal, 21 (1971), 185-200.

Avigad, Nahman. [929] "Depository of Inscribed Ossuaries in the Kidron Valley, Israel Exploration Journal, 12 (1962), 1-12.

Avigad, Nahman. [930] "The Epitaph of a Royal Steward from Siloam Village," Israel Exploration Journal, 3 (1953), 137-152.

Avigad, Nahman. [931] "Holy Places and Everlasting Monuments," Ariel, 23 (1969), 25-32.

Avigad, Nahman. [932] "Jewish Rock-Cut Tombs in Jerusalem and in the Judaean Hill Country," in Eretz-Israel: Archaeological, Historical, and Geographical Studies, 8. Jerusalem: Israel Exploration Society, 1967, 119-142 (Hebrew), 72* (English summary).

Avigad, Nahman. [933] "A Jewish Tomb-Cave on Mt. Scopus," Qadmoniot, 1 (1968), 37-38 (Hebrew).

Avigad, Nahman. [934] "The Rock-Carved Facades of the Jerusalem Necropolis," Israel Exploration Journal, 1 (1950-1951), 96-106.

Avigad, Nahman. [935] "The second Tomb Inscription of the Royal Steward," Israel Exploration Journal, 5 (1955), 163-166.

Avigad, Nahman. [936] "The Tomb of a Nazirite on Mount Scopus," in Y. Yadin (ed.), Jerusalem Revealed: Archaeology in the Holy City, 1968-1974. New Haven and London: Yale University Press and the Israel Exploration Society, 1976, 66-67.

Avigad, Nahman. [937] "The Tombs around Jerusalem," in J. Aviram (ed.), Jerusalem through the Ages. Jerusalem: Israel Exploration Society, 1968, 49-61 (Hebrew), 60 (English summary).

Avigad, Nahman. [938] "The Tombs in Jerusalem," in M. Avi-Yonah (ed.), Encyclopedia of Archaeological Excavations in the Holy Land, 2. Englewwod Cliffs, NJ: Prentice-Hall, 1976, 627-641.

Bagatti, Bellarmino. [939] "Jérusalem," Revue biblique, 61 (1954), 568-570; 63 (1956), 76-77. [Tombs at Dominus Flevit.]

Bagatti, Bellarmino. [940] "Nuovi apporti archeologici al 'Dominus Flevit' (Oliveto)," Studii Biblici Franciscani, Liber Annuus, 19 (1969), 194-236.

Bagatti, Bellarmino. [941] "Ritrovamento di una tomba pitturata sull' Oliveto," Studii Biblici Franciscani, Liber Annuus, 24 (1974), 170-187.

Bagatti, Bellarmino. [942] "Scavo di un monastero al 'Dominus Flevit,'" Studii Biblici Franciscani, Liber Annuus, 6 (1955-1956), 240-270.

6/Tombs and Related Materials

Bagatti, Bellarmino. [943] "Scoperta di un cimitero giudeo-cristiano al 'Dominus Flevit,'" Studii Biblici Franciscani, Liber Annuus, 3 (1952-1953), 149-184.

Bagatti, Bellarmino and Milik, J. T. [944] Gli scavi del 'Dominus Flevit' (Monte Oliveto-Gerusalemme), 1: La necropoli del periodo Romano. Studium Biblicum Franciscanum, Collectio Major, 13. Jerusalem: Franciscan Printing Press, 1958, 187 + 23 pp.

Bagatti, Bellarmino and Milik, J. T. [945] "Nuovi scavi al 'Dominus Flevit' (Monte Oliveto-Gerusalemme)," Studii Biblici Franciscani, Liber Annuus, 4 (1953-1954), 247-276.

Bahat, Dan. [946] "Tombs of the Second Temple Period in Jerusalem: Burial Caves on Giv'at Hamivtar," Atiqot (Hebrew Series), 8 (1982), 35-40 (Hebrew with English summary).

Bahat, Dan. [947] "Tombs of the Second Temple Period in Jerusalem: Two Burial Caves at Sderot Ben-Zvi," Atiqot (Hebrew Series), 8 (1982), 66-68 (Hebrew with English summary).

Bahat, Dan and Ben-Ari, M. [948] "Excavations in Zahal-Square," Qadmoniot, 5 (1972), 118-119 (Hebrew).

Barag, Dan. [949] "A Jewish Burial-Cave on Mt. Scopus," in Eretz-Israel: Archaeological, Historical, and Geographical Studies, 11. Jerusalem: Israel Exploration Society, 1973, 101-103 (Hebrew), 25*-26* (English summary).

Barkay, Gabriel. [950] "The Divine Name Found in Jerusalem," Biblical Archaeology Review, 9/2 (March/April, 1983), 14-19.

Barkay, Gabriel. [951] "Excavations on the Slope of Himmon Valley in Jerusalem," Qadmoniot, 17 (1984), 94-108 (Hebrew). [English summary in Old Testament Abstracts, 8 (1985), 220-221.]

Barkay, Gabriel. [952] Ketef Hinnom: A Treasure Facing Jerusalem's Walls. Jerusalem: The Israel Museum, 1986, 31 pp (English) + 37 pp. (Hebrew).

Barkay, Gabriel. [953] "Le nom divin découvert à Jérusalem," Le Monde de la Bible, 30 (Au.-Sept.-Oct., 1983), 53-54.

Barkay, Gabriel. [954] "St. Andrew's Church, Jerusalem," Israel Exploration Journal, 26 (1976), 57-58.

Barkay, Gabriel and Kloner, Amos. [955] "Burial Caves North of Damascus Gate, Jerusalem," Israel Exploration Journal, 26 (1976), 55-57.

Barkay, Gabriel and Kloner, Amos. [956] "Jerusalem Tombs from the Days of the First Temple," Biblical Archaeology Review, 12/2 (March/April, 1986), 22-39.

Barkay, Gabriel; Mazar, Amihay; and Kloner, Amos. [957] "The Northern Cemetery of Jerusalem in First Temple Times," Qadmoniot, 8 (1975), 71-76.

6/Tombs and Related Materials

Barnett, R. D. [958] "Reminiscences of the Temple of Herod: The Ossuary of Nicanor, in Illustrations of Old Testament History. London: British Museum, rev. edn., 1968, 83-86.

Barnett, R. D. [959] "The Tomb of Shebna, a Royal Steward, " in Illustrations of Old Testament History. London: British Museum, rev. edn., 1968, 66-67.

Barrois, A.-G. (=Georges Augustin). [960] "La Sépultures des morts," in Manuel d' archéologie biblique, 2. Paris: Picard, 1953, 274-323.

Barrois, Georges Augustin. [961] "Tombs of the Kings," in Interpreter's Dictionary of the Bible, 4. New York: Abingdon, 1962, 668-669.

Barton, George. [962] "Researches of the American School in Palestine, 1: The Tombs of the Judges, and a Neighboring Tomb Hitherto Unexplored," Journal of Biblical Literature, 22 (1903), 164-176. [= Tombs of the Sanhedrin.]

Ben-Ari, M. See Bahat, Dan and Ben-Ari, M. [948]

Ben-Arieh, Sara. See Netzer, Ehud and Ben-Arieh, Sara. [1107]

Ben-Arieh, Sarah. [963] "Tombs of the Second Temple Period: A Burial Cave at Giv'at Ram," Atiqot (Hebrew Series), 8 (1982), 65 (Hebrew with English summary).

Ben-Arieh, Sarah. [964] "Tombs of the Second Temple Period: A Burial Cave on Mt. Scopus," Atiqot (Hebrew Series), 8 (1982), 59-60 (Hebrew with English summary).

Benayahu, M. [965] "Funerary Rites in Jerusalem," Sinai, 92 (1985), 58-65 (Hebrew).

Benoit, Pierre. See Rahmani, L. Y.; Avigad, Nahman; and Benoit, Pierre. [1126]

Benoit, Pierre. [966] "L' inscription grecque du tombeau de Jason," Israel Exploration Journal, 17 (1967), 112-113.

Berman, Ariel. See Tsaferis, Vassilios and Berman, Ariel. [1200]

Birch, W. F. [967] "The City and Tomb of David," Palestine Exploration Fund, Quarterly Statement, (1881), 94-97.

Birch, W. F. [968] "The City and Tomb of David on Ophel (so-called)," Palestine Exploration Fund, Quarterly Statement, (1911), 187-189.

Birch, W. F. [969] "David's Tomb and the Siloam Tunnel," Palestine Exploration Fund, Quarterly Statement, (1898), 161-167.

Birch, W. F. [970] "The Entrance to the Tomb of David," Palestine Exploration Fund, Quarterly Statement, (1883), 155.

Birch, W. F. [971] "It Is Required to Find the Entrance to the Tomb of David," Palestine Exploration Fund, Quarterly Statement, (1881), 97-100.

6/Tombs and Related Materials

Birch, W. F. [972] "Nehemiah's Wall and David's Tomb," Palestine Exploration Fund. Quarterly Statement, (1879), 176-179.

Birch, W. F. [973] "The Sepulchres of David and of the Kings of Judah," Palestine Exploration Fund. Quarterly Statement, (1877), 195-204.

Birch, W. F. [974] "Scheme for Finding the Sepulchre of David," Palestine Exploration Fund. Quarterly Statement, (1899), 273-276.

Birch, W. F. [975] "The Sepulchres of David on Ophel," Palestine Exploration Fund. Quarterly Statement, (1895), 261-263.

Birch, W. F. [976] "The Tomb of David," Palestine Exploration Fund. Quarterly Statement, (1879), 172-176.

Birch, W. F. [977] "The Tomb of David in the City of David," Palestine Exploration Fund. Quarterly Statement, (1883), 150-155.

Birch, W. F. [978] "The Tomb of David, Zion, and Josephus," Palestine Exploration Fund. Quarterly Statement, (1880), 167-170.

Briend, Jacques. [979] "La sépulture d' un crucifié," Bible et Terre Sainte, 133 (1971), 6-10.

Büchler, Adolpf. [980] "La pureté lévitique de Jérusalem et les tombeaux des prophètes," Revue des études juives, 62 (1911), 201-215.

Burrows, Millar. [981] "The Byzantine Tombs in the Garden of the Jerusalem School," Bulletin of the American Schools of Oriental Research, 47 (1932), 28-35.

Cassuto-Salzmann M. [982] "Una interessante iscrizone de Gerusalemme," Bibbia et Oriente, 19 (1977), 27-29. [On the Giv'at ha-Mivtar inscription.]

Chaplin, Thomas. [983] "Tomb at Jerusalem," Palestine Exploration Fund. Quarterly Statement, (1876), 61-62.

Clermont-Ganneau, Charles. [984] "Ancient Tombs North-East of Jerusalem," in C. Warren and C. R. Conder (eds.), The Survey of Western Palestine, 5: Jerusalem. London: Palestine Exploration Fund, 1884, 297-301.

Clermont-Ganneau, Charles. [985] "At Selwân," in Archaeological Researches in Palestine during the Years 1873-1874, 1. Trans. by Aubrey Stewart. London: Palestine Exploration Fund, 1899, 304-324.

Clermont-Ganneau, Charles. [986] "The Cemetery of Mâmillâ," in Archaeological Researches in Palestine during the Years 1873-1874, 1. Trans. by Aubrey Stewart. London: Palestine Exploration Fund, 1899, 279-290.

Clermont-Ganneau, Charles. [987] "Jérusalem-- Tombeaux antiques réputés judïco-chrétiens," Bulletin d' archéologie chrétienne, 2nd ser., 5 (1874), 175-179.

Clermont-Ganneau, Charles. [988] "Jewish Ossuaries and Sepulchres in the Neighbourhood of Jerusalem," in Archaeological Researches in Palestine during the Years 1873-1874, 1. Trans. by Aubrey Stewart. London: Palestine Exploration Fund, 1899, 381-454.

Clermont-Ganneau, Charles. [989] "Judaeo-Christian Sarcophagi with Inscriptions Found on the Mount of Offence," Palestine Exploration Fund, Quarterly Statement, (1874), 7-10.

Clermont-Ganneau, Charles. [990] "Notes on Certain New Discoveries at Jerusalem: Greek Inscriptions in the So-Called Tomb of the Prophets," Palestine Exploration Fund, Quarterly Statement, (1871), 104.

Clermont-Ganneau, Charles. [991] "The Sepulchres of Kerm esh Sheik and the Ground to the North-East of Jerusalem," in Archaeological Researches in Palestine during the Years 1873-1874, 1. Trans. by Aubrey Stewart. London: Palestine Exploration Fund, 1899, 248-254.

Clermont-Ganneau, Charles. [992] "The Tomb of Absalom," in C. Warren and C. R. Conder (eds.), The Survey of Western Palestine, 5: Jerusalem. London: Palestine Exploration Fund, 1884, 294-295.

Clermont-Ganneau, Charles. [993] "Tombs of the Prophets," in Archaeological Researches in Palestine during the Years 1873-1874, 1. Trans. by Aubrey Stewart. London: Palestine Exploration Fund, 1899, 345-380.

Clermont-Ganneau, Charles. [994] "The So-Called Tomb of Simon the Just," in Archaeological Researches in Palestine during the Years 1873-1874, 1. Trans. by Aubrey Stewart. London: Palestine Exploration Fund, 1899, 267-270.

Clermont-Ganneau, Charles. [995] Les tombeaux de David et des rois de Juda et le tunnel-aqueduc de Siloé. Paris: Imprimerie Nationale, 1897, 48 pp. Also in Recueil d' archéologie orientale, 2. Paris: Leroux, 1898, 254-294.

Cole, Dan. [996] "Where is King David's Tomb?" Biblical Archaeology Review, 9/4 (July/Aug., 1983), 73.

Communication du Service des Antiquités: [997] "Jérusalem: Giv'at HaMivtar, inscription araméenne," Revue biblique, 78 (1971), 428-429.

Conder, Claude R. [998] "Jewish Traditions in Jerusalem," Palestine Exploration Fund, Quarterly Statement, (1882), 142-146. [Tomb of Simon the Just.]

Conder, Claude R. [999] "Masonry Tombs," Palestine Exploration Fund, Quarterly Statement, (1876), 151-152.

Conder, Claude R. [1000] "Notes on Jerusalem," Palestine Exploration Fund, Quarterly Statement, (1880), 101-103. [Tombs of the Kings.]

Conder, Claude R. [1001] "Notes on Jerusalem: Tombs of the Kings," Palestine Exploration Fund, Quarterly Statement, (1879), 101-102.

Conder, Claude R. [1002] "Rock-Cut Tombs," Palestine Exploration Fund, Quarterly Statement, (1876), 17-20.

Corbo, Virgilio. [1003] "Dans la vallée de Josaphat: Le culte de Saint Jacques et le tombeau des Beni Hezir à Jérusalem," Bible et Terre Sainte, 56 (1963), 20-23.

Corbo, Virgilio. [1004] "Mort et Sépulture de St. Jacques," in Saint Jacques le Mineur: Premier eveque de Jérusalem. Jerusalem: Terre Sainte de Custodie Franciscaine, 1962, 59-75.

Cross, Frank M. [1005] "A Note on a Burial Inscription from Mt. Scopus," Israel Exploration Journal, 33 (1983), 245-246.

Dalman, Knut Olaf. [1006] "Über die Felsengrab im Hinnomtale bei Jerusalem," Zeitschrift des deutschen Palästina-Vereins, 62 (1939), 190-208.

Davies, D. and Kloner, Amos. [1007] "A Burial Cave of the Late Israelite Period on the Slopes of Mt. Zion," Qadmoniot, 11 (1978), 16-19 (Hebrew). [English summary in Old Testament Abstracts, 2 (1979), 13.]

Decroix, J. [1008] "La tombe de la fille du Pharaon," Bible et Terre Sainte, 116 (1969), 5.

Dickie, Archibald C. [1009] "Report on Tomb Discovered near 'Tombs of the Kings,'" Palestine Exploration Fund, Quarterly Statement, (1896), 305-310.

Dickson, Gladys. [1010] "The Tomb of Nicanor of Alexandria," Palestine Exploration Fund, Quarterly Statement, (1903), 326-332.

Dinkler, E. [1011] "Comments on the History of the Symbol of the Cross," Journal for Theology and the Church, 1 (1965), 124-146. [Relates to Talpioth ossuaries.]

Diringer, David. [1012] "Le iscrizioni della zona di Silwan," in Le iscrizioni antico-ebraiche Palestinesi. Florence: Monnier, 1934, 81-110

Duncan, J. Garrow. [1013] "A Leaden Ossuary," Palestine Exploration Fund, Quarterly Statement, (1925), 65-67.

Feigin, Samuel. [1014] "The Meaning of Ariel," Journal of Biblical Literature, 39 (1920), 131-137. [= necropolis; city of David.]

Ferembach, Denise. [1015] "Note sur deux crânes trouvés à Jérusalem dans une sépulture d' époque romaine," in Eretz-Israel: Archaeological, Historical, and Geographical Studies, 6. Jerusalem: Israel Exploration Society, 1960, 7*-8*.

Figueras, P. [1016] Decorated Jewish Ossuaries. Documenta et monumenta orientis antiqui, 20. Leiden: Brill, 1983, 122 pp.

Finegan, Jack. [1017] "Tombs," in The Archeology of the New Testament: The Life of Jesus and the Beginning of the Early Church. Princeton: Princeton University Press, 1969, 181-202.

Fishwick, Duncan. [1018] "The Talpioth Ossuaries Again," New Testament Studies, 10 (1963/1964), 49-61.

Flecker, E. [1019] "The Sepulchre of Shebna," Palestine Exploration Fund, Quarterly Statement, (1884), 178-181.

Flinders-Petrie, William M. [1020] "Notes on Places Visited in Jerusalem: Silwan," Palestine Exploration Fund, Quarterly Statement, (1890), 157-159.

Flinders-Petrie, William M. [1021] "The Tomb-Cutters Cubit at Jerusalem," Palestine Exploration Fund, Quarterly Statement, (1892), 28-35.

Foerster, G. [1022] "Architectural Fragments from 'Jason's Tomb' Reconsidered," Israel Exploration Journal, 28 (1978), 152-156.

Gafni, Isaiah. [1023] "Reinterment in the Land of Israel: Notes on the Origin and Development of the Custom," in L. I. Levine (ed.), Jerusalem Cathedra, 1. Jerusalem: Yad Izhaq Ben-Zvi Institute / Detroit: Wayne State University Press, 1981, 96-104.

Galling, Kurt. [1024] "Ein Etagen-Pilaster-Grab im Norden von Jerusalem," Zeitschrift des deutschen Palästina-Vereins, 59 (1936), 111-123.

Galling, Kurt. [1025] "Die Nekropole von Jerusalem," Palästinajahrbuch, 32 (1936), 73-101.

Gath, Joseph and Rahmani, L. Y. [1026] "Roman Tombs at Manahat, Jerusalem," Israel Exploration Journal, 27 (1977), 209-214.

Geraty, Lawrence. [1027] "A Thrice Repeated Ossuary Inscription from French Hill, Jerusalem," Bulletin of the American Schools of Oriental Research, 219 (1975), 73-78.

Germer-Durand, Joseph. [1028] "Épigraphie chrétienne de Jérusalem: Épitaphes, objets divers," Revue biblique, 1 (1892), 560-588.

Geva, Hillel. See Reich, Ronny and Geva, Hillel. [1128-1130]

Gildemeister, J. [1029] "Ghassanidengräber vor Jerusalem" Zeitschrift des deutschen Palästina-Vereins, 3 (1880), 147-148.

Gonen, Rivka. [1030] "Was the Site of the Jerusalem Temple Originally a Cemetery?" Biblical Archaeology Review, 11/3 (May/June, 1985), 44-55.

Goodenough, Erwin R. [1031] "The Jewish Tombs of Palestine, / The Contents of the Jewish Tombs in Palestine," in Jewish Symbols in the Greco-Roman Period, 1: The Archaeological Evidence from Palestine. New York: Pantheon, 1953, 61-177.

Gressmann, Hugo. [1032] "Ein prähistorisches Grab auf dem Grundstück der Kaiserin Auguste Viktoria-Stiftung bei Jerusalem," Palästinajahrbuch, 3 (1907), 72-75.

Gustafsson, Berndt. [1033] "The Oldest Graffiti in the History of the Church," New Testament Studies, 3 (1956/1957), 65-69. [The Talpioth ossuaries.]

Haas, N. [1034] "Anthropological Observations on the Skeletal Remains from Giv'at ha-Mivtar," Israel Exploration Journal, 20 (1970), 38-59.

Hamilton, R. W. and Husseini, S. A. S. [1035] "Shaft Tombs on the Nablus Road, Jerusalem," Quarterly of the Department of Antiquities in Palestine, 4 (1935), 170-174.

Har-El, Menashe. [1036] "Necropolis Hills," in This is Jerusalem. Jerusalem: Canaan, 1977, 124-151.

Holland, T. A. [1037] "A Study of Palestinian Iron Age Baked Clay Figurines with Special Reference to Jerusalem: Cave I," Levant, 9 (1977), 121-155.

Hornstein, C. A. [1038] "Newly Discovered Tomb on Mount Scopus," Palestine Exploration Fund, Quarterly Statement, (1900), 75-76.

Hueso, Vicente Vilar. [1039] "Onomástica neotestamentaria y símbolos crístianos en el cemeterio de 'Dominus Flevit,'" Estudios bíblicos, 18 (1959), 285-291.

Husseini, S. A. S. See Hamilton, R. W. and Husseini, S. A. S. [1035]

Jeremias, Joachim. [1040] Heiligengräber in Jesu Umwelt (Mt. 23. 29; Lk. 11. 47): Eine Untersuchung zur Volksreligion der Zeit Jesu. Göttingen: Vandenhoeck and Ruprecht, 1958, 155 pp.

Jotham-Rothschild, Julius. [1041] "The Tombs of Sanhedria," Palestine Exploration Quarterly, (1952), 23-38; (1954), 16-22.

Kahane, P. [1042] "Pottery Types from the Jewish Ossuary-Tombs round Jerusalem: An Archaeological Contribution to the Problem of the Hellenization of Jewry in the Herodian Period," Israel Exploration Journal, 2 (1952), 125-139.

Kane, J. P. [1043] "By No Means 'The Earliest Records of Christianity'--with an Emended Reading of the Talpioth Inscription IEOUS IOU," Palestine Exploration Quarterly, (1971), 103-108.

Kane, J. P. [1044] "The Ossuary Inscriptions of Jerusalem," Journal of Semitic Studies, 23 (1978), 268-282.

Katzenstein, H. J. [1045] "The Royal Steward (asher -'al ha-bayith)," Israel Exploration Journal, 10 (1960), 152-155.

Kloner, Amos. See Barkay, Gabriel and Kloner, Amos. [955-956]

Kloner, Amos. See Barkay, Gabriel; Mazar, Amihay; and Kloner, Amos. [957]

Kloner, Amos. See Davies, D. and Kloner, Amos. [1007]

Kloner, Amos. [1046] "A Burial-Cave of the Second Temple Period," in Y. Yadin (ed.), Jerusalem Revealed: Archaeology in the Holy City, 1968-1974. New Haven and London: Yale University Press and the Israel Exploration Society, 1976, 69-70.

Kloner, Amos. [1047] "The Burial-Cave of the Second Temple Period at Giv'at ha-mivtar," Qadmoniot, 5 (1972), 108-109 (Hebrew).

Kloner, Amos. [1048] "A Burial-Cave of the Second Temple Period at Giv'at Hamivtar, Jerusalem," in A. Oppenheimer, U. Rappaport, and M. Stern (eds.), Jerusalem in the Second Temple Period: Abraham Schalit Memorial Volume. Jerusalem: Yad Izhaq Ben-Zvi Institute, 1980, 191-224 (Hebrew), xii-xiii (English summary).

Kloner, Amos. [1049] "Burial Caves in Ha'Ari Street, Jerusalem," in Eretz-Israel: Archaeological, Historical, and Geographical Studies, 15. Jerusalem: Israel Exploration Society, 1981, 401-405 (Hebrew), 88* (English summary).

Kloner, Amos. [1050] "A Monument of the Second Temple Period West of the Old City of Jerusalem," in Eretz-Israel: Archaeological, Historical, and Geographical Studies, 18. Jerusalem: Israel Exploration Society, 1985, 58-64 (Hebrew), 67* (English summary).

Kloner, Amos. [1051] "An Ossuary from Jerusalem Decorated with a Monumental Façade Motif," Qadmoniot, 17 (1984), 121-123 (Hebrew). [English summary in Old Testament Abstracts, 8 (1985), 226.]

Kloner, Amos. [1052] "A Painted Tomb on the Mount of Olives," Qadmoniot, 8 (1975), 27-30 (Hebrew).

Kloner, Amos. [1053] "Rock-Cut Tombs in Jerusalem," Bulletin of the Anglo-Israel Archeological Society, (1982/1983), 37-40.

Kloner, Amos. [1054] "A Tomb of the Second Temple Period at French Hill, Jerusalem," Israel Exploration Journal, 30 (1980), 99-108.

Kloner, Amos. [1055] "Tombs of the Second Temple Period: A Burial Cave on Mt. Scopus," Atiqot (Hebrew Series), 8 (1982), 57-58 (Hebrew with English summary).

Kon, Maximillian. [1056] The Tombs of the Kings. With an Introduction by E. L. Sukenik. Tel-Aviv: Dvir, 1947, 87 pp.

Kraeling, Carl H. [1057] "Christian Burial Urns?" Biblical Archaeologist, 9 (1946), 16-20. [The Talpioth ossuaries.]

Krauss, Samuel. [1058] "La double inhumation chez les juifs," Revue des études juives, 97 (1934), 1-34.

Kuhn, Heinz-W. [1059] "Der Gekreuzigte von Giv'at ha-Mivtar: Bilanz einer Entdeckung," in C. Anderson (ed.), Theologia Crucis - Signum Crucis (Festschrift Erich Dinkler). Tübingen: Mohr, 1979, 303-334.

Kuhn, Heinz-W. [1060] "Der Gekreuzigte von Giv'at ha-Mivtar: Korrektur eines Versehens in der Erstausgabe," Zeitschrift für die neutestamentlich Wissenschaft, 69 (1978), 118-122.

Lagrange, Marie-Joseph. [1061] "Lettre de Jérusalem," Revue biblique, 1 (1892), 439-456. [Christian tombs; inscriptions.]

Landman, L. [1062] "Hall of Reckoning outside Jerusalem," Jewish Quarterly Review, 61 (1971), 199-211.

Lemaire, André. [1063] "Une tombe du Récent Bronze au Mont des Oliviers," Studii Biblici Franciscani, Liber Annuus, 5 (1954/1955), 261-298.

Lidzbarski, M. [1064] "An Inscribed Jewish Ossuary," Palestine Exploration Fund, Quarterly Statement, (1913), 84-85.

Lidzbarski, M. [1065] "The Jewish-Aramaic Inscriptions at the Tomb near Silwan," Palestine Exploration Fund, Quarterly Statement, (1909), 73.

Lifshitz, Baruch. [1066] "L' exhortation à la jouissance de la vie dans une inscription tombale juive à Jérusalem," Revue biblique, 73 (1966), 248-255. [From Jason's tomb.]

Loffreda, Stanislao. [1067] "Due tombe a Betania presso le Suore della Nigrizia," Studii Biblici Franciscani, Liber Annuus, 19 (1969), 349-366.

Loffreda, Stanislao. [1068] "The Late Chronology of Some Rock-Cut Tombs of the Selwan Necropolis, Jerusalem," Studii Biblici Franciscani, Liber Annuus, 23 (1973), 7-36.

Loffreda, Stanislao. [1069] "Il monolita di Siloe: Monumento incompiuto del periodo ellenistico-romano," Studii Biblici Franciscani, Liber Annuus, 16 (1965/1966), 85-126.

Loffreda, Stanislao. [1070] "La tomba n. 3 presso le Suore della Nigrizia à Betania," Studii Biblici Franciscani, Liber Annuus, 24 (1974), 143-169.

Luciani, F. [1071] "Le tombe di Siloe," Bibbia e Oriente, 10 (1968), 135-140.

Macalister, R. A. Stewart. [1072] "Additional Notes on Tombs in the Wâdy er Rabâbi," Palestine Exploration Fund, Quarterly Statement, (1903), 170-171.

Macalister, R. A. Stewart. [1073] "Further Observations on the Ossuary of Nicanor of Alexandria," Palestine Exploration Fund, Quarterly Statement, (1905), 253-257.

Macalister, R. A. Stewart, [1074] "Mughâret el-'Anab," Palestine Exploration Fund, Quarterly Statement, (1904), 246-248. [The so-called "Cave of the Grapes."]

Macalister, R. A. Stewart. [1075] "The Newly-Discovered Tomb North of Jerusalem, Palestine Exploration Fund, Quarterly Statement, (1902), 118-120.

Macalister, R. A. Stewart. [1076] "The Nicophorieh Tomb," Palestine Exploration Fund, Quarterly Statement, (1901), 397-402.

Macalister, R. A. Stewart. [1077] "The Pachomios Inscription in Wâdy er-Rabâbi," Palestine Exploration Fund, Quarterly Statement, (1903), 173-175.

Macalister, R. A. Stewart. [1078] "A Peculiar Rock-Cutting in the Kedron Valley," Palestine Exploration Fund, Quarterly Statement, (1902), 247-248.

Macalister, R. A. Stewart. [1079] "On a Rock-Tomb North of Jerusalem," Palestine Exploration Fund, Quarterly Statement, (1900), 54-61.

Macalister, R. A. Stewart. [1080] "The Rock-Cut Tombs in Wâdy er-Rabâbi," Palestine Exploration Fund, Quarterly Statement, (1900), 225-248; (1901), 145-158, 215-226.

Macalister, R. A. Stewart. [1081] "A Tomb with Aramaic Inscriptions near Silwan," Palestine Exploration Fund, Quarterly Statement, (1908), 341-342.

Macalister, R. A. Stewart. [1082] "On a Tomb beside the Bethlehem Road," Palestine Exploration Fund, Quarterly Statement, (1902), 244-245.

Macalister, R. A. Stewart. [1083] "An Unpublished Inscription in the Northern Necropolis of Jerusalem," Palestine Exploration Fund, Quarterly Statement, (1904), 255-257.

Maisler, B. (= Mazar, Benjamin) [1084] "Cypriote Pottery at a Tomb-Cave in the Vicinity of Jerusalem," American Journal of Semitic Languages and Literatures, 49 (1933), 248-253.

Maisler, B. (= Mazar, Benjamin) [1085] "A Hebrew Ossuary Inscription," Palestine Exploration Fund, Quarterly Statement, (1931), 171-172.

Mancini, Ignazio. [1086] "The Jewish Christian Burial Ground of 'Dominus Flevit,'" in Archaeological Discoveries Relative to the Judaeo-Christians. Studium Biblicum Franciscanum, Collectio Minor, 10. Jerusalem: Franciscan Printing Press, Jerusalem: Franciscan Printing Press, 1970, 47-64.

Mantell, A. M. [1087] "Jerusalem: The Bakoosh Hill," Palestine Exploration Fund, Quarterly Statement, (1882), 165-166.

Mayer, Leo A. [1088] "A Tomb in the Kidron Valley Containing Ossuaries with Hebrew Graffiti Names," Bulletin of the British School of Archaeology in Jerusalem, 5 (1924), 56-60.

Mayer, Leo A. [1089] "A Tomb in the Nahalath Ahim Quarter, Jerusalem," Proceedings of the Jewish Palestine Exploration Society, 1, 2-4 (1925), 40-42.

Mazar, Amihay. See Barkay, Gabriel; Mazar, Amihay; and Kloner, Amos. [957]

Mazar, Amihay. [1090] "Iron Age Burial Caves North of the Damascus Gate," Israel Exploration Journal, 26 (1976), 1-8.

Mazar, Amihay. [1091] "Tombs of the Second Temple Period: A Burial Cave on French Hill," Atiqot (Hebrew Series), 8 (1982), 41-45 (Hebrew with English summary).

Mazar, Benjamin. See Maisler, B. (= Mazar, Benjamin) [1084-1085]

Mazar, Benjamin. [1092] "The Necropolis of Jerusalem," in The Mountain of the Lord. Garden City, NY: Doubleday, 1975, 223-231.

Mazar, Benjamin. [1093] "Royal Tombs in the City of David," in The Mountain of the Lord. Garden City, NY: Doubleday, 1975, 183-189.

Merrill, Selah. [1094] "An Immense Charnel House," Palestine Exploration Fund, Quarterly Statement, (1903), 153-155.

Meyers, Eric M. [1095] Jewish Ossuaries: Reburial and Rebirth, Secondary Burials in their Near Eastern Setting. Rome: Pontifical Biblical Institute, 1971, 120 pp.

Meyers, Eric M. [1096] "Secondary Burials in Palestine," Biblical Archaeologist, 33 (1970), 2-29.

Milik, J. T. See Bagatti, Bellarmino and Milik, J. T. [944-945]

Milik, J. T. [1097] "Nuovi scavi ad 'Dominus Flevit:' Iscrizioni sugli ossuari," Studii Biblici Franciscani, Liber Annuus, 4 (1954), 260-276.

Milik, J. T. [1098] "Trois tombeaux juifs récemment découverts au Sud-Est de Jérusalem," Studii Biblici Franciscani, Liber Annuus, 7 (1956/1957), 232-267.

Møller-Christensen, Vilhelm. [1099] "Skeletal Remains from Giv'at Ha-Mivtar," Israel Exploration Journal, 26 (1976), 35-38.

Naveh, Joseph. [1100] "An Aramaic Consolatory Burial Inscription," Atiqot (English Series), 14 (1980), 55-59.

Naveh, Joseph. [1101] "An Aramaic Tomb Inscription Written in Paleo-Hebrew Script," Israel Exploration Journal, 23 (1973), 82-92.

Naveh, Joseph. [1102] "New Inscriptions on Ossuaries from Northern Jerusalem," in Eretz-Israel: Archaeological, Historical, and Geographical Studies, 10. Jerusalem: Israel Exploration Society, 1971, 188-190 (Hebrew).

Naveh, Joseph. [1103] "A New Tomb-Inscription from Giv'at Hamivtar," in Y. Yadin (ed.), Jerusalem Revealed: Archaeology in the Holy City, 1968-1974. New Haven and London: Yale University Press and the Israel Exploration Society, 1976, 73-74

Naveh, Joseph. [1104] "The Ossuary Inscriptions from Giv'at Ha-Mivtar," Israel Exploration Journal, 20 (1970), 33-37.

Negbi, Ora and Oran, Eliézer. [1105] "Jérusalem: Colline française," Revue biblique, 77 (1970), 572-573.

Netzer, Ehud. [1106] "Herod's Family Tomb in Jerusalem," Biblical Archaeology Review, 9/3 (May/June, 1983), 51-59.

Netzer, Ehud and Ben-Arieh, Sara. [1107] "Remains of an Opus Reticulatum Building in Jerusalem," Israel Exploration Journal, 33 (1983), 163-175.

Nubani, Hamdi. [1108] "Mamilla Cemetary: Historical Tombstones in Arabic," Annual of the Department of Antiquities of Jordan, 3 (1956), 8-14.

Ollendorf, Franz. [1109] "Two Mamluk Tomb-Chambers in Western Jerusalem," Israel Explorqation Journal, 32 (1982), 245-250.

Oran, Eliézer. See Negbi, Ora and Oran, Eliézer. [1105]

Oran, Eliézer. [1110] "Jérusalem: Colline française," Revue biblique, 78 (1971), 429-430.

Orfali, Gaudence. [1111] "Un hypogée juif à Bethphagé," Revue biblique, 32 (1923), 253-260.

Pfennigsdorf, E. [1112] "Die Aussenanlagen der sogenannt Königsgräber (Kubur es-Salatin) bei Jerusalem," Zeitschrift des deutschen Palästina-Vereins, 27 (1904), 173-187.

Puech, E. [1113] "Inscriptions funéraires palestiniennes: Tombeau de Jason et ossuaires," Revue biblique, 90 (1983), 481-533.

Puech, E. [1114] "Ossuaires inscrits d' une tombe du Mont des Oliviers," Studii Biblici Franciscani, Liber Annuus, 32 (1982), 355-372.

Rahmani, L. Y. See Gath, Joseph and Rahmani, L. Y. [1026]

Rahmani, L. Y. [1115] "Ancient Jerusalem's Funerary Customs and Tombs," Biblical Archaeologist, 44 (1981), 171-177, 229-235; 45 (1982), 43-53, 109-119.

Rahmani, L. Y. [1116] "Jason's Tomb," Israel Exploration Journal, 17 (1967), 61-100.

Rahmani, L. Y. [1117] "Jerusalem's Tomb Monuments on Jewish Ossuaries," Israel Exploration Journal, 18 (1968), 220-225.

Rahmani, L. Y. [1118] "Jewish Rock Cut Tombs in Jerusalem," Atiqot (English Series), 3 (1961), 100-101.

Rahmani, L. Y. [1119] "A Jewish Rock-Cut Tomb on Mt. Scopus," Atiqot (English Series), 14 (1980), 49-54.

Rahmani, L. Y. [1120] "A Jewish Tomb on Shahin Hill, Jerusalem," Israel Exploration Journal, 8 (1958), 101-105.

Rahmani, L. Y. [1121] "Jewish Tombs in the Romema Quarter of Jerusalem," in Eretz-Israel: Archaeological, Historical, and Geographical Studies, 8. Jerusalem: Israel Exploration Society, 1967, 186-192 (Hebrew), 74* (English summary).

Rahmani, L. Y. [1122] "Ossuaries and Bone-Gathering in the Late Second Temple Period," Qadmoniot, 11 (1978), 102-112 (Hebrew). [English summaries in Old Testament Abstracts, 2 (1979), 208-209 and New Testament Abstracts, 24 (1980),53.]

Rahmani, L. Y. [1123] "Roman Tombs in Nahal Raqafot, Jerusalem," Atiqot (English Series), 11 (1976), 77-88.

Rahmani, L. Y. [1124] "Roman Tombs in Shemuel Ha-Navi Street, Jerusalem," in Eretz-Israel: Archaeological, Historical, and Geographical Studies, 6. Jerusalem: Israel Exploration Society, 1960, 68-72 (Hebrew), 28*-29* (English summary).

Rahmani, L. Y. [1125] "Tombs of the Second Temple Period: A Tomb and a Columbarium on Shemuel Hanavi Street," Atiqot (Hebrew Series), 8 (1982), 61-64 (Hebrew with English summary).

Rahmani, L. Y.; Avigad, Nahman; and Benoit, Pierre. [1126] "The Tomb of Jason," Atiqot (Hebrew Series), 4 (1964), 1-40 (Hebrew with English summary).

Rak, Y. See Arensburg, B. and Rak, Y. [923-924]

Reed, William L. [1127] "Tomb," in Interpreter's Dictionary of the Bible, 4. New York: Abingdon, 1962, 663-668.

Reich, Ronny and Geva, Hillel. [1128] "Five Jewish Burial-Caves on Mount Scopus," Qadmoniot, 5 (1972), 110-111 (Hebrew).

Reich, Ronny and Geva, Hillel. [1129] "Five Jewish Burial-Caves on Mount Scopus," in Y. Yadin (ed.), Jerusalem Revealed: Archaeology in the Holy City, 1968-1974. New Haven and London: Yale University Press and the Israel Exploration Society, 1976, 67-69.

Reich, Ronny And Geva, Hillel. [1130] "Tombs of the Second Temple Period: Burial Caves on Mt. Scopus," Atiqot (Hebrew Series), 8 (1982), 53-56 (Hebrew with English summary).

Reifenberg, Adolf. [1131] "A Newly Discovered Hebrew Inscription of the Pre-Exilic Period," Journal of the Palestine Oriental Society, 2 (1948), 134-137.

Rosenthal, E. S. [1132] "The Giv'at Ha-Mivtar Inscription," Israel Exploration Journal, 23 (1973), 72-81.

Sa'ad, Y. [1133] "A Bronze Age Tomb group from Heblat el Amud, Silwan Village Lands," Annual of the Department of Antiquities of Jordan, 8-9 (1964), 77-80.

St. Clair, George. [1134] "Nehemiah's Wall and the Royal Sepulchres," Palestine Exploration Fund, Quarterly Statement, (1888), 288-289

St. Clair, George. [1135] "Sepulchres of the Kings," Palestine Exploration Fund, Quarterly Statement, (1888), 48-50.

Saller, Sylvester J. [1136] "The Archaeological Setting of the Shrine of Bethphage: The Tombs," Studii Biblici Franciscani, Liber Annuus, 11 (1960/1961), 208-250.

Saller, Sylvester J. [1137] "Ancient Rock-Cut Burial Chambers at Bethany," Studii Biblici Franciscani, Liber Annuus, 1 (1951), 191-226.

Saller, Sylvester J. [1138] The Excavations at Dominus Flevit (Mount of Olives, Jerusalem), 2: The Jebusite Burial Place. Studium Biblicum Franciscanum,

Collectio Major, 13. Jerusalem: Franciscan Printing Press, Jerusalem: Franciscan Printing Press, 1964, 197 pp.

Saller, Sylvester J. [1139] "Recent Archaeological Work in Palestine: At Bethphage," Studii Biblici Franciscani, Liber Annuus, 14 (1963/1964), 282-284.

Saller, Sylvester J. [1140] "The Tombs of Dominus Flevit," in J. Aviram (ed.), Jerusalem through the Ages. Jerusalem: Israel Exploration Society, 1968, 39-41.

de Saulcy, L. Félicien J. C. [1141] "Inscription du tombeau dit de Saint Jacques," Revue archéologique, (1865/A), 137-153, 398-405.

Savignac, M.-R. [1142] "Inscription romaine et sépultures au Nord de Jérusalem," Revue biblique, 13 (1904), 90-92.

Savignac, M.-R. [1143] "Noveaux ossuaris juifs avec graffites," Revue biblique, 34 (1925), 253-266.

Schick, Conrad. [1144] "Another Rock-Cut Chapel at Silwân," Palestine Exploration Fund, Quarterly Statement, (1890), 252-256.

Schick, Conrad. [1145] "Another Rock-Cut Tomb," Palestine Exploration Fund, Quarterly Statement, (1898), 82-83.

Schick, Conrad. [1146] "Discoveries North of Damascus Gate," Palestine Exploration Fund, Quarterly Statement, (1889), 116-117.

Schick, Conrad. [1147] "Discovery of Rock-Hewn Chapels at Silwân," Palestine Exploration Fund, Quarterly Statement, (1890), 16-18.

Schick, Conrad. [1148] "Excavations on the Rocky Knoll North of Jerusalem," Palestine Exploration Fund, Quarterly Statement, (1893), 298-299.

Schick, Conrad. [1149] "Katakomben auf dem Ölberg," Zeitschrift des deutschen Palästina-Vereins, 12 (1889), 193-199.

Schick, Conrad. [1150] "More Discoveries at Silwân," Palestine Exploration Fund, Quarterly Statement, (1891), 11-13.

Schick, Conrad. [1151] "Die neuaufgefundenen Felsengräber neben der Jeremiasgrotte bei Jerusalem," Zeitschrift des deutschen Palästina-Vereins, 9 (1886), 74-78.

Schick, Conrad. [1152] "Neu aufgedeckte Gräber in Jerusalem," Zeitschrift des deutschen Palästina-Vereins, 16 (1893), 202-205.

Schick, Conrad. [1153] "Newly-Discovered Rock Block with Tombs," Palestine Exploration Fund, Quarterly Statement, (1897), 105-107.

Schick, Conrad. [1154] "A Newly-Discovered Rock-Cut Tomb at Aceldama," Palestine Exploration Fund, Quarterly Statement, (1890), 248-249.

Schick, Conrad. [1155] "Newly-Discovered Rock-Cut Tomb near Bethany," Palestine Exploration Fund, Quarterly Statement, (1890), 249-252.

Schick, Conrad. [1156] "The Newly-Discovered Rock-Cut Tombs close to the Jeremiah Grotto near Jerusalem," Palestine Exploration Fund, Quarterly Statement, (1886), 155-157.

Schick, Conrad. [1157] "Notes from Jerusalem," Palestine Exploration Fund, Quarterly Statement, (1887), 151-154. [Tombs on the Mount of Olives.]

Schick, Conrad. [1158] "Recent Discoveries at the Nicophorieh," Palestine Exploration Fund, Quarterly Statement, (1892), 115-120.

Schick, Conrad. [1159] "Remarkable Rock-Cut Tomb in 'Wâdy el-Jôz,'" Palestine Exploration Fund, Quarterly Statement, (1892), 13-16.

Schick, Conrad. [1160] "A Remarkable Tomb," Palestine Exploration Fund, Quarterly Statement, (1887), 112-115.

Schick, Conrad. [1161] "The (So-Called) Tombs of the Kings at Jerusalem," Palestine Exploration Fund, Quarterly Statement, (1897), 182-188.

Schick, Conrad. [1162] "The Tombs of the Prophets," Palestine Exploration Fund, Quarterly Statement, (1893), 128-132.

Schick, Conrad. [1163] "Tomb in Wâdy Yasûl," Palestine Exploration Fund, Quarterly Statement, (1887), 215-216.

Schick, Conrad. [1164] "Tombs and Ossuaries at Rujm el Kahakin," Palestine Exploration Fund, Quarterly Statement, (1891), 201-204.

Schultze, Victor. [1165] "Sarkophage und Grabinschrift aus Jerusalem," Zeitschrift des deutschen Palästina-Vereins, 4 (1881), 9-17.

Schur, Nathan. [1166] "Tomb of Absalom, / Tomb of Jehoshafat, / Grotto of St. James, / Tomb of Zacharias, / Tombs of the Kings, / Tombs of the Judges, / Tomb of Simon the Just," in Jerusalem in Pilgrims and Travellers' Accounts: A Thematic Bibliography of Western Christian Itineraries, 1300-1917. Jerusalem: Ariel, 1980, 31-32, 48-50.

Schwabe, M. [1167] "Eine judische Grabinschrift vom Ophelhügel in Jerusalem," Zeitschrift des deutschen Palästina-Vereins, 55 (1932), 238-241.

Séjourné, Paul-M. [1168] "Hypogée judéo-grec découvert au Scopas," Revue biblique, 9 (1900), 106-112.

Sekeles, Eliezer. See Zias, Joseph and Sekeles, Eliezer. [1230]

Shanks, Hershel. [1169] "New Analysis of the Crucified Man," Biblical Archaeology Review, 11/6 (Nov./ dec., 1985), 20-21.

Simons, Jan. [1170] "The Royal Necropolis," in Jerusalem in the Old Testament: Researches and Theories. Leiden: Brill, 1952, 194-225.

Smith, Patricia. [1171] "Human Skeletal Remains from the Abba Cave," Israel Exploration Journal, 27 (1977), 121-124.

Smith, Patricia and Zias, Joseph. [1172] "Skeletal Remains from the Late Hellenistic French Hill Tomb," Israel Exploration Journal, 30 (1980), 109-115.

Smith, Robert H. [1173] "Cross Marks on Jewish Ossuaries," Palestine Exploration Quarterly, (1974), 53-66.

Smith, Robert H. [1174] "An Early Roman Sarcophagus of Palestine and its School," Palestine Exploration Quarterly, (1973), 71-82. [On a Jerusalem workshop.]

Smith, Robert H. [1175] "A Middle Bronze II Tomb from the Vicinity of Jerusalem," Annual of the Department of Antiquities, Jordan, 15 (1970), 17-19.

Sokoloff, M. [1176] "The Giv'at ha-Mivtar Aramaic Tomb Inscription in Palaeo-Hebrew Script and its Historical Implications," Immanuel, 10 (1980), 38-46.

Stauffer, Ethelbert. [1177] "Zu den Kreuzeszeichen von Talpioth," Zeitschrift für die neutestamentliche Wissenschaft, 43 (1950/1951), 262.

Stern, Ephraim. [1178] "Dwellings and Graves," in A. Malamat (ed.), World History of the Jewish People, 4/2: The Age of the Monarchies: Culture and Society. Jerusalem: Massada, 1979, 265-278.

Steve, M.-A. See Vincent, Louis-Hugues and Steve, M.-A. [1219]

Strange, James F. [1179] "Late Hellenistic and Herodian Ossuary Tombs at French Hill, Jerusalem," Bulletin of the American Schools of Oriental Research, 219 (1975), 39-67.

Stutchbury, Howard E. [1180] "Excavations in the Kidron Valley," Palestine Exploration Quarterly, (1961), 101-113.

Sukenik, Eleazar L. See Kon, Maximillian. [1056]

Sukenik, Eleazar L. [1181] "The Earliest Records of Christianity," American Journal of Archaeology, 51 (1947), 351-365. [The Talpioth ossuaries.]

Sukenik, Eleazar L. [1182] "Funerary Tablet of Uzziah, King of Judah," Palestine Exploration Fund, Quarterly Statement, (1931), 217-221; (1932), 106-107.

Sukenik, Eleazar L. [1183] "A Jewish Hypogeum near Jerusalem," Journal of the Palestine Oriental Society, 8 (1928), 113-121; 9 (1929), 45-49.

Sukenik, Eleazar L. [1184] "A Jewish Tomb in the Kedron Valley," Palestine Exploration Quarterly, (1937), 126-130.

Sukenik, Eleazar L. [1185] Jüdische Gräber Jerusalems um Christi Geburt, Vortrag gehalten am 6. Januar 1931 in der archäologischen Gesellschaft, Berlin. Jerusalem, 1931, 23 pp.

Sukenik, Eleazar L. [1186] "Tomb Discovered in the 'Mahanaim' Quarter, Jerusalem: Description of the Tomb and Ossuaries," Proceedings of the Jewish Palestine Exploration Society, 1, 2-4 (1925), 30-31.

Sukenik, Eleazar L. [1187] "A Tomb in the Hebrew University Premises," Proceedings of the Jewish Palestine Exploration Society, 1, 2-4 (1925), 43-45.

Sukenik, Eleazar L. [1188] "Verschlusssstein mit Inschrift aus einer Grabhöle bei Jerusalem," Zeitschrift des deutschen Palästina-Vereins, 55 (1932), 124-128.

Sussman, Vardi. [1189] "Tombs of the Second Temple Period: A Burial Cave in the Valley of the Cross," Atiqot (Hebrew Series), 8 (1982), 69 (Hebrew with English summary).

Sussman, Vardi. [1190] "Tombs of the Second Temple Period: A Burial Cave near Augusta Victoria," Atiqot (Hebrew Series), 8 (1982), 46-48 (Hebrew with English summary).

Testa, Emmanuele. [1191] "The Graffiti of Tomb 21 at Bethphage," Studii Biblici Franciscani, Liber Annuus, 11 (1960/1961), 251-287.

Tzaferis, Vassilios. [1192] "The 'Abba' Burial Cave in Jerusalem," Atiqot (Hebrew Series), 7 (1974), 61-64 (Hebrew with English summary).

Tzaferis, Vassilios. [1193] "The Burial of Simeon the Temple Builder (Jewish Tomb-Caves at Giv'at Hamivtar, Jerusalem)," Qadmoniot, 1 (1968), 137-138 (Hebrew).

Tzaferis, Vassilios. [1194] "The Burial of Simon the Temple Builder," in Y. Yadin (ed.), Jerusalem Revealed: Archaeology in the Holy City, 1968-1974. New Haven and London: Yale University Press and the Israel Exploration Society, 1976, 71-72.

Tzaferis, Vassilios. [1195] "Chronique archéologique: Jérusalem," Revue biblique, 76 (1969), 568-569. [On the tombs at Giv'at ha-mivtar.]

Tzaferis, Vassilios. [1196] "Crucifixion: The Archaeological Evidence," Biblical Archaeology Review, 11/1 (Jan./Feb., 1985), 44-53.

Tzaferis, Vassilios. [1197] "Jewish Graves from the Time of Herod in North East Jerusalem," in Proceedings of the Fifth World Congress of Jewish Studies, Jerusalem, 1969, 1. Jerusalem: World Union of Jewish Studies, n. d., 1-4 (Hebrew), 221 (English summary).

Tzaferis, Vassilios. [1198] "Jewish Tombs at or near Giv'at Ha-Mivtar," Israel Exploration Journal, 20 (1970), 18-32.

Tsaferis, Vassilios. [1199] "Tombs of the Second Temple Period: Rock-Cut Tombs on Mt. Scopus," Atiqot (Hebrew Series), 8 (1982), 49-52 (Hebrew with English summary).

Tsaferis, Vassilios and Berman, Ariel. [1200] "Tombs of the Second Temple Period: A Burial Cave in Meqor Hayim," Atiqot (Hebrew Series), 8 (1982), 70-73 (Hebrew with English summary).

Ussishkin, David. [1201] "The Necropolis from the Time of the Kingdom of Judah at Silwan, Jerusalem," Biblical Archaeologist, 33 (1970), 34-46.

Ussishkin, David. [1202] "On the Shorter Inscription from the 'Tomb of the Royal Steward,'" Bulletin of the American Schools of Oriental Research, 196 (1969), 16-22.

Ussishkin, David. [1203] "A Recently Discovered Monolithic Tomb in Siloam," Qadmoniot, 3 (1970), 25-26 (Hebrew).

Ussishkin, David. [1204] "A Recently Discovered Monolithic Tomb in Siloam," in Y. Yadin (ed.), Jerusalem Revealed: Archaeology in the Holy City, 1968-1974. New Haven and London: Yale University Press and the Israel Exploration Society, 1976, 63-65.

Ussishkin, David. [1205] "The Rock Called Peristereon," Israel Exploration Journal, 24 (1974), 70.

Ussishkin, David. [1206] "Siloé: La nécropole," Revue biblique, 77 (1970), 573-576.

Van Berchem, Max. [1207] "Épitaphe arabe de Jérusalem," Revue biblique, 9 (1900), 288-290.

Vincent, Louis-Hugues. [1208] "Une grande sépulture sacerdotale à Jérusalem," in Memorial Joseph Chaine. Bibliothèque de la Faculté Catholique de Théologie de Lyon, 5. Lyon: Facultés Catholiques, 1950, 385-397.

Vincent, Louis-Hugues. [1209] "Hypogée antique dans la nécropole septenrionale de Jerusalem," Revue biblique, 10 (1901), 448-452.

Vincent, Louis-Hugues. [1210] "Un hypogée cananéen à Béthanie," Revue biblique, 23 (1914), 438-441.

Vincent, Louis-Hugues. [1211] "Un hypogée juif," Revue biblique, 8 (1899), 297-304.

Vincent, Louis-Hugues. [1212] "Hypogée romain au nord de Jérusalem," Revue biblique, 18 (1909), 112-117.

Vincent, Louis-Hugues. [1213] "Une nécropole gréco-romaine à Jérusalem," Revue biblique, 9 (1900), 603-607.

Vincent, Louis-Hugues. [1214] "Un nouvel ossuaire juif," Revue biblique, 11 (1902), 276-277.

Vincent, Louis-Hugues. [1215] "Noveaux ossuaires judéo-grecs," Revue biblique, 11 (1902), 103-107.

Vincent, Louis-Hugues. [1216] "Ossuaires juifs," Revue biblique, 16 (1907), 410-414.

Vincent, Louis-Hugues. [1217] "Le tombeau et ossuaires du mont des Oliviers," Revue biblique, 11 (1902), 277-280.

Vincent, Louis-Hugues. [1218] "Le tombeau des prophètes," Revue biblique, 10 (1901), 72-88.

Vincent, Louis-Hugues and Steve, M.-A. [1219] "Les nécropoles," in Jérusalem de l' Ancien Testement, 1. Paris: Gabalda, 1954, 313-371.

H. B. S. W. [1220] "The Sepulchres of the Kings: Who Were Buried in Them?" Palestine Exploration Fund, Quarterly Statement, (1882), 266-269.

Walls, Archibald G. [1221] "The Mausoleum of the Amir Kilani," Levant, 7 (1975), 39-76.

Walls, Archibald G. [1222] "The Mausoleum of the Amir Kilani: Restored Elevations," Levant, 9 (1977), 168-173.

Warren, Charles. [1223] "The Tomb of David," Palestine Exploration Fund, Quarterly Statement, (1875), 102-103.

Wilson, Charles W. [1224] "The Tombs of the Prophets, 'Kabur el-'Anaba,' at Jerusalem," Palestine Exploration Fund, Quarterly Statement, (1901), 309-317.

Wilson, Charles W. [1225] "Two Latin Epitaphs," Palestine Exploration Fund, Quarterly Statement, (1903), 271.

Wright, Theodore F. [1226] "The Isaiah Inscription," Palestine Exploration Fund, Quarterly Statement, (1907), 162.

Yadin, Yigael. [1227] "Epigraphy and Crucifixion," Israel Exploration Journal, 23 (1973), 18-22.

Yeivin, Samuel. [1228] "The Sepulchers of the Kings of the House of David," Journal of Near Eastern Studies, 7 (1948), 30-45.

Zias, Joseph. See Smith, Patricia and Zias, Joseph. [1172]

Zias, Joseph. [1229] "A Rock-Cut Tomb in Jerusalem," Bulletin of the American Schools of Oriental Research, 245 (1982), 53-56.

Zias, Joseph and Sekeles, Eliezer. [1230] "The Crucified Man from Giv'at ha-Mivtar: A Reappraisal," Israel Exploration Journal, 35 (1985), 22-27.

Seven

Jerusalem Before David

Aharoni, Yohanan. [1231] "The El-Amarna Period," in The Land of the Bible. A Historical Geography. Philadelphia: Westminster, revised and enlarged edn., 1979, 169-176.

Aharoni, Yohanan. [1232] "The Execration Texts," in The Land of the Bible. A Historical Geography. Philadelphia: Westminster, revised and enlarged edn., 1979, 144-147.

Albright, William F. [1233] "The Amarna Letters," in J. B. Pritchard (ed.), Ancient Near Eastern Texts Relating to the Old Testament. Princeton: Princeton University Press, 1955, 483-490.

Albright, William F. [1234] "The Amarna Letters from Palestine," in Cambridge Ancient History, 2/2. Cambridge: Cambridge University Press, 3rd edn., 1975, 98-116.

Albright, William F. [1235] "New Egyptian Data on Palestine in the Patriarchal Period," Bulletin of the American Schools of Oriental Research, 81 (1941), 16-21.

Albright, William F. [1236] "Palestine in the Earliest Historical Period," Journal of the Palestine Oriental Society, 2 (1922), 110-139.

Alt, Albrecht. [1237] "Die asiatischen Gefahrzonen in den Ächtungstexten der 11 Dynastie," Zeitschrift für ägyptische Sprache und Altertumskunde, 63 (1927), 39-45. Also in Kleine Schriften zur Geschichte des Volkes Israel, 3. Munich: Beck'sche Verlagsbuchhandlung, 1959, 49-56.

Alt, Albrecht. [1238] "Herren und Herrensitze Palästinas im Anfang des zweiten Jahrtausends v. Chr.," Zeitschrift des deutschen Palästina-Vereins, 64 (1941), 21-39. Also in Kleine Schriften zur Geschichte des Volkes Israel, 3. Munich: Beck'sche Verlagsbuchhandlung, 1959, 57-71.

Alt, Albrecht. [1239] "Neues über Palästina aus dem Archiv Amenophis IV," Palästinajahrbuch, 20 (1924), 22-41. Also in Kleine Schriften zur Geschichte des Volkes Israel, 3. Munich: Beck'sche Verlagsbuchhandlung, 1959, 158-175.

Astour, Michael. [1240] "Political and Cosmic Symbolism in Genesis 14 and in its Babylonian Sources, in A. Altman (ed.), Biblical Motifs. Brandeis University Studies and Texts, 3. Cambridge, MA: Harvard University Press, 1966, 65-112.

7/Jerusalem Before David

Bar-Yosef, Ofer. [1241] "Jerusalem, Pre-History: The Site in the Valley of Rephaim," in M. Avi-Yonah (ed.), Encyclopedia of Archaeological Excavations in the Holy Land, 2. Englewood Cliffs, NJ: Prentice-Hall, 1976, 579-580.

Barrois, Georges Augustin. [1242] "Jebus," in Interpreter's Dictionary of the Bible, 2. New York: Abingdon, 1962, 807-808.

Barton, George A. [1243] "A Liturgy for the Celebration of the Spring Festival at Jerusalem in the Age of Abraham and Melchizedek," Journal of Biblical Literature, 53 (1934), 61-78.

Busink, Th. A. [1244] "Die Jebusiterstadt: Urusalem," in Der Tempel von Jerusalem, 1: Der Tempel Salomos. Leiden: Brill, 1970, 77-89.

Campbell, Edward J., Jr. [1245] "The Amarna Letters and the Amarna Period," Biblical Archaeologist, 23 (1960), 2-22.

Cassuto, Umberto. [1246] "Jerusalem in the Pentateuch," in Eretz-Israel: Archaeological, Historical, and Geographical Studies, 3. Jerusalem: Israel Exploration Society, 1954, 15-17 (Hebrew), i (English summary).

Cassuto, Umberto. [1247] "Jerusalem in the Pentateuch," in Biblical and Oriental Studies, 1. Trans. by I. Abrahams. Jerusalem: Magnes, 1973, 71-78.

Clay, A. T. [1248] "The Amorite Name Jerusalem," Journal of the Palestine Oriental Society, 1 (1920/1921), 28-32.

Dhorme, Édouard. [1249] "Les pays bibliques au temps d' el-Amarna," Revue biblique, 17 (1908), 500-519; 18 (1909), 50-73, 368-385.

Driver, S. R. [1250] "Jebus, Jebusi, Jebusite," in J. Hastings (ed.), Dictionary of the Bible, 2. New York: Scribner's, 1899, 554-555.

Emerton, J. A. [1251] "The Riddle of Genesis XIV," Vetus Testamentum, 21 (1971), 403-

Fisher, Loren R. [1252] "Abraham and His Priest-King," Journal of Biblical Literature, 81 (1962), 264-270.

Gonen, Rivka. [1253] "Was the Site of the Jerusalem Temple Originally a Cemetery?" Biblical Archaeology Review, 11/3 (May/June, 1985), 44-55.

Gray, John. [1254] "An Amorite City-State," in A History of Jerusalem. New York: Praeger, 1969, 65-79.

Gray, John. [1255] "Shalem (God)," Interpreter's Dictionary of the Bible, 4. New York: Abingdon, 1962, 303-304.

Hunt, Ignatius. [1256] "Recent Melkizedek Study," in J. L. McKenzie (ed.), Current Catholic Thought. St. Mary's Theology Series, 1. New York: Herder and Herder, 1962, 21-33.

Johnson, Robert F. [1257] "Adoni-bezek," Interpreter's Dictionary of the Bible, 1. New York: Abingdon, 1962, 47.

Kallai, Zechariah. and Tadmor, Hayim. [1258] "Bit Ninurta = Beth Horon-- On the History of the Kingdom of Jerusalem in the Amarna Period," in Eretz-Israel: Archaeological, Historical, and Geographical Studies, 9. Jerusalem: Israel Exploration Society, 1969, 138-147 (Hebrew), 138* (English summary).

Kenyon, Kathleen M. [1259] "The Jerusalem of the Jebusites and of David," in Jerusalem: Excavating 3000 Years of History. New York: McGraw-Hill, 1967, 19-53.

Kenyon, Kathleen M. [1260] "Jerusalem of the Jebusites and of David," in Royal Cities of the Old Testament. London: Barrie and Jenkins, 1971, 25-35.

Kenyon, Kathleen M. [1261] "Pre-Israelite Jerusalem," in Digging Up Jerusalem. New York: Praeger, 1974, 76-97.

Lewy, Julius. [1262] "The sulman Temple in Jerusalem," Journal of Biblical Literature, 59 (1940), 519-522.

Luria, Ben-Zion. [1263] "Bezek and Adonibezek," Beth Miqra, 28 (1983/1984), 7-13 (Hebrew). [English summary in Old Testament Abstracts, 7 (1984), 166.]

Maisler, B. (= Mazar, Benjamin) [1264] "Das vordavidische Jerusalem," Journal of the Palestine Oriental Society, 10 (1930), 181-191.

Mallon, Alexis, [1265] "Jérusalem et les documents égyptiene," Journal of the Palestine Oriental Society, 8 (1928), 1-6.

Mazar, Benjamin. See Maisler, B. (= Mazar, Benjamin) [1264]

Mazar, Benjamin. [1266] "Biblical Jerusalem until the Time of David," in The Mountain of the Lord. Garden City, NY: Doubleday, 1975, 40-50.

Mazar, Benjamin. [1267] "Remnants in the City of David: The Earliest Settlement," in The Mountain of the Lord. Garden City, NY: Doubleday, 1975, 153-166.

Miller, J. Maxwell. [1268] "Jebus and Jerusalem: A Case of Mistaken Identity," Zeitschrift des deutschen Palästina-Vereins, 90 (1974), 115-127.

Muhly, James D. [1269] "Ur and Jerusalem Not Mentioned in Ebla Tablets Says Ebla Expedition Scholar," Biblical Archaeology Review, 9/6 (1983), 74-75.

"Il Periodo del bronzo nella cittè e regione di Gerusalemme," [1270] Bibbia e Oriente, 7 (1965), 205-208.

Priebatsch, Hans Y. [1271] "Jerusalem und die Brunnenstrasse Merneptahs," Zeitschrift des deutschen Palästina-Vereins, 91 (1975), 18-29.

Reid, Stephen B. [1272] "Jebus," in Harper's Bible Dictionary. San Francisco: Harper and Row, 1985, 449-450.

Rosen, H. B. [1273] "Arawna-- Non-Hittite?" Vetus Testamentum, 5 (1955), 318-320.

Rosenberg, Roy A. [1274] "The God Sedeq," Hebrew Union College Annual, 36 (1965), 161-177.

Rosenberg, Roy A. [1275] "Sedheq (God)," in Interpreter's Dictionary of the Bible, Supplementary Volume. Nashville: Abingdon, 1976, 800.

Rosenberg, Roy A. [1276] "Shalem (God)," in Interpreter's Dictionary of the Bible, Supplementary Volume. Nashville: Abingdon, 1976, 820-821.

Saller, Sylvester J. [1277] "Jerusalem and its Surroundings in the Bronze Age," Studii Biblici Franciscani. Liber Annuus, 12 (1961/1962), 146-176.

Schatz, Werner. [1278] Genesis 14. Eine Untersuchung. Europäische Hochschulschriften, 23/2. Bern: Herbert Lang / Frankfort: Peter Lang, 1979, 384 pp.

Schmitt, John J. [1279] "Pre-Israelite Jerusalem," in W. W. Hallo and J. B. White (eds.), Scripture in Context: Essays on the Comparative Method. Pittsburgh: Pickwick, 1980, 101-121.

Schunck, Klaus. [1280] "Juda und Jerusalem in vor- und frühisraelitischer Zeit," in K. H. Bernhardt (ed.), Schalom: Studien zu Glaube und Geschichte Israels (Festschrift Alfred Jepsen). Stuttgart: Calwer, 1971, 50-57.

Smith, Robert H. [1281] "Abram and Melchizedek (Gen 14, 18-20)," Zeitschrift für die alttestamentliche Wissenschaft, 77 (1965), 129-153.

Stekelis, M. [1282] "Rephaim-Baq'a: A Palaeolithic Station in the Vicinity of Jerusalem," Journal of the Palestine Oriental Society, 21 (1948), 80-97.

Steve, M.-A. See Vincent, Louis-Hugues and Steve, M.-A. [1287]

Tadmor, Hayim See Kallai, Zechariah and Tadmor, Hayim. [1258]

Thompson, Thomas L. [1283] "The Early West Semites in Palestine and Syria," in The Historicity of the Patriarchal Narratives: The Quest for the Historical Abraham. Beihefte zur Zeitschrift für die alttestamentliche Wissenschaft, 133. Berlin: de Gruyter, 1974, 89-117.

Thureau-Dangin, M. [1284] "Le nom du prince de Jérusalem au temps d' el-Amarna," in L.-H. Vincent (ed.), Mémorial Lagrange. Paris: Gabalda, 1940, 27-28.

Vincent, Louis-Hugues. [1285] "Abraham à Jérusalem," Revue biblique, 58 (1951), 360-371.

Vincent, Louis-Hugues. [1286] "Site primitif de Jérusalem et son évolution initiale," Revue biblique, 65 (1958), 547-567.

Vincent, Louis-Hugues and Steve, M.-A. [1287] "Le nom et les origines jusqu' à la conquête davidique," in Jérusalem de l' Ancien Testament, 3. Paris: Gabalda, 1956, 611-632.

Weinstein, James M. [1288] "Egyptian Relations with Palestine in the Middle Kingdom Period," Bulletin of the American Schools of Oriental Research, 217 (1975), 1-16.

Weippert, Manfred. [1289] "Lú-ad-da-a-ni in den Briefen des Abduheba von Jerusalem an den Pharao," in K. Bergerhof, M. Dietrich, and O. Luretz (eds.), Ugarit Forschungen, 6. Internationales Jahrbuch für die Altertumskunde Syrien-Palästinas. Neukirchen-Vluyn: Neukirchener Verlag / Kevelaer: Butzon and Bercker, 1974, 415-419.

Weir, C. J. Mullo. [1290] "Letters from Tel El-Amarna," in D. W. Thomas (ed.), Documents from Old Testament Times. London: Nelson, 1958, 38-45.

Wilson, John A. [1291] "The Execration of Asiatic Princes," in J. B. Pritchard (ed.), Ancient Near Eastern Texts Relating to the Old Testament. Princeton: Princeton University Press, 1955, 328-329.

Yeivin, Samuel. [1292] "Jerusalem in the Egyptian Sources," in Judah and Jerusalem: The Twelfth Archaeological Convention. Jerusalem: Israel Exploration Society, 1957, 33 (Hebrew), iv (English summary).

Zimmerli, Walther. [1293] "Abraham und Melchisedek," in F. Maass (ed.), Das Ferne und Nahe Wort. Beihefte zur Zeitschrift für die alttestamentliche Wissenschaft, 105. Berlin: de Gruyter, 1967, 225-264.

Eight

Jerusalem During the Biblical Period, to 587 B. C.

Alt, Albrecht. See Wallis, Gerhard. [1366]

Alt, Albrecht. [1294] "Archäologische Fragen zur Baugeschichte von Jerusalem und Samaria in der israelitischen Königszeit," in Kleine Schriften zur Geschichte des Volkes Israel, 3. Munich: Beck'sche Verlagsbuchhandlung, 1959, 303-325.

Avi-Yonah, Michael. [1295] "Jerusalem: David and the First Temple Period," in Encyclopaedia Judaica, 9. Jerusalem: Macmillan, 1971, 1381-1384. Also in Israel Pocket Library: Jerusalem. Jerusalem: Keter, 1973, 9-17.

Avigad, Nahman. [1296] "The Period of the First Temple," in Discovering Jerusalem. Nashville: Thomas Nelson, 1983, 23-60.

Bahat, Dan. [1297] "Early History until 586 B. C. E.," in Carta's Historical Atlas of Jerusalem: An Illustrated Survey. Jerusalem: Carta, 1983, 12-19.

Barnes, William Emory. [1298] "David's 'Capture' of the Jebusite 'Citadel," Expositor, (1914, A), 29-39.

Ben-Dov, Meir. [1299] "Remains from the Kingdom of Judah," in In the Shadow of the Temple: The Discovery of Ancient Jerusalem. Translated by Ina Friedman. Jerusalem: Keter / New York: Harper and Row, 1982, 31-55.

Briend, Jacques. [1300] "Jérusalem dans l' Ancien Testament," Bible et Terre Sainte, 114 (1969), 6-16.

Broshi, Magen. [1301] "The Expansion of Jerusalem in the Reigns of Hezekiah and Manasseh," Israel Exploration Journal, 24 (1974), 21-26.

Burrows, Millar. [1302] "Jerusalem," in Interpreter's Dictionary of the Bible, 2. New York: Abingdon, 1962, 843-866, esp. 847-853.

Busink, Th. A. [1303] "Jerusalem und die Salomburg," in Der Tempel von Jerusalem, 1: Der Tempel Salomos. Leiden: Brill, 1970, 77-161.

Conder, Claude R. [1304] "Jerusalem of the Kings," Palestine Exploration Fund, Quarterly Statement, (1884), 20-29.

Donner, Herbert. [1305] "Jerusalem," in K. Galling (ed.), Biblisches Realexikon. Tübingen: Mohr (Siebeck), 2nd edn., 1977, 157-165.

Eisman, Michael. [1306] "A Tale of Three Cities," Biblical Archaeologist, 41 (1978), 47-60. [Ancient Athens, Jerusalem, and Rome.]

Elitzur, Yoel. [1307] "The Josiade Reform in the Light of Archaeology: The Stone Mounds in the West of the City," in P. Peli (ed.), Proceedings of the Fifth World Congress of Jewish Studies, 1969, 1. Jerusalem: World Union of Jewish Studies, n.d., 92-97 (Hebrew), 233-234 (English summary).

Flanagan, James W. [1308] "The Relocation of the Davidic Capital," Journal of the American Academy of Religion, 47 (1979), 223-244.

Fohrer, Georg. [1309] "Zion-Jerusalem in the Old Testament," in G. Friedrich (ed.), Theological Dictionary of the New Testament, 7. Grand Rapids, MI: Eerdmans, 1971, 293-319.

Galling, Kurt. [1310] "Jerusalem," in Biblisches Reallexikon. Handbuch zum Alten Testament, 1. Tübingen: Mohr (Siebeck), 1937, 297-307.

Goldschmidt-Lehman, Ruth P. [1311] "Jerusalem in First Temple Times, Selected Bibliography," in L. I. Levine (ed.), Jerusalem Cathedra, 2. Jerusalem: Yad Izhaq Ben-Zvi Institute / Detroit: Wayne State University Press, 1982, 328-351.

Guthe, Hermann. [1312] "Jerusalem unter der davidischen Dynastie," in J. J. Herzog (ed.), Realencyklopädie für protestantische Theologie und Kirche, 8. Leipzig: Hinrichs'sche Buchhandlung, 1900, 676-682.

Harrison, Roland K. [1313] "Jerusalem, Old Testament," in E. M. Blaiklock and R. K. Harrison (eds.), The New International Dictionary of Biblical Archaeology. Grand Rapids: Zondervan, 1983, 265-270.

Hauer, Christian. [1314] "Jerusalem, the Stronghold, and Rephaim," Catholic Biblical Quarterly, 32 (1970), 571-578.

Haag, Herbert. [1315] "Jerusalemer Profanbauten in den Psalmen," Zeitschrift des deutschen Palästina-Vereins, 93 (1977), 87-96.

Kallai-Kleinman, Zechariah. [1316] "Jerusalem-- in Judah or in Benjamin?" in Judah and Jerusalem: The Twelfth Archaeological Convention. Jerusalem: Israel Exploration Society, 1957, 34-36 (Hebrew), v (English summary).

Kenyon, Kathleen M. [1317] "Biblical Jerusalem," Expedition, 5 (1962), 32-35.

Kenyon, Kathleen M.. [1318] "David's Jerusalem," in Digging Up Jerusalem. New York: Praeger, 1974, 98-106.

Kenyon, Kathleen M. [1319] "The Divided Monarchy: Jerusalem as the Capital of Judah," in Jerusalem: Excavating 3000 Years of History. New York: McGraw-Hill, 1967, 63-77.

Kenyon, Kathleen M. [1320] "Israelite Jerusalem," in J. A. Sanders (ed.), Near Eastern Archaeology in the Twentieth Century (Festschrift Nelson Glueck). Garden City, NY: Doubleday, 1970, 232-253.

Kenyon, Kathleen M. [1321] "Jerusalem at the Time of Solomon," in Digging Up Jerusalem. New York: Praeger, 1974, 107-128.

Kenyon, Kathleen M. [1322] "Jerusalem of the Jebusites and of David," in Royal Cities of the Old Testament. London: Barrie and Jenkins, 1971, 25-35.

Kenyon, Kathleen M. [1323] "The Kingdom of Judah and its Capital Jerusalem," in Digging Up Jerusalem. New York: Praeger, 1974, 129-143.

Kenyon, Kathleen M. [1324] "The Last Century of the Kingdom of Judah," in Digging Up Jerusalem. New York: Praeger, 1974, 144-165.

Kenyon, Kathleen M. [1325] "The Last Century of Royal Jerusalem," in Jerusalem: Excavating 3000 Years of History. New York: McGraw-Hill, 1967, 78-104.

Kenyon, Kathleen M. [1326] "The Last Years of the Monarchies of Judah and Israel," in Royal Cities of the Old Testament. London: Barrie and Jenkins, 1971, 129-150. [Jerusalem, 145-150.]

Kenyon, Kathleen M. [1327] "The Later History of the Royal Cities," in Royal Cities of the Old Testament. London: Barrie and Jenkins, 1971, 111-128. [Jerusalem, 111-124.]

Kenyon, Kathleen M. [1328] "Solomonic Jerusalem," in Royal Cities of the Old Testament. London: Barrie and Jenkins, 1971, 36-52.

Kenyon, Kathleen M. [1329] "The United Monarchy," in Archaeology in the Holy Land. London: Ernest Benn / New York: Norton, 1979, 233-257. [Jerusalem, 233-243.]

Klein, H. Arthur. See Klein, Mina C. and Klein, H. Arthur. [1330]

Klein, Mina C. and Klein, H. Arthur. [1330] Temple Beyond Time: The Story of the Site of Solomon's Temple at Jerusalem. New York: Van Nostrand Reinhold, 1970, 23-62.

Kosmala, Hans. [1331] "Jerusalem," in B. Reicke and L. Rost (eds.), Biblisch-Historisches Handwörterbuch, 2. Göttingen: Vanderhoeck and Ruprecht, 1964, 820-850.

Laperrousaz, Ernest-Marie. [1332] "L' extension préexilique sur la colline occidentale, Revue des études juives, 134 (1975), 3-30.

Legendre, A. [1333] "Jérusalem," in F. Vigouroux (ed.), Dictionnaire de la Bible, 3. Paris: Letouzey et Ané, 1926, 1317-1396.

McClellan, Thomas L. [1334] "Towns to Fortresses: Urban Life in Judah from 8th to 7th Century B. C.," in P. J. Achtemeir (ed.), Society of Biblical Literature 1978 Seminar Papers, 1. Missoula, MT: Scholars Press, 1978, 277-286.

May, Herbert G. [1335] "Jerusalem in Old Testament Times," in Oxford Bible Atlas. New York: Oxford University Press, 3rd edn. revised by John Day, 1984, 80-81.

Mazar, Benjamin. [1336] "David's Reign in Hebron and the Conquest of Jerusalem," in D. J. Silver (ed.), In the Time of Harvest: Essays in Honor of Abba Hillel Silver. New York: Macmillan, 1963, 235-244.

Mazar, Benjamin. [1337] "Hezekiah's Achievments," in The Mountain of the Lord. Garden City, NY: Doubleday, 1975, 175-180.

Mazar, Benjamin. [1338] "In the Days of the Monarchy," in The Mountain of the Lord. Garden City, NY: Doubleday, 1975, 50-60.

Mazar, Benjamin. [1339] "The Jebusite Stronghold and King David," in The Mountain of the Lord. Garden City, NY: Doubleday, 1975, 166-174.

Mazar, Benjamin. [1340] "Jerusalem in Biblical Times," in L. I. Levine (ed.), Jerusalem Cathedra, 2. Jerusalem: Yad Izhaq Ben-Zvi Institute / Detroit: Wayne State University Press, 1982, 1-24.

Mazar, Benjamin. [1341] "Jerusalem in the Biblical Period," Qadmoniot, 1 (1968), 3-12 (Hebrew).

Mazar, Benjamin. [1342] "Jerusalem in the Biblical Period," in M. Avi-Yonah (ed.), Encyclopedia of Archaeological Excavations in the Holy Land, 2. Englewood Cliffs, NJ: Prentice-Hall, 1976, 580-591.

Mazar, Benjamin. [1343] "Jerusalem in the Biblical Period," in Y. Yadin (ed.), Jerusalem Revealed: Archaeology in the Holy City, 1968-1974. New Haven and London: Yale University Press and the Israel Exploration Society, 1976, 1-8.

Mazar, Benjamin. [1344] "King's Chapel and Royal City," in Judah and Jerusalem: The Twelfth Archaeological Convention. Jerusalem: Israel Exploration Society, 1957, 25-32 (Hebrew), v (English summary).

Mazar, Benjamin. [1345] "Remnants in the City of David: Hezekiah's Achievements," in The Mountain of the Lord. Garden City, NY: Doubleday, 1975, 175-180.

Noth, Martin. [1346] "Jerusalem and the Northern Kingdom," in J. Aviram (ed.), Jerusalem through the Ages. Jerusalem: Israel Exploration Society, 1968, 33-38.

Paton, Lewis B. [1347] Jerusalem in Bible Times. Chicago: University of Chicago Press, 1908, 162 pp.

Penna, Angelo. [1348] "Gerusalemme nella realtà quotidiana (Periodo veterotestamentario)," in M. Borrmans, et al. (eds.), Gerusalemme. Brescia: Paideia, 1982, 53-80.

Peters, F. E. [1349] "Holy Land, Holy City," in Jerusalem: The Holy City in the Eyes of Chroniclers, Visitors, Pilgrims, and Prophets from the Days of Abraham to the Beginning of the Modern Period. Princeton: Princeton University Press, 1985, 3-41.

Prignaud, J. [1350] "Scribes et graveurs à Jérusalem 700 av. J.-C.," in R. Moorey and P. Parr (eds.), Archaeology in the Levant: Essays for Kathleen Kenyon. Warminster: Aris and Phillipps, 1978, 136-148.

Procksch, Otto. [1351] "Das Jerusalem Jesajas," Palästinajahrbuch, 26 (1930), 12-40.

Rian, D. [1352] Den hellige Stad, 1: Jerusalem i bibelsk tid. Sjalombok, 10. Oslo: Luther Rorlag, 1977, 140 pp.

Schein, Bruce. [1353] "Jerusalem," Harper's Bible Dictionary. San Francisco: Harper and Row, 1985, 463-473.

Scippa, Vincenzo. [1354] "Davide conquista Gerusalemme," Bibbia e Orient, 27 (1985), 65-76.

Shanks, Hershel. [1355] The City of David: A Guide to Biblical Jerusalem. Tel Aviv: Bazak, 1973, 126 pp.

Simons, Jan. [1356] Jerusalem in the Old Testament: Researches and Theories. Studia Francisci Scholten Memoriae Dicta, 1. Leiden: Brill, 1952, 517 pp.

Smith, George Adam. [1357] Jerusalem: The Topography, Economics, and History from the Earliest Times to A. D. 70, 2 vols. New York: Armstrong / London: Hodder and Stoughton, 1907-1908, 498 + 631 pp. Reprinted with prolegomenon by S. Yeivin, New York: KTAV, 2 vols. in 1, 1972. Reprinted in two vols: 1. Topography, Economics and Historical Geography; 2. History from the Earliest Times to A. D. 70. Jerusalem: Ariel / Warminster, England: Aris and Phillips, 1979, 498 + 631 pp.

Steve, M.-A. See Vincent, Louis-Hugues and Steve, M.-A. [1365]

Stoebe, Hans-Joachim. [1358] "Die Einnahme Jerusalem und der sinnôr," Zeitschrift des deutschen Palästina-Vereins, 73 (1957), 73-99.

Sukenik, Eleazar L. [1359] "An Account of David's Capture of Jerusalem," Journal of the Palestine Oriental Society, 8 (1928), 12-16.

Thomas, D. Winton. [1360] "Jerusalem in the Lachish Ostraca," Palestine Exploration Quarterly, (1946), 86-91.

Tsevat, Matitiahu. [1361] "Jerushalem / J^{e}rushalayim," in G. J. Botterweck, J. Ringren, and H.-J. Fabry (eds.), Theologisches Wörterbuch zum Alten Testament, 3. Stuttgart: Kohlhammer, 1982, 930-939.

Ussishkin, David. [1362] "The Camp of the Assyrians," Israel Exploration Journal, 29 (1979), 137-142.

Vincent, Louis-Hugues. [1363] "Jérusalem," in H. Cazelles and A. Feuillet (eds.), Supplément au Dictionnaire de la Bible, 4. Paris: Letouzey et Ané, 1949, 897-966.

Vincent, Louis-Hughes. [1364] "Le Sinnor dans la prise de Jérusalem (II Sam. v, 8)," Revue biblique, 33 (1924), 357-370.

Vincent, Louis-Hugues and Steve, M.-A. [1365] "De David à l' exil," in Jérusalem de l' Ancien Testament, 3. Paris: Gabalda, 1956, 633-654.

Wallis, Gerhard. [1366] "Jerusalem und Samaria als Königstädte: Auseinandersetzung mit der These Albrecht Alts," Vetus Testamentum, 26 (1976), 480-496.

Watson, W. G. E. [1367] "David Ousts the City Ruler of Jebus," Vetus Testamentum, 20 (1970), 501-502.

Yeivin, Shmuel. See Smith, George Adam. [1357]

Nine

The Theology/Mythology of the City and the Sanctuary

Ahlström, Gosta W. [1368] Aspects of Syncretism in Israelite Religion. Horae Soederblominae, 5. Lund: Gleerup, 1963, 97 pp.

Ahlström, Gosta W. [1369] "Der Prophet Nathan und der Tempelbau," Vetus Testamentum, 11 (1961), 113-127.

Alonso Schökel, Luis. See Strus, Andrej and Alonso Schökel, Luis. [1511]

Andreasen, Niels-Erik. [1370] "Town and Country in the Old Testament," Encounter, 42 (1981), 259-275.

Bauer, Johannes B. [1371] "Zion's Flüsse, Ps. 45 (46), 5," in J. B. Bauer and J. Marböck (eds.), Memoria Jerusalem (Festschrift Franz Sauer). Graz: Akademische Druck-u. Verlagsanstalt, 1977, 59-91.

Beaucamp, Evode. [1372] "Psaume 87: A la Jérusalem nouvelle," Laval Théologique et Philosophique, 35 (1979), 279-288.

Berry, George. [1373] "The Glory of YHWH and the Temple," Journal of Biblical Literature, 56 (1937), 115-117.

Beuker, W. A. M. [1374] "God's Presence in Salem: A Study of Psalm 76," in A. Ridderbos-Boersma (ed.), Loven en geloven (Festschrift N. H. Ridderbos). Amsterdam: Ton Bolland, 1975, 135-150.

Böcher, Otto. [1375] "Die heilige Stadt im Völkerkreig: Wandlungen eines apokalyptischen Schemas," in O. Betz, K. Haacher, and M. Martin (eds.), Josephus-Studien: Untersuchungen zu Josephus dem antiken Judentum und dem Neuen Testament (Festschrift Otto Michel). Göttingen: Vandenhoeck and Ruprecht, 1974, 55-76.

Böhl, Felix. [1376] Über das Verhältnis von Shetija-Stein und Nabel der Welt in der Kosmologonie der Rabbinen," Zeitschrift der deutschen Morgenländischen Gesellschaft, 124 (1974), 253-270.

Bratcher, Dennis R. [1377] "Pilgrimage," in Harper's Bible Dictionary. San Francisco: Harper and Row, 1985, 798-799.

Brueggemann, Walter. [1378] "Presence of God, Cultic," in Interpreter's Dictionary of the Bible, Supplementary Volume. Nashville: Abingdon, 1976, 680-683.

Buis, Pierre. [1379] "Jérusalem, un chaud rouillé," Études théologiques et religieuses, 56 (1981), 446-448.

Buis, Pierre. [1380] "Le Seigneur libère les hommes: Psaume 76," Études théologiques et religieuses, 55 (1980), 412-415.

Caspari, Wilhelm. [1381] "Tabur (Nabel)," Zeitschrift der deutschen Morgenländischen Gesellschaft, 86 (1933), 49-65.

Causse, Antonin. [1382] "De la Jérusalem terrestre à la Jérusalem céleste," Revue d' histoirie et de philosophie religieuses, 27 (1947), 12-36.

Causse, Antonin. [1383] "Le mythe de la nouvelle Jérusalem du Deutéro-Esaie à la IIIe Sibylle," Revue d' histoirie et de philosophie religieuses, 18 (1938), 377-414.

Causse, Antonin. [1384] "La vision de la nouvelle Jérusalem (Esaie lx) et la signification sociologique des assemblees de fete et des pelerinages dans l' orient semitique," Mélanges syriens, 2. Bibliothèque archéologique et historique, 30. Paris: Guethner, 1939, 739-750.

Child, Brevard. [1385] Myth and Reality in the Old Testament. London: SCM, 2nd edn., 1960, 83-93.

Clements, Ronald E. [1386] God and Temple: The Idea of the Divine Presence in Ancient Israel. Oxford: Blackwell, 1965, 163 pp.

Clements, Ronald E. [1387] Isaiah and the Deliverence of Jerusalem: A Study in the Interpretation of Prophecy in the Old Testament. Sheffield: University of Sheffield, 1980, 131 pp.

Clements, Ronald E. [1388] "Temple and Land: A Significant Aspect of Israel's Worship," Transactions of the Glasgow University Oriental Society, 19 (1961/1962), 16-28.

Clements, Ronald E. [1389] "The Prophecies of Isaiah and the Fall of Jerusalem in 587 B. C.," Vetus Testamentum, 30 (1980), 421-436.

Clifford, Richard J. [1390] The Cosmic Mountain in Canaan and the Old Testament. Harvard Semitic Monographs, 4. Cambridge, MA: Harvard University Press, 1972, 221 pp.

Clifford, Richard J. [1391] "The Temple and the Holy Mountain," in T. Madsen (ed.), The Temple in Antiquity: Ancient Records and Modern Perspectives. Religious Studies Monograph Series, 9. Provo, UT: Brigham Young University Press, 1984, 107-124.

Cohen, Chayim. [1392] "The 'Widowed' City," Journal of the Ancient Near Eastern Society of Columbia University, 5 (1973), 75-81.

Cohn, Robert L. [1393] "The Mountains and Mt. Zion," Judaism, 26 (1977), 97-115.

Cohn, Robert L. [1394] "Mountains in the Biblical Cosmos," in The Shape of Sacred Space: Four Biblical Studies. American Academy of Religion Studies in Religion, 23. Chico, CA: Scholars Press, 1981, 43-61.

Colunga, Alberto. [1395] "Jerusalén, la ciudad del Gran Rey," Estudios Bíblicos, 14 (1955), 255-279.

Cucchi, Francesco. [1396] "La nuova Gerusalemme nella visione profetica del dopo-esilio (raccolta di testi)," in S. Gozzo (ed.), La distruzione di Gerusalemme del 70: nei suoi riflessi storico-letterari. Assisi: Studio Teologico "porziuncolo," 1971, 57-68.

Davies, G. Henton. [1397] "Presence of God," in Interpreter's Dictionary of the Bible, 3. New York: Abingdon, 1962, 874-875.

Ehrlich, Ernst Ludwig. [1398] Die Kultsymbolik im Alten Testament und im nachbiblischen Judentum. Symbolik der Religionen, 3. Stuttgart: Hiersemann, 1959, 143 pp.

Fisher, Loren R. [1399] "The Temple Quarter," Journal of Semitic Studies, 8 (1963), 34-41.

Fitzgerald, Aloysius. [1400] "BTWLT and BT as Titles for Capital Cities," Catholic Biblical Quarterly, 37 (1975), 167-183.

Fitzgerald, Aloysius. [1401] "The Mythological Background for the Presentation of Jerusalem as a Queen and False Worship as Adultery in the Old Testament," Catholic Biblical Quarterly, 34 (1972), 403-416.

Fohrer, Georg. [1402] "Zion-Jerusalem im Alten Testament," in Studien zur alttestamentlichen Theologie und Geschichte (1949-1966). Beihefte zur Zeitschrift für die alttestamentliche Wissenschaft, 115. Berlin: de Gruyter, 1969, 195-241.

Fohrer, Georg. [1403] "Zion-Jerusalem in the Old Testament," in G. Friedrich (ed.), Theological Dictionary of the New Testament, 7. Grand Rapids, MI: Eerdmans, 1971, 292-319.

Franco, Ettore. [1404] "Gerusalemme in Is. 40-66," in M. Borrmans, et al. (eds.), Gerusalemme. Brescia: Paideia, 1982, 143-152.

Freedman, David N. [1405] "A Letter to the Readers," Biblical Archaeologist, 40 (1977), 46-48. [Argues that YHWH's celestial temple remained at Sinai throughout Biblical times.]

Fretheim, Terence E. [1406] "The Priestly Document: Anti-Temple?" Vetus Testamentum, 18 (1968), 313-329.

Fullerton, Kemper. [1407] "The Stone of Foundation," American Journal of Semitic Languages and Literatures, 37 (1920/1921), 1-12.

Görg, Manfred. [1408] "Die Gattung des sogenannten Tempelweihespruchs (I Kgs. 8, 12f)," in K. Bergerhof, M. Dietrich, and O. Luretz (eds.), Ugarit-Forschungen, 6. Internationales Jahrbuch für die Altertumskunde Syrien-Palästinas. Neukirchen-Vluyn: Neukirchener Verlag / Kevelaer: Butzon and Bercker, 1974, 55-63.

Goldman, Bernard. [1409] The Sacred Portal: A Primary Symbol in Ancient Judaic Art. Detroit: Wayne State University Press, 1966, 215 pp.

Gray, George Buchanan. [1410] "The Heavenly Temple and the Heavenly Altar," The Expositor, 5 (1908), 385-402, 530-546.

Hadey, Jean. [1411] "Jéremie et la temple: le conflit de la parole prophetique et de la tradition religieuse: Jér. 7: 1-15; 26: 1-19," Études théologiques et religieuses, 54 (1979), 438-443.

Hamerton-Kelly, R. G. [1412] "The Temple and the Origin of Jewish Apocalyptic," Vetus Testamentum, 20 (1970), 1-15.

Hamilton, R. W. [1413] "Jerusalem: Patterns of Holiness," in R. Moorey and P. Parr (eds.), Archaeology in the Levant: Essays for Kathleen Kenyon. Warminster: Aris and Phillips, 1978, 194-201.

Hamlin, E. John. [1414] "The Meaning of 'Mountains and Hills' in Isa. 41: 14-16," Journal of Near Eastern Studies, 13 (1954), 185-190.

Haran, Menahem. [1415] "The Divine Presence in the Israelite Cult and Cultic Institutions," Biblica, 50 (1969), 251-267.

Hayes, John H. [1416] "The Tradition of Zion's Inviolability," Journal of Biblical Literature, 82 (1963), 419-426.

Hertzberg, Hans Wilhelm. [1417] "Der heilige Fels und das Alte Testament," Journal of the Palestine Oriental Society, 12 (1932), 32-42.

Hollis, Frederick J. [1418] "The Sun-Cult and the Temple at Jerusalem," in S. H. Hooke (ed.), Myth and Ritual. London: Oxford University Press, 1933, 87-110.

Hooke, Samuel H. [1419] "The Corner-Stone of Scripture," in The Siege Perilous: Essays in Biblical Anthropology and Kindred Subjects. London: SCM, 1956, 235-249.

Hubmann, Franz D. [1420] "Der 'Weg' zum Zion: Literar- und stilkritische Beobachtungen zu Jes. 35: 8-10," in J. B. Bauer and J. Marböck (eds.), Memoria Jerusalem (Festschrift Franz Sauer). Graz: Akademische Druck-u. Verlagsanstalt, 1977, 29-41.

Jeremias, Jörg. [1421] "Lade und Zion: Zur Entstehung der Ziontradition," in H. W. Wolff (ed.), Probleme biblischer Theologie (Festschrift Gerhard von Rad). Munich: Kaiser Verlag, 1971, 183-198.

Jeremias, Jörg. [1422] Theophanie: Die Geschichte einer alttestamentlichen Gattung. Wissenschaftliche Monographien zum Alten und Neuen Testament, 10. Neukirchen-Vluyn: Neukirchener Verlag, 1965, 182 pp.

Jeremias, Johannes. [1423] Der Gottesberg, ein Beitrag zum Verständnis der biblischen Symbolsprache. Gütersloh: Bertelmann, 1919, 199 pp.

Jones, Douglas. [1424] "The Traditio of the Oracles of Isaiah of Jerusalem," Zeitschrift für die alttestamentliche Wissenschaft, 67 (1955), 226-246.

Junker, Hubert. [1425] "Sancta Civitas, Jerusalem Nova: Eine formcritische und überlieferungsgeschichtliche Studie zu Is. 2," in H. Gross and F. Musser (eds.), Ekklesia (Festschrift Matthias Wehr). Trier theologische Studien, 15. Trier: Paulinus Verlag, 1962, 17-33.

Kapelrud, Arvid S. [1426] "Temple Building: A Task for Gods and Kings," Orientalia, 32 (1963), 56-62.

Keel, Othmar. [1427] "God in the Temple," in The Symbolism of the Biblical World: Ancient Near Eastern Iconography and the Book of Psalms. Translated by T. J. Hallett. New York: Seabury, 1978, 179-201.

Kelly, Sidney. [1428] "Psalm 46: A Study in Imagery," Journal of Biblical Literature, 89 (1970), 305-312.

Kraus, Hans-Joachim. [1429] "Das Heiligtum und der Gottesdienst: Die Zion-Theologie," in Theologie der Psalmen. Neukirchen-Vluyn: Neukirchener Verlag, 1979, 94-103.

Krinetzki, Leo. [1430] "Zur Poetik und Exegese von Ps. 48," Biblische Zeitschrift, 4 (1960), 70-97.

Lach, Stanislaw. [1431] "Versuch einer neuen Interpretation der Zionshymnen," in W. Zimmerli, et al. (eds.), Interantional Organization for the Study of the Old Testament, Congress Volume, Göttingen, 1977. Supplements to Vetus Testamentum, 29. Leiden: Brill, 1978, 149-164.

Levenson, Jon D. [1432] "From Temple to Synagogue: I Kings 8," in B. Halpern and J. Levenson (eds.), Traditions in Transformation: Turning Points in Bbilical Faith. Winona Lake, IN: Eisenbrauns, 1981, 143-166.

Levenson, Jon D. [1433] Sinai and Zion: An Entry into the Jewish Bible. Minneapolis, MN: Winston-Salem, 1985.

Levenson, Jon D. [1434] "The Temple and the World," Journal of Religion, 64 (1984), 275-298.

Levine, Baruch. [1435] "On the Presence of God in Biblical Religion," in J. Neusner (ed.), Religions in Antiquity: Essays in Memory of E. R. Goodenough. Leiden: Brill, 1968, 71-87.

Lignée, Hubert. [1436] The Temple of Yahweh. Baltimore: Helicon, 1966,128 pp.

Lindblom, Johannes. [1437] "Der Eckstein in Jes. 28, 16," in Interpretationes ad vetus testamentum pertinentes Sigmundo Mowinckel septuagenario missae. Oslo: Forlaget Land Ogkirke, 1955, 123-132.

Lundquist, John M. [1438] "The Common Temple Ideology of the Ancient Near East," in T. Madsen (ed.), The Temple in Antiquity: Ancient Records and Modern Perspectives. Religious Studies Monograph Series, 9. Provo, UT: Brigham Young University Press, 1984, 53-76.

Lundquist, John M. [1439] "The Legitimatizing Role of the Temple in the Origin of the State," in K. H. Richards (ed.), Society of Biblical Literature Seminar Papers Series, 21. Chico, CA: Scholars Press, 1982, 271-297.

Lundquist, John M. [1440] "What is a Temple? A Preliminary Typology" in H. B. Huffmon, F. A. Spina, and A. R. Green (eds.), The Quest for the Kingdom of God: Essays in Honor of G. E. Mendenhall. Winona Lake, IN: Eisenbrauns, 1983, 205-219.

McCarter, P. Kyle. [1441] "The Ritual Dedication of the City of David in 2 Samuel 6," in C. L. Meyers and M. O'Connor (eds.), The Word of the Lord Shall Go Forth: Essays in Honor of David Noel Freedman. American Schools of Oriental Research, Special Volume Series, 1. Winona Lake: Eisenbrauns, 1983, 273-278.

McKelvey, R. J. [1442] "The Foundation-Stone in Zion," in The New Temple: The Church in the New Testament. London: Oxford University Press, 1969, 188-192.

McKenzie, John L. [1443] "The Presence in the Temple: God as Tenant" in L. E. Frizzell (ed.), God and His Temple. South Orange, NJ: Seton Hall University, Institute for Judaeo-Christian Studies, 1980, 30-38.

Mackenzie, R. A. F. [1444] "The City and Israelite Religion," Catholic Biblical Quarterly, 25 (1963), 60-70.

Maertens, Thierry. [1445] Jérusalem, Cité de Dieu (Psaumes 120-138). Lumiere et Vie, 3. Bruges: Abbaye de Saint-André, 1954, 149 pp.

Maigret, Jacques. [1446] "Jérusalem, ses poètes, ses prophètes," Bible et Terre Sainte, 114 (1969), 5.

Maigret, Jacques. [1447] "Le Temple au coeur de la Bible," Le Monde de la Bible, 13 (1980), 3-5.

Marböck, Johannes. [1448] "Des Gebet um die Rettung Zions Sir. 36, 1-22 (G: 33, 1-13a; 36, 16b-22) im Zusammenhang der Geschichtsschau Ben Siras," in J. B. Bauer and J. Marböck [eds.], Memoria Jerusalem [Festschrift Franz Sauer]. Graz: Akademische Druck-u. Verlagsanstalt, 1977, 93-115.

Martin-Achard, Robert. [1449] "Esaïe liv et la nouvelle Jérusalem," in Interantional Organization for the Study of the Old Testament, Congress Volume, Vienna, 1980. Supplements to Vetus Testamentum, 32. Leiden: Brill, 1981, 238-262.

May, Herbert G. [1450] "The Departure of the Glory of Yahweh," Journal of Biblical Literature, 56 (1937), 309-321.

May, Herbert G. [1451] "Some Aspects of Solar Worship at Jerusalem," Zeitschrift für die alttestamentliche Wissenschaft, 55 (1937), 269-281.

Merendino, Rosario [1452] "Jes. 49, 14-26: Jahwes Bekenntnis zu Sion und die neue Heilszeit," Revue biblique, 89 (1982), 321-369.

Merrill, A. L. [1453] "Psalm 23 and the Jerusalem Tradition," *Vetus Testamentum*, 15 (1965), 354-360.

Mettinger, Tryggve N. D. [1454] *The Dethronement of Sabaoth: Studies in the Shem and Kabod Theologies*. *Coniectanea Biblica, Old Testament Series*, 18. Lund: Gleerup, 1982, 158 pp.

Mettinger, Tryggve N. D. [1455] "YHWH SABAOTH-- The Heavenly King on the Cherubim Throne, " in T. Ishida (ed.), *Studies in the Period of David and Solomon and Other Esays*. Winona Lake, IN: Eisenbrauns, 1982, 109-138.

Metzger, Martin. [1456] "Himmlische und irdische Wohnstatt Jahwes," in K. Bergerhof, et al. (eds.), *Ugarit-Forschungen*, 2. *Internationales Jahrbuch für die Altertumskunde Syrien-Palästinas*. Neukirchen-Vluyn: Neukirchener Verlag / Kevelaer: Butzon and Bercker, 1970, 139-158.

Milgrom, Jacob. [1457] "Sancta Contagion and Altar/City/Asylum," in *Interantional Organization for the Study of the Old Testament, Congress Volume, Vienna,1980*. *Supplements to Vetus Testamentum*, 32. Leiden: Brill, 1981, 278-310.

Miller, Patrick D. Jr. [1458] "Psalm 127-- The House that Yahweh Builds," *Journal for the Study of the Old Testament*, 22 (1982), 119-132.

Molin, Georg. [1459] "Das Motiv vom Chaoskampf im alten Orient und in den Traditionen Jerusalems und Israels," J. B. Bauer and J. Marböck (eds.), *Memoria Jerusalem* (Festschrift Franz Sauer). Graz: Akademische Druck-u. Verlagsanstalt, 1977, 13-28.

Montgomery, James A. [1460] "The Holy City and Gehenna," *Journal of Biblical Literature*, 27 (1908), 24-47.

Montgomery, James A. [1461] "Paronomasia on the Name Jerusalem," *Journal of Biblical Literature*, 49 (1930), 277-282.

Morgenstern, Julian. [1462] *The Fire upon the Altar*. Chicago: Quadrangle, 1963, 132 pp.

Morgenstern, Julian. [1463] "Fire upon the Altar Once Again," *Encounter*, 26 (1965), 215-224.

Morgenstern, Julian. [1464] "The Gates of Righteousness," *Hebrew Union College Annual*, 6 (1929), 1-37.

Müller, Hans-Peter. [1465] "Die kultische Darstellung der Theophanie," *Vetus Testamentum*, 14 (1964), 183-191.

Noth, Martin. [1466] "Jerusalem and the Israelite Tradition," in *The Laws of the Pentateuch and other Studies*. Edinburgh: Oliver and Boyd, 1966, 132-144.

Offord, Joseph. [1467] "The Mountain Throne of Jahveh," *Palestine Exploration Fund, Quarterly Statement,* (1919), 39-45.

Ollenburger, Ben C. [1468] Zion, the City of the Great King: A Theological Symbol of the Jerusalem Cult. Journal for the Study of the Old Testament, Supplement Series, 41. Sheffield: JSOT Press, 1986, 240 pp.

Otto, Eckart. [1469] "El und Jhwh in Jerusalem: Historische und theologische Aspekte einer Religionsintegration," Vetus Testamentum, 30 (1980), 316-329.

Otzen, Benedikt. [1470] "Traditions and Structures of Isaiah 24-27," Vetus Testamentum, 24 (1974), 196-206.

Palmer, Martin. [1471] "The Cardinal Points in Psalm 48," Biblica, 46 (1945), 357-358.

Patai, Raphael. [1472] Man and Temple in Ancient Jewish Myth and Ritual. New York: KTAV, 2nd edn., 1967, 247 pp.

Peter, Adalbert. [1473] "Der Segensstrom des endzeitlichen Jerusalem: Herkunft und Bedeutung eines prophetischen Symbols," in F. Scholz (ed.), Miscellanea Fuldensia: Beitrage aus Geschichte, Theologie, Seelsorge (Festschrift Adolf Bolte). Fulda: Parzeller, 1966, 109-134.

Petersen, Claus. [1474] Mythos im Alten Testament: Bestimmung des Mythosbegriffs und Untersuchung der mythischen Elemente in den Psalmen. Beihefte zur Zeitschrift für die alttestamentliche Wissenschaft, 157. Berlin: de Gruyter, 1982, 279 pp.

Pfeifer, Claude J. [1475] "Sing for Us the Songs of Zion: The Jerusalem Psalms," The Bible Today, 97 (1978), 1690-1696.

Porteous, Norman W. [1476] "Jerusalem-Zion: The Growth of a Symbol," in A. Kuschke (ed.), Verbannung und Heimkehr. Tübingen: Mohr (Siebeck), 1961, 235-252. Reprinted and updated in N. W. Porteous, Living the Mystery: Collected Essays. Oxford: Blackwell, 1963, 93-111.

Rabe, Virgil W. [1477] "Israelite Opposition to the Temple," Catholic Biblical Quarterly, 29 (1967), 228-233.

von Rad, Gerhard. [1478] Die Weissagungen von dem neuen Jerusalem," in Theologie des Alten Testaments, 2. Munich: Kaiser Verlag, 1960, 305-309. English translation by D. M. G. Stalker in Old Testament Theology, 2. New York: Harper and Row, 1965, 292-297.

von Rad, Gerhard. [1479] "Der Zion," in Theologie des Alten Testaments, 2. Munich: Kaiser Verlag, 1960, 166-179. English translation by D. M. G. Stalker in Old Testament Theology, 2. New York: Harper and Row, 1965, 155-169.

Roberts, J. J. M. [1480] "The Davidic Origin of the Zion Tradition," Journal of Biblical Literature, 92 (1973), 329-344.

Roberts, J. J. M. [1481] "Isaiah 33: An Isaianic Elaboration of the Zion Tradition," in C. L. Meyers and M. O'Connor (eds.), The Word of the Lord Shall Go Forth: Essays in Honor of David Noel Freedman. American Schools of

Oriental Research, Special Volume Series, 1. Winona Lake: Eisenbrauns, 1983, 15-25.

Roberts, J. J. M. [1482] "Mount Zaphon," Interpreter's Dictionary of the Bible, Supplementary Volume. Nashville: Abingdon, 1976, 977.

Roberts, J. J. M. [1483] "The Religio-Political Setting of Psalm 47," Bulletin of the American Schools of Oriental Research, 221 (1976), 129-132.

Roberts, J. J. M. [1484] "Zion in the Theology of the Davidic-Solomonic Empire," in T. Ishida (ed.), Studies in the Period of David and Solomon and Other Essays. Winona Lake, IN: Eisenbrauns, 1982, 93-108.

Roberts, J. J. M. [1485] "Zion Tradition," in Interpreter's Dictionary of the Bible, Supplementary Volume. Nashville: Abingdon, 1976, 985-987.

Robinson, A. [1486] "Zion and Saphon in Ps. XLVIII. 3," Vetus Testamentum, 24 (1974), 118-123.

Rost, Leonhard. [1487] "Die Gerichtshoheit am Heiligtum," in A. Kuschke and E. Kutsch (eds.), Archäologie und Altes Testament (Festschrift Kurt Galling). Tübingen: Mohr (Siebeck), 1970, 225-231.

Rost, Leonhard. [1488] "Die Stadt im Alten Testament," Zeitschrift des deutschen Palästina-Vereins, 97 (1981), 129-138.

Rust, H. [1489] "Warum Jeruschalajim?" Theologische Literaturzeitung, 74 (1949), 627-629. [Dual form of name reflects earthly and heavenly cities.]

Schäfer, Peter. [1490] "Tempel und Schöpfung: Zur Interpretation einiger Heiligtumstraditionen in der rabbinischen Literatur," in Studien zur Geschichte und Theologie des Rabbinischen Judentums. Leiden: Brill, 1978, 122-133.

Schick, Conrad. [1491] "Jerusalem nach Ps. 122. 3," Zeitschrift des deutschen Palästina-Vereins, 16 (1893), 206-208.

Schmid, Herbert. [1492] "Jahwe und die Kulttraditionem von Jerusalem," Zeitschrift für die alttestamentliche Wissenschaft, 67 (1955), 168-197.

Schmid, Herbert. [1493] "Die Wurzeln des Zionismus im Alten Testament," in P. von der Osten-Sacken (ed.), Zionismus: Befreiungsbewegung des jüdischen Volkes. Berlin: Institute Kirche und Judentum, 1977, 23-29.

Schmidt, Hans. [1494] Der heilige Fels in Jerusalem: Eine archäologische und religionsgeschichtliche Studie. Tübingen: Mohr (Siebeck), 1933. 102 pp.

Schmidt, Helmut. [1495] Israel, Zion, und die Völker. Marburg: Goerich and Weiershaeuser, 1968.

Schmidt, Karl-Ludwig. [1496] "Jerusalem als Urbild und Abbild," in O. Fröbe-Kapteyn (ed.), Aus der Welt der Urbilder: Sonderband für C. G. Jung zum 15. Geburtstag. Eranos Jahrbuch, 18. Zürich: Rhein Verlag, 1950, 207-248.

Schmidt, Werner Hans. [1497] "Safon, Norden," in E. Jenni and C. Westermann (eds.), Theologische Handwörterbuch zum Alten Testament, 2. Munich: Kaiser Verlag, 1979, 575-582.

Schmitt, John J. [1498] "The Motherhood of God and Zion as Mother, " Revue biblique, 92 (1985), 557-569.

Schreiner, Josef. [1499] Sion-Jerusalem, Jahwes Königssitz: Theologie der heiligen Stadt im Alten Testament. Studien zum Alten und Neuen Testament, 7. Munich: Kösel, 1963, 312 pp.

Schunck, Klaus-Dietrich. [1500] "Zentralheiligtum, Grenzheiligtum und 'Höhenheiligtum' in Israel," Numen, 18 (1971), 132-140.

Simon, Marcel. [1501] "La prophétie de Nathan et le temple," Revue d' histoirie et de philosophie religieuses, 32 (1952), 41-58.

Soggin, J. Alberto. [1502] "Der offiziell geförderte Synkretismus in Israel während des 10. Jahrhunderts," Zeitschrift für die alttestamentliche Wissenschaft, 78 (1966), 179-204.

Sperber, Daniel. [1503] "On Sealing the Abysses," Journal of Semitic Studies, 11 (1966), 168-174.

Sperling, S. David. [1504] "Navel of the Earth," in Interpreter's Dictionary of the Bible, Supplementary Volume. Nashville: Abingdon, 1976, 621-623.

Sprecafico, Ambrogio. [1505] "Gerusalemme, città di pace e di giustizia," in M. Borrmans, et al. (eds.), Gerusalemme. Brescia: Paideia, 1982, 81-98.

Steck, Odil H. [1506] "Jerusalemer Vorstellungen vom Frieden und ihre Abwandlungen in der Prophetie des alten Israel," in G. Liedke (ed.), Freiden-Bible-Kirche. Stuttgart: Ernst Klett Verlag, 1972, 75-95.

Stinespring, William F. [1507] "No Daughter of Zion," Encounter, 26 (1965), 133-141.

Stinespring, William F. [1508] "Zion, Daughter of," in Interpreter's Dictionary of the Bible, Supplementary Volume. Nashville: Abingdon, 1976, 985.

Stolz, Fritz. [1509] Strukturen und Figuren im Kult von Jerusalem: Studien zur altorientalischen vor- und frühisaelitischen Religion. Beihefte zur Zeitschrift für die alttestamentliche Wissenschaft, 18. Berlin: de Gruyter, 1970, 235 pp.

Stolz, Fritz. [1510] "Zion," in E. Jenni and C. Westermann (eds.), Theologische Handwörterbuch zum Alten Testament, 2. Munich: Kaiser Verlag, 1979, 543-551.

Struz, Andrej and Alonso Schökel, Luis. [1511] "Salmo 122: Canto al nombre de Jerusalén," Biblica, 61 (1980), 234-250.

Talmon, Shemaryahu. [1512] "The Biblical Concept of Jerusalem," Journal of Ecumenical Studies, 8 (1971), 300-316. Also in J. M. Oestrreicher and A. Sinai (eds.), Jerusalem. New York: John Day, 1974, 189-204.

Talmon, Shemaryahu. [1513] "Har," in G. J. Botterweck and H. Ringgren (eds.), Theological Dictionary of the Old Testament, 3. Grand Rapids: Eerdmans, 1978, 427-447.

Talmon, Shemaryahu. [1514] "The 'Navel of the Earth' and the Comparative Method," in A. Merrill and T. Overholt (eds.), Scripture in History and Theology (Festschrift C. Rylaarsdam). Pittsburg: Pickwick, 1977, 243-268.

Terrien, Samuel. [1515] "The Omphalos Myth and Hebrew Religion," Vetus Testamentum, 20 (1970), 315-338.

Testa, Emmanuele. [1516] "La 'Gerusalemme cleste,' dall' Antico Oriente alla Bibbia e alla Liturgia," Bibbia e Oriente, 1 (1959), 47-50.

Turner, Harold W. [1517] "Phenomenological Analysis: The Sacred Place and its Biblical Versions," in From Temple to Meeting House: The Phenomenology and Theology of Places of Worship. The Hague: Mouton, 1979, 1-154.

Van der Born, A. [1518] "Zum Tempelweihspruch (I Kg VIII, 12f)," Oudtestamentische Studiën, 14 (1965), 235-244.

de Vaux, Roland. [1519] "Jerusalem and the Prophets," in H. M. Orlinsky (ed.), Interpreting the Prophetic Tradition. Cincinnati: Hebrew Union College Press, 1969, 275-300.

de Vaux, Roland. [1520] "Jérusalem et les Prophètes," Revue biblique, 73 (1966), 481-509.

de Vaux, Roland. [1521] "Le lieu que Yahwé a choisi pour y établir son nom," in F. Maass (ed.), Das Ferne und nahe Wort (Festschrift Leonhard Rost). Beihefte zur Zeitschrift für die alttestamentliche Wissenschaft, 105. Berlin: Töpelmann, 1967, 219-228.

Vriezen, Th. C. [1522] Jahwe en zijn Stad. Amsterdam: Uitgevers, 1962, 26 pp.

Wales, H. G. Quaritch. [1523] "The Sacred Mountain in the Old Asiatic Religions," Journal of the Royal Asiatic Society, (1953), 23-30.

Wanke, Gunther. [1524] Die Ziontheologie der Korachiten. Beihefte zur Zeitschrift für die alttestamentliche Wissenschaft, 97. Berlin: Töpelmann, 1966. 120 pp.

Weinfeld, Moshe. [1525] "Cult Centralization in Israel in the Light of a Neo-Babylonian Analogy," Journal of Near Eastern Studies, 23 (1964), 202-212.

Weinfeld, Moshe. [1526] "Zion and Jerusalem as Religious and Political Capital: Ideology and Utopia." in R. E. Friedman (ed.), The Poet and the Historian: Essays in Literary and Historical Criticism. Harvard Semitic Studies, 26. Chico, CA: Scholars Press, 1983, 75-115.

Weippert, H. [1527] "'Der Ort, den Jahwe erwählen wird, um dort seiner Namen wohnen zu lassen:' Die Geschichte einer alttestamentlichen Formel," Biblische Zeitschrift, 24 (1980), 76-94.

Welten, Peter. [1528] "Kulthöhe und Jahwetempel," Zeitschrift des deutschen Palästina-Vereins, 88 (1972), 19-37.

Wensinck, Arent Jan. [1529] The Ideas of the Western Semites Concerning the Navel of the Earth. Amsterdam: Johannes Müller, 1916, 65 pp.

Westphal, Gustav. [1530] Jahwes Wohnstätten nach den Anschauungen der alten Hebräer. Beihefte zur Zeitschrift für die alttestamentliche Wissenschaft, 15. Giessen: Töpelmann, 1908, 280 pp.

Wildberger, Hans. [1531] "Die Völkerwallfahrt zum Zion, Jes III, 1-5," Vetus Testamentum, 7 (1957), 62-81.

Willesen, F. [1532] "The Cultic Situation of Ps. LXXIV," Vetus Testamentum, 2 (1952), 289-306.

Wilshire, Leland Edward. [1533] "The Servant-City: A New Interpretation of the Servant Songs of Deutero-Isaiah," Journal of Biblical Literature, 94 (1975), 356-367.

Wolverton, W. I. [1534] "The Meaning of Zion in the Psalms," Anglican Theological Review, 47 (1965), 16-33.

Youngblood, Ronald. [1535] "Ariel, 'City of God,'" in A. I. Katsh and L. Nemoy (eds.), Essays on the Occasion of the Seventieth Anniversary of the Dropsie University. Philadelphia: Dropsie University, 1979, 457-462.

Ten

The Kingship of YHWH and The Throne of David

Abramsky, Shaul. [1536] "The Chronicler's View of King Solomon," in Eretz-Israel: Archaeological, Historical, and Geographical Studies, 16. Jerusalem: Israel Exploration Society, 1982, 3-14 (Hebrew), *252 (English summary).

Ahlström, Gosta W. [1537] "Die Königsideologie in Israel: Ein Diskussionsbeitrag," Theologische Zeitschrift, 18 (1962), 205-210.

Ahlström, Gosta W. [1538] Psalm 89: Eine Liturgie aus dem Ritual des leidenden Königs. Lund: Gleerup, 1959, 228 pp.

Ahlström, Gosta W. [1539] Royal Administration and National Religion in Ancient Palestine. Studies in the History of the Ancient Near East, 1. Leiden: Brill, 1982, 112 pp.

Ahlström, Gosta W. [1540] "Solomon, the Chosen One," History of Religions, 8 (1969), 93-110.

Ahuvia, A. [1541] "'Behold a King Will Reign in Righteousness-- A Study of the Royal Ideal according to the Criterion of Reality," Beth Miqra, 29 (1983/1984), 26-36 (Hebrew). [English summary in Old Testament Abstracts, 7 (1984), 188.]

Alt, Albrecht. [1542] "Gedanken über das Königtum Jahwes," in Kleine Schriften zur Geschichte des Volkes Israel, 1. Munich: Beck'sche Verlagsbuchhandlung, 1953, 345-357.

Alt, Albrecht. [1543] "Jesaja 8, 23-9, 6: Befreiungsnacht und Krönungstag," in W. Baumgartner, et al. (eds.), Festschrift Alfred Bertholet. Tübingen: Mohr (Siebeck), 1950, 29-49. Also in Kleine Schriften zur Geschichte des Volkes Israel, 2. Munich: Beck'sche Verlagsbuchhandlung, 1953, 206-225.

Alt, Albrecht. [1544] "Das Königtum in den Reichen Israel und Juda," Vetus Testamentum, 1 (1951), 2-22. Also in Kleine Schriften zur Geschichte des Volkes Israel, 2. Munich: Beck'sche Verlagsbuchhandlung, 1953, 116-134.

Alt, Albrecht. [1545] "The Monarchy in the Kingdoms of Israel and Judah," in Essays on Old Testament History and Religion. Oxford: Basil Blackwell, 1966, 239-259.

Anderson, G. W. See Bentzen, Aage. [1546]

Bentzen, Aage. [1546] King and Messiah. Edited by G. W. Anderson. London: Lutterworth, 1955; 2nd edn., Oxford: Blackwell, 1970, 118 pp.

Bernhardt, Karl-Heinz. [1547] Das Problem der altorientalischen Königsideologie im Alten Testament unter besonderer Berücksichtigung der Geschichte der Psalmenexegese dargestellt und kritisch gewürdigt. Supplements to Vetus Testamentum, 8. Leiden: Brill, 1961, 351 pp.

Bic, Milos. [1548] "Das erste Buch des Psalters: Eine Thronbesteigungsfestliturgie," in The Sacral Kingship: Contributions to the Central Theme of the VIIIth International Congress for the History of Religions (Rome, April, 1955). Studies in the History of Religions, Supplement to Numen, 4. Leiden: Brill, 1959, 316-332.

Bourke, Joseph. [1549] "The Ideal King of Judah," Scripture, 11 (1959), 97-110.

Braun, Roddy L. [1550] "Solomon, the Chosen Temple Builder," Journal of Biblical Literature, 95 (1976), 581-590.

Braun, Roddy L. [1551] "Solomonic Apologetic in Chronicles," Journal of Biblical Literature, 92 (1973), 503-516.

Bright, John. [1552] "Yahweh's Election of Mt. Zion and of David," in Covenant and Promise: The Prophetic Understanding of the Future in Pre-Exilic Israel. Philadelphia: Westminster, 1976, 49-77.

Brueggeman, Walter. [1553] "David and His Theologian," Catholic Biblical Quarterly, 31 (1969), 484-498.

Campbell, Anthony F. [1554] "Psalm 78: A Contribution to the Theology of Tenth Century Israel," Catholic Biblical Quarterly, 41 (1979), 51-79.

Carlson, Rolf August. [1555] David, the Chosen King: A Traditio-Historical Approach to the Second Book of Samuel. Stockholm: Almqvist and Wiksell, 1964, 304 pp.

Clifford, Richard J. [1556] "In Zion and David a New Beginning: An Interpretation of Psalm 78," in B. Halpern and J. D. Levenson (eds.), Traditions in Transformation: Turning Points in Bilical Faith. Winona Lake, IN: Eisenbrauns, 1981,121-141.

Cooke, Gerald. [1557] "The Israelite King as Son of God," Zeitschrift für die alttestamentliche Wissenschaft, 73 (1961), 202-225.

Cooper, Alan. [1558] "Ps. 24: 7-10: Mythology and Exegesis," Journal of Biblical Literature, 102 (1983), 37-60.

Coppens, Joseph. [1559] "Les apports du psaume CX (Vulg. CIX) à l' idéologie royale Israelite," in The Sacral Kingship: Contributions to the Central Theme of the VIIIth International Congress for the History of Religions (Rome, April, 1955). Studies in the History of Religions, Supplement to Numen, 4. Leiden: Brill, 1959, 333-348.

Coppens, Joseph. [1560] "La royauté de Yahve dans le psautier," Ephemerides Theologicae Lovanienses, 53 (1977), 297-362.

Crim, Keith. [1561] The Royal Psalms. Richmond, VA: John Knox, 1962, 127 pp.

Cross, Frank M. [1562] "The Ideologies of Kingship in the Era of Empire: Conditional Covenant and Eternal Decree," in Canaanite Myth and Hebrew Epic. Cambridge, MA: Harvard University Press, 1973, 219-273.

Cross, Frank M. and Freedman, David Noel. [1563] "A Royal Song of Thanksgiving," Journal of Biblical Literature, 72 (1953), 15-34.

Dietrich, Walter. [1564] "Gott als König: Zur Frage nach der theologischen und politischen Legitimität religiöser Begriffsbildung," Zeitschrift für Theologie und Kirche, 77 (1980), 251-268.

Donner, Herbert. [1565] "Adoption oder Legitimation? Erwägung zur Adoption im Alten Testament auf dem Hintergrund der altorientalischen Recht," Oriens Antiquus, 8 (1969), 87-119.

Dürr, Lorenz. [1566] Psalm 110 im Lichte der neueren altorientalischen Forschungen. Münster: Aschendorf, 1929, 26 pp.

Eaton, J. H. [1567] Kingship and the Psalms. Studies in Biblical Theology, 2/32. London: SCM, 1976, 227 pp.; 2nd edn., The Biblical Seminar, 3. Sheffield: JSOT Press, 1986, 240 pp.

Eissfeldt, Otto. [1568] "Jahwe als König," Zeitschrift für die alttestamentliche Wissenschaft, 46 (1928), 81-105. Also in Kleine Schriften, 1. Tübingen: Mohr (Siebeck), 1962, 172-193.

Eissfeldt, Otto. [1569] "The Promise of Grace to David in Isaiah 55: 1-5," in B. W. Anderson and W. Harrelson (eds.), Israel's Prophetic Herritage: Essays in Honor of James Muilenburg. New York: Harper, 1962, 196-207.

Eissfeldt, Otto. [1570] "Psalm 132," in Die Welt des Orients, 2 (1954-1959), 480-483. Also in Kleine Schriften, 3. Tübingen: Mohr (Siebeck), 1966, 481-483.

Engnell, Ivan. [1571] Studies in Divine Kingship in the Ancient Near East. Uppsala: Almquist and Wiksells, 1943; 2nd edn., Oxford: Blackwell, 1967, 261 pp.

Fohrer, Georg. [1572] "Der Vertrag zwischen König und Volk in Israel," Zeitschrift für die alttestamentliche Wissenschaft, 71 (1959), 1-22.

de Fraine, Jean. [1573] L' aspect religieux de la royauté israélite: L' institution monarchique dans l' Ancien Testament et dans les textes mésopotamiens. Analecta Biblica, 3. Rome Pontifical Biblical Institute, 1954, 425 pp.

de Fraine, Jean. [1574] "Monarchia e teocrazia in Israel," Bibbia e oriente, 1 (1959), 4-11.

de Fraine, Jean. [1575] "La royaute de Yahve dans les textes concernant l' arche," in International Organization for the Study of the Old Testament, Volume du Congrès, Genève, 1965. Supplements to Vetus Testamentum, 15. Leiden: Brill, 1966, 134-149.

Frankfort, Henri. [1576] Kingship and the Gods: A Study of Ancient Near Eastern Religion as the Integration of Society and Nature. Chicago: University of Chicago Press, 1948, 444 pp.

Freedman, David Noel. See Cross, Frank M. and Freedman, David Noel. [1563]

Gadd, Cyril J. [1577] Ideas of Divine Rule in the Ancient East. The Schweich Lectures, 1945. London: Geoffrey Cumberlege / Oxford University Press, 1948, 101 pp.

von Gall, August. [1578] Basileia tou Theou: Eine religionsgeschichtliche Studie zur vorkirchlichen Eschatologie. Heidelberg: Winter, 1926, 491 pp.

von Gall, August. [1579] "Über die Herkunft der Bezeichnung Jahwes als König," in K. Marti (ed.), Studien zur Semitischen Philologie und Religionsgeschichte Julius Wellhausen. Giessen: Töpelmann, 1914, 147-160.

Galling, Kurt. [1580] "Königlich und nichtkönigliche Stifter beim Tempel von Jerusalem," Zeitschrift des deutschen Palästina-Vereins, 68 (1946/51), 134-142.

Gese, Hartmut. [1581] "Der Davidsbund und die Zionservwählung, Zeitschrift für Theologie und Kirche, 61 (1964), 10-26.

Gilbert, M. and Pisano, S. [1582] "Psalm 110 (109), 5-7," Biblica, 61, (1980), 343-356.

Görg, Manfred. [1583] Gott-König-Reden in Israel und Ägypten. Beiträge zur Wissenschaft vom Alten und Neuen Testament, 105. Stuttgart: Kohlhammer, 1975, 295 pp.

Goodall, Terence. [1584] "Motifs of the Royal Ideology," in N. Brown (ed.), Essays in Faith and Culture. Sydney: Catholic Institute, 1979, 145-156.

Goodenough, Erwin R. [1585] "Kingship in Early Israel," Journal of Biblical Literature, 48 (1929), 169-205.

Gray, John. [1586] "The Kingship of God in the Prophets and the Psalms," Vetus Testamentum, 11 (1961), 1-29.

Grønbaeck, J. H. [1587] "Kongens Kultiske Funktion i det Forexilske Israel," Dansk Teologiske Tidskrift, 20 (1956), 1-16.

Gunneweg, A. H. J. [1588] "Sinaibund und Davidsbund," Vetus Testamentum, 10 (1960), 335-341.

Halpern, Baruch. [1589] The Constitution of the Monarchy in Israel. Harvard Semitic Monographs, 25. Chico, CA: Scholars Press, 1981, 410 pp.

Harrelson, Walter. [1590] "Nonroyal Motifs in the Royal Eschatology," in B. W. Anderson and W. Harrelson (eds.), Israel's Prophetic Heritage: Essays in Honor of James Muilenburg. New York: Harper, 1962, 147-165.

Hooke, Samuel H. (ed.) [1591] Myth, Ritual, and Kingship: Essays on the Theory and Practice of Kingship in the Ancient Near East and in Israel. Oxford: Clarendon Press, 1958, 308 pp.

Ishida, Tomoo. [1592] The Royal Dynasties in Ancient Israel: A Study on the Foundation and Development of Royal-Dynastic Ideology. Beihefte zur Zeitschrift für die alttestamentliche Wissenschaft, 142. Berlin: de Gruyter, 1977, 211 pp.

James, E. O. [1593] "The Sacred Kingship," in Myth and Ritual in the Ancient Near East. London: Thames and Hudson, 1958, 80-112.

Jefferson, Helen G. [1594] "Psalm 93," Journal of Biblical Literature, 71 (1952), 155-160.

Johnson, Aubrey. R. [1595] "Divine Kingship and the Old Testament," Expository Times, 62 (1950), 36-42.

Johnson, Aubrey. R. [1596] "Hebrew Conceptions of Kingship, in S. H. Hooke (ed.), Myth, Ritual, and Kingship: Essays on the Theory and Practice of Kingship in the Ancient Near East and in Israel. Oxford: Clarendon Press, 1958, 204-235.

Johnson, Aubrey. R. [1597] "The Role of the King in the Jerusalem Cultus," in S. H. Hooke (ed.), The Labyrinth: Further Studies in the Relation between Myth and Ritual in the Ancient World. London: SPCK, 1935, 71-111.

Johnson, Aubrey. R. [1598] Sacral Kingship in Ancient Israel. Cardiff: University of Wales Press, 2nd edn., 1967, 154 pp.

Keel, Othmar. [1599] "The King," in The Symbolism of the Biblical World: Ancient Near Eastern Iconography and the Book of Psalms. New York: Seabury, 1978, 243-306.

Kenik, Helen Ann. [1600] "Code of Conduct for the King," Journal of Biblical Literature, 95 (1976), 391-403.

Kissane, H. G. [1601] "The Interpretation of Psalm 110," Irish Theological Quarterly, 21 (1954), 103-114.

Klein, Hans. [1602] "Zur Auslegung von Psalm 2," Theologische Beiträge, 10 (1979), 63-71.

Köhler, Ludwig. [1603] "Jahwä malak," Vetus Testamentum, 3 (1953), 188-189.

Kraus, Hans-Joachim. [1604] Die Königsherrschaft Gottes im Alten Testament: Untersuchungen zur den Liedern von Jahwes Thronbesteigung. Beiträge zur historischen Theologie, 13. Tübingen: Mohr (Siebeck), 1951, 155 pp.

Kruse, Heinz. [1605] "David's Covenant," Vetus Testamentum, 35 (1985), 139-164.

Kruse, Heinz. [1606] "Psalm cxxxii and the Royal Zion Festival," Vetus Testamentum, 33 (1983), 279-297.

Kutsch, E. [1607] "Die Dynastie von Gottes Gnaden," Zeitschrift für Theologie und Kirche, 58 (1961), 137-153.

Lemaire, André. [1608] "Crise et effondrement de la monarchie davidique," Revue biblique, 45 (1936), 161-183.

Levenson, Jon D. [1609] "The Davidic Covenant in Modern Interpretation," Catholic Biblical Quarterly, 41 (1979), 205-219.

Lipínski, Edouard. [1610] "L' hymn à Yahwé Roi au Psaume 22, 28-32," Biblica, 50 (1969), 153-168.

Lipínski, Edouard. [1611] Le poemè royal du Psaume LXXXIX, 1-5, 20, 38. Cahiers de la Revue Biblique, 6. Paris: Gabalda, 1967, 109 pp.

Lipínski, Edouard. [1612] "Les psaumes de la Royauté de Yahwé dans l' Exegèse moderne," in Le Psautier. Orientalia et Biblica Lovaniensia, 4. Louvain: Louvain University, 1962, 133-272.

Lipínski, Edouard. [1613] La royauté de Yahwé dans le poésie et le culte de l' ancien Israël. Brussels: Koninklijke Academie, 1965, 560pp.

Lipínski, Edouard. [1614] "Yahweh mâlak," Biblica, 44 (1963), 405-460.

Lods, Adolphe. [1615] "La divinisation du roi dans l' Orient méditeranéen et ses pépercussions dans l' ancien Israël," Revue d' histoirie et de philosophie religieuses, 10 (1930), 209-221.

Maag, Victor. [1616] "Malkût Yhwh," in International Organization for the Study of the Old Testament, Congress Volume, Oxford, 1959. Supplements to Vetus Testamentum, 7. Leiden: Brill, 1960, 129-153.

McCarthy, Dennis J. [1617] "Compact and Kingship: Stimuli for Hebrew Covenant Thinking," in T. Ishida (ed.), Studies in the Period of David and Solomon and Other Essays. Winona Lake, IN: Eisenbrauns, 1982, 75-92.

McCarthy, Dennis J. [1618] "2 Samuel 7 and the Structure of the Deuteronomic History," Journal of Biblical Literature, 84 (1965), 131-138.

McCullough, W. Stewart. [1619] "'The Enthronment of Yahweh' Psalms," in E. C. Hobbs (ed.), A Stubborn Faith: Papers on the Old Testament and Related Subjects (W. A. Irwin Festschrift). Dallas: Southern Methodist University Press, 1956, 53-61.

Maly, Eugene H. [1620] "God and King in Ancient Israel," The Bible Today, 100 (1979), 1893-1900.

Mann, Thomas W. [1621] "The Davidic Empire," in Divine Presence and Guidance in Israelite Traditions: The Typology of Exaltation. Baltimore: Johns Hopkins Press, 1977, 213-230.

Mendenhall, George E. [1622] "The Monarchy," Interpretation, 29 (1975), 155-170.

Mettinger, Tryggve N. D. [1623] King and Messiah: The Civil and Sacral Legitimation of the Israelite Kings. Coniectanae biblica, Old Testament Series, 8. Lund: Gleerup, 1976, 342 pp.

Mettinger, T. N. D. [1624] "The Last Words of David: A Study of Structure and Meaning in II Samuel 23: 1-7," Svensk Exegetisk Årsbok, 41/42 (1976/1977), 147-156.

Michel, Diethelm. [1625] "Studien zu den Sogenannten Thronbesteigungspsalmen," Vetus Testamentum, 6 (1956), 40-68.

Morgenstern, Julian. [1626] "The Cultic Setting of the 'Enthronment Psalms,'" Hebrew Union College Annual, 35 (1964), 1-42.

du Mortier, Jean-Bernard. [1627] "Un ritual d' intronisation: Le Ps lxxxix, 2-38," Vetus Testamentum, 22 (1972), 176-197.

Mowinckel, Sigmund. [1628] "The Ancient Israelite Conception of the King," in The Psalms in Israel's Worship, 1. Oxford: Blackwell, 1962, 50-60.

Mowinckel, Sigmund. [1629] "The Ideal of Kingship in Ancient Israel," in He That Cometh. New York: Abingdon, n.d., 21-95.

Mowinckel, Sigmund. [1630] "General Oriental and Specific Israelite Elements in the Israelite Conception of the Sacral Kingdom," in The Sacral Kingship: Contributions to the Central Theme of the VIIIth International Congress for the History of Religions (Rome, April, 1955). Studies in the History of Religions, Supplement to Numen, 4. Leiden: Brill, 1959, 283-293.

Mowinckel, Sigmund. [1631] Zum israelitischen Neujahrfest und zur Deutung der Thronbesteigungspsalmen. Avhandlinger utgitt av Det Norske Videnskaps-Akademi i Oslo, 2. Hist.-Filos. Klasse. 1952; Oslo: Dybwad, 1985, 68 pp.

Mowinckel, Sigmund. [1632] "'Die Letzten Worte Davids:' II Sam 23. 1-7," Zeitschrift für die alttestamentliche Wissenschaft, 45 (1927), 30-58.

Mowinckel, Sigmund. [1633] Psalmenstudien, 2. Das Thronbesteigungsfest Jahwäs und der Ursprung der Eschatologie. Skrifter utgitt av Det Norske Videnskaps-Akademi i Osl, 2. Hist.-Filos. Klasse, 6. Oslo: Dybwad, 1922; Amsterdam: Schippers, 1961, 347 pp.

Muilenburg, James. [1634] "Psalm 47," Journal of Biblical Literature, 63 (1944), 235-256.

Mullen, E. Theodore, Jr. [1635] "The Divine Witness and the Davidic Royal Grant," Journal of Biblical Literature, 102 (1983), 207-218.

Neufeld, Edward. [1636] "The Emergence of a Royal Urban Society in Ancient Israel," Hebrew Union College Annual, 31 (1960), 31-53.

von Nordheim, Eckhard. [1637] "König und Tempel: Der Hintergrund des Tempelbauverbotes in 2 Samuel vii," Vetus Testamentum, 27 (1977), 434-453.

North, Christopher R. [1638] "The Old Testament Estimate of Monarchy," American Journal of Semitic Languages and Literatures, 48 (1931), 1-19.

North, Christopher R. [1639] "The Religious Aspect of Hebrew Kingship," Zeitschrift für die alttestamentliche Wissenschaft, 50 (1932), 8-38.

North, Robert. [1640] "Theology of the Chronicler," Journal of Biblical Literature, 82 (1963), 369-381.

Noth, Martin. [1641] "David and Israel in II Samuel VII," in The Laws in the Pentateuch and Other Studies. Edinburgh: Oliver and Boyd, 1966, 250-259.

Noth, Martin. [1642] "God, King, and Nation in the Old Testament," in The Laws in the Pentateuch and Other Studies. Edinburgh: Oliver and Boyd, 1966, 145-178.

Noth, Martin. [1643] "Gott, Konig, Volk im Alten Testament," Zeitschrift für Theologie und Kirche, 47 (1950), 157-191.

Ollenburger, Ben C. [1644] Zion, The City of the Great King: A Theological Symbol of the Jerusalem Cult. Journal for the Study of the Old Testament, Supplement Series, 41. Sheffield: JSOT Press, 1986, 240 pp.

Patai, Raphael. [1645] "Hebrew Installation Rites," Hebrew Union College Annual, 20 (1947), 143-225.

Peterca, Vladimir. [1646] "Die Verwendung des verbs BHR für Salomo in den Büchern der Chronik," Biblische Zeitschrift, 28 (1985), 94-96.

Pisano, S. See Gilbert, M. and Pisano, S. [1582]

Porter, J. R. [1647] "The Interpretation of 2 Samuel vi and Psalm cxxxii," Journal of Theological Studies, 5 (1954), 161-173.

Poulssen, Niek. [1648] König und Tempel im Glaubenszeugnis des Alten Testamentes. Stuttgart Biblische Monographien, 3.Stuttgart: Katholisches Bibelwerk, 1967, 220 pp.

Poulssen, Niek. [1649] "Rex et templum in Israël," Verbum Domini, 40 (1962), 264-269.

Quintens, W. [1650] "La vie du roi dans le Psaume 21," Biblica, 59 (1978), 516-541.

von Rad, Gerhard. [1651] "Israel's Anointed," in Old Testament Theology, 1. English translation by D. M. G. Stalker. New York: Harper and Bros., 1962, 306-354.

von Rad, Gerhard. [1652] "Das judäische Königsritual," Theologische Literaturzeitung, 72 (1947), 211-216. Reprinted in Gesammelte Studien zum Alten Testament, 1. Munich: Chr. Kaiser Verlag, 1958, 205-213.

von Rad, Gerhard. [1653] "The Royal Ritual in Judah," in The Problem of the Hexateuch and Other Essays. New York: McGraw-Hill, 1966, 222-231.

Ridderbos, J. [1654] "Jahwäh malak," Vetus Testamentum, 4 (1954), 87-89.

Ringgren, Helmer. [1655] "Behold Your King Comes," Vetus Testamentum, 24 (1974), 207-211.

Roberts, J. J. M. [1656] "The Davidic Origin of the Zion Tradition," Journal of Biblical Literature, 92 (1973), 329-344.

Roberts, J. J. M. [1657] "The Religio-Political Setting of Psalm 47," Bulletin of the American Schools of Oriental Research, 221 (1976), 129-132.

Roberts, J. J. M. [1658] "Zion in the Theology of the Davidic-Solomonic Empire," in T. Ishida (ed.), Studies in the Period of David and Solomon and Other Essays. Winona Lake, IN: Eisenbrauns, 1982, 93-108.

Rosenthal, Erwin. I. J. [1659] "Some Aspects of the Hebrew Monarchy," Journal of Jewish Studies, 9 (1958), 1-18. Reprinted in Studia Semitica, 1. Cambridge: University Press, 1971, 3-20.

Rost, Leonhard. [1660] "Sinaibund und Davidsbund," Theologische Literaturzeitung, 72 (1947), 129-134.

Rost, Leonhard. [1661] Die Überlieferung von der Thronnachfolge Davids. Beiträge zur Wissenschaft von Alten und Neuen Testament, 3/6. Stuttgart: Kohlhammer, 1926, 142 pp. English translation, The Succession to the Throne of David. Trans. by M. D. Rutter and D. M. Gunn, with an introduction by Edward Ball. Historic Texts and Interpreters in Biblical Scholarship, 1. Sheffield: Almond Press, 1982, 133 pp.

Runnalls, Donna. [1662] "The King as Temple Builder: A Messianic Typology," in E. J. Furcha (ed.), Spirit within Structure: Essays in Honor of George Johnston. Pittsburgh Theological Monograph Series, n. s. 3. Allison Park, PA: Pickwick, 1983, 15-37.

Sarna, Nahum. [1663] "Psalm 89: A Study in Inner Biblical Exegesis," in A. Altman (ed.), Biblical and Other Studies. Brandeis University Studies and Texts, 1. Cambridge: Harvard University Press, 1963, 29-46.

Schmidt, Hans. [1664] Die Thronfahrt Jahwes am Fest der Jahreswende im alten Israel. Sammlung Gemeinverständlicher Vorträge und Schriften, 122. Tübingen: Mohr (Siebeck), 1927, 55 pp.

Schmidt, Werner Hans. [1665] Königtum Gottes in Ugarit und Israel: Zur Herkunft der Königsprädikation Jahwes. Beihefte zur Zeitschrift für die alttestamentliche Wissenschaft, 80. Berlin: Töpelmann, 1966, 90 pp.

Seybold, Klaus. [1666] Das davidische Königtum im Zeugnis der Propheten. Forschungen zur Religion und Literatur des Alten und Neuen Testaments, 107. Göttingen: Vanderhoeck & Ruprecht, 1972, 183 pp.

Soggin, J. Alberto. [1667] "Der Beitrag des Königtums zur altisraelitischen Religion," Studies in the Religion of Ancient Israel. Supplements to Vetus Testamentum, 23. Leiden: Brill, 1972, 9-26.

Soggin, J. Alberto. [1668] "Gott als König in der biblischen Dichtung: Bermerkungen zu den YHWH mlk-Psalmen," in Proceedings of the Fifth World Congress of Jewish Studies, Jerusalem, 1969,1. Jerusalem: World Union of Jewish Studies, 1972, 126-133.

Soggin, J. Alberto. [1669] Das Königtum in Israel. Beihefte zur Zeitschrift für die alttestamentliche Wissenschaft, 104. Berlin: Töpelmann, 1967, 167 pp.

Soggin, J. Alberto. [1670] "mlk, moeloek, König," in E. Jenni and C. Westermann (eds.), Theologisches Handwörterbuch zum Alten Testament, 1. Munich: Chr. Kaiser Verlag, 1971, 908-920.

Szikszai, Stephan. [1671] "King, Kingship," in Interpreter's Dictionary of the Bible, 3. New York: Abingdon, 1962, 11-17.

Tadmor, Hayim. [1672] "'The People' and the Kingship in Ancient Israel: The Role of Political Institutions in the Biblical Period," in H. H. Ben-Sasson and S. Ettinger (eds.), Jewish Society through the Ages. New York: Schocken, 1971, 46-68.

Tadmor, Hayim. [1673] "Traditional Institutions and the Monarchy: Social and Political Tensions in the Time of David and Solomon," in T. Ishida (ed.), Studies in the Period of David and Solomon and Other Essays. Winona Lake, IN: Eisenbrauns, 239-257.

Talmon, Shemaryahu. [1674] "Kingship and Ideology of the State," in A. Malamat (ed.), The Age of the Monarchies: Culture and Society. World History of the Jewish People, 4/2. Jerusalem: Masadda Press, 1979, 3-26.

Tsevat, Matitiahu. [1675] "The House of David in Nathan's Prophecy," Biblica, 46 (1965), 353-356.

Tsevat, Matitiahu. [1676] "King, God as," in Interpreter's Dictionary of the Bible, Supplementary Volume. Nashville: Abingdon, 1976, 515-516.

Tsevat, Matitiahu. [1677] "The Steadfast House," in The Meaning of the Book of Job and Other Essays. New York: KTAV, 1980, 101-117.

Tsevat, Matitiahu. [1678] "Studies in the Book of Samuel, 3. The Steadfast House, What Was David Promised in 2 Samuel 7: 11b-16?" Hebrew Union College Annual, 34 (1963), 71-82.

Ulrichsen, Jarl H. [1679] "YHWH MALAK: Einige Sprachliche Beobachtungen," Vetus Testamentum, 27 (1977), 361-374.

Van den Bussche, Henri. [1680] Le texte de la prophetie de Nathan sur la dynastie davidique. Analecta Lovanienses Biblica et Orientalia, 2/7. Louvain: Imprimerie Orientiste, 1948, 45 pp.

de Vaux, Roland. [1681] "The King of Israel, Vassal of Yahweh," in The Bible and the Ancient Near East. Garden City: Doubleday, 1971, 152-166.

de Vaux, Roland. [1682] "The Person of the King," in Ancient Israel: Its Life and Institutions. New York: McGraw-Hill, 1961, 100-114.

de Vaux, Roland. [1683] "Le roi d' Israël, vassal de Yahvé," in Bible et Orient. Paris: Cerf, 1967, 287-301.

Veijola, Timo. [1684] Die ewige Dynastie. David und die Ensthehung seiner Dynastie nach der deuteronomistischen Darstellung. Annales Academiae Scientiarum Fennicae, B, 193. Helsinki: Suomalainen Tiedeakatemia, 1975, 164 pp.

Veijola, Timo. [1685] Das Königtum in der Beurteilung der deuteronomistischen Historiographie. Annales Academiae Scientiarum Fennicae, B, 198. Helsinki: Suomalainen Tiedeakatemia, 1977, 147 pp.

Wales, H. G. Quaritch. [1686] The Mountain of God: A Study in Early Kingship. London: Bernard Quaritch, 1953.

Wallis, Gerhard. [1687] "Jerusalem und Samaria als Königsstadte, Vetus Testamentum, 26 (1976), 480-496.

Weinfeld, Moshe. [1688] "Covenant, Davidic," Interpreter's Dictionary of the Bible, Supplementary Volume. Nashville: Abingdon, 1976, 188-192.

Weinfeld, Moshe. [1689] "The Covenant of Grant in the Old Testament and in the Ancient Near East," Journal of the American Oriental Society, 90 (1970), 184-203.

Weinfeld, Moshe. [1690] "The Covenants with Abraham and David, the Royal Grant," in G. J. Botterweck and H. Ringgren (eds.), Theological Dictionary of the Old Testament, 2. English translation by J. T. Willis. Grand Rapids: Eerdmans, 1975, 270-272.

Weiser, Artur. [1691] "Die Legitimation des Königs David," Vetus Testamentum, 16 (1966), 325-354.

Weiser, Artur. [1692] "Die Tempelbaukreise unter David," Zeitschrift für die alttestamentliche Wissenschaft, 77 (1965), 153-167.

Welten, Peter. [1693] "Königsherrschaft Jahwes und Thronbesteigung: Bemerkungen zu ürledigten Fragen," Vetus Testamentum, 32 (1982), 297-310.

Widengren, Geo. [1694] "King and Covenant," Journal of Semitic Studies, 2 (1957), 1-32.

Widengren, Geo. [1695] Sakrales Königtum im Alten Testament und in Judentum. Stuttgart: Kohlhammer, 1955, 127 pp.

Wildberger, Hans. [1696] "Die Thronnamen des Messias, Jes. 9, 5b," Theologische Zeitschrift, 16 (1960), 314-332.

Wyatt, Nicolas. [1697] "'Araunah the Jebusite' and the Throne of David," Studia Theologica, 39 (1985), 39-53.

Yeivin, Samuel. [1698] "Social, Religious, and Cultural Trends in Jerusalem under the Davidic Dynasty," Vetus Testamentum, 3 (1953), 149-166.

Eleven

YHWH's Sanctuary: Traditions of the Pre-Solomonic Cultus / Tent, Ark, and Cherubim

Abrahams, Israel. [1699] "Tabernacle," in Encyclopaedia Judaica, 15. Jerusalem: Macmillan, 1971, 679-687.

Aharoni, Yohanan. [1700] "From Shiloh to Jerusalem," in J. Aviram (ed.), Jerusalem through the Ages. Jerusalem: Israel Exploration Society, 1968, 85-95 (Hebrew), 61 (English summary).

Ahlström, Gosta. W. [1701] "The Travels of the Ark: A Religio-Political Composition," Journal of Near Eastern Studies, 43 (1984), 141-149.

Albright, William F. [1702] "What Were the Cherubim?" Biblical Archaeologist, 1 (1938), 1-3. Reprinted in G. E. Wright and D. N. Freedman (eds.), Biblical Archaeologist Reader. Garden City: Doubleday, 1961, 95-97.

Alt, Albrecht. [1703] "Zelte und Hütten," in H. Junker and J. Botterweck (eds.), Alttestamentliche Studien (F. Nötscher Festschrift). Bonner Biblische Beiträge, 1. Bonn: Peter Hanstein, 1950, 16-25. Reprinted in Kleine Schriften zur Geschichte des Volkes Israel, 3. Munich: Beck'sche Verlagsbuchhandlung, 1959, 233-242.

Andrews, S. J. [1704] "The Worship in the Tabernacle Compared with that of the Second Temple," Journal of Biblical Literature, 5 (1886), 56-68.

Armerding, Carl E. See Lotz, Wilhelm; Kyle, Melvin G.; and Armerding, Carl E. [1784]

Arnold, William R. [1705] Ephod and Ark: A Study in the Records and Religion of the Ancient Hebrews. Harvard Theological Studies, 3. Cambridge, MA: Harvard University Press, 1917, 170 pp.

Barnett, R. D. [1706] "Cherubim and the Temple of Solomon," in Illustrations of Old Testament History. London: British Museum, 1966, 44-45.

Ben-Ori, Z. [1707] "The Ark of Testimony and its Parts," Beth Miqra, 27 (1981/1982), 214-221 (Hebrew). [English summary in Old Testament Abstracts, 6 (1983), 33.]

Ben-Ori, Z. [1708] "The Posts of the Tabernacle Court," Beth Miqra, 26 (1981), 148-158 (Hebrew). [English summary in Old Testament Abstracts, 4 (1980/1981), 211.]

Bentzen, Aage. [1709] "The Cultic Use of the Story of the Ark in Samuel," Journal of Biblical Literature, 67 (1948), 37-53.

Benzinger, Immanuel. [1710] "Tabernacle," in T. K. Cheyne and J. S. Black (eds.), Encyclopaedia Biblica, 4. New York: Macmillan, 1903, 4861-4875.

Bernhardt, Karl-Heinz. [1711] "Lade," in B. Reicke and L. Rost (eds.), Biblisch-Historisches Handwörterbuch, 2. Göttingen: Vanderhoeck and Ruprecht, 1964, 1038-1041.

Blekinsopp, Joseph. [1712] "Gibeon and the Ark: A Hypothesis," in Gibeon and Israel: The Role of Gibeon and the Gibeonites in the Political and Religious History of Early Israel. Society for Old Testament Study, Monograph Series, 2. Cambridge: Cambridge University Press, 1972, 65-83.

Blekinsopp, Joseph. [1713] "Kiriath-Jearim and the Ark," Journal of Biblical Literature, 88 (1969), 143-156.

Bovet, F. [1714] "Sur le Tabernacle," Revue d' histoirie et de philosophie religieuses, n. s., 21 (1933), 277-280.

Brown, John P. [1715] "The Ark of the Covenant and the Temple of Janus: The Magico-Military Numen of the State in Jerusalem and Rome," Biblische Zeitschrift, 30 (1986), 20-35.

Budde, Karl. [1716] "Ephod und Lade," Zeitschrift für die alttestamentliche Wissenschaft, 39 (1921), 1-42.

Budde, Karl. [1717] "Die ursprüngliche Bedeutung der Lade Jahwe's," Zeitschrift für die alttestamentliche Wissenschaft, 21 (1901), 193-197.

Budde, Karl. [1718] "War die Lade Jahwes ein leerer Thron?" Theologische Studien und Kritiken, 79 (1906), 489-507.

Caldecott, W. Shaw. [1719] The Tabernacle: Its History and Structure. Philadelphia: Union Press, 2nd edn., 1906, 236 pp.

Campbell, Anthony F. [1720] The Ark Narrative (1 Sam 4-6; 2 Sam 6): A Form-Critical and Traditio-Historical Study. Society of Biblical Literature Dissertation Series, 16. Missoula, MT: Scholars Press, 1975, 282 pp.

Cheyne, Thomas K. [1721] "Ark of the Covenant," in T. K. Cheyne and J. S. Black (eds.), Encyclopaedia Biblica, 1. New York: Macmillan, 1899, 300-310.

Clifford, Richard J. [1722] "The Tent of El and the Israelite Tent of Meeting," Catholic Biblical Quarterly, 33 (1971), 221-227.

Couard, Ludwig. [1723] "Die religiös-nationale Bedeutung der Lade Jahwes," Zeitschrift für die alttestamentliche Wissenschaft, 12 (1897), 53-90.

Cross, Frank M. [1724] "The Cultus of the Israelite League," in Canaanite Myth and Hebrew Epic. Cambridge: Harvard University Press, 1973, 77-144.

Cross, Frank M. [1725] "The Tabernacle," Biblical Archaeologist, 10 (1947), 45-68. Reprinted in D. N. Freedman and G. E. Wright (eds.), Biblical Archaeologist Reader. Garden City: Doubleday, 1961, 201-228.

Cross, Frank M. [1726] "The Priestly Tabernacle in the Light of Recent Research," in A. Biran (ed.), Temples and High Places in Biblical Times. Jerusalem: Hebrew Union College, 1981, 169-180. Also in T. Madsen (ed.), The Temple in Antiquity: Ancient Records and Modern Perspectives. Religious Studies Monograph Series, 9. Provo, UT: Brigham Young University Press, 1984, 27-30.

Davies, G. Henton. [1727] "The Ark of the Covenant," Annual of the Swedish Theological Institute, 5 (1966/1967), 30-47.

Davies, G. Henton. [1728] "Ark of the Covenant," in Interpreter's Dictionary of the Bible, 1. New York: Abingdon, 1962, 222-226.

Davies, G. Henton. [1729] "The Ark in the Psalms," in F. F. Bruce (ed.), Promise and Fulfillment (S. H. Hooke Festschrift). Edinburgh: T. & T. Clark, 1963, 51-61.

Davies, G. Henton. [1730] "Tabernacle," in Interpreter's Dictionary of the Bible, 4. New York: Abingdon, 1962, 498-506.

Dhorme, Édouard. [1731] "Le nom des Chérubins," in Recueil Édouard Dhorme: Études et orientales. Paris: Imprimerie Nationale, 1951, 671-683.

Dhorme, Édouard and Vincent, Louis-Hugues. [1732] "Les Chérubins," Revue biblique, 35 (1926), 328-358, 481-495.

Dibelius, Martin. [1733] Die Lade Jahves: Eine religionsgeschichtliche Untersuchung. Forschungen zur Religion und Literatur des Alten und Neuen Testament, 7. Göttingen: Vanderhoeck and Ruprecht, 1906, 128 pp.

Dürr, Lorenz. [1734] "Ursprung und Bedeutung der Bundeslade," Bonner Zeitschrift für Theologie und Seelsorge, 1 (1924), 17-24.

Dus, Jan. [1735] "Die Analyse zweier Ladeerzählungen des Josuabuches (Jos. 3-4 und 6)," Zeitschrift für die alttestamentliche Wissenschaft, 72 (1960), 107-134.

Dus, Jan. [1736] "Der Brauch der Ladewanderung im alten Israel," Theologische Zeitschrift, 17 (1961), 1-16.

Dus, Jan. [1737] "The Dreros Bilingual and the Tabernacle of the Ancient Israelites,: Journal of Semitic Studies, 10 (1965), 55-57.

Dus, Jan. [1738] "Die Erzählung über den Verlust der Lade, 1 Sam 4," Vetus Testamentum, 13 (1963), 333-337.

Dus, Jan. [1739] "Herabfahrung Jahwes auf die Lade und Entziehung der Feuerwolke," Vetus Testamentum, 19 (1969), 290-311.

Dus, Jan. [1740] "Noch zum Brauch der Ladewanderung," Vetus Testamentum, 13 (1963), 126-132.

Dus, Jan. [1741] "Die Thron- und Bundeslade," Theologische Zeitschrift, 20 (1964), 241-251.

Dus, Jan. [1742] "Zur bewegten Geschichte der israelitischen Lade," Annali, Instituto Orientali de Napoli, 41 (1981), 351-383.

Eckart, Otto. [1743] "Silo und Jerusalem," Theologische Zeitschrift, 32 (1976), 65-77.

Eerdmans, B. D. [1744] "Sojourn in the Tent of Jahu," Oudtestamentlische Studien, 1 (1942), 1-16.

Eissfeldt, Otto. [1745] "Kultzelt und Tempel," in H. Gese and H. P. Rüger (eds.), Wort und Geschichte (Karl Elliger Festschrift). Neukirchen-Vluyn: Neukirchener Verlag, 1973, 51-55. Reprinted in Kleine Schriften, 6. Tübingen: Mohr (Siebeck), 1979, 1-7.

Eissfeldt, Otto. [1746] "Lade und Gesetztafeln," Theologische Zeitschrift, 16 (1960), 281-284. Reprinted in Kleine Schriften, 3. Tübingen: Mohr (Siebeck), 1966, 526-529.

Eissfeldt, Otto. [1747] "Lade und Stierbild," Zeitschrift für die alttestamentliche Wissenschaft, 58 (1940/1941), 190-215. Reprinted in Kleine Schriften, 2. Tübingen: Mohr (Siebeck), 1963, 282-305.

Eissfeldt, Otto. [1748] "Die Lade Jahwes in Geschichtserzählung, Sage und Lied," Altertum, 14 (1968), 131-145. Reprinted in Kleine Schriften, 5. Tübingen: Mohr (Siebeck), 1973, 77-93.

Eissfeldt, Otto. [1749] "Silo und Jerusalem," in International Organization for the Study of the Old Testament, Volume du Congrès,1956. Supplements to Vetus Testamentum, 4. Leiden: Brill, 1957, 138-147. Reprinted in Kleine Schriften, 3. Tübingen: Mohr (Siebeck), 1966, 417-425.

Fretheim, Terence E. [1750] "The Ark in Deuteronomy," Catholic Biblical Quarterly, 30 (1968), 1-14.

Fretheim, Terence E. [1751] "Psalm 132: A Form Critical Study," Journal of Biblical Literature, 86 (1967), 289-300.

Galling, Kurt. [1752] "Lade Jahwes," in Die Religion in Geschichte und Gegenwart, 3. Tübingen: Mohr (Siebeck), 2nd edn., 1929, 1449-1450.

Görg, Manfred. [1753] "Ein architectonischer Fachausdruck in der Priesterschrift: Zur Bedeutung von 'eden," Vetus Testamentum, 33 (1983), 334-338.

Görg, Manfred. [1754] Das Zelt der Begegnung: Untersuchung zur Gestalt der Sakralen Zelttraditionen Altisraels. Bonner Biblische Beiträge, 27. Bonn: Hanstein, 1967, 174 pp.

Gooding, D. W. [1755] The Account of the Tabernacle: Translation and Textual Problems of the Greek Exodus. Texts and Studies, n. s. 6. Cambridge: Cambridge University Press, 1959, 115 pp.

Gressmann, Hugo. [1756] Die Lade Jahwes und das Allerheiligste des salomonischen Tempels. Beiträge zur Wissenschaft vom Alten Testament, 2/1. Berlin: Kohlhammer, 1920, 72 pp.

Grintz, Yehoshua. M. [1757] "Ark of the Covenant," in Encyclopaedia Judaica, 3. Jerusalem: Macmillan, 1971, 459-465.

Gutmann, Joseph. [1758] "The History of the Ark," Zeitschrift für die alttestamentliche Wissenschaft, 83 (1971), 22-30.

Haran, Menahem. [1759] "The Ark and the Cherubim: Their Symbolic Significance in Biblical Ritual," Israel Exploration Journal, 9 (1959), 30-38, 89-94.

Haran, Menahem. [1760] "The Ark of the Covenant and the Cherubs," in Eretz-Israel: Archaeological, Historical, and Geographical Studies, 5. Jerusalem: Israel Exploration Society, 1958, 83-90 (Hebrew), 88* (English summary).

Haran, Menahem. [1761] "The Complex of Ritual Acts Performed inside the Tabernacle," in C. Rabin (ed.), Studies in the Bible. Scripta Hierosolymitana, 8. Jerusalem: Magnes Press, 1961, 272-302.

Haran, Menahem. [1762] "The Disappearance of the Ark," Israel Exploration Journal, 13 (1963), 46-58.

Haran, Menahem. [1763] "The Nature of the 'ohel mô'edh in Pentateuchal Sources," Journal of Semitic Studies, 5 (1960), 50-65.

Haran, Menahem. [1764] "The Priestly Image of the Tabernacle," Hebrew Union College Annual, 36 (1965), 191-226.

Haran, Menahem. [1765] "Shiloh and Jerusalem: The Origin of the Priestly Tradition in the Pentateuch," Journal of Biblical Literature, 81 (1962), 14-24.

Hartmann, Richard. [1766] "Zelt und Lade," Zeitschrift für die alttestamentliche Wissenschaft, 37 (1917/1918), 209-244.

Hilliers, Delbert R. [1767] "Ritual Procession of the Ark and Psalm 132," Catholic Biblical Quarterly, 30 (1968), 48-55.

Hurowitz, Victor (= Avigdor). [1768] "The Priestly Account of Building the Tabernacle," Journal of the American Oriental Society, 105 (1985), 21-30.

Irwin, W. H. [1769] "Le sanctuaire central israélite avant l' établissement de la monarchie," Revue biblique, 72 (1965), 161-184.

Jeremias, Jörg. [1770] "Lade und Zion: Zur Entstehung der Ziontradition," in H. W. Wolff (ed.), Probleme biblischer Theologie (Gerhard von Rad Festschrift). Munich: Kaiser Verlag, 1971, 183-198.

Kapelrud, Arvid. S. [1771] "The Gates of Hell and the Guardian Angels of Paradise," Journal of the American Oriental Society, 70 (1950), 151-156.

Kennedy, A. R. S. [1772] "Ark of the Covenant," in James Hastings (ed.), Dictionary of the Bible, 1. New York: Scribner's, 1898, 149-151.

Kennedy, A. R. S. [1773] "Tabernacle," in James Hastings (ed.), Dictionary of the Bible, 4. New York: Scribner's, 1898, 653-668.

Kennett, R. H. [1774] "Ark," in James Hastings (ed.), Encyclopaedia of Religion and Ethics, 1. New York: Scribner's, 1928, 791-793.

Kiene, Paul F. [1775] The Tabernacle of God in the Wilderness of Sinai. Grand Rapids: Zondervan, 1977, 176 pp.

Koch, Klaus. [1776] "'ohel," in G. J. Botterwick and H. Ringgren (eds.), Theological Dictionary of the Old Testament, 1. Grand Rapids: Eerdmans, 1977, corrected edn., 118-130.

Kuschke, Arnulf. [1777] "Die Lagervorstellung der priesterschriftlichen Erzählung," Zeitschrift für die alttestamentliche Wissenschaft, 63 (1951), 74-105.

Kutsch, Ernst. [1778] "Lade Jahwes," in Die Religion in Geschichte und Gegenwart, 4. Tübingen: Mohr (Siebeck), 3rd edn., 1960, 197-199.

Kutsch, Ernst. [1779] "Zelt," in Die Religion in Geschichte und Gegenwart, 6. Tübingen: Mohr (Siebeck), 3rd edn., 1962, 1893-1894.

Kyle, Melvin G. See Lotz, Wilhelm; Kyle, Melvin G.; and Armerding, Carl E. [1784]

Lesétre, Henri. [1780] "Arche d' Alliance," in F. Vigouroux (ed.), Dictionnaire de la Bible, 1. Paris: Letouzey et Ané, 1895, 912-923.

Lesétre, Henri. [1781] "Tabernacle," in F. Vigouroux (ed.), Dictionnaire de la Bible, 5. Paris: Letouzey et Ané, 1922, 1951-1961.

Levine, Baruch A. [1782] "The Descriptive Tabernacle Texts of the Pentateuch," Journal of the American Oriental Society, 85 (1965), 307-318.

Levine, Moshe. [1783] The Tabernacle: Its Structure and Utinsels. London: Soncino Press, 1969, 144 pp.

Lotz, Wilhelm; Kyle, Melvin G.; and Armerding, Carl E. [1784] "Ark of the Covenant," in G. W. Bromily (ed.), International Standard Bible Encyclopedia, 1. Grand Rapids: Eerdmans, 1979, 291-294.

McKane, William. [1785] "The Earlier History of the Ark," Transactions of the Glasgow University Oriental Society, 21 (1965/1966), 68-76.

Maier, Johann. [1786] Das altisraelitische Ladeheiligtum. Beihefte zur Zeitschrift für die alttestamentliche Wissenschaft, 93. Berlin: Töpelmann, 1965.

May, Herbert G. [1787] "The Ark: A Miniature Temple," American Journal of Semitic Languages and Literatures, 52 (1936), 215-234.

Mettinger, Tryggve N. D. [1788] "YHWH SABAOTH-- The Heavenly King on the Cherubim Throne," in T. Ishida (ed.), Studies in the Period of David and Solomon and Other Essays. Winona Lake, IN: Eisenbrauns, 1982, 109-138.

Meyers, Carol L. [1789] The Tabernacle Menorah. American Schools of Oriental Research Dissertation Series, 2. Missoula, MT: Scholars Press, 1976, 243 pp.

Milgrom, Jacob. [1790] "The Shared Custody of the Tabernacle and a Hittite Analogy," Journal of the American Oriental Society, 90 (204-209.

Miller, Parrick D., Jr. and Roberts, J. J. M. [1791] The Hand of the Lord: A Reassessment of the 'Ark Narrative' of 1 Samuel. Johns Hopkins Near Eastern Studies. Baltimore: Johns Hopkins University Press, 1977, 119 pp.

Morgenstern, Julian. [1792] "The Ark, the Ephod and the 'Tent of Meeting,'" Hebrew Union College Annual, 17 (1942/1943), 153-266; 18 (1944), 1-52.

Morgenstern, Julian. [1793] The Ark, the Ephod and the "Tent of Meeting." Cincinnati: Hebrew Union College Press, 1945, 166 pp.

Morgenstern, Julian. [1794] "The Tent of Meeting," Journal of the American Oriental Society, 38 (1918), 125-139.

Nielsen, Eduard. [1795] "Some Reflections on the History of the Ark," in International Organization for the Study of the Old Testament, Congress Volume, Oxford, 1959. Supplements to Vetus Testamentum, 7. Leiden: Brill, 1960, 61-74.

Pfeiffer, Robert H. [1796] "Cherubim," Journal of Biblical Literature, 41 (1922), 249-250.

Porter, Joshua R. [1797] "Ark," in Harper's Dictionary of the Bible. San Francisco: Harper and Rowe, 1985, 63-64.

Porter, Joshua R. [1798] "Tabernacle," in Harper's Dictionary of the Bible. San Francisco: Harper and Rowe, 1985, 1013-1014.

Rabe, Virgil W. [1799] "The Identity of the Priestly Tabernacle," Journal of Near Eastern Studies, 25 (1966), 132-134.

von Rad, Gerhard. [1800] "The Tent, the Ark, and the Glory of God," in Old Testament Theology, 1. New York: Harper, 1962, 234-241.

von Rad, Gerhard. [1801] "Zelt und Lade," Neue Kirchliche Zeitschrift, 42 (1931), 478-498. Reprinted in Gesammelte Studien zum Alten Testament, 1. Munich: Kaiser Verlag, 1958, 109-129.

Randellini, Lino. [1802] "La Tenda e l' Arca nella tradizione del Vecchio Testamento," Studii Biblici Franciscani, Liber Annuus, 13 (1962/1963), 163-189.

Reicke, Bo. [1803] "Stiftshütte," in B. Reicke and L. Rost (eds.), Biblisch-Historisches Handwörterbuch, 3. Göttingen: Vanderhoeck and Ruprecht, 1966, 1871-1875.

Reimpell, W. [1804] "Der Ursprung der Lade Jahwes," Orientalistische Literaturzeitung, 19 (1916), 326-331.

Roberts, J. J. M. See Miller, Patrick D., Jr and Roberts, J. J. M. [1791]

Robertson, Edward. [1805] "The Altar of Earth (Exod. xx, 24-26)," Journal of Jewish Studies, 1 (1948), 12-21.

Rost, Leonhard. [1806] "Die Wohnstätte des Zeugnisses," in J. Hermann (ed.), Festschrift F. Baumgärtel. Erlanger Forschungen, reihe A: Geisteswissenshaften, 10. Erlangen, 1959, 158-165.

Schmidt, Hans. [1807] "Kerubenthron und Lade," in H. Schmidt (ed.), Eucharisterion für H. Gunkel, 1. Forschungen zur Religion und Literatur des Alten und Neuen Testaments, n. f., 19/1 (36/1). Göttingen: Vanderhoeck and Ruprecht, 1923, 120-144.

Schmidt, Werner H. [1808] "Mishkan als Ausdruck für die Kultsprache," Zeitschrift für die alttestamentliche Wissenschaft, 75 (1963), 91-92.

Schmitt, Rainer. [1809] Zelt und Lade als Thema alttestamentlicher Wissenschaft. Gütersloh: Gütersloher Verlagshaus, 1972, 342 pp.

Sellin, Ernst. [1810] "Das Zelt Jahwes," Alttestamentliche Studien für R. Kittel. Beiträge zur Wissenschaft zum Alten Testament, 13. Leipzig: Hinrich's, 1913, 168-192.

de Tarragon, Jean M. [1811] "David et l' arche: 2 Sam 6," Revue biblique, 86 (1979), 514-523.

de Tarragon, Jean M. [1812] "La kapporet est-elle une fiction ou un élément du culte tardif?" Revue biblique, 88 (1981), 5-12.

Torczyner, Harry. See Tur-Sinai, N. H. [1814]

Torczyner, Harry. [1813] Die Bundeslade und die Anfänge der Religion Israels. Berlin: Philo, 2nd edn., 1930, 22 pp.

Tur-Sinai, N. H. [1814] "The Ark of God at Beit Shemesh (1 Sam vi) and Peres 'Uzza (2 Sam vi; 1 Chron xiii)," Vetus Testamentum, 1 (1951), 275-286.

de Vaux, Roland. [1815] "Arche d' alliance et Tent de réunion," in A la Recontre de Dieu (Mémorial Albert Gelin). Bibliothèque de la Faculté Catholique de Théologie de Lyon, 8. Le Puy: Xavier Mappus, 1961, 55-70. Reprinted in Bible et Orient. Paris: Cerf, 1967, 261-176.

de Vaux, Roland. [1816] "Ark of the Covenant and Tent of Reuinion," in The Bible and the Ancient Near East. Garden City: Doubleday, 1971, 136-151.

de Vaux, Roland. [1817] "Les chérubins et l' arche d' alliance, les sphinx gardiens et les trônes divins dans l' Ancien Orient," in Bible et Orient. Paris: Cerf, 1967, 231-259.

de Vaux, Roland. [1818] "The Desert Sanctuary: The Tent; The Ark of the Covenant," in Ancient Israel: Its Life and Institutions. New York: McGraw-Hill, 1961, 294-302.

Vincent, Louis-Hugues. See Dhorme, Édouard and Vincent, Louis-Hugues. [1732]

Wiener, Harold M. [1819] "The Position of the Tent of Meeting," Expositor, (1912, A), 476-480.

Worden, T. [1820] "The Ark of the Covenant," Scripture, 5/4 (1952), 82-90.

Woudstra, Marten H. [1821] The Ark of the Covenant from Conquest to Kingship. Philadelphia: Presbyterian and Reformed, 1965, 152 pp.

Zobel, Hans-Jürgen. [1822] "'arôn," in G. J. Botterwick and H. Ringgren (eds.), Theological Dictionary of the Old Testament, 1. Grand Rapids: Eerdmans, 1977, corrected edn., 363-374.

Twelve

YHWH'S Sanctuary: Solomon's Temple

Abel, Félix-M. and Barrois, Georges Augustin. [1823] "Dédicace d' un Temple à Jérusalem," Revue biblique, 40 (1931), 292-294.

Aharoni, Yohanan. [1824] "Israelite Temples in the Period of the Monarchy," in P. Peli (ed.), Proceedings of the Fifth World Congress of Jewish Studies, 1969, 1. Jerusalem: World Union of Jewish Studies, n. d., 69-74.

Aharoni, Yohanan. [1825] "The Solomonic Temple, the Tabernacle and the Arad Sanctuary," in H. A. Hoffner (ed.), Orient and Occident: Essays Presented to Cyrus Gordon. Alter Orient und Alten Testament, 22. Kevelaer: Butzon and Bercker, 1973, 1-8.

Aharoni, Yohanan. [1826] "Temples, Semitic," in Interpreter's Dictionary of the Bible, Supplementary Volume. Nashville: Abingdon, 1976, 874-875.

Albouy, A. [1827] Jérusalem et les Sanctuaires de la Judée. Paris: Firmin-Didot, 1894, 302 pp.

Albright, William F. [1828] "The Babylonian Temple-Tower and the Altar of Burnt-Offering," Journal of Biblical Literature, 39 (1920), 137-142.

Albright, William F. [1829] "Two Cressets from Marisa and the Pillars of Jachin and Boaz," Bulletin of the American Schools of Oriental Research, 85 (1942), 18-27.

Albright, William F. [1830] "The Place of the Temple of Solomon in the History of Israelite Religion," in Archaeology and the Religion of Israel. Garden City: Doubleday, 5th edn.,1969, 138-150.

Albright, William F. and Wright, G. Ernest. [1831] "Comments on Professor Garber's Article," Journal of Biblical Literature, 78 (1958), 129-132.

Andrae, Walter. [1832] Das Gotteshaus und die Urformen des Bauens im alten Orient. Berlin: Hans Schoetz, 1930, 89 pp.

Bagnani, Gilbert. [1833] "The Molten Sea of Solomon's Temple," in W. S. McCullough (ed.), The Seed of Wisdom: Essays in Honor of T. J. Meek. Toronto: University of Toronto Press, 1964, 114-117.

Bardtke, Hans. [1834] "Der Tempel von Jerusalem," Theologische Literaturzeitung, 97 (1972), 801-810.

Barnes, W. Emery. [1835] "Jachin and Boaz," Journal of Theological Studies, 5/19 (1904), 447-451.

Barrois, Georges Augustin. See Abel, Félix-M. and Barrois, Georges Augustin. [1823]

Barrois, Georges Augustin. [1836] "Cultes et sanctuaires Israélites: Les sanctuaires," in Manuel d' archéologie biblique, 2. Paris: Picard, 1953, 426-456.

Barton, George A. [1837] "Temple of Solomon," in The Jewish Encyclopedia, 12. New York: Funk and Wagnalls, 1905, 98-101.

Benzinger, Immanuel. [1838] "Temple," in T. K. Cheyne and J. S. Black (eds.), Encyclopaedia Biblica, 4. New York: Macmillan, 1903, 4923-4948.

Bertrand, Alexandre. [1839] "L' enceinte du Haram-ech-chérif et le Temple de Salomon: analyse d' un mémoire de M. de Saulcy," Revue archéologique, n. s. 7 (1863), 12-31.

Bertrand, Alexandre. [1840] "Le Temple de Jérusalem-- opinion de M. de Vogüe," Revue archéologique, n. s. 9 (1864), 428-433.

Bruston, Ch. [1841] "L' Inscription des deux colonnes du Temple de Salomon," Zeitschrift für die alttestamentliche Wissenschaft, 42 (1924), 153-154.

Busink, Th. A. [1842] "Les origines du Temple de Salomon," Jaarbericht ex Oriente Lux, 17 (1963), 165-192.

Busink, Th. A. [1843] Der Tempel von Jerusalem, 1. Der Tempel Salomos. Leiden: Brill, 1970, 699 pp.

Carreira, José Nunes. [1844] O plano e arquitectura do templo de Salomäo à luz dos paralelos orientais. Porto: Depositaria, Livraria Tavares Martins, 1969, 140 pp.

Cazelles, Henri. [1845] "Le Temple de Salomon," Le Monde de la Bible, 13 (March-April, 1980), 6-7.

Chaplin, Thomas. [1846] "The Stone of Foundation and the Site of the Temple," Palestine Exploration Fund, Quarterly Statement, (1876), 23-28.

Chaplin, Thomas and Warren, Charles. [1847] "Even Hash-Sheteyah," Palestine Exploration Fund, Quarterly Statement, (1875), 182-183.

Chipiez, Charles and Perrot, Georges. [1848] Le Temple de Jérusalem et la maison du Bois-Liban: Restitués d' apres Ezéchiel et le livres des Rois. Paris: Hachette, 1889.

Cole, Harris F. G. [1849] Concerning Solomon's Temple. London: Roberts, 1920, 75 pp.

Comay, Joan. [1850] The Temple of Jerusalem with the History of the Temple Mount. New York: Holt, Rinehart and Winston, 1975, 279 pp.

Davey, C. J. [1851] "Temples of the Levant and the Buildings of Solomon," Tyndale Bulletin, 31 (1980), 107-146.

Davies, T. Witton. [1852] "Temple," in James Hastings (ed.), Dictionary of the Bible, 4. New York: Scribner's, 1898, 695-716.

Delcor, Mathias. [1853] "Le trésor de la maison de Yahweh, des origines à l' exil," Vetus Testamentum, 12 (1962), 351-377.

Dever, William G. [1854] "Monumental Architecture in Ancient Israel in the Period of the United Monarchy," in T. Ishida (ed.), Studies in the Period of David and Solomon. Winona Lake, IN: Eisenbrauns, 1982, 269-306.

Dever, William G. See Paul, Shalom M. and Dever William G. [1939]

Donner, Herbert. [1855] "Der Felsen und der Tempel," Zeitschrift des deutschen Palästina-Vereins, 93 (1977), 1-11.

Friedman, Richard. [1856] "The Tabernacle in the Temple," Biblical Archaeologist, 43 (1980), 241-248.

Friedrich, Thomas. [1857] Tempel und Palast Salomo's, Denkmäller phönicischer Kunst. Innsbruck: Wagnerschen Universitäts-Buchhandlung, 1887, 72 pp.

Fritz, Volkmar. [1858] Tempel und Zelt: Studien zum Tempelbau in Israel und zu dem Zeltheiligtum der Priesterschrift. Wissenschaftliche Monographïen zum Alten und Neuen Testament, 47. Neukirchen: Neukirchener Verlag, 1977, 208 pp.

Gadegaard, Niels H. [1859] "On the So-Called Burnt Offering Altar in the Old Testament," Palestine Exploration Quarterly, (1978), 33-45.

Galling, Kurt. [1860] "Das Allerheiligste in Salomos Tempel, ein christlicher 'Thoraschrein:' Zwei archäeologische Bermerkungen," Journal of the Palestine Oriental Society, 12 (1932), 43-48.

Galling, Kurt. [1861] "Altar," in Interpreter's Dictionary of the Bible, 1. New York: Abingdon, 1962, 96-100.

Galling, Kurt. [1862] Der Altar in den Kulturen des alten Orients, eine archäologische Studie. Berlin: Karl Curtius, 1925, 108 pp.

Galling, Kurt. [1863] "Incense Altar," Interpreter's Dictionary of the Bible, 2. New York: Abingdon, 1962, 699-700.

Galling, Kurt. [1864] "Königlich und nichtkönigliche Stifter beim Tempel von Jerusalem," Zeitschrift des deutschen Palästina-Vereins, 68 (1946/51), 134-142.

Galling, Kurt. [1865] "Zur Lokalisierung von Debir," Zeitschrift des deutschen Palästina-Vereins, 70 (1954), 135-141.

Galling, Kurt. [1866] "Tempel," in Die Religion in Geschichte und Gegenwart, 5. Tübingen: Mohr (Siebeck), 2nd edn., 1931, 1040-1046.

Galling, Kurt. [1867] "Tempel," in Die Religion in Geschichte und Gegenwart, 6. Tübingen: Mohr (Siebeck), 3rd ed., 1962, 681-686.

Galling, Kurt. [1868] "Tempelgeräte in Israel," in Die Religion in Geschichte und Gegenwart, 6. Tübingen: Mohr (Siebeck), 3rd edn., 1962, 686-687.

Garber, Paul L. See Albright, William F. and Wright, G. Ernest. [1831]

Garber, Paul L. See Howland, E. G. [1888]

Garber, Paul L. [1869] "Reconsidering the Reconstruction of Solomon's Temple," Journal of Biblical Literature, 78 (1958), 122-129, 132-133.

Garber, Paul L. [1870] "Reconstructing Solomon's Temple," Biblical Archaeologist, 14 (1951), 2-24.

Garber, Paul L. [1871] "A Reconstruction of Solomon's Temple," in Archaeological Institute of America: Archaeological Discoveries in the Holy Land. New York: Crowell, 1967, 101-111.

Garber, Paul L. [1872] "A Reconstruction of Solomon's Temple," Archaeology, 5 (1952),165-172.

Gehman, Henry S. See Montgomery, James A. and Gehman, Henry S. [1920]

Gervitz, Stanley. [1873] "Jachin and Boaz," in Harper's Dictionary of the Bible. San Francisco: Harper and Row, 1985, 443.

Görg, Manfred. [1874] "Zur Dekoration des Leuchters," Biblische Notizen: Beiträge zur exegetischen Diskussion, 15 (1981), 21-29.

Görg, Manfred. [1875] "Lexikalisches zur Beschreibung des salomonischen Palastbezirks (i Kön 7, 1-12)," Biblische Notizen: Beiträge zur exegetischen Diskussion, 11 (1980), 7-13.

Görg, Manfred. [1876] "Weiteres zur Gestalt des Tempelbaus," Biblische Notizen: Beiträge zur exegetischen Diskussion, 13 (1980), 22-25.

Görg, Manfred. [1877] "Zur Dekoration der Tempelsaülen," Biblische Notizen: Beiträge zur exegetischen Diskussion, 13 (1980), 17-21.

Görg, Manfred. [1878] "Zwei bautechnische Begriffe in I Kön 6, 9," Biblische Notizen: Beiträge zur exegetischen Diskussion, 10 (1979), 12-15.

Gooding, D. W. [1879] "An Impossible Shrine," Vetus Testamentum, 15 (1965), 405-420.

Gooding, D. W. [1880] "Temple Specifications: A Dispute in Logical Arrangement between the MT and the LXX," Vetus Testamentum, 17 (1967), 143-172.

Gray, John. [1881] "The Building and Dedication of the Temple," in I and II Kings: A Commentary. London: SCM Press, 2nd edn., 1970, 149-238.

Grintz, Yehoshua. M. and Yadin, Yigael. [1882] "Temple: First Temple," in Encyclopaedia Judaica, 15. Jerusalem: Macmillan, 1971, 943-955.

de Groot, J. [1883] *Die Altäre des salomonischen Tempelhofes*. *Beiträge zur Wissenschaft vom Alten Testament*, n. f. 6. Stuttgart: Kohlhammer, 1924, 88 pp.

Gutmann, Joseph (ed.). [1884] *The Temple of Solomon: Archaeological Fact and Medieval Tradition in Christian, Islamic, and Jewish Art*. *Religion and the Arts*, 3. Missoula, MT: Scholars Press, 1976, 198 pp.

Haak, Robert D. [1885] "The 'Shoulder' of the Temple," *Vetus Testamentum*, 33 (1983), 271-278.

Hachlili, Rahel and Merhav, Rivkah. [1886] "The Menorah in First and Second Temple Times in the Light of the Sources and Archaeology," in *Eretz-Israel: Archaeological, Historical, and Geographical Studies*, 18. Jerusalem: Israel Exploration Society, 1985, 256-267 (Hebrew), 74* (English summary).

Hertzberg, Hans Wilhelm. [1887] "Der heilige Fels und das Alte Testament," *Journal of the Palestine Oriental Society*, 12 (1932), 32-42.

Howland, E. G. [1888] *Solomon's Temple: A Reconstruction Based on the Howland-Garber Model*. Ohio, 1950, 48 pp.

Isserlin, B. S. J. [1889] "Israelite Architectural Planning and the Question of the Level of Secular Learning in Ancient Israel," *Vetus Testamentum*, 34 (1984), 169-178.

Kaufman, Asher. [1890] "Where the Ancient Temple of Jerusalem Stood," *Biblical Archaeology Review*, 9/2 (1983), 40-59.

Keel, Othmar. [1891] "The Temple: Place of Yahweh's Presence and Sphere of Life," in *Symbolism of the Biblical World: Ancient Near Eastern Iconography and the Book of Psalms*. New York: SEabury, 1978, 111-176.

Kennedy, A. R. S. and Snaith, Norman. H. [1892] "Temple," in James Hastings (ed.), *Dictionary of the Bible*, revised edn. by F. C. Grant and H. H. Rowley. New York: Scribner's, 1963, 961-968.

Kenyon, Kathleen M. [1893] "The Mystery of the Horses of the Sun at the Temple Entrance," *Biblical Archaeology Review*, , 4/2 (1978), 8-9.

Kenyon, Kathleen M. [1894] "New Evidence on Solomon's Temple," in *Mélanges offerts à M. Maurice Dunand*, 2. *Mélanges de l' Université Saint-Joseph*, 46. Beirut: Université Saint-Joseph, 1972, 137-149.

Kenyon, Kathleen M. [1895] "Solomon and the Building of the Temple," in *Jerusalem: Excavating 3,000 Years of History*. New York: McGraw-Hill, 1967, 54-62.

Kittel, Rudolf. [1896] "Der heilige Fels auf dem Moria: Seine Geschichte und seine Altäre," in *Studien zur hebräischen Archäologie und Religionsgeschichte*. *Beiträge zur Wissenschaft vom Alten Testament*, 1. Leipzig, 1908, 1-96.

Klein, H. Arthur. See Klein, Mina C. and Klein, H. Arthur. [1897]

Klein, Mina C. and Klein, H. Arthur. [1897] "Solomon in All his Glory-- and the Temple," in Temple beyond Time: The Story of the Site of Solomon's Temple at Jerusalem. New York: Van Nostrand Reinhold, 1970, 35-49.

Klingele, Otto Heinrich. [1898] "Der Tempel von Jerusalem," Das Heilige Land, 90 (1958), 77-91.

Kornfeld, Walter. [1899] "Der Symbolismus der Tempelsäulen," Zeitschrift für die alttestamentliche Wissenschaft, 74 (1962), 50-57.

Kuschke, Arnulf. [1900] "Tempel," in K. Galling (ed.), Biblisches Reallexikon (BRL^2). Tübingen: Mohr (Siebeck), 1927, 333-342.

Kuschke, Arnulf. [1901] "Der Tempel Salomos und der 'syrische Tempeltypus,'" in F. Maass (ed.), Des Ferne und nahe Wort (Festschrift Leonhard Rost). Beihefte zur Zeitschrift für die alttestamentliche Wissenschaft, 105. Berlin: Töpelmann, 1967, 124-132.

Laperrousaz, Ernest-Marie. [1902] "A-t-on dégagé l' angle sud-est du 'Temple de Salomon?'" Syria, 50 (1973), 355-399.

Lemaire, André. [1903] "Une inscription paleo-hebraique sur grenade en ivorie," Revue biblique, 88 (1981), 236-239.

Lemaire, André. [1904] "Probable Head of Priestly Scepter from Solomon's Temple Surfaces in Jerusalem," Biblical Archaeology Review, 10/1 (Jan./Feb., 1984), 24-29.

Lesétre, Henri. [1905] "Temple," in F. Vigouroux (ed.), Dictionnaire de la Bible, 5. Paris: Letouzey et Ané, 1922, 2024-2078.

Lods, Adolphe. [1906] "Les cuisines du temple de Jerusalem," Revue de l' Histoire des Religions, 127 (1944), 30-54.

McKay, John W. [1907] "Further Light on the Horses and Chariot of the Sun in the Jerusalem Temple (2 Kings 23: 11)," Palestine Exploration Quarterly, (1973), 167-169.

Margueron, Jean. [1908] "Les origins syriennes du Temple de Jérusalem," Le Monde de la Bible, 20 (Aug.-Sept., 1981), 31-33.

May, Herbert G. [1909] "The Two Pillars before the Temple of Solomon," Bulletin of the American Schools of Oriental Research, 88 (1942), 19-27.

Mayer, Hannes. [1910] "Das Bauholz des Tempels Salomos," Biblische Zeitschrift, n. f. 11 (1967), 53-66.

Mazar, Benjamin. [1911] "The Temple Mount and the Temple: The First Temple," in The Mountain of the Lord. Garden City: Doubleday, 1975, 96-103.

Merhav, Rivka. See Hachlili, Rahel and Merhav, Rivkah. [1886]

Meyers, Carol L. [1912] "Altar," in Harper's Dictionary of the Bible. San Francisco: Harper and Row, 1985, 22-24.

Meyers, Carol L. [1913] "The Elusive Temple," Biblical Archaeologist, 45 (1982), 33-41.

Meyers, Carol L. [1914] "Jachin and Boaz in Religious and Political Perspective," Catholic Biblical Quarterly, 45 (1983), 167-178. Also in T. Madsen (ed.), The Temple in Antiquity: Ancient Records and Modern Perspectives. Religious Studies Monograph Series, 9. Provo, UT: Brigham Young University Press, 1984, 135-150.

Meyers, Carol L. [1915] "Menorah," Interpreter's Dictionary of the Bible, Supplementary Volume. Nashville: Abingdon, 1976, 586-587.

Meyers, Carol L. [1916] "The Temple," in Harper's Dictionary of the Bible. San Francisco: Harper and Row, 1985, 1021-1032.

Meyers, Carol L. [1917] "Was there a Seven-Branched Lampstand in Solomon's Temple?" Biblical Archaeology Review, 5/5 (1979), 46-57.

Möhlenbrink, Kurt. [1918] Der Tempel Salomos. Eine Untersuchung seiner Stellung in der Sakralarchitektur des alten Orients. Beiträge zur Wissenschaft vom Alten und Neuen Testament, 4/7. Stuttgart: Kohlhammer, 1932, 160 pp.

Mommert, C. [1919] Topographie des alten Jerusalem, 2: Der Salomonische Tempel- und Palastbezirk auf Moriah. Leipzig: Haberland, 1903.

Montgomery, James A. and Gehman, Henry S. [1920] A Critical and Exegetical Commentary on the Book of Kings. International Critical Commentary. Edinburgh: T. and T. Clark, 1951, 140-184.

Mowinckel, Sigmund. [1921] "A quel moment le culte de Yahvé à Jérusalem est-il officiellement devenu un culte sans images," Revue d' histoirie et de philosophie religieuses, (1929), 197-216.

Mowinckel, Sigmund. [1922] "Wann wurde der Jahwäkultus in Jerusalem offiziell bildos," Acta Orientalia, 8 (1930), 257-279.

Mulder, Martin J. [1923] "Einige Bemerkungen zur Beschreibung des Libanonwaldhaus in I Reg 7, 2f," Zeitschrift für die alttestamentliche Wissenschaft, 88 (1976), 99-105.

Myers, Jacob M. [1924] "Building the Temple," in II Chronicles. Anchor Bible. Garden City: Doubleday, 1965, 8-44.

Myers, Jacob M. [1925] "David and the Founding of the Temple," in I Chronicles. Anchor Bible. Garden City: Doubleday, 1965, 77-200.

Myres, J. L. [1926] "King Solomon's Temple and Other Buildings and Works of Art," Palestine Exploration Quarterly, (1948), 14-41.

Obbink, H. Th. [1927] "The Horns of the Altar in the Semitic World, Especially in Yahwism," Journal of Biblical Literature, 56 (1937), 43-49.

Ottosson, Magnus. [1928] "hêkhal," in G. J. Botterweck and H. Ringgren (eds.), Theological Dictionary of the Old Testament, 3. Grand Rapids: Eerdmans, 1978, 382-388.

Ouellette, Jean. [1929] "'Atumim in I Kings 6: 4," Bulletin of the Institute of Jewish Studies, (1974), 99-102.

Ouellette, Jean. [1930] "The Basic Structure of Solomon's Temple and Archaeological Research," in J. Gutmann (ed.), The Temple of Solomon. Religion and the Arts. MIssoula, MT: Scholars Press, 1976, 7-11.

Ouellette, Jean. [1931] "Jachin and Boaz," Interpreter's Dictionary of the Bible, Supplementary Volume. Nashville: Abingdon, 1976, 469.

Ouellette, Jean. [1932] "The Solomonic Debir According to the Hebrew Text of I Kings 6," Journal of Biblical Literature, 89 (1970), 338-343.

Ouellette, Jean. [1933] "Temple of Solomon," in Interpreter's Dictionary of the Bible, Supplementary Volume. Nashville: Abingdon, 1976, 872-874.

Ouellette, Jean. [1934] "Le vestibule du Temple de Salomon était-il un Bit Hilâni?" Revue biblique, 76 (1969), 365-378.

Ouellette, Jean. [1935] "Yasia' and sela'ot: Two Mysterious Structures in Solomon's Temple," Journal of Near Eastern Studies, 31 (1972), 187-191.

Pailloux, X. [1936] Monographie du temple de Salomon. Paris: Roger and Chemovitz, 1885, 516 pp.

Parrot, André. [1937] The Temple of Jerusalem. Studies in Biblical Archaeology, 5. New York: Philosophical Library, 1955; London: SCM, 1957, 112 pp; reprinted, Westport, CN: Greenwood Publishers, 1985.

Parunak, H. Van Dyke. [1938] "Was Solomon's Temple Aligned to the Sun?" Palestine Exploration Quarterly, (1978), 29-33.

Paul, Shalom M. and Dever, William G. [1939] "Cultic Structures," in Biblical Archaeology. New York: Quadrangle, 1974, 54-83.

Perrot, Georges. See Chipiez, Charles and Perrot, Georges. [1848]

Pronobis, C. [1940] "Der Tempel zu Jerusalem: Seine Masse und genaue Lage," Das Heilige Land, 70 (1926), 197-211; 71 (1927), 8-32.

Robins, E. C. [1941] The Temple of Solomon: A Review of the Various Theories Respecting its Form and Style of Architecture. London: Whithaker, 1887.

Rowton, M. B. [1942] "The Date of the Founding of Solomon's Temple," Bulletin of the American Schools of Oriental Research, 119 (1950), 20-22.

Rüger, Hans Peter. [1943] "Tempel," in B. Reicke and L. Rost (eds.), Biblisch-Historisches Handwörterbuch, 3. Göttingen: Vanderhoeck and Ruprecht, 1966, 1940-1947.

Rupprecht, Konrad. [1944] "Nachrichten von Erweiterung und Renovierung des Tempels in 1 Könige 6," Zeitschrift des deutschen Palästina-Vereins, 88 (1972), 38-52.

Rupprecht, Konrad. [1945] Der Tempel von Jerusalem: Gründung Salomos oder jebusitisches Erbe? Beihefte zur Zeitschrift für die alttestamentliche Wissenschaft, 144. Berlin: Walter de Gruyter, 1976, 109 pp.

Rupprecht, Konrad. [1946] "Die Zuverlässigkeit der Überlieferung von Salomos Tempelgründung," Zeitschrift für die alttestamentliche Wissenschaft, 89 (1977), 205-214.

de Saulcy, L. Félicien J. C. See Bertrand, Alexandre. [1839]

Schmid, Herbert. [1947] "Der Tempelbau Salomos in religionsgeschichtlicher Sicht," in A. Kuschke and E. Kutsch (eds.), Archäologie und Altes Testament: Festschrift für Kurt Galling. Tübingen: Mohr (Siebeck), 1970, 241-250.

Schmidt, Hans. [1948] Der heilige Fels in Jerusalem: Eine archäologische und religionsgeschichtliche Studie. Tübingen: Mohr (Siebeck), 1933, 102 pp.

Schreiber, A. [1949] "La légende de l' emplacement du Temple de Jérusalem," Revue des études juives, 109 (1949), 103-108.

Schult, Hermann. [1950] "Zum Bauverfahren in 1 Könige 6, 7," Zeitschrift des deutschen Palästina-Vereins, 88 (1972), 53-54.

Schult, Hermann. [1951] "Der Debir im salomonischen Tempel," Zeitschrift des deutschen Palästina-Vereins, 80 (1964), 46-54.

Schwartz. A. [1952] "Die Schatzkammer des Tempels zu Jerusalem," Monatsschrift für Wissenschaft des Judentums, 63 (1919), 227-252.

Scott, R. B. Y. [1953] "The Pillars Jachin and Boaz," Journal of Biblical Literature, 58 (1939), 143-149.

Shupak, Nili. [1954] "Jachin and Boaz," in Encyclopaedia Judaica, 15. Jerusalem: Macmillan, 1971, 1186-1189.

Skehan, Patrick W. [1955] "Wisdom's House," Catholic Biblical Quarterly, 29 (1967), 468-486. [Suggests that the literary structure of the Book of Proverbs follows the design of the Temple.]

Snaith, Norman H. See Kennedy, A. R. S. and Snaith, Norman H. [1892]

Snijders, L. A. [1956] "L' Orientation du Temple de Jérusalem," in P. A. H. de Boer (ed.), Oudtestamentische Studien, 14. Leiden: Brill, 1965, 214-234.

Sperber, Daniel. [1957] "The History of the Menorah," Journal of Jewish Studies, 16 (1965), 135-159.

Stade, Bernhard. [1958] "Die Kesselwagen des salomonischen Tempels," Zeitschrift für die alttestamentliche Wissenschaft, 21 (1901), 145-190.

Stade, Bernhard. [1959] "Der Text des Berichtes über Salomos Bauten, 1 Kö. 5-7," Zeitschrift für die alttestamentliche Wissenschaft, 3 (1883), 129-177.

Stamm, Johann Jakob. [1960] "Zum Altargesetz im Bundesbuch," Theologische Zeitschrift, 1 (1945), 304-306.

Stendebach, Franz Josef. [1961] "Altarformen vom kanaanäisch-israelitischen Raum," Biblische Zeitschrift, 20 (1976), 180-196.

Steve, M. A See Vincent, Louis-Hugues and Steve, M. A. [1978]

Stinespring, William F. [1962] "Temple, Jerusalem," Interpreter's Dictionary of the Bible, 4. New York: Abingdon, 1962, 534-560.

Strange, John. [1963] "The Idea of Afterlife in Ancient Israel: Some Remarks on the Iconography in Solomon's Temple," Palestine Exploration Quarterly, (1985), 35-40.

Tenz, J. M. [1964] "Position of the Altar of Burnt Sacrifice in the Temple of Jerusalem," Palestine Exploration Fund, Quarterly Statement, (1910), 137-139.

Thomsen, H. C. [1965] "The Right of Entry to the Temple in the Old Testament," in Transactions of the Glasgow University Oriental Society, 21 (1965-1966), 25-34.

Thomsen, H. C. [1966] "A Row of Cedar Beams," Palestine Exploration Quarterly, (1960), 57-63.

Ussishkin, David. [1967] "Building IV in Hamath and the Temple of Solomon and Tel Tayanat," Israel Exploration Journal, 16 (1966), 104-110.

Ussishkin, David. [1968] "King Solomon's Palace and Building 1723 in Megiddo," Israel Exploration Journal, 16 (1966), 174-186.

Ussishkin, David. [1969] "King Solomon's Palaces," Biblical Archaeologist, 36 (1973), 78-105.

Vattioni, Francesco. [1970] "Il velo del tempio e i Cherubini," Revista biblica, 7 (1959), 67-68.

de Vaux, Roland. [1971] "Notes sur le Temple de Salomon," in Bible et Orient. Paris: Cerf, 1967, 303-315.

de Vaux, Roland. [1972] "The Temple at Jerusalem," in Ancient Israel: Its Life and Institutions. New York: McGraw-Hill, 1961, 312-330.

Vincent, Louis-Hugues. [1973] "Une Antechambre du palais de Salomon," Revue biblique, 14 (1905), 258-265.

Vincent, Louis-Hugues. [1974] "Les bassins roulants du Temple de Salomon," in Miscellanea Biblica B. Ubach. Scripta et Documenta, 1. Montserrat, 1953, 147-159.

Vincent, Louis-Hugues. [1975] "Le Caractère du Temple Salomonien," in Melanges bibliques rédigés en l' honneur de André Robert. Travaux de l' Institute Catholique de Paris, 4. Paris: Bloud and Gay, 1957, 137-148.

Vincent, Louis-Hugues. [1976] "De la tour de Babel au Temple," Revue biblique, 53 (1946), 403-440.

Vincent, Louis-Hugues. [1977] "La Description du Temple de Salomon. Notes exégétiques sur 1 Rois VI," Revue biblique, 16 (1907), 515-542.

Vincent, Louis-Hugues and Steve, M. A. [1978] "Le Temple de Salomon," in Jérusalem de l' Ancien Testament, 2. Paris: Gabalda, 1956, 373-431.

Vogt, Ernst. [1979] "Vom Tempel zur Felsendom," Biblica, 43 (1962), 23-64.

de Vogüé, Melchior. See Bertrand, Alexandre. [1840]

Wainright, J. A. [1980] "Zoser's Pyramid and Solomon's Temple," Expository Times, 91 (1980), 137-140.

Warren, Charles. See Chaplin, Thomas and Warren, Charles. [1847]

Waterman, Leroy. See Wright, G. Ernest. [1988]

Waterman, Leroy. [1981] "The Damaged 'Blueprints' of the Temple of Solomon," Journal of Near Eastern Studies, 2 (1943), 284-294.

Waterman, Leroy. [1982] "A Rebuttal [to G. Ernest Wright]," Journal of Near Eastern Studies, 7 (1948), 54-55.

Waterman, Leroy. [1983] "The Treasuries of Solomon's Private Chapel," Journal of Near Eastern Studies, 6 (1947), 161-163.

Watson, Charles M. [1984] "The Position of the Altar of Burnt Sacrifice in the Temple of Solomon," Palestine Exploration Fund, Quarterly Statement, (1910), 15-22.

Wiener, Harold M. [1985] The Altars of the Old Testament. Beigabe zur orientalischen Literatur-Zeitung. Leipzig: Hinrichs, 1927, 34 pp.

Wolff, Odilo. [1986] Der Tempel von Jerusalem und seine Maasse. Graz: Styria, 1887, 104 pp.

Wolff, Odilo. [1987] Der Tempel von Jerusalem: Eine kunsthistorische Studie über seine Masse und Proportionen. Wien: Schroll, 1913, 100 pp.

Wright, G. Ernest. See Albright, William F. and Wright, G. Ernest. [1831]

Wright, G. Ernest. See Waterman, Leroy. [1982]

Wright, G. Ernest. [1988] "Dr. Waterman's View Concerning the Solomonic Temple," Journal of Near Eastern Studies, 7 (1948), 53.

Wright, G. Ernest (ed.) [1989] "The Significance of the Temple in the Ancient Near East," Biblical Archaeologist, 7 (1944), 41-88. Reprinted in G. E. Wright and D. N. Freedman (eds.), The Biblical Archaeologist Reader. Garden City: Doubleday, 1961, 145-200.

Wright, G. Ernest. [1990] "Solomon's Temple Resurrected," Biblical Archaeologist, 4 (1941), 17-31.

Wright, G. Ernest. [1991] "The Stevens' Reconstruction of the Solomonic Temple," Biblical Archaeologist, 18 (1955), 41-44.

Wylie, C. C. [1992] "On King Solomon's Molten Sea," Biblical Archaeologist, 12 (1949), 86-90.

Yadin, Yigael. See Grintz, Yehoshua M. and Yadin, Yigael. [1882]

Yarden, Leon. [1993] The Tree of Light: A Study of the Menorah, the Seven - Branched Lampstand. Ithaca, NY: Cornell University Press, 1971, 162 pp.

Yeiven, Samuel. [1994] "Jachin and Boaz," in Eretz-Israel: Archaeological, Historical, and Geographical Studies, 5. Jerusalem: Israel Exploration Society, 1958, 97-104 (Hebrew), 89* (English summary).

Yeivin, Samuel. [1995] "Jachin and Boaz," Palestine Exploration Quarterly, (1959), 6-22.

Yeivin, Samuel. [1996] "Solomon's Temple," in J. Aviram (ed.), Jerusalem through the Ages. Jerusalem: Israel Exploration Society, 1968, 12-26 (Hebrew), 58-59 (English summary).

Yeivin, Samuel. [1997] "Was there a High Portal in the First Temple?" Vetus Testamentum, 14 (1964), 331-343.

Zuidhof, Albert. [1998] "King Solomon's Molten Sea and (π)," Biblical Archaeologist, 45 (1982), 179-184.

Thirteen

YHWH'S Sanctuary: Cultic Functionaries and Cultic Activities

Abba, Raymond. [1999] "The Origin and Significance of Hebrew Sacrifice," Biblical Theology Bulletin, 7 (1977), 123-138.

Abba, Raymond. [2000] "Priests and Levites in Ezekiel," Vetus Testamentum, 28 (1978), 1-9.

Abba, Raymond. [2001] "Priests and Levites," in Interpreter's Dictionary of the Bible, 3. New York: Abingdon, 1962, 876-889.

Ahlström, Gosta W. [2002] "Some Remarks on Prophet and Cult," in J. Coert Rylaarsdam (ed.), Transitions in Biblical Scholarship. Essays in Divinity, 6. Chicago: University of Chicago Press, 1968, 113-129.

Allan, N. [2003] "The Identity of the Jerusalem Priesthood during the Exile," The Heythrop Journal, 23 (1982), 259-269.

Armerding, Carl E. [2004] "Were David's Sons Really Priests?" in G. F. Hawthorne (ed.), Current Issues in Biblical and Patristic Interpretation: Studies in Honor of Merrill C. Tenney. Grand Rapids: Eerdmans, 1975, 75-86.

Auerbach, Elias. [2005] "Die Feste im alten Israel," Vetus Testamentum, 8 (1958), 1-18.

Auerbach, Elias. [2006] "Die Herkunft der Sadokiden," Zeitschrift für die alttestamentliche Wissenschaft, 49 (1931), 327-328.

Bartlett, John R. [2007] "Zadok and His Successors at Jerusalem," Journal of Theological Studies, 19 (1968), 1-18.

Bentzen, Aage. [2008] "Zur Geschichte der Sadokiden," Zeitschrift für die alttestamentliche Wissenschaft, , 51 (1933), 173-176.

Bergman, Jan; Ringgren, Helmer; and Lang, Bernhard. [2009] "zabhach," in G. J. Botterwick and H. Ringgren (eds.), Theological Dictionary of the Old Testament, 4. Grand Rapids: Eerdmans, 1980, 8-29.

Bertholet, Alfred. [2010] "Opfer, 1: Religionsgeschichtlich," in Die Religion in Geschichte und Gegenwart, 4. Tübingen: Mohr (Siebeck), 2nd edn., 1930, 704-711.

Bertholet, Alfred. [2011] "Zum Verständniss der alttestamentlichen Opfergedanken," Journal of Biblical Literature, 49 (1930), 218-233.

de Boer, P. A. H. [2012] "An Aspect of Sacrifice," in Studies in the Religion of Ancient Israel. Supplements to Vetus Testamentum, 23. Leiden: Brill, 1972, 27-47.

Botterweck, G. Johannes. See Kedar-Kopfstein, Benjamin and Botterweck, G. Johannes. [2079]

Bowman, John. [2013] "Ezekiel and the Zadokite Priesthood," Transactions of the Glasgow University Oriental Society, 16 (1957), 1-14.

Box, G. H. [2014] "The Temple Service," in T. K. Cheyne and J. S. Black (eds.), Encyclopaedia Biblica, 4. New York: Macmillan, 1903, 4948-4956.

Budde, Karl. [2015] "Das Deuteronomium und die Reform König Josias," Zeitschrift für die alttestamentliche Wissenschaft, 44 (1926), 177-224.

Budde, Karl. [2016] "Die Herkunft Sadok's," Zeitschrift für die alttestamentliche Wissenschaft, 52 (1934), 42-50.

Castelot, John J. [2017] "Religious Institutions of Israel," in R. E. Brown, J. A. Fitzmyer, and R. E. Murphy (eds.), The Jerome Biblical Commentary. Englewood Cliffs, NJ: Prentice-Hall, 1968, 703-735.

Chopineau, J. [2018] "Les Prophetes et le temple," Le Monde de la Bible, 13 (1980), 10-13.

Clements, Ronald E. [2019] "Deuteronomy and the Jerusalem Cult Tradition," Vetus Testamentum, 15 (1965), 300-312.

Cody, Aelred. [2020] A History of Old Testament Priesthood. Analecta Biblica, 35. Rome: Pontifical Biblical Institute, 1969, 216 pp.

Cohen, Martin A. [2021] "The Role of the Shilonite Priesthood in the United Monarchy of Ancient Israel," Hebrew Union College Annual, 35 (1965), 59-98.

Corney, Richard W. [2022] "Zadok the Priest," in Interpreter's Dictionary of the Bible, 4. New York: Abingdon, 1962, 928-929.

Cross, Frank M. [2023] "The Priestly Houses of Early Israel," in Canaanite Myth and Hebrew Epic. Cambridge: Harvard University Press, 1973, 195-215.

Daniel, Suzanne. [2024] Recherches sur le vocabulaire du culte dans la Septante. Études et Commentaires, 61. Paris: Klincksieck, 1966, 428 pp.

Delcor, Mathias. [2025] "Rites pour l' obtention de la pluie à Jérusalem et dans le Proche-Orient," Revue d' histoire des religions, 178 (1970), 117-132.

Del Medico, H. E. [2026] "Melchisédech," Zeitschrift für die alttestamentliche Wissenschaft, 69 (1957), 160-170.

Dussaud, René. [2027] Les origines cananéenes du sacrifice israélite. Paris: Leroux, 1921, 334 pp.; 2nd edn., 1941.

Eaton, J. H. [2028] Vision in Worship: The Relation of Prophecy and Liturgy in the Old Testament. London: SPCK, 1981, 115 pp.

Eichrodt, Walther. [2029] Theology of the Old Testament, 1. Translated by J. A. Baker. Philadelphia: Westminster, 1961, 98-177.

Eissfeldt, Otto. [2030] "Opfer, 2A: Im AT," in Die Religion in Geschichte und Gegenwart, 4. Tübingen: Mohr (Siebeck), 2nd edn., 711-717.

Elbogen, I. [2031] Der jüdische Gottesdienst in seiner geschichtlichen Entwicklung. Leipzig: Gustav Fock, 1913, 619 pp.

Elhorst, H. J. [2032] "Die deuteronomischen Jahresfeste," Zeitschrift für die alttestamentliche Wissenschaft, 42 (1924), 136-145.

Emerton, J. A. [2033] "Priests and Levites in Deuteronomy," Vetus Testamentum, 12 (1962), 129-138.

Feuchtwang, D. [2034] "Das Wasseropfer und die damit verbundenen Zeremonien," Monatsschrift für Geschichte und Wissenschaft des Judentums, 54 (1910), 535-552, 713-729; 55 (1911), 43-63.

Frymer-Kensky, Tivka. [2035] "Pollution, Purification, and Purgation in Biblical Israel," in C. L. Meyers and M. O'Connor (eds.), The Word of the Lord Shall Go Forth: Essays in Honor of David Noel Freedman. American Schools of Oriental Research, Special Volume Series, 1. Winona Lake: Eisenbrauns, 1983, 399-414.

Gammie, John. [2036] "Loci of the Melchizedek Tradition," Journal of Biblical Literature, 90 (1971), 385-396.

Gaster, Moses. [2037] "Sacrifice (Jewish)," in James Hastings (ed.), Encyclopaedia of Religion and Ethics, 11. New York: Scribner's, 1928, 24-29.

Gaster, Theodore H. [2038] "Sacrifices and Offerings," in Interpreter's Dictionary of the Bible, 4. New York: Abingdon, 1962, 147-159.

Gaster, Theodore H. [2039] "The Service of the Sanctuary: A Study in Hebrew Survivals," in Mélanges Syriens offerts à Monsieur René Dussaud, 2. Paris: Geuthner, 1939, 577-582.

Gates, Owen H. [2040] "The Relation of Priests to Sacrifice before the Exile," Journal of Biblical Literature, 27 (1908), 67-92.

Gottlieb, Hans. [2041] "Amos and Jerusalem," Vetus Testamentum, 17 (1967), 430-463.

Gray, George Buchanan. [2042] Sacrifice in the Old Testament. Oxford: Clarendon, 1925, 434 pp. Reprinted with an introduction by B. A. Levine, New York: KTAV, 1971.

Gray, John. [2043] "Cultic Affinities between Israel and Ras Shamra," Zeitschrift für die alttestamentliche Wissenschaft, 62 (1950), 207-220.

Greenberg, Moshe. [2044] "A New Approach to the History of the Israelite Priesthood," *Journal of the American Oriental Society*, 70 (1950), 41-47.

Grimes, Ronald L. [2045] "Sources for the Study of Ritual," *Religious Studies Review*, 10 (1984), 134-145.

Gunneweg, A. H. J. [2046] *Leviten und Priester: Hauptlinien der Traditionbildung und Geschichte des israelitisch-jüdischen Kultpersonals*. *Forschungen zur Religion und Literatur des Alten und Neuen Testaments*, 89. Göttingen: Vanderhoeck and Rupprecht, 1965, 225 pp.

Haldar, Alfred. [2047] *Associations of Cult Prophets among the Ancient Semites*. Uppsala: Almqvist and Wiksell, 1945, 247 pp.

Haran, Menahem. [2048] "The Gibeonites, the Nethinim and the Servants of Solomon," in *Judah and Jerusalem: The Twelfth Archaeological Convention*. Jerusalem: Israel Exploration Society, 1957, 37-45 (Hebrew), v (English summary).

Haran, Menahem. [2049] "The Passover Sacrifice," in *Studies in the Religion of Ancient Israel*. *Supplements to Vetus Testamentum*, 23. Leiden: Brill, 1972, 86-116.

Haran, Menahem. [2050] "Priest, Temple, and Worship," *Tarbiz*, 48 (1979), 175-185 (Hebrew). [English summary in *Old Testament Abstracts*, 5 (1982), 177.]

Haran, Menahem. [2051] "Priesthood, Temple, Divine Service: Some Observations on Institutions and Practices of Worship," in R. Ahroni (ed.), *Biblical and Other Studies in Honor of Robert Gordis*. *Hebrew Annual Review*, 7. Columbus: Ohio University Press, 1983, 121-135.

Haran, Menahem. [2052] "Priests and Priesthood," in *Encyclopaedia Judaica*, 13. Jerusalem: Macmillan, 1971, 1069-1086.

Haran, Menahem. [2053] *Temples and Temple-Service in Ancient Israel: An Inquiry into the Character of Cult Phenomena and the Historical Setting of the Priestly School*. Oxford: Clarendon Press, 1978, 394 pp.

Haran, Menahem. [2054] "The Uses of Incense in the Ancient Israelite Ritual," *Vetus Testamentum*, 10 (1960), 113-129.

Hardy, E. R. [2055] "The Date of Psalm 110," *Journal of Biblical Literature*, 64 (1945), 385-390.

Harrelson, Walter. [2056] *From Fertility Cult to Worship*. Garden City: Doubleday, 1969, 138 pp.

Hauer, Christian , Jr. [2057] "Who was Zadok?" *Journal of Biblical Literature*, 82 (1963), 89-94.

Hauer, Christian, Jr. [2058] "David and the Levites," *Journal for the Study of the Old Testament*, 23 (1982), 33-54.

Hecht, Richard D. [2059] "Studies on Sacrifice, 1970-1980," Religious Studies Review, 8 (1982), 253-259.

Hentschke, Richard. [2060] "Opfer, 2: Im AT," in Die Religion in Geschichte und Gegenwart, 4. Tübingen: Mohr (Siebeck), 3rd edn., 1960, 1641-1647.

Hertzberg, Hans Wilhelm. [2061] "Die Melchisedek Traditionen," Journal of the Palestine Oriental Society, 7 (1928), 169-179.

Hooke, Samuel H. [2062] The Origins of Early Semitic Ritual. Schweich Lectures of the British Academy, 1935. London: Humphrey Milford/ Oxford University Press, 1938, 74 pp.

Hooke, Samuel H. (ed.) [2063] Myth and Ritual. London: Humphrey Milford/Oxford University Press, 1933, 204 pp.

Hooke, Samuel H. [2064] "The Theory and Practice of Substitution," Vetus Testamentum, 2 (1952), 2-17.

Horst, Friedrich. [2065] "Die Kultusreform des Königs Josia (II Reg. 22-23)," Zeitschrift der deutschen Morgenländischen Gesellschaft, 77 (1923), 220-238.

James, Edwin Oliver. [2066] The Nature and Function of Priesthood: A Comparative and Anthropological Study. London: Thames and Hudson, 1955, 336 pp.

James, Edwin Oliver. [2067] Origins of Sacrifice: A Study in Comparative Religion. London: J. Murray, 1933; 2nd edn., 1937; reprinted, New York: Kennicat Press, 1971, 313 pp.

James, Edwin Oliver. [2068] "Aspects of Sacrifice in the Old Testament," Expository Times, 50 (1938/1939), 151-155.

Jefferson, Helen G. [2069] "Is Psalm 110 Canaanite?" Journal of Biblical Literature, 73 (1954), 152-156.

Johnson, Aubrey R. [2070] The Cultic Prophet and Israel's Psalmody. Cardiff: University of Wales Press, 1979, 467 pp.

Johnson, Aubrey R. [2071] The Cultic Prophet in Ancient Israel. Cardiff: University of Wales, 1944; 2nd edn., 1962, 91 pp.

Join-Lambert, Michel. [2072] "Les pèlerinages en Israël," in M. Simon et als. (eds.), Les pèlerinages de l' antiquité biblique et classique à l' occident médieval. Études d' histoire des religions, 1. Paris: Paul Geunther, 1973, 55-62.

Jones, Douglas. [2073] "The Cessation of Sacrifice after the Destruction of the Temple in 586 B. C.," Journal of Theological Studies, 14 (1963), 12-31.

Jones, Douglas. [2074] "Priests and Levites," in James Hastings (ed.), Dictionary of the Bible, revised edn. by F. C. Grant and H. H. Rowley. New York: Scribner's, 1963, 793-797.

Judge, H. G. [2075] "Aaron, Zadok, and Abiathar," Journal of Theological Studies, 7 (1956), 70-74.

Kapelrud, Arvid S. [2076] "The Role of the Cult in Old Israel," in J. P. Hyatt (ed.), The Bible in Modern Scholarship. Nashville: Abingdon, 1965, 45-56. [With responses by H. G. May and B. Vawter.]

Katzenstein, H. J. [2077] "Some Remarks on the Lists of the Chief Priests of the Temple of Solomon," Journal of Biblical Literature, 81 (1962), 377-384.

Kaufmann, Yehzkel. [2078] "The Cult," in The Religion of Israel. Chicago: University of Chicago Press, 1960, 101-121.

Kedar-Kopfstein, Benjamin and Botterweck, G. Johannes. [2079] "chag," in G. J. Botterwick and H. Ringgren (eds.), Theological Dictionary of the Old Testament, 4. Grand Rapids: Eerdmans, 1980, 201-213.

Keel, Othmar. [2080] "Man before God," in The Symbolism of the Biblical World. New York: Seabury Press, 1978, 307-355.

Kellermann, Diether. [2081] "'asham," in G. J. Botterwick and H. Ringgren (eds.), Theological Dictionary of the Old Testament, 1. Grand Rapids: Eerdmans, rev. edn., 1977, 429-437.

Kennett, Robert Hatch. [2082] "The Origin of the Aaronite Priesthood," Journal of Theological Studies, o. s. 9 (1905), 161-186.

Kidner, Derek. [2083] "Sacrifice-- Metaphors and Meaning," Tyndale Bulletin, 33 (1982), 119-136.

Knierim, Rolph. [2084] "'asham," in E. Jenni and C. Westermann (eds.), Theologische Handwörterbuch zum Alten Testament, 1. Munich: Chr. Kaiser Verlag, 1971, 251-257.

König, Ed. [2085] "The Priests and the Levites in Exekiel XLIV. 7-15," Expository Times, 12 (1901), 300-303.

Kraus, Hans-Joachim. [2086] "Das Heiligtum und der Gottesdienst," in Theologie der Psalmen. Biblischer Kommentar Altes Testament, 15/3. Neukirchen-Vluyn: Neukirchener Verlag, 1979, 88-133.

Kraus, Hans-Joachim. [2087] Worship in Israel: A Cultic History of the Old Testament. Translated by Geoffrey Buswell. Richmond: John Knox Press, 1966, 246 pp.

Kruse, Heinz. [2088] "Psalm CXXXII and the Royal Zion Festival," Vetus Testamentum, 33 (1983), 279-297.

Lang, Bernhard. See Bergman, Jan; Ringgren, Helmer: and Lang, Bernhard. [2009]

Lesétre, Henri. [2089] "Sacrifice," in F. Vigouroux (ed.), Dictionnaire de la Bible, 5. Paris: Letouzey et Ané, 1922, 1311-1337.

Levine, Baruch. See Gray, George Buchanan. [2042]

Levine, Baruch. [2090] "Cult," in Encyclopaedia Judaica, 5. Jerusalem: Macmillan, 1971, 1155-1162.

Levine, Baruch. [2091] In the Presence of the Lord: A Study of Cult and Some Cultic Terms in Ancient Israel. Studies in Judaism in Late Antiquity, 5. Leiden: Brill, 1974, 154 pp.

Levine, Baruch. [2092] "Priests," in Interpreter's Dictionary of the Bible, Supplementary Volume. Nashville: Abingdon, 1976, 687-690.

Lods, Adolphe. [2093] "Éléments anciens et éléments modernes dans le rituel du sacrifice israélite," Revue d' historie et de philosophie religieuses, 8 (1928), 399-411.

Loisy, Alfred. [2094] "La Notion de sacrifice dans l' antiquité israélite," Revue de Histoire et de Littérature Religieuses, n. s. 1 (1910), 1-30.

Maag, Victor. [2095] "Erwägungen zur deuteronomischen Kultzentralisation," Vetus Testamentum, 6 (1956), 10-18.

Macalister, R. A. Stewart. [2096] "Sacrifice (Semitic)," in James Hastings (ed.), Encyclopaedia of Religion and Ethics, 11. New York: Scribner's, 1928, 31-38.

McCarter, P. Kyle. [2097] "The Ritual Dedication of the City of David in 2 Samuel 6," in C. L. Meyers and M. O'Connor (eds.), The Word of the Lord Shall Go Forth: Essays in Honor of David Noel Freedman. American Schools of Oriental Research, Special Volume Series, 1. Winona Lake: Eisenbrauns, 1983, 273-278.

McCarthy, Dennis J. [2098] "Further Notes on the Symbolism of Blood and Sacrifice," Journal of Biblical Literature, 92 (1973), 205-210.

McCarthy, Dennis J. [2099] "The Symbolism of Blood and Sacrifice," Journal of Biblical Literature, 88 (1969), 166-176.

McCready, Wayne O. [2100] "Priests and Levites," in G. W. Bromiley (ed.), The International Standard Bible Encyclopedia, 3. Grand Rapids: Eerdmans, 1986, 965-970.

MacRae, George W. [2101] "The Meaning and Evolution of the Feast of Tabernacles," Catholic Biblical Quarterly, 22 (1960), 251-276.

Martin-Achard, Robert. [2102] Essai biblique sur les fêtes d' Israël. Geneva: Labor et Fides, 1974, 166 pp.

May, Herbert G. See Kapelrud, Arvid S. [2076]

Médebielle, A. [2103] "La Symbolisme du sacrifice expiatoire en Israël," Biblica, 2 (1921), 141-169, 273-302.

Meek, Theophile J. [2104] "Aaronites and Zadokites," American Journal of Semitic Languages and Literatures, 45 (1929), 149-166.

Meek, Theophile J. [2105] "The Origin of the Hebrew Priesthood," in Hebrew Origins. New York: Harper, rev. edn., 1950, 119-147.

Metzinger, Adalbert. [2106] "Die Substitutions-theorie," Biblica, 21 (1940), 159-187.

Milgrom, Jacob. [2107] "The Alleged Wave-Offering in Israel and in the Ancient Near East," Israel Exploration Journal, 22 (1972), 33-38.

Milgrom, Jacob. [2108] Cult and Conscience: The Asham and the Priestly Doctrine of Repentance. Studies in Judaism in Late Antiquity, 18. Leiden: Brill, 1976, 173 pp.

Milgrom, Jacob. [2109] "Day of Atonement," in Encyclopaedia Judaica, 5. Jerusalem: Macmillan, 1971, 1384-1387.

Milgrom, Jacob. [2110] "Israel's Sanctuary: The Priestly 'Picture of Dorian Gray,'" Revue biblique, 83 (1976), 390-399.

Milgrom, Jacob. [2111] "Kipper," Encyclopaedia Judaica, 10. Jerusalem: Macmillan, 1971, 1039-1044.

Milgrom, Jacob. [2112] "Sacrifices and Offerings, OT," in Interpreter's Dictionary of the Bible, Supplementary Volume. Nashville: Abingdon, 1976, 763-741.

Milgrom, Jacob. [2113] "The Shared Custody of the Tabernacle and a Hittite Analogy," Journal of the American Oriental Society, 90 (1970), 204-209.

Milgrom, Jacob. [2114] "Sin-Offering or Purification-Offering?" Vetus Testamentum, 21 (1971), 237-239.

Milgrom, Jacob. [2115] Studies in Levitical Terminology. Berkely: University of California Press, 1970, 110 pp.

Milgrom, Jacob. [2116] "Two Kinds of hattat," Vetus Testamentum, 26 (1976), 333-337.

Möhlenbrink, Kurt. [2117] "Die levitischen Überlieferungen des Alten Testaments," Zeitschrift für die alttestamentliche Wissenschaft, n. s. 11 (1934), 184-231.

Moore, George F. [2118] "Sacrifice," in T. K. Cheyne and J. S. Black (eds.), Encyclopaedia Biblica, 4. New York: Macmillan, 1903, 4183-4233.

Moraldi, Luigi. [2119] Espiazione sacrificale e riti espiatori nell' ambiente biblico e nell' Antico Testamento. Analecta Biblica, 5. Rome: Pontifical Biblical Institute, 1956, 304 pp.

Moraldi, Luigi. [2120] "Terminologia cultuale israelitica," Rivista degli Studi Orientali, 32 (1957), 321-337.

Morgenstern, Julian. [2121] "A Chapter in the History of the Highpriesthood," American Journal of Semitic Languages and Literatures, 55 (1938), 1-24, 183-197, 360-377.

Mowinckel, Sigmund. [2122] Psalmenstudien, 3. Kultprophetie und prophetische Psalmen. Oslo: Jacob Dybwad, 1923, 118 pp.

Mowinckel, Sigmund. [2123] The Psalms in Israel's Worship, 2 vols. Translated by D. R. Ap-Thomas. Oxford: Blackwell, 1962, 246 + 303 pp.

Murray, Robert. [2124] "Prophecy and the Cult," in R. Coggins, A. Phillips, and M. Knibb (eds.), Israel's Prophetic Tradition: Essays in Honour of Peter R. Ackroyd. Cambridge: Cambridge University Press, 1982, 200-216.

Nicholson, Ernest. [2125] "The Centralization of the Cult in Deuteronomy," Vetus Testamentum, 13 (1963), 380-389.

Nicholson, Ernest. [2126] "Josiah's Reformation and Deuteronomy," Transactions of the Glasgow University Oriental Society, 20 (1965), 77-84.

Nickolsky, N. M. [2127] "Pascha im Kulte des jerusalemischen Tempels," Zeitschrift für die alttestamentliche Wissenschaft, 45 (1927), 171-190, 241-253.

North, Christopher R. [2128] "Sacrifice," in Alan Richardson (ed.), A Theological Wordbook of the Bible. New York: Macmillan, 1956, 206-213.

North, Christopher R. [2129] "Sacrifice in the Old Testament," Expository Times, 47 (1935/1936), 250-254.

North, Francis S. [2130] "Aaron's Rise to Powqer," Zeitschrift für die alttestamentliche Wissenschaft, 66 (1954), 191-199.

Oesterley, W. O. E. [2131] "Early Hebrew Festival Rituals," in S. H. Hooke (ed.), Myth and Ritual. London: Humphrey Milford/Oxford University Press, 1933, 111-146.

Oesterley, W. O. E. [2132] Sacrifices in Ancient Israel, their Origin, Purposes and Development. London: Hodder and Stoughton, 1937, 320 pp.

Olyan, Saul. [2133] "Zadok's Origins and the Tribal Politics of David," Journal of Biblical Literature, 101 (1982), 177-193.

O'Rourke, William J. [2134] "Israelite Sacrifice," American Ecclesistical Review, 149 (1963), 259-274.

Paterson, William P. [2135] "Sacrifice," in James Hastings (ed.), Dictionary of the Bible, 4. New York: Scribner's, 1898, 329-343.

Pedersen, Johannes. [2136] Israel, It's Life and Culture, 3-4. Oxford: Geoffrey Cumberlege/Oxford University Press, 1940, 150-465.

Peters, John P. [2137] "A Jerusalem Processional," Journal of Biblical Literature, 39 (1920), 52-59.

Plöger, Otto. [2138] "Priester und Prophet," Zeitschrift für die alttestamentliche Wissenschaft, 63 (1951), 157-192.

Polk, Timothy. [2139] "The Levites in the Davidic-Solomonic Empire," Studia Biblica et Theologica, 9 (1979), 3-22.

Porter, Joshua R. [2140] "Levites," in *Harper's Bible Dictionary*. San Francisco: Harper and Row, 1985, 557-558.

Rainey, Anson. [2141] "The Order of Sacrifices in Old Testament Ritual Texts," *Biblica*, 51 (1970), 485-498.

Rainey, Anson. [2142] "Sacrifice," in *Encyclopaedia Judaica*, 14. Jerusalem: Macmillan, 1971, 599-607.

Rattray, Susan. [2143] "Worship," in *Harper's Bible Dictionary*. San Francisco: Harper and Row, 1985, 1143-1147.

Rehm, Merlin D. [2144] "Zadok the Priest," in *Interpreter's Dictionary of the Bible*, Supplementary Volume. Nashville: Abingdon, 1976, 976-977.

Rentdorff, R. [2145] *Studien zur Geschichte des Opfers im alten Israel*. *Wissenschaftliche Monographien zum Alten und Neuen Testament*, 24. Neukirchen: Neukirchener Verlag, 1967, 277 pp.

Ringgren, Helmer. See Bergman, Jan; Ringgren, Helmer; and Lang, Bernhard. [2009]

Robinson, H. Wheeler. [2146] "Hebrew Sacrifice and Prophetic Symbolism," *Journal of Theological Studies*, o. s. 43 (1942), 129-139.

Rost, Leonhard. [2147] "Erwägungen zum israelitischen Brandopfer," in J. Hempel (ed.), *Von Ugarit nach Qumran: Beiträge zur alttestamentlichen und altorientalichen Forschung* (Festschrift Otto Eissfeldt). *Beihefte zur Zeitschrift für die alttestamentliche Wissenschaft*, 77. Berlin: Töpelmann, 1958, 177-183.

Rost, Leonhard. [2148] *Studien zum Opfer im alten Israel*. *Beiträge zur Wissenschaft vom Alten und Neuen Testament*, 6/13. Stuttgart: Kohlhammer, 1981, 96 pp.

Rowley, H. H. [2149] "Hezekiah's Reform and Rebellion," *Bulletin of the John Rylands Library*, 44 (1961/1962), 395-431. Reprinted in *Men of God*. London: Nelson, 1963, 98-132.

Rowley, H. H. [2150] "The Meaning of Sacrifice in the Old Testament," *Bulletin of the John Rylands Library*, 33 (1950/1951), 74-110. Reprinted in *From Moses to Qumran: Studies in the Old Testament*. New York: Association Press, 1963, 67-107.

Rowley, H. H. [2151] "Melchizedek and Zadok," in W. Baumgartner et al. (eds.), *Festschrift Alfred Bertholet*. Tübingen: Mohr (Siebeck), 1950, 461-472.

Rowley, H. H. [2152] "Ritual and the Hebrew Prophets," *Journal of Semitic Studies*, 1 (1956), 338-360. Reprinted in *From Moses to Qumran: Studies in the Old Testament*. New York: Association Press, 1963, 111-138; also in S. H. Hooke (ed.), *Myth, Ritual and Kingship*. Oxford: Clarendon Press, 1958, 236-260.

Rowley, H. H. [2153] *Worship in Ancient Israel, Its Form and Meaning*. Philadelphia: Fortress Press, 1967 / London: S. P. C. K., 1967, 307 pp.

Rowley, H. H. [2154] "Zadok and Nehushtan," Journal of Biblical Literature, 58 (1939), 113-141.

Saydon, P. [2155] "Sin-Offering and Tresspass Offering," Catholic Biblical Quarterly, 8 (1946), 393-398.

Scheneker, Adrien. [2156] "koper et expiation," Biblica, 63 (1982), 32-46.

Schiffman, Lawrence H. [2157] "Priests," in Harper's Bible Dictionary. San Francisco: Harper and Row, 1985, 821-823.

Schmidt, Martin Anton. [2158] Prophet und Tempel: Ein Studie zum Problem der Gottesnähe im Alten Testament. Zollikon-Zürich: Evangelischer Verlag, 1948, 276 pp.

Smith, W. Robertson. [2159] The Religion of the Semites: The Fundamental Institutions. New York: Meridian Books, 1956, 507 pp. (Originally published in 1899 as Lectures on the Religion of the Semites.)

Snaith, Norman H. [2160] The Jewish New Year Festival. London: S. P. C. K., 1947, 230 pp.

Snaith, Norman H. [2161] "Sacrifice in the Old Testament," Vetus Testamentum, 7 (1957), 308-317.

Snaith, Norman H. [2162] "The Sin-Offering and the Guilt-Offering," Vetus Testamentum, 15 (1965), 78-80.

Snaith, Norman H. [2163] "The Sprinkling of Blood," Expository Times, 82 (1970/1971), 23-24.

Snaith, Norman H. [2164] "The Verbs zabah and shahat," Vetus Testamentum, 25 (1975), 242-246.

Steinmueller, John E. [2165] "Sacrificial Blood in the Bible," Biblica, 40 (1959), 556-567.

Stevenson, Willim B. [2166] "Hebrew 'Olah and Zebach Sacrifices," in W. Baumgartner et al. (eds.), Festschrift Alfred Bertholet. Tübingen: Mohr (Siebeck), 1950, 488-497.

Szörényi, Andreas. [2167] Psalmen und Kult im Alten Testament (Zur Formsgeschichte des Psalmen). Budapest: Sankt Stefans Gesellschaft, 1961, 571 pp.

Thompson, R. J. [2168] Penitence and Sacrifice outside the Levitical Law: An Examination of the Fellowship Theory of Early Israelite Sacrifice. Leiden: Brill, 1963, 287 pp.

Thomson, H. C. [2169] "The Significance of the Term 'Asham in the Old Testament," Transactions of the Glasgow University Oriental Society, 14 (1953), 20-26.

Todd, E. W. [2170] "The Reforms of Hezekiah and Josiah," Scottish Journal of Theology, 9 (1956), 288-293.

Urie, D. M. L. [2171] "Sacrifice among the Western Semites," Palestine Exploration Quarterly, (1949), 67-82.

Van Hoonacker, Albin. [2172] "La Date de l' introduction de l' encens dans le culte de Jahvé," Revue biblique, 23 (1914), 161-187.

Van Hoonacker, Albin. [2173] "Les Prêtres et les lêvites dans le livre d' Ezechiel," Revue biblique, 8 (1899), 177-205.

de Vaux, Roland. [2174] "Religious Institutions," in Ancient Israel; Its Life and Institutions. New York: McGraw-Hill, 1961, 271-517.

de Vaux, Roland. [2175] Studies in Old Testament Sacrifice. Cardiff: University of Wales Press, 1964, 120 pp.

Vawter, Bruce. See Kapelrud, Arvid S. [2076]

Vincent, Louis-Hugues. [2176] "Les Rites du balancement (tenoûphâh) et du prélèvement (teroûmâh) dans le sacrifice de communion de l' AT," in Mélanges Syriens offerts à Monsieur René Dussaud, 2. Paris: Geuthner, 1939, 267-272.

Weiser, Artur. [2177] "Zur Frage nach den Beziehungen der Psalmen zum Kult: Die Darstellung der Theophanie in dem Psalmen und im Festkult," in W. Baumgartner et al. (eds.), Festschrift Alfred Bertholet. Tübingen: Mohr (Siebeck), 1950, 513-531. Reprinted in Glaube und Geschichte im Alten Testament. Göttingen: Vanderhoeck and Ruprecht, 1961, 303-321.

Welch, Adam C. [2178] "When Was the Worship of Israel Centralised at the Temple?" Zeitschrift für die alttestamentliche Wissenschaft, 43 (1925), 250-255.

Wellhausen, Julius. [2179] "History of the Ordinances of Worship," in Prolegomenon to the History of Ancient Israel. New York: Meridian, 1957, 17-167. [Originally published in 1878.]

Wendel, Adolf. [2180] Das Opfer in der altisraelitischen Religion. Leipzig: Pfeiffer, 1927, 238 pp.

Wenham Gordon J. [2181] "Deuteronomy and the Central Sanctuary," Tyndale Bulletin, 22 (1971), 103-118.

Wenham, Gordon J. [2182] "Were David's Sons Priests?" Zeitschrift für die alttestamentliche Wissenschaft, 87 (1975), 79-82.

Wilson, Robert R. [2183] "Prophecy in Israel: The Judaean Tradition," in Prophecy and Society in Ancient Israel. Philadelphia: Fortress Press, 1980, 253-295.

Wright, David P. [2184] "Feasts, Festivals, and Fasts," in Harper's Bible Dictionary. San Francisco: Harper and Row, 1985, 305-307.

Yerkes, R. K. [2185] Sacrifice in Greek and Roman Religion and in Early Judaism. Hale Lectures, 1951. New York: Scribner's, 1952, 267 pp.

Fourteen

The City and Temple of Ezekiel's Vision

Bertholet, Alfred. [2186] "Die Fertige Ordnung der künftigen Dinge (Hesekiel's Verfassungsentwurf), Cap. 40-48," in Das Buch Hesekiel. Kurzer Hand-Kommentar zum Alten Testament, 12. Freiburg / Leipzig / Tübingen: Mohr (Siebeck), 1897, 195-252.

Bewer, Julius A. [2187] "Vision of the New Jerusalem," in The Prophets. Harper's Annotated Bible Series. New York: Harper & Bros., 1949, 438-467.

Busink, Th. A. [2188] "Der Ezechielische Tempelentwurf," in Der Tempel von Jerusalem von Salomo bis Middot, 2: Von Ezechiel bis Middot. Leiden: Brill, 1980, 701-775.

Chary, T. [2189] "Le Temple d' Ezéchiel," Le Monde de la Bible, 40 (1985), 34-38.

Cooke, George A. [2190] "Some Considerations on the Text and Teaching of Ezekiel 40-48," Zeitschrift für die alttestamentliche Wissenschaft, 42 (1924), 105-115.

Cooke, George A. [2191] "The Temple and the Community of the Future," in A Critical and Exegetical Commentary on the Book of Ezekiel. The International Critical Commentary. Edinburgh: T. & T. Clark, 1936, 425-541.

Douglas, George C. M. [2192] "Ezekiel's Temple," Expository Times, 9 (1897/1898), 365-367, 420-422, 468-470, 515-518.

Douglas, George C. M. [2193] "Ezekiel's Vision of the Temple," Expository Times, 14 (1902/1903), 365-368, 424-427.

Eichrodt, Walther. [2194] "The Temple and its Ordinances; The Land and the People in the New Israel of the Time of Salvation," in Ezekiel: A Commentary. Old Testament Library. Trans. by C. Quin. Philadelphia: Westminster, 1970, 530-594.

Eichrodt, Walther. [2195] "Der neue Tempel in der Heilsoffung Hesekiels," in F. Maass (ed.), Das Ferne und nahe Wort: Festschrift für Leonhard Rost. Beihefte zur Zeitschrift für die alttestamentliche Wissenschaft, 105. Berlin: Töpelmann, 1967, 37-48.

Eichrodt, Walther. [2196] "Tempel und Tempelsatzungen, Land und Volk im Israel der Heilziet," in Der Prophet Hesekiel, Kapitel 19-48. Das Alte Testament Deutsch, 22/2. Göttingen: Vandenhoeck & Ruprecht, 1966, 372-421.

Eisemann, Moshe. [2197] Ezekiel: A New Translation with a Commentary Anthologized from Talmudic, Midrashic, and Rabbinic Sources, 3: The Third Temple. Artscroll Tanak Series. Brooklyn: Mesorah , 1980, 603-763 pp.

Elliger, Karl. [2198] "Die grossen Tempelsakristeien im Verfassungsentwurf des Ezechiel (42: 1ff)," in Festschrift für Albrecht Alt: Geschichte und Alten Testament. Tübingen: Mohr (Siebeck), 1953, 79-102.

Farrar, Frederic W. [2199] "The Last Nine Chapters of Ezekiel," The Expositor, 3rd ser., 9 (1889), 1-15.

Galling, Kurt. [2200] "Die Beschreibung des Heiligtums," in G. Fohrer (ed.), Ezechiel. Handbuch zum Alten Testament, 13. Tübingen: Mohr (Siebeck), 1955, 220-241.

Galling. Kurt. [2201] "Die Beschreibung des Kultortes." in A. Bertholet (ed.), Hesekiel. Handbuch zum Alten Testament, 13. Tübingen: Mohr (Siebeck), 1936, 135-155.

Gese, Hartmut. [2202] Der Verfassungsentwurf des Ezechiel (Kap. 40-48) traditionsgeschichtlichen Untersucht. Beiträge zur historischen Theologie, 25. Tübingen: Mohr (Siebeck), 1957, 192 pp.

Greenberg, Moshe. [2203] "The Design and Themes of Ezekiel's Program of Restoration," Interpretation, 38 (1984), 181-208.

Howie, Carl G. [2204] "The East Gate of Ezekiel's Temple Enclosure and the Solomonic Gateway of Megiddo," Bulletin of the American Schools of Oriental Research, 117 (1950), 13-19.

Hurwitz, Avi. [2205] "The Term lishkat sharîm (Ez. 40:44) and its Position in the Cultic Terminology of the Temple," in Eretz-Israel, 14. Jerusalem: Israel Exploration Society, 1978, 100-104 (Hebrew), 126* (English summary).

Jeremias, Joachim. [2206] "Hesekieltempel und Serubbabeltempel," Zeitschrift für die alttestamentliche Wissenschaft, 52 (1934), 109-112.

Kühn, Ernst. [2207] "Ezechiels Gesicht vom Tempel der Vollendungszeit, Kap. 40-42; 43: 13-17; 46: 19-24," Theologische Studien und Kritiken, 55 (1882), 601-688.

Levenson, Jon D. [2208] Theology of the Program of Restoration of Ezekiel 40-48. Harvard Semitic Monographs, 10. Missoula, MT: Scholars Press, 1976, 176 pp.

Levy, Abraham J. (ed.) [2209] Rashi's Copmmentary on Ezekiel 40-48. Edited on the basis on 11 Manuscripts. Philadelphia: Dropsie College Publications, 1931, 122 pp.

Lofthouse, William F. [2210] "The City and the Sanctuary," Expository Times, 34 (1922/1923), 198-202.

Macholz, Georg Christian. [2211] "Noch einmal: Planungen für den Wiederaufbau nach der Katastrophe von 587 (Erwägungen zum Schlussteil der sog. 'Verfassungsentwurf des Hesekiel')," Vetus Testamentum, 19 (1969), 322-352.

Mackay, Cameron. [2212] "The City and the Sanctuary," Expository Times, 34 (1922/1923). 475-476.

Mackay, Cameron. [2213] "The City and the Sanctuary: Ezekiel 48," Princeton Theological Review, 20 (1922), 399-417.

Mackay, Cameron. [2214] "The City of Ezekiel's Oblation," Princeton Theological Review, 21 (1923), 372-388.

Mackay, Cameron. [2215] "The Key to the Old Testament (Ezek. 40-48)," Church Quarterly Review, 199 (1935), 173-196.

Mackay, Cameron. [2216] "Prolegomena to Ezekiel 40-48," Expository Times, 55 (1943/1944), 292-295.

Maier, Johann. [2217] "Die Hofanlagen im Tempel-Entwurf des Ezechiel im Licht der 'Tempelrolle' von Qumran," in J, A. Emerton (ed.), Prophecy (Festschrift Georg Fohrer). Beihefte zur Zeitschrift für die alttestamentliche Wissenschaft, 150. Berlin: De Gruyter, 1980, 55-68.

May, Herbert G. [2218] "Ezekiel, Exegesis: Vision of the Restored Community (40:1-48:35)," The Interpreter's Bible, 6. New York: Abingdon, 1956, 282-338.

Molin, Görg. [2219] "Holonoth 'atumoth bei Ezechiel," Biblische Zeitschrift, 15 (1971), 250-253.

Niditch, Susan. [2220] "Ezekiel 40-48 in a Visionary Context," Catholic Biblical Quarterly, 48 (1986), 208-224.

Pfeifer, Claude J. [2221] "Ezekiel and the New Jerusalem," The Bible Today, 18 (1980), 22-27.

Pohl, Alfred. [2222] "Der verschlossene Tor, Ez. 44: 1-3," Biblica, 13 (1932), 90-92, 201.

Rosenau, William. [2223] "Harel und Ha-Ariel: Ezechiel 43: 15-16," Monatsschrift für Geschichte und Wissenschaft des Judentums, 65 (1921), 350-356.

Rost, Paul. [2224] "Der Altar Ezechiels, Kap. 43: 13-17," in Altorientalische Studien (Bruno Meissner Festschrift). Mitteilungen der altorientalischen Gesellschaft, 4. Leipzig: Harrassowitz, 1928/1929, 170-174.

Soares, Theodore G. [2225] "Ezekiel's Temple," The Biblical World, 14 (1899), 93-103.

Steve, M.-A. See Vincent, Louis-Hugues and Steve, M.-A. [2228]

Thomson, Clive A. [2226] "The Necessity of Blood Sacrifices in Ezekiel's Temple," Biblical Studies, 123 (1966), 237-248.

Vincent, Louis-Hugues. [2227] "L' autel des holocaustes et le caractère du temple d' Ézéchiel," Analecta Bollandiana, 67 (1949), 7-20.

Vincent, Louis-Hugues and Steve, M.-A. [2228] "Le temple d' Ézéchiel," in Jérusalem de l' Ancien Testament, part 2. Paris: Gabalda, 1956, 471-495.

Zimmerli, Walther. [2229] Ezechiel. Biblischer Kommentar, Altes Testament, 13/2. Neukirchen-Vluyn: Neukirchener Verlag, 1969, 976-1249.

Zimmerli, Walther. [2230] "Ezechieltempel und Salomostadt," in Hebräische Wortforschung (Festschrift Walter Baumgartner). Vetus Testamentum, Supplement, 16. Leiden: Brill, 1967, 389-414.

Zimmerli, Walther. [2231] "The Great Vision of the New Temple and the Land," in Ezekiel, 2: A Commentary on the Book of the Prophet Ezekiel. Hermeneia: A Critical and Historical Commentary on the Bible. Philadelphia: Fortress Press, 1983, 325-553.

Zimmerli, Walther. [2232] "Jerusalem in der Sicht des Ezechielbuches," in C. L. Meyers and M. O'Connor (eds.), The Word of the Lord Shall Go Forth: Essays in Honor of David Noel Freedman. American Schools of Oriental Research, Special Volume Series, 1. Winona Lake: Eisenbrauns, 1983, 415-426.

Zimmerli, Walther. [2233] "Planungen für den Wiederaufbau nach der Katastrophe von 587," Vetus Testamentum, 18 (1968), 229-255.

Fifteen

The Babylonian Destruction of Jerusalem

Aharoni, Yohanan. [2234] "The Latter Days of the Judaean Kingdom," in The Land of the Bible. A Historical Geography. Westminster, revised and enlarged edn., 1979, 385-423.

Auerbach, Elias. [2235] "Wann eroberte Nebukadnezar Jerusalem?" Vetus Testamentum, 11 (1961), 128-136.

Barnett, R. D. [2236] "The End of Assyria, the Fall of Nineveh, and the Capture of Jerusalem," in Illustrations of Old Testament History. London: British Museum, 1966; reprinted with revisions, 1968, 70-75.

Bartlett, John R. [2237] "Edom and the Fall of Jerusalem, 587 B. C.," Palestine Exploration Quarterly, (1982), 13-24.

Bickerman, Elias. [2238] "Nebuchadnezzar and Jerusalem," in S. W. Baron and I. E. Barzilay (eds.) Proceedings of the American Academy of Jewish Research, Jubilee Volume, 1. New York: Columbia, 1979, 69-85.

Blenkinsopp, Joseph. [2239] "Abraham and the Righteous of Sodom," Journal of Jewish Studies, 33 (1982), 119-132. [Considers final redaction of Genesis 18: 23-32 as midrash on the fall of Jerusalem, with Sodom being code-name for Jerusalem.]

Bright, John. [2240] "The Neo-Babylonian Empire and the Last Days of Judah," in A History of Israel. Philadelphia: Westminster, 3rd edn., 1981, 324-339.

Brunet, Gilbert. [2241] "La prise de Jérusalem sous Sédécias," Revue d' histoire des religions, 167 (1965), 157-176.

Cazelles, Henri. [2242] "587 ou 586?" in C. L. Meyers and M. O'Connor (eds.), The Word of the Lord Shall Go Forth: Essays in Honor of David Noel Freedman. American Schools of Oriental Research, Special Volume Series, 1. Winona Lake: Eisenbrauns, 1983, 427-435.

Clements, Ronald E. [2243] "The Prophecies of Isaiah and the Fall of Jerusalem in 587 B. C.," Vetus Testamentum, 30 (1980), 421-436.

Finegan, Jack. [2244] "Nebuchadnezzar and Jerusalem," Journal of Bible and Religion, 25 (1957), 203-205.

Freedman, David N. [2245] "The Babylonian Chronicle," Biblical Archaeologist, 19 (1956), 50-60. Reprinted in G. E. Wright and D. N. Freedman (eds.), Biblical Archaeologist Reader. Garden City: Doubleday, 1961, 113-127.

Harrelson, Walter. [2246] "Guilt and Rites of Purification Related to the Fall of Jerusalem in 587 B. C.," in Proceedings of the XIth International Congress of the International Association for the History of Religions, 2. Leiden: Brill, 1968, 73-74.

Hyatt, J. Philip. [2247] "New Light on Nebuchadnezzar and Judean History," Journal of Biblical Literature, 75 (1956), 277-284.

Jones, Douglas. [2248] "The Cessation of Sacrifice after the Destruction of the Temple in 586 B. C.," Journal of Theological Studies, 15 (1964), 12-31.

Kenyon, Kathleen M. [2249] "The Destruction of Jerusalem and the End of the Monarchy of Judah," in Digging Up Jerusalem. New York: Praeger, 1974, 166-171.

Kutsch, Ernst. [2250] "Das Jahr der Katastrophe, 587 v. Chr: Kritische Erwägungen zur neueren chronologischen Versuchen," Biblica, 55 (1974), 520-545.

L' Duhaime, Jean. [2251] "Le verset 8 du psaume 51 et la destruction de Jérusalem," Eglise et Théologie, 13 (1982), 35-56.

Malamat, Abraham. [2252] "A Further Note on Nebuchadrezzar's Palestinian Campaigns," in Judah and Jerusalem: The Twelfth Archaeological Convention. Jerusalem: Israel Exploration Society, 1957, 73-78 (Hebrew), v (English summary).

Malamat, Abraham. [2253] "The Last Kings of Judah and the Destruction of Jerusalem," in Jerusalem through the Ages. Jerusalem: Israel Exploration Society, 1968, 27-48 (Hebrew), 59 (English summary).

Malamat, Abraham. [2254] "The Last Years of the Kingdom of Judah," Journal of Near Eastern Studies, 9 (1950), 218-227.

Malamat, Abraham. [2255] "The Last Years of the Kingdom of Judah," in A. Malamat (ed.), The Age of the Monarchies: Political History. World History of the Jewish People, 4/1. Jerusalem: Masadda Press, 1979, 205-221.

Malamat, Abraham. [2256] "A New Record of Nebuchadnezzar's Palestinian Campaign," Israel Exploration Journal, 6 (1956), 246-256.

Malamat, Abraham. [2257] "The Twilight of Judah in the Egyptian-Babylonian Maelstrom," International Organization for the Study of the Old Testament, Congress Volume, Edinburgh, 1974. Supplements to Vetus Testamentum. Leiden: Brill, 1975, 123-145.

Noth, Martin. [2258] "The Age of Assyrian and Neo-Babylonian Power," in The History of Israel. New York: Harper and Row, 2nd edn., 1960, 253-299.

Noth, Martin. [2259] "Catastrope de Jérusalem en l' an 587 avant Jésus-Christ et sa signification pour Israël," Revue d' histoirie et de philosophie religieuses, 33 (1953), 80-102.

Noth, Martin. [2260] "Die Einnahme von Jerusalem im Jahre 597 v. Chr.," Zeitschrift des deutschen Palästina-Vereins, 74 (1958), 133-157.

Noth, Martin. [2261] "The Jerusalem Catastrophe of 587 B. C. and its Significance for Israel," in The Laws of the Pentateuch and Other Studies. Edinburgh: Oliver and Boyd, 1966, 260-280.

Oded, Bustenay. [2262] "The Last Days of Judah and the Destruction of Jerusalem (609-586 B. C. E.)," in J. H. Hayes and J. M. Miller (eds.), Israelite and Judaean History. London: SCM Press, 1977, 469-476.

Oppenheim, A. Leo. [2263] "Babylonian and Assyrian Historical Texts," in J. B. Pritchard (ed.), Ancient Near Eastern Texts Relating to the Old Testament. Princeton: Princeton University Press, 1955, 265-317.

Oppenheim, A. Leo. [2264] "Babylonian and Assyrian Historical Texts," in J. B. Pritchard (ed.), The Ancient Near East: Supplementary Texts and Pictures Relating to the Old Testament. Princeton: Princeton University Press, 1969, 556-567.

Orlinsky, Harry M. [2265] "The Destruction of the First Temple and the Babylonian Exile in the Light of Archaeology," in Essays in Biblical Culture and Bible Translation. New York: KTAV, 1974, 144-161.

Robinson, Theodore H. [2266] "The Fall of Jerusalem," in A History of Israel, 1: From the Exodus to the Fall of Jerusalem, 586 B. C. Oxford: Clarendon Press, 1957, 429-464.

Schedl, Claus. [2267] "Nochmals des Jahr der Zerstörung Jerusalems, 587 oder 586?" Zeitschrift für die alttestamentliche Wissenschaft, 74 (1962), 209-213.

Singer, Suzanne. [2268] "Found in Jerusalem: Remains of the Babylonian Siege," Biblical Archaeology Review, 2/1 (March, 1976), 7-10.

Vogt, Ernst. [2269] "Bermerkungen über das Jahr der Eroberung Jerusalem," Biblica, 56 (1975), 223-230.

Vogt, Ernst. [2270] "Die neubabylonische Chronik über die Schlacht bei Karkemisch und die Einnahme von Jerusalem," International Organization for the Study of the Old Testament, Volume du Congress, 1956. Supplements to Vetus Testamentum, 4. Leiden: Brill, 1957, 66-96.

Wiseman, Donald J. [2271] The Babylonian Chronicle," in D. W. Thomas (ed.), Documents from Old Testament Times. New York: Harper and Row, 1958, 75-83.

Wiseman, Donald J. [2272] Chronicles of Chaldean Kings (626-556 B. C.) in the British Museum. London: British Museum, 1956, 100 pp.

Sixteen

Jerusalem During the Second Temple Period / The City and Sanctuary in Jewish Thought

Abel, Félix-M. [2273] "Le siège de Jérusalem par Pompeé," Revue biblique, 54 (1947), 56-74.

Aharoni, Yohanan and Avi-Yonah, Michael. [2274] "Herod's Building in Jerusalem," in The Macmillan Bible Atlas. New York: Macmillan, 1968, 139 (map 221).

Aharoni, Yohanan and Avi-Yonah, Michael. [2275] "Jerusalem in the Days of the Return, ca. 440 B. C.," in The Macmillan Bible Atlas. New York: Macmillan, 1968, 108 (map 170).

Aharoni, Yohanan and Avi-Yonah, Michael. [2276] "Pompey's Siege of Jerusalem, 63 B. C.," in The Macmillan Bible Atlas. New York: Macmillan, 1968, 135 (map 215).

Alberti, O. [2277] Jerusalem und seine grosse Zeit: Leben und Kultur in der Heiligen Stadt zur Zeit Christi. Würzburg: Arena Verlag, 2nd edn., 1978, 313 pp.

von Alten, Baron. [2278] "Die Antonia und ihre Umgebungen," Zeitschrift des deutschen Palästina-Vereins, 1 (1878), 61-100.

Amir, Yehoshua. [2279] "Philo's Version of the Pilgrimage to Jerusalem," in A. Oppenheimer, U. Rappaport, and M. Stern (eds.), Jerusalem in the Second Temple Period (Abraham Schalit Memorial Volume). Jerusalem: Yad Izhak Ben-Zvi, 1980, 154-165 (Hebrew), ix-x (English summary).

Amiran, Ruth and Eitan, Avraham. [2280] "Herod's Palace," Israel Exploration Journal, 22 (1972), 50-51.

Appelbaum, Shimon. [2281] "A Fragment of a New Hellenistic Inscription from the Old City of Jerusalem," in A. Oppenheimer, U. Rappaport, and M. Stern (eds.), Jerusalem in the Second Temple Period (Abraham Schalit Memorial Volume). Jerusalem: Yad Izhak Ben-Zvi, 1980, 47-60 (Hebrew), iii (English summary).

Ariel, Donald T. [2282] "A Survey of Coin Finds in Jerusalem (until the end of the Byzantine Period)," Studii Biblici Franciscani, Liber Annuus, 32 (1982), 273-326.

Avi-Yonah, Michael. See Aharoni, Yohanan and Avi-Yonah, Michael. [2274-2276]

Avi-Yonah, Michael. [2283] "Jérusalem du temps d' Hérode," Bible et Terre Sainte, 117 (1970), 7-13.

Avi-Yonah, Michael. [2284] "Jerusalem in the Hellenistic and Roman Periods," in The Herodian Period. World History of the Jewish People, 7. New Brunswick: Rutgers University Press, 1975, 207-249.

Avi-Yonah, Michael. [2285] "Jerusalem in the Second Temple Period," Qadmoniot, 1 (1968), 19-27 (Hebrew).

Avi-Yonah, Michael. [2286] "Jerusalem in the Second Temple Period," in Encyclopedia of Archaeological Excavations in the Holy Land, 2. Englewood Cliffs, NJ: Prentice-Hall, 1976, 599-610.

Avi-Yonah, Michael. [2287] "Jerusalem of the Second Temple Period," in Y. Yadin (ed.), Jerusalem Revealed: Archaeology in the Holy City, 1968-1974. New Haven and London: Yale University Press and the Israel Exploration Society, 1976, 9-13.

Avi-Yonah, Michael. [2288] "Jewish Art and Architecture in the Hasmonean and Herodian Periods," in The Herodian Period. World History of the Jewish People, 7. New Brunswick: Rutgers University Press, 1975, 250-263.

Avi-Yonah, Michael and Stern, Menahem. [2289] "Jerusalem: Second Temple Period," in Encyclopaedia Judaica, 9. Jerusalem: Macmillan, 1971, 1384-1405.

Avigad, Nahman. [2290] "The Architecture of Jerusalem in the Second Temple Period," Qadmoniot, 1 (1968), 28-36 (Hebrew).

Avigad, Nahman. [2291] "The Architecture of Jerusalem in the Second Temple Period," in Y. Yadin (ed.), Jerusalem Revealed: Archaeology in the Holy City, 1968-1974. New Haven and London: Yale University Press and the Israel Exploration Society, 1976, 14-20.

Avigad, Nahman. [2292] "How the Wealthy Lived in Herodian Jerusalem," Biblical Archaeology Review, 2/4 (December, 1976), 1, 23-35.

Avigad, Nahman. [2293] "Jerusalem Flourishing: A Craft Center for Stone, Pottery, and Glass," Biblical Archaeology Review, 9/6 (Nov./Dec., 1983), 48-65.

Avigad, Nahman. [2294] "More Evidence on the Judean Post-Exilic Stamps: Ceramic Evidence for Dating the YRSLM Stamps," Israel Exploration Journal, 24 (1974), 54-58.

Avigad, Nahman. [2295] "Period of the Second Temple," in Discovering Jerusalem. Nashville: Nelson, 1983, 65-204.

Avigad, Nahman. [2296] "Remains of Jewish Art Found in the Upper City of Jerusalem," Qadmoniot, 3 (1970), 27-29 (Hebrew).

Bahat, Dan. [2297] "David's Tower and its Name in Second Temple Times," in Eretz-Israel: Archaeological, Historical, and Geographical Studies, 15. Jerusalem: Israel Exploration Society, 1981, 396-400 (Hebrew), 88* (English summary).

Bahat, Dan. [2298] "The Second Temple Period, 538 B. C. E. - 70 C. E.," in Carta's Historical Atlas of Jerusalem. Jerusalem: Carta, 1983, 20-31.

Ben-Dov, Meir. [2299] "Archaeological Excavation Near the Temple Mount," Christian News from Israel, 22 (1972), 135-142.

Ben-Dov, Meir. [2300] "Daily Life in the Second Temple Period, / Public Buildings and Institutions," in In the Shadow of the Temple: The Discovery of Ancient Jerusalem. Jerusalem: Keter / New York: Harper and Row, 1985, 148-183.

Ben-Dov, Meir. [2301] "Herodian Jerusalem Revisited," Christian News from Israel, 26/3-4 (1978), 138-142.

Ben-Dov, Meir. [2302] "The Persian and Hasmonaean Eras," in In the Shadow of the Temple: The Discovery of Ancient Jerusalem. Jerusalem: Keter / New York: Harper and Row, 1985, 56-71.

Ben-Dov, Meir. [2303] "The Seleucid Akra-- South of the Temple," in Cathedra: For the History of Eretz-Israel and its Yishuv, 18 (1981), 22-35 (Hebrew). [For summary in English, see In the Shadow of the Temple: The Discovery of Ancient Jerusalem. Jerusalem: Keter / New York: Harper and Row, 1985, 65-71.]

Benoit, Pierre. [2304] "L' Antonia d' Hérode le Grand et le forum oriental d' Aelia Capitolina," Harvard Theological Review, 64 (1971), 135-167. Reprinted with some updating in Exégèse et théologie, 4. Paris: Cerf, 1982, 311-346. [The Roman remains at the Ecce Homo arch belong to the eastern forum of Aelia Capitolina and not Herod's Antonia fortress.]

Benoit, Pierre. [2305] "The Archaeological Reconstruction of the Antonia Fortress," in Y. Yadin (ed.), Jerusalem Revealed: Archaeology in the Holy City, 1968-1974. New Haven and London: Yale University Press and the Israel Exploration Society, 1976, 87-89.

Benoit, Pierre. [2306] "De la fortresse Antonia: La reconstitution archéologique," Australian Journal of Biblical Archaeology, 1/6 (1973), 16-22.

Benoit, Pierre. [2307] "Reconstitution archéologique de l' Antonia," Bible et Terre Sainte, 159 (1974), 2-5.

Bickerman, Elias. [2308] "La charte séleucide de Jérusalem," Revue des études juives, 100 (1935), 4-35. Revised version in Studies in Jewish and Christian History, 2. Leiden: Brill, 1980, 44-85.

Bickerman, Elias. [2309] "Héliodore au temple de Jérusalem," in Studies in Jewish and Christian History, 2. Leiden: Brill, 1980, 159-191.

Bickerman, Elias. [2310] "Une proclamation séleucide relative au temple de Jérusalem," Syria, 25 (1946-1948), 67-85. Revised version in Studies in Jewish and Christian History, 2. Leiden: Brill, 1980, 86-104.

Bickerman, Elias. [2311] "Der seleukidische Freibrief für Jerusalem," in A. Schalit (ed.), Zur Josephus-Forschung. Darmstadt: Wissenschaftliche Buchgesellschaft, 1973, 205-240.

Birch, W. F. [2312] "The Levelling of the Akra," Palestine Exploration Fund, Quarterly Statement, (1903), 353-355.

Böhl, Felix. [2313] Über das Verhältnis von Shetija-Stein und Nabel der Welt in der Kosmologonie der Rabbinen," Zeitschrift der deutschen Morgenländischen Gesellschaft, 124 (1974), 253-270.

Bonfil, R. [2314] "Judah and Jerusalem in the Letter of Aristeas," Beth Miqra, 17 (1972), 131-142, 260 (Hebrew).

Briend, Jacques. [2315] "Jérusalem depuis l' exil jusqu' au roi Hérode," Bible et Terre Sainte, 117 (1970), 2-5.

Broshi, Magen. [2316] "Estimating the Population of Ancient Jerusalem," Biblical Archaeology Review, 4/2 (1978), 10-15.

Broshi, Magen. [2317] "La population de l' ancienne Jérusalem," Revue biblique, 82 (1975), 5-14.

Broshi, Magen. [2318] "The Population of Western Palestine in the Roman-Byzantine Period," Bulletin of the American Schools of Oriental Research, 236 (1979), 1-10.

Burrows, Millar. [2319] "Jerusalem," in Interpreter's Dictionary of the Bible, 2. New York: Abingdon, 1962, 843-866, esp. 853-866.

Byatt, Anthony. [2320] "Josephus and Population Numbers in First Century Palestine," Palestine Exploration Quarterly, (1973), 51-60.

Cerny, Edward A. [2321] "Jerusalem: Palace of Herod the Great," Catholic Biblical Quarterly, , 4 (1942), 258-261.

Clermont-Ganneau, Charles. [2322] "Découverte à Jérusalem d' une Synagogue de l' époque hérodienne," Syria, 1 (1920), 190-197.

Clermont-Ganneau, Charles. [2323] "The Royal Caves," in Archaeological Researches in Palestine during the Years 1873-1874, 1. Translated by Aubrey Stewart. London: Palestine Exploration Fund, 1896, 239-246.

Conder, Claude R. [2324] "Herod the Great," in The City of Jerusalem. London: John Murray, 1909, 108-138.

Constantinou, V. H. [2325] "The Fortress of Akra," Christian News from Israel, 23 (1972), 97-99.

Cook, Stanley A. [2326] "The Synagogue of Theodotus at Jerusalem," Palestine Exploration Fund, Quarterly Statement, (1921), 22-23.

Cornfeld, Gaalya (general editor) with Mazar, Benjamin and Maier, Paul L. (consulting editors). [2327] "Description of Jerusalem," in Josephus, The Jewish War: Newly Translated with Extensive Commentary and Archaeological Background Illustrations. Grand Rapids: Zondervan, 1982, 331-346.

Cross, Frank M. [2328] "An Aramaic Ostracon of the Third Century B. C. E. from Excavations in Jerusalem," in Eretz-Israel: Archaeological, Historical, and Geographical Studies, 15. Jerusalem: Israel Exploration Society, 1981, 67*-69*

Daniélou, Jean. [2329] "La symbolique du Temple de Jérusalem chez Philon et Josèphe," in Le symbolisme cosmique des monuments religieux. Serie Orientale Roma, 14. Rome: Is. M. E. O., 1957, 83-90.

Eitan, Avraham. See Amiran, Ruth and Eitan, Avraham. [2280]

Ellis, Frank T. [2330] "Mosaics on Mt. Zion," Palestine Exploration Fund, Quarterly Statement, (1891), 309-310.

Emmanuele da S. Marco. [2331] "Lo pseudo-Aristea e il Siracida (Ecclo 50) sulla cittadella e il tempio de Gerusalemme," in S. Gozzo (ed.), La distruzione di Gerusalemme del 70: nei suoi riflessi storico-letterari. Atti del V Convegno biblico francescano, Roma, 22 sett., 1969. Collectio Assisiensis, 8. Assisi: Studio Teologico "porziuncolo," 1971, 194-207.

Finegan, Jack. [2332] "The Tower of David," in Archeology of the New Testament: The Life of Jesus and the Beginnings of the Early Church. Princeton: Princeton University Press, 1969, 133-134.

Flusser, David. [2333] "Jerusalem in the Literature of the Second Temple Period," Emmanuel: Bulletin of Religious Thought and Research in Israel, 6 (1976), 43-46.

Fohrer, Georg and Lohse, Eduard. [2334] "Sión, Hierousalém, Hierosólyma, Hierosolymítes," in G. Friedrich (ed.), Theological Dictionary of the New Testament, 7. Grand Rapids: Eerdmans, 1971, 292-338.

Ford, J. Massyngberde. [2335] "The Heavenly Jerusalem and Orthodox Judaism," in E. Bammel; C. K. Barrett; and W. D. Davies (eds), Donum gentilicium: New Testament Studies in Honour of David Daube. Oxford: Clarendon Press, 1978, 215-226.

Galling, Kurt. [2336] "Die Halle des Schreibers: Ein Beitrag zur Topographie der Akropolis von Jerusalem," Palästinajahrbuch, 27 (1931), 51-57.

Galling, Kurt. [2337] "Die terpole des Alexander Jannäus," in J. Hempel and L. Rost (eds.), Von Ugarit nach Qumran (Festschrift Otto Eissfeldt). Berlin: Töpelmann, 1958, 49-62.

Geva, Hillel. [2338] "The Tower of David-- Phasael or Hippicus?" Israel Exploration Journal, 31 (1981), 57-65.

Golan, D. [2339] "Josephus, Alexander's Visit to Jerusalem, and Modern Historiography," in U. Rappaport (ed.), Josephus Flavius, Historian of Eretz-Israel in the Hellenistic-Roman Period. Jerusalem, 1982, 29-55.

Gray, John. [2340] "The House of Herod," in A History of Jerusalem. New York: Praeger, 1969, 150-168.

Har-El, Menashe. [2341] "Jerusalem during the Second Temple Period," in This is Jerusalem. Jerusalem: Canaan, 1977, 79-102.

Husseini, S. A. S. [2342] "An Unfinished Monolith Column in Mahneh Yehuday Quarter, Jerusalem," Quarterly of the Department of Antiquities in Palestine, 5 (1935/1936), 1-2.

Ita of Sion, Sr. Marie. [2343] "The Antonia Fortress," Palestine Exploration Quarterly, (1968), 140-142.

Jeremias, Joachim. [2344] "Economic Conditions in the City of Jerusalem; Economic Status," in Jerusalem in the Time of Jesus: An Investigation into the Economic and Social Conditions during the New Testament Period. Trans. by F. H. and C. H. Cave. Philadelphia: Fortress Press, 1969, 3-144.

Jeremias, Joachim. [2345] "Die Einwohnerzahl Jerusalems zur Zeit Jesu," Zeitschrift des deutschen Palästina-Vereins, 66 (1943), 24-31.

Kasher, A. [2346] "Jerusalem as a 'Metropolis' in Philo's National Consciousness," Cathedra: For the History of Eretz-Israel and its Yishuv, 11 (1979), 45-56 (Hebrew).

Kenyon, Kathleen M. [2347] "Herodian and New Testament Jerusalem," in Jerusalem: Excavating 3,000 Years of History. New York: McGraw-Hill, 1967, 138-154.

Kenyon, Kathleen M. [2348] "Jerusalem in the First Century A. D. down to the End of Jewish Jerusalem," in Digging Up Jerusalem. New York: Praeger, 1974, 236-264.

Kenyon, Kathleen M. [2349] "The Jerusalem of Herod Agrippa and the Destruction," in Jerusalem: Excavating 3,000 Years of History. New York: McGraw-Hill, 1967, 155-186.

Kenyon, Kathleen M. [2350] "Jerusalem of Herod the Great and of the New Testament," in Digging Up Jerusalem. New York: Praeger, 1974, 205-235.

Kenyon, Kathleen M. [2351] "Post-Exilic Jerusalem," in Jerusalem: Excavating 3,000 Years of History. New York: McGraw-Hill, 1967, 105-137.

Kenyon, Kathleen M. [2352] "The Post-Exilic Period," in Digging Up Jerusalem. New York: Praeger, 1974, 172-187.

Kindler, Arie. [2353] Coins of the Land of Israel: A Collection of the Bank of Israel, A Catalogue. Jerusalem: Keter, 1974, 138 pp.

Laperrousaz, Ernest-Marie. [2354] "Angle Sud-Est du "Temple de Salomon' ou vestiges de l' Acra des Séleucides?" Syria, 52 (1975), 241-259.

Laperrousaz, Ernest-Marie. [2355] "Encore l' Acra des Séleucides, et nouvelles remarques sur les pierres à bossage préhérodiennes de Palestine," Syria, 56 (1979), 99-144.

Lapp, Paul. [2356] "Ptolemaic Stamped Handles from Judah," Bulletin of the American Schools of Oriental Research, 172 (1963), 22-35. ["Jerusalem" seals.]

La Sor, William S. [2357] "Herodian Jerusalem," in G. W. Bromiley (ed.), International Standard Bible Encyclopedia, 2. Grand Rapids: Eerdmans, 1982, 1022-1026.

Lohse, Eduard. See Fohrer, Georg and Lohse, Eduard. [2334]

Lohse, Eduard. [2358] "Die römischen Staathalter in Jerusalem," Zeitschrift des deutschen Palästina-Vereins, 74 (1958), 69-78.

McKelvey, R. J. [2359] "The Foundation-Stone in Zion," in The New Temple: The Church in the New Testament. London: Oxford University Press, 1969, 188-192. [Rabbinic traditions on the Foundation Stone of the Temple.]

Mackowski, Richard M. [2360] Jerusalem, City of Jesus: An Exploration of the Traditions, Writings, and Remains of the Holy City from the Time of Christ. Grand Rapids: Eerdmans, 1980, 221 pp.

Mackowski, Richard M. [2361] "Some 'New' Place Names in Herodian Jerusalem," Biblische Zeitschrift, 29 (1985), 262-267.

Magen, Y. [2362] "Jerusalem as a Center for the Production of Stoneware in the Herodian Period," Qadmoniot, 17 (1984), 124-127 (Hebrew). [English summary in Old Testament Abstracts, 8 (1985), 249-250.]

Maier, Paul L. See Cornfeld, Gaalya with Mazar, Benjamin and Maier, Paul L. [2327]

Ma'oz, Zvi Uri. [2363] "On the Hasmonean and Herodian Town-Plan of Jerusalem," in Eretz-Israel: Archaeological, Historical, and Geographical Studies, 18. Jerusalem: Israel Exploration Society, 1985, 46-57 (Hebrew), 66*-67* (English summary).

Marie Ita de Sion, Sr. See Ita of Sion, Sr. Marie. [2343]

Marmorstein, Abraham. [2364] "The Inscription of Theodotus," Palestine Exploration Fund, Quarterly Statement, (1921), 23-28.

Maurer, Christian. [2365] "Der Struthionteich und der Burg Antonia," Zeitschrift des deutschen Palästina-Vereins, 80 (1964), 137-149.

Mazar, Benjamin. See Cornfeld, Gaalya with Mazar, Benjamin and Maier, Paul L. [2327]

Mazar, Benjamin. [2366] "The Archaeological Excavations near the Temple Mount," in Y. Yadin (ed.), Jerusalem Revealed: Archaeology in the Holy City, 1968-1974. New Haven and London: Yale University Press and the Israel Exploration Society, 1976, 25-40.

Mazar, Benjamin. [2367] "Découverts archéologiques près des murs du Temple, La Terre Sainte, 8-9 (1973), 222-232.

Mazar, Benjamin. [2368] "Excavations near Temple Mount Reveal Splendors of Herodian Jerusalem," Biblical Archaeology Review, 6/4 (1980), 44-59.

Mazar, Benjamin. [2369] "The Excavations South and West of the Temple Mount in Jerusalem: The Herodian Period," Biblical Archaeologist, 33 (1970), 47-60.

Mazar, Benjamin. [2370] "Herod's Period," in The Mountain of the Lord. Garden City, NY: Doubleday, 1975, 75-87.

Mazar, Benjamin. [2371] "Herodian Jerusalem in the Light of the Excavations South and Southwest of the Temple Mount," Israel Exploration Journal, 28 (1978), 230-237.

Mazar, Benjamin. [2372] "Jerusalem in Post-Exilic Times," in The Mountain of the Lord. Garden City, NY: Doubleday, 1975, 60-64.

Mazar, Benjamin. [2373] "Jerusalem in the Hellenistic Period / The Hasmoneans," in The Mountain of the Lord. Garden City, NY: Doubleday, 1975, 64-74.

Mazar, Benjamin. [2374] "Jerusalem of Hellenistic and Hasmonean Times," in The Mountain of the Lord. Garden City, NY: Doubleday, 1975, 201-204.

Mazar, Benjamin. [2375] "Nehemiah's Vital Evidence on the City of David," in The Mountain of the Lord. Garden City, NY: Doubleday, 1975, 190-201.

Mazar, Benjamin. [2376] "Rediscovering the Lower City of the Herodian Period," in The Mountain of the Lord. Garden City, NY: Doubleday, 1975, 204-216.

Meshorer, Ya'akov. [2377] Ancient Jewish Coinage, 2 vols. Dix Hills, NY: Amphora Books, 1985, 184 pp., 56 pls. + 295 pp., 36 pls.

Meshorer, Ya'akov. [2378] Jewish Coins of the Second Temple Period. Tel-Aviv: Am Hassefer and Massada, 1967, 184 + 32.

Mickley, Paul. [2379] "Jerusalem zur Zeit Christi," Palästinajahrbuch, 7 (1911), 35-72.

Mor, Menachem and Rappaport, Uriel. [2380] "A Survey of 25 Years (1960-1985) of Israeli Scholarship on Jewish History in the Second Temple Period (539 B. C. E. - 135 C. E.)," Biblical Theology Bulletin, 16 (1986), 56-72. [A bibliographical survey.]

Morgenstern, Julian. [2381] "Jerusalem-- 485 B. C.," Hebrew Union College Annual, 27 (1956), 101-179; 28 (1957), 15-47; 31 (1960), 1-29.

Netzer, Ehud et al. [2382] "Symposium: Herod's Building Projects: State Necessity or Personal Need?" in L. I. Levine (ed.), Jerusalem Cathedra, 1. Jerusalem: Yad Izhaq Ben-Zvi Institute / Detroit: Wayne State University Press, 1981, 48-50.

Nikiprovetzki, Valentin. [2383] "La spiritualisation des sacrifices et le culte sacrificiel au Temple de Jérusalem chez Philon d' Alexandri," Semitica, 17 (1967), 97-116.

Noth, Martin. [2384] "The Life of the Jerusalem Religious Community in the Persian Period," in The History of Israel. New York: Harper and Row, 2nd edn., 1960, 337-345.

Oppenheimer, Aharon. [2385] "Benevolent Societies in Jerusalem," in A. Oppenheimer; U. Rappaport; and M. Stern (eds.), Jerusalem in the Second Temple Period: Abraham Schalit Memorial Volume. Jerusalem: Yad Izhaq Ben-Zvi, 1980, 178-190 (Hebrew), xi-xii (English summary).

Oppenheimer, Aharon; Rappaport, Uriel; and Stern, Menahem (eds.). [2386] Jerusalem in the Second Temple Period: Abraham Schalit Memorial Volume. Jerusalem: Yad Izhaq Ben-Zvi, 1980, 488 pp. (Hebrew), xxviii pp. (English summaries).

Peters, F. E. [2387] "Jews and Greeks in Jerusalem," in Jerusalem: The Holy City in the Eyes of Chroniclers, Visitors, Pilgrims, and Prophets from the Days of Abraham to the Beginnings of Modern Times. Princeton: Princeton University Press, 1985, 176-214.

Rajak, T. [2388] "Roman Intervention in a Seleucid Siege of Jerusalem?" Greek, Roman, and Byzantine Studies, 22 (1981), 65-81.

Rappaport, Uriel. See Mor, Menachem and Rappaport, Uriel. [2380]

Rappaport, Uriel. See Oppenheimer, Aharon; Rappaport, Uriel; and Stern, Menahem (eds.). [2386]

Safrai, Shmuel. [2389] "The Heavenly Jerusalem," Ariel, 23 (1969), 11-16.

Safrai, Shmuel. [2390] "Pilgrimage: Second Temple Period / Post-Temple Period," in Encyclopaedia Judaica, 13. Jerusalem: Macmillan, 1971, 510-514.

Safrai, Shmuel. [2391] "Pilgrimage to Jerusalem at the End of the Second Temple Period," in O. Michel, et al. (eds.), Studies on the Jewish Background of the New Testament. Assen, Netherlands: Van Gorcum, 1969, 12-21.

Safrai, Shmuel. [2392] "Pilgrimage to the Temple at the Time of the Second Temple," Emmanuel: Bulletin of Religious Thought and Research in Israel, 5 (1975), 51-62.

Safrai, Shmuel. [2393] Wallfahrt im Zeitalter des Zweiten Tempels. Forschungen zum jüdisch-christlichen Dialog, 3. Neukirchen-Vluyn: Neukirchener-Verlag, 1981, 331 pp.

Schäfer, Peter. [2394] "Tempel und Schöpfung: Zur Interpretation einiger Heiligtumstraditionen in der rabbinischen Literatur," in Studien zur Geschichte und Theologie des Rabbinischen Judentums. Leiden: Brill, 1978, 122-133.

Schick, Conrad. [2395] "Ausdehnung der Stadt Jerusalem und ihre Einwohnerzahl zur Zeit des 2. Tempels," Jerusalem, 1 (1881), 83-103.

Schick, Conrad. [2396] "Der Davidsthurm in Jerusalem. Neu untersucht gemmesen und gezeichnet," Zeitschrift des deutschen Palästina-Vereins, 1 (1878), 226-237

Schick, Conrad. [2397] "Herod's Amphitheatre," Palestine Exploration Fund, Quarterly Statement, (1887), 161-166.

Seeligman, J. A. [2398] "Jerusalem in Jewish-Hellenistic Thought," in Judah and Jerusalem: The Twelfth Archaeological Convention. Jerusalem: Israel Exploration Society, 1957, 192-208 (Hebrew), viii (English summary).

di Segni, Riccardo. [2399] "Gerusalemme nella tradizione religiosa giudaica dell' età post-bíblíca," in M. Bormans (ed.), Gerusalemme. Brescia: Paideia, 1982, 99-110.

Shotwell, Willis. [2400] "The Problem of the Syrian Akra," Bulletin of the American Schools of Oriental Research, 176 (1964), 10-19.

Sisti, Adalberto. [2401] "Il governo della Città Santa sotto i Seleucidi," in M. V, 70)," in M. Borrmans (ed.), Gerusalemme. Brescia: Paideia, 1982, 153-162.

Sperber, Daniel. [2402] "Social Legislation in Jerusalem during the Latter Part of the Second Temple Period," Journal for the Study of Judaism, 6 (1975), 86-95.

Spiess, F. [2403] "Die königliche Halle des Herods im Tempel von Jerusalem," Zeitschrift des deutschen Palästina-Vereins, 15 (1892), 234-256.

Stern, Menahem. See Avi-Yonah, Michael and Stern, Menahem. [2289]

Stern, Menahem. See Oppenheimer, Aharon; Rappaport, Uriel; and Stern, Menahem (eds.). [2386]

Stern, Menahem. [2404] "'Jerusalem, the Most Famous of the Cities of the East' (Pliny, Natural History, V, 70)," in A. Oppenheimer, U. Rappaport, and M. Stern (eds.), Jerusalem in the Second Temple Period: Abraham Schalit Memorial Volume. Jerusalem: Yad Izhaq Ben-Zvi, 1980, 257-270 (Hebrew), xv (English summary).

Steve, M.-A. See Vincent, Louis-Hugues and Steve, M.-A. [2417-2420]

Sukenik, Eleazar L. [2405] "The 'Jerusalem' and the 'City' Stamps on Jar Handles," Journal of the Palestine Oriental Society, 13 (1933), 226-231.

Tcherikover, Victor. [2406] "Was Jerusalem a 'Polis,'" Israel Exploration Journal, 14 (1964), 61-78.

Tsafrir, Yoram. [2407] "The Location of the Seleucid Akra in Jerusalem," Qadmoniot, 5 (1972), 125-126 (Hebrew).

Tsafrir, Yoram. [2408] "The Location of the Seleucid Akra in Jerusalem," Revue biblique, 82 (1975), 501-521. Also in Y. Yadin (ed.), Jerusalem Revealed: Archaeology in the Holy City, 1968-1974. New Haven and London: Yale University Press and the Israel Exploration Society, 1976, 85-86.

Ubigli, L. Rosso. [2409] "Dalla 'Nuova Gerusalemme' alla 'Gerusalemme Celeste'-- Contributo per la comprensiòne dell' Apocalillica," Henoch, 3 (1981), 69-80.

Uhrbach, Ephraim M. [2410] "Heavenly and Earthly Jerusalem," in J. Aviram (ed.), Jerusalem through the Ages. Jerusalem: Israel Exploration Society, 1968, 156-171 (Hebrew), 64 (English summary).

Vincent, Louis-Hugues. [2411] "Acra," Revue biblique, 43 (1934), 205-235.

Vincent, Louis-Hugues. [2412] "L' Antonia, palais primitif d' Hérode," Revue biblique, 61 (1954), 87-107.

Vincent, Louis-Hugues. [2413] "Aux cavernes royales," Revue biblique, 34 (1925), 587-588.

Vincent, Louis-Hugues. [2414] "Découverte de la 'Synagogue des affranchis' à Jérusalem," Revue biblique, 30 (1921), 247-277.

Vincent, Louis-Hugues. [2415] "Jérusalem d' apres la lettre d' Aristée," Revue biblique, 17 (1908), 520-532; 18 (1909), 555-575.

Vincent, Louis-Hugues. [2416] "Vestiges hérodiene près de la citadelle," Revue biblique, 10 (1910), 418-420.

Vincent, Louis-Hugues and Steve, M.-A. [2417] "L' exile et la restauration," in Jérusalem de l' Ancien Testament, 3. Paris: Gabalda, 1956, 655-576.

Vincent, Louis-Hugues and Steve, M.-A. [2418] "Fortresses: 1. Acra; 2. L' Antonia, Les palais," Jérusalem de l' Ancien Testament, 1. Paris: Gabalda, 1954, 175-236.

Vincent, Louis-Hugues and Steve, M.-A. [2419] "Jérusalem à l' époque hérodienne et jusqu' à la première révolte (63 av.-66 ap. J. C.)," in Jérusalem de l' Ancien Testament, 3. Paris: Gabalda, 1956, 699-725.

Vincent, Louis-Hugues and Steve, M.-A. [2420] "De la restauration postexilique à Hérode," in Jérusalem de l' Ancien Testament, 3. Paris: Gabalda, 1956, 677-698.

Watzinger, Carl. [2421] "Herodes der Grosse," in Denkmäler Palästinas, 2. Leipzig: Hinrichs'sche Buchhandlung, 1935, 31-78.

Wilkinson, John. [2422] "The City Plan," in Jerusalem as Jesus Knew It: Archaeology as Evidence. London: Thames and Hudson, 1978, 53-65.

Wilkinson, John. [2423] "The Streets of Jerusalem," Levant, 7 (1975), 118-136.

Seventeen

Zerubbabel's Temple

Abel, Félix-M. [2424] "La reconstruction du Temple de Jérusalem," in Histoirie de la Palestine, 1. Paris: Le Coffre, 1952, 372-379.

Ackroyd, Peter R. [2425] "The Temple Vessels-- A Continuity Theme," in Studies in the Religion of Ancient Israel. Supplements to Vetus Testamentum, 23. Leiden: Brill, 1972, 166-181.

Ahlström, Gosta W. [2426] Joel and the Temple Cult of Jerusalem. Leiden: Brill, 1971, 151 pp.

Anderson, Francis I. [2427] "Who Built the Second Temple?" Australian Biblical Review, 6 (1958), 1-35.

Brand, J. [2429] "Some Remarks on the Second Temple Edifice," Tarbiz, 29 (1960), 210-217 (Hebrew). [English summary in New Testament Abstracts, 5 (1960/1961), 75.]

Braun, Roddy L. [2430] "The Message of Chronicles: Rally Round the Temple," Concordia Theological Monthly, 42 (1971), 502-514.

Bright, John. [2431] "The Restoration of the Jewish Community in Palestine; / The Completion of the Temple," in A History of Israel. Philadelphia: Westminster, 3rd edn., 1981, 360-372.

Busink, Th. A. [2432] "Der Tempel Serubbabels," in Der Tempel von Jerusalem bis Herodes, 2: Von Ezechiel bis Middot. Leiden: Brill, 1980, 776-841.

Clermont-Ganneau, Charles. [2433] "The Veil of the Temple of Jerusalem at Olympia," Palestine Exploration Fund, Quarterly Statement, (1878), 79-81.

Doran, Robert. [2434] Temple Propaganda: The Purpose and Character of 2 Maccabees. Catholic Biblical Quarterly Monograph Series, 12. Washington, DC: Catholic Biblical Association of America, 1981, 124 pp.

Dunand, Maurice. [2435] "Byblos, Sidon, Jérusalem: Monuments apparentés des temps achémenides," in International Organization for the Study of the Old Testament, Congress Volume, 1968. Supplements to Vetus Testamentum, 17. Leiden: Brill, 1969, 64-70.

Eissfeldt, Otto. [2436] "Eine Einschmelzstelle am Tempel zu Jerusalem," in Kleine Schriften, 2. Tübingen: Mohr (Siebeck), 1963, 107-109.

Fernández, Andreas. [2437] "El Profeta Ageo 2, 15-18 y la fundación del segundo templo," Biblica, 2 (1921), 206-215.

Fohrer, Georg. [2438] "Kritik an Tempel: Kultus und Kultusausübung in nachexilischer Zeit," in A. Kuschke and E. Kutsch (eds.), Archäologie und Altes Testament (Festschrift Kurt Galling). Tübingen: Mohr (Siebeck), 1970, 101-116.

Fujita, Shozo. [2439] "Temple Theology in the Second Book of Maccabees," The Bible Today, 64 (1973), 1066-1071.

Galling, Kurt. [2440] "Serubbabel und der Hohepriester beim Wiederaufbau des Tempels in Jerusalem," in Studien zur Geschichte Israels im persischen Zeitalter. Tübingen: Mohr (Siebeck), 1964, 127-148.

Galling, Kurt. [2441] "Serubbabel und der Wiederaufbau des Tempels in Jerusalem," in A. Kuschke (ed.), Verbannung und Heimkehr: Beiträge zur Geschichte und Theologie Israels im 6. und 5. Jahrhundert v. Chr. (Festschrift Wilhelm Rudolph). Tübingen: Mohr (Siebeck), 1961, 67-96.

Galling, Kurt. [2442] "Der Tempelschatz nach Berichten und Urkunden im Buche Esra," Zeitschrift des deutschen Palästina-Vereins, 60 (1937), 177-183.

Gelston, A. [2443] "The Foundation of the Second Temple," Vetus Testamentum, 16 (1966), 232-235.

Gese, Hartmut. [2444] "Zur Geschichte der Kultsänger am zweiten Tempel," in O. Betz (eds.), Abraham unser Vater: Juden und Christen im Gespräch über die Bibel (Festschrift Otto Michel). Leiden: Brill, 1963, 222-234.

Halpern, Baruch. [2445] "The Ritual Background of Zerubbabel's Temple Song," Catholic Biblical Quarterly, 40 (1978), 167-190.

Hamerton-Kelly, Robert G. [2446] "The Temple and the Origins of Jewish Apocalyptic," Vetus Testamentum, 20 (1970), 1-15.

Hanson, Paul. [2447] "The Origins of the Post-Exilic Hierocracy," in The Dawn of Apocalyptic. Philadelphia: Fortress Press, 1975, 209-279.

Imbert, J. [2448] "Le temple reconstruit par Zorobabel," Le Muséon, 7 (1888), 77-87, 221-235, 302-314, 584-592; 8 (1889), 51-66, 520-521.

Ivry, Alfred L. [2449] "Nehemiah 6, 10: Politics and the Temple," Journal for the Study of Judaism, 3 (1972), 35-45.

Japhet, Sara. [2450] "Sheshbazzar and Zerubbabel against the Background of the Historical and Religious Tendencies of Ezra-Nehemiah," Zeitschrift für die alttestamentliche Wissenschaft, 95 (1983), 218-229.

Le Bas, Edwin E. [2451] "Zechariah's Climax to the Career of the Corner-Stone," Palestine Exploration Quarterly, (1951), 139-155.

Le Bas, Edwin E. [2452] "Zechariah's Enigmatical Contribution to the Corner-Stone," Palestine Exploration Quarterly, (1950), 102-122.

Luria, Ben-Zion. [2453] "The Temple Mount at the Time of the Return to Zion," Beth Miqra, 26 (1981), 206-218 (Hebrew). [English summary in Old Testament Abstracts, 5 (1982), 45-46.]

Lutz, Hans-Martin. [2454] Jahwe, Jerusalem und die Völker: Vorgeschichte von Sach 12, 1-8 und 14, 1-5. Wissenschaftliche Monographien zum Alten und Neuen Testament, 27. Neukirchen: Neukirchener Verlag, 1968, 237 pp.

Mackay, Cameron. [2455] "Zechariah's Relation to Ezek. 40-48," Evangelical Quarterly, 40 (1968), 197-210.

Madsen, Truman. [2456] "The Temple and the Restoration," in in T. Madsen (ed.), The Temple in Antiquity: Ancient Records and Modern Perspectives. Religious Studies Monograph Series, 9. Provo, UT: Brigham Young University Press, 1984, 1-18.

de Moor, Fl. [2457] "Le temple reconstruit par Zorobabel," Le Muséon, 8 (1889), 364-371, 467-473, 514-551; 9 (1890), 5-15.

Noth, Martin. [2458] "The Re-establishment of the Sanctuary and the Cultus in Jerusalem," in The History of Israel. New York: Harper and Row, 2nd edn., 1960, 300-316.

Petersen, David L. [2459] "Zechariah's Visions: A Theological Perspective," Vetus Testamentum, 34 (1984), 195-206.

Petersen, David L. [2460] "Zerubbabel and Jerusalem Temple Reconstruction," Catholic Biblical Quarterly, 36 (1974), 366-372.

Petitjean, Albert. [2461] "La mission de Zorobbabel et la reconstruction du Temple, Zach. iii, 8-10," Ephemerides Theologicae Lovanienses, 42 (1966), 40-71.

Petitjean, Albert. [2462] Les oracles du Proto-Zacharie. Un programme de restauration pour la communauté juive apres l' exile. Etudes Bibliques. Paris: Gabalda, 1969, 502 pp.

Porten, Bezalel. [2463] "Temple: Temple of Zerubbabel," in Encyclopaedia Judaica, 15. Jerusalem: Macmillan, 1971, 955-958.

von Rad, Gerhard. [2464] "The Prophets of the Later Persian Period and the Prophecies of the New Jerusalem," in Old Testament Theology, 2. New York: Harper and Row, 1965, 278-300.

Sellin, Ernst. [2465] "Der Stein des Sacharja," Journal of Biblical Literature, 50 (1931), 242-249.

Seybold, Klaus. [2466] Bilder zum Tempelbau: Die Visionen des Propheten Sacharja. Stuttgarter Bibelstudien, 70. Stuttgart: Verlag Katholisches Bibelwerk, 1974, 128 pp.

Siebeneck, Robert T. [2467] "Messianism of Aggeus and Proto-Zacharias," Catholic Biblical Quarterly, 19 (1957), 312-318.

Steck, Odil H. [2468] "Zu Haggai 1: 2-11," Zeitschrift für die alttestamentliche Wissenschaft, 83 (1971), 355-379.

Stinespring, William F. [2469] "Temple, Jerusalem: The Temple of Zerubbabel," in Interpreter's Dictionary of the Bible, 4. New York: Abingdon, 1962, 547-550.

Torrey, Charles C. [2470] "The Foundry of the Second Temple at Jerusalem," Journal of Biblical Literature, 55 (1936), 247-260.

Van Hoonacker, Albin. [2471] "Zorobabel et le second temple," Le Muséon, 10 (1891), 379-397, 489-515, 634-644.

de Vaux, Roland. [2472] "Les décrets de Cyrus et de Darius sur la reconstruction du Temple," Revue biblique, 46 (1937), 29-57. English version, "The Decrees of Cyrus and Darius on the Rebuilding of the Temple," in The Bible and the Ancient Near East. Garden City: Doubleday, 1971, 63-96.

Welten, Peter. [2473] "Lade-Tempel-Jerusalem: Zur Theologie der Chronikbücher," in O. Kaiser (ed.), Textgemäss: Aufsätze und Beiträge zur Hermeneutik des Alten Testaments (Festschrift Ernst Würthwein). Göttingen: Vanderhoeck and Ruprecht, 1979, 169-183.

Wright, John Stafford. [2474] The Buiding of the Second Temple. The Tyndale Old Testament Lecture, 1958. London: Tyndale Press, 1958, 20 pp.

Eighteen

Herod's Temple

Abecassis, A. [2475] "Les Pharisiens et le Temple," Le Monde de la Bible, 13 (1980), 39-40.

Aucler, Paul. [2476] "Le Temple de Jérusalem au temps de N.-S. Jésus Christ," Revue biblique, 7 (1898), 193-206.

Avi-Yonah, Michael. [2477] "The Facade of Herod's Temple: An Attempted Reconstruction," in J. Neusner (ed.), Religions in Antiquity: Essays in Memory of E. R. Goodenough. Leiden: E. J. Brill, 1968, 327-335.

Avi-Yonah, Michael and Safrai, Shmuel. [2478] "Temple: Second Temple," in Encyclopaedia Judaica, 15. Jerusalem: Macmillan, 1971, 958-983.

Bagatti, Bellarmino. [2479] "La posizione del tempio erodiano di Gerusalemme," Biblica, 46 (1965), 428-444.

Bammel, Ernst. [2480] "Nicanor and His Gate," Journal of Jewish Studies, 7 (1956), 77-78.

Barnett, R. D. [2481] "Reminiscences of Herod's Temple," Christian News from Israel, 12/3 (1961), 14-20.

Barrois, A. -G. (= Georges Augustin). [2481A] "Le Temple d' Hérode," in Manuel d' Archéologie biblique, 1. Paris: Picard, 1953, 449-452.

Barton, George A. [2482] "Temple of Herod," in Jewish Encyclopedia,1. New York: Funk and Wagnalls, 1905, 85-89.

Baumgarten, Joseph M. [2483] "Exclusions from the Temple: Proselytes and Agrippa I," Journal of Jewish Studies, 33 (1982), 215-225.

Belleli, L. [2484] "The High Priest's Procession on the Day of Atonement," Jewish Quarterly Review, 17 (1904-1905), 163-167.

Ben-Dov, Meir. [2485] "Herod's Monumental Enterprise, / The Walls of the Temple Mount, / The First Overpass in History, / The Gates of the Temple Mount," in In the Shadow of the Temple: The Discovery of Ancient Jerusalem. Jerusalem: Keter / New York: Harper and Row, 1985, 148-183.

Ben-Dov, Meir. [2486] "Temple of Herod," in Interpreters Dictionary of the Bible, Supplementary Volume. Nashville: Abingdon, 1976, 870-872.

Benzinger, Immanuel. [2487] "The Temple of Herod," in T. K. Cheyne and J. S. Black (eds.), Encyclopaedia Biblica, 4. London: A. and C. Black, 1903, 4943-4948.

Berto, P. [2488] "Le Temple de Jérusalem," Revue des études juives, 59 (1910), 14-35, 161-187; 60 (1911), 1-23.

"Beth Habbechereh, or The Chosen House," [2489] Palestine Exploration Fund, Quarterly Statement, (1885), 29-56, 140-147, 184-196. [Translation of Maimonides on the Temple.]

Bickerman, Elias. [2490] "The Warning Inscriptions of Herod's Temple," in Studies in Jewish and Christian History, 2. Leiden: Brill, 1980, 210-224. [Revision of article published originally in Jewish Quarterly Review, 37 (1946/1947), 387-405.]

Billerbeck, Paul. [2491] "Ein Tempelgottesdienst in Jesu Tagen," Zeitschrift für die neutestamentliche Wissenschaft, 55 (1964), 1-17.

Black, Matthew. See Schürer, Emil. [2630]

Blackman, P. See Middoth: [2603]

Bonsirven, Joseph. [2492] "Le Temple et ses liturgies," in Le Judaisme au Temps de Jésus-Christ, 2. Paris: G. Beauchesne, 1935, 107-136.

Briend, Jacques. [2493] "Le Temple d' Hérode le Grand," Le Monde de la Bible, 13 (1980), 12-13.

Büchler, Adolpf. [2494] "The Fore-Court of Women and the Brass Gate in the Temple of Jerusalem," Jewish Quarterly Review, 10 (1898) 678-718.

Büchler, Adolpf. [2495] "Zur Geschichte der Tempelmusik und der Tempelpsalmen," Zeitschrift für die alttestamentliche Wissenschaft, 19 (1899) 96-133, 329-344; 20 (1900), 97-135.

Büchler, Adolpf. [2496] "The Nicanor Gate and the Brass Gate," Jewish Quarterly Review, 11 (1899) 46-63.

Büchler, Adolpf. [2497] "On the History of the Temple Worship in Jerusalem," in I. Brodie and J. Rabbinowitz (eds.), Studies in Jewish History. London: Oxford University Press, 1956, 24-63.

Büchler, Adolpf. [2498] Die Priester und der Cultus im letzten Jahrzehnt des Jerusalemischen Tempels. Vienna: Israel-Theologische Lehranstalt, 1895, 207 pp.

Büchler, Adolpf. [2499] "The Visits of Gentiles to the Temple," Jewish Quarterly Review, n.s. 17 (1926/1927), 31-38.

Busink, Th. A. [2500] "Der Herodianische Tempel," in Der Tempel von Jerusalem von Salomo bis Middot, 2: Von Ezechiel bis Middot. Leiden: E. J. Brill, 1980, 1017-1251.

Busink, Th. A. [2501] "Der Tempel nach dem Traktat Middot," in Der Tempel von Jerusalem von Salomos bis Middot, 2: Von Ezechial bis Middot. Leiden: E. J. Brill, 1980, 1592-1574.

Busink, Th. A. [2502] "Untergang der Jerusalemer Tempels," in Der Tempel von Jerusalem von Salomos bis Middot, 2: Von Ezechiel bis Middot. Leiden: E. J. Brill, 1980, 1433-1528.

Caldecott, W. Shaw. [2503] Herod's Temple: Its New Testament Associations and its Actual Structure. London: C. H. Kelly, 1913 / Philadelphia: Union, 1914, 395 pp.

Caldecott, W. Shaw. [2504] The Second Temple in Jerusalem: Its History and its Structure. London: John Murray, 1908, 396 pp.

Caldecott, W. Shaw. [2505] "The Temple Spoils Represented on the Arch of Titus," Palestine Exploration Fund, Quarterly Statement, (1906), 306-315.

Celada, B. [2506] "El velo del Templo," Cultura Biblica, 15/159 (1958), 109-112.

Chaplin, Thomas. [2507] "The Stone of Foundation and the Site of the Temple," Palestine Exploration Fund, Quarterly Statement, (1876), 23-28.

Clark, Kenneth. [2508] "Worship in the Jerusalem Temple after A.D. 70," New Testament Studies, 6 (1960), 269-280; reprinted in The Gentle Bias and Other Essays. Leiden: E. J. Brill, 1980, 9-20.

Clermont-Ganneau, Charles. See St. Clair, George. [2624]

Clermont-Ganneau, Charles. [2509] "A Column of Herod's Temple," in Archaeological Researches in Palestine during the Years 1873-1874, 1. Translated by Aubrey Stewart. London: Palestine Exploration Fund, 1896, 254-258.

Clermont-Ganneau, Charles. [2510] "Discovery of a Tableau from Herod's Temple," Palestine Exploration Fund, Quarterly Statement, (1871), 132-133.

Clermont-Ganneau, Charles. [2511] "The 'Gate of Nicanor' in the Temple in Jerusalem," Palestine Exploration Fund, Quarterly Statement, (1903), 125-131.

Clermont-Ganneau, Charles. [2512] "La 'porte de Nicanor' du Temple de Jérusalem," Recueil d' Archéologie Orientale, 5 (1903), 334-340.

Clermont-Ganneau, Charles. [2513] "Une stèle du Temple de Jérusalem," Revue Archéologiques, 13th year, 23 (1872A), 214-234, 290-296.

Clermont-Ganneau, Charles. [2514] "The Veil of the Temple," in C. Warren and C. R. Conder, The Survey of Western Palestine, 5: Jerusalem. London: Palestine Exploration Fund, 1884, 340-341.

Cohen, J. [2515] "Les pèlerinages au Temple de Jérusalem," Le Monde de la Bible, 13 (1980), 29-32.

Conder, Claude R. [2516] "Age of the Temple Wall: Pilasters of the West Haram Wall," Palestine Exploration Fund, Quarterly Statement, (1877), 135-137.

Conder, Claude R. [2517] "Herod's Temple," in The City of Jerusalem. London: John Murray, 1909, 123-132.

Conder, Claude R. [2518] "The High Sanctuary of Jerusalem," Transactions of the Royal Institute of British Architects, (1879), 25-60.

Conder, Claude R. [2519] "Notes on Colonel Wilson's Paper on the Masonry of the Haram Wall," Palestine Exploration Fund, Quarterly Statement, (1880), 91-97.

Conder, Claude R. [2520] "Supposed Cliff in the Haram," Palestine Exploration Fund, Quarterly Statement, (1881), 56-60.

Corbett, Spencer. [2521] "Some Observations on the Gateways to the Herodian Temple in Jerusalem," Palestine Exploration Quarterly, (1952) 7-14.

Cornfeld, Gaalya (general editor) with Mazar, Benjamin and Maier, Paul L. (consulting editors). [2522] "Description of the Temple," in Josephus, The Jewish War. Newly Translated with Extensive Commentary and Archaeological Background Illustrations. Grand Rapids: Zondervan, 1982, 346-364.

Cornfeld, Gaalya. [2523] The Mystery of the Temple Mount: New Guidebook to Discovery. Tel Aviv/New York: Bazak Israel Guidebook Publishers, 1972. 112 pp.

Dalman, Gustaf. [2524] "Der Felsen als Fundament des Altars," in Neue Petra-Forschungen und der heilige Felsen von Jerusalem. Leipzig: J. C. Hinrichs'sche Buchhandlung, 1912, 137-145.

Dalman, Gustaf. [2525] "Der zweite Tempel zu Jerusalem," Palästinajahrbuch, 5 (1909), 29-57.

Danby, Herbert. See Middoth: [2604]

Danby, Herbert. See Moses ben Maimon: [2606]

Daniélou, Jean. [2526] "La Symbolique du Tempel de Jérusalem chez Philon et Josèphe," in Le Symbolisme Cosmique des Monuments Religieux. Rome: Is. M.E.O., 1957, 83-90.

Davies, T. Witton. [2527] "Herod's Temple," in James Hastings (ed.), Dictionary of the Bible, 4. New York: Scribner's, 1898, 711-716.

Demsky, Aaron. [2528] "The Trumpeter's Inscription from the Temple Mount," in Eretz-Israel, 18. Jerusalem: Israel Exploration Society, 1985, 40-42 (Hebrew), 66* (English summary).

Derenbourg, Joseph. [2529] "Une stèle du Tempel d'Hérode," Journal Asiatique, 6th ser., 20 (1872), 178-195.

Doeve, J. W. [2530] "Le domaine du Temple de Jérusalem," in W. van Unnik (ed.), La littérature juive entre Tenach et Mischna: quelques problemes. Recherches bibliques, 9. Leiden: Brill, 1974, 118-163.

Donner, Herbert. [2531] "Der Felsen und der Tempel," Zeitschrift des deutschen Palästina-Vereins, 93 (1977), 1-11.

Dussaud, René. [2532] "Des Fouilles à entreprendre sur l'emplacement du Temple de Jérusalem," Revue de l`Histoire des Religions, 79 (1919), 319-327.

Edersheim, Alfred. [2533] The Temple, its Ministry and Services as they Were at the Time of Jesus Christ. Boston: Bradley and Woodruff, rev. edn., 1904. Reprinted: Grand Rapids: Eerdmans, 1951. 367 pp.

Eisenstein, J. D. [2534] "Temple, Plan of Second," in The Jewish Encyclopedia, 12. New York: Funk and Wagnalls, 1905, 89-92.

Eisenstein, J. D. [2535] "Temple, Administration and Service of," in The Jewish Encyclopedia, 12. New York: Funk and Wagnalls, 1905, 81-85.

Eisenstein, J. D. [2536] "Temple in Rabbinical Literature," in The Jewish Encyclopedia, 12. New York: Funk and Wagnalls, 1905, 92-97.

Eltester, Walther. [2537] "Der Siebenarmige Leuchter und der Titus-bogen," in W. Eltester (ed.), Judentum, Urchristentum, Kirche (Festschrift Joachim Jeremias). Berlin: A Töpelmann, 1960, 62-76.

Falk, Zev. [2538] "The Law of Temple and Priests in the Halakah," in P. Peli (ed.), Proceedings of the Fifth World Congress of Jewish Studies, 1969, 1. Jerusalem: World Union of Jewish Studies, n. d. [1972], 105-109 (Hebrew), 236-237 (English summary).

Finegan, Jack. [2539] "The Pinacle of the Temple, / The Double Gate, / The Triple Gate, / The Golden Gate, / Robinson's Arch, /Wilson's Arch," in Archeology of the New Testament: The Life of Jesus and the Beginnings of the Early Church. Princeton: Princeton University Press, 1969, 125-132.

Finegan, Jack. [2540] "Plan of the Temple of Herod, / Fragment of a Warning Inscription from Herod's Temple," in Archeology of the New Testament: The Life of Jesus and the Beginnings of the Early Church. Princeton: Princeton University Press, 1969, 117-120.

Fleming, James. [2541] "The Uncovered Gate beneath Jerusalem's Golden Gate," Biblical Archaeology Review, 9/1 (Jan.-Feb., 1983), 24-37.

Galling, Kurt. [2542] "Die Halle des Schreibers," Palästinajahrbuch, 27 (1931), 51-57.

Galling, Kurt. [2543] "Herodianischer Tempel," in Religion in Geschichte und Gegenwart, 5. Tübingen: J. C. B. Mohr (Siebeck), 1931, 1045-1046.

Gese, Hartmut. [2544] "Zur Geschichte der Kultsänger am zweiten Tempel," in Abraham unser Vater (Festschrift O. Michel). Arbeiten zur Geschichte des Spätjudentums und Urchristentum, 5. Leiden: Brill, 1963, 222-234.

Goldschmidt-Lehmann, Ruth P. [2545] "The Second (Herodian) Temple, Selected Bibliography," in L. I. Levine, (ed.), Jerusalem Cathedra, I. Jerusalem: Ben-Zvi Institute, 1981, 336-358.

Graetz, H. [2546] "Die Höfe und Thore des zwetien Tempels: Eine archäologische Untersuchung," Monatsschrift für Geschichte und Wissenschaft des Judenthums, 25 (1876), 385-397.

Graetz, H. [2547] "Die musikalischen Instrumente im jerusalemischen Tempel und der musikalische Chor der Leveiten," Monatsschrift für Geschichte und Wissenschaft des Judenthums, 30 (1881), 241-259.

Grafman, R. [2548] "Herod's Foot and Robinson's Arch," Israel Exploration Journal, 20 (1970), 60-66.

Grünhut, L. [2549] "Der Raum des Tempels nach Estori hap-Parchi," Zeitschrift des deutschen-Palästina Vereins, 31 (1908), 281-296.

Gutmann, Joseph. [2550] "A Note on the Temple Menorah," Zeitschrift für die neutestamentliche Wissenschaft, 60 (1969), 289-291.

Guttman, Alexander. [2551] "The End of the Jewish Sacrificial Cult," Hebrew Union College Annual, 38 (1967), 137-148.

Hachlili, Rahel and Merhav, Rivkah. [2552] "The Menorah in First and Second Temple Times in the Light of the Sources and Archaeology," in Eretz-Israel, 18. Jerusalem: Israel Exploration Society, 1985, 256-267 (Hebrew), 74* (English summary).

Hanauer, James Edward. [2553] "Cuttings in the Rock in the Haram Area," Palestine Exploration Fund, Quarterly Statement, (1891), 206-207.

Hanauer, James Edward. [2554] "A Subterranean Passage in Solomon's Stables," Palestine Exploration Fund, Quarterly Statement, (1891), 204-205.

Heinemann, Joseph. [2555] "Prayer in the Temple," in Prayer in the Talmud: Forms and Patterns. Berlin: Walter de Gruyter, 1977, 123-138.

"The Herodian Temple, according to the Treatise Middoth and Flavius Josephus," [2556] Palestine Exploration Fund, Quarterly Statement, (1886), 92-113. Appears to be an English translation of Hildesheimer, Israel. [2558]

Herr, Moshe David. [2557] "Jerusalem, the Temple and its Cult: Reality and Concepts in Second Temple Times," in A. Oppenheimer, U. Rappaport, and M. Stern (eds.), Jerusalem in the Second Temple Period: Abraham Schalit Memorial Volume. Jerusalem: Yad Izhaq Ben-Zvi, 1980, 166-177 (Hebrew), X-XI (English summary).

Hildesheimer, Israel. [2558] Die Beschreibung des Herodianischen Tempels im Tractate Middoth und bei Flavius Josephus. Berlin: Rabbiner-seminar, 1877, 32 pp.

Hoenig, Sidney. [2559] "The Suppositious Temple-Synagogue," Jewish Quarterly Review, 54 (1963/64), 115-131. Also in J. Guttman (ed.), The Synagogue: Studies in Origins, Archaeology and Architecture. New York: KTAV, 1975, 55-131.

Hollis, Frederick J. [2560] The Archaeology of Herod's Temple, with a Commentary on the Tractate Middoth. London: J. M. Dent, 1934, 366 pp.

Holtzmann, Oskar. [2561] "Tore und Terrassen des herodianischen Tempels," Zeitschrift für neutestamentliche Wissenschaft, 9 (1908), 71-74.

Holzinger, Heinrich. [2562] "Der Schaubrottisch des Titusbogens," Zeitschrift für die alttestamentliche Wissenschaft, 21 (1901), 341-342.

Hull, Edward. [2563] "Where are the Sacred Vessels of the Temple?" Palestine Exploration Fund, Quarterly Statement, (1896), 344.

Iliffe, J. H. [2564] "The Thanatos Inscription from Herod's Temple: Fragments of a Second Copy," Quarterly of the Department of Antiquities in Palestine. 6 (1938), 1-3.

Isaac, Benjamin. [2565] "A Donation for Herod's Temple in Jerusalem," Israel Exploration Journal, 33 (1983), 86-92.

Isaac, Benjamin. [2566] "A Donation for Herod's Temple in Jerusalem," in Eretz-Israel, 18. Jerusalem: Israel Exploration Society, 1985, 1-4 (Hebrew), 65* (English summary).

Isenberg, Sheldon R. [2567] "Power through Temple and Torah in Greco-Roman Palestine," in J. Neusner (ed.), Christianity, Judaism, and Other Greco-Roman Cults: Studies for Morton Smith at Sixty, 2. Leiden: Brill, 1975, 24-52.

Jacobson, David M. [2568] "Ideas Concerning the Plan of Herod's Temple," Palestine Exploration Quarterly, (1980), 33-40.

Jeremias, Joachim. [2569] "The Clergy," in Jerusalem in the Time of Jesus: An Investigation into Economic and Social Conditions during the New Testament Period. Translated by F. H. and C. H. Cave. Philadelphia: Fortress Press, 1969, 147-221.

Jeremias, Joachim. [2570] "The Unique Character of Jerusalem as an Attraction to Travellers from Abroad / The Number of Pilgrims at the Passover / On Calculating the Number of Festival Pilgrims," in Jerusalem in the Time of Jesus: An Investigation into Economic and Social Conditions during the New Testament Period. Philadelphia: Fortress Press, 1969, 73-84.

Jeremias, Joachim and Schneider, Alfons Maria. [2571] "Das westliche Sudtor des herodianischen Tempels," Zeitschrift des deutschen Palästina-Vereins, 65 (1942), 112-121. Reprinted in J. Jeremias, Abba: Studien zur neutestamentlichen Theologie und Zeitgeschichte. Gottingen: Vandenhoeck and Ruprecht, 1966, 353-360.

Kaufman, Asher. [2572] "Determining the Length of the Medium Cubit," Palestine Exploration Quarterly, (1984), 120-132. [Concerned primarily with author's theory on the location of the Temple.]

Kaufman, Asher. [2573] "The Eastern Wall of the Second Temple of Jerusalem Revealed," Biblical Archaeologist, 44 (1981), 108-115.

Kaufman, Asher. [2574] "New Light on the Ancient Temple of Jerusalem," Christian News from Israel, 27/2 (1979), 54-58.

Kaufman, Asher. [2575] "New Light upon Zion: The Plan and Precise Location of the Second Temple," Ariel, 43 (1977), 63-99.

Kaufman, Asher. [2576] "A Note on Artistic Representations of the Second Temple of Jerusalem," Biblical Archaeologist, 47 (1984), 253-254.

Kaufman, Asher. [2577] "Temple," in Encyclopaedia Judaica, 17, Supplement. Jerusalem: Keter, n.d. [1981], 577-580.

Kaufman, Asher. [2578] "Temple," in Encyclopaedia Judaica Yearbook, 1975/6. Jerusalem: Encyclopaedia Judaica, 1976, 393-397.

Kaufman, Asher. [2579] "Where the Ancient Temple of Jerusalem Stood," Biblical Archaeology Review, 9/2 (March/April, 1983), 40-59.

Kennedy, A. R. S. [2580] "Some Problems of Herod's Temple," Expository Times, 20 (1908/1909), 24-27, 66-69, 181-183, 270-273.

Kennedy, A. R. S. and Snaith, Norman H. [2581] "The Temple of Herod," in James Hastings (ed.), Dictionary of the Bible, revised edn. by F. C. Grant and H. H. Rowley. New York: Scribners, 1963, 965-968.

Klein, H. Arthur. See Klein, Mina C. and Klein, H. Arthur. [2582]

Klein, Mina C. and Klein, H. Arthur. [2582] "The Great Temple Rises (22-4 B.C.E.)," in Temple beyond Time: The Story of the site of Solomon's Temple at Jerusalem. New York: Van Nostrand Reihold, 1970, 94-99.

Klimowsky, Ernst W. [2583] "Symbols on Ancient Jewish Coins / Religious Symbols on Ancient Jewish Coins," in On Ancient Palestinian and Other Coins: Their Symbolism and Metrology. Numismatic Studies and Researches, 7. Tel Aviv: Israel Numismatic Society, 1974, 21-50.

Kon, Maxmilian. [2584] "The Menorah of the Arch of Titus," Palestine Exploration Quarterly, (1950), 25-30.

Lagrange, Marie-Joseph. [2585] "Comment s'est formée l'enciènte du Temple de Jérusalem," Revue biblique, 2 (1893), 90-113.

Lande-Nash, Irene. [2586] "Der herodianische Tempel," in 3000 Jahre Jerusalem: Eine Geschichte der Stadt von den Anfängen bis zur Eroberung durch die Kreuzfahrer. Tübingen: Verlag Ernst Wamuth, 1964, 101-11.

de Langhe, Robert. [2587] "L'autel d' or du Temple de Jérusalem," Biblica, 40 (1959), 476-494. Also in Studia biblica et orientalia Analecta biblica, 10. Rome: Pontifical Biblical Institute, 1959, 342-360.

Legasse, Simon. [2588] "Les voiles du Temple de Jérusalem," Revue biblique, 87 (1980), 560-589.

Lesetre, Henri. [2589] Le Temple de Jérusalem. Paris: G. Beauchesne, 1912, 216 pp.

Lesetre, Henri. [2590] "Le Temple d'Hérode," in F. Vigouroux (ed.), Dictionnaire de la Bible, vol. 5/2. Paris: Letouzey et Ané, 1912, 2051-2074.

Lewittes, M. See Moses ben Maimon: [2607]

Lieberman, Saul. [2591] "The Temple: Its Layout and Procedure," in Hellenism in Jewish Palestine. New York: Jewish Theological Seminary of America, 1950, 164-179.

Lohse, Eduard. [2592] "Temple and Synagogue," in H. J. Schultz (ed.), Jesus in His Time. Philadelphia: Fortress Press, 1971, 75-83.

Mackowski, Richard M. [2593] "The City of the Temple," in Jerusalem, City of Jesus: An Exploration of the Traditions, Writings, and Remains of the Holy City from the Time of Christ. Grand Rapids: Eerdmans, 1980, 113-137.

Magen, Yizhaq. [2594] "Bet Ha-Mesibah in the Temple Scroll and in the Mishnah," in Eretz-Israel, 17. Jerusalem: Israel Exploration Society, 1984, 226-235 (Hebrew), 10* (English Summary).

Magen, Yizhaq. [2595] "The Gates of the Temple Mount according to Josephus and the Mishnah (Middot)," Cathedra: History of Eretz-Israel, 14 (1980), 41-53 (Hebrew).

Maier, Johann. [2596] "Religionsgeschichtliche Aspekte Frühjudischer Institutionen: Tempel und Tempelkult," in J. Maier and J. Schreiner (eds.), Literatur und Religion des Frühjudentums. Würzburg: Echter Verlag / Gutersloh: Verlaghaus Gerd Mohn, 1973, 371-390.

Maier, Paul. See Cornfeld, Gaalya with Mazar, Benjamin and Maier, Paul L. [2522]

Manns, Fréderic. [2597] "A Priest's Day in the Temple of Jerusalem," The Holy Land, 5/3 (1985), 139-146.

Mantel, Hugo. [2598] "The Highpriesthood and the Sanhedrin in the time of the Second temple," in M. Avi-yonah (ed.), World History of the Jewish People, 7: The Herodian Period. New Brunswick: Rutgers University Press, 1975, 264-281.

Mazar, Benjamin. See Cornfeld, Gaalya with Mazar, Benjamin and Maier, Paul L. [2522]

Mazar, Benjamin. [2599] "Exploration of the Wilson Arch and the Northern Extension of the Western Wall," in The Mountain of the Lord. Garden City, NY: Doubleday, 1975, 217-222.

Mazar, Benjamin. [2600] "Herod's Temple / Functions of the Outer Walls and Gates of the Temple Mount," in The Mountain of the Lord. Garden City: Doubleday, 1975, 106-152.

Mazar, Benjamin. [2601] "The Royal Stoa on the Southern Part of the Temple Mount," in S. Baron and I. E. Barzilay (eds.), Proceedings of the American Academy for Jewish Research, Jubilee Volume (1928/29-1978/79), 2. New York: Columbia University Press, 1980, 381-387. Also in H. Shanks and B. Mazar (eds.), Recent Archaeology in the Land of Israel. Washington, DC: Biblical Archaeology Society / Jerusalem: Israel Exploration Society, 1985, 141-147.

Merhav, Rivkah. See Hachlili, Rahel and Merhav, Rivkah. [2552]

Meyers, Carol L. [2602] "The Temple," in Harper's Dictionary of the Bible. San Francisco: Harper & Row, 1985, 1021-1032.

Middoth. See Busink, Th. A. [2501]

Middoth: See "The Herodian Temple, according to the Treatise Middoth and Flavius Josephus," [2556]

Middoth: See Hildesheimer, Israel. [2558]

Middoth: See Hollis, Frederick J. [2560]

Middoth: See "The Tract 'Middoth' - On the Measurements of the Temple, Literally Translated from the Mishna," [2655]

Middoth: [2603] Hebrew Text, English translation and notes in P. Blackman, Mishnayoth, 5: Kodashim. New York: Judaica Press, 1965, 501-533.

Middoth: [2604] English translation with brief explanatory notes in H. Danby, The Mishnah. London: Oxford University Press, 1933, 589-598.

"Middoth, or the Measurements of the Temple, with the Commentary of Rabbi Obadiah of Bartenora," [2605] Palestine Exploration Fund, Quarterly Statement, (1886), 224-228; (1887), 60-63, 116-128, 132.

Millar, F. See Schürer, Emil. [2630]

Moses ben Maimon: See "Beth Habbechereh, or The Chosen House," [2489]

Moses ben Maimon: See Wischnitzer, Rachel. [2670]

Moses ben Maimon: [2606] The Book of Offerings, translated from the Hebrew by H. Danby. Yale Judaica Series, 4. New Haven: Yale University Press, 1950, 307 pp.

Moses ben Maimon: [2607] The Book of Temple Service, translated from the Hebrew by M. Lewittes. Yale Judaica Series, 17. New Haven: Yale University Press, 1957, 525 pp.

Muehsam, Alice. [2608] Coin and Temple: A Study of the Architectural Representation in Ancient Jewish Coins. Leiden: Brill, 1966, 70 pp.

Narkiss, Bezalel. [2609] "The Scheme of the Sanctuary from the Time of Herod the Great," Journal of Jewish Art, 1 (1974), 6-14.

Nickelsburg, George W. E. and Stone, Michael. [2610] "Temple and Cult," in Faith and Piety in Early Judaism: Texts and Documents. Philadelphia: Fortress Press, 1983, 51-88.

Oesterley, W. O. E. [2611] "Herod's Temple," in T. H. Robinson and W. O. E. Oesterley, A History of Israel, 2: From the Fall of Jerusalem, 586 B.C. to the Bar Koknba Revolt, A.D. 135. Oxford: Clarendon Press, 1932, 376-378.

Parrot, André. [2612] "Herod's Temple," in The Temple of Jerusalem. Studies in Biblical Archaeology, 5. New York: Philosophical Library, 1955; London: SCM Press, 1957; reprinted, Westport, CN: Greenwood Publishers, 1985, 76-100.

Pelletier, André. [2613] "Le Grand Rideau du vestibule du Temple de Jérusalem," Syria, 35 (1958), 218-226.

Pelletier, André. [2614] "Le 'voile' du temple de Jérusalem est-il devenu la 'Portière' du temple d'Olympie? (IMac., I, 22 et Pausanius,V, 12, 4)," Syria, 32 (1955), 289-307.

Pelletier, André. [2615] "Le 'voile du Temple' de Jérusalem en termes de métier," Revue des études grecques, 77 (1964), 70-75.

Rabello, Alfred M. [2616] "The 'Lex de Templo Hiersolymitano,' Prohibiting Gentiles from Entering Jerusalem's Sanctuary," Christian News from Israel, 21/3 (1970), 28-32; 21/4 (1970), 28-32.

Reinach, Salomon. [2617] "L'Arc de Titus," Revue des études juives, 20 (1890), lxv-xci.

Rengstorf, Karl H. [2618] "Erwägungen zur Frage des Landbesitzes des zweiten Tempels in Judäa und seiner Verwaltung," in S. Wagner (ed.), Bibel und Qumran (Festschrift Hans Bardtke). Berlin: Evangelische Haupt-Bibelgesselschaft, 1968, 156-175.

Renov, Israel. [2619] "A View of Herod's Temple from Nicanor's Gate in a Mural Panel of the Dura-Europas Synagogue," Israel Exploration Journal, 20 (1970), 67-72, with editor's note, by M. Avi-Yonah, 73-74.

Rofé, Y. [2620] "The Site of Our Holy Temple-- the Location of the Temple at the Southern End of the the Temple Mount," Niv Hamidrashia, 13 (1978/1979), 166-186 (Hebrew), 105-113 (plans and English summary).

Rothkoff, Aaron. [2621] "Sacrifice: Second Temple Period," in Encyclopaedia Judaica, 14. Jerusalem: Macmillan, 1971, 607-615.

Safrai, Shmuel. See Avi-Yonah, Michael and Safrai, Shmuel. [2478]

Safrai, Shmuel. [2622] "The Temple," in S. Safrai and M. Stern (ed.), The Jewish People in the First Century, 2. Compendia rerum iudaicarum ad novum testamentum, I/2. Assen / Amsterdam: Van Gorcum, 1976, 865-907.

Safrai, Shmuel. [2623] "The Temple and the Divine Service," in M. Avi-Yonah, (ed.), World History of the Jewish People,7: The Herodian Period. New Brunswick: Rutgers University Press, 1975, 282-337.

St. Clair, George. [2624] "Note on M. Ganneau's Discovery of an Inscribed Stone of the Temple of Jerusalem," Palestine Exploration Fund, Quarterly Statement, (1871), 172-173.

Schaffer, Shaul. [2625] Israel's Temple Mount: The Jews Magnificent Sanctuary. Jerusalem: S. Schaffer, 1975, 299 pp.

Schick, Conrad. [2626] "Discoveries in 'Solomon's Stables,'" Palestine Exploration Fund, Quarterly Statement, (1891), 198-199.

Schick, Conrad. [2627] "The Newly Discovered Arch in 'Solomon's Stables,'" Palestine Exploration Fund, Quarterly Statement, (1891), 200-201.

Schick, Conrad. [2628] Die Stiftschütte der Tempel in Jerusalem und der Tempelplatz der Jetztzeit. Berlin: Weidmannsche Buchhandlung, 1896, 363 pp.

Schmidt, Hans. [2629] "Der Fels im Tempel des Herodes," in Der heilige Fels in Jerusalem: Eine archäologische und religionsgeschichtliche Studie. Tübingen: Mohr (Siebeck), 1933, 17-39.

Schneider, Alfons Maria. See Jeremias, Joachim and Schneider, Alfons Maria. [2571]

Schürer, Emil. [2630] "Priesthood and Temple Worship," in The History of the Jewish People in the Age of Jesus Christ (175 B.C. - A.D. 135), 2. New English version revised and edited by G. Vermes and F. Millar (literary editor, P. Vermes; organizing editor, M. Black). Edinburgh: T. + T. Clark, 1979, 237-313.

Schürer, Emil. [2631] "Die Thura oder Pule oraia (Acts 3, 2 v. 10)," Zeitschrift für neuentestamentiche Wissenschaft, 7 (1906), 51-68.

Schürer, Emil. [2632] "Der Versammlungsort der Grossen Synedriums: Ein Beitrag zur Topographie des herodianischen Tempels," Theologische Studien und Kritiken, 51 (1878), 608-626.

Schwartz, Daniel R. [2633] "Viewing the Holy Utinsels (P. Ox. V, 840)," New Testament Studies, 32 (1986), 153-159.

Schwarz, Adolf. [2634] "Die Schatzkammer des Tempels in Jerusalem," Monatsschrift für Geschichte und Wissenschaft, 63 (1919), 227-252.

Simon, Marcel. [2635] "On Josephus, War, V, 5, 7," Jewish Quarterly Review, 13 (1901) 547-48.

Simons, Jan. [2636] "The Problem of the Temple," in Jerusalem in the Old Testament: Researches and Theories. Leiden: Brill, 1952, 381-436.

Simpson, William. [2637] "Robinson's Arch," Palestine Exploration Fund, Quarterly Statement, (1869/70), 46-48.

Simpson, William, [2638] "The Temple and the Mount of Olives," Palestine Exploration Fund, Quarterly Statement, (1897), 307-308.

Simpson, William. [2639] "Where are the Sacred Vessels of the Temple?" Palestine Exploration Fund, Quarterly Statement, (1897), 77-80.

Snaith, Norman H. See Kennedy, A. R. S. and Snaith, Norman H. [2581]

Spiess, F. [2640] "Die königliche Halle des Herodes im Temple von Jerusalem," Zeitschrift des deutschen Palästina-Vereins, 15 (1892), 234-256.

Spiess, F. [2641] Der Tempel zu Jerusalem während des letzten Jahrhunderts seines Bestandes nach Josephus. Berlin: C. Habel, 1880, 36 pp.

Starcky, J. [2642] "Le Temple hérodien et les sanctuaires orientaux," Le Monde de la Bible, 13 (1980), 14-18.

Stauffer, Ethelbert. [2643] "Das Tor des Nikanor," Zeitschrift für neuentestamentliche Wissenschaft, 44 (1952/53), 44-66.

Stein, Murray. [2644] "How Herod Moved Gigantic Blocks to Construct Temple Mount," Biblical Archaeology Review, 7/3 (1981), 42-46.

Stern, Menahem. [2645] "Priests and Priesthood: From the Beginning of the Hellenistic Period to the Destruction of the Temple," in Encyclopaedia Judaica, 13. Jerusalem: Macmillan, 1971, 1086-1088.

Steve, M.-A. See Vincent, Louis-Hugues and Steve, M.-A. [2659-2660]

Stinespring, William F. [2646] "Temple, Jerusalem: The Temple of Herod," in Interpreter's Dictionary of the Bible, 4. New York: Abingdon, 1962, 550-560.

Stinespring, William F. [2647] "Temple Research in Jerusalem," Duke Divinity School Review, 29 (1964), 85-101.

Stinespring, William F. [2648] "Wilson's Arch and the Masonic Hall, Summer, 1966," Biblical Archaeologist, 30 (1967), 27-31.

Stinespring, William F. [2649] "Wilson's Arch Revisited," Biblical Archaeologist, 29 (1966), 27-36.

Stone, Michael. See Nickelsburg, George W. E. and Stone, Michael. [2610]

"Tamid, or the Continual Service, with the Commentary of Rabbi Obadiah of Bartenora," [2650] Palestine Exploration Fund, Quarterly Statement, (1886), 199-130, 213-223.

Taylor, W. R. [2651] "A Jerusalem Forgery of the Balustrade Inscription of Herod's Temple," Journal of the Palestine Oriental Society, 13 (1933), 137-139.

Taylor, W. R. [2652] "A Second Forgery of the Balustrade Inscription of Herod's Temple, Journal of the Palestine Oriental Society, 16 (1936), 37-38.

Tenz, J. M. [2653] "Position of the Altar of Burnt Sacrifice in the Temple of Jerusalem," Palestine Exploration Fund, Quarterly Statement, (1910), 137-139.

Townsend, John T. [2654] "The Jerusalem Temple in the First Century," in L. E. Frizzell (ed.), God and His Temple. South Orange, NJ: Seton Hall University, Institute for Judaeo-Christian Studies, 1980, 48-65.

"The Tract 'Middoth' - On the Measurements of the Temple, Literally Translated from the Mishna," [2655] Palestine Exploration Fund, Quarterly Statement, (1872), 12-19.

Vajda, G. [2656] "La description du Temple de Jérusalem d' apres le K. al-Masalik wal-mamalik d' al-Muhallabi-- ses éléments bibliques et rabbiniques, Journal asiatique, 247 (1959), 193-202.

Van der Muelen, H. E. Faber. [2657] "One or Two Veils in Front of the Holy of Holies?" Theologica Evangelica, 18 (1985), 22-27.

Vermes, G. See Schürer, Emil. [2630]

Vermes, P. See Schürer, Emil. [2630]

Vincent, Louis-Hugues. [2658] "Le Temple Hérodien d'après la Mishnah," Revue biblique, 61 (1954), 5-35, 398-418.

Vincent, Louis-Hugues and Steve, M.-A. [2659] "Le Temple d' Hérode," in Jérusalem de l'Ancien Testament, 2. Paris: Gabalda, 1956, 432-470.

Vincent, Louis-Hugues and Steve, M.-A. [2660] "Le Temple herodien a'près la Misnah," Jérusalem de l'Ancien Testament, 2. Paris: Gabalda, 1956, 496-523.

Vogt, Ernst. [2661] "Vom Tempel zum Felsendom," Biblica, 55 (1974), 23-64.

de Vogüé, Melchior. [2662] Le Temple de Jérusalem: Monographie du Haram-ech-Chérif, suive d'un essai sur la topographie de la Ville Sainte. Paris: Noblet and Baudry, 1864-1865, 146 pp.

Walker, Norman. [2663] "The Riddle of the Ass's Head, and the Question of a Trigram," Zeitschrift für die alttestamentliche Wissenschaft, 75 (1963), 225-227.

Warren, Charles. [2664] "The Temple of Herod," Palestine Exploration Fund, Quarterly Statement, (1875), 97-101.

Warren, Charles. [2665] "Notes on Colonel Wilson's Paper on the Masonry of the Haram Wall," Palestine Exploration Fund, Quarterly Statement, (1880), 159-166.

Watson, Charles M. [2666] "The Position of the Altar of Burnt Sacrifice in the Temple of Jerusalem," Palestine Exploration Fund, Quarterly Statement, (1910), 15-22.

Watson, Charles M. [2667] "The Site of the Temple," Palestine Exploration Fund, Quarterly Statement, (1896), 47-60, 226-228.

Wiesenberg, Ernest. [2668] "The Nicanor Gate," Journal of Jewish Studies, 3 (1952), 14-29. [cf. "corrections" in Journal of Jewish Studies, 4 (1953), 91.]

Wilson, Charles W. See Conder, Claude R. [2519]

Wilson, Charles W. See Warren, Charles. [2665]

Wilson, Charles W. [2669] "The Masonry of the Haram Wall," Palestine Exploration Fund, Quarterly Statement, (1880), 9-65.

Wischnitzer, Rachel. [2670] "Maimonides' Drawings of the Temple," Journal of Jewish Art, 1 (1974), 16-27.

Wrightson, T. [2671] "On the Relation of Certain Arch Springings Found Within the Area of the Temple of Jerusalem," Palestine Exploration Fund, Quarterly Statement, (1891), 219-224.

Zeitlin, Solomon. [2672] "The Temple," in The Rise and Fall of the Judaean State, 1. Philadelphia: Jewish Publication Society, 2nd edn., 1968, 256-268.

Zeitlin, Solomon. [2673] "The Temple and Worship," Jewish Quarterly Review, n.s. 51 (1961), 209-241.

Zeitlin, Solomon. [2674] "There was no Court of Gentiles in the Temple Area," Jewish Quarterly Review, 56 (1965-1966), 88.

Zeitlin, Solomon. [2675] "There was no Synagogue in the Temple," Jewish Quarterly Review, 53 (1962/63), 168-169.

Zeitlin, Solomon. [2676] "The Warning Inscription of the Temple," Jewish Quarterly Review, 38 (1947/1948), 111-116.

Zimmerman, Michael A. "Tunnel Exposes New Areas of Temple Mount," Biblical Archaeology Review, 7 / 3 (1981), 33-41.

Nineteen

The Essenes and Jerusalem

Allegro, John M. [2678] "Florilegium." in Discoveries in the Judaean Desert, 5: Qumrân Cave 4, I. Oxford: Clarendon Press, 1968, 53-57., pl XXI. [On 4Q 174.] For corrections, see Strugnell, John. [2747]

Allegro, John M. [2679] The Treasure of the Copper Scroll. Garden City, NY: Doubleday, 1960, 191 pp. [Topography.] For corrections, see Milik, J. T. [2731]

Baillet, Maurice. [2680] "Description de la Jérusalem nouvelle," in M. Baillet, J. T. Milik, and R. de Vaux, Discoveries in the Judaean Desert, 3: Les 'Petites Grottes' de Qumrân. Oxford: Clarendon Press, 1962. Textes, 84-89; Planches, XVI. [On 2Q 24.]

Baillet, Maurice. [2681] "Fragments araméens de Qumrân 2, Description de la Jérusalem nouvelle," Revue biblique, 62 (1955), 222-245.

Barthélemy, D. and Milik, J. T. [2682] "'Description de la Jérusalem nouvelle' (?)," in Discoveries in the Judaean Desert, 1: Qumrân Cave I. Oxford: Clarendon Press, 1955, 134-135; pl. XXXI. [On 1Q 32.]

Baumgarten, Joseph M. [2683] "Sacrifices and Worship among the Jewish Sectaries of the Dead Sea (Qumrân) Scrolls," Harvard Theological Review, 46 (1953), 141-159.

Ben-Yashar, Menachem. [2684] "Noch zum Miqdash 'Adam in 4Q Florilegium," Revue de Qumrân, 10 (1981), 587-588.

Betz, Otto. [2685] "Le ministère cultuel dans la secte de Qumrân et dans le Christianisme," in La secte de Qumrân et les origines du Christianisme. Recherches bibliques, 4. Paris: Descelée de Brouwer, 1959,163-202.

Brooke, George J. [2686] Exegesis at Qumrân: 4Q Florilegium in its Jewish Context. Journal for the Study of the Old Testament, Supplement Series, 29. Sheffield: JSOT Press, 1985, 390 pp.

Burgmann, Hans. [2687] "Das Kultmahl der Qumrangemeinde und der politische Gegensatz zum Makkabäer Jonathan," Theologische Zeitschrift, 27 (1971), 385-398. [Cult meal as protest against liturgy of Jerusalem Temple.]

Callaway, Phillip. [2688] "Exegetisch Erwägung zur Tempelrolle XXIX, 7-10," Revue de Qumran, 12/45 (1985), 95-104.

Carmignac, Jean. [2689] "Le document de Qumrân sur Melkisédeq," Revue de Qumran, 7 (1970), 343-378.

Cullmann, Oscar. [2690] "L' opposition contre le Temple de Jérusalem, motif commun de la théologie johannique et du monde ambiant, " New Testament Studies, 5 (1958/1959), 157-173. ["monde ambiant" = Qumrân.]

Cullmann, Oscar. [2691] "A New Approach to the Interpretation of the Fourth Gospel," Expository Times, 71 (1959), 39-43. English version of Cullmann, Oscar. [2690]

Dagut, M. H. [2692] "The Habbakuk Scroll and Pompey's Capture of Jerusalem," Biblica, 32 (1951), 542-548.

Davies, Philip R. [2693] "The Ideology of the Temple in the Damascus Document," Journal of Jewish Studies, 33 (1982), 287-301.

Delcor, M. [2694] "Repas cultuels esséniens et thérapeutes. Thiases et Haburoth," Revue de Qumrân, 6/23 (1968), 401-425. [Demurs on meals as cultic acts among Essenes and related groups.]

Dupont-Sommer, A. [2695] "Les rouleaux de cuivre trouvés à Qumrân," Revue d' histoire des religions, 151 (1957), 22-36. [Topography.]

Eldar, Yishai. [2696] "An Essene Quarter on Mt. Zion?" Christian News from Israel, 26/1 (1976), 53-54.

Finkel, Asher. [2697] "The Theme of God's Presence and the Qumrân Temple Scroll," in L. E. Frizzell (ed.), God and His Temple. South Orange, NJ: Seton Hall University Institute for Judaeo-Christian Studies, 1980, 39-47.

Fiorenza, Elizabeth Schüssler. [2698] "Cultic Language in Qumrân and in the New Testament," Catholic Biblical Quarterly, 38 (1976), 159-177.

Fitzmyer, Joseph. [2699] "Further Light on Melchizedek from Qumrân Cave 11," Journal of Biblical Literature, 86 (1967), 25-41.

Flusser, David. [2700] "Two Notes on the Midrash on 2 Sam. vii: 1. The Temple 'Not Made with Hands' in the Qumrân Doctrine," Israel Exploration Journal, 9 (1959), 99-104. [On 4Q Florilegium.]

Gärtner, Bertil. [2701] The Temple and the Community in Qumrân and the New Testament: A Comparative Study in the Temple Symbolism of the Qumrân Texts and the New Testament. Society for New Testament Studies Monograph Series, 1. Cambridge: Cambridge University Press, 1965, 164 pp.

Garciá Martínez, Florentino. [2702] "4Q 'Amram B, I, 4: ¿Melki-Resha' o Melki-Sedeq?" Revue de Qumran, 12/45 (1985), 111-114.

Garciá Martínez, Florentino. [2703] "El rollo de Temple: Traduccion y notas," Estudios Bíblicos, 36 (1977), 247-292.

Greenfield, Jonas C. [2704] "The Small Caves of Qumrân," Journal of the American Oriental Society, 89 (1969), 128-141. Includes critique of Milik, J. T. [2728]

Hayward, Robert. [2705] "The Jewish Temple at Leontopolis: A Reconsideration," Journal of Jewish Studies, 33 (1982), 429-443. [Relates to Essene understanding of Jerusalem's temple and priesthood.]

Horgan, Maurya P. [2706] "A Lament over Jerusalem (4Q179)," Journal of Semitic Studies, 19 (1973), 222-234.

Jeremias, Joachim. [2707] "The Copper Scroll from Qumrân," Expository Times, 71 (1959/1960), 227-228. [On the topography of the Pool of Bethesda.]

Jeremias, Joachim. [2708] "Die Kuperrolle von Qumran and Bethesda," in Abba: Studien zur neutestamentlichen Theologie und Zeitgeschichte. Göttingen: Vandenhoeck und Ruprecht, 1966, 361-364.

Jeremias, Joachim and Milik, J. T. [2709] "Remarques sur le rouleau cuivre de Qumrân," Revue biblique, 67 (1960), 220-223. [Topography.]

de Jonge, M. and Van der Woude, Adam S. [2710] "11Q Melchizedek and the New Testament," New Testament Studies, 12 (1965/1966), 301-326.

Jongeling, B. [2711] "Publication provisoire d' un fragment provenant de la grotte 11 de Qumrân (11 Q Jér Nouv ar)," Journal for the Study of Judaism, 1 (1970), 58-64, 185-186.

Klinzing, Georg. [2712] Die Umdeutung des Kultus in der Qumran Gemeinde und in Neuen Testament. Studien zum Umwelt des Neuen Testaments, 7. Göttingen: Vandenhoeck und Ruprecht, 1971, 248 pp.

Lehmann, Manfed R. [2713] "Identification of the Copper Scroll Based on its Technical Terms," Revue de Qumrân, 5/17 (1964), 97-105. [On the hidden treasures as caches for future temple-rebuilding.]

Levine, Baruch A. [2714] "The Temple Scroll: Aspects of its Historical Provenance and Literary Character," Bulletin of the American Schools of Oriental Research, 232 (1978), 2-23.

Licht, Jacob. [2715] "An Ideal Town Plan from Qumrân-- the Description of the New Jerusalem," Israel Exploration Journal, 29 (1979), 45-59.

Mc Cready, W. O. [2716] "The Sectarian Status of Qumrân: The Temple Scroll," Revue de Qumrân, 11 (1983), 183-191.

Mackowski, Richard M. [2717] "Some 'New' Place Names in Herodian Jerusalem," Biblische Zeitschrift, 29 (1958), 262-267. [Suggests, inter alia, that the name Essene may derive from Sion and that the designation Sion for the southwestern hill may derive from it having been the Essene quarter.]

Mc Nicol, A. J. [2718] "The Eschatological Temple in the Qumrân Pesher 4Q Florilegium 1: 1-7," Ohio Journal of Religious Studies, 5 (1977), 133-141.

Magen, Isaac. [2719] "Bet Ha-Mesibah in the Temple Scroll and in the Mishnah," in Eretz-Israel: Archaeological, Historical, and Geographical Studies, 17. Jerusalem: Israel Exploration Society, 1984, 226-235 (Hebrew), 10* (English summary).

Maier, Johann. [2720] Die Tempelrolle vom Toten Meer, übersetzt und erläutert. Munich: Reinhardt, 1978, 128 pp.

Maier, Johann. [2721] The Temple Scroll: An Introduction, Translation, and Commentary. Journal for the Study of the Old Testament, Supplement Series, 34. Sheffield: Journal for the Study of the Old Testament Press, 1985, 147 pp. Revision and updating of the German edition, with cross-references to Yadin, Yigael. [2761]

Milgrom, Jacob. [2722] "Challenge to Sun-Worship Interpretation of Temple Scroll's Gilded Staircase," Biblical Archaeology Review, 11/1 (Jan./Feb., 1985), 70-73.

Milgrom, Jacob. [2723] "'Sabbath' and 'Temple City' in the Temple Scroll," Bulletin of the American Schools of Oriental Research, 232 (1978), 25-27.

Milgrom, Jacob. [2724] "Studies in the Temple Scroll," Journal of Biblical Literature, 97 (1978), 501-523.

Milgrom, Jacob. [2725] "The Temple Scroll," Biblical Archaeologist, 41 (1978), 105-120.

Milik, J. T. See Barthélemy, D. and Milik, J. T. [2682]

Milik, J. T. See Jeremias, Joachim and Milik, J. T. [2709]

Milik, J. T. [2726] "4Q Visions de 'Amram et une citation d' Origène," Revue biblique, 79 (1972), 77-97. [Angleic Melchizedek tradition.]

Milik, J. T. [2727] "The Copper Document from Cave III of Qumrân: Translation and Commentary," Annual of the Department of Antiquities of Jordan, 4/5 (1960), 137-155. [Topography.]

Milik, J. T. [2728] "Description de la Jérusalem nouvelle," in M. Baillet, J. T. Milik, and R. de Vaux, Discoveries in the Judaean Desert, 3: Les 'Petites Grottes' de Qumrân. Oxford: Clarendon Press, 1962. Textes, 184-193; Planches, XL-XLI. [On 5Q 15.]

Milik, J. T. [2729] "Milkî-sedeq et Milkî-resha' dans les anciens écrits juifs et chrétiens," Journal of Jewish Studies, 23 (1972), 95-144.

Milik, J. T. [2730] "Notes d' épigraphie et de topographie palestiniennes, VIII: Traité des vases (mskt klym)," Revue biblique, 66 (1959), 567-575.

Milik, J. T. [2731] "Le rouleau de cuivre provenant de la grotte 3Q (3Q 15): Commentaire et texte," in M. Baillet, J. T. Milik, and R. de Vaux, Discoveries in the Judaean Desert, 3: Les 'Petites Grottes' de Qumrân. Oxford: Clarendon Press, 1962. Textes, 211-302; Planches, XLIII-LXXI. [Topography.]

Milik, J. T. [2732] "Le rouleau de cuivre de Qumrân (3Q 15): Traduction et commentaire topographique," Revue biblique, 66 (1959), 321-357, esp. 344-354. [Topography.]

Mowinckel, Sigmund. [2733] "The Copper Scroll-- An Apocryphon," Journal of Biblical Literature, 76 (1957), 261-265. [An apocryphon relating to the hidden treasures of Solomon's temple.]

Newsom, Carol. [2734] Songs of the Sabbath Service, a Critical Edition. Harvard Semitic Studies, 27. Atlanta: Scholars Press, 1985, 476 pp.

Nolland, John. [2735] "A Misleading Statement of the Essene Attitude to the Temple," Revue de Qumrân, 9 (1978), 555-562.

Pixner, Bargil. [2736] "An Essene Quarter on Mt. Zion?" in E. Testa, I. Mancini, and M. Piccirillo (eds.), Studia Hierosolymitana in onore del P. Bellarmino Bagatti, 1: Studia archeologici. Studium Biblicum Franciscanum, Collectio Major, 22. Jerusalem: Franciscan Printing Press, 1976, 245-284.

Pixner, Bargil. [2737] "Das Essenerquartier in Jerusalem und dessen Einfluss auf die Urkirche," Das Heilige Land, 113/2 (1981), 3-14.

Pixner, Bargil. [2738] "Unravelling the Copper Scroll Code: A Study on the Topography of 3Q 15," Revue de Qumrân, 11 (1983), 323-261.

Ringgren, Helmer. [2739] "The Cult," in The Faith of Qumrân: Theology of the Dead Sea Scrolls. Philadelphia: Fortress Press, 1963, 214-229.

Robinson, Stephen E. [2740] "The Testament of Adam and the Angelic Liturgy," Revue de Qumrân, 12/45 (1985), 105-110. [On the administration and liturgy of the Jerusalem Temple as influence on Jewish angelology.]

Sanders, J. A. [2741] "Apostrophe to Zion," in The Psalms Scroll of Qumrân Cave 11. Discoveries in the Judaean Desert, 4. Oxford: Clarendon Press, 85-89.

Schwartz, Daniel R. [2742] "The Three Temples of 4Q Florilegium," Revue de Qumrân, 10 (1979), 83-91.

Silberman, Lou A. [2743] "A Note on the Copper Scroll," Vetus Testamentum, 10 (1960), 77-79.

Smith, Morton. [2744] "The Case of the Gilded Staircase: Did the Dead Sea Sect Worship the Sun?" Biblical Archaeology Review, 10/5 (Sept./Oct., 1984), 50-55.

Smith, Morton. [2745] "Helios in Palestine," in Eretz-Israel: Archaeological, Historical, and Geographical Studies, 16. Jerusalem: Israel Exploration Society, 1982, 199*-214*.

Strugnell, John. [2746] "The Angelic Liturgy at Qumrân, 4Q Serek Shirôt 'Olat Hashshabat," in International Organization for the Study of the Old Testament: Congress Volume, 1959. Supplements to Vetus Testamentum, 7. Leiden: Brill, 1960, 318-345.

Strugnell, John. [2747] "Notes en marge du volume V des 'Discoveries in the Judaean Desert of Jordan,'" Revue de Qumrân, 7 (1970), 163-276, esp. 220-225. [on 4Q 174].

Teicher, J. L. [2748] "Priests and Sacrifices in the Dead Sea Scrolls," Journal of Jewish Studies, 5 (1954), 93-9.

Van der Ploeg, J. [2749] "The Meals of the Essenes," Journal of Semitic Studies, 2 (1957), 163-175.

Van der Woude, Adam S. See de Jonge, M. and Van der Woude, Adam S. [2710]

Van der Woude, Adam S. [2750] "Fragmente einer Rolle der Lieder für das Sabbatopfer aus Höhle XI von Qumran (11Q Sir Sab)," in Von Kanaan bis Kerala (Festschrift J. P. M. Van der Ploeg). Kevelaer-Neukirchen-Vluyn: Butzon und Bercker, Neukirchener Verlag, 1982, 311-337. [The Angelic Liturgy.]

Van der Woude, Adam S. [2751] "Melchisedek als himmlische Erlösergestalt in den neugefundenen eschatologischen Midrashim aus Qumran Höhle XI," Oudtestamentische Studiën, 14 (1965), 354-373.

Van der Woude, Adam S. [2752] "De Tempel van Qumran," Nederlands Theologisch Tijdschrift, 34 (1980), 177-190, 281-293.

Wallace, David H. [2753] "The Essenes and Temple Sacrifice," Theologische Zeitschrift, 13 (1957), 335-338.

Wills, Lawrence. See Wilson, Andrew M. and Wills, Lawrence. [2755]

Wilms, F.-E. [2754] "Blutige Opfer oder Opfer der Lippen: Eine Alternative der Theologie von Qumran," Archiv für Liturgiewissenschaft, 25 (1983), 121-137.

Wilson, Andrew M. and Wills, Lawrence. [2755] "Literary Sources of the Temple Scroll," Harvard Theological Review, 75 (1982), 275-288.

Yadin, Yigael. [2756] "The Gate of the Essenes and the Temple Scroll," Qadmoniot, 5 (1972), 129-130.

Yadin, Yigael. [2757] "The Gate of the Essenes and the Temple Scroll," in Y. Yadin (ed.), Jerusalem Revealed: Archaeology in the Holy City, 1968-1974. New Haven and London: Yale University Press and the Israel Exploration Society, 1976, 90-91.

Yadin, Yigael. [2758] "Le rouleau du Temple," in M. Delcor (ed.), Qumrân. Sa piété, sa théologie et son milieu. Bibliotheca Ephemeridum Theologicarum Lovaniensium, 46. Paris-Gembloux: Duculot, 1978, 115-119.

Yadin, Yigael. [2759] "The Temple Scroll," in D. N. Freedman and J. C. Greenfield (eds.), New Directions in Biblical Archaeology. Garden City, NY: Doubleday, 1969, 139-148. Originally published in Biblical Archaeologist, 30 (1967), 135-139.

Yadin, Yigael. [2760] "The Temple Scroll," in J. Aviram (ed.), Jerusalem through the Ages. Jerusalem: Israel Exploration Society, 1968, 72-84 (Hebrew), 60-61 (English summary).

Yadin, Yigael. [2761] The Temple Scroll, 3 vols. Jerusalem: Israel Exploration Society, 1983, 1098 pp.

Yadin, Yigael. [2762] "The Temple Scroll: The Longest and Most Recently Discovered Dead Sea Scroll," Biblical Archaeology Review, 10/5 (Sept./Oct., 1984), 33-49.

Twenty

The Jewish Revolt Against Rome and the Destruction of Jerusalem, A. D. 70

Abel, Félix-M. [2763] "Siège de Jérusalem et achèvement de la conquête," in *Histoire de la Palestine*, 2. Paris: Lecoffre, 1952, 22-43.

Abel, Félix-M. [2764] "Topographie du siège de Jérusalem en 70," *Revue biblique*, 56 (1949), 238-258.

Aberbach, Moses. [2765] "The Conflicting Accounts of Josephus and Tacitus concerning Cumanus' and Felix' Terms of Office," *Jewish Quarterly Review*, 40 (1949/1950), 1-14.

Aberbach, Moses. [2766] *The Roman-Jewish War (66-70 A. D.): Its Origins and Consequences*. London: Golub, 1966, 80 pp.

Aharoni, Yohanan and Avi-Yonah, Michael. [2767] "The Siege of Jerusalem in the Year 70 A. D.," in *The Macmillan Bible Atlas*. New York: Macmillan, 1968, 160-161; map 256.

Alon, Gedalyahu. [2768] "The Burning of the Temple," in *Jews, Judaism, and the Classical World: Studies in Jewish History in the Times of the Second Temple and Talmud*. Jerusalem: Magnes Press, 1977, 252-269.

Alon, Gedalyahu. [2769] "The Impact of the Great Defeat," in *The Jews in Their Land in the Talmudic Age*, 1. Jerusalem: Magnes Press, 1980, 41-55.

Amitaï, L. K. [2770] [Pseudonym of Lehman Kahn] *Vae victis, Romains et Juifs: Étude critique sur les rapports publices et privés qui ont existé entre les Romains et les Juifs jusqu' à la prise de Jérusalem par Titus*. Paris: Fishbacher, 1894, 136 pp.

Appelbaum, Shimon. [2771] "The Struggle for the Soil and the Revolt of 66-73 C. E.," in *Eretz-Israel: Archaeological, Historical, and Geographical Studies*, 12. Jerusalem: Israel Exploration Society, 1975, 125-128 (Hebrew), 122*-123* (English summary).

Appelbaum, Shimon. [2772] "The Zealots: The Case for Revaluation," *Journal of Roman Studies*, 61 (1971), 156-170.

Arranz, Miguel. [2773] "La liturgie pénitentielle juive après la destruction du Temple," in A. Pistoia (ed.), *Liturgie et rémission des péchés. Conferences Saint-Serge, Paris, 1973*. Rome: Edizioni Liturgische, 1975, 39-55.

Avi-Yonah, Michael. See Aharoni, Yohanan and Avi-Yonah, Michael. [2767]

Avigad, Nahman. [2774] "The Burnt House," in Discovering Jerusalem. Nashville: Nelson, 1983, 120-139.

Avigad, Nahman. [2775] "Jerusalem in Flames-- The Burnt House Captures a Moment in Time," Biblical Archaeology Review, 9/6 (Nov./Dec., 1983), 66-72.

Ayali, M. [2776] "Gotte und Israels Trauer über die Zerstörung des Tempels," Kairos, 23 (1981), 215-231.

Baer, Y. [2777] "Jerusalem in the Times of the Great Revolt (Based on Source Criticism of Josephus and Talmudic-Midrashic Legends of the Temple Destruction)," Zion, 36, (1971), 127-190 (Hebrew with English summary). [English summary also in New Testament Abstracts, 18 (1973/1974), 87.]

Barnett, P. W. [2778] "The Jewish Sign Prophets-- A. D. 40-70-- Their Intentions and Origins," New Testament Studies, 27 (1980/1981), 679-697.

Baumbach, G. [2779] "Die Zealoten-- ihre geschichtliche und religionspolitische Dedeutung," Bibel und Liturgie, 41 (1968), 2-25.

Ben-Shammai, M. H. [2780] "The Legends of the Destruction of the Temple among the Paintings of the Dura Synagogue," Bulletin of the Jewish Palestine Exploration Society, 9 (1942), 93-97 (Hebrew).

Betz, Otto. [2781] "Stadt und Gegenstadt: Ein Kapitel zelotischer Theologie," in B. Benzing, O. Böcher, and G. Mayer (eds.), Wort und Wirklichkeit, 1: Geschichte und Religionswissenschaft (Festschrift Ludwig Rapp). Meisenheim am Glan: Verlag Hain, 1976, 96-109.

Bilde, Per. [2782] "The Causes of the Jewish War according to Josephus," Journal for the Study of Judaism, 10 (1979), 179-202.

Bilde, Per. [2783] "The Roman Emperor Gaius (Caligula)'s Attempt to Erect His Statue in the Temple of Jerusalem," Studia Theologica, 32 (1978), 67-93.

Black, Matthew. [2784] "Judas of Galilee and Josephus's 'Fourth Philosophy,'" in O. Betz, K. Haacker, and M. Hengel (eds.), Josephus-Studien: Untersuchungen zu Josephus, dem antiken Judentum und dem Neuen Testament (Festschrift Otto Michel). Göttingen: Vandenhoeck and Ruprecht, 1974, 45-54.

Bogaert, Pierre-Maurice. [2785] "Les réactions juives après la ruine de Jérusalem: L' Apocalypse de Baruch," Le Monde de la Bible, 29 (1983), 19-20.

Bogaert, Pierre-Maurice. [2786] "Ruine de Jérusalem et les apocalypses juives après 70," in H. Cazelles (ed.), Apocalypses et théologie de l' espérance. Association Catholique Française pour l' étude de la Bible. Congress de Toulouse, 1975 (Festschrift Louis Monloubou). Paris: Cerf, 1977, 123-141.

Borg, Marc. [2787] "The Currency of the Term 'Zealot.'" Journal of Theological Studies, 22 (1971), 504-512.

Brandon, Samuel G. F. [2788] "The Fall of Jerusalem, A. D. 70," History Today, 8 (1958), 248-255.

Brandon, Samuel G. F. [2789] "The Fall of Jerusalem, A. D. 70," in Religion in Ancient History: Studies in Ideas, Men and Events. London: George Allen and Unwin, 1973, 268-281.

Brandon, Samuel G. F. [2790] The Fall of Jerusalem and the Christian Church: A Study of the Effects of the Jewish Overthrow of A. D. 70 on Christianity. London: S. P. C. K., 1951, 284 pp.

Brandon, Samuel G. F. [2791] "Jerusalem, A. D. 70," History Today, 20 (1970), 814-816.

Brandon, Samuel G. F. [2792] "Sicarii," Encyclopaedia Judaica, 14. Jerusalem: Macmillan, 1971, 1491-1492.

Brandon, Samuel G. F. [2793] "Zealots," Encyclopaedia Judaica, 16. Jerusalem: Macmillan, 1971, 947-950.

Brandon, Samuel G. F. [2794] "The Zealots: The Jewish Resistance against Rome, A. D. 6-73," in Religion in Ancient History: Studies in Ideas, Men and Events. London: George Allen and Unwin, 1973, 282-297.

Brauer, George C., Jr. [2795] Judaea Weeping: The Jewish Struggle against Rome from Pompey to Masada, 63 B. C. to A. D. 73. New York: Crowell, 1970, 296 pp.

Bruce, Frederick F. [2796] "Tacitus on Jewish History," Journal of Semitic Studies, 29 (1984), 33-44.

Büchler, Adolpf. [2797] "On the Provisioning of Jerusalem in the Year 69-70 C. E.," in I. Brodie and J. Rabbowitz (eds.), Studies in Jewish History. London: Oxford University Press, 1956, 98-125.

Cagnet, René. [2798] "Sur l' armé romaine au siège de Jérusalem," Revue des études juives, 22 (1891), 28-58.

Conder, Claude R. [2799] "The Fall of Jerusalem," in The City of Jerusalem. London: John Murray, 1909, 159-187.

Cornfeld, Gaalya (general editor) with Mazar, Benjamin and Maier, Paul L. [2800] Josephus, The Jewish War, Newly Translated with Extensive Commentary and Archaeological Background Illustrations. Grand Rapids: Zondervan, 1982, 526 pp.

Daoust, Joseph. [2801] "L' arc de Titus," Bible et Terre Sainte, 118 (1970), 10-14.

Daoust, Joseph. [2802] "La guerre juive selon Tacite," Bible et Terre Sainte, 118 (1970), 4-7.

Du Buit, M. [2803] "Les réactions juives après la ruine de Jérusalem," Bible et Terre Sainte, 117 (1970), 15-18.

Echegaray, Joaquín González. [2804] "La guarnicion romana de Judea en los tiempos de N. T.," Estudios Bíblicos, 36 (1977), 57-84.

Farmer, William R. [2805] Maccabees, Zealots, and Josephus: An Inquiry into Jewish Nationalism in the Greco-Roman Period. New York: Columbia University Press, 1956, 239 pp.

Fuks, Gideon. [2806] "Again on the Episode of the Gilded Shields at Jerusalem," Harvard Theological Review, 75 (1982), 503-507.

Furneaux, Rupert. [2807] The Roman Siege of Jerusalem. New York: Hart-Davis, 1973, 223 pp.

Gichon, Mordecai. [2808] "Cestius Gallus's Campaign in Judaea," Palestine Exploration Quarterly, (1981), 39-62.

Gichon, Mordecai. [2809] "Cestius Gallus's March on Jerusalem, 66 C. E.," in A. Oppenheimer, U. Rappaport, and M. Stern (eds.), Jerusalem in the Second Temple Period: Abraham Schalit Memorial Volume. Jerusalem: Yad Izhaq Ben-Zvi, 1980, 283-319 (Hebrew), xvii=xviii (English Summary).

Giet, Stanislas. [2810] "Les épisodes de la guerre juive," Revue des sciences religieuses, 26 (1952), 325-362.

Goldenberg, Robert. [2811] "Early Rabbinic Explanations for the Destruction of Jerusalem," Journal of Jewish Studies, 33 (1982), 517-525.

Goodman, Martin. [2812] "The First Jewish Revolt: Social Conflict and the Problem of Debt," Journal of Jewish Studies, 33 (1982), 417-427.

Gozzo, Serafino (ed.). [2813] La distruzione di Gerusalemme del 70: nei suoi riflessi storico-letterari. Atti del V Convegno biblico francescano, Roma, 22 sett., 1969. Collectio Assisiensis, 8. Assisi: Studio Teologico "porziuncolo," 1971, 222 pp.

Gray, B. C. [2814] "The Movements of the Jerusalem Church during the First Jewish War," Journal of Ecclesiastical History, 24 (1973), 1-7.

Gray, John. [2815] "The Great Divide," in A History of Jerusalem. New York: Praeger, 1969, 168-193.

Gry, Léon. [2816] "La ruine du Temple par Titus-- quelques traditions juives plus anciennes et primitives à la base de Pesikta Rabbathi XXVI," Revue biblique, 55 (1948), 215-226.

Hayward, C. T. R. [2817] "The Fourth Philosophy: Sicarii and Zealots," in E. Schürer, The History of the Jewish People in the Age of Jesus Christ (175 B. C. - A. D. 135), 2. New English version revised and edited by G. Vermes and F. Miller (literary editor, P. Vermes; organizing editor, M. Black). Edinburgh: T. & T. Clark, 1979, 598-606.

Hengel, Martin. [2818] Die Zealoten: Untersuchungen zür jüdischen Freiheits--Bewegung in der Zeit von Herodes I bis 70 n. Chr. Arbeiten zur Geschichte des Spätjudentums und Urchristentums, 1.Leiden: Brill, 1961, 406 pp.

Hengel, Martin. [2819] "Zealoten und Sikarier: Zur Frage der Einheit und Vielfalt der jüdischen Befreiungsbewegung 6-74 n. Chr.," in O. Betz, K. Haacker, and M. Hengel (eds.), Josephus-Studien: Untersuchungen zu Josephus, dem antiken Judentum und dem Neuen Testament (Festschrift Otto Michel). Göttingen: Vandenhoeck and Ruprecht, 1974, 175-196.

Horsley, Richard A. [2820] "Ancient Jewish Banditry and the Revolt against Rome, A. D. 66-70," Catholic Biblical Quarterly, 43 (1981), 409-432.

Horsley, Richard A. [2821] "Josephus and the Bandits," Journal for the Study of Judaism, 10 (1979), 37-63.

Horsley, Richard A. [2822] "Menahem in Jerusalem: A Brief Messianic Episode among the Sicarii-- Not 'Zealot Messianism,'" Novum Testamentum, 27 (1985), 334-348.

Horsley, Richard A. [2823] "The Sicarii: Ancient Jewish Terrorists," Journal of Religion, 59 (1979), 435-458.

Horsley, Richard A. [2824] "The Zealots: Their Origin, Relationship and Importance in the Jewish Revolt," Novum Testamentum, 28 (1986), 159-192.

Israel, Gérard and Lebar, Jacques. [2825] When Jerusalem Burned. New York: William Morrow, 1973, 177 pp.

Kadman, Leo. [2826] "The Coinage of the Jewish War," in Israel Numismatic Society: The Dating and Meaning of Ancient Jewish Coins and Symbols. Numismatic Studies and Researches, 2. Jerusalem: Schocken, 1958, 42-61.

Kadman, Leo. [2827] The Coins of the Jewish War of 66-73 C. E. Corpus Nummorum Palaestinensium, 3. Jerusalem: Schocken, 1960, 203 pp.

Kahn, Lehman. See Amitaï, L. K. [2770]

Kasher, A. (ed.). [2828] The Great Jewish Revolt: Factors and Circumstances Leading to its Outbreak. Jerusalem: Zalman Shazar Center, 1983, 438 pp. (Hebrew). [English summary in New Testament Abstracts, 29 (1985), 229.]

Kennard, J. Spenser. [2829] "Judas of Galilee and His Clan," Jewish Quarterly Review, 36 (1945/1946), 281-286.

Kenyon, Kathleen M. [2830] "The Jerusalem of Herod Agrippa and the Roman Destruction," in Jerusalem: Excavating 3,000 Years of History. New York: McGraw-Hill, 1967, 155-186.

Kindler, Arie. [2831] "The Jewish War against Rome (66-70 C. E.)," in Coins of the Land of Israel: A Collection of the Bank of Israel, A Catalogue. Jerusalem: Keter, 1974, 52-57.

Kingdon, H. Paul. [2832] "The Origins of the Zealots," New Testament Studies, 19 (1972/1973), 74-81.

Kingdon, H. Paul. [2833] "Who Were the Zealots and their Leaders in A. D. 66?" New Testament Studies, 17 (1970/1971), 62-72.

Klein, H. Arthur. See Klein, Mina C. and Klein, H. Arthur. [2834]

Klein, Mina C. and Klein, H. Arthur. [2834] "The Great Revolt in Judea and Destruction of the Temple (29-75 C. E.)," in Temple beyond Time: The Story of the Site of Solomon's Temple at Jerusalem. New York: Van Nostrand Reinhold, 1970, 107-115.

Kolenkow, Anitra B. [2835] "The Fall of the Temple and the Coming of the End: The Spectrum and Process of Apocalyptic Argument in 2 Baruch and Other Authors," in K. H. Richards (ed.), Society of Biblical Literature, Seminar Papers Series, 21. Chico, CA: Scholars Press, 1982, 243-250.

Kraeling, Carl H. [2836] "The Episode of the Roman Standards at Jerusalem," Harvard Theological Review, 35 (1942), 263-289.

Leaney, A. R. C. [2837] "The First Jewish Revolt," in J. H. Hayes and M. Miller (eds.), Israelite and Judaean History. London, SCM, 1977, 653-663.

Lebar, Jacques. See Israel, Gérard and Lebar, Jacques. [2825]

Levine, L. I. [2838] "The Zealots at the End of the Second Temple Period as a Historiographical Problem," Cathedra: History of Eretz-Israel, 1 (1976), 39-48 (Hebrew).

Lewin, Thomas. [2839] The Siege of Jerusalem by Titus. London: Lonman, Green, Longmans, Robert, and Green, 1863, 499 pp.

Loftus, Francis. [2840] "The Anti-Roman Revolts of the Jews and the Galileans," Jewish Quarterly Review, 68 (1977), 78-98.

Maier, Johann. [2841] "Die alttestamentlich-jüdischen Voraussetzungen der Zealotenbewegungen, Bibel und Kirche, 37 (1982), 82-89.

Maier, Paul L. See Cornfeld, Gaalya (general editor) with Mazar, Benjamin and Maier, Paul L. [2800]

Maier, Paul L. [2842] "Episode of the Golden Roman Shields at Jerusalem," Harvard Theological Review, 62 (1969), 111-114.

Mazar, Benjamin. See Cornfeld, Gaalya (general editor) with Mazar, Benjamin and Maier, Paul L. [2800]

Mertens, Aurélius. [2843] "L' assedio di Gerusalemme a opera di Tito nel 70 D. C.," Bibbia e Oriente, 12 (1970), 264-272.

Mertens, Aurélius. [2844] "O assédio de Jerusalém por Tito no ano 70 d. C.," Revista de Cultura Biblica, 9 (1972), 135-146.

Meshorer, Ya'akov. [2845] "The Jewish War," in Ancient Jewish Coinage, 2: Herod the Great through Bar Cochba. Dix Hills, NY: Amphora Books, 1985, 96-131.

Meshorer, Ya'akov. [2846] "The Coins of the War of the Jews against the Romans, 66-70 C. E.," in Jewish Coins of the Second Temple Period. Tel-Aviv: Am Hassefer and Massada, 1967, 88-91.

Momigliano, A. See Stevenson, G. H. and Momigliano, A. [2886]

Momigliano, A. [2847] "The Siege and Fall of Jerusalem," in The Cambridge Ancient History, 10: The Augustan Empire, 44 B. C. - A. D. 70. Cambridge: Cambridge University Press, 1934, 861-865.

Montefiore, Hugh. [2848] "Sulpicius Severus and Titus' Council of War," Historia, 11 (1962), 156-170.

Mueller, James R. [2849] "The Apocalypse of Abraham and the Destruction of the Second Jewish Temple," in K. H. Richards (ed.), Society of Biblical Literature, Seminar Papers Series, 21. Chico, CA: Scholars Press, 1982, 341-349.

Mulder, H. [2850] De verwoesting van Jeruzalem en haar gefolgen. Amsterdam: Ton Bolland, 1977, 148 pp. [Reactions to the fall of Jerusalem by Jews, Christians, and pagans.]

Nataf, G. [2851] "Les Zélotes et la chute du Temple," Le Monde de la Bible, 13 (1980), 36-37.

Nedava, J. [2852] "Who Were the Biryoni?" Jewish Quarterly Review, 63 (1973), 317-322.

Neusner, Jacob. [2853] "Judaism after the Destruction of the Temple," in J. H. Hayes and M. Miller (eds.), Israelite and Judaean History. London, SCM, 1977, 663-667.

Neusner, Jacob. [2854] "Judaism beyond Catastrophe: The Destruction of the Temple and the Renaisance of Torah," in Judaism in the Beginning of Christianity. Philadelphia: Fortress Press, 1984, 89-99.

Neusner, Jacob. [2855] "Judaism in a Time of Crisis: Four Responses to the Destruction of the Second Temple," Judaism, 21 (1972), 313-327.

Nevin, J. C. [2856] "The Siege of Jerusalem: Diary of the Principal Events Connected with the Memorable Siege of Jerusalem by Titus, drawn from Josephus, with Some Accompanying Notes and Observations," Palestine Exploration Fund, Quarterly Statement, (1907), 34-42.

Nikiprowetzky, Valentin. [2857] "Sicaires et Zélotes, une reconsideration," Semitica, 23 (1973), 51-64.

Noth, Martin. [2858] "The Insurrections against Rome and the End of Israel," in The History of Israel. New York: Harper and Row, 2nd. ed., 1960, 432-454.

Oesterley, W. O. E. [2859] "From the Death of Agrippa I to the Outbreak of the Jewish War, / The Jewish War," in T. H. Robinson and W. O. E. Oesterley, A History of Israel, 2.: From the Fall of Jerusalem, 586 B. C., to the Bar Kokhba Revolt, A. D. 135. Oxford: Clarendon Press, 425-451.

Peters, F. E. [2860] "Not a Stone upon a Stone: The Destruction of the Holy City," in Jerusalem: The Holy City in the Eyes of Chroniclers, Visitors, Pilgrims, and Prophets from the Days of Abraham to the Beginnings of Modern Times. Princeton: Princeton University Press, 1985, 88-130.

Prigent, Pierre. [2861] La fin de Jérusalem. Archéologie biblique, 17. Neuchâtel: Delachaux et Niestlé, 1969, 158 pp.

Prigent, Pierre. [2862] "Préhistoire d' une guerre religieuse," Bible et Terre Sainte, 118 (1970), 2-3.

Rappaport, Uriel. [2863] "Jewish-Pagan Relations and the Revolt against Rome in 66-70 C. E.," in L. I. Levine (ed.), Jerusalem Cathedra, 1. Jerusalem: Yad Izhaq Ben-Zvi Institute / Detroit: Wayne State University Press, 1981, 81-95.

Rappaport, Uriel. [2864] "John of Gischala: From Galilee to Jerusalem," Journal of Jewish Studies, 33 (1982), 479-493.

Reifenberg, Adolf. [2865] "The First Revolt (66-70 A. D.)," in Ancient Jewish Coins. Jerusalem: Rubin Mass, 6th edn., 1973, 28-33.

Rengstorf, Karl H. [2866] "Der Glanz von Jabne: Rabban Jochanan ben Zakkai und die Rettung des Judentums nach der Zerstörung Jerusalems," in E. Graf (ed.), Festschrift Werner Caskel zum siebzigsten Geburtstag. Leiden: Brill, 1968, 233-244.

Rhoads, David M. [2867] Israel in Revolution: 6-74 C. E.: A Political History Based on the Writings of Josephus. Philadelphia: Fortress Press, 1976, 199 pp.

Roth, Cecil. [2868] "The Constitution of the Jewish Republic of 66-70," Journal of Semitic Studies, 9 (1964), 295-319.

Roth, Cecil. [2869] "The Debate on the Royal Sacrifices, A. D. 66," Harvard Theological Review, 53 (1960), 93-97.

Roth, Cecil. [2870] "The Historical Implications of the Jewish Coinage of the First Revolt," Israel Exploration Journal, 12 (1962), 33-46.

Roth, Cecil. [2871] "An Ordinance against Images in Jerusalem," Harvard Theological Review, 49 (1956), 169-177.

Roth, Cecil. [2872] "The Pharisees in the Jewish Revolution of 66-73," Journal of Semitic Studies, 7 (1962), 63-80.

Roth, Cecil. [2873] "The Zealots-- a Jewish Religious Sect," Judaism, 8 (1959), 33-40.

Roth, Cecil. [2874] "The Zealots in the War of 66-73," Journal of Semitic Studies, 4 (1959), 332-355.

Rubenstein, Richard L. [2875] "The Fall of Jerusalem and the Birth of Holocaust Theology," in R. Jospe and S. Z. Fishman (eds.), Go and Study: Essays and Studies in Honor of Alfred Jospe. Washington, DC: B'nai Brith Hillel Foundations, 1980, 223-240.

Safrai, Shmuel. [2876] "Vespasian's Campaigns of Conquest in Judea," in A. Oppenheimer, U. Rappaport, and M. Stern (eds.), Jerusalem in the Second Temple Period: Abraham Schalit Memorial Volume. Jerusalem: Yad Izhaq Ben-Zvi, 1980, 320-339 (Hebrew), xviii=xix (English Summary).

Saldarini, Anthony J. [2877] "Varieties of Rabbinic Response to the Destruction of the Temple," in K. H. Richards (ed.), Society of Biblical Literature, Seminar Papers Series, 21. Chico, CA: Scholars Press, 1982, 437-458.

de Saulcy, L. Félicien J. C. [2878] Les derniers jours de Jérusalem. Paris: Hachette, 1866, 437 pp.

Schoeps, Hans-Joachim. [2879] "Die Tempelzerstörung des Jahres 70 in der jüdischen Religionsgeschichte" in Coniectanea Neotestmentica, 6. Uppsala: Seminarium Neotestamenticum Upsaliense, 1942, 1-45. Also in Aus Frühchristlicher Zeit. Tübingen: Mohr (Siebeck), 1950, 144-183.

Smallwood, E. Mary. [2880] "Bandits, Terrorists, Sicarii and Zealots," in G. A. Williamson (trans.), Josephus: The Jewish War. Harmondsworth: Penguin, rev. edn., 1981, 461-462.

Smallwood, E. Mary. [2881] "High Priests and Politics in Roman Palestine," Journal of Theological Studies, 13 (1962), 14-34.

Smallwood, E. Mary. [2882] "The War of A. D. 66-70," in The Jews under Roman Rule. Leiden: Brill, 1981, 293-330.

Smith, Morton. [2883] "Zealots and Sicarii: Their Origins and Relations," Harvard Theological Review, 64 (1971), 1-19.

Stern, Menahem. [2884] "Sicarii and Zealots," in M. Avi-Yonah and Z. Baras (eds), World History of the Jewish People, 8: Society and Religion in the Second Temple Period. Jerusalem: Massada, 1977, 263-301.

Stern, Menahem. [2885] "Zealots," in Encyclopaedia Judaica Yearbook, 1973. Jerusalem: Macmillan, 1971, 135-152.

Steve, M.-A. See Vincent, Louis-Hugues and Steve, M.-A. [2895]

Stevenson, G. H. and Momigliano, A. [2886] "Rebellion within the Empire," in The Cambridge Ancient History, 10: The Augustan Empire, 44 B. C. - A. D. 70. Cambridge: Cambridge University Press, 1934, 840-890.

Stone, Michael E. [2887] "Reactions to Destruction of the Second Temple: Theology, Perception, and Conversion," Journal for the Study of Judaism, 12 (1981), 195-204.

Testa, Emmanuele. [2888] "Reazione della correnti religiose giudaich e cristiane sulla distruzione di Gerusalemme," Rivista Biblica, 21 (1973), 301-324.

Testa, Emmanuele. [2889] "Riflessi letterari della distruzione di Gerusalemme (I-II) secolo d C.," in S. Gozzo (ed.), La distruzione di Gerusalemme del 70: nei suoi riflessi storico-letterari. Assisi: Studio Teologico "porziuncolo," 1971, 15-32.

Testa, Emmanuele. [2890] "Lo schema letterario sulla distruzione del tempio e di Gerusalemme," Studii Biblici Franciscani, Liber Annuus, 24 (1974), 265-316.

Thoma, Clemens. [2891] "Auswirkungen des jüdischen Krieges gegen Rom (66-70/73 n. Chr.) auf das rabbinische Judentum," Biblische Zeitschrift, 12 (1968), 30-54.

Toaff, Elio R. [2892] "La distruzione di Gerusalemme nella letteratura rabbinico-talmudica," in Gozzo (ed.), La distruzione di Gerusalemme del 70: nei suoi riflessi storico-letterari. Assisi: Studio Teologico "porziuncolo," 1971, 33-41.

Uhsadel, Walter. [2893] "Predigt zum Gedächtnistage der Zerstörung Jerusalems," in O. Betz, M. Hengel, and P. Schmidt (eds.), Abraham unser Vater: Juden und Christen im Gesprach über die Bibel, Festchrift für Otto Michel. Leiden: Brill, 1963, 459-466.

Ussishkin, David. [2894] "The Camp of the Assyrians in Jerusalem," Israel Exploration Journal, 29 (1979), 137-142.

Vincent, Louis-Hugues and Steve, M.-A. [2895] "Le siège de l' an 70," in Jérusalem de l' Ancien Testament, 3. Paris: Gabalda, 1956, 726-752.

Weiler, I. [2896] "Titus und die Zerstörung des Tempels von Jerusalem-- Absicht oder Zufall?" Klio-Beiträge zur Alten Geschichte, 50 (1968), 139-158.

Windisch, Hans. [2897] "Der Untergang Jerusalems (Anno 70) im Urtheil der Christen und Juden," Theologische Tijdschrift, 48 (1914), 519-550.

Zeitlin, Solomon. [2898] A Note on the Chronology of the Destruction of the Second Temple," Jewish Quarterly Review, 37 (1946/1947), 165-167.

Zeitlin, Solomon. [2899] "Zealots and Sicarii," Journal of Biblical Literature, 81 (1962), 395-398.

Twenty-One

Roman Jerusalem from A. D. 70 to Constantine / The Bar Kokhba Revolt

Abel, Félix-M. [2900] "Construction d' Aelia Capitolina," in Histoire de la Palestine, 2. Paris: Lecoffre, 1952, 97-102.

Abramsky, Samuel. [2901] "Bar Kokhba," in Encyclopaedia Judaica, 4. Jerusalem: Macmillan, 1971, 228-239.

Aharoni, Yohannan. See Avigad, Nahman; Aharoni, Yohannan; Bar-Adon, P.; and Yadin, Yigael. [2913-2914]

Aleksandrov, G. S. [2902] "The Role of 'Aqiba in the Bar-Kokhba Rebellion," Revue des études juives, 132 (1973), 65-77.

Alon, Gedaliah. [2903] "Judaea under Roman Occupation," in The Jews in their Land in the Talmudic Age, 1. Jerusalem: Magnes Press, 1980, 56-85.

Appelbaum, Shimon. [2904] "The Agrarian Question and the Revolt of Bar Kokhba," in Eretz-Israel: Archaeological, Historical, and Geographical Studies, 8. Jerusalem: Israel Exploration Society, 1967, 283-287 (Hebrew), 77* (English summary).

Appelbaum, Shimon. [2905] Prolegomena to the Study of the Second Jewish Revolt (A. D. 132-135). Biblical Archaeological Reports Supplementary Series, 7. Oxford: British Archaeological Reports, 1967, 100 pp.

Appelbaum, Shimon. [2906] "The Second Jewish Revolt (A. D. 131-35)," Palestine Exploration Quarterly, (1984), 35-41.

Appelbaum, Shimon. [2907] "Tineius Rufus and Julius Severus," in A. Oppenheimer and U. Rappaport, The Bar-Kokhva Revolt: A New Approach. Jerusalem: Yad Izhaq Ben-Zvi, 1984, 133-139 (Hebrew), xi-xii (English summary).

Avi-Yonah, Michael. [2908] "Aelia Capitolina," in Encyclopedia of Archaeological Excavations in the Holy Land, 2. Englewood Cliffs, NJ: Prentice-Hall, 1976, 610-613.

Avi-Yonah, Michael. [2909] "A Fragment of a Latin Inscription from the Excavations in the Old City of Jerusalem," in Eretz-Israel: Archaeological, Historical, and Geographical Studies, 9. Jerusalem: Israel Exploration Society, 1969, 175-176 (Hebrew), 139* (English summary).

Avi-Yonah, Michael. [2910] "Jerusalem: Roman Period," Encyclopaedia Judaica, 9. Jerusalem: Macmillan, 1971, 1405-1406. Also in Israel Pocket Library: Jerusalem. Jerusalem: Keter, 1973, 38-42.

Avi-Yonah, Michael. [2911] "When Did Judea Become a Consular Province?" Israel Exploration Journal, 23 (1972), 209-213. [re. Jewish uprising in the time of Trajan.]

Avigad, Nahman. [2912] "The Roman City," in Discovering Jerusalem. Nashville: Thomas Nelson, 1980, 205-207.

Avigad, Nahman; Aharoni, Yohannan; Bar-Adon, P.; and Yadin, Yigael. [2913] "The Expedition to the Judean Desert, 1960," Israel Exploration Journal, 11 (1961), 3-52.

Avigad, Nahman; Aharoni, Yohannan; Bar-Adon, P.; Yadin, Yigael; et al. [2914] "The Expedition to the Judean Desert, 1961," Israel Exploration Journal, 12 (1962), 167-262.

Bagatti, Bellarmino. [2915] "Jerusalem from the Beginnings of Christianity to the Council of Nicea," in The Church from the Gentiles in Palestine. History and Archaeology. Studium Biblicum Franciscanum, Collectio Minor, 4. Jerusalem: Franciscan Printing Press, 1971, reprinted, 1984, 5-28.

Bahat, Dan. [2916] "Aelia Capitolina (135-330 C. E.)," in Carta's Historical Atlas of Jerusalem. Jerusalem: Carta, 1973, 18-21.

Bahat, Dan. [2917] "The Roman Period, 70-330 C. E.," in Carta's Historical Atlas of Jerusalem: An Illustrated History. Jerusalem: Carta, 1983, 34-39.

Bar-Adon, P. See Avigad, Nahman; Aharoni, Yohannan; Bar-Adon, P.; and Yadin, Yigael. [2913-2914]

Barag, Dan. [2918] "Brick Stamp-Impressions of the Legio X Fretensis," in Eretz-Israel: Archaeological, Historical, and Geographical Studies, 8. Jerusalem: Israel Exploration Society, 1967, 168 (Hebrew), 73* (English summary).

Barag, Dan. [2919] "Brick Stamp Inscription of the Legio X Fretensis," Bonner Jahrbücher, 167 (1967), 244-267.

Barag, Dan. [2920] "The Countermarks of the Legio Decima Fretensis," in A. Kindler (ed.), The Patterns of Monetary Development in Phoenicia and Palestine in Antiquity. Proceedings of the International Numismatic Convention, Jerusalem, 27-31 December 1963. Tel-Aviv: Schocken, 1967, 117-125.

Barag, Dan. [2921] "A Note on the Geographical Distribution of Bar Kokhba Coins," Israel Numismatic Journal, 4 (1980), 30-33.

Beer, M. [2922] "Shimon Bar Yohai and Jerusalem," in A. Oppenheimer, U. Rappaport, and M. Stern (eds.), Jerusalem in the Second Temple Period: Abraham Schalit Memorial Volume. Jerusalem: Yad Izhaq Ben-Zvi, 1980, 361-375 (Hebrew), xxi (English summary).

Ben-Dov, Meir. [2923] "Roman Jerusalem," in In the Shadow of the Temple: The Discovery of Ancient Jerusalem. Jerusalem: Keter/ New York: Harper and Row, 1985, 184-205.

Ben-Shalom, Israel. [2924] "Events and Ideology of the Yavneh Period as Indirect Causes of the Bar-Kokhva Revolt," in A. Oppenheimer and U. Rappaport, The Bar-Kokhva Revolt: A New Approach. Jerusalem: Yad Izhaq Ben-Zvi, 1984, 1-12 (Hebrew), i-ii (English summary). [On the slogan "May the Temple be built speedily" in the dialectic of Pharisaic scholarship and its importance for the Bar Kokhba revolt.]

Benoit, Pierre. [2925] "L' Antonia d' Hérode le Grand et le forum oriental d' Aelia Capitolina," Harvard Theological Review, 64 (1971), 135-167. Reprinted with some updating in Exégèse et théologie, 4. Paris: Cerf, 1982, 311-346.

Bietenhard, H. [2926] "Die Freiheitskriege der Juden unter des Kaisern Trajen und Hadrian und der messianische Tempelbau," Judaica, 4 (1948), 57-77, 81-108, 161-185.

Birnbaum, Solomon. [2927] "Akiba and Bar-Kosba," Palestine Exploration Quarterly, (1968), 137-138.

Birnbaum, Solomon. [2928] "Bar Kokhba and Akiba," Palestine Exploration Quarterly, (1954), 23-32.

Bowersock, G. W. [2929] "A Roman Perspective on the Bar Kokhba Revolt," in W. S. Green (ed.), Approaches to Ancient Judaism, 2. Brown Judaic Studies, 9. Chico, CA: Scholars Press, 1980, 131-141.

Chen, Doren; Margalit, Sh.; and Solar, Giora. [2930] "An Ancient Street in the Christian Quarter in Jerusalem," Holy Land Review, 4/2-4 (Summer-Winter, 1978), 61-63.

Chen, Doren; Margalit, Sh.; and Solar, Giora. [2931] "Jerusalem (quartier chrétien), 1977," Revue biblique, 85 (1978), 419-421.

Clermont-Ganneau, Charles. [2932] "Discovery of a Fragment of an Imperial Inscription at Jerusalem," Palestine Exploration Fund, Quarterly Statement, (1884), 194.

Clermont-Ganneau, Charles. [2933] "Head of an Imperial or Royal Statue," in Archaeological Researches in Palestine during the Years 1873-1874, 1. Translated by Aubrey Stewart. London: Palestine Exploration Fund, 1896, 259-206.

Clermont-Ganneau, Charles. [2934] "Notes on Certain New Discoveries at Jerusalem: Roman Inscriptions," Palestine Exploration Fund, Quarterly Statement, (1871), 103-104.

Clermont-Ganneau, Charles. [2935] "The Statue of Hadrian Placed in the Temple at Jerusalem," Palestine Exploration Fund, Quarterly Statement, (1874), 207-210.

Clermont-Ganneau, Charles. [2936] "The Vase of Bezetha," Palestine Exploration Fund, Quarterly Statement, (1874), 264-269.

Conder, Claude R. [2937] "The Roman City," in The City of Jerusalem. London: John Murray, 1909, 188-207.

Dalton, J. N. and Davis, Ebenezer. [2938] "On the Latin Inscription Found by D. Bliss behind the Gate of Neby Daûd," Palestine Exploration Fund, Quarterly Statement, (1896), 133-152.

Davis, Ebenezer. See Dalton, J. N. and Davis, Ebenezer. [2938]

Efron, Joshua. [2939] "Bar-Kokhva in the Light of the Palestinian and Babylonian Talmudic Traditions," in A. Oppenheimer and U. Rappaport, The Bar-Kokhva Revolt: A New Approach. Jerusalem: Yad Izhaq Ben-Zvi, 1984, 47-105 (Hebrew), v-vii (English summary).

Finegan, Jack. [2940] "Latin Inscription of Hadrian on Stone Built into Southern Temple Enclosure Wall," in Archeology of the New Testament: The Life of Jesus and the Beginnings of the Early Church. Princeton: Princeton University Press, 1969, 122-123.

Fishman-Duker, Rivkah. [2941] "The Bar-Kokhva Rebellion in Christian Sources," in A. Oppenheimer and U. Rappaport, The Bar-Kokhva Revolt: A New Approach. Jerusalem: Yad Izhaq Ben-Zvi, 1984, 233-242 (Hebrew), xviii (English summary).

Fitzgerald, Gerald. [2942] "Palestine in the Roman Period, 63 B. C. - A. D. 324," Palestine Exploration Quarterly, (1956), 38-48.

Fitzmyer, Joseph A. [2943] "The Bar Cochba Period," in Essays on the Semitic Background to the New Testament. Missoula, MT: Scholars Press, 1974, 305-354.

Fulco, William J. [2944] "The Bar Kokhba Rebellion: Puzzling Evidence," The Bible Today, 64 (1973), 1041-1045. [Numismatic materils.]

Gafni, Isaiah. [2945] "The Status of Eretz Israel in Reality and in Jewish Consciousness following the Bar-Kokhva Uprising," in A. Oppenheimer and U. Rappaport, The Bar-Kokhva Revolt: A New Approach. Jerusalem: Yad Izhaq Ben-Zvi, 1984, 224-232 (Hebrew), xvii (English summary).

Geiger, J. [2946] "The Ban on Circumcision and the Bar-Kokhba Revolt," Zion, 41 (1976), 139-147 (Hebrew). [English summary in New Testament Abstracts, 21 (1977), 305.]

Germer-Durand, Joseph. [2947] "Aelia Capitolina," Revue biblique, 1 (1892), 369-387.

Germer-Durand, Joseph. [2948] "Antiquités romaines trouvées a Jérusalem," Revue biblique, 3 (1894), 237-259.

Germer-Durand, Joseph. [2949] "Épigrapie palestinienne: un miliaire romain," Revue biblique, 3 (1894), 613-614.

Germer-Durand, Joseph. [2950] "Inscription romaine à Jérusalem," Revue biblique, 4 (1895), 239.

Geva, Hillel. [2951] "The Camp of the Tenth Legion in Jerusalem: An Archaeological Reconsideration," Israel Exploration Journal, 34 (1984), 239-254.

Gibbon, H. H. Clifford. See Offord, Joseph and Gibbon, H. H. Clifford. [2990]

Gibbon, H. H. Clifford. [2952] "Further Note on Inscriptions Relating to Roman Campaigns in Palestine," Palestine Exploration Fund, Quarterly Statement, (1911), 192-194.

Gichon, Mordecai. [2953] "The Bar Kokhba War: A Colonial Uprising against Imperial Rome (131/2-135 C. E.)," Revue Internationale d' Histoire Militaire, 42 (1979), 82-97.

Gichon, Mordecai and Isaac, Benjamin. [2954] "A Flavian Inscription from Jerusalem," Israel Exploration Journal, 24 (1974), 117-123.

Goodblatt, David. [2955] "The Title Nasi' and the Ideological Background of the Second Revolt," in A. Oppenheimer and U. Rappaport, The Bar-Kokhva Revolt: A New Approach. Jerusalem: Yad Izhaq Ben-Zvi, 1984, 113-132 (Hebrew), vii-ix (English summary).

Gunther, John. [2956] "The Epistle of Barnabas and the Final Rebuilding of the Temple," Journal for the Study of Judaism, 7 (1976), 143-151.

Harris, Rendel. [2957] "Hadrian's Decree of Expulsion of the Jews from Jerusalem," Harvard Theological Review, 19 (1926), 199-206.

Helms, S. W. [2958] "The Jerusalem Ship: ISIS MYRIONYMOS and the True Cross," International Journal of Nautical Archaeology and Underwater Exploration, 9 (1980), 105-120. [Corrects the reading of DOMINE IVIMUS of the ship-inscription in the foundation of the Holy Sepulchre; a pagan sailor's ex voto from the Hadrianic period.]

Herr, M. D. [2959] "The Causes of the Bar-Kokhba War," Zion, 43 (1978), 1-11 (Hebrew, with English summary).

Isaac, Benjamin. See Gichon, Mordecai and Isaac, Benjamin. [2954]

Isaac, Benjamin. [2960] "The Revolt of Bar-Kokhva as Described by Cassius Dio and other Revolts against the Romans in Greek and Latin Literature," in A. Oppenheimer and U. Rappaport, The Bar-Kokhva Revolt: A New Approach. Jerusalem: Yad Izhaq Ben-Zvi, 1984, 106-112 (Hebrew), vii-viii (English summary).

Isaac, Benjamin. [2961] "Roman Colonies in Judea: The Foundation of Aelia Capitolina," in A. Oppenheimer, U. Rappaport, and M. Stern (eds.), Jerusalem in the Second Temple Period: Abraham Schalit Memorial Volume. Jerusalem: Yad Izhaq Ben-Zvi, 1980, 340-360 (Hebrew), xx (English summary).

Isaac, Benjamin and Oppenheimer, Aharon. [2962] "The Revolt of Bar Kokhba: Ideology and Modern Scholarship," Journal of Jewish Studies, 36 (1985), 33-60.

Jeffrey, George. [2963] "Roman Remains Found on the Anglican College Ground, Jerusalem," Palestine Exploration Fund, Quarterly Statement, (1898), 35.

Jonas, Rudolf. [2964] "Titus (Flavius Vespasian) and (Flavius Claudius) Julian: Two Gem Portraits from the Jerusalem Area," Palestine Exploration Quarterly, (1971), 9-12.

Kadman, Leo. [2965] The Coins of Aelia Capitolina. Corpus Nummorum Palaestinensium, 1. Jerusalem: Universitas, 1956, 191 pp.

Kadman, Leo. [2966] "When Was Aelia Capitolina Named 'Commodiana' and By Whom?" Israel Exploration Journal, 9 (1959), 137-140.

Kanael, Baruch. [2967] "Notes on the Dates Used During the Bar Kokhba Revolt," Israel Exploration Journal, 21 (1971), 39-46.

Kenyon, Kathleen M. [2968] "Roman and Byzantine Jerusalem," in Jerusalem: Excavating 3,000 Years of History. New York: McGraw-Hill, 1967, 187-193.

Kindler, Arie. [2969] "The Bar Kokhba Revolt (132-135 C. E.)," in Coins of the Land of Israel: A Collection of the Bank of Israel, a Catalogue. Jerusalem: Keter, 1974, 58-93.

Kindler, Arie. [2970] "The Coinage of the Bar Kokhba War," in Israel Numismatic Society: The Dating and Meaning of Ancient Jewish Coins and Symbols. Numismatic Studies and Researches, 2. Jerusalem: Schocken, 1958, 62-80.

Kindler, Arie. [2971] "The Roman Administration in Eretz Israel after the Destruction of the Second Temple (70 C. E.), / The Imperial 'Judaea Capta' Issues, / Denarii of Hadrian (117-138 C. E.), / Colonia Aelia Capitolina," in Coins of the Land of Israel: A Collection of the Bank of Israel. A Catalogue. Jerusalem: Keter, 1974, 107-128.

Luria, Ben-Zion. [2972] "Did the Jews Make Pilgrimage to Jerusalem and Did They Settle There after the Bar Kokhba Rebellion? Beth Miqra, 19 (1974), 309-336, 457-458 (Hebrew).

Mantel, Hugo. [2973] "The Causes of the Bar Kokhba War," Jewish Quarterly Review, 58 (1968), 224-242, 274-296.

Margalit, Sh. See Chen, Doren; Margalit, Sh.; and Solar, Giora. [2930-2931]

Mazar, Benjamin. [2974] "Archaeological Discovery in Jerusalem after A. D. 70: The Roman Period," in The Mountain of the Lord. Garden City, NY: Doubleday, 1975, 232-244.

Meshorer, Ya'akov. [2975] "The Bar Cochba War," in Ancient Jewish Coinage, 2: Herod the Great through Bar Cochba. Dix Hills, NY: Amphora Books, 1985, 132-165.

Meshorer, Ya'akov. [2976] "The Coins of the Bar Cochba War, 132-135 C. E.," in Jewish Coins of the Second Temple Period. Tel-Aviv: Am Hassefer and Massada, 1967, 92-101.

Meshorer, Ya'akov. [2977] "The Perforated Dinar of Bar Kokhba," in A. Kindler (ed.), The Patterns of Monetary Development in Phoenicia and Palestine in

Antiquity. Proceedings of the International Numismatic Convention, Jerusalem, 27-31 December 1963. Tel-Aviv: Schocken, 1967, 209-211.

Meyshan. Josef. [2978] "The Legion which Reconquered Jerusalem in the War of Bar Kochba (A. D. 132-135)," Palestine Exploration Quarterly, 90 (1958), 19-26. [Numismatic evidence; Fifth Legion Macedonica.]

Mildenberg, Leo. [2979] "Bar Kokhba Coins and Documents," Harvard Studies in Classical Philology, 84 (1980), 311-355.

Mildenberg, Leo. [2980] "Bar Kokhba in Jerusalem?" Schweizer Münzblätter, 27/105 (1977), 1-6.

Mildenberg, Leo. [2981] The Coinage of the Bar Kokhba War. New York: Garland Publishing Co., 1985, 396 pp.

Mildenberg, Leo. [2982] "The Monetary System of the Bar Kokhba Coinage," in A. Kindler (ed.), The Patterns of Monetary Development in Phoenicia and Palestine in Antiquity. Proceedings of the International Numismatic Convention, Jerusalem, 27-31 December 1963. Tel-Aviv: Schocken, 1967, 41-49.

Milik, J. T. [2983] "Textes hébreux et araméens," in P. Benoit, J. T. Milik, and R. de Vaux (eds.), Les Grottes de Murabba'ât. Discoveries in the Judaean Desert, 2. Oxford: Clarendon, 1961, Texte, 67-205.

Mor, Menahem and Rappaport, Uriel. [2984] "Bibliography of the Bar-Kokhva Revolt (1960-1983)," in A. Oppenheimer and U. Rappaport, The Bar-Kokhva Revolt: A New Approach. Jerusalem: Yad Izhaq Ben-Zvi, 1984, 243-251.

Muesham, Alice. [2985] Coin and Temple: A Study of the Architectural Representation on Ancient Jewish Coins. Leiden: Brill, 1966, 70 pp.

Murray, A. S. [2986] "Latin Inscription in the Wall of Neby Daud, Jerusalem," Palestine Exploration Fund, Quarterly Statement, (1895), 130.

Offord, Joseph. [2987] "Fresh Light on Hadrian's Jewish War," Palestine Exploration Fund, Quarterly Statement, (1919), 37-38.

Offord, Joseph. [2988] "A MS of Homer at Jerusalem," Palestine Exploration Fund, Quarterly Statement, (1912), 158.

Offord, Joseph. [2989] "A New-Found Inscription Concerning Hadrian's Jewish War," Palestine Exploration Fund, Quarterly Statement, (1916), 38-40.

Offord, Joseph and Gibbon, H. H. Clifford. [2990] "Recently Found Inscriptions Relating to the Roman Campaigns in Palestine," Palestine Exploration Fund, Quarterly Statement, (1911), 91-97.

Oppenheimer, Aharon. See Isaac, Benjamin and Oppenheimer, Aharon. [2962]

Oppenheimer, Aharon. [2991] "The Bar Kokhba Revolt," Immanuel: A Bulletin of Religious Thought and Research in Israel, 14 (1982), 58-76.

Oppenheimer, Aharon and Rappaport, Uriel. [2992] The Bar-Kokhva Revolt: A New Approach. Jerusalem: Yad Izhaq Ben-Zvi, 1984, 254 pp. (Hebrew) + xviii pp. (English summaries).

Rabello, Alfredo M. [2993] "The Edicts on Circumcision as a Factor in the Bar-Kokhva Revolt," in A. Oppenheimer and U. Rappaport, The Bar-Kokhva Revolt: A New Approach. Jerusalem: Yad Izhaq Ben-Zvi, 1984, 27-46 (Hebrew), iv-v (English summary).

Rappaport, Uriel. See Mor, Menahem and Rappaport, Uriel. [2984]

Rappaport, Uriel. See Oppenheimer, Aharon and Rappaport, Uriel. [2992]

Reifenberg, Adolf. [2994] "Second Revolt of the Jews (A. D. 132-135)," in Ancient Jewish Coins. Jerusalem: Rubin Mass, 6th edn. 1973, 33-38.

Safrai, Shmuel. [2995] "The Status of Provincia Judaea after the Destruction," Zion, 27 (1962), 216-222 (Hebrew with English summary).

Schäfer, Peter. [2996] "Aqiva and Bar Kokhba," in W. S. Green (ed.), Approaches to Ancient Judaism, 2. Brown Judaic Studies, 9. Chico, CA: Scholars Press, 1980, 113-130.

Schäfer, Peter. [2997] Der Bar Kokhba-Aufstand: Studien zum zweiten jüdischen Krieg gegen Rom. Texte und Studien zum Antiken Judentum, 1. Tübingen: Mohr (Siebeck), 1981, 271 pp.

Schäfer, Peter. [2998] "The Causes of the Bar Kokhba Revolt," in Studies in Aggadah, Targum and Jewish Liturgy (Joseph Heinemann Memorial Volume). Jerusalem, 1981, 74-94.

Schick, Conrad. [2999] "Inscription of the Xth Legion Fretensis," Palestine Exploration Fund, Quarterly Statement, (1898), 158.

Solar, Giora. See Chen, Doren; Margalit, Sh.; and Solar, Giora. [2930-2931]

Spijkerman, Auguste. [3000] "Observations on the Coinage of Aelia Capitolina," Studii Biblici Franciscani, Liber Annuus, 14 (1963/1964), 245-260.

Spijkerman, Auguste. [3001] "A Supplemental Study of the Coinage of Aelia Capitolina," Studii Biblici Franciscani, Liber Annuus, 7 (1956/1957), 145-164.

Steve, M. A. See Vincent, Louis-Hugues and Steve, M. A. [3009]

Stinespring, William F. [3002] "Hadrian in Palestine," Journal of the American Oriental Society, 59 (1939), 360-365.

Sukenik, Eleazar L. [3003] "Some Unpublished Coins of Aelia Capitolina," Jewish Quarterly Review, 38 (1947), 157-160.

Syme, R. [3004] "Antonius Saturninus," Journal of Roman Studies, 68 (1978), 12-21. [On Latin inscription found near the Temlpe Mount.]

Trifon, Dalia Ben-Haim. [3005] "Some Aspects of Internal Politics Connected with the Bar-Kokhva Revolt," in A. Oppenheimer and U. Rappaport, The Bar-Kokhva Revolt: A New Approach. Jerusalem: Yad Izhaq Ben-Zvi, 1984, 13-26 (Hebrew), iii (English summary).

Verdier, P. [3006] "La colonne de Colonia Aelia Capitolina et l' imago clipeata du Christ Helios," Cahiers Archéologique, 23 (1974), 17-40.

Vincent, Louis-Hugues. [3007] "Aelia Capitolina," in Jérusalem Nouvelle, 1. Paris: Gabalda, 1914, 1-88.

Vincent, Louis-Hugues. [3008] "Timbres romains," Revue biblique, 19 (1910), 261-265.

Vincent, Louis-Hugues and Steve, M. A. [3009] "Du siège de 70 à la fondation d' Aelia Capitolina," in Jérusalem de l' Ancien Testament, 3. Paris: Gabalda, 1956, 753-782.

Wilson, Charles W. [3010] "The Camp of the Tenth Legion at Jerusalem and the City of Aelia," Palestine Exploration Fund, Quarterly Statement, (1905), 138-144.

Yadin, Yigael. See Avigad, Nahman; Aharoni, Yohannan; Bar-Adon, P.; and Yadin, Yigael. [2913-2914]

Yadin, Yigael. [3011] Bar-Kokhba: The Rediscovery of the Legendary Hero of the Last Jewish Revolt. London: Weidenfeld and Nicholson and New York: Random House, 1971, 271 pp.

Yadin, Yigael. [3012] The Finds from the Bar-Kokhba Period in the Cave of the Letters. Judean Desert Series, 1. Jerusalem: Israel Exploration Society, 1963, 273 pp. + 108 pls.

Yadin, Yigael. [3013] "More on the Letters of Bar Kochba," Biblical Archaeologist, 24 (1961), 86-95. Also in E. F. Campbell, Jr. and D. N. Freedman (eds.), The Biblical Archaeologist Reader, 3. Garden City, NY: Doubleday, 1970, 270-278.

Yadin, Yigael. [3014] "New Discoveries in the Judean Desert," Biblical Archaeologist, 24 (1961), 34-50. Also in E. F. Campbell, Jr. and D. N. Freedman (eds.), The Biblical Archaeologist Reader, 3. Garden City, NY: Doubleday, 1970, 254-269..

Zangemeister, Karl. [3015] "Römische Inschrift von Jerusalem," Zeitschrift des deutschen Palästina-Vereins, 10 (1887), 49-53; 11 (1888), 138.

Twenty-Two

Jewish Presence in Jerusalem From Julian II to Modern Times / Jerusalem in Jewish Thought

Adler, Cyrus. [3016] Memorandum on the Western Wall, Submitted to the Special Commision of the League of Nations on Behalf of the Rabbinate, the Jewish Agency for Palestine, the Jewish Community of Palestine (Knesseth Israel) and the Central Agudath Israel of Palestine. Jerusalem, 1930, 75 pp. / Philadelphia: Dropsie College Publications, 1930, 103 pp.

Adler, Marcus N. [3017] The Itinerary of Benjamin of Tudela: Critical Text, Translation, and Commentary. London: H. Frowde, 1907, 89 pp.; reprinted, London: Philipp Feldheim, 1965.

Adler, Marcus N. [3018] "Jewish Pilgrims to Palestine," Palestine Exploration Fund, Quarterly Statement, (1894), 288-300.

Amram, David. [3019] "A Further Example of Paronomasia on Jerusalem," Journal of Biblical Literature, 49 (1930), 429.

Andrews, Fannie Fern. [3020] "The Wailing Wall," in The Holy Land under Mandate, 2. New York: Houghton Mifflin, 1931, 223-289.

Aner, Zeev. See Ben-Dov, Meir; Naor, Mordechai; and Aner, Zeev. [3045]

Arazi, Simon. See Ben-Arieh, Yehoshua; Arazi, Simon; Yablovitch, Moshe. [3044]

Arce, Augustín. [3021] "The Location of David's Tomb According to the Itinerary of Benjamin of Tudela," in Jerusalem in the Middle Ages, Selected Papers. Jerusalem: Yad Izhaq Ben-Zvi, 1979, 112-121 (Hebrew), xiii-xiv (English summary). English summary also in "From the Hebrew Press: Jerusalem in the Middle Ages, Selected Papers," in L. I. Levine (ed.), Jerusalem Cathedra, 2. Jerusalem: Yad Izhaq Ben-Zvi Institute / Detroit: Wayne State University Press, 1982, 321.

Arce, Augustín. [3022] "Restricciones impuestas a los judios en Jerusalen (1534)," Sefarad, 17 (1957), 49-72.

Arce, Augustín. [3023] "Restrictions upon the Freedom of Movement of Jews in Jerusalem (15th-16th Centuries)," in Jerusalem in the Middle Ages, Selected Papers. Jerusalem: Yad Izhaq Ben-Zvi, 1979, 206-220 (Hebrew), xix (English summary). English summary also in "From the Hebrew Press: Jerusalem in the Middle Ages, Selected Papers," in L. I. Levine (ed.), Jerusalem Cathedra, 2. Jerusalem: Yad Izhaq Ben-Zvi Institute / Detroit: Wayne State University Press, 1982, 323.

Arce, Augustín. [3024] "El sepulcro de David en un texte de Benjamin de Tudela (1169)," Sefarad, 23 (1963), 105-115.

Auerbach, Jacob. [3025] "Western Wall," in Encyclopaedia Judaica, 16. Jerusalem: Macmillan, 1971, 467-472.

Avi-Yonah, Michael. [3026] "The Eternal City," Ariel, 23 (1969), 5-10. Also in Israel Yearbook, 1970. Tel Aviv: Israel Yearbook Publications, 1970, 223-232.

Avitsur, Shmuel. [3027] "Jewish Craftsmanship and Industry at the Time of Mandate in Jerusalem," in M. Friedman, B.-Z. Yehoshua, and Y. Tobi (eds.), Chapters in the History of the Jewish Community in Jerusalem, 2. Jerusalem: Yad Izhaq Ben-Zvi, 1976, 266-285 (Hebrew), xvii-xix (English summary).

Avitsur, Shmuel. [3028] "The Jewish Quarter of the Old City of Jerusalem," in Y. Ben-Porat, B.-Z. Yehoshua, and A. Kedar (eds.), Chapters in the History of the Jewish Community in Jerusalem, 1. Jerusalem: Yad Izhaq Ben-Zvi, 1973, 9-43 (Hebrew).

Bacher, W. [3029] "Statements of a Contemporary of the Emperor Julian on the Rebuilding of the Temple," Jewish Quarterly Review, 10 (1898), 168-172.

"Back to Sanity in Jerusalem: Reconstruction of the Jewish Quarter," [3030] The Architectural Review, 152 (July, 1972), 41-43.

Bahat, Dan. [3031] Jerusalem: Selected Plans of Historical Sites and Monumental Buildings. Jerusalem: Ariel Publishing House, 1980, passim, esp. 35-41.

Bahat, Dan. [3032] "Jewish Quarter," in Carta's Historical Atlas of Jerusalem: An Illustrated History. Jerusalem: Carta, 1983, 87.

Baras, Zvi. [3033] "Jewish-Christian Disputes and Conversions in Jerusalem," in Jerusalem in the Middle Ages, Selected Papers. Jerusalem: Yad Izhaq Ben-Zvi, 1979, 27-38 (Hebrew), viii-ix (English summary). English summary also in "From the Hebrew Press: Jerusalem in the Middle Ages, Selected Papers," in L. I. Levine (ed.), Jerusalem Cathedra, 2. Jerusalem: Yad Izhaq Ben-Zvi Institute / Detroit: Wayne State University Press, 1982, 319.

Barnai, Ya'acov. [3034] "The Mugrabi Community in Jerusalem in the 19th Century," in Y. Ben-Porat, B.-Z. Yehoshua, and A. Kedar (eds.), Chapters in the History of the Jewish Community in Jerusalem, 1. Jerusalem: Yad Izhaq Ben-Zvi, 1973, 129-140 (Hebrew).

Barnai, Ya'acov. [3035] "The Regulations (taqanot) of Jerusalem in the Eighteenth Century as a Source on the Sociey, Economy, and Daily Activities of the Jewish Community," in A. Cohen (ed.), Jerusalem in the Early Ottoman Period. Jerusalem: Yad Izhaq Ben-Zvi, 1979, 271-316 (Hebrew), xiv-xvi (English summary).

Bartur, R. [3036] "Episodes in the Relations of the American Consulate in Jerusalem with the Jewish Community in the 19th Century (1856-1906)," Cathedra: For the History of Eretz-Israel and its Yishuv, 5 (1977), 109-143 (Hebrew).

Bartura, Avraham. [3037] "On the History of 'Batei Machse," in Y. Ben-Porat, B.-Z. Yehoshua, and A. Kedar (eds.), Chapters in the History of the Jewish

Community in Jerusalem, 1. Jerusalem: Yad Izhaq Ben-Zvi, 1973, 122-128 (Hebrew).

Bashan, Eliezer. [3038] "A Document Dated 5384 (1624) concerning a Dispute on Lending Money to Christians in Jerusalem," in M. Friedman, B.-Z. Yehoshua, and Y. Tobi (eds.), Chapters in the History of the Jewish Community in Jerusalem, 2. Jerusalem: Yad Izhaq Ben-Zvi, 1976, 77-96 (Hebrew), ix (English summary).

Bashan, Eliezer. [3039] "A German Source on the Ashkenazi Community in Jerusalem in the 1830's," in A. Cohen (ed.), Jerusalem in the Early Ottoman Period. Jerusalem: Yad Izhaq Ben-Zvi, 1979, 317-322 (Hebrew), xvi-xvii (English summary).

Bayer, Bathja. See Narkiss, Bezalel and Bayer, Bathja. [3196]

Ben-Arieh, Yehoshua. [3040] "The First Jewish Quarters Erected Outside the Old City Walls in the 1880's," Cathedra: For the History of Eretz-Israel and its Yishuv, 2 (1976), 20-58 (Hebrew).

Ben-Arieh, Yehoshua. [3041] "The Growth of the Jewish Community of Jerusalem in the 19th Century," in Y. Ben-Porat, B.-Z. Yehoshua, and A. Kedar (eds.), Chapters in the History of the Jewish Community in Jerusalem, 1. Jerusalem: Yad Izhaq Ben-Zvi, 1973, 80-121 (Hebrew).

Ben-Arieh, Yehoshua. [3042] "The Jewish Community before Expansion beyond the Old City Walls (1800-1870), / The Jewish Community of Jerusalem at the End of the Ottoman Period (1870-1914)," in Jerusalem in the 19th Century: The Old City. Jerusalem: Yad Izhaq Ben-Zvi / New York: St. Martin's, 1984, 265-389.

Ben-Arieh, Yehoshua. [3043] "The Process of the Jewish Community's Emergence from within Jerusalem's Walls at the End of the Ottoman Period," in A. Shinan (ed.), Proceedings of the Sixth World Congress of Jewish Studies, 2. Jerusalem: World Union of Jewish Studies, 1975, 239-315.

Ben-Arieh, Yehoshua; Arazi, Simon; Yablovitch, Moshe. [3044] "The Jewish Quarter in the Old City: Site, Growth, and Expansion in the Nineteenth Century," in M. Friedman, B.-Z. Yehoshua, and Y. Tobi (eds.), Chapters in the History of the Jewish Community in Jerusalem, 2. Jerusalem: Yad Izhaq Ben-Zvi, 1976, 9-51 (Hebrew), vii (English summary).

Ben-Dov, Meir; Naor, Mordechai; and Aner, Zeev. [3045] The Western Wall. Jerusalem: Ministry of Defense Publishing House, 1983, 245 pp.

Ben-Eliezer, Shimon. [3046] Destruction and Renewal: The Synagogues of the Jewish Quarter. Jerusalem: Rubin Mass, 1973, 64 pp.

Ben-Porat, Yehuda; Yehoshua, Ben-Zion.; and Kedar, Ahron (eds.). [3047] Chapters in the History of the Jewish Community in Jerusalem, 1. Jerusalem: Yad Izhaq Ben-Zvi, 1973, 337 pp. (Hebrew).

Ben-Sasson, Hayim H. [3048] "The Image of Eretz-Israel in the View of Jews Arriving There in the Late Middle Ages," in M. Ma'oz (ed.), Studies on

Palestine During the Ottoman Period. Jerusalem: Magnes Press, 1975, 103-110.

Ben-Zvi, Izhak. [3049] "Eretz Israel under Ottoman Rule, 1517-1917," in L. Finkelstein (ed.), The Jews: Their History, Culture, and Religion, 1. New York: Harper and Row, 3rd edn., 1960, 602-689; New York: Schocken Books, 4th edn., 399-486.

Ben-Zvi, Izhaq. [3050] "The Jews in Jerusalem under Ottoman Rule till the End of the 18th Century," in Judah and Jerusalem: The Twelfth Archaeological Convention. Jerusalem: Israel Exploration Society, 1957, 110-128 (Hebrew), viii (English summary).

Ben-Zvi, Izhaq. [3051] "Under Ottoman Rule, 1517-1917," in D. Ben-Gurion (ed.), The Jews in their Land. Garden City, NY: Doubleday, 1974, 224-269.

Bentwich, Norman. [3052] "Jerusalem," in Palestine of the Jews, Past, Present, and Future. London: Kegan Paul, Trench, Trubner and Co., 1919, 100-128.

Benvenisti, Meron. [3053] "The Western Wall and the Jewish Quarter," in Jerusalem: The Torn City. Minneapolis: University of Minnesota Press, 1976, 305-322.

Berkovits, Eliezer. [3054] "From the Temple to Synagogue and Back," Judaism, 8 (1959), 303-311.

Bickermann, Elias. [3055] "The Civic Prayer for Jerusalem," Harvard Theological Review, 55 (1962), 163-185. Revised version in Studies in Jewish and Christian History, 2. Leiden: Brill, 1980, 290-312.

Blanchetière, François. [3056] "Julian philhellène, philosémite, antichétien: L' affaire du temple de Jérusalem," Journal of Jewish Studies, 31 (1980), 61-81.

Braslavi, Joseph. [3057] "Pilgrimages to the Mount of Olives in the Middle Ages," in J. Aviram (ed.), Jerusalem through the Ages. Jerusalem: Israel Exploration Society, 1968, 120-144 (Hebrew), 63 (English summary).

Brock, Sebastian P. [3058] "A Letter Attributed to Cyril of Jerusalem on the Rebuilding of the Temple," Bulletin of the American Schools of Oriental Research, 40 (1977), 267-286.

Brock, Sebastian P. [3059] "The Rebuilding of the Temple under Julian: A New Source," Palestine Exploration Quarterly, (1976), 103-107.

Broshi, Magen. [3060] "Jewish Jerusalem throughout the Ages," in Discussing Jerusalem: From the Procedings of the Seminar Held at the Van-Leer Jerusalem Foundation. Jerusalem: Israel Academic Committee on the Middle East, 1972, 38 pp.

Brownrigg, Ronald. See Hollis, Christopher and Brownrigg, Ronald. [3145]

Carmoly, E. [3061] Itineraires de la Tera Sainte des XIIIe, XIVe, XVe, XVIe et XVIIe siècle, traduits de l' hébreu et accompagnes de tables, de cartes et d' éclairissements. Brussels: Vandale, 1847, 572 pp.

Cassuto, D. [3062] "Four Sephardi Synagogues in the Old City," in Y. Yadin (ed.), Jerusalem Revealed: Archaeology in the Holy City, 1968-1974. New Haven and London: Yale University Press and the Israel Exploration Society, 1976, 122-123.

Cassuto, D. [3063] "Four Sephardi Synagogues in the Old City," Qadmoniot, 5 (1972), 135-137 (Hebrew).

Charif, Ruth and Simcha, Raz. [3064] Jerusalem, the Eternal Bond: An Unbroken Link with the Jewish People. Tel Aviv: Don Pulishing House, 1977, 96 pp.

Chavel, Charles B. (ed.). [3065] "Prayer at the Ruins of Jerusalem," in Ramban (Nachmanides): Writings and Discourses, 2. New York: Shilo, 1978, 697-725.

Christie, W. M. [3066] "The Wailing Wall at Jerusalem," Expository Times, 42 (1930/1931), 176-180.

Cohen, Amnon. [3067] "Demographic Changes in the Jewish Comunity of Jerusalem in the Sixteenth Century on the Basis of Turkish and Arabic Sources," in Jerusalem in the Early Ottoman Period. Jerusalem: Yad Izhaq Ben-Zvi, 1979, 93-111 (Hebrew), ix-x (English summary).

Cohen, Amnon. [3068] "Development Projects in Jerusalem under Early Ottoman Rule," Cathedra: For the History of Eretz-Israel and its Yishuv, 8 (1978), 179-187 (Hebrew).

Cohen, Amnon. [3069] Jewish Life under Islam: Jerusalem in the Sixteenth Century. Cambridge, MA: Harvard University Press, 1984, 267 pp.

Cohen, Amnon. [3070] "Local Trade, International Trade and Government Involvement in Jerusalem During the Early Ottoman Period," Asian and African Studies: Journal of the Israel Oriental Society, 12 (1978), 5-12.

Cohen, Amnon. [3071] "New Evidence on Demographic Change: The Jewish Community in Sixteenth Century Jerusalem," in R. Mantran (ed.), Memorial Omer Lûfti Barkan. Paris, 1980, 57-64.

Cohen, Amnon. [3072] "On the Realities of the Millet System: Jerusalem in the Sixteenth Century," in B. Braude and B. Lewis (eds.), Christians and Jews in the Ottoman Empire, 2: The Arabic- Speaking Lands. New York/London: Holmes and Meier, 7-18.

Cohen, Amnon. [3073] Ottoman Documents on the Jewish Community of Jerusalem in the Sixteenth Century. Jerusalem: Yad Izhaq Ben-Zvi, 1976, 100 pp. (Turkish texts with Hebrew translations) + xxii pp (English summary).

Cohen, Amnon. [3074] "Sixteenth Century Egypt and Palestine: The Jewish Connection as Reflected in the Sijill of Jerusalem," in A. Cohen and G. Baer (eds), Egypt and Palestine: A Millenium of Association (868-1948). New York: St. Martin's Press / Jerusalem: Ben Zvi Institute, 1984, 232-240.

Cohen, Shaye J. D. [3075] "The Temple and the Synagogue," in T. Madsen (ed.), The Temple in Antiquity: Ancient Records and Modern Perspectives.

Religious Studies Monograph Series, 9. Provo, UT: Brigham Young University Press, 1984, 151-174.

Cohn, Eric W. [3076] "Second Thoughts about the Perforated Stone on the Haram of Jerusalem," Palestine Exploration Quarterly, (1982), 143-146.

Cohn, Robert L. [3077] "Jerusalem: The Senses of a Center," Journal of the American Academy of Religion, 66 (1978), 63.

Comay, Joan. [3078] "The Western Wall," in The Temple of Jerusalem. New York: Holt, Rinehart, and Winston, 1975, 234-263.

Cornfeld, Gaalyah. [3079] "The Western Wall," in The Mystery of the Temple Mount. Tel Aviv: Bazak, 1972, 68-87.

Cragg, Kenneth. See Davies, William D. [3085]

Curtis, John B. [3080] "An Investigation of the Mount of Olives in the Judaeo-Christian Tradition," Hebrew Union College Annual, 28 (1957), 137-177.

Dalman, Gustaf. [3081] "Gegenwärtiger Bestand der judischen Colonien in Palästina: Die Umgebung von Jerusalem," Zeitschrift des deutschen Palästina-Vereins, 16 (1893), 196-197.

David, Abraham. [3082] "The Historical Significance of the 'Elders' Mentioned in the Letters of R. Obadia of Bertinoro," in Jerusalem in the Middle Ages, Selected Papers. Jerusalem: Yad Izhaq Ben-Zvi, 1979, 221-243 (Hebrew), xx (English summary). [On the leadership of the Jewish community of Jerusalem in the late 15th century.]

David, Abraham. [3083] "A Letter from Jerusalem from the Early Ottoman Period in Eretz-Yisrael," in A. Cohen (ed), Jerusalem in the Early Ottoman Period. Jerusalem: Yad Izhaq Ben-Zvi, 1979, 39-60 (Hebrew), vii-viii (English summary).

David, Abraham. [3084] "The Vice-Nagid of Jerusalem in the 15th and Early 16th Century," Zion, 85 (1980), 327-331 (Hebrew), xxvii-xxviii (English summary).

Davies, William D. [3085] "Symposium: The Territorial Dimensions of Judaism, Introductory Reflections, with Responses from K. Cragg, D. N. Freedman, A. Hertzberg, J. Neusner, K. Stendahl, R. J. Werblowsky, and J. S. Whale," in Midstream, 29/3 (March, 1983), 32-43.

Davies, William D. [3086] "The Territorial Dimension of Judaism," in D. Y. Hadidian (ed.), Intergerini Parietis Septum: Essays Presented to Markus Barth on His Sixty-Fifth Birthday. Pittsburgh: Pickwick, 1981, 61-96.

Davies, William D. [3087] The Territorial Dimension of Judaism. Berkeley: University of California Press, 1982, 168 pp.

Dinur, B. Z. [3088] "Aliya Inscriptions on the Temple Mount from the Early Times of the Arabic Conquest," Zion, 21 (1956), 50-65 (Hebrew).

Dinur, B. Z. [3089] "An Inscription on the Temple Mount from the Early Arab Period," in Judah and Jerusalem: The Twelfth Archaeological Convention. Jerusalem: Israel Exploration Society, 1957, 85-89 (Hebrew), vii (English summary). [Graffito of a Jewish pilgrim.]

Di Segni, Riccardo. [3090] "Gerusalemme nella tradizione religiosa giudaica dell' età post-bíblíca, " in M. Borrmans (ed.), Gerusalemme. Brescia: Paideia, 1982, 99-110.

Dorgelès, R. [3091] "The Wailing Wall," The Menorah Journal, 15 (1928), 362-368.

Druyan Nitza. [3092] "Yemenite Immigrants in Jerusalem: A Historical Survey of the Community from 1881-1914," in E. Shaltiel (ed.), Jerusalem in the Modern Period: Yaacov Herzog Memorial Volume. Jerusalem: Yad Izhaq Ben-Zvi and Ministry of Defense, 1981, 212-226 (Hebrew), vi-vii (English summary).

Dutheil, Michel; Vardi, Méir; and Neherm André. [3093] "Jérusalem, témoignages," in E. Amado Levy-Valensi and J. Halpérin (eds.), Israel dans la conscience juive: Données et debats 7e et 9e Colloques d' Intellectuels juifs de Langue Française. Paris: Presses Universitaires de France, 1971, 291-311.

Eliashar, Eliahu. [3094] "The Rabbi Yohanan Ben Zakkai Synagogues," in Y. Ben-Porat, B.-Z. Yehoshua, and A. Kedar (eds.), Chapters in the History of the Jewish Community in Jerusalem, 1. Jerusalem: Yad Izhaq Ben-Zvi, 1973, 61-79 (Hebrew).

Eliav, Mordechai. [3095] "Das deutsche Konsulat in Jerusalem und die jüdische Bevölkerung in Erez-Israel während des 19. Jahrhunderts," Bulletin des Leo Baeck Instituts, 11/43 (1968), 157-192.

Eliav, Mordechai. [3096] "The German Consulate in Jerusalem and the Jews in Jerusalem," Zionism, 1 (1970), 57-83.

Eliav, Mordechai. [3097] "German Interests and the Jewish Community in Nineteenth Century Palestine," M. Ma'oz (ed.), Studies on Palestine during the Ottoman Period. Jerusalem: Magnes Press, 1975, 423-441.

Eliav, Mordechai. [3098] "The Jewish Community in Jerusalem in the Late Ottoman Period (1815-1914)," in E. Shaltiel (ed.), Jerusalem in the Modern Period: Yaacov Herzog Memorial Volume. Jerusalem: Yad Izhaq Ben-Zvi and Ministry of Defense, 1981, 132-173 (Hebrew), iv (English summary).

Eliav, Mordechai. [3099] Die Juden Palästinas in der deutschen Politik, 2 vols. Tel Aviv: Tel Aviv University / Hakibbutz Hameuhad, 1973.

Eliav, Mordechai. [3100] "Notes on the Development of the 'Old Yishuv' in the 19th Century," in Y. Ben-Porat, B.-Z. Yehoshua, and A. Kedar (eds.), Chapters in the History of the Jewish Community of Jerusalem, 1. Jerusalem: Yad Izhaq Ben-Zvi, 1973, 44-60 (Hebrew).

Farhi, David. [3101] "Documents on the Attitude of the Ottoman Government Towards the Jewish Settlement in Palestine after the Revolution of the Young Turks," in M. Ma'oz (ed.), Studies on Palestine During the Ottoman Period. Jerusalem: Magnes Press, 1975, 190-210.

Feliks, Yehuda. [3102] "Flora and Fauna on the Kotel Ma'aravi (Western Wall)," in M. Friedman, B.-Z. Yehoshua, and Y. Tobi (eds.), Chapters in the History of the Jewish Community in Jerusalem, 2. Jerusalem: Yad Izhaq Ben-Zvi, 1976, 317-321 (Hebrew), xxi-xxii (English summary).

Feliks, Yehuda. [3103] "Flora and Fauna at the Wall," in M. Ben-Dov, M. Naor, and Z. Aner (eds.), The Western Wall. Jerusalem: Ministry of Defense Publishing House, 1983, 205-211.

Fishof, I. [3104] "'Jerusalem above My Chief Joy:' Depictions of Jerusalem in Italian Ketubot," Journal of Jewish Art, 9 (1982), 61-75.

Ford, J. Massyngberde. [3105] "The Heavenly Jerusalem and Orthodox Judaism," in E. Bammel; C. K. Barrett; and W. D. Davies (eds.), Donum gentilicium: New Testament Studies in Honour of David Daube. Oxford: Clarendon Press, 1978, 215-226.

Frankel, E. [3106] "Jérusalem: Projet de restauration urbaine; quartier juif de la vieille ville," L' Architecture d' Aujour-d'hui, 153 (1970), 66-69.

Freedman, David N. See Davies, William D. [3085]

Friedman, Irving. [3107] "The Sacred Space of Judaism," Parabola, 3/11 (1978), 20-23.

Friedman, Menahem. [3108] "On the Structure of Community Leadership and the Rabbinate in the 'Old Ashkenazi Yishuv' towards the End of the Ottoman Rule," in Y. Ben-Porat, B.-Z. Yehoshua, and A. Kedar (eds.), Chapters in the History of the Jewish Community in Jerusalem, 1. Jerusalem: Yad Izhaq Ben-Zvi, 1973, 273-288 (Hebrew).

Friedman, Menahem; Yehoshua, Ben-Zion; and Tobi, Yosef (eds.). [3109] Chapters in the History of the Jewish Community in Jerusalem, 2. Jerusalem: Yad Izhaq Ben-Zvi, 1976, 344 pp. (Hebrew) + xxii pp. (English summaries).

Gafni, Shlomo S. and Van der Heyden, A. [3110] "The Western Wall / Synagogues and the Orthodox Quarters," in The Glory of Jerusalem. Cambridge: Cambridge University Press, 1982, 28-35.

Gil, Moshe. [3111] "Aliya and Pilgrimage in the Early Arab Period," in L. I. Levine (ed.), Jerusalem Cathedra, 3. Jerusalem: Yad Izhaq Ben-Zvi Institute / Detroit: Wayne State University Press, 1983, 163-173.

Gil, Moshe. [3112] "Christian and Jewish Donations and Foundations for the Benefit of Jerusalem during the Early Muslim Period (638-1099)," Cathedra: For the History of Eretz-Israel and its Yishuv, 18 (1981), 57-72 (Hebrew).

Gil, Moshe. [3113] "The Jewish Quarter of Jerusalem (A. D. 638-1099) according to Cairo Geniza Documents and Other Sources," Journal of Near Eastern Studies, 41 (1982), 261-278.

Gil, Moshe. [3114] "The Scroll of Evyatar as an Historical Source for the Struggle of the Jerusalem Yeshiva during the Second Half of the Eleventh Century-- A New Reading of the Scroll," in Jerusalem in the Middle Ages, Selected Papers.

Jerusalem: Yad Izhaq Ben-Zvi, 1979, 39-106 (Hebrew), ix-xii (English summary). English summary also in "From the Hebrew Press: Jerusalem in the Middle Ages, Selected Papers," in L. I. Levine (ed.), Jerusalem Cathedra, 2. Jerusalem: Yad Izhaq Ben-Zvi Institute / Detroit: Wayne State University Press, 1982, 319-320.

Gilbert, Martin. [3115] "Jerusalem and the Jewish Search for a Secure Haven, 1000 A. D. - 1600," in Jerusalem History Atlas. New York: Macmillan, 1977, 22-23.

Gilbert, Martin. [3116] "Jerusalem: Holy City, City of Pilgrimage since 1000 B. C." in Jerusalem History Atlas. New York: Macmillan, 1977, 21.

Gilbert, Martin. [3117] "A Jewish Journey to Jerusalem, 1479," in Jerusalem History Atlas. New York: Macmillan, 1977, 33.

Gilbert, Martin. [3118] "The Jewish Quarter of the Old City in 1865," in Jerusalem History Atlas. New York: Macmillan, 1977, 50-51.

Gilbert, Martin. [3119] "The Jews of Jerusalem under Ottoman Rule, 1517-1831," in Jerusalem History Atlas. New York: Macmillan, 1977, 30-31.

Gilbert, Martin. [3120] "The Return of the Jews to Jerusalem, 1200-1841," in Jerusalem History Atlas. New York: Macmillan, 1977, 26-27.

Gilbert, Martin. [3121] "The 'Wailing Wall' under Ottoman Rule, 1517-1917," in Jerusalem History Atlas. New York: Macmillan, 1977, 34-35.

Goldman, Bernard. [3122] The Sacred Portal: A Primary Symbol in Ancient Judaic Art. Detroit: Wayne State University, 1966, 215 pp.

Goldschmidt-Lehmann, Ruth P. [3123] "Jerusalem and its Jews, 1517-1799: A Classified, Selected Bibliography," in A. Cohen (ed.), Jerusalem in the Early Ottoman Period. Jerusalem: Yad Izhaq Ben-Zvi, 1979, 435-453.

Goldschmidt-Lehmann, Ruth P. [3124] "The Jews in Medieval Jerusalem-- A Selected Bibliography," in Jerusalem in the Middle Ages, Selected Papers. Jerusalem: Yad Izhaq Ben-Zvi, 1979, 279-286 (Hebrew).

Goldschmidt-Lehmann, Ruth P. [3125] "The Western Wall: Selected Bibliography," Cathedra: For the History of Eretz-Israel and its Yishuv, 12 (1979), 207-225.

Green, Arthur. [3126] "Sabbath as Temple: Some Thoughts on Space and Time in Judaism," in R. Jospe and S. Z. Fishman (eds.), Go and Study: Essays in Honor of Alfred Jospe. Washington, DC: B'nai Brith Hillel Foundations, 1980, 287-305.

Grunwald, Kurt. [3127] "Jewish Schools under Foreign Flags in Ottoman Palestine," in M. Ma'oz (ed.), Studies on Palestine During the Ottoman Period. Jerusalem: Magnes Press, 1975, 164-174.

Gutmann, Joseph (ed.). [3128] The Temple of Solomon: Archaeological Fact and Medieval Tradition in Christian, Islamic and Jewish Art. Religion and the Arts, 3. Missoula, MT: Scholars Press, 1976, 198 pp.

Guttmann, Alexander. [3129] "Jerusalem in Tannaitic Law," Hebrew Union College Annual, 40/41 (1969/1970), 251-275.

Ha'cohen, Mordechai. [3130] "Sanctity, Law and Customs," in M. Ben-Dov, M. Naor, and Z. Aner (eds.), The Western Wall. Jerusalem: Ministry of Defense Publishing House, 1983, 79-97.

Halevy, Shoshana. [3131] "Clarifying the Development of Jerusalem outside the Walls," in Y. Ben-Porat, B.-Z. Yehoshua, and A. Kedar (eds.), Chapters in the History of the Jewish Community in Jerusalem, 1. Jerusalem: Yad Izhaq Ben-Zvi, 1973, 141-153 (Hebrew).

Halevy, Shoshana. [3132] "The Establishment of the Kollel Ungarn (Neturei Karta) and Batei Ungarn," in E. Shaltiel (ed.), Jerusalem in the Modern Period: Yaacov Herzog Memorial Volume. Jerusalem: Yad Izhaq Ben-Zvi and Ministry of Defense, 1981, 227-254 (Hebrew), vii-viii (English summary).

Halkin, Abraham S. [3133] Zion in Jewish Literature. New York: Herzl Press, 1961, 135 pp.

Halper, Jeff. [3134] "Oriental Jewish Communities in Jerusalem during the Century Preceding Statehood: Economic Sources of Ethnic Stratification," in E. Shaltiel (ed.), Jerusalem in the Modern Period: Yaacov Herzog Memorial Volume. Jerusalem: Yad Izhaq Ben-Zvi and Ministry of Defense, 1981, 279-301 (Hebrew), ix-x (English summary).

Hanauer, James Edward. [3135] "The Churches of St. Martin and St. John the Evangelist," Palestine Exploration Fund, Quarterly Statement, (1893), 301-305. [On the site of Ramban's synagogue; on Jewish-Arab relations.]

Hanauer, James Edward. [3136] "Julian's Attempt to Restore the Temple," Palestine Exploration Fund, Quarterly Statement, (1902), 389-392.

Har-El, Menashe. [3137] "The Jewish Presence in Jerusalem throughout the Ages," Christian News from Israel, 21/1 (1970), 25-30. Also in J. M. Oestrreicher and A. Sinai (eds.), Jerusalem. New York: John Day, 1974, 137-147.

Har-El, Menashe. [3138] "The Jewish Quarter in the Old City," in This is Jerusalem. Jerusalem: Canaan Publishing Co., 1977, 275-292.

Hayim, Abraham. [3139] "Additional Documents on the Relations of the Sephardi Community with the Ottoman Authorities and the Arab Population of Jerusalem," in M. Friedman, B.-Z. Yehoshua, and Y. Tobi (eds.), Chapters in the History of the Jewish Community in Jerusalem, 2. Jerusalem: Yad Izhaq Ben-Zvi, 1976, 216-238 (Hebrew), xiv-xvi (English summary).

Hayim, Abraham. [3140] "The Archives of the Council of the Sephardic Community in Jerusalem as a Source for the History of the Jewish Community in Palestine under Ottoman Rule," in M. Ma'oz (ed.), Studies on Palestine During the Ottoman Period. Jerusalem: Magnes Press, 1975, 557-561.

Hertzberg, Arthur. See Davies, William D. [3085]

Hertzberg, Arthur. [3141] "Judaism and the Land of Israel," Judaism, 19 (1970), 423-434. Also in J. Neusner (ed.), Understanding Jewish Theology: Classical Issues and Modern Perspectives. New York: KTAV, 1973, 75-88.

Heschel, Abraham J. [3142] "Jerusalem-- a Charismatic City," in Israel: An Echo of Eternity. New York: Farrar, Straus and Giroux, 1969, 5-38.

Hirschberg, H. Z. [3143] "The Temple Mount in Jewish and Mohammedan Traditions," in J. Aviram (ed.), Jerusalem through the Ages. Jerusalem: Israel Exploration Society, 1968, 109-119 (Hebrew), 62-63 (English summary).

Hirschberg, J. W. [3144] "The Remains of an Ancient Synagogue on Mt. Zion," in Y. Yadin (ed.), Jerusalem Revealed: Archaeology in the Holy City, 1968-1974. New Haven and London: Yale University Press and the Israel Exploration Society, 1976, 116-117.

Hollis, Christopher and Brownrigg, Ronald. [3145] "Jewish Holy Places," in Holy Places: Jewish, Christian, and Muslim Monuments in the Holy Land. New York: Praeger, 1969, 13-72.

Holtz, Avraham. [3146] The Holy City: Jews on Jerusalem. New York: Norton, 1970, 187 pp.

Holtz, Avraham. [3147] "Jerusalem-- City of Visions and Prayers," in L. Finkelstein (ed.), The Samuel Friedland Lectures, 1967-1974. New York: Jewish Theological Seminary, 1974, 41-50.

"Hurva Synagogue," [3148] Architectural Forum, 137 (July-Aug., 1972), 68-69.

Hyamson, Albert M. [3149] The British Consulate in Jerusalem in Relation to the Jews of Palestine, 1838-1914, 2 vols. London: The Jewish Historical Society of London, 1939-41.

International Commision for the Wailing Wall: [3150] The Rights and Claims of Moslems and Jews in Connection with the Wailing Wall at Jerusalem. Beirut: Institute for Palestine Studies, 1968, 93 pp.

Irwin, Patrick. [3151] "Bishop Alexander and the Jews of Jerusalem," in W. Sheils (ed.), Persecution and Toleration: Papers Read at the 22nd and 23rd Meetings of the Ecclesiastical Historical Society. Oxford: Blackwell, 1984, 317-327.

Izrael, Rami. [3152] Quartertour: Walking Tour of the Jewish Quarter. Jerusalem: Hamakor Press, n. d., 48 pp.

"Jerusalem in Judaism: Halakah, Aggadah, and Liturgy," [3153] in Encyclopaedia Judaica, 9. Jerusalem: Macmillan, 1971, 1553-1563. Reprinted in Israel Pocket Library: Jerusalem. Jerusalem: Keter Books, 279-297.

Joseph, Asher. See Schaffer, Shaul in conjunction with Joseph, Asher. [3240]

Kaniel, Yehoshua. [3154] "Cultural and Religious Cooperation between the Ashkenazim and the Sephardim in the 19th Century in Jerusalem," in Y. Ben-Porat, B.-Z. Yehoshua, and A. Kedar (eds.), Chapters in the History of the

Jewish Community in Jerusalem, 1. Jerusalem: Yad Izhaq Ben-Zvi, 1973, 289-300 (Hebrew).

Kaniel, Yehoshua. [3155] "Organizational and Economic Contentions between Communities in Jerusalem in the Nineteenth Century," in M. Friedman, B.-Z. Yehoshua, and Y. Tobi (eds.), Chapters in the History of the Jewish Community in Jerusalem, 2. Jerusalem: Yad Izhaq Ben-Zvi, 1976, 97-126 (Hebrew), x-xi (English summary).

Kaplan, Zvi. [3156] "Temple Mount," in Encyclopaedia Judaica, 15. Jerusalem: Macmillan, 1971, 988-994. [In Jewish thought and sentimentality.]

Kasher, Menahem M. [3157] The Western Wall: Its Meaning in the Thought of the Sages. New York: Judaica Press, 1972, 171 pp.

Katzburg, Nathaniel. [3158] "Cultural Conflicts in the Jewish World and the 'Yishuv' in Jerusalem in the 19th Century," in Y. Ben-Porat, B.-Z. Yehoshua, and A. Kedar (eds.), Chapters in the History of the Jewish Community in Jerusalem, 1. Jerusalem: Yad Izhaq Ben-Zvi, 1973, 301-309 (Hebrew).

Kaufmann, David. [3159] "Zur Geschichte der Aschkenasim-Gemeinde in Jerusalem während des 17. Jahrhunderts," Jerusalem, 4 (1892), 25-52.

Kedar, Ahron. See Ben-Porat, Yehuda; Yehoshua, Ben-Zion; and Kedar, Ahron (eds.). [3047]

Kedar, Benjamin Z. [3160] "The Jewish Community of Jerusalem in the Thirteenth Century," Tarbiz, 41 (1971), 82-94 (Hebrew), vi-vii (English summary).

Kedar, Benjamin Z. [3161] "The Jews of Jerusalem, 1187-1267, and the Role of Nahmanides in the Re-Establishment of their Community." in Jerusalem in the Middle Ages. Selected Papers. Jerusalem: Yad Izhaq Ben-Zvi, 1979, 122-136 (Hebrew), xiv-xv (English summary). English summary found also in "From the Hebrew Press: Jerusalem in the Middle Ages, Selected Papers," in L. I. Levine (ed.), Jerusalem Cathedra, 2. Jerusalem: Yad Izhaq Ben-Zvi Institute / Detroit: Wayne State University Press, 1982, 321-322.

Khayyat, Shimon. [3162] "Additional Documents on the Jewish Settlement in Jerusalem during the Ottoman Period," Sefarad, 42 (1982), 113-128.

Khayyat, Shimon. [3163] "New Sources on the Jewish Community in Jerusalem during the Ottoman Period," Hebrew Union College Annual, 51 (1980), 1*-8* (Hebrew section).

Kopp, Clemens. [3164] "Der Tempelplatz unter Julian," Das Heilige Land, 91 (1959), 17-24.

Krinsky, C. H. [3165] "Representations of the Temple before 1500," Journal of the Warburg and Courtauld Institutes, 33 (1970), 1-19.

Kroyanker, David and Wahrman, Dror. [3166] Jerusalem Architecture. Periods and Styles: The Jewish Quarters and Public Buildings outside the Old City Walls, 1860-1914. Jerusalem: Domino Press, 1983, 362 pp. [Includes studies of Me'a She'arim, Batei Ungarn, Batei Neitin, Mishkenot Sha'ananim and Yemin

Moshe, Sha'arei Hessed, Nahalat Shiva, Mazkeret Moshe and Ohel Moshe, Beit David, Even Israel, Batei Rand, Batei Braude, Knesset Yisrael, Ohel Shlomo, Sha'arei Yerushalayim, Batei Seidhoff, the Bukharan Quarter, and Zichron Moshe.]

Kurzweil, B. [3167] "Agnon's Jerusalem," Ariel, 23 (1969), 43-45.

La Sor, William. [3168] "The Sanctity of the Mount of Olives," Christian News from Israel, 13/3-4 (1962), 16-23.

Levinson, N. Peter. [3169] "Tempel und Synagoge," in Die Kultusymbolik im Alten Testament und im nachbiblischen Judentum. Symbolik der Religionen, 17. Stuttgart: Hiersemann, 1972, 15-45

Lewy, Yohanan. [3170] "Julian the Apostate and the Building of the Temple," in L. I. Levine (ed.), Jerusalem Cathedra, 3. Jerusalem: Yad Izhaq Ben-Zvi Institute / Detroit: Wayne State University Press, 1983, 70-96.

Lind, N. F. [3171] "Return of the Gaddites: Reminiscences of the American Colony and the Yemenite Jews in Jerusalem," Palestine Exploration Quarterly, (1973), 151-160.

Linder, Amnon. [3172] "Jerusalem as a Focal Point in the Conflict between Judaism and Christianity," in B. Z. Kedar (ed.), Jerusalem in the Middle Ages, Selected Papers. Jerusalem: Yad Izhaq Ben-Zvi, 1979, 5-26 (Hebrew), vii-viii (English summary).

Loewe, L. (ed.). [3173] The Diaries of Sir Moses and Lady Montefiòre. London: Griffith, Farran, Okeden, and Welsh, 1890, 363 pp.

Lohse, Eduard. [3174] "Zion-Jerusalem in Post-Biblical Judaism," in G. Friedrich (ed.), Theological Dictionary of the New Testament, 7. Grand Rapids: Eerdmans, 1971. 319-327.

Luncz, Abraham M. (ed.). [3175] Jerusalem Yearbook for the Diffusion of an Accurate Knowledge of Ancient and Modern Palestine, 1. Vienna: Georg Brög, 1882, 194 pp., esp. 20-82, 103-114. Facsimile edition with forward by Zev Vilnay, Jerusalem: Carta, 1982.

Luria, Ben-Zion. [3176] "The Western Wall," Dor le Dor, 6 (1978), 141-146, 198-203; 7 (1979), 35-40, 84-88, 136-139, 193-197.

Madmoni, Zion. [3177] "The Settlement of Yemenite Jews in Silwan," in Y. Ben-Porat, B.-Z. Yehoshua, and A. Kedar (eds.), Chapters in the History of the Jewish Community in Jerusalem, 1. Jerusalem: Yad Izhaq Ben-Zvi, 1973, 250-259 (Hebrew).

Mamluk, Gershon. [3178] "Jerusalem-- City of Three Religions?" Midstream, 26/7 (Aug./Sept., 1980), 7-9.

Mann, Jacob. [3179] The Jews in Egypt and in Palestine under the Fatimid Caliphs: A Contribution to their Political and Communal History Based Chiefly on Genizah Material Hitherto Unpublished, 2 vols. Oxford: Oxford University Press, 1969, 280 + 427 pp.

Mann, Jacob. [3180] "The Karaite Settlement in Palestine (til the First Crusade): 1. The Karaite Authors and Scholars of Jerusalem; 2. The Karaite Nesiim of Jerusalem; 3. The Social Relations and Strife between Rabbanites and Karaites in Jerusalem," in Texts and Studies in Jewish History and Literature, 2: Karaitica. Philadelphia: Jewish Publication Society, 1935, 3-66 = appendixes with source materials, 67-283.

Mann, Jacob. [3181] "A Tract by an Early Karaite Settler in Jerusalem," Jewish Quarterly Review, 12 (1922), 257-298.

Ma'oz, Moshe. [3182] "Changes in the Position of the Jewish Communities of Palestine and Syria in the Mid-Nineteenth Century," in M. Ma'oz (ed.), Studies on Palestine During the Ottoman Period. Jerusalem: Magnes Press, 1975, 142-163.

Ma'oz, Moshe. [3183] "Jerusalem in the Last Hundred Years of Turkish Ottoman Rule," in Y. Ben-Porat, B.-Z. Yehoshua, and A. Kedar (eds.), Chapters in the History of the Jewish Community in Jerusalem, 1. Jerusalem: Yad Izhaq Ben-Zvi, 1973, 260-272 (Hebrew).

Margoliouth, Moses. [3184] A Pilgrimage to the Land of My Fathers, 2. London: Bentley, 1850, 299-366.

Marmorstein, Emile. [3185] "European Jews in Muslim Palestine," Middle Eastern Studies, 11 (1975), 74-87. Also in E. Kedourie and S. G. Haim (eds.), Palestine and Israel in the 19th and 20th Centuries. London: Frank Cass, 1982, 1-14.

Matthews, Charles D. [3186] "The Wailing Wall and al-Buraq: Is the 'Wailing Wall' in Jerusalem the 'Wall of al-Buraq' of Moslem Tradition?" The Muslim World, 22 (1932), 331-339. [Negative.]

Mayer, Leo A. [3187] "Hebräische Inschriften im Haram zu Jerusalem," Zeitschrift des deutschen Palästina-Vereins, 53 (1930), 222-229.

Menes, Abraham. [3188] "Tempel und Synagoge," Zeitschrift für die alttestamentliche Wissenschaft, 50 (1932), 268-276.

Metzger, Thérèes. [3189] "Les objets du culte, le Sanctuaire du Désert et le Temple de Jérusalem, dans les Bibles Hébraîques médievales enlumineés, en Orient et en Espagne," Bulletin of the John Rylands Library, 52 (1969/1970), 397-436; 53 (1970/1971), 167-209.

Meyer, Martin A. [3190] "Jerusalem: Modern," in The Jewish Encyclopedia, 7. New York: Funk and Wagnalls, 1905, 150-157.

Millás, Vallicrosa, J. M. [3191] "Origenes de la localizacion de la tumba de David en el Santo Cenáculo," Estudios Eclesiásticos, 34 (1960), 595-602.

Montefiòre, Moses. See Loewe, L. (ed.). [3173]

Montgomery, James A. [3192] "'The Place' as an Appelation of Deity," Journal of Biblical Literature, 24 (1905), 17-26.

Motzkin, A. L. [3193] "A Thirteenth Century Jewish Physician in Jerusalem: A Geniza Portrait," Muslim World, 60 (1970), 344-349.

Nahon, S. A. [3194] "Ritual Articles in the Synagogues," in E. Reiner, The Yochanan Ben Zakkai Four Sephardi Synagogues. Jerusalem: Israel Comunications, 1977, 46-47.

Naor, Mordechai. See Ben-Dov, Meir; Naor, Mordechai; and Aner, Zeev. [3045]

Narkiss, Bezalel. [3195] "Temple in the Arts," in Encyclopaedia Judaica, 15. Jerusalem: Macmillan, 1971, 984-988.

Narkiss, Bezalel and Bayer, Bathja. [3196] "Jerusalem in the Arts," in Encyclopaedia Judaica, 9. Jerusalem: Macmillan, 1971, 1577-1591. Reprinted in Israel Pocket Library: Jerusalem. Jerusalem: Keter Books, 1973, 326-348.

Nau, F. [3197] "Deux episodes de l' histoire juive sous Théodore II (423 et 438) d' après la vie de Barsauma le Syrien," Revue des études juives, 83 (1927), 184-206.

Neher, André. See Dutheil, Michel; Vardi, Méir; and Neher, André. [3093]

Netzer, Ehud. [3198] "Reconstruction of the Jewish Quarter in the Old City," in Y. Yadin (ed.), Jerusalem Revealed: Archaeology in the Holy City, 1968-1974. New Haven and London: Yale University Press and the Israel Exploration Society, 1976, 118-121.

Netzer, Ehud. [3199] "Reconstruction of the Jewish Quarter in the Old City, Jerusalem," Qadmoniot, 5 (1972), 132-135 (Hebrew).

Neusner, Jacob. See Davies, William D. [3085]

Neusner, Jacob. [3200] "Map without Territory: Mishnah's System of Sacrifice and Sanctuary," History of Religions, 19 (1979), 103-127.

Noy, Dov. [3201] "Folk Tales about the Western Wall," in M. Ben-Dov, M. Naor, and Z. Aner (eds.), The Western Wall. Jerusalem: Ministry of Defense Publishing House, 1983, 99-119.

Parfitt, Tudor. [3202] "The Jewish Presence in Jerusalem, 1800-1881: Jerusalem before Zionism," in P. Schneider and G. Wigoder (eds.), Jerusalem Perspectives: A Nineteenth and Twentieth Century Outline of the Holy City. Arundel, West Susex: London Rainbow Group, 1976, 5-10.

Partin, Harry B. [3203] "Pilgrimage to Jerusalem: Jewish, Christain, Muslim," Encounter, 46 (1985), 15-35.

Paul, Shalom M. [3204] "Jerusalem-- A City of Gold," Israel Exploration Journal, 17 (1967), 259-263.

Paul, Shalom M. [3205] "Jerusalem of Gold-- A Song and an Ancient Crown," Biblical Archaeology Review, 3/4 (Dec., 1977), 38-40.

Paulker, Fred. See Sperber, Daniel. [3254]

Peli, Pinchas. [3206] "The Meaning of Jerusalem in the Jewish Religion," in Israel Yearbook, 1980. Tel Aviv: Israel Yearbook Publications, 1980, 197-199.

Phillips, Charles R., III. [3207] "Julian's Rebuilding of the Temple: A Sociological Study of Religious Competition," in P. J. Achtemeir (ed.), Society of Biblical Literature 1979 Seminar Papers. Missoula, MT: Scholars Press, 1979, 167-172.

Pinkerfeld, Jacob. [3208] "'David's Tomb,' Notes on the History of the Building," Bulletin of the Louis M. Rabinowitz Fund for the Exploration of Ancient Synagogues, 3. Jerusalem: Hebrew University, Department of Archaeology, 1960, 41-43.

Pinkerfeld, Jacob. [3209] "Synagogues in the Old City," in Judah and Jerusalem: The Twelfth Archaeological Convention. Jerusalem: Israel Exploration Society, 1957, 105-109 (Hebrew), vi (English summary).

Popper, William. [3210] "Pilgrimage (Hebrew and Jewish)," in James Hastings (ed.), Encyclopaedia of Religion and Ethics, 10. New York: Scribner's, 1928, 23-24.

Prawer, Joshua. [3211] "Jerusalem in the Christian and Jewish Perspectives of the Early Middle Ages," in Gli ebrei nell' alto mediovo. Spoleto, 1980, 739-814.

Prawer, Joshua. [3212] "Jerusalem in Jewish and Christian Thought of the Early Middle Ages," Cathedra: For the History of Eretz-Israel and its Yishuv, 17 (1980), 40-72 (Hebrew).

Prawer, Joshua. [3213] "Jewish Quarters in Jerusalem," Israel Museum News, 12 (1977), 80-91.

Prawer, Joshua. [3214] "Jewish Resettlement in Crusader Jerusalem," Ariel, 19 (1967), 60-66.

Prawer, Joshua. [3215] "Notes on the History of the Jews in the Latin Kingdom of Jerusalem," Immanuel: A Bulletin of Religious Thought and Research in Israel, 9 (1979), 81-86.

Rabinowitz, Louis I. [3216] "Israel and Jerusalem," in Israel Pocket Library: Jewish Values. Jerusalem: Keter Books, 1974, 304-310.

Razhabi, Yehuda. [3217] "'Zechor le-Avraham'-- the Diary of Rabbi Avraham Alnadaf: A History of the Yemenite Community of Jerusalem," in M. Friedman, B.-Z. Yehoshua, and Y. Tobi (eds.), Chapters in the History of the Jewish Community in Jerusalem, 2. Jerusalem: Yad Izhaq Ben-Zvi, 1976, 144-191 (Hebrew), xii-xiii (English summary).

"Reconstruction du quartier juif à Jérusalem," [3218] L' architecture d' aujourd' hui, 169 (Sept., 1973), 44-47.

Reiner, Elchanan. [3219] The Yochanan Ben Zakkai Four Sephardi Synagogues. Jerusalem: Israel Comunications, 1977, 47 pp.

Riesner, Rainer. [3220] "More on King David's Tomb," Biblical Archaeology Review, 9/6 (Nov./Dec., 1983), 20, 80-81.

Robinson, Ira. [3221] "Messianic Prayer Vigils in Jerusalem in the Early Sixteenth Century," Jewish Quarterly Review, 72 (1981), 32-42.

Rosenau, Helen. [3222] "Architecture of Nicolaus de Lyra's Temple Illustrations and the Jewish Tradition," Journal of Jewish Studies, 25 (1974), 294-304.

Rosenau, Helen. [3223] "Some Aspects of the Pictorial Influence of the Jewish Temple," Palestine Exploration Fund, Quarterly Statement, (1936), 157-162.

Rosenau, Helen. [3224] Vision of the Temple: The Image of the Temple in Judaism and Christianity. London: Oresko Books, 1979, 192 pp.

Rosenfeld, Alvin H. [3225] "Testament of Stone," Midstream, 21/6 (June/July, 1975), 29-37.

Roshwald, Mordecai, [3226] "Jerusalem, a Portrait," Judaism, 32 (1983), 103-107.

Rosovsky, Nitza. [3227] "The Jewish Quarter," in Jerusalemwalks. New York: Holt, Rinehart, and Winston, 1982, 229-274.

Rozen, Micah. [3228] "The Incident of the Converted Boy-- A Chapter in the History of the Jews in Seventeenth Century Jerusalem," Cathedra: For the History of Eretz-Israel and its Yishuv, 14 (1980), 66-80 (Hebrew).

Rozen, Minna. [3229] "On the Relationship between the Jewish Communities of Jerusalem and Safed in the Seventeenth Century," in A. Cohen (ed.), Jerusalem in the Early Ottoman Period. Jerusalem: Yad Izhaq Ben-Zvi, 1979, 152-195 (Hebrew), xi-xii (English summary).

Rozen, Minna. [3230] "The Relations between Egyptian Jewry and the Jewish Community of Jerusalem in the Seventeenth Century," in A. Cohen and G. Baer (eds), Egypt and Palestine: A Millenium of Association (868-1948). New York: St. Martin's Press / Jerusalem: Ben Zvi Institute, 1984, 251-265.

Rozin, Mordechai. [3231] Mishkenot Sha'ananim. Jerusalem: Jerusalem Foundation, 1974, 47 pp.

Russell, Kenneth W. [3232] "The Earthquake of May 19, A. D. 363," Bulletin of the American Schools of Oriental Research, 238 (1980), 47-64. [Relates to Julian II and the rebuilding of the temple.]

Safrai, Shmuel. [3233] "The Heavenly Jerusalem," Ariel, 23 (1969), 11-16.

Safrai, Shmuel. [3234] "The Holy Congregation in Jerusalem," in D. Asheri and I. Shatzman (eds.), Studies in History, 1972. Scripta Hierosolymitana, 23. Jerusalem: Magnes Press, 1972, 62-78.

Safrai, Shmuel. [3235] "Pilgrimage: Second Temple Period / Post-Temple Period," in Encyclopaedia Judaica, 13. Jerusalem: Macmillan, 1971, 510-514.

Safrai, Shmuel. [3236] "Pilgrimage to Jerusalem after the Destruction of the Second Temple," in A. Oppenheimer, U. Rappaport, and M. Stern (eds.), Jerusalem in the Second Temple Period: Abraham Schalit Memorial Volume. Jerusalem: Yad Izhaq Ben-Zvi, 1980, 376-393 (Hebrew), xxi-xxii (English summary).

Safran, Alexandre. [3237] Israel dans le temps et dans l' espace: thèmes fondamentaux de la spiritualité juive. Paris: Payot, 1980, 403 pp.

Safran, Alexandre. [3238] "Jérusalem, coeur d' Israël, coeur du monde," in E. Amado Lévy-Valensi, et al. (eds.), Mélanges André Neher. Paris: Librairie Adrien Maisonneuve, 1975, 127-135.

Schäfer, Peter. [3239] "Tempel und Schöpfung: Zur Interpretation einiger Heiligtumstraditionen in der rabbinischen Literatur," in Studien zur Geschichte und Theologie des Rabbinischen Judentums. Kairos, 16. Leiden: Brill, 1974, 122-133.

Schaffer, Shaul in conjunction with Joseph, Asher. [3240] "A History of the Western Wall-- HaKotel HaMaaravi / Customs and Prayers at the Western Wall / From Legend / An International Commission for the Wailing Wall," in Israel's Temple Mount: The Jew's Magnificent Sanctuary. English editor, A. Feuchtwanger. Jerusalem: Achva Press, 1975, 137-264.

Schein, Sylvia. [3241] "The Custodia Terrae Sanctae and the Image of the Jews of Jerusalem in the Late Middle Ages," Cathedra: For the History of Eretz-Israel and its Yishuv,19 (1981), 47-54 (Hebrew).

Schein, Sylvia. [3242] "La Custodia Terrae Sanctae franciscaine et les Juifs de Jérusalem à la fin du moyen âge," Revue des études juives, 141 (1982), 369-377.

Schick, Conrad. [3243] "A Remarkable Stone in the Jewish Quarter, Jerusalem," Palestine Exploration Fund, Quarterly Statement, (1897), 120-121.

Schmelz, Uziel O. [3244] "Development of the Jewish Population of Jerusalem during the Last Hundred Years," Jewish Journal of Sociology, 2 (1960), 56-73.

Schmelz, Uziel O. [3245] "The Jewish Population of Jerusalem," Jewish Journal of Sociology, 6 (1964), 243-263.

Schmelz, Uziel O. [3246] "Some Demographic Peculiarities of the Jews of Jerusalem in the Nineteenth Century," in M. Ma'oz (ed.), Studies on Palestine During the Ottoman Period. Jerusalem: Magnes Press, 1975, 119-141; also in M. Friedman, B.-Z. Yehoshua, and Y. Tobi (eds.), Chapters in the History of the Jewish Community in Jerusalem, 2. Jerusalem: Yad Izhaq Ben-Zvi, 1976, 52-76 (Hebrew), viii-ix (English summary).

Schmelzer, Menahem. [3247] "Travelers and Travels to Eretz-Israel: Jewish Travelers," in Encyclopaedia Judaica, 15. Jerusalem: Macmillan, 1971, 1351-1354.

Schur, Nathan. [3248] "The Jewish Community of Jerusalem in the 16th-18th Centuries according to Christian Chronicles and Travel Descriptions," in A.

Cohen (ed.), Jerusalem in the Early Ottoman Period. Jerusalem: Yad Izhaq Ben-Zvi, 1979, 343-434 (Hebrew), xix-xx (English summary).

Schur, Nathan. [3249] "The Jews," in Jerusalem in Pilgrim and Travellers' Accounts: A Thematic Bibliography of Western Christian Itineraries, 1300-1917. Jerusalem: Ariel, 1980, 55-69.

Shohat, A. [3250] "The Jews in Jerusalem in the Eighteenth Century," Cathedra: For the History of Eretz-Israel and its Yishuv, 13 (1979), 3-45 (Hebrew).

Silk, Dennis. [3251] Retrievements: A Jerusalem Anthology. Jerusalem: Israel Universities Press, 1968, 100 pp.

Simcha, Raz. See Charif, Ruth and Simcha, Raz. [3064]

Simon, Rita J. [3252] "A Profile of the Ultra-Orthodox Community in Mea Shearim," in Continuity and Change: A Study of Two Ethnic Communities in Israel. Cambridge: Cambridge University Press, 1978, 79-96.

Smith, Jonathan. [3253] "Earth and the Gods," Journal of Religion, 49 (1969), 103-127.

Sperber, Daniel. [3254] Midrash Yerushalayim: A Metaphysical History of Jerusalem. Calligraphy by Fred Paulker. Jerusalem: World Zionist Organization, 1982, 120 pp.

Starobinski-Safran, Esther. [3255] "Aspects de Jérusalem dans les écrits rabbiniques," Revue de théologie et de philosophie, 112 (1980), 151-162.

Stendahl, Krister. See Davies, William D. [3085]

Tamar, D. [3256] "The Letter of the Sages of Jerusalem of 1455," Sinai, 86 (1979/1980), 55-61 (Hebrew).

Tanai, Dan. [3257] "The Ben-Zakkai Synagogues-- Reconstruction and Restoration," in Y. Yadin (ed.), Jerusalem Revealed: Archaeology in the Holy City, 1968-1974. New Haven and London: Yale University Press and the Israel Exploration Society, 1976, 124-126.

Tanai, Dan. [3258] "From the 'Ramban' to the 'Hurva'-- Reconstruction of Synagogues in the Old City," in Y. Ben-Porat, B.-Z. Yehoshua, and A. Kedar (eds.), Chapters in the History of the Jewish Community in Jerusalem, 1. Jerusalem: Yad Izhaq Ben-Zvi, 1973, 217-236 (Hebrew).

Tanai, Dan. [3259] "Notes on the Restoration of the Sephardi Synagogues," in E. Reiner, The Yochanan Ben Zakkai Four Sephardi Synagogues. Jerusalem: Israel Comunications, 1977, 35-45.

Tanai, Dan. [3260] "The 'Ramban' (Nachmanides) Synagogue," in M. Friedman, B.-Z. Yehoshua, and Y. Tobi (eds.), Chapters in the History of the Jewish Community in Jerusalem, 2. Jerusalem: Yad Izhaq Ben-Zvi, 1976, 286-301 (Hebrew), xix-xx (English summary).

Tobi, Yosef. See Friedman, Menahem; Yehoshua, Ben-Zion; and Tobi, Yosef (eds.). [3109]

Tobi, Yosef. [3261] "Mishkenot-- the First Yemenite Quarter in Jerusalem," in Y. Ben-Porat, B.-Z. Yehoshua, and A. Kedar (eds.), Chapters in the History of the Jewish Community in Jerusalem, 1. Jerusalem: Yad Izhaq Ben-Zvi, 1973, 202-216 (Hebrew).

Tobi, Yosef. [3262] "Yemenite-Sephardi Relations in Jerusalem (1882-1908)," in M. Friedman, B.-Z. Yehoshua, and Y. Tobi (eds.), Chapters in the History of the Jewish Community in Jerusalem, 2. Jerusalem: Yad Izhaq Ben-Zvi, 1976, 192-215 (Hebrew), xiii-xiv (English summary).

Urbach, Ephraim M. [3263] "Heavenly and Earthly Jerusalem," in J. Aviram (ed.), Jerusalem through the Ages. Jerusalem: Israel Exploration Society, 1968, 156-171 (Hebrew), 64 (English summary).

Van der Heyden, A. See Gafni, Shlomo S. and Van der Heyden, A. [3110]

Vardi, Méir. See Dutheil, Michel; Vardi, Méir; and Neher, André. [3093]

Vilnay, Zev. See Luncz, Abraham M. (ed.). [3175]

Vilnay, Zev. [3264] "Jerusalem-- the Beginnings of the New City (1860-1917)," in Y. Ben-Porat, B.-Z. Yehoshua, and A. Kedar (eds.), Chapters in the History of the Jewish Community in Jerusalem, 1. Jerusalem: Yad Izhaq Ben-Zvi, 1973, 154-177 (Hebrew).

Vilnay, Zev. [3265] "The Jewish Quarter in Old Jerusalem and its Synagogues," in J. Aviram (ed.), Jerusalem through the Ages. Jerusalem: Israel Exploration Society, 1968, 203-234 (Hebrew), 66 (English summary).

Vilnay, Zev. [3266] Legends of Jerusalem. Philadelphia: Jewish Publication Society, 1973, 338 pp.

Vilnay, Zev. [3267] "Pictures of Jerusalem and its Holy Places," in Eretz-Israel: Archaeological, Historical, and Geographical Studies, 6. Jerusalem: Israel Exploration Society, 149-161 (Hebrew), 37* (English summary).

Vilnay, Zev. [3268] "Qadmoniot Yerushalayim: Jerusalem in the Talmud and Midrash," Beth Miqra, 15 (1969), 115-124 (Hebrew).

Wahrman, Dror. See Kroyanker, David and Wahrman, Dror. [3166]

Wallenstein, M. [3269] "An Insight into the Sefardi Community of Jerusalem in 1855," Zion, 43 (1978), 75-96.

Weinstein, Menahem. [3270] "The Religious and Social Life of Jerusalem in the 18th Century," in Y. Ben-Porat, B.-Z. Yehoshua, and A. Kedar (eds.), Chapters in the History of the Jewish Community in Jerusalem, 1. Jerusalem: Yad Izhaq Ben-Zvi, 1973, 178-188 (Hebrew).

Werblowsky, R. J. See Davies, William D. [3085]

Werblowsky, Z. J. (= R. J. Zwi). [3271] "Jerusalem-- The Metropolis of All the Countries," in J. Aviram (ed.), Jerusalem through the Ages. Jerusalem: Israel Exploration Society, 1968, 172-178 (Hebrew), 64 (English summary).

Werblowsky, R. J. Zwi. [3272] The Meaning of Jerusalem to Jews, Christians, and Muslims. Jerusalem: Israel Universities Study Group for Middle Eastern Affairs, rev. edn., 1978, 16 pp. Published originally in Jaarbericht Ex Orient Lux, 23 (1975), 423-439.

Whale, J. S. See Davies, William D. [3085]

Wiesel, Elie. [3273] A Beggar in Jerusalem, a Novel. New York: Random House, 1970, 211 pp. Published originally as Le Mendiant de Jérusalem, récit. Paris: Éditions du Seuil, 1968, 189 pp. [Literature.]

Wilhelm, K. [3274] Roads to Zion: Four Centuries of Travelers Reports. New York: Schocken, 1948, 117 pp.

Wischnitzer, R. [3275] "Maimonides' Drawings of the Temple," Journal of Jewish Art, 1 (1974), 16-27.

Yablovitch, Moshe. See Ben-Arieh, Yehoshua; Arazi, Simon; Yablovitch, Moshe. [3044]

Yehoshua, Ben-Zion. See Ben-Porat, Yehuda; Yehoshua, Ben-Zion; and Kedar, Ahron (eds.). [3047]

Yehoshua, Ben-Zion. See Friedman, Menahem; Yehoshua, Ben-Zion; and Tobi, Yosef (eds.). [3109]

Yehuda, Shamir. [3276] "Mystic Jerusalem," Studia Mystica, 3/2 (1980), 50-60.

Yeshaia, Samuel B. [3277] "Jerusalén y sus comunidades sefaraditas," in I. M. Hassan (ed.), Actas del primer simposio de sefardies, (Madrid, 1-6 Junio de 1964.). Madrid: Instituto 'Arias Montano' 1970, 95-105.

Ziv, Shaul. [3278] "New Documents on the History of the Maughrabi Community in Jerusalem," in M. Friedman, B.-Z. Yehoshua, and Y. Tobi (eds.), Chapters in the History of the Jewish Community in Jerusalem, 2. Jerusalem: Yad Izhaq Ben-Zvi, 1976, 127-143 (Hebrew), xi-xii (English summary).

Twenty-Three

Jerusalem in the New Testament

A. General

Brandon, Samuel G. F. [3279] "The Effect of the Destruction of Jerusalem in A. D. 70 on Primitive Christian Soteriology," in The Sacred Kingship: Contributions to the Central Theme of the VIIIth International Congress for the History of Religions (Rome, April 1955). Studies in the History of Religions, Supplement to Numen, 4. Leiden: Brill, 1959, 471-477.

Brandon, Samuel G. F. [3280] The Fall of Jerusalem and the Christian Church: A Study of the Effects of the Jewish Overthrow of A. D. 70 on Christianity. London: S. P. C. K., 1951, 284 pp.

Burrows, E. [3281] "The Name of Jerusalem," in E. F. Sutcliffe (ed.), The Gospel of the Infancy and Other Biblical Essays. London: Burns, Oates, 1940, 118-123.

Davies, William D. [3282] The Gospel and the Land: Early Christianity and Jewish Territorial Doctrine. Berkeley: University of California Press, 1974, 521 pp.

Davies, William D. [3283] "Jerusalem and the Land in the Christian Tradition," in M. H. Tanenbaum and R. J. Z. Werblowsky (eds.), The Jerusalem Colloquium on Religion, Peoplehood, Nation, and Land, Jerusalem, 1970. Jerusalem: Truman Research Institute, 1972, 115-154.

Davies, William D. [3284] "Jérusalem et la terre dans la tradition chrétienne," Revue d' histoirie et de philosophie religieuses, 55 (1975), 491-533.

Elliott, James K. [3285] "Jerusalem in Acts and the Gospels," New Testament Studies, 23 (1976) 462-469.

Gray, B. C. [3286] "The Movements of the Jerusalem Church during the First Jewish War, Journal of Ecclesiastical History, 24 (1973), 1-7.

Gunther, J. J. [3287] "The Fate of the Jerusalem Church: The Flight to Pella," Theologische Zeitschrift, 29 (1973), 81-94.

Hartmann, L. [3288] "Hierosolyma / Ierousalem, Jerusalem," in H. Balz and G. Schneider (eds.), Exegetisches Wörterbuch zum Neun Testament, 2. Stuttgart: Kohlhammer, 1981, 432-439.

Hydahl, Niels. [3289] "Die Versuchung auf der Zinne des Tempels (Matth. 4, 5-7 = Luk. 4, 9-12)," Studia Theologica, 15 (1961), 113-127.

Jeremias, Joachim. [3290] "Die 'Zinne' des Tempels (Mt. 4. 5; Lk. 4.9)," Zeitschrift des deutschen Palästina-Vereins, 59 (1936), 195-208.

Jeremias, Joachim. [3291] "*Ierousalem* / *Hierosolyma*," *Zeitschrift für die neutestamentliche Wissenschaft*, 65 (1974), 273-276.

Kremers, H. [3292] "Jesus in Jerusalem," in A. Oppenheimer, U. Rappaport, and M. Stern (eds.), *Jerusalem in the Second Temple Period: Abraham Schalit Memorial Volume*. Jerusalem: Yad Izhaq Ben-Zvi, 1980, 136-153 (Hebrew), viii-ix (English summary).

Laconi, Mauro. [3293] "Gerusalemme e la liturgia del tempio nel quarto vangelo," in M. Borrmans (ed.), *Gerusalemme*. *Atti della XXVI Settimana Biblica, Associazione Biblica Italiana*. Brescia: Paideia, 1982, 251-260.

Lohse, Eduard. [3294] "Zion-Jerusalem in the New Testament," in G. Friedrich (ed.), *Theological Dictionary of the New Testament*, 7. Grand Rapids: Eerdmans, 1971, 327-338.

May, G. Lacey. [3295] "Temple or Shrine?" *Expository Times*, 62 (1949/1950), 346-347. [On distinction betwen *naós* and *hierón* in the New Testament.]

Michaelis, Wilhelm. [3296] "*skené*," in G. Friedrich (ed.), *Theological Dictionary of the New Testament*, 7. Grand Rapids: Eerdmans, 1971, 368-381.

Michel, O. [3297] "*naós*," in G. Kittel (ed.), *Theological Dictionary of the New Testament*, 4. Grand Rapids: Eerdmans, 1967, 880-890.

Michel, O. [3298] "*oikos*," in G. Friedrich (ed.), *Theological Dictionary of the New Testament*, 5. Grand Rapids: Eerdmans, 1967, 119-159.

de la Potterie, Ignace. [3299] "Les deux noms de Jérusalem dans les Actes des Apôtres," *Biblica*, 63 (1982), 153-187.

de la Potterie, Ignace. [3300] "Les deux noms de Jérusalem dans l' évangile de Luc," *Revue des sciences religieuses*, 69 (1981), 57-70.

Schelke, Karl H. [3301] "Jerusalem und Rom im Neuen Testament," *Theologie und Glaube*, 40 (1950), 97-119.

Schrenk, Gottlob. [3302] "*hierón*," in G. Kittel (ed.), *Theological Dictionary of the New Testament*, 3. Grand Rapids: Eerdmans, 1965, 230-247.

Schütz, Roland. [3303] "*Ierousalem* und *Ierosolyma* im Neuen Testament," *Zeitschrift für die neutestamentliche Wissenschaft*, 11 (1910), 169-187.

Sylva, Dennis D. [3304] "Ierousalem and Hierosolyma in Luke-Acts," *Zeitschrift für die neutestamentliche Wissenschaft*, 74 (1983), 207-221.

Trummer, Peter. [3305] "Die Bedeutung Jerusalems für die ntl. Chronologie," in J. B. Bauer and J. Marböck (eds.), *Memoria Jerusalem* (Festschrift Franz Sauer). Graz: Akademische Druck- u. Verlagsanstalt, 1977, 129-142.

Van Iersel, Bas. [3306] "The Finding of Jesus in the Temple: Some Observations on the Original Form of Luke ii, 41-51a," *Novum Testamentum*, 4 (1960), 161-173.

Van Unnik, W. C. [3307] Tarsus or Jerusalem? The City of Paul's Youth. London: Epworth, 1962, 76 pp. [Jerusalem.]

Winter, Paul. [3308] "'Nazareth' and 'Jerusalem' in Luke chs. I and II," New Testament Studies, 3 (1957), 136-142.

Winter, Paul. [3309] "Note on Salem-Jerusalem," Novum Testamentum, 3 (1957), 151-152.

23. B. The Topography of the Gospels and Acts

Aharoni, Johanan and Avi-Yonah, Michael. [3310] "Jesus' Trial, Judgment and Crucifixion," in The Macmillan Bible Atlas. New York: Macmillan, 1968, 149, map 236.

Avi-Yonah, Michael. See Aharoni, Johanan and Avi-Yonah, Michael. [3310]

Bahat, Dan. [3311] "Jerusalem at the Time of Jesus," in Carta's Historical Atlas of Jerusalem: An Illustrated History. Jerusalem: Carta, 1983, 32-33.

Bailey, Loyd R. [3312] "Gehenna," in Interpreter's Dictionary of the Bible, Supplementary Volume. Nashville: Abingdon, 1976, 353-354.

Bernard, John H. [3313] "Akeldama," in James Hastings (ed.), Dictionary of Christ and the Gospels, 1. New York: Scribner's, 1906, 40-41.

Bruce, Frederick F. [3314] "Bethany, / Jerusalem, / The Temple," in Jesus and Paul, Places they Knew. Nashville: Nelson, 1981, 45-63.

Burrows, Millar. [3315] "Jerusalem," in Interpreter's Dictionary of the Bible, 2. New York: Abingdon, 1962, 843-866. [860-863 = "Lifetime of Jesus;" 863-865 = "Apostolic Period to the Death of Agrippa I."]

Charles, R. H. [3316] "Gehenna," in James Hastings (ed.), Dictionary of the Bible, 2. New York: Scribner's, 1898, 119-120.

Clark, Kenneth W. [3317] "Akeldama," in Interpreter's Dictionary of the Bible, 1. New York: Abingdon, 1962, 73-74.

Conder, Claude R. [3318] "The Gospel Sites," in The City of Jerusalem. London: John Murray, 1909, 139-158.

Cruickshank, William. [3319] "Jerusalem," in J. Hastings (ed.), Dictionary of the Apostolic Church, 1. New York: Scribner's, 1922, 634-640.

Dalman, Gustaf. [3320] Sacred Sites and Ways: Studies in the Topography of the Gospels. New York: Macmillan, 1935, 397 pp.

Finegan, Jack. [3321] "Jerusalem," in The Archaeology of the New Testament: The Life of Jesus and the Beginning of the Early Church. Princeton: Princeton University Press, 109-177.

Frank, Harry T. [3322] "Events of the Passion Week, / Jerusalem in the Time of Jesus Christ," in Hammond's Atlas of Bible Lands. Maplewood, NJ: Hammond, 1984, 28-29.

Gaster, Theodore H. [3323] "Gehenna," in Interpreter's Dictionary of the Bible, 2. New York: Abingdon, 1962, 361-362.

Henderson, Archibald. [3324] "Akeldama," in James Hastings (ed.), Dictionary of the Bible, 1. New York: Scribner's, 1898, 59.

Jeremias, Joachim. [3325] "géenna," in G. Kittel (ed.), Theological Dictionary of the New Testament, 1. Translated by G. W. Bromiley. Grand Rapids: Eerdmans, 1964, 657-658.

Kopp, Clemens. [3326] Die heiligen Stätten der Evangelien. Regensburg: Friedrich Pustet, 1959, 504 pp.

Kopp, Clemens. [3327] The Holy Places of the Gospels. New York: Herder and Herder, 1963, 424 pp. [Abridgment of the German edition.]

La Sor, William S. [3328] "Jerusalem in the Time of Christ and the Apostles," in G. W. Bromiley (ed.), International Standard Bible Encyclopedia, 2. Grand Rapids: Eerdmans, 1982, 1026-1029.

Livio, Jean-Bernard. [3329] "Sur les pas de Jésus a Jérusalem," Bible et Terre Sainte, 117 (1970), 16-19.

Loffreda, Stanislao. [3330] "Recenti scoperte archeologiche a Gerusalemme: La Gerusalemme del Nuova Testamento," Rivista Biblica, 17 (1969), 175-192.

Mackowski, Richard. [3331] Jerusalem, City of Jesus: An Exploration of the Traditions, Writings, and Remains of the Holy City from the Time of Christ. Grand Rapids: Eerdmans, 1980, 221 pp.

Mare, W. Harold. [3332] "Jerusalem, New Testament," in E. M. Blaiklock and R. K. Harrison (eds.), The New International Dictionary of Biblical Archaeology. Grand Rapids: Zondervan, 1983, 261-265.

Martin, I. [3332A] Six New Testament Walks in Jerusalem. New York: Harper and Row, 1986, 240 pp.

Masterman, Ernest W. Gurney. [3333] "Jerusalem," in James Hastings (ed.), Dictionary of Christ and the Gospels, 1. New York: Scribner's, 1906, 849-859.

May, Herbert G. [3334] "Jerusalem in New Testament Times," in Oxford Bible Atlas. New York: Oxford University Press, 3rd edn. revised by John Day, 1984, 96-97.

Montgomery, James A. [3335] "The Holy City and Gehenna," Journal of Biblical Literature, 27 (1908), 24-47.

Morales Gomez, G. [3336] "Jerusalén-Jerosálima en el vocabulario y la geografia," Revista Catalana de Teología, 7 (1982), 131-186.

Oesterley, W. O. E. [3337] "Temple," in James Hastings (ed.), Dictionary of Christ and the Gospels, 2. New York: Scribner's, 1906, 708-713.

Sanday, William. [3338] Sacred Sites of the Gospels. Oxford: Clarendon, 1903, 126 pp.

Schick, Conrad. [3339] "Aceldama," Palestine Exploration Fund, Quarterly Statement, (1892), 283-289.

Schick, Conrad. [3340] "Durch welches Thor ist Jesus am Palmsonntag in Jerusalem eingezogen?" Zeitschrift des deutschen Palästina-Vereins, 22 (1899), 94-101.

Wilkinson, John. [3341] Jerusalem as Jesus Knew It: Archaeology as Evidence. London: Thames and Hudson, 1978, 208 pp.

See also 29/The Church of the Holy Sepulchre; 30/Rival Sites for Golgotha and the Tomb of Jesus; 31/The Churches of Mt. Sion; 32/The Churches of Gethsemane, the Mount of Olives, and Bethany; 33/The Pool of Bethesda and the Church of St. Anne; and 34/The Pretorium and the Way of the Cross.

23. C. Theological Judgments on the City and Sanctuary

Bachmann, M. [3342] Jerusalem und der Tempel: Die geographischen-theologischen Elemente in der lukanischen Sicht des jüdischen Kultzentrums. Beiträge zur Wissenschaft vom Alten und Neuen Testament, 109. Stuttgart: Kohlhammer, 1980, 402 pp.

Baltzer, Klaus. [3343] "The Meaning of the Temple in the Lukan Writings," Harvard Theological Review, 58 (1965), 263-277.

Barnard, L. W. [3344] "The Testimonium concerning the Stone in the New Testament and the Epistle of Barnabas," in F. L. Cross (ed.), Studia Evangelica, 3. Papers Presented to the Second International Congress on New Testament Studies, 2: The New Testament Message. Texte und Untersuchungen zur Geschichte der altchristliche Literatur, 88. Berlin: Akademie-Verlag, 1964, 306-313.

Barrett, Charles K. [3345] "The House of Prayer and the Den of Theives," in E. E. Ellis (ed.), Jesus und Paulus (Festschrift Georg Kümmel). Göttingen: Vandenhoeck and Ruprecht, 1975, 13-20.

Barrois, Georges Augustin. [3346] Jesus Christ and the Temple. New York: St. Vladimir Seminary Press, 1980, 164 pp.

Bergmeier, Roland. [3347] "Jerusalem, du hochgebaute Stadt," Zeitschrift für die neutestamentliche Wissenschaft, 75 (1984), 86-106.

Biguzzi, G. [3348] "Gesù, il discepolo e Gerusalemme nel vangelo di Marco," Revista Biblica, 29 (1981), 177-186.

Bobichon, Marius. [3349] "Fille de Sion," Bible et Terre Sainte, 114 (1969), 16.

Bobichon, Marius. [3350] "Du Temple au Cénacle," Bible et Terre Sainte, 98 (1968), 2-5.

Bockel, Pierre. [3351] "Jésus et le Temple: Il parlait du sanctuaire de son corps," Bible et Terre Sainte, 122 (1970), 16-18.

Boswell, R. B. [3352] "Destroying and Rebuilding the Temple," Expository Times, 26 (1914/1915), 140-141.

Braumann, Georg. [3353] "Die lukanische Interpretation der Zerstörung Jerusalems," Novum Testamentum, 6 (1963), 120-127.

Braun, F.-M. [3354] "L' expulsion des vendeurs du Temple (Mat XXI, 12-17, 23-24, Mc. XI, 15-19, 27-33, Lc. XIX, 45-XX, 8, Jo. II, 13-22)," Revue biblique, 38 (1929), 178-200.

Brodie, L. T. [3355] "A New Temple and a New Law: The Unity and Chronicler-based Nature of Luke 1: 1-4: 22a," Journal for the Study of the New Testament, 5 (1979), 21-45.

Bruce, Frederick F. [3356] "Paul and Jerusalem," Tyndale Bulletin, 19 (1968), 3-25.

Buchanan, George W. [3357] "Mark 11: 15-19: Brigands in the Temple," Hebrew Union College Annual, 30 (1959), 169-177; 31 (1960), 103-105.

Burkitt, F. Crawford. [3358] "The Cleansing of the Temple," Journal of Theological Studies, 25 (1923/1924), 386-390.

Buse, Ivor. [3359] "The Cleansing of the Temple in the Synoptics and John," Expository Times, 70 (1958/1959), 22-24.

Butin, J.-D. [3360] "Les Evangiles et la ruine de Jérusalem," Le Monde de la Bible, 29 (1983), 45-47.

Caird, George B. [3361] "The Mind of Christ, Attitude to Institutions: The Temple," Expository Times, 62 (1950/1951), 259-261.

Caldecott, A. [3362] "The Significance of the 'Cleansing of the Temple,'" Journal of Theological Studies, 24 (1923), 382-386.

Casalegno, A. [3363] Gesù e il Tempio: Studio redazionale di Luca-Atti. Brescia: Morcelliana, 1984, 257 pp.

Cheetham, F. P. [3364] "'Destroy this Temple and in Three Days I will Raise It Up' (St. John ii, 19)," Journal of Theological Studies, 24 (1922/1923), 315-317.

Chronis, Harry L. [3365] "The Torn Veil: Cultus and Chronology in Mark 15: 37-39," Journal of Biblical Literature, 101 (1982), 97-114.

Cipriani, Settimio. [3366] "Illa quae sursum est Jerusalem," in M. Borrmans (ed.), Gerusalemme. Atti della XXVI Settimana Biblica, Associazione Biblica Italiana. Brescia: Paideia, 1982, 219-236.

Comblin, J. [3367] "La ville bien-aimee," Vie Spirituelle, 112 (1965), 631-648.

Cooke, F. A. [3368] "The Cleansing of the Temple," Expository Times, 63 (1951/1952), 321-322.

Corsani, Bruno. [3369] "Gerusalemme nell' opera lucana," in M. Borrmans (ed.), Gerusalemme. Atti della XXVI Settimana Biblica, Associazione Biblica Italiana. Brescia: Paideia, 1982, 13-26.

Cothenet, Edouard. [3370] "Attitude de l' église naissante à l' égard du Temple de Jérusalem," in A. Pistoia and A. M. Triacca (eds.), Liturgie et l'église particulière et liturgie de l' église universelle. Conférences Saint-Serge XXIIe Semaine d' Études Liturgiques, Paris, 1975. Rome: Liturgiche, 1977, 89-111.

Cullmann, Oscar. [3371] "A New Approach to the Interpretation of the Fourth Gospel," Expository Times, 71 (1959), 8-12, 39-43. English version of Cullmann, Oscar. [3372]

Cullmann, Oscar. [3372] "L' opposition contre le Temple de Jérusalem, motif commun de la théologie johannique et du monde ambiant," New Testament Studies, 5 (1958/1959), 157-173.

Cullmann, Oscar. [3373] "Von Jesus zum Stephanuskreis und zum Johannesevangelium," in E. E. Ellis (ed.), Jesus und Paulus (Festschrift Georg Kümmel). Göttingen: Vandenhoeck and Ruprecht, 1975, 44-56.

Culpeper, R. Alan. [3374] "Mark 11: 15-19," Interpretation, 34 (1980), 176-181.

Dawsey, James M. [3375] "Confrontation in the Temple (Luke 19: 45-20: 47)," Perspectives in Religious Studies, 11 (1984), 153-165.

Derrett, J. Duncan. [3376] "The Lukan Christ and Jerusalem: teleioumai (Lk. 13, 32)," Zeitschrift für die neutestamentliche Wissenschaft, 75 (1985), 36-43.

Derrett, J. Duncan. [3377] "The Zeal of the House and the Cleansing of the Temple," Downside Review, 95/319 (1977), 79-94.

De Souza, B. [3378] "The Coming of the Lord, 3: The Destruction of Jerusalem in Lk 21," Studii Biblici Franciscani, Liber Annuus, 20 (1970), 196-208.

Dodd, Charles H. [3379] "The Fall of Jerusalem and the Abomination of Desolation," Journal of Roman Studies, 37 (1947), 47-54.

Doeve, J. W. [3380] "Purification du Temple et dessèchement du figuier," New Testament Studies, 1 (1954/1955), 297-308.

Dubarle, André-Marie. [3381] "Le signe du Temple (Jo ii, 19)," Revue biblique, 48 (1939), 21-44.

Dupont, Jacques. [3382] "Il n'en sera pas laissé pierre sur pierre (Marc xiii, 2, Luc xix, 44)," Biblica, 52 (1971), 301-320.

Dupont, Jacques. [3383] "Ruine du Temple et la fin des temps dans le discours de Marc 13," in H. Cazzelles (ed.), Apocalypses et theologie de l' espérance. Association Catholique Française pour l' Étude de la Bible, Congress de Toulouse, 1975 (Festschrift Louis Monoloubou). Paris: Cerf, 1977, 207-269.

Eppstein, Victor. [3384] "The Historicity of the Gospel Account of the Cleansing of the Temple," Zeitschrift für die neutestamentliche Wissenschaft, 55 (1964), 42-58.

Evans, C. A. [3385] "'He Set His Face:' A Note on Luke 9: 51," Biblica, 63 (1982), 545-548.

Fascher, Erich. [3386] "Jerusalems Untergang in der urchristlichen und altkirchlichen Überlieferung," Theologische Literaturzeitung, 89 (1964), 81-98.

Feuillet, André. [3387] "Le discours de Jésus sur la ruine du Temple d' apres Marc xiii et Luc xxi, 2-36," Revue biblique, 55 (1948), 481-502; 56 (1049), 61-92.

Flanagan, Neal M. [3388] "Mark and the Temple Cleansing," The Bible Today, 63 (1972), 980-984.

Flückiger, Felix. [3389] "Luk. 21, 20-24 und die Zerstörung Jerusalems," Theologische Zeitschrift, 28 (1972), 385-390.

Flusser, David. [3390] "The Liberation of Jerusalem: A Prophecy in the New Testament," in Eretz-Israel: Archaeological, Historical, and Geographical Studies, 10. Jerusalem: Israel Exploration Society, 1971, 226-236 (Hebrew), xvii (English summary).

Gari-Jaune, Lorenzo. [3391] "'Desacralizzazione' neotestmentaria del tempio di Gerusalemme," in S. Gozzo (ed.), La distruzione di Gerusalemme del 70: nei suoi riflessi storico-letterari. Assisi: Studio Teologico "por ziuncolo," 1971, 135-144.

Gaston, Lloyd. [3392] No Stone on Another: Studies in the Significance of the Fall of Jerusalem in the Synoptic Gospels. Supplements to Novum Testamentum, 23. Leiden: Brill, 1970, 537 pp.

Gaston, Lloyd. [3393] "Paul and Jerusalem," in P. Richardson and J. Hurd (eds.), From Jesus to Paul: Essays in Honor of Francis Wright Beare. Waterloo, Ont.: Wilfrid Laurier University Press, 1984, 61-72.

Giblin, Charles H. [3394] The Destruction of Jerusalem according to Luke's Gospel: A Historical-Theological Model. Analecta Biblica, 107. Rome: Biblical Institute Press, 1985, 123 pp.

Glasson, T. F. [3395] "Davidic Links with the Betrayal of Jesus," Expository Times, 85 (1973/1974), 118-119. [On reference to the Kidron valley in John 18: 1.]

Goguel, Maurice. [3396] "La parole de Jésus sur la destruction et la reconstruction du Temple," in Congrès d' Histoire du Christianisme (Jubilé Alfred Loisy), 1. Paris: Rieder, 1928, 117-136.

Hamilton, Neil Q. [3397] "Temple Cleansing and Temple Bank," Journal of Biblical Literature, 83 (1964), 365-372.

Hannay, Thomas. [3398] "The Temple," Scottish Journal of Theology, 3 (1950), 278-287.

Hatch, William H. P. [3399] "An Allusion to the Destruction of Jerusalem in the Fourth Gospel," Expositor, ser. 8, 17 (1919), 194-197.

Hiers, Richard. [3400] "Purification of the Temple: Preparation for the Kingdom of God," Journal of Biblical Literature, 90 (1971), 82-90.

Hoffmann, Richard A. [3401] "Das Wort Jesu von der Zerstörung und dem Wiederaufbau des Tempels," in Neutestamentliche Studien Georg Heinrice zu seinem 70 Geburtstag. Untersuchungen zum Neuen Testament, 6. Leipzig, 1914, 130-139.

Horbury, William. [3402] "New Wine in Old Wine Skins, 9: The Temple," Expository Times, 86 (1974), 36-42.

Horbury, William. [3403] "The Temple Tax," in E. Bammel and C. Moule (eds.), Jesus and the Politics of His Day. Cambridge: Cambridge University Press, 1984, 265-286.

Hudry-Clergeon, J. [3404] "Jésus et le Sanctuaire: Étude de Jn. 2, 12-22," Nouvelle Revue Théologique, 105 (1983), 535-548.

de Jonge, M. [3405] "De berichten over het schewren van het voorhangel bij Jezus' doot in der synoptische evangeliën," Nederlands Theologisch Tijdschrift, 21 (1966), 90-97.

de Jonge, M. [3406] "Het motief van het gescheurde voorhangsel van der Tempel in een aantal vroegchristlijke geschriften," Nederlands Theologisch Tijdschrift, 22 (1967), 257-276.

Juel, Donald. [3407] Messiah and Temple: The Trial of Jesus in the Gospel of Mark. Society of Biblical Literature Dissertation Series, 31. Missoula, MT: Scholars Press, 1977, 223 pp.

Käser, Walter. [3408] "Exegetische und theologische Erwägungen zur Seligpreisung der Kinderlosen, Lc 23, 29b," Zeitschrift für die neutestamentliche Wissenschaft, 54 (1963), 240-254.

Lamarche, Paul. [3409] "La mort du Christ et le voile du Temple selon Marc," Nouvelle revue théologique, 96 (1974), 583-599.

Lancellotti, Angelo. [3410] "La distruzione di Gerusalemme e del suo tempio nel discorso eschatologico secondo una recente interpretatzione," in S. Gozzo (ed.), La distruzione di Gerusalemme del 70: nei suoi riflessi storico-letterari. Assisi: Studio Teologico "porziuncolo," 1971, 69-78.

Léon-Dufour, Xavier. [3411] "Le signe du Temple selon saint Jean," Revue des sciences religieuses, 39 (1951/1952), 155-175.

Lightfoot, Robert H. [3412] "The Cleansing of the Temple in St. John's Gospel," Expository Times, 60 (1948/1949), 64-68.

Lindeskog, Gösta. [3413] "The Veil of the Temple," in Coniectanae Neotestamentica, 11: In honorem A. Fridrichsen. Lund: Gleerup, 1947, 132-137.

Lohmeyer, Ernst. [3414] Kultus und Evangelium. Göttingen: Vandenhoeck and Ruprecht, 1942, 128 pp.

Lohmeyer, Ernst. [3415] Lord of the Temple: A Study of the Relation betwen Cult and Gospel. Edinburgh: Oliver and Boyd, 1961, 116 pp.

Lohmeyer, Ernst. [3416] "Die Reinigung des Tempels," Theologische Blätter, 20 (1941), 257-264.

Lührmann, Dieter. [3417] "Markus 14: 55-64: Christologie und Zerstörung des Tempels im Markusevangelium," New Testament Studies, 27 (1981), 457-474.

Manson, T. W. [3418] "The Cleansing of the Temple," Bulletin of the John Rylands Library, 33 (1950/1951), 271-282.

Mendner, Siegfried. [3419] "Die Tempelreinigung," Zeitschrift für die neutestamentliche Wissenschaft, 47 (1956), 93-112.

Montefiore, Hugh. [3420] "Jesus and the Temple Tax," New Testament Studies, 11 (1964/1965), 60-71.

Neyrey, Jerome H. [3421] "Jesus Address to the Women of Jerusalem (Lk. 23, 27-31): A Prophetic Judgment Oracle," New Testament Studies, 29 (1983), 74-86.

Nibley, Hugh. [3422] "Christian Envy of the Temple," Jewish Quarterly Review, 50 (1959/1960), 97-123, 229-240.

Plooij, D. [3423] "Jesus and the Temple," Expository Times, 42 (1930/1931), 36-40.

Prete, Benedetto. [3424] "Origine de logion, 'Non conviene che un profeta perisca fuori di Gerusalemme' (Lc. 13, 33 b)," in M. Borrmans (ed.), Gerusalemme. Atti della XXVI Settimana Biblica, Associazione Biblica Italiana. Brescia: Paideia, 1982, 181-200.

Provera, Mario. [3425] "Gerusalemme nella vita e pensiero di Paolo," Bibbia e Oriente, 28 (1986), 111-120.

Reicke, Bo. [3426] "Synoptic Problems on the Destruction of Jerusalem," in D. E. Aune (ed.), Studies in New Testament and Early Christian Literature. Leiden: Brill, 1972, 121-134.

Rengstorf, Karl H. [3427] "Die Stadt der Mörder (Mt. 22, 7)," in W. Altester (ed.), Judentum, Urchristentum, Kirche (Festschrift Joachim Jeremias). Berlin: Töpelmann, 1960, 106-129.

Salas, Antonio. [3428] "Oráculo contra Jerusalén (Lc xix, 41-44)," Ciudad de Dios, 178 (1965), 270-292.

Sawyer, John F. A. [3429] "The Temple at Jerusalem," in From Moses to Patmos: New Perspectives in Old Testament Study. London: S. P. C. K., 1977, 57-71.

Schnellbächer, Ernest L. [3430] "The Temple as Focus of Mark's Theology," Horizons in Biblical Theology, 5/2 (1983), 95-112.

Simon, Marcel. [3431] "Retour du Christ et reconstruction du Temple dans la pensée chrétienne primative," in Aux soures de la tradition chrétienne: Mélanges offerts à M. Maurice Goguel à l' occasion de son soixante-dixìeme anniversaire. Neuchâtel: Delachaux et Niestlé, 1950, 247-257. Also in Recherches d' Histoire Judéo-Chrétienne. Paris / La Haye: Mouton, 1962, 9-19.

Simon, Marcel. [3432] "Saint Stephen and the Jerusalem Temple," Journal of Ecclesiastical History, 2 (1951), 127-142.

Simson, P. [3433] "The Drama of the City of God: Jerusalem in Luke's Gospel," Scripture, 15 (1963), 65-80.

Stano, Gaetano. [3434] "La distruzione di Gerusalemme dell' anno 70e l' esegesi di Dan 9, 24-27 (Mt 24, 15; Mc 13, 14)," in S. Gozzo (ed.), La distruzione di Gerusalemme del 70: nei suoi riflessi storico-letterari. Assisi: Studio Teologico "por ziuncolo," 1971, 79-110.

Sylva, Dennis D. [3435] "The Temple Curtain and Jesus' Death in the Gospel of Luke," Journal of Biblical Literature, 105 (1986), 239-250.

Taylor, Vincent. [3436] "A Cry from the Siege: A Suggestion Regarding a Non-Markan Oracle Embeded in Luke 21: 20-36," Journal of Theological Studies, 26 (1924/1925), 136-144.

Telford, William R. [3437] The Barren Temple and the Withered Tree. Journal for the Study of the New Testament, Supplement Series, 1. Sheffield: JSOT Press, 1980, 319 pp.

Testa, Emmanuele. [3438] "La Nouva Sion," Studii Biblici Franciscani, Liber Annuus, 22 (1972), 48-73.

Theissen, Gerd. [3439] "Die Tempelweissagung Jesu," Theologische Zeitschrift, 32 (1976), 144-158.

Trocmé, Étienne. [3440] "L' expulsion des marchands du Temple," New Testament Studies, 15 (1968/1969), 1-22.

Trocmé, Étienne. [3441] "Jésus Christ et le Temple: Éloge d' un naïf," Revue d' histoirie et de philosophie religieuses, 44 (1964), 245-251.

Van den Bussche, Henri. [3442] "Le signe du Temple (Jean 2, 13-22)," Bible et vie chrétienne, 20 (1957/1958), 92-100.

Van der Kwaak, H. [3443] "Die Klage über Jerusalem (Matth. xxiii, 37-39)," Novum Testamentum, 8 (1966), 156-170.

Van der Waal, C. [3444] "The Temple in the Gospel according to Luke," in W. van Unnik (ed.), Essays on the Gospel of Luke and Acts: Proceedings of the 9th Meeting of Die Nuwe-Testamentiese Werkgemeenskap van Suid Afrika. Pretoria: University of Pretoria, 1973, 49-59.

Walter, Nikolaus. [3445] "Tempelzerstörung und synoptische Apokalypse," Zeitschrift für die neutestamentliche Wissenschaft, 57 (1966), 38-49.

Watty, William W. [3446] "Jesus and the Temple-- Cleansing or Cursing?" Expository Times, 93 (1981/1982), 235-239.

Weinert, Francis D. [3447] "The Meaning of the Temple in Luke-Acts," Biblical Theology Bulletin, 11 (1981), 85-89.

Weinert, Francis D. [3448] "Luke, the Temple, and Jesus' Saying about Jerusalem's Abandoned House (Luke 13: 34-35)," Catholic Biblical Quarterly, 44 (1982), 68-76.

de Young, James C. [3449] Jerusalem in the New Testament: The Significance of the City in the History of Redemption and in Eschatology. Kampen: J. H. Kok, 1960, 168 pp.

Young, Frances M. [3450] "Temple Cult and Law in Early Christianity: A Study in the Relationship between Jews and Christians in the Early Centuries," New Testament Studies, 19 (1973), 325-338.

Zehrer, Franz. [3451] "Gedanken zum Jerusalem-Motiv im Lukasevangelium," in J. B. Bauer and J. Marböck (eds.), Memoria Jerusalem (Festschrift Franz Sauer). Graz: Akademische Druck-u-Verlagsanstalt, 1977, 117-127.

23. D. Heavenly City and Sanctuary

Bardy, Gustave. [3452] "Melchisédech dans la tradition patristique," Revue biblique, 35 (1926), 496-509; 36 (1927), 25-45.

Beet, J. Agar. [3453] "Another Solution of Revelation XX-XXII," Expository Times, 26 (1914/1915), 217-220.

Biguzzi, G. [3454] "Mc 14, 58: Un tempio acheiropoietos," Revista Biblica, 26 (1978), 225-240.

Böcher, Otto. [3455] "Die heilige Stadt im Völker-krieg: Wandlungen eines apokalyptischen Schemas," in O. Betz, K. Haacker, and M. Hengel (eds.), Josephus-Studien: Untersuchungen zu Josephus, dem antiken Judentum und dem Neuen Testament (Festschrift Otto Michel). Göttingen: Vandenhoeck and Ruprecht, 1974, 55-76.

Campbell, Ken M. [3456] "The New Jerusalem in Matthew 5: 14," Scottish Journal of Theology, 31 (1978), 335-363.

Charles, R. H. [3457] "A Solution of the Chief Difficulties in Revelation XX-XXIII," Expository Times, 26 (1914/1915), 54-57, 119-123.

Cody, Aelred. [3458] Heavenly Sanctuary and Liturgy in the Epistle to the Hebrews. St. Meinrad, IN: Grail, 1960, 227 pp.

Comblin, J. [3459] "La liturgie de la Nouvelle Jérusalem (Apoc. XXI, 1-XXII, 5)," Ephemerides theologicae lovanienses, 29 (1953), 15-40.

Davies, J. H. [3460] "The Heavenly Work of Christ in Hebrews," in F. L. Cross (ed.), Studia Evangelica, 4. Papers Presented to the Third International Congress on the New Testament, 1: The New Testament Scriptures. Berlin: Akademie-Verlag, 1968, 384-389.

Del Alamo, M. [3461] "Las medidas de la Jerusalen celeste (Apoc. 21, 16)," Cultura biblica, 3 (1946), 136-138.

Du Brul, Peter. [3462] "Jerusalem in the Apocalypse of John," in D. Burrell, P. Du Brul, and W. Dalton (eds.), Jerusalem: Seat of Theology. Yearbook of the Ecumenical Institute for Theological Research, 1981/1982. Tantur, Jerusalem: Ecumenical Institute for Theological Research, 1982, 55-77.

Fitzmyer, Joseph. [3463] "'Now this Melchizedek. . ." (Heb. 7, 1)," Catholic Biblical Quarterly, 25 (1963), 305-321.

Fransen, Irénée. [3464] "Jesus pontife parfait due parfait sanctuaire (Epitre aux Hebreux)," Bible et vie chretienne, 20 (1957/1958), 79-91.

Gaechter, Paul. [3465] "The Original Sequence of Apocalypse 20-22," Theological Studies, 10 (1949), 485-521. [Millennial Jerusalem and Eternal Jerusalem in two descriptions of the heavenly Jerusalem.]

Georgi, Dieter. [3466] "Die Visionen vom himmlischen Jerusalem in Apk. 21 und 22," in D. Lührmann and G. Strecker (eds.), Kirche (Festschrift Günther Bornkamm). Tübingen: Mohr (Siebeck), 1980, 351-372.

Grigsby, Bruce. [3467] "Gematria and John 21: 11-- Another Look at Ezekiel 47: 10," Expository Times, 95 (1983/1984), 177-178.

Hofius, Otfried. [3468] "Das 'erste' und das 'zweite' Zelt: Ein Beitrag zur Auslegung von Hbr 9, 1-10," Zeitschrift für die neutestamentliche Wissenschaft, 61 (1970), 271-277.

Hofius, Otfried. [3469] Der Vorhang vor dem Thron Gottes: Eine exegetisch-religionsgeschichtliche Untersuchung zu Hebräer 6, 19 f und 10, 19 f. Wissenschaftliche Untersuchungen zum Neuen Testament, 14. Tübingen: Mohr (Siebeck), 1972, 122 pp.

Horton, Fred L., Jr. [3470] The Melchizedek Tradition: A Critical Examination of the Sources to the Fifth Century A. D. and in the Epistle to the Hebrews. Cambridge: Cambridge University Press, 1976, 192 pp.

Hurst, Lincoln D. [3471] "Eschatology and 'Platonism' in the Epistle to the Hebrews," in K. H. Richards (ed.), Society of Biblical Literature 1984 Seminar Papers. Chico, CA: Scholars Press, 1984, 41-74. [Heavenly tent as cosmic sanctuary not Platonic ideal.]

Johnsson, William G. [3472] "The Cultus of Hebrews in Twentieth Century Scholarship," Expository Times, 89 (1977/1978), 104-108.

Johnsson, William G. [3473] "The Pilgrimage Motif in the Book of Hebrews," Journal of Biblical Literature, 97 (1978), 239-251.

de Jonge, M and Van der Woude, Adam S. [3474] "11Q Melchizedek and the New Testament," New Testament Studies, 12 (1965/1966). 301-326.

Läpple, A. [3475] "'Das neue Jerusalem:' Die Eschatologie der Offenbarung des Johannes, Bibel und Kirche, 39 (1984), 75-81.

McQueen, D. H. [3476] "The New Jerusalem and Town Planning," Expositor, 9/2 (1924), 220-226. [The New Jerusalem of the Apocalypse.]

MacRae, George W. [3477] "Heavenly Temple and Eschatology in the Letter to the Hebrews," Semeia, 12 (1978), 179-199.

MacRae, George W. [3478] "A Kingdom that Cannot be Shaken: The Heavenly Jerusalem in the Letter to the Hebrews," in P. Bonnard, G. MacRae, and J. Cobb (eds.), Spirituality and Ecumenism. Yearbook of the Ecumenical Institute for Theological Research, 1979/1980. Tantur, Jerusalem: Ecumenical Institute for Theological Research, 1980, 27-40.

Moe, Olaf. [3479] "Das irdische und das himmlische Heiligtum: Zur Auslegung von Hebr. 9, 4 f," Theologische Zeitschrift, 9 (1953), 23-29.

Müller, W. [3480] Die Heilige Stadt: Roman Quadrata, himmlisches Jerusalem und die Mythe vom Weltnabel. Stuttgart: Kohlhammer, 1961, 304 pp.

Muntingh, L. M. [3481] "'The City which Has Foundations:' Hebrews 11: 8-10 in the Light of the Mari Texts," in I. H. Eybers, (ed.), De fructo oris sui: Essays in Honour of Adrianus van Selms. Leiden: Brill, 1971, 108-120.

Northcote, H. [3482] "A Solution to the Chief Difficulties in Revelation XX-XXII," Expository Times, 26 (1914/1915), 426-428.

Prigent, Pierre. [3483] "Une trace de liturgie judéochrétienne dans le chapitre XXI de l' Apocalypse de Jean," Revue des sciences religieuses, 60 (1972), 163-172.

Riley, W. [3484] "Temple Imagery and the Book of Revelation: Ancient Near Eastern Temple Ideology and Cultic Resonances in the Apocalypse," Proceedings of the Irish Biblical Association, 6 (1982), 81-102.

Sabourin, Léopold. [3485] "Liturgie du Sanctuaire et de la Tent Véritable (Heb. viii, 2)," New Testament Studies, 18 (1971/1972), 87-90.

Sabourin, Léopold. [3486] "Scrificium ut liturgia in Epistula ad Hebraeos," Verbum Domini, 46 (1968), 235-258.

Sisti, Adalberto. [3487] "Le due alleanze (Gal 4, 21-31)," Bibbia e Oriente, 11 (1969), 25-32, esp. 31-32 on "Gerusalemme superna."

Swetnam, James. [3488] "The Greater and More Perfect Tent: A Contribution to the Discussion of Hebrews ix, 11," Biblica, 47 (1966), 91-106.

Thompson, Leonard. [3489] "Cult and Eschatology in the Apocalypse of John," Journal of Religion, 49 (1969), 330-350.

Thüsing, W. [3490] "Die Vision des 'Neuen Jerusalem' (Apk 21, 1-22) als Verheissung und Gottesverkündigung," Trierer Theologische Zeitschrift, 77 (1968), 17-34.

Van der Woude, Adam S. See de Jonge, M. and Van der Woude, Adam S. [3474]

Van der Woude, Adam S. [3491] "Melchizedek," Interpreter's Dictionary of the Bible, Supplementary Volume. Nashville: Abingdon, 1976, 585-586.

Vanhoye, Albert. [3492] "Le Christ, grand-prétre selon Héb. 2, 17-18," La nouvelle revue théologique, 91 (1969), 449-474.

Vanhoye, Albert. [3493] "Par la Tente plus grande et plus parfaite (Heb. ix, 11)," Biblica, 46 (1965), 1-28.

Vanhoye, Albert. [3494] "L' utilisation du livre d' Ézechiel dans l' Apocalypse," Biblica, 43 (1962), 436-476.

Vanni, Ugo. [3495] "Gerusalemme nell' Apocalisse," in M. Borrmans (ed.), Gerusalemme. Atti della XXVI Settimana Biblica, Associazione Biblica Italiana. Brescia: Paideia, 1982, 27-52.

Watson, W. [3496] "The New Jerusalem," Expository Times, 25 (1913/1914), 454-457.

Zeilinger, Franz. [3497] "Das himmlische Jerusalem: Untersuchungen zur Bildersprache der Johannesapokalypse und des Hebräerbriefs," in J. B. Bauer and J. Marböck (eds.), Memoria Jerusalem (Festschrift Franz Sauer). Graz: Akademische Druck-u-Verlagsanstalt, 1977, 143-165.

23. E. The Church as Temple

Amiot, François. [3498] "Temple," in X. Léon-Dufour (ed.), Dictionary of Biblical Theology. New York: Seabury, 1973, 594-597.

Best, Ernest. [3499] "The Building in Christ," in One Body in Christ: A Study in the Relationship of the Church to Christ in the Epistles of the Apostle Paul. London: S. P. C. K., 1955, 160-168.

Betz, Otto. [3500] "Felsenmann und Felsengemeinde (Eine Paralle zu Mt. 16. 17-19 in den Qumranpsalmen)," Zeitschrift für die neutestamentliche Wissenschaft, 48 (1957), 49-77.

Betz, Otto. [3501] "Le ministère cultuel dans la secte de Qumrân et dans le Christianisme," in La secte de Qumrân et les origines du Christianisme. Recherches bibliques, 4. Paris: Descelée de Brouwer, 1959, 163-202.

Bruce, Frederick F. [3502] "New Wine in Old Wine Skins: 3. The Corner Stone," Expository Times, 84 (1972/1973), 231-235.

Bultmann, Rudolf. [3503] "Die Frage nach der Echtheit von Mt. 16, 17-19," Theologische Blätter, 20 (1941), 265-279.

Burch, Vacher. [3504] "The 'Stone' and the 'Keys' (Mt. 16: 18f)," Journal of Biblical Literature, 52 (1933), 147-152.

Clowney, Edmund P. [3505] "The Final Temple," Westminster Theological Journal, 35 (1973), 156-189.

Cole, Robert Alan. [3506] The New Temple: A Study in the Origins of the Catechetical 'Form' of the Church in the New Testament. London: Tyndale Press, 1950, 55 pp.

Coppens, Joseph. [3507] "The Spiritual Temple in the Pauline Letters and its Background," in E. A. Livingstone (ed.), Studia Evangelica, 6. Papers Presented to the Fourth International Congress on New Testament Studies Held at Oxford, 1969. Texte und Untersuchungen, 112. Berlin: Akademie-Verlag, 1973, 53-66.

Du Buit, M. [3508] "Les rochers se fendirent," Bible et Terre Sainte, 149 (1973), 7-8.

Fiorenza, Elisabeth Schüssler. [3509] "Cultic Language in Qumran and in the New Testament, Catholic Biblical Quarterly, 38 (1976), 159-177.

Fraeyman, M. [3510] "La Spiritualisation de l' idée de Temple dans les épîtres pauliniennes," Ephemerides theologicae lovanienses, 33 (1947), 378-412.

Gärtner, Bertil. [3511] The Temple and the Community in Qumran and the New Testament. Society for New Testament Studies Monograph Series, 1. Cambridge: Cambridge University Press, 1965, 164 pp.

Gaston, Lloyd. [3512] "The Theology of the Temple: The New Testament Fulfillment of the Promise of Old Testament Heilsgeschichte," in F. Christ (ed.), Oikonomia: Heilsgeschichte als Thema der Theologie (Festschrift Oscar Cullmann). Hamburg / Bergstedt: Herbert Reich, 1967, 32-41.

Hamman, Adalbert. [3513] "Prière et culte chez Saint Paul," Studii Biblici Franciscani, Liber Annuus, 8 (1957/1958), 289-308.

Hamman, Adalbert. [3514] "Prière et culte dans la Lettre de Saint-Jacques," Ephemerides theologicae lovanienses, 34 (1958), 35-47.

Jeremias, Joachim. [3515] "Der Eckstein," Angelos, 1 (1925), 65-70.

Jeremias, Joachim. [3516] "Eckstein-Schlussstein," Zeitschrift für die neutestamentliche Wissenschaft, 36 (1937), 154-157.

Jeremias, Joachim. [3517] "Kephalè gonìas-akrogoviaios," Zeitschrift für die neutestamentliche Wissenschaft, 29 (1930), 264-280.

Klinzing, Georg. [3518] Die Umdeutung des Kultus in der Qumran Gemeinde und in Neuen Testament. Studien zum Umwelt des Neuen Testaments, 7. Göttingen: Vandenhoeck and Ruprecht, 1971, 248 pp.

Le Bas, Edwin E. [3519] "Was the Corner-Stone of Scripture a Pyramidion?" Palestine Exploration Quarterly, (1946), 103-115.

Lignée, Hubert. [3520] The Living Temple. Baltimore: Helicon, 1966, 107 pp.

McKelvey, R. J. [3521] "Christ the Cornerstone," New Testament Studies, 8 (1961/1962), 352-359.

McKelvey, R. J. [3522] The New Temple: The Church in the New Testament. Oxford Theological Monographs. Oxford: Oxford University Press, 1969, 238 pp.

McKelvey, R. J. [3523] "'Temple' in the New Testament," in J. D. Douglas (ed.), The New Bible Dictionary. Grand Rapids: Eerdmans, 1962, 1247-1250.

MacRae, George W. [3524] "Building the House of the Lord," American Ecclesiastical Review, 140 (1959), 361-376.

Moule, C. F. D. [3525] "Sanctuary and Sacrifice in the Church of the New Testament," Journal of Theological Studies, 1 (1950), 29-41.

Nikiprowetzky, Valentin. [3526] "Le Noveau Temple: A propos ouvrage récent," Revue des études juives, 130 (1971), 1-30.

Nikiprowetzky, Valentin. [3527] "Temple et communeauté," Revue des études juives, 126 (1967), 7-25.

Pfammatter, Josef. [3528] Die Kirche als Bau: Ein exegetisch-theologische Studie zur Ekklesiologie der Paulusbriefe. Rome: Gregoriana, 1960, 196 pp.

Sabourin, Léopold. [3529] "Novum Templum," Verbum Domini, 47 (1969), 65-82.

Seidensticker, Philipp. [3530] Lebendiges Opfer (Röm 12, 1): Ein Beitrag zur Theologie des Apostels Paulus. Neutestamentliche Abhandlungen, 20/ 1-3. Münster: Aschendorff, 1954, 347 pp.

Turner, Harold W. [3531] "The New Temple of the New Testament," in From Temple to Meetinghouse: The Phenomenology and Theology of Places of Worship. The Hague: Mouton, 1979, 106-130.

Wenschkewitz, Hans. [3532] Die Spiritualisierung der Kultusbegriffe: Tempel, Priester, und Opfer im Neuen Testament. Angelos: Archiv für neuentestamentliche Zeitschrift und Kulturkunde, 4. Leipzig: Pfeiffer, 1932, 166 pp.

Zimmer, Robert G. [3533] "The Temple of God," Journal of the Evangelical Theological Society, 18 (1975), 41-46.

Twenty-Four

Jerusalem in Christian Thought, Art, and Sentimentality

Albaric, Michel. [3534] "Entre Babylone et Jérusalem: Pour une théologie de la ville," Bible et Terre Sainte, 117 (1970), 22-23.

Atiyeh, G. N. [3535] "Jerusalem in Medieval Christian Thought," Studies in Comparative Religion, 13 (1979), 167-175.

Baggati, Bellarmino and Testa, Emmanuele. [3536] Corpus Scriptorum de Ecclesia Matre, 4: Gerusalemme, La Redenzione secondo la Tradizione biblica dei SS. Padri. Studium Biblicum Franciscanum, Collectio Major, 26. Jerusalem: Franciscan Printing Press, 1982, 214 pp.

Borger, Hugo. [3537] "Die mittelalterliche Stadt als Abbild des himmlischen Jerusalem," in E. Reimbold (ed.), Symbolon: Jahrbuch für Symbolforschung, 2. Cologne: Weinand Verlag, 1974, 21-48.

Bouyer, L. [3538] "Jérusalem, la Sainte Cité," La Vie Spirituelle, 86 (1952), 367-377.

Bredero, Adriaan H. [3539] "Jérusalem dans l' occident médiéaval," in P. Gallais and Y. J. Riou (eds.), Mélanges offerts à René Crozet, 1. Poitiers: Société d' Études Médiéavales, 1966, 259-271.

Brennan, Joseph P. [3540] "Jerusalem-- A Christian Perspective," in in J. M. Oestrreicher and A. Sinai (eds.), Jerusalem. New York: John Day, 1974, 226-232.

Brunot, Amédée. [3541] "Rome, miroir de Jérusalem," Bible et Terre Sainte, 168 (1975), 8-15.

Campos, Julio. [3542] "La 'Ciudad de Dios' según la mente y sentir de los Padres de la Iglesia," Ciudad de Dios, 184 (1971), 495-579.

Cardini, Franco. [3543] "Crusade and 'Presence of Jerusalem' in Medieval Florence," in B. Z. Kedar, et al. (eds.), Outremer: Studies in the Crusading Kingdom of Jerusalem. Jerusalem: Ben-Zvi Institute, 1982, 332-346.

Castelot, John J. [3544] "Jesus and the City," The Bible Today, 49 (1970), 24-28.

Colli, A. [3545] "La Gerusalemme celeste nei cicli apocalittici altomedievali e l' affresco di San Pietro al monte di Civate," Cahiers Archéologique, 30 (1982), 107-124.

Congar, Yves M.-J. [3546] The Mystery of the Temple. Wetminster, MD: Newman Press, 1962, 322 pp.

Dalmais, I.-H. [3547] "Le souvenir du Temple dans la liturgie chrétienne," Bible et Terre Sainte, 122 (1970), 6-7.

Daoust, Joseph. [3548] "La cité de Jérusalem à Rouen," Bible et Terre Sainte, 140 (1972), 22.

Daoust, Joseph. [3549] "Jérusalem dans Rome: 1. L' église Sainte Pudentienne; 2. Saint Étienne le rond," Bible et Terre Sainte, 103 (1968), 11-16, 19.

Davis, Moshe. [3550] "The Holy Land in American Spiritual History," in M. Davis (ed.), With Eyes Toward Zion: Scholars Colloquium on America-Holy Land Studies. New York: Arno Press, 1977, 3-33.

Diebner, B. [3551] "Die Orientierung des Jerusalemer Tempels und die 'Sacred Direction' der frühchristlichen Kirchen," Zeitschrift des deutschen Palästina-Vereins, 87 (1971), 153-166.

Dougherty, James. [3552] The Fivesquare City: The City in Religious Imagination. Notre Dame, IN: University of Notre Dame Press, 1980, 167 pp.

Dougherty, James. [3553] "The Sacred City and the City of God," Augustinian Studies, 10 (1979), 81-90.

Dubois, M. J. [3554] "The Meaning of Jerusalem for Christians," in Israel Yearbook, 1982. Tel Aviv: Israel Yearbook Publications, 1982, 168-178.

Dubois, M. J. [3555] "What Jerusalem Really Means for Christians," The Holy Land, 2/1 (Spring, 1982), 36-47.

Du Buit, M. [3556] "Le signe de Jérusalem," Bible et Terre Sainte, 105 (1968), 19.

Dynes, W. [3557] "The Medieval Cloister as Portico of Solomon," Gesta: International Center of Medieval Art, 12/1-2 (1973), 61-69.

Ellul, Jacques. [3558] The Meaning of the City. Grand Rapids: Eerdmans, 1970, 209 pp.

Fascher, Erich. [3559] "Jerusalems Untergang in der urchristlichen und altkirchlichen Überlieferung," Theologische Literaturzeitung, 89 (1964), 81-98.

Féret, H.-M. [3560] "L' église dans l' histoire et la Jérusalem céleste," in L' Apocalypse de Saint Jean. Paris: Corrêa, 1946, 212-261.

Ferriére, Cinette. [3561] "Jérusalem en esprit et en vérité," Bible et Terre Sainte, 122 (1970), 20-21.

Fransen, Irénée. [3562] "Les chemins de Jérusalem," Bible et Terre Sainte, 105 (1968), 18.

Frizzell, Lawrence E. [3563] "Jerusalem: City of God and of His People," The Bible Today, 97 (1978), 1670-1676.

Garcia del Valle, C. [3564] Jerusalén, un siglo de oro de vida litúrgica. Madrid: Edic. Stadium, 1968, 300 pp.

Gatti Perer, M. L. and Pizzolato, L. F. (eds.). [3565] La Gerusalemme celeste: Immagini della Gerusalemme celeste dal III al XIV secolo. Milan: Vita e Pensiero, 1983, 304 pp.

Geffré, C. and Jossua, J. P. [3566] "Jerusalem: Some Reflections on a City That is 'Unique and Universal' for the Monotheistic Religions," in True and False Universality of Christianity. Concilium, 35. New York: Seabury, 1980, 113-125.

Gelin, A. [3567] "Jérusalem dans le Dessein de Dieu," La Vie Spirituelle, 86 (1952), 353-366.

Gourgues, M. [3568] "L' an prochain à Jérusalem. Approche concrete de l' espérance biblique," La Vie Spirituelle, 134 (1980), 610-630.

Gousset, M.-Th. [3569] "Un aspect du symbolisme des encensoirs romans: La Jérusalem céleste," Cahiers Archéologique, 30 (1982), 81-106.

Gousset, M.-Th. [3570] "La représentation de la Jérusalem céleste à l' epougue carolingienne," Cahiers Archéologique, 23 (1974), 47-60.

Grelot, Pierre. See Join-Lambert, Michel and Grelot, Pierre. [3576]

Gutman, Joseph (ed.). [3571] The Temple of Solomon: Archaeological Fact and Medieval Tradition in Christian, Islamic and Jewish Art. Religion and the Arts, 3. Missoula, MT: Scholars Press, 1976, 198 pp.

Hamdani, Abbas. [3572] "Columbus and the Recovery of Jerusalem," Journal of the American Oriental Society, 99 (1979), 39-48.

Handy, Robert T. [3573] "Sources for Understanding American Christian Attitudes toward the Holy Land, 1800-1959," in M. Davis (ed.), With Eyes Toward Zion: Scholars Colloquium on America-Holy Land Studies. New York: Arno Press, 1977, 34-56.

Handy, Robert T. [3574] "Studies in the Interrelationship between America and the Holy Land: A Fruitful Field for Interdisciplinary and Interfaith Cooperation," Journal of Church and State, 13 (1971), 283-301. Reprinted in J. E. Wood, Jr. (ed.), Jewish-Christian Relations in Today's World. Waco, TX: Markham Press, 1971, 106-123.

Handy, Robert T. [3575] "Zion in American Christian Movements," in M. Davis (ed.), Israel: Its Role in Civilization. New York: Harper and Brothers, 1956, 284-297.

Join-Lambert, Michel and Grelot, Pierre. [3576] "Vers la Jérusalem Nouvelle," in X. Léon-Dufour (ed.), Vocabulaire de Théologie Biblique. Paris: Cerf, 1962, 483-487.

Jossua, J. P. See Geffré, C. and Jossua, J. P. [3566]

Konrad, Robert. [3577] "Das himmlische und das irdische Jerusalems im mittelalterischen Denken: Mystische Vorstellung und geschichtliche Wirkung," in C. Bauer, L. Boehm, and M. Müller (eds.), Speculum historiale: Geschicht im Spiegel von Geschichtsschreibung und Geschichtsdeutung (Festschrift Johannes Spörl). Freiburg: Alber, 1967, 523-540.

Krinsky, C. H. [3578] "Representations of the Temple of Jerusalem before 1500," Journal of the Warburg and Courtland Institutes, 33 (1970), 1-19.

Lamirande, É. [3579] "Le thème de la Jérusalem céleste chez Saint Ambroise," Revue des Études Augustiniennes, 29 (1983), 209-232.

L' Atrebate, Dominique. [3580] "Monjoie! La découverte de Jérusalem," Bible et Terre Sainte, 103 (1968), 17.

Linder, Amnon. [3581] "Jerusalem as a Focal Point in the Conflict between Judaism and Christianity," in B. Z. Kedar (ed.), Jerusalem in the Middle Ages. Selected Papers. Jerusalem: Yad Izhaq Ben-Zvi, 1979, 5-26 (Hebrew), vii-viii (English summary). English summary also in "From the Hebrew Press: Jerusalem in the Middle Ages, Selected Papers (Yad Izhaq Ben-Zvi, Jerusalem, 1979," in L. I. Levine (ed.), Jerusalem Cathedra, 2. Jerusalem: Yad Izhaq Ben-Zvi Institute / Detroit: Wayne State University Press, 1982, 318.

Mc Kenzie, Leon. [3582] "Of Rocks and Stones and Temples Rare," The Bible Today, 23 (1966), 1522-1527.

Mähl, S. [3583] "Jerusalem im mittelalterlichen Sicht," Welt als Geschichte, 22 (1962), 11-26.

Maigret, Jacques. [3584] "La demeure de Dieu avec les hommes," Bible et Terre Sainte, 122 (1970), 4-5.

Maigret, Jacques. [3585] "Jérusalem, Source d' eau vive," Bible et Terre Sainte, 101 (1968), 2-4.

Martin-Achard, Robert. [3586] "Jérusalem perdue et retrouvée," Foi et Vie, 63 (1964), 244-247.

Martini, Carlo M. [3587] "Gerusalemme: Storia, mistero, profezia," in M. Borrmans (ed.), Gerusalemme. Atti della XXVI Settimana Biblica, Associazione Biblica Italiana. Brescia: Paideia, 1982, 1-12.

Mees, Michael. [3588] "Der geistige Tempel: Einige Überlegungen zu Klemens von Alexandrien," Vetera Christianorum, 1 (1964), 83-89.

Mehnert, Gottfried. [3589] "Jerusalem als religiöses Phanomen in neuerer Zeit," in G. Müller (ed.), Glaube, Geist, Geschichte (Festschrift E. Benz). Leiden: Brill, 1967, 160-174.

Minear, Paul. [3590] "Holy People, Holy Land, Holy City," Interpretation, 37 (1983), 18-31.

Neri, Damiano. [3591] Il S. Sepolcro riprodotto in Occidente. Jerusalem: Franciscan Printing Press, 1971, 142 pp. [In Western art and architecture.]

Pellett, D. C. [3592] "Jerusalem the Golden: From the Earthly to the Heavenly Holy City," Encounter, 34 (1973), 272-281.

Pizzolata, L. F. See Gatti Perer, M. L. and Pizzolato, L. F. [3565]

Poleman, R. [3593] "Jérusalem d' en Haut," La Vie Spirituelle, 108 (1963), 637-659.

Prawer, Joshua. [3594] "Christianity between Heavenly and Earthly Jerusalem," in J. Aviram (ed.), Jerusalem through the Ages. Jerusalem: Israel Exploration Society, 1968, 179-192 (Hebrew), 65 (English summary).

Prawer, Joshua. [3595] "Jerusalem in Jewish and Christian Thought of the Early Middle Ages," Cathedra: History of Eretz-Israel, 17 (1980), 40-72 (Hebrew).

Prawer, Joshua. [3596] "Jerusalem in the Christian and Jewish Perspectives of the Early Middle Ages," in Gli ebrei nell' alto mediova. Spoleto, 1980, 739-814.

Provera, Mario. [3597] "Jerusalen en los escritos de San Jeronimo," Tierra Santa, 61 (May-June, 1986), 147-150.

Rose, André. [3598] "Jérusalem dans l' année liturgique," La Vie Spirituelle, 86 (1952), 389-403.

Rosenau, Helen. [3599] The Ideal City in Its Architectural Evolution. Boston: Book and Art Shop / Bristol, UK: Western Printing Services, 1959, 168 pp.

Rosenau, Helen. [3600] Vision of the Temple: The Image of the Temple in Judaism and Christianity. London: Oresko Books, 1979, 192 pp.

Rousse, Jacques. [3601] "J' ai tant aimé Jérusalem!" La Vie Spirituelle, 132 (1978), 454-457.

Rousseau, O. [3602] "Quelques textes patristiques sur la Jérusalem Céleste," La Vie Spirituelle,

Rusche, H. [3603] "Himmlisches Jerusalem," in J. Höfer and K. Rahner (eds.), Lexikon für Theologie und Kirche, 5. Freiburg: Verlag Herder, 1960, 367-368.

Sarno, R. A. [3604] "Rebuilding the Temple," The Bible Today, 45 (1969), 2799-2804.

Schreckenberg, H. [3605] "The Destruction of the Second Temple as Reflected in Christian Art," in A. Oppenheimer, U. Rappaport, and M. Stern (eds.), Jerusalem in the Second Temple Period: Abraham Schalit Memorial Volume. Jerusalem: Yad Izhaq Ben-Zvi, 1980, 394-414 (Hebrew), xxii-xxiii (English summary).

Stookey, L. H. [3606] "Gothic Cathedral as the Heavenly Jerusalem: Liturgical and Theological Sources," Gesta: International Center of Medieval Art, 8/1 (1969), 35-41.

Testa, Emmanuele. See Baggati, Bellarmino and Testa, Emmanuele. [3536]

Testa, Emmanuele. [3607] "La nuova Sion," Studii Biblici Franciscani, Liber Annuus, 22 (1972), 48-73.

Walsh, Michael F. [3608] "The New Jerusalem: Where God Lives Today," The Bible Today, 97 (1978), 1677-1682.

Wardi, Chaim. [3609] "[Jerusalem:] The Christian Perspective," Ariel, 23 (1969), 22-24.

Werblowsky, R. J. Z. [3610] "Bernard of Clairvaux, the Templars and the Significance of the Holy Land," in Eretz-Israel: Archaeological, Historical, and Geographical Studies, 10. Jerusalem: Israel Exploration Society, 1971, 143-145 (Hebrew), xiii (English summary).

Werblowsky, R. J. Z. [3611] The Meaning of Jerusalem to Jews, Christians, and Muslims. Jerusalem: Israel Universities Study Group for Middle Eastern Affairs, revised edn., 1978, 16 pp. Published originally as "Jerusalem, Holy City of Three Religions," in Jaarbericht Ex Orient Lux, 23 (1975), 423-439.

Winchester, Dean of. [3612] "Dante and Jerusalem," Church Quarterly Review, 110 (1930), 252-270.

Twenty-Five

Byzantine Jerusalem

Abel, Félix-M. [3613] "Eudocie et son premier vôyage a Jérusalem, / Installation d' Eudocie a Jérusalem, / Eudocie régit la Palestine de 444 a 460," in Histoire de la Palestine, 2. Paris: Lecoffre, 1952, 331-337.

Abel, Félix-M. [3614] "Jean de Jérusalem," in Histoire de la Palestine, 2. Paris: Lecoffre, 1952, 305-311.

Abel, Félix-M. [3615] "Jérusalem," in F. Cabrol and H. Leclerq (eds.), Dictionnaire d' Archéologie et de Liturgie. Paris: Letouzey et Ané, 1927, 7/2, 2304-2374.

Abel, Félix-M. [3616] "Le patriarche Juvénal de Jérusalem d' apres sa plus récent monographie," Proche-Orient Chrétien, 1 (1951), 305-317.

Abel, Félix-M. [3617] [Review and summary of C. S. Kekelidze's publication in Russian of 7th century Georgian liturgy from Jerusalem.] Revue biblique, 23 (1914), 453-462.

Abel, Félix-M. [3618] "Saint Cyrille de Jérusalem," in Histoire de la Palestine, 2. Paris: Lecoffre, 1952, 284-289.

Alexander, Spain. [3619] "Studies in Constantinian Church Architecture," Revista di Archeologia Cristiana, 47 (1971), 281-330; 49 (1973), 33-44.

Arce, Augustín. [3620] Itinerario de la virgen Egeria (381-384), edición critica del texto latino, variantes, traducción anotada, documentos auxiliares amplia introducción, planos y notas. Biblioteca de autores cristianos, 416. Madrid: La Editorial Catolica, 1980, 353 pp.

Armstrong, Gregory T. [3621] "Fifth and Sixth Century Church Buildings in the Holy Land," Greek Orthodox Theological Review, 14 (1969), 17-30.

Armstrong, Gregory T. [3622] "Imperial Church Buildings and Church-State Relations, A. D. 313-363," Church History, 36 (1967), 3-17.

Armstrong, Gregory T. [3623] "Imperial Church Buildings in the Holy Land in the Fourth Century," Biblical Archaeologist, 30 (1967), 90-102.

Avi-Yonah, Michael. [3624] "Byzantine Jerusalem," in Encyclopaedia Judaica, 9. Jerusalem: Macmillan, 1971, 1406-1408. Also in Israel Pocket Library: Jerusalem. Jerusalem: Keter, 1973, 43-47.

Avi-Yonah, Michael. [3625] "Jerusalem: The Byzantine Period," in Encyclopedia of Archaeolocial Excavations in the Holy Land, 2. Englewood Cliffs, NJ: Prentice-Hall, 1976, 613-626.

Avi-Yonah, Michael. [3626] "The Madeba Map," in Atlas of Israel. Jerusalem: Survey of Israel Ministry of Labour / Amsterdam: Elsevier, 1970, section I/1.

Avi-Yonah, Michael. [3627] "The Madeba Mosaic Map," in Eretz-Israel: Archaeological, Historical, and Geographical Studies, 2. Jerusalem: Israel Exploration Society, 1953, 129-156.

Avi-Yonah, Michael. [3628] The Madeba Mosaic Map. Jerusalem: Israel Exploration Society, 1954, 70 + 10 + 10 pp.

Avi-Yonah, Michael. [3629] "Mosaic Pavements in Palestine," in Art in Ancient Palestine. Collected and prepared for republication by H. Katzenstein and Y. Tsafrir. Jerusalem: Magnes Press, 1981, 283-382, esp. 309-325, 356-357, 378-379. [Jerusalem; primarily Byzantine remains.] Originally published in Quarterly of the Department of Antiquities of Palestine, 2 (1932), 136-181; 3 (1933), 26-27, 49-73; 4 (1935), 187-193.

Avigad, Nahman. [3630] "A Building Inscription of Justinian and the 'Nea' Church in Jerusalem," Qadmoniot, 10 (1977), 80-83 (Hebrew).

Avigad, Nahman. [3631] "A Building Inscription of the Emperor Justinian and the Nea in Jerusalem," Israel Exploration Journal, 27 (1977), 145-151.

Avigad, Nahman. [3632] "Byzantine Jerusalem," Discovering Jerusalem. Nashville: Thomas Nelson, 1983, 208-246. [Cardo Maximus, 213-229; Nea Church, 229-246.]

Avigad, Nahman. [3633] "Die Entdeckung der 'Nea' gegennten Marienkirche in Jerusalem," Antike Welt: Zeitschrift für Archaeologie und Kulturgeschichte, 10/3 (1979), 31-35.

Avigad, Nahman. [3634] "Jérusalem (Quartier juif)-- 1975-1977," Revue biblique, 85 (1978), 421-423. [On the Nea.]

Bagatti, Bellarmino. [3635] "The Church from the Council of Chalcedon to the Persian Occupation (451-614)," in The Church from the Gentiles in Palestine, History and Archaeology. Studium Biblicum Franciscanum, Collectio Minor, 4. Jerusalem: Franciscan Printing Press, 1971; reprinted, 1984, 85-125, esp. 85-90 ("the Patriarchs of Jerusalem").

Bagatti, Bellarmino. [3636] "The Church from the Council of Nicea to that of Chalcedon (325-451)" in The Church from the Gentiles in Palestine, History and Archaeology. Studium Biblicum Franciscanum, Collectio Minor, 4. Jerusalem: Franciscan Printing Press, 1971; reprinted, 1984, 46-84, esp. 48-49 ("the Bishops of Jerusalem"), 56-57 (the churches in Jerusalem).

Bagatti, Bellarmino. [3637] "Le origini della tradizione dei Luoghi Santi in Palestina," Studii Biblici Franciscani, Liber Annuus, 14 (1963/1964), 32-64, esp. 32-44.

Bagatti, Bellarmino. [3638] "Il 'tempio di Gerusalemme' dal II all' VIII secolo," Biblica, 43 (1962), 1-21. For French version see Bagatti, Bellarmino. [3640]

Bagatti, Bellarmino. [3639] Recherches sur le site du Temple de Jérusalem (Ier - VIIer siècle). Studium Biblicum Franciscanum, Collectio Minor, 22. Jerusalem:

Franciscan Printing Press,1979, 75 pp. + 45 pls. [Articles previously published in Italian in *Studii Biblici Franciscani, Liber Annuus,* 8 (1958), 309-352; *Biblica*, 43 (1962), 1-21; *Biblica*, 46 (1965), 428-444-- "Adaptation française" by A. Storme.]

Bagatti, Bellarmino. [3640] "Resti romani nell' area della Flagellazione in Gerusalemme," *Studii Biblici Franciscani, Liber Annuus,* 8 (1958), 309-352. For French version see Bagatti, Bellarmino. [3640]

Bahat, Dan. [3641] "The Byzantine Period (330-638 C. E.)," in *Carta's Historical Atlas of Jerusalem: An Illustrated History*. Jerusalem: Carta, 1983, 40-47.

Bain, R. Nisbet. [3642] "Armenian Description of the Holy Places in the Seventh Century," *Palestine Exploration Fund, Quarterly Statement,* (1896), 346-349.

Baldi, Donatus. [3643] *Enchiridion Locorum Sanctorum: Documenta S. Evangelii Loca Respicientia*. Jerusalem: Franciscan Printing Press, 1935, 2nd edn., 1955, reprinted 1982, 788 pp. [References in the Church Fathers and the liturgy to the holy places of the Gospels.]

Barsottelli, L. [3644] "I Luoghi Santi evangelici di Gerusalemme e la tradizone fino a Constantino," *Euntes Docete*, 25 (1972), 266-271.

Baumstark, A. [3645] "Darstellungen früchristlicher Sakralbauten Jerusalems auf einem Mailänder Elfenbeindiptychon," *Oriens Christianus*, n. s. 4 (1914), 64-75.

Baumstark, A. [3646] "Die Heiligtümer des byzantinischen Jerusalem nach einer übersehenen Urkunde," *Oriens Christianus,* 5 (1905), 227-289.

Ben-Dov, Meir. [3647] "Discovery of the Nea Church-- Jewel of Byzantine Jerusalem," *Christian News from Israel*, 226/2 (1977), 86-90.

Ben-Dov, Meir. [3648] "Found after 1400 Years-- the Magnificent Nea," *Biblical Archaeology Review,* 3/4 (Dec., 1977), 32-36.

Ben-Dov, Meir. [3649] "Jerusalem under Christian Rule, / The Age of Byzantine Splendor, / The Byzantine Residential Quarter," in *In the Shadow of the Temple: The Discovery of Ancient Jerusalem*. Jerusalem: Keter / New York: Harper and Row, 1985, 206-271.

Ben-Dov, Meir. [3650] "More on the Nea Church," *Biblical Archaeology Review,* 4/1 (March, 1978), 48-49.

Bernard, John H. [3651] "The Pilgrimage of S. Sylvia of Aquitana to the Holy Places (circa 385 A. D.)," in *The Library of the Palestine Pilgrims' Text Society*, 1. New York: AMS Press, 1971, 1-50. [Originally published in 1891.] [= Egeria.]

Bernard, John H. [3652] "Theodosius on the Topography of the Holy Land (A. D. 530)," in *The Library of the Palestine Pilgrims' Text Society*, 2. New York: AMS Press, 1971, 3-19. [Originally published in 1893.]

Bernard, John H. and Lewis, T. Hayter. [3653] "The Churches of Constantine at Jerusalem: Being Translations from Eusebius and the Early Pilgrims with an Introduction and Explanatory Notes and Drawings," in The Library of the Palestine Pilgrims' Text Society, 1. New York: AMS Press, 1971, i-xxix, 1-38. [Originally published in 1887.]

Bliss, Frederick J. See Schick, Conrad and Bliss, Frederick J. [3763]

Bliss, Frederick J. and Dickie, Archibald C. [3654] "The Church at the Pool of Siloam," in Excavations at Jerusalem, 1894-1897. London: Palestine Exploration Fund, 1898, 178-210.

Bori, Pier Cesare. [3655] "La référence à la communauté de Jérusalem dans les sources chrétiennes orientalis et occidentalis jusqu' au Ve siècle," Istina, 19 (1974), 31-48.

Bredy, Michel. [3656] "Mamila ou Maqulla: La prise de Jérusalem et ses conséquences selon la récension alexandrine des Annales d' Eutychès," Oriens Christianus, 65 (1981), 62-86. [Persian conquest of A. D. 614.]

Brooks, E. W. [3657] "An Armenian Visitor to Jerusalem in the Seventh Century," English Historical Review, 11 (1896), 93-97.

Broshi, Magen. [3658] "Evidence of Earliest Christian Pilgrimage to the Holy Land Comes to Light in the Holy Sepulchre Church," Biblical Archaeology Review, 3/4 (Dec., 1977), 42-44. [The "Jerusalem Ship" / DOMINE IVIMUS inscription.]

Broshi, Magen. [3659] "The Population of Western Palestine in the Roman-Byzantine Period," Bulletin of the American Schools of Oriental Research, 236 (1979), 1-10.

Broshi, Magen. [3660] "Standards of Street Widths in the Roman-Byzantine Period," Israel Exploration Journal, 27 (1977), 232-235.

Brownlow, Canon. [3661] "The Hodoeporicon of St. Willibald (circa 754 A. D.)," in The Library of the Palestine Pilgrims' Text Society, 3. New York: AMS Press, 1971, i-x, 1-58. [Originally published in 1895.]

Capelle, B. [3662] "La fête de la Vierge à Jérusalem au Ve siècle," Muséon, (1943), 1-33. Also in Travaux liturgiques, 3. Louvain: Abbaye du Mont-César, 1968, 280-301.

Cardman, Francine. [3663] "Fourth Century Jerusalem: Religious Geography and Christian Tradition," in P. Henry (ed.), Schools of Thought in the Christian Tradition (Festschrift Jaroslav Pelikan). Philadelphia: Fortress Press, 1984, 49-64.

Cardman, Francine. [3664] "The Rhetoric of Holy Places: Palestine in the Fourth Century," in E. A. Livingstone (ed.), Studia Patristica, 17/1. Elmsford, NY: Pergamon Press, 1982, 18-25.

Chen, Doren. [3665] "Dating the Cardo Maximus in Jerusalem," Palestine Exploration Quarterly, (1982), 43-45.

Chen, Doren. [3666] "On the Golden Gate in Jerusalem and the Baptistery at Emmaus-Nicopolis," Zeitschrift des deutschen Palästina-Vereins, 97 (1981), 171-177.

Chitty, D. J. [3667] "Jerusalem after Chalcedon, A. D. 451-518," The Christian East, 2/1 (1952), 22-32.

Cignelli, L. [3668] "Il pellegrinaggio in Terra Santa (nei Padri della Chiesa)," La Terra Santa, 55 (1979), 180-187.

Clark, Elizabeth A. [3669] "Claims on the Bones of St. Stephen: The Partisans of Melania and Eudocia," Church History, 51 (1982), 141-156.

Clermont-Ganneau, Charles. [3670] "The Mâdeba Mosaic," Palestine Exploration Fund, Quarterly Statement, (1897), 213-225.

Clermont-Ganneau, Charles. [3671] "The Taking of Jerusalem by the Persians, A. D. 614," Palestine Exploration Fund, Quarterly Statement, (1898), 36-54.

Colbi, Paul S. [3672] "A Byzantine Empress, Benefactress of the Holy Land," Holy Land Review, 5/1-2 (Spring-Summer, 1979), 50-53. [Eudokia.]

Conant, K. J. [3673] "The Holy Sites at Jerusalem in the First to Fourth Centuries," Proceedings of the American Philosophical Association, 102/1 (1958), 14-24.

Conder, Claude R. [3674] "The Byzantines," in The City of Jerusalem. London: John Murray, 1909, 208-232.

Conybeare, F. C. [3675] "Antiocus Strategos' Account of the Sack of Jerusalem in A. D. 614," English Historical Review, 25 (1910), 502-517.

Couret, Comte A. [3676] La Palestine sous les empereurs grecs, 326-636. Grenoble: F. Allier, 1869, 276 pp.

Couret, Comte A. [3677] La prise de Jérusalem par les Perses en 614, Trois documents nouveaux. Orléans: Herluison Académie de Sainte-Croix, 1896, 46 pp.

Crawley-Boevey, A. W. [3678] "The Churches of Constantine," Palestine Exploration Fund, Quarterly Statement, (1907), 215-220.

Crowfoot, John W. [3679] Early Churches in Palestine. The Schweich Lectures of the British Academy, 1937. London: Oxford University Press, 1941, 166 pp.

Dalmais, I.-H. [3680] "Sophrone, pèlerin, poète des Lieux saints," Bible et Terre Sainte, 103 (1968), 10.

Daoust, Joseph. [3681] "Dame Éthérie aux Lieux saints," Bible et Terre Sainte, 103 (1968), 6-9. [= Egeria.]

Daoust, Joseph. [3682] "Eusèbe de Césarée et l' église judéo-chrétienne de Jérusalem," Bible et Terre Sainte, 161 (1974), 18-19.

Daoust, Joseph. [3683] "La gauloise Stercoria git ici: Une rouennaise au Moyen-Orient en 342," Bible et Terre Sainte, 98 (1968), 22-23.

Daoust, Joseph. [3684] "Robert le diable à Jérusalem," Bible et Terre Sainte, 101 (1968), 20-22.

Daoust, Joseph. [3685] "Sainte Croix en Jérusalem," Bible et Terre Sainte, 168 (1975), 16-17.

Daoust, Joseph. [3686] "Le voyage de Jérome et Paula," Bible et Terre Sainte, 148 (1973), 6-20.

Dashian, P. J. [3687] "Anhang," Zeitschrift des deutschen Palästina-Vereins, 24 (1901), 165-171. [On the Armenian memorial mosaic found near the Damascus Gate.]

Davies, J. G. [3688] "The Peregrination Egeriae and the Ascension," Virgiliae Christianae, 8 (1954), 93-100.

Deltombe, F.-L. [3689] "Arculf, le gaulois," Bible et Terre Sainte, 103 (1968), 4-5.

Díaz y Díaz, M. See Maraval, P. and Díaz y Díaz, M. [3735]

Dickie, Archibald C. See Bliss, Frederick J. and Dickie, Archibald C. [3654]

Dickie, Archibald C. [3690] "Architectural Notes on Remains of Ancient Church at Pool of Siloam," Palestine Exploration Fund, Quarterly Statement, (1897), 26-29.

Dickie, Archibald C. [3691] "The Lower Church of St. John, Jerusalem," Palestine Exploration Fund, Quarterly Statement, (1899), 43-45.

Dickson, J. See Schick, Conrad and Dickson, J. [3764]

Donner, Herbert. [3692] Pilgerfahrt ins Heilige Land: Die ältesten Berichte christlicher Palästinapilger (4.-7. Jdt.). Stuttgart: KBW, 1979, 435 pp.

Downey, Glanville. [3693] "From the Pagan City to the Christian City," Greek Orthodox Theological Review, 10/1 (1964), 121-139.

Drake, H. A. [3694] "Coptic Version of the Discovery of the Holy Sepulchre," Greek, Roman, and Byzantine Studies, 20 (1979), 381-392.

Drake, H. A. [3695] "Eusebius on the True Cross," Journal of Ecclesiastical History, 36 (1985), 1-22.

Drake, H. A. [3696] "The Return of the Holy Sepulchre," Catholic Historical Review, 70 (1984), 263-267.

Feldman, Jennie. [3697] "Restoring the Main Thoroughfare of Byzantine Jerusalem," Christian News from Israel, special issue (June, 1985), 26-27.

Finegan, Jack. [3698] "The Pool of Siloam," in The Archeology of the New Testament: The Life of Jesus and the Beginning of the Early Church.

Princeton: Princeton University Press, 1969, 114-115. [On the Byzantine churches at the pool.]

Fletcher, R. A. [3699] "Celebrations at Jerusalem on March 25th in the Sixth Century," in Studia Patristica, 5/3. Texte und Untersuchungen, 80. Berlin: Akademie-Verlag, 1962, 30-34.

Fransen, Irénée. [3700] "Tu es de Jérusalem," Bible et Terre Sainte, 100 (1968), 3-4.

Garitte, Gerardo. [3701] Expugnationis hierosolymae, A. D. 614, recensiones arabicae. Corpus scriptorum christianorum orientalium. Louvain: Secrétariat du Corpus SCO, 1973-1974, 340-341, 347-348.

Germer-Durand, Joseph. [3702] "Épigraphie chrétienne de Jérusalem," Revue biblique, 1 (1892), 560-588.

Geyer, Paul. [3703] Itinera hiersolymitanae, saeculi IV-VIII. Corpus scriptorum ecclesiasticorum latinorum, 39. Vindobonae: F. Tempsky / Lipsiae: G. Freytag, 1898, 480 pp.

Gingras, G. E. [3704] Egeria: Diary of a Pilgrimage. Ancient Christian Writers, 38. New York: Newman, 1970, 287 pp.

Gold, Victor R. [3705] "The Mosaic Map of Madeba," Biblical Archaeologist, 21 (1958), 50-71. Also in E. F. Campbell, Jr. and D. N. Freedman (eds.), Biblical Archaeologist Reader, 3. Garden City, NY: Doubleday, 1970, 366-389.

Gray, John. [3706] "The Metropolis of Christendom," in A History of Jerusalem. New York: Praeger, 1969, 194-209.

Grumel, V. [3707] "La reposition de la Vraie Croix à Jérusalem par Héraclius," in P. Wirth (ed.), Polychordia (Festschrift F. Dölger). Byzantinische Forschungen, 1. Amsterdam: A. M. Hakkert, 1967, 139-149.

Guthe, Hermann. [3708] "Das Stadtbild Jerusalems auf der Mosaikkarte von Madeba," Zeitschrift des deutschen Palästina-Vereins, 28 (1905), 120-130.

Hamilton, R. W. [3709] "Jerusalem in the Fourth Century," Palestine Exploration Quarterly, (1952), 83-90.

Hanauer, James Edward. [3710] "Was There a Street of Columns in Jerusalem?" Palestine Exploration Fund, Quarterly Statement, (1891), 318-319.

Harvey, A. E. [3711] "Melito and Jerusalem," Journal of Theological Studies, 17 (1966), 401-404.

Holum, Kenneth G. [3712] "Hadrian and St. Helena: Imperial Travelers and the Origins of Christian Pilgrimage," Byzantine Studies Conference: Abstracts of Papers, 10 (1984), 1-2.

Honigmann, E. [3713] "Juvenal of Jerusalem," Dumbarton Oaks Papers, 5. Canbridge, MA: Harvard University Press,1950, 209-279.

Hunt, E. D. [3714] Holy Land Pilgrimage in the Later Roman Empire, A. D. 312-460. Oxford: Clarendon Press, 1982, 269 pp.

Hunt, E. D. [3715] "Palladius of Helenopolis: A Party and Its Supporters in the Church of the Late Fourth Century, 1. Jerusalem," Journal of Theological Studies, 24 (1973), 456-466.

Hunt, E. D. [3716] "St. Silvia of Aquitane: The Role of a Theodosian Pilgrim in the Society of East and West," Journal of Theological Studies, 23 (1972), 351-373.

Hurley, G. [3717] "The Sixty Martyrs of Jerusalem," Greek, Roman, and Byzantine Studies, 18 (1977), 369-374.

Hurst, Thomas R. [3718] "Pilgrimage and Holy Sites," Byzantine Studies Conference: Abstracts of Papers, 10 (1984), 33.

Itinerari et alia geographica: Itineraria Hierosolymitana. [3719] Corpus Christianorum, Series Latina, 175-176. Turnholti: Typographi Brepols Editores Pontificii, 1965, 280 pp.

Join-Lambert, Michel. [3720] "Christian Jerusalem," in Jerusalem. London: Elek Books / New York: Putnam's, 1958, 102-145.

Kekelidze, C. S. See Abel, Félix-M. [3617]

Kenyon, Kathleen M. [3721] "Roman and Byzantine Jerusalem," in Jerusalem: Excavating 3,000 Years of History. New York: McGraw-Hill, 1967, 187-193.

Kohler, C. See Molinier, Augustus and Kohler, C. [3741]

Kretschmar, Georg. [3722] "Festkalendar und Memorialstätten Jerusalems in altkirchlicher Zeit," Zeitschrift des deutschen Palästina-Vereins, 87 (1971), 167-205.

Lagrange, Marie-Joseph. [3723] "Jérusalem d' apres la mosaïque de Mâdeba," Revue biblique, 6 (1897), 450-458.

Lassus, J. [3724] "L' empereur Constantin, Eusèbe et les Lieux saints," Revue d' histoire des religions, 171 (1967), 135-144.

Leclercq, Henri. [3725] "Pèlerinages aux Lieux saints," in F. Cabrol and H. Leclercq (eds.), Dictionnaire d' Archéologie et de Liturgie, 14/1. Paris: Letouzey et Ané, 1939, 65-176.

Leconte, René. [3726] "Le pèlerin de Bordeaux," Bible et Terre Sainte, 103 (1968), 2-4.

Leeb, H. [3727] Die Gesänge im Gemeindegottesdienst von Jerusalem vom 5. bis 8. Jahrhundert. Wiener Beiträge zur Theologie, 28. Wien: Herder, 1970, 312 pp.

Lewis, T. Hayter. See Bernard, John H. and Lewis, T. Hayter. [3653]

Lewis, T. Hayter. See Stewart, Aubrey; Wilson, Charles W.; and Lewis, T. Hayter. [3777]

Lewis, T. Hayter. [3728] "Byzantine Capital Found in the Haram Area," Palestine Exploration Fund, Quarterly Statement, 19 (1887), 59-60.

Linder, A. [3729] "Jerusalem between Judaism and Christianity in the Byzantine Period," Cathedra: For the History of Eretz-Israel and its Yishuv, 11 (1979), 110-119 (Hebrew).

Macalister, R. A. Stewart. [3730] "The Lost Inscription of Eugenos in the Wady er-Rababi," Palestine Exploration Fund, Quarterly Statement, (1900), 101-102.

Macalister, R. A. Stewart. [3731] "Some New Inscriptions from Jerusalem and its Neighbourhood," Palestine Exploration Fund, Quarterly Statement, (1907), 234-239.

McCarthy, M. C. [3732] "Pilgrimages: Early Christian," in New Catholic Encyclopedia, 11. New York: McGraw-Hill, 1967, 362-365.

Macpherson, James R. [3733] "The Pilgrimage of Arculfus in the Holy Land (about the Year 670)," in The Library of the Palestine Pilgrims' Text Society, 3. New York: AMS Press, 1971, i-xx, 1-91. [Originally published in 1895.]

Macpherson, James R. [3734] "The Venerable Bede concerning the Holy Places," in The Library of the Palestine Pilgrims' Text Society, 3. New York: AMS Press, 1971, 67-87. [Originally published in 1895.]

Maraval, P. and Díaz y Díaz, M. [3735] Egérie, Journal de voyage: Introduction, texte critique, traduction, notes, index et cartes. Sources chrétiennes, 296. Paris: Cerf, 1982, 400 pp.

Mazar, Benjamin. [3736] "Archaeological Discovery in Jerusalem after A. D. 70: Byzantium and Jerusalem," in The Mountain of the Lord. Garden City, NY: Doubleday, 1975, 244-260.

Meimaris, Y. E. [3737] "Two Unpublished Greek Inscriptions," Studii Biblici Franciscani, Liber Annuus, 30 (1980), 225-232.

Milani, Celestina. [3738] Itinerarium Antonini Placentini: Un viaggio in Terra Santa del 560-570 d. C. Milan: Vita e pensiero, 1977, 324 pp.

Milik, J. T. [3739] "Notes d' epigraphie et topographie palestiniennes, 9: Sanctuaires chrétiens de Jérusalem a l' epoque arabe (VIIe-Xe s.)," Revue biblique, 67 (1960), 354-367, 550-591.

Milik, J. T. [3740] La Topographie de Jérusalem vers la fin de l' Époque byzantine. Beirut: Imprimerie Catholique, 1961, 62 pp. [Originally published in Mélanges de l' Université Saint-Joseph (Beyrouth), 37 (1960-1961), 127-189.]

Mohrmann, Christine. See Van der Meer, F. and Mohrmann, Christine. [3788]

Molinier, Augustus. See Tobler, Titus and Molinier, Augustus. [3786]

Molinier, Augustus and Kohler, C. [3741] Itinera Hierosolymitana et descriptiones Terrae Sanctae bellis sacris anteriora et Latina lingua exarata, 2 . Publications de la Société de l' Orient Latin, série géographie, 4. Genevae: J.-G. Fick, 1885, 267 pp.

Moore, Elinor A. [3742] The Ancient Churches of Old Jerusalem: The Evidence of the Pilgrims. London: Constable / Beirut: Khayats, 1961, 121 pp.

Mucznik, Sonia. See Ovadia, Asher and Mucznik, Sonia. [3749-3750]

Murray, A. S. [3743] "The Mosaic with Armenian Inscription from near the Damascus Gate, Jerusalem," Palestine Exploration Fund, Quarterly Statement, (1895), 126-127.

Narkiss, Bezalel. [3744] "The Armenian Treasures of Jerusalem: Mosaic Pavements," in B. Narkiss (ed.) in collaboration with M. E. Stone, Armenian Art Treasures of Jerusalem. Jerusalem: Massada Press, 1979, 21-28.

Nebenzahl, Kenneth. [3744A] "Madaba Mosaic Map," in Maps of the Holy Land: Images of Terra Sancta through Two Millennia. New York: Abbeville Press, 1986, 24-25, pl. 5.

O'Callaghan, R. T. [3745] "Madeba (Carte de)," in H. Cazelles (ed.), Supplément au Dictionnaire de la Bible, 5. Paris: Letouzey et Ané, 1957, 624-704, esp. 656-666.

Orlandi, Tito. [3746] Eudoxia and the Holy Sepulchre: A Constantinian Legend in Coptic. Testi e documente per lo studio dell' antichita, 67. Milan: Cisalpino-Goliardica, 1980, 191 pp.

Ovadia, Asher. [3747] "Byzantine Churches in the Holy Land," Christian News from Israel, 19/1-2 (May, 1968), 48-62.

Ovadia, Asher. [3748] Corpus of the Byzantine Churches in the Holy Land. Theophaneia: Beiträge zur Religions- und Kirchengeschichte des Altertums, 22. Bonn: Peter Hanstein Verlag, 1970, 223 pp. + 74 pls.

Ovadia, Asher and Mucznik, Sonia. [3749] "The Jerusalem Orpheus-- A Pagan or Christian Figure?" in A. Oppenheimer, U. Rappaport, and M. Stern (eds.), Jerusalem in the Second Temple Period: Abraham Schalit Memorial Volume. Jerusalem: Yad Izhaq Ben-Zvi, 1980, 415-433 (Hebrew), xxiii-xxiv (English summary).

Ovadia, Asher and Mucznik, Sonia. [3750] "Orpheus from Jerusalem-- Pagan or Christian Image?" in L. I. Levine (ed.), Jerusalem Cathedra, 1. Jerusalem: Yad Izhaq Ben-Zvi Institute / Detroit: Wayne State University Press, 1981, 152-166.

Ovadia, Asher and de Silva, Carla Gomez. [3751] "Supplementum to the Corpus of the Byzantine Churches in the Holy Land," Levant, 13 (1981), 200-261; 14 (1982), 122-170.

Owsepian, Archdiakonus. [3752] "Mosaik mit armenischer Inschrift im norden Jerusalems," Zeitschrift des deutschen Palästina-Vereins, 18 (1895), 88-90.

Peters, F. E. [3753] "Mother of All the Churches," in Jerusalem: The Holy City in the Eyes of Chroniclers, Visitors, Pilgrims, and Prophets from the Days of Abraham to the Beginnings of Modern Times. Princeton: Princeton University Press, 1985, 131-175.

Renoux, Charles. [3754] "Les ministres du culte à Jérusalem au IVe et au Ve siècle," in A. Pistoia and A. M. Triacca (eds.), L' assemblée liturgique et les différents rôles dans l' assemblée: Conference Saint-Serge 23e semaine d' étues liturgiques, 1976. Rome: Edizioni Liturgiche, 1977, 253-267.

Rhétoré, J. [3755] "La prise de Jérusalem par les Perses d' apres un document nouveau," Revue biblique, 6 (1897), 458-463.

Rosen, Baruch. [3756] "Reidentified Animals in the 'Orpheus Mosaic' from Jerusalem," Israel Exploration Journal, 34 (1984), 182-183.

Rozemond, Keetje. [3757] "Jean Mosch, Patriarche de Jérusalem en exil (614-634)," Vigiliae Christianae, 31 (1977), 60-67.

Rubin, Ze'ev. [3758] "The Church of the Holy Sepulchre and the Conflict between the Sees of Caesarea and Jerusalem," in L. I. Levine (ed.), Jerusalem Cathedra, 2. Jerusalem: Yad Izhaq Ben-Zvi Institute / Detroit: Wayne State University Press, 1982, 79-105.

Rubin, Ze'ev. [3759] "The Tenure of Maximos, Bishop of Jerusalem, and the Conflict between Caesarea and Jerusalem during the Fourth Century," Cathedra: For the History of Eretz-Israel and its Yishuv, 31 (1984), 31-42 (Hebrew).

Runciman, Steven. [3760] "Pilgrimages to Palestine before 1095," in K. M. Setton (ed.), History of the Crusades, 1. Philadelphia: University of Pennsylvania, 1958, 68-78.

Schick, Conrad. [3761] "The Church at the Pool of Shiloah," Palestine Exploration Fund, Quarterly Statement, (1897), 109-113.

Schick, Conrad. [3762] "The Columbarium or Cistern East of the Zion Gate," Palestine Exploration Fund, Quarterly Statement, (1898), 79-81. [Later identified as the Nea church.]

Schick, Conrad and Bliss, Frederick J. [3763] "Discovery of a Beautiful Mosaic with Armenian Inscription North of Jerusalem," Palestine Exploration Fund, Quarterly Statement, (1894), 257-261.

Schick, Conrad and Dickson, J. [3764] "A Recently Discovered Mosaic at Jerusalem," Palestine Exploration Fund, Quarterly Statement, (1901), 233-234. [The "Jerusalem Orpheus."]

Schneider, A. M. [3765] "Das Itinerarum des Epiphanius Hagiopolita," Zeitschrift des deutschen Palästina-Vereins, 63 (1940), 143-154.

von Schönborn, Christoph. [3766] Sophrone de Jérusalem, Vie monastique et confession dogmatique. Théologie historique, 20. Paris: Beauchesne, 1972, 260 pp.

Séjourne, Paul-M. [3767] "Une inscription grecque sur les murs de Jérusalem," Revue biblique, 3 (1894), 260-262.

de Silva, Carla Gomez. See Ovadia, Asher and de Silva, Carla Gomez. [3751]

Siméon, Vailhé. [3768] "Sophrone le Sophiste et Sophrone le Patriarche," Revue de l' orient chrétien, 7 (1902), 360-385; 8 (1903), 32 -69, 356-387.

Simon, Marcel. [3769] "Les pèlerinages dans l' antiquité chretienne," in Les pèlerinages de l' antiquité biblique et classique à l' occident médiéval. Études d' histoire des religions, 1. Paris: Paul Geuthner, 1973, 95-116.

Stegensek, Augustin. [3770] "Die Kirchenbauten Jerusalems im vierten Jahrhundert in bildicher Darstellung," Oriens Christianus, n. s. 1 (1911), 272-285.

Stewart, Aubrey. [3771] "Eutychii Annales," in The Library of the Palestine Pilgrims' Text Society, 11. New York: AMS Press, 1971, 35-68. [Originally published in 1895.]

Stewart, Aubrey. [3772] "The Pilgrimage of the Holy Paula by St. Jerome," in The Library of the Palestine Pilgrims' Text Society, 1. New York: AMS Press, 1971, i-viii, 1-16. [Originally published in 1887.]

Stewart, Aubrey and Wilson, Charles W. [3773] "The Epitome of S. Eucherius about Certain Holy Places (circ. A. D. 530)," in The Library of the Palestine Pilgrims' Text Society, 2. New York: AMS Press, 1971, i-vi, 7-23. [Originally pblished in 1890.]

Stewart, Aubrey and Wilson, Charles W. [3774] "Itinerary from Bordeaux to Jerusalem: 'The Bordeaux Pilgrim,'" in The Library of the Palestine Pilgrims' Text Society, 1. New York: AMS Press, 1971, i-xii, 1-68. [Originally published in 1887.]

Stewart, Aubrey and Wilson, Charles W. [3775] "The Letter of Paula and Eustochium to Marcella about the Holy Places (386 A. D.)," in The Library of the Palestine Pilgrims' Text Society, 1. New York: AMS Press, 1971, i-vii, 1-16. [Originally published in 1889.]

Stewart, Aubrey and Wilson, Charles W. [3776] "Of the Places Visited by Antoninus Martyr (circ, 560-570 A. D.)," in The Library of the Palestine Pilgrims' Text Society, 2. New York: AMS Press, 1971, i-viii, 1-44. [Originally published in 1896.]

Stewart, Aubrey; Wilson, Charles W.; and Lewis, T. Hayter. [3777] "Of the Buildings of Justinian by Procopius (circa 560 A. D.)," The Library of the Palestine Pilgrims' Text Society, 2. New York: AMS Press, 1971, i-ix, 1-178, esp. 138-143 (on the Nea). [Originally published in 1896.]

Stone, Michael E. See Narkiss, Bezalel. [3744]

Stone, Michael E. [3778] "Epigraphica Armeniaca Hierosolymitana," in Annual of Armenian Linguistics, 1 (1980), 51-68; 2 (1981), 71-81. [Armenian inscriptions of the 4th-12th centuries.]

Stone, Michael E. [3779] "An Armenian Pilgrim to the Holy Land in the Early Byzantine Era," Revue des Études Arméniennes, 18 (1984), 173-178.

Stone, Michael E. [3780] "Holy Land Pilgrimage of Armenians before the Arab Conquest," Revue biblique, 93 (1986), 93-110.

Storme, Albert. [3781] Les pèlerins célébres de Terre Sainte. Jerusalem: Franciscan Printing Press, 1984, 72 pp.

Strange, James F. [3782] "Archaeology and Pilgrims in the Holy Land and Jerusalem," Bulletin of the American Schools of Oriental Research, 245 (1982), 75-79.

Strzygowski, Joseph. [3783] "Das neugefundene Orpheus-Mosaik in Jerusalem," Zeitschrift des deutschen Palästina-Vereins, 24 (1901), 139-165.

Telfer, W. [3784] "Constantine's Holy Land Plan," in Studia Patristica, 1. Texte und Untersuchungen, 63. Berlin: Akademie-Verlag, 1957, 696-700.

Thomsen, Peter. [3785] "Das Stadtbild Jerusalems auf der Mosaikkarte von Madeba," Zeitschrift des deutschen Palästina-Vereins, 52 (1929), 149-174, 192-219.

Tobler, Titus and Molinier, Augustus. [3786] Itinera Hierosolymitana et descriptiones Terrae Sanctae bellis sacris anteriora et Latina lingua exarata, 1/1-2 . Publications de la Société de l' Orient Latin, série géographie, 1-2. Genèvae: J.-G. Fick, 1879, 418 pp.

Trombley, F. R. [3787] "A Note on the See of Jerusalem and the Synodal List of the Sixth Oecumenical Council (680-681)," Byzantion, 53 (1983), 632-638.

Van der Meer, F. and Mohrmann, Christine. [3788] "The Holy Places in Jerusalem," in M. F. Hedlund and H. H. Rowley (eds.), Atlas of the Early Christian World. London: Nelson, 1958, 321-322.

Vincent, Louis-Hugues. [3789] "Une mosaïque byzantine à Jérusalem," Revue biblique, 10 (1901), 436-444. [The "Jerusalem Orpheus."]

Vincent, Louis-Hugues. [3790] "La mosaïque d' Orphée," Revue biblique, 11 (1902), 100-103.

Watson, Charles M. [3791] "Commemoratorium de casis dei vel Monasteriis," Palestine Exploration Fund, Quarterly Statement, (1913), 23-33.

Watson, Charles M. [3792] "Notes on the Churches of Jerusalem Founded before A. D. 1099," Palestine Exploration Fund, Quarterly Statement, (1917, 165-171.

Watson, Charles M. [3793] "The Site of the Church of St. Mary at Jerusalem, Built by the Emperor Justinian," Palestine Exploration Fund, Quarterly Statement, (1903), 250-257, 344-353.

Weitzmann, Kurt. [3794] "Loca santa and the Representational Arts of Palestine," in Dumbarton Oaks Papers, 28. Washington, DC: Dumbarton Oaks Center for Byzantine Studies, 1974, 31-55.

Wilkinson, John. [3795] "Architectural Procedures in Byzantine Palestine," Levant, 13 (1981), 156-172.

Wilkinson, John. [3796] "Arculf's Plan of the Holy Places," in Jerusalem Pilgrims before the Crusades. Jerusalem: Ariel, 1977, 193-197.

Wilkinson, John. [3797] "At Siloam," in Jerusalem as Jesus Knew It. London: Thames and Hudson, 1978, 104-108. [On the Byzantine churches at Siloam.]

Wilkinson, John. [3798] "Christian Pilgrims in Jerusalem during the Byzantine Period," Palestine Exploration Quarterly, (1976), 75-101.

Wilkinson, John. [3799] Egeria's Travels to the Holy Land. London: S. P. C. K., 1971; rev. edn., Jerusalem: Ariel / Warminster, England: Aris and Phillips, 1981, 354 pp. [Includes translations of The Letter of King Abgar, Egeria's Travels, The Pilgrim of Bordeaux, Eusebius on the Buildings on Golgotha, Pseudo-Cyril's Mystagogical Lecture on the Eucharist, Valarius' Letter in Praise of the Life of the Most Blessed Egeria, and Peter the Deacon's Book on the Holy Places.]

Wilkinson, John. [3800] "The Gazetteer," in Jerusalem Pilgrims before the Crusades. Jerusalem: Ariel, 1977, 148-178. [Encyclopaedia of the holy sites of Byzantine Jerusalem.]

Wilkinson, John. [3801] "The Jerusalem Buildings," in Egeria's Travels to the Holy Land. Jerusalem: Ariel / Warminster, England: Aris and Phillips, rev. edn.,1981, 36-53.

Wilkinson, John. [3802] Jerusalem Pilgrims before the Crusades. Jerusalem: Ariel, 1977, 225 pp. [Includes translations of Jerome, Letter 108 (on Paula); Eucharius, Letter to Faustus; Brevarius (A Short Account of Jerusalem); Theodosius, Topography of the Holy Land; Cosmas Indicopleustes, Christian Topography; Procopius of Caesarea, Buidings; Piacenza Pilgrim, Travels; Sophronius of Jerusalem, Anacreontica; Adomnan, The Holy Places; Epiphanius the Monk, The Holy City and the Holy Places; Jacinthus the Presbyter, Pilgrimage; Hugeburc's Life of Willibald; Commemoratorium; Dicuil, The Measurement of the World; Bernard the Monk, A Journey to the Holy Places and Babylon; Photius, Question 107 to Amphilochius; and Rodulf Glaber, History.]

Wilson, Charles W. See Stewart, Aubrey and Wilson, Charles W. [3773-3776]

Wilson, Charles W. See Stewart, Aubrey; Wilson, Charles W.; and Lewis, T. Hayter. [3777]

Wilson-Kastner, Patricia. [3803] "Egeria," in A Lost Tradition: Women Writers of the Early Church. Washington, DC: University Presses of America, 1981, 71-134.

Windisch, Hans. [3804] "Die ältesten christlichen Palästinapilger," Zeitschrift des deutschen Palästina-Vereins, 48 (1925), 145-158.

Winkler, G. [3805] "Einige Randbemerkungen zum österlichen Gottesdienst in Jerusalem von 4. bis 8 Jahrhundert," Orientalia Christianus Periodica, 39 (1973), 481-490.

Wright, Thomas. [3806] Early Travels in Palestine. London: H. G. Bohn, 1848; reprinted, New York: KTAV, 1968, 1-31.

See also 29/The Church of the Holy Sepulchre; 31/The Churches of Mt. Sion; 32/The Churches of Gethsemane, the Mount of Olives, and Bethany; 33/The Pool of Bethesda and the Church of St. Anne; and 35/The Church of St. Stephen.

Twenty-Six

Crusader Jerusalem

Abel, Félix-M. [3807] "Lettre d' un Templier trouvé récemment à Jérusalem," Revue biblique, 35 (1926), 288-295.

Ashtour, E. And Hirschberg, H. Z. [3808] "Jerusalem: Crusader Period," in Encyclopaedia Judaica, 9. Jerusalem: Macmillan, 1971, 1415- 1418. Also in Israel Pocket Library: Jerusalem. Jerusalem: Keter, 1973, 60-68.

Avigad, Nahman. [3809] "Muslim and Crusader Remains," in Discovering Jerusalem. Nashville, Thomas Nelson, 1983, 247-257.

Babcock, Emily A. and Krey, A. C. [3810] William of Tyre: A History of Deeds Done beyond the Sea, 2 vols. Records of Civilizatation, 35. New York: Columbia University Press, 1943, 556 + 553 pp.

Bahat, Dan. [3811] "The Church of Mary Magdalene and its Quarter," in Eretz-Israel: Archaeological, Historical, and Geographical Studies, 18. Jerusalem: Israel Exploration Society, 1985, 5-7 (Hebrew),65* (English summary).

Bahat, Dan. [3812] "The Crusader Period,1099-1187," in Carta's Historical Atlas of Jerusalem: An Illustrated History. Jerusalem: Carta, 1983, 54-61.

Bahat, Dan. [3813] "A Smithy in a Crusader Church," Biblical Archaeology Review, 6/2 (March-April, 1980), 46-49.

Bahat, Dan and Ben-Ari, M. [3814] "Excavations at Tancred's Tower," in Y. Yadin (ed.), Jerusalem Revealed: Archaeology in the Holy City, 1968-1974. New Haven and London: Yale University Press and the Israel Exploration Society, 1976, 109-110.

Bahat, Dan and Reich, Ronny. [3815] "Une église médiévale dans le quartier juif," Revue biblique, 93 (1986), 111-114. [Church of St. Thomas of the Germans.]

Bahat, Dan and Solar, Giora. [3816] "Une église croisée récemment découverte à Jérusalem," Revue biblique, 85 (1978), 72-80.

Bahat, Dan and Solar, Giora. [3817] "A Newly Found Crusader Church in Jerusalem," in B. Kedar (ed.), Jerusalem in the Middle Ages. Selected Papers. Jerusalem: Yad Izhaq Ben-Zvi, 1979, 347-356 (Hebrew), xxvi (English summary).

Baldwin, Marshall W. (ed.). [3818] The First Hundred Years. K. M. Setton (gen. ed.), History of the Crusades, 1. Philadelphia: University of Pennsylvania Press, 1958, 694 pp.

Baras, Zvi. [3819] "Jewish-Christian Disputes and Conversions in Jerusalem," in B. Z. Kedar (ed.), Jerusalem in the Middle Ages, Selected Papers. Jerusalem: Yad Izhaq Ben-Zvi, 1979, 27-38 (Hebrew), viii-ix (English summary). English summary also in "From the Hebrew Press: Jerusalem in the Middle Ages, Selected Papers," in L. I. Levine (ed.), Jerusalem Cathedra, 2. Jerusalem: Yad Izhaq Ben-Zvi Institute / Detroit: Wayne State University Press, 1982, 319.

Ben-Ami, Ahron. [3820] Social Change in a Hostile Environment: The Crusader's Kingdom of Jerusalem. Princeton: Princeton University Press, 1969, 193 pp.

Ben-Ari, M. See Bahat, Dan and Ben-Ari, M. [3814]

Ben-Dov, Meir. [3821] "A Cross on the Temple Mount," in In the Shadow of the Temple: The Discovery of Ancient Jerusalem. Jerusalem: Keter / New York: Harper and Row, 1985, 342-353.

Benvenisti, Meron. [3822] "Jerusalem," in The Crusaders in the Holy Land. Jerusalem: Israel Universities Press, 1970, 49-73.

Besant, Walter and Palmer, E. H. [3823] Jerusalem: The City of Herod and Saladin. London: Chatto and Windus / Philadelphia: J. B. Lippincott, 4th edn. enlarged, 1899, 532 pp. [Mostly about Jerusalem and the Crusades; see esp. 155-528.]

Blyth, Estelle. [3824] "The Taking of Jerusalem, 15th July, 1099," Palestine Exploration Fund, Quarterly Statement, (1922), 172-178.

Boase, T. S. R. [3825] "Ecclesiastical Art in the Crusading States in Palestine and Syria: Architecture and Sculpture, in K. M. Setton (gen. ed.), History of the Crusades, 4: H. W. Hazard (ed.), Art and Architecture of the Crusader States. Madison, WI: University of Wisconsin Press, 1977, 69-116.

Brentjes, Burchard. [3826] "Der 'Felsendom' auf Kreuzfahrerminiaturen," in A. Hadidi (ed.), Studies in the History and Archaeology of Jordan, 1. Amman: Department of Antiquities, 1982, 357-359.

Buchthal, H. [3827] Miniature Painting in the Latin Kingdom of Jerusalem. Oxford: Oxford University Press, 1957, 156 pp.

Clermont-Ganneau, Charles. [3828] "Distinctive Character of Crusading Masonry" in C. Warren and C. R. Conder, The Survey of Western Palestine, 5: Jerusalem. Palestine Exploration Fund, 1884, 296-297.

Clermont-Ganneau, Charles. [3829] "The Distinctive and Specific Character of Crusading Masonry" in Archaeological Researches in Palestine during the Years 1873-1874, 1. Translated by Aubrey Stewart. London: Palestine Exploration Fund, 1896, 1-47.

Clermont-Ganneau, Charles. [3830] "John of La Rochelle's Epitaph," in Archaeological Researches in Palestine during the Years 1873-1874, 1. Translated by Aubrey Stewart. London: Palestine Exploration Fund, 1896, 230-232.

Clermont-Ganneau, Charles. [3831] "St. Anne's Market and Abbey," in Archaeological Researches in Palestine during the Years 1873-1874, 1. Translated by Aubrey Stewart. London: Palestine Exploration Fund, 1896, 116-126,

Clermont-Ganneau, Charles. [3832] "Tomb and Portrait of a Crusading Bishop of Palestine Contemporary with St. Louis," in Archaeological Researches in Palestine during the Years 1873-1874, 1. Translated by Aubrey Stewart. London: Palestine Exploration Fund, 1896, 269-274

Clermont-Ganneau, Charles. [3833] "The Tomb of Philippe d' Aubingné," in Archaeological Researches in Palestine during the Years 1873-1874, 1. Translated by Aubrey Stewart. London: Palestine Exploration Fund, 1896, 106-112.

Clermont-Ganneau, Charles. [3834] "The Tombstone of Jean de Valenciennes," in Archaeological Researches in Palestine during the Years 1873-1874, 1. Translated by Aubrey Stewart. London: Palestine Exploration Fund, 1896, 276-279.

Clermont-Ganneau, Charles. [3835] "Seal of the Crusading Hospital of St. Lazarus at Jerusalem," Palestine Exploration Fund, Quarterly Statement, (1901), 109-114.

Clifton, Lord Bishop of. [3836] "The Pilgrimage of Saewulf to Jerusalem (1102, 1103 A. D.)," in The Library of the Palestine Pilgrims' Text Society, 4. New York: AMS Press, 1971, i-viii, 1-55. [Originally published in 1896.]

Conder, Claude R. See Stewart, Aubrey and Conder, Claude R. [3936-3937]

Conder, Claude R. [3837] "The City of Jerusalem (1220 A. D.)," in The Library of the Palestine Pilgrims' Text Society, 6. New York: AMS Press, 1971, i-viii, 1-69. [Originally published in 1896.]

Conder, Claude R. [3838] "The Latin Kingdom," in The City of Jerusalem. London: John Murray, 1909, 275-307.

Conder, Claude R. [3839] The Latin Kingdom of Jerusalem, 1099-1291 A. D. London: Palestine Exploration Fund, 1897, 443 pp.

Conder, Claude R. [3840] "Mason's Marks," Palestine Exploration Fund, Quarterly Statement, (1883), 130-133.

Conder, Claude R. [3841] "The Muristan," Palestine Exploration Fund, Quarterly Statement, (1875), 77-81.

Daoust, Joseph. [3842] "L' hospitalité des chevaliers de Saint-Jean," Bible et Terre Sainte, 160 (1974), 19.

Duncalf, Frederic. [3843] "Some Influences of Oriental Environment in the Kingdom of Jerusalem," American Historical Association Annual Report, 6 (1914), 137-146.

Englezakis, B. [3844] "Jean le Chrysostomite: Patriarche de Jérusalem au XIIe siècle," Byzantion, 43 (1973), 506-508.

Enlart, Désiré Louis Camile. [3845] Les monuments des croisés dans le royaume de Jérusalem: Architecture religieuse et civile, 4 vols. Paris: P. Geuthner, 1925-1928, 217 pp. + 100 pls. + 541 pp. + 95 pls.

Folda, Jaroslav. [3846] "Aspects of Crusader Fresco Painting in the Latin Kingdom of Jerusalem," in Byzantine Studies Conference: Abstracts of Papers, 2 (1976), 12-13.

Folda, Jaroslav. [3847] "Crusader Art and Architecture: A Photographic Essay," in K. M. Setton (gen. ed.), History of the Crusades, 4: H. W. Hazard (ed.), Art and Architecture of the Crusader States. Madison, WI: University of Wisconsin Press, 1977, 281-354.

Folda, Jaroslav. [3848] "A Fourth Capital from the Chapel of the Repose in Jerusalem," Levant, 15 (1983), 194-195.

Folda, Jaroslav. [3849] "Three Crusader Capitals in Jerusalem," Levant, 10 (1978), 139-155.

France, J. [3850] "Unknown Account of the Capture of Jerusalem," English Historical Review, 87 (1972), 771-783.

Gabrieli, Francesco. [3851] Arab Historians of the Crusades. Selected and Translated from the Arabic Sources. Berkeley: University of California Press, 1969, 362 pp.

Gilbert, Martin. [3852] "Crusader Jerusalem" in Jerusalem History Atlas. New York: Macmillan, 1977, 24-25.

Goitein, S. D. [3853] "Contemporary Letters on the Capture of Jerusalem by the Crusaders," Journal of Jewish Studies, 3 (1952), 162-177.

Goitein, S. D. [3854] "Geniza Sources for the Crusader Period: A Survey," in B. Z. Kedar, H. E. Mayer, and R. C. Smail (eds.), Outremer: Studies in the Crusading Kingdom of Jerusalem (Festschrift Joshua Prawer). Jerusalem: Ben-Zvi Institute, 1982, 306-322.

Goitein, S. D. [3855] "New Sources on Palestine in Crusader Days," in Eretz-Israel: Archaeological, Historical, and Geographical Studies, 4. Jerusalem: Israel Exploration Society, 1956, 147 (Hebrew), x (English summary).

Grabois, Aryeh. [3856] "Christian Pilgrims in the Thirteenth Century and the Latin Kingdom of Jerusalem: Buchard of Mount Zion," in B. Z. Kedar, et al. (eds.), Outremer: Studies in the Crusading Kingdom of Jerusalem. Jerusalem: Ben-Zvi Institute, 1982, 285-296.

Grabois, Aryeh. [3857] "Le pèlerin occidental en Terre Sainte à l' époque des croisades: La relation de pèlerinage de Jean de Wurtzbourg," in B. Jeanneau (ed.), Études de civilisation médiévale (IXe-XIIe siècles): Melanges offerts à Edmond-René Labande. Poitiers: Études Supérieures de Civilisation Médiéval, 1974, 367-376.

Gray, John. [3858] "The Crescent and the Cross," in A History of Jerusalem. New York: Praeger, 1969, 228-259.

Grousset, René. [3859] Histoire des croisades et du royaume franc de Jérusalem, 3 vols. Paris: Libraire Plon et Nourrit, 1934-1936, 698 + 921 + 874 pp.

Hamilton, Bernard. [3860] "Rebuilding Zion: The Holy Places of Jerusalem in the Twelfth Century," in D. Baker (ed.), Renaissance and Renewal in Christian History: Papers Read at the Fifteenth and Sixteenth Winter Meeting of the Ecclesiastical History Society. Studies in Church History, 14. Oxford: Blackwell, 1977, 105-116.

Hamilton, Bernard. [3861] "Women in the Crusader States: The Queens of Jerusalem, 1100-90," in D. Baker (ed.), Medieval Women (Festschrift Rosalind M. Y. Hill). Studies in Church History, subsidia, 1. Oxford: Blackwell,1978, 143-174.

Hanauer, James Edward. [3862] "The Churches of St. Martin and St. John the Evangelist," Palestine Exploration Fund, Quarterly Statement, (1893), 301-305.

Hanauer, James Edward. [3863] "St Martin's Church and Other Medieval Remains," Palestine Exploration Fund, Quarterly Statement, (1893), 141-142.

Hanauer, James Edward. [3864] "The Tomb of Philip d' Aubigné at Jerusalem," Palestine Exploration Fund, Quarterly Statement, (1887), 76-78.

Heydenreich, Ludwig H. [3865] "Ein Jerusalem-Plan aus der Zeit der Kreuzfahrer," in A. von Euw (ed.), Miscellanea Pro Arte (Festschrift Hermann Schnitzler). Düsseldorf: Schwann, 1965, 83-90.

Hill, Joyce. [3866] "From Rome to Jerusalem: An Icelandic Itinerary of the Mid-Twelfth Century," Harvard Theological Review, 76 (1983), 175-203.

Hill, Rosalind. [3867] Gesta francorum et aliorum Hierosolimitanorum: The Deeds of the Franks and Other Pilgrims to Jerusalem. London: Thomas Nelson, 1962, 113 pp. [Latin text and English translation.]

Hirschberg, H. Z. See Ashtour, E. And Hirschberg, H. Z. [3808]

Jacoby, Zehavia. [3868] "A Newly Discovered Crusader Fragment in Jerusalem," Israel Exploration Journal, 30 (1980), 202-204.

Jacoby, Zehavia. [3869] "Tomb of Baldwin V, King of Jerusalem (1185-1186) and the Workshop of the Temple Area," Gesta: International Center of Medieval Art, 18/2 (1979), 3-14.

Jacoby, Zehavia. [3870] "Workshop of the Temple Area in Jerusalem in the Twelfth Century: Its Origin, Evolution, and Impact," Zeitschrift für Kunstgeschichte, 45 (1983), 325-394.

Join-Lambert, Michel. [3871] "The Latin Kingdom of Jerusalem (1099-1291)," in Jerusalem. London: Elek Books / New York: Putnam's, 1958, 211-221.

Joranson, E. [3872] "The Great Pilgrimage of 1064-1065," in L. J. Paetow (ed.), The Crusades and Other Historical Essays, Presented to D. C. Munro. New York: Crofts, 1928, 3-43.

Kedar, Benjamin Z. [3873] "The Patriarch Eraclius," in B. Z. Kedar, H. E. Mayer, and R. C. Smail (eds.), Outremer: Studies in the Crusading Kingdom of Jerusalem (Festschrift Joshua Prawer). Jerusalem: Ben-Zvi Institute, 1982, 177-204.

Kenaan, Nurith. [3874] "Local Christian Art in Twelfth Century Jerusalem," Israel Exploration Journal, 23 (1973), 167-175, 221-229.

Kenaan, Nurith. [3875] "A Local Trend in Crusader Art in Jerusalem," in Y. Yadin (ed.), Jerusalem Revealed: Archaeology in the Holy City, 1968-1974. New Haven and London: Yale University Press and the Israel Exploration Society, 1976, 114-115.

Klein, H. Arthur. See Klein, Mina and Klein, H. Arthur. [3876]

Klein, Mina and Klein, H. Arthur. [3876] "Crusaders and Crusader Kings in Jerusalem (1095-1171 C. E.)," in Temple beyond Time: The Story of the Site of Solomon's Temple at Jerusalem. New York: Van Nostrand Reinhold, 1970, 147-156.

Kraemer, Jörg. [3877] "Der Sturz des Königreichs Jerusalem (583/1187) in der Darstellung des 'Imad ad Din al-Katib al-Isfahani," Der Islam: Zeitschrift für Geschichte und Kultur der islamischen Orients, 30 (1952), 1-38.

Krey, A. C. See Babcock, Emily A. and Krey, A. C. [3810]

Krueger, E. W. [3878] "Der Muristan in Jerusalem und seine Kirchen," Im Lande der Bibel, 19/2 (1973), 5-10.

Kühn, Fritz. [3879] Geschichte der ersten lateinischen Patriarchen von Jerusalem. Leipzig: Kühn, 1886.

Leskien, A. [3880] "Die Pilgerfahrt des russischen Abtes Daniel ins heilige Land, 1113-1115," Zeitschrift des deutschen Palästina-Vereins, 7 (1884), 17-64.

Le Strange, Guy. [3881] "Idrîsî's Description of Jerusalem in 1154," Palestine Exploration Fund, Quarterly Statement, (1888), 31-35.

Macpherson, James R. [3882] "Fetellus (circa 1130 A. D.)," in The Library of the Palestine Pilgrims' Text Society, 5. New York: AMS Press, 1971, 1-58. [Originally published in 1896.]

Mandonnet, P. [3883] "Fra Ricoldo de Monte-Croce," Revue biblique, 2 (1893), 44-61, 182-202, 584-607.

Martin, J. P. P. [3884] "Les premiers princes croisés et les Syriens jacobites de Jérusalem," Journal asiatique, 8th ser., 12 (1888), 471-490; 13 (1889), 33-79.

Massé, Henri. [3885] "Pris de Jérusalem," in 'Imâd ad-Dîn al-Isfahâni (519-597/1125-1201): Conquête de la Syrie et de la Palestine par Saladin. Académie des Inscriptions et Belles-Lettres. Documents relatifs a l' histoire des Croisades. Paris: P. Geuthner, 1972, 44-63.

Mayer, Hans Eberhard. [3886] "Jérusalem et Antioche au temps de Baudouin II," Comptes rendus de l' Académie des Inscriptions et Belles-Lettres, (1980), 717-733.

Mayer, Hans Eberhard. [3887] Kreuzzüge und lateinischer Osten. London: Variorum, 1983, 332 pp. [12 studies in German, 2 in English.]

Mayer, Hans Eberhard. [3888] "Latins, Muslims and Greeks in the Latin Kingdom of Jerusalem," History, 63 (1978), 175-192.

Mayer, Hans Eberhard. [3889] Probleme des lateinischen Königreich Jerusalem. London: Variorum, 1983, 356 pp. [8 studies in German, English, and French.]

Mayer, Hans Eberhard. [3890] "Studies in the History of Queen Melisende of Jerusalem," Dumbarton Oaks Papers, 26. Washington, DC: Dumbarton Oaks Research Library and Collection, 1972, 93-182.

Mazar, Benjamin. [3891] "Archaeological Discovery in Jerusalem after A. D. 70: Jerusalem of Crusader Times," in The Mountain of the Lord. Garden City, NY: Doubleday, 1975, 274-279.

Michelant, Henri and Raynaud, Gaston. [3892] Itinéraires à Jérusalem et descriptions de la Terre Sainte, rédiges en français aux IXe-XIIIe siècles. Publications de la Société de l' orient latin, Série Géographie, 3. Genéve: J.-G. Fick, 1882, 281 pp.

Munro, Dana C. [3893] The Kingdom of the Crusaders. New York: Appleton-Century, 1935, 216 pp.

Nebbia, Thomas. See Shor, Frank and Nebbia, Thomas. [3930]

Nebenzahl, Kenneth. [3893A] "Early Twelfth-Century Crusader Map of Jerusalem," in Maps of the Holy Land: Images of Terra Sancta through Two Millennia. New York: Abbeville Press, 1986, 11, fig. 5.

Nebenzahl, Kenneth. [3893B] "Situs Hierusalem: Map of Jerusalem, ca. 1100," in Maps of the Holy Land: Images of Terra Sancta through Two Millennia. New York: Abbeville Press, 1986, 32, pl. 9.

Ovadiah, Asher. [3894] "A Crusader Church in the Jewish Quarter of Jerusalem," in Eretz-Israel: Archaeological, Historical, and Geographical Studies, 11. Jerusalem: Israel Exploration Society, 1973, 208-212 (Hebrew), 29* (English summary).

Ovadiah, Asher. [3895] "A Restored Crusader Church in the Jewish Quarter," Christian News from Israel, 25/3 (1975), 150-153.

Palmer, E. H. See Besant, Walter and Palmer, E. H. [3823]

Peters, F. E. [3896] "Coming of the Crusade, / Jerusalem under the Latin Cross," in Jerusalem: The Holy City in the Eyes of Chroniclers, Visitors, Pilgrims, and Prophets from the Days of Abraham to the Beginnings of Modern Times. Princeton: Princeton University Press, 1985, 251-332.

"The Pilgrimage of the Abbot Daniel," [3897] Palestine Exploration Fund, Quarterly Statement, 20 (1888), 35-39.

Prawer, Joshua, [3898] "The Armenians in Jerusalem under the Crusades," in M. E. Stone (ed.) Armenian and Biblical Studies. Jerusalem: St. James Press, 1976, 222-236.

Prawer, Joshua. [3899] "A Contribution to the Medieval Topography of Jerusalem--the Crusader Conquest of 1099," in Eretz-Israel: Archaeological, Historical, and Geographical Studies, 17. Jerusalem: Israel Exploration Society, 1984, 312-324 (Hebrew), 13*-14* (English summary).

Prawer, Joshua. [3900] "Crusader Cities," in Medieval City, in Honour of R. S. Lopez. New Haven: Yale University Press, 1977, 179-199.

Prawer, Joshua. [3901] Crusader Institutions. Oxford: Clarendon Press, 1980, 519 pp.

Prawer, Joshua. [3902] The Crusaders' Kingdom: European Colonization in the Middle Ages. New York: Praeger, 1972, 587 pp.

Prawer, Joshua. [3903] "Jerusalem, Capital of the Crusader Kingdom," in Judah and Jerusalem: The Twelfth Archaeological Convention. Jerusalem: Israel Exploration Society, 1957, 90-104 (Hebrew), vii (English summary).

Prawer, Joshua. [3904] "Jerusalem in Crusader Days," Qadmoniot, 1 (1968), 3-12 (Hebrew).

Prawer, Joshua. [3905] "Jerusalem in Crusader Days," in Y. Yadin (ed.), Jerusalem Revealed: Archaeology in the Holy City, 1968-1974. New Haven and London: Yale University Press and the Israel Exploration Society, 1976, 102-108.

Prawer, Joshua. [3906] "Jewish Resettlement in Crusader Jerusalem," Ariel, 19 (1967), 60-66.

Prawer, Joshua. [3907] "Notes on the History of the Jews in the Latin Kingdom of Jerusalem," Immanuel: A Bulletin of Religious Thought and Research in Israel, 9 (1979), 81-86.

Prawer, Joshua. [3908] "The Settlement of the Latins in Jerusalem," Speculum, 27 (1952), 490-503.

Prawer, Joshua. [3909] The World of the Crusaders. London: Weidenfeld and Nicolson, 1972, 160 pp.

Pringle, R. Denys. [3910] "Les édifices ecclésiastiques du royaume latin de Jérusalem," Revue biblique, 89 (1982), 92-98. [A comprehensive catalogue.]

Pringle, R. Denys. [3911] "Some Approaches to the Study of Crusader Masonry Marks in Palestine," Levant, 13 (1981), 173-199.

Raynaud, Gaston. See Michelant, Henri and Raynaud, Gaston. [3892]

Reich, Ronny. See Bahat, Dan and Reich, Ronny. [3815]

Riant, P. [3912] Expéditions et pèlerinages scandinaves en Terre Sainte au temps des Croisades. Paris: Lainé et Harvard, 1865.

Richard, Jean. [3913] The Latin Kingdom of Jerusalem, 2 vols. Amsterdam, NY: North Holland Publishing Co., 1979, 514 pp.

Riley-Smith, Jonathan. [3914] The Knights of St. John in Jerusalem and Cyprus. A History of the Order of the Hospital of St. John of Jerusalem, 1.New York: St. Martins's Press, 1967, 553 pp.

Röhricht, Reinhold. [3915] Geschichte des Königreichs Jerusalem (1100-1291). Innsbruck: Wagner, 1898, 1105 pp.

Röhricht, Reinhold. [3916] "Syria Sacra," Zeitschrift des deutschen Palästina-Vereins, 10 (1887), 1-48.

Röhricht, Reinhold. [3917] "Zur Geschichte der Kirche S. Maria Latina in Jerusalem," Neues Archiv der Gesellschaft für ältere deutsche Geschichtskunde, 14 (1889), 203-206.

Rotermund, Ernst. [3918] "Das Jerusalem des Burchard vom Berge Sion," Zeitschrift des deutschen Palästina-Vereins, 35 (1912), 1-27, 57-85.

Runciman, Steven. [3919] A History of the Crusades, 1: The First Crusade and the Foundation of the Kingdom of Jerusalem; 2. The Kingdom of Jerusalem and the Frankish East, 1100-1187. Cambridge: Cambridge University Press, 1951-1952, 377 + 523 pp.

de Sandoli, Sabino. [3920] "Bethany: Millicent Builds a Monastery," Holy Land Review, 6/1-4 (Spring-Winter, 1980), 23-24.

de Sandoli, Sabino. [3921] Corpus inscriptionum crucesignatorum Terrae-Sanctae (1099-1291). Studium Biblicum Franciscanum, Collectio Major, 21. Jerusalem: Franciscan Printing Press,1974, 351 pp.

de Sandoli, Sabino. [3922] Itinera hierosolymitana crucesignatorum (saec. XII-XIII). Textus latina cum versione italica, 1: Tempore primi belli sacri; 2. Tempore regum francorum, 100-1187; 3. Tempore recuperationis Terrae Sanctae, 1187-1244; 4. Tempore regni latini extremo, 1250-1291. Studium Biblicum Franciscanum, Collectio Major, 24. Jerusalem: Franciscan Printing Press, 1978-1984, 381 + 498 + 580 + 513 pp.

Savage, H. L. [3923] "Pilgrimage and Pilgrim Shrines in Palestine and Syria after 1095," in K. M. Setton (gen. ed.), History of the Crusades, 4: H. W. Hazard (ed.), Art and Architecture of the Crusader States. Madison, WI: University of Wisconsin Press, 1977, 36-68.

Schein, Sylvia. [3924] "The Patriarchs of Jerusalem in the Late Thirteenth Century," in B. Z. Kedar, H. E. Mayer, and R. C. Smail (eds.), Outremer: Studies in the Crusading Kingdom of Jerusalem (Festschrift Joshua Prawer). Jerusalem: Ben-Zvi Institute, 1982, 297-305.

Schick, Conrad. [3925] "The Ancient Churches in the Muristan," Palestine Exploration Fund, Quarterly Statement, (1901), 51-53. [Includes plans of the Maria Major.]

Schick, Conrad. [3926] "Crusading Ruins on Mount Scopus," Palestine Exploration Fund, Quarterly Statement, (1889), 114-116.

Schick, Conrad. [3927] "Church of the Knights of St. John," Palestine Exploration Fund, Quarterly Statement, (1872), 100.

Schick, Conrad. [3928] "The Muristan, or the Site of the Hospital of St. John of Jerusalem," Palestine Exploration Fund, Quarterly Statement, (1902), 42-56.

Schick, Conrad. [3929] "St. Martin's Church at Jerusalem," Palestine Exploration Fund, Quarterly Statement, (1893), 283-286.

Shor, Frank and Nebbia, Thomas. [3930] "Crusader Road to Jerusalem: Conquest of the Holy City," National Geographic, 124/6 (December, 1963), 838-855.

Sivan, Emmanuel. [3931] "Palestine during the Crusades (1099-1291)," in M. Avi-Yonah (ed.), A History of the Holy Land. London: Weidenfeld and Nicolson, 1969, 223-256.

Solar, Giora. See Bahat, Dan and Solar, Giora. [3816-3817]

Stewart, Aubrey. [3932] "Anonymous Pilgrims, I-VIII (11th and 12th centuries)," in The Library of the Palestine Pilgrims' Text Society, 6. New York: AMS Press, 1971, 1-86. [Originally published in 1894.]

Stewart, Aubrey. [3933] "The History of Jerusalem, A. D. 1180, by Jacques de Vitry," in The Library of the Palestine Pilgrims' Text Society, 11. New York: AMS Press, 1971, i-vi, 1-128. [Originally published in 1896.]

Stewart, Aubrey. [3934] "The Pilgrimage of Johannes Phocas in the Holy Land (in the year 1185 A. D.)," in The Library of the Palestine Pilgrims' Text Society, 5. New York: AMS Press, 1971, i-iv, 5-36. [Originally published in 1896.]

Stewart, Aubrey. [3935] "Theoderich's Description of the Holy Places (circa 1172 A. D.)," in The Library of the Palestine Pilgrims' Text Society, 5. New York: AMS Press, 1971, i-ix, 1-82. [Originally published in 1896.]

Stewart, Aubrey and Conder, Claude R. [3936] "Buchard of Mount Sion, A. D. 1280," in The Library of the Palestine Pilgrims' Text Society, 12. New York: AMS Press, 1971, i-vi, 1-136. [Originally published in 1896.]

Stewart, Aubrey and Conder, Claude R. [3937] "Marino Santo's Secrets for True Crusaders to Help Them Recover the Holy Land, Written in A. D. 1321," in The Library of the Palestine Pilgrims' Text Society, 12. New York: AMS Press, 1971, i-xii, 1-73. [Originally published in 1896.]

Stewart, Aubrey and Wilson, Charles W. [3938] "Description of the Holy Land by John of Würzburg (A. D. 1160-1170)," in The Library of the Palestine Pilgrims' Text Society, 5. New York: AMS Press, 1971, i-xii, 1-72. [Originally published in 1896.]

Stone, Michael E. [3939] "Epigraphica Armeniaca Hierosolymitana," in Annual of Armenian Linguistics, 2. Cleveland, 1981, 71-81. [Armenian inscriptions of the 9th-12th centuries.]

Storme, Albert. [3940] Les pèlerins célébres de Terre Sainte. Jerusalem: Franciscan Printing Press, 1984, 72 pp.

Stryzgowski, Joseph. [3941] "Ruins of Tombs of the Latin Kings on the Haram in Jerusalem," Speculum, 11 (1936), 499-508.

Tasso, Torquato. [3942] Jerusalem Delivered. Being a tranlation into English verse by Edward Fairfax of Tasso's Gerusalemme Liberata with an introduction by John C. Nelson. New York: G. P. Putnam's Sons, n. d., 446 pp. [Literature.]

Tobler, Titus. [3943] Descriptiones Terrae Sanctae, ex saeculo VIII, IX, XII et XV. New York: G. Olms, 1974, 539 pp. [Originally published in 1874.]

Tobler, Titus. [3944] Theodorici libellus de Locis Sanctis editus circa A. D. 1172. Cui accedunt breviores aliquot descriptiones Terra Sanctae. St. Gallen: Huber / Paris: Frank, 1865.

Vincent, Louis-Hugues. [3945] "L' église Ste Marie latine la petite," Revue biblique, 10 (1901), 100-103.

Volz, Paul. [3946] "Das Jerusalem der Kreuzfahrer," Palästinajahrbuch, 3 (1907), 56-71.

Watson, Charles M. [3947] "The Christian Kingdom," in The Story of Jerusalem. New York: Dutton, 1912, 168-208.

Williams, Robert. [3948] "Crosses on the Dome of the Rock," Palestine Exploration Fund, Quarterly Statement, (1913), 179-183.

Wilson, Charles W. See Stewart, Aubrey and Wilson, Charles W. [3938]

Wilson, Charles W. [3949] "The Pilgrimage of the Russian Abbot Daniel in the Holy Land, 1106-1107 A. D.," in The Library of the Palestine Pilgrims' Text Society, 4. New York: AMS Press, 1971, i-xv, 1-109. [Originally published in 1895.]

Wright, Thomas. [3950] Early Travels in Palestine. London: H. G. Bohn, 1848; reprinted New York: KTAV, 1968, 31-62.

See also 29/The Church of the Holy Sepulchre; 31/The Churches of Mt. Sion; 32/The Churches of Gethsemane, the Mount of Olives, and Bethany; 33/The Pool of Bethesda and the Church of St. Anne; and 35/The Church of St. Stephen.

Twenty-Seven

Jerusalem as Goal of Christian Pilgrimage

Adler, Nikolaus. [3951] "Des Magister Johannes von Frankfort Beschreibung seiner Palästinafahrt mit den Pfalzgrafen Ludwig III, 1426/27," Das Heilige Land, 86 (1954), 1-10.

Adler, Nikolaus. [3952] "Des Magister Johannes von Frankfort Dankansprache in Venedig nach der Rückkehr aus Palästina im Jahre 1427," Das Heilige Land, 90, (1958), 68-76.

Adler, Nikolaus. [3953] "Die Pilgerfahrt des Pfalzgrafen Ludwig III und die Franziskaner vom Hl. Lande," Studii Biblici Franciscani, Liber Annuus, 13 (1962/1963), 319-322.

Adrichem, Christiaan van. [3954] A Briefe Description of Hierusalem by Christianus Adrichomius. Amsterdam: Theatrum Orbis Terrarum / New York: Da Capo Press, 1969, 112 pp. [16th century cartographer; for use by pilgrims, but based on literary sources.]

Agate, L. D. [3955] "Pilgrimage (Christian)," in James Hastings (ed.), Encyclopaedia of Religion and Ethics, 10. New York: Scribner's, 1928, 18-23.

Altmann, Wilhelm. [3956] "Die Beschreibung der heiligen Stätten von Jerusalem in Eberhard Windecke's Denkwürdigkeiten über das Zeitalter Kaiser Sigmund's," Zeitschrift des deutschen Palästina-Vereins, 16, (1893), 188-192.

d' Anglure, Baron. [3957] Le saint voyage de Jérusalem, 1395. Bibliothèque catholique de voyages et de romans: Série des voyages. Paris: Au Bureau de la Bibliothèque, 1858, 222 pp.

Arce, Augustín. [3958] Itinario a Jerusalén 1703-1704, de Fray Eugenio de San Francisco. Jerusalem: Franciscan Printing Press, 1940, 98 pp.

Arce, Augustín. [3959] Expediciones de España a Jerusalén, 1673-1842. Jerusalem: Franciscan Printing Press, 1958, 460 pp.

Ashtour, E. [3960] "Travelers and Travels to Erez-Israel: Christian Travelers," in Encyclopaedia Judaica, 15. Jerusalem: Macmillan, 1971, 1354-1357.

Atiya, Aziz S. [3961] "Pilgrims and Propagandists in the Fourteenth / Fifteenth Century," in The Crusade in the Later Middle Ages. London: Butler and Tanner, 1938; reprinted, New York: Kraus, 1965, 155-230.

Atkinson, Clarissa. [3962] Mystic and Pilgrim: The 'Book' and the World of Margery Kempe. Ithaca: Cornell University Press, 1983, 241 pp.

Bagatti, Bellarmino. See Bellorini, T. and Hoade, Eugene. [3965-3968]

27/Christian Pilgrimage

Bagatti, Bellarmino. [3963] Fra Niccolò da Poggibonsi: Libro d' Oltramare (1346-1350). Studium Biblicum Franciscanum, Collectio Major, 2. Jerusalem: Franciscan Printing Press, 1945, 168 pp. Italian text of A. Bacchi, revised and annotated; For companion volume with English translation see Bellorini, T. and Hoade, Eugene. [3967]

Bassan, Fernande. [3964] Chateaubriand et la Terre Sainte. Paris: Presses Universitaires, 1959, 280 pp.

Bellorini, T. and Hoade, Eugene. [3965] Fra Bernardino Amico: Plans of the Sacred Edifices of the Holy Land, with preface and notes by B. Bagatti. Studium Biblicum Franciscanum, Collectio Major, 10. Jerusalem: Franciscan Printing Press, 1953, 147 pp. + 47 drawings.

Bellorini, T. and Hoade, Eugene. [3966] Fra Francesco Suriano: Treatise on the Holy Land, with preface and notes by B. Bagatti. Studium Biblicum Franciscanum, Collectio Major, 8. Jerusalem: Franciscan Printing Press, 1949; reprinted, 1983, 255 pp.

Bellorini, T. and Hoade, Eugene. [3967] Fra Niccolò of Poggibonsi: A Voyage beyond the Sea (1346-1350), with preface and notes by B. Bagatti. Studium Biblicum Franciscanum, Collectio Major, 2. Jerusalem: Franciscan Printing Press, 1945, 144 p..

Bellorini, T. and Hoade, Eugene. [3968] Gucci and Sigoli Frescobaldi: Visit to the Holy Places of Egypt, Sinai, and Syria in 1384, with preface and notes by B. Bagatti. Studium Biblicum Franciscanum, Collectio Minor, 6. Jerusalem: Franciscan Printing Press, 1948, 207 pp.

Benoit, Pierre. See Kaeppeli, Thomas and Benoit, Pierre. [4010]

Benoit, Pierre. [3969] "Die Gnade Jerusalems: Die geistliche Bedeutung der heilige Stätten und der Pilgerschaft," Das Heilige Land, 106 (1974), 26-31.

Bernard, John H. [3970] "Guide-Book to Jerusalem (circ. 1350)," in The Library of the Palestine Pilgrims' Text Society, 6. New York: AMS Press, 1971, 1-44. [Originally published in 1894.]

Besnard, A.-M. [3971] "Le sens de nos pèlerinages," Bible et Terre Sainte, 122 (1970), 18-20.

Bidot, G. [3972] "Théologie du pèlerinage," La Terre Sainte, (Spring, 1955), 11-13.

Bockel, Pierre. [3973] "Le pèlerinage de S.S. Paul VI en Terre Sainte," Bible et Terre Sainte, 61 (1964), 22-23.

Brehier, L. [3974] "Charlemagne et la Palestine," Revue historique, 157 (1928), 227-291.

Browne, R. A. [3975] The Holy Jerusalem Voyage of Ogier VIII, Seigneur d' Anglure. Gainsville, FL: Florida University Press, 1975, 163 pp.

Butler-Bowden, W. [3976] The Book of Margery Kempe, a Modern Version. New York: Devin-Adair, 1954, 243 pp.

Canova, G. [3977] "Un canto copto per il pellegrinaggio a Gerusalemme," Oriente Moderno, 60 (1980), 85-94.

Castelar, Emilie. [3978] "Le voyage de Saint Ignace de Loyola à Jérusalem" Revue internationale, 2 (1884), 145-168.

Chateaubriand, François Auguste René. See Bassan, Fernande. [3964]

Chateaubriand, François Auguste René. [3979] Itinéraire de Paris à Jérusalem. Edition critique en deux volumes avec un avant-propos, une bibliographie, des notes, par Emile Malakis, 2 vols. Paris: "Les Belles Lettres" / Baltimore: Johns Hopkins University Press, 1946, 407 + 492 pp.

Chateaubriand, François Auguste René. [3980] Journal de Jérusalem. Notes inédites publiées par G. Moulinier et A. Outrey. Cahiers Chateaubriand, 2. Paris: E. Bélin, 1950, 192 pp.

Chateaubriand, François Auguste René. [3981] Travels to Jerusalem and the Holy Land, through Egypt, 2 vols. Trans. by Frederic Shoberl. London: H. Colburn, 3rd ed., 1835.

Clarisse, Fernand. [3982] "Itinéraires, Voyage de Jérusalem du P. Bernardin Surius," La Terre Sainte, (April, 1965), 112-118.

Cohen, E. [3983] "The Pilgrim Artists," Ariel, 23 (1969), 46-51.

Colbi, Saul P. [3984] "La ripresa dei pellegrinaggi dopo la fine del regno crociato," La Terra Santa, 62 (July-August, 1986), 149-151.

Collis, Louise. [3985] Memoirs of a Medieval Woman: The Life and Times of Margery Kemp. New York: Harper and Row, 1983, 270 pp. [Originally published as The Apprentice Saint. London: Thomas Y. Crowell, 1964.]

Compain, M. [3986] "Les objets de pèlerinage," Bible et Terre Sainte, 170 (1975), 17-18.

Conder, Claude R. [3987] "Zuallardo's Traavels," Palestine Exploration Fund, Quarterly Statement, (1902), 97-105.

Conrady, Ludwig. [3988] Vier rheinische Palästina-Pilgerschriften des XIV, XV, und XVI Jahrhunderts. Wiesbaden: Feller and Geeks, 1882, 370 pp.

Couderc, C. [3989] Journal de voyage à Jérusalem de Louis de Rochechouart évêque de Saintes (1461). Paris: Leroux, 1893, 107 pp. Published also in Revue d' orient Latin, 1 (1893), 168-274.

Crawley-Boevey, A. W. [3989A] "Map and Description of Jerusalem by Christian Van Adrichem (1533-1585),"Palestine Exploration Fund, Quarterly Statement, (1909), 64-68. [Map/drawng of the city in the early Ottoman period (ca. 1486); indication of pilgrimage sites.]

Dannenfeldt, K. H. [3990] "Leonhard Rauwolf: A Lutheran Pigrim in Jerusalem, 1575," Archiv für Reformationsgeschichte, 55 (1964), 18-36.

Dannenfeldt, K. H. [3991] Leonhard Rauwolf: Sixteenth Century Physician, Botonist, and Traveller. Cambridge, MA: Harvard University Press, 1968, 321 pp. [Jerusalem, 153-176, 195-203.]

Daoust, Joseph. [3992] "Le chanoine Mésenge aux Lieux saints," Bible et Terre Sainte, 105 (1968), 12-17; 108 (1969), 22-23.

Daoust, Joseph. [3993] "La vie quotitienne à Jérusalem au XVIe siècle," Bible et Terre Sainte, 111 (1969), 22-23. [From the pilgrimage of Mésenge.]

Decroix, J. [3994] "Un guide des Lieux-Saints au XVe siècle," Bible et Terre Sainte, 105 (1968), 8.

Deluz, C. [3995] "Prìer à Jérusalem: Permanence et évolution d' après quelques récits de pèlerins occidentaux du XVe siècles," in La prière au moyen âge. Paris: Champion, 1981, 187-210.

Drinkwater, C. H. [3996] "Palestine Pilgrim's Certificate," Palestine Exploration Fund, Quarterly Statement, (1897), 81-82.

Dumoulin, Anne. [3997] "Towards a Psychological Understanding of the Pilgrim," Lumen Vitae, 32 (1977), 108-114.

Fiej, J. M. [3998] "Le pèlerinage des Nestoriens et Jacobites à Jérusalem," Cahiers de Civilization Médiévale, 12 (1969), 113-126.

Foster, William. [3999] The Travels of John Sanderson in the Levant, 1584-1602, with His Autobiography and Selections from His Correspondence. London: Hakluyt Society, 1931, 2nd ser., no. 67, 332 pp.

G. M. F. G. [4000] "A Sixteenth Century Pilgrim," Palestine Exploration Fund, Quarterly Statement, (1930), 91-97.

de Galbert, Oronce; Maurice, Charles; and Storme, Albert. [4001] "Le pèlerinage du sieur François de Ferrus à Jérusalem en 1585," La Terre Sainte, (Sept.-Oct., 1985), 219-230.

Gilbert, Martin. [4002] "A Christian Pilgrimage of 1670," in Jerusalem History Atlas. New York: Macmillan, 1977, 38-39.

Glikson, Yvonne and Hyman, Semah C. [4003] "Christian Pilgrimages," in Encyclopaedia Judaica, 13. Jerusalem: Macmillan, 1971, 514-519.

Graham, Stephen. [4004] With the Russian Pilgrims to Jerusalem. London: Thomas Nelson, n. d. [ca 1913], 253 pp.

de Groër, Georgette. See Heers, Jacques and de Groër, Georgette. [4006]

von Harff, Arnold. [4005] The Pilgrimage of Arnold von Harff, Knight from Cologne, through Italy, Syria, Egypt, Ethiopia, Nubia, Palestine, Turkey, France and Spain, which He Accomplished in the Years 1496 to 1499. London: The Hakluyt Society, 2nd ser., no. 94, 325 pp.

Heers, Jacques and de Groër, Georgette. [4006] Itinéraire d' Anselme Adorno en Terre Sainte (1470-1471). Paris: Centre Nationale de la Recherche Scientifique, 1978.

Heyd, W. [4007] "Les consulats établis en Terre Sainte au moyen-âge pour la protection des pèlerins," in Archives de l' Orient Latin, 2. Paris: Société de l' Orient Latin / Ernest Leroux, 1884, 355-364.

Hoade, Eugene. See Bellorini, T. and Hoade, Eugene. [3965-3968]

Hoade, Eugene. [4008] Western Pilgrims: The Itineraries of Fr. Simon Fitzsimons (1322-23), a Certain English Gentleman (1344-45), Thomas Brygg (1392), and Notes on Other Authors and Pilgrims. Studium Biblicum Franciscanum, Collectio Major, 18. Jerusalem: Franciscan Printing Press, 1952; reprinted 1970, 117 pp.

Howell, David. See Maundrell, Henry. [4022]

Hyman, Semah C. See Glikson, Yvonne and Hyman, Semah C. [4003]

"Itinerario al Santo Sepolcro del secolo XIV," [4009] Studia Orientalia Christiana, 2 (1957), 141-171.

Kaeppeli, Thomas and Benoit, Pierre. [4010] "Une pèlerinage Dominicain inédit du XIVe siècle," Revue biblique, 62 (1955), 513-540. [Humbert de Dijon, 1332.]

de Khitrowo, B. [4011] Itinéraires russes en orient, traduit pour la Sociét´de l' orient latin. Publications de la Société de l' orient latin, Série Géogeraphie, 5. Genève: J.-G. Fick, 1889, 334 pp.

Kraus, J. A. [4012] "Ein 500 jähriger Bericht aus Jerusalem," Das Heilige Land, 87 (1955), 10-15.

Labande, E. R. [4013] "Pilgrimages: Medieval and Modern," in New Catholic Encyclopedia, 11. New York: McGraw-Hill, 1967, 365-372.

Livio, Jean-Bernard. [4014] "Aujourd'hui si vous montez à Jérusalem," Bible et Terre Sainte, 103 (1968), 18-19.

Loftie, W. J. [4015] The Oldest Diarie of Englysshe Travel: Being the Hitherto Unpublished Narrative of the Pilgrimage of Sir Richard Torkington to Jerusalem in 1517. London: Field and Tuer, 1884, 72 pp.

Luke, Harry C. See Pink, H. L. and Luke, Harry C. [4031]

Luke, Harry C. [4016] "Extracts from the Diary of a Franciscan Pilgrim of the Sixteenth Century," in Jerusalem, 1920-1922. London: Murray, 1924, 41-45.

Macalister, R. A. Stewart. [4017] "The Pilgrimage of Symon Simeonis," Palestine Exploration Fund, Quarterly Statement, (1912), 153-156.

Macalister, R. A. Stewart. [4018] "Rauwolff's Travels in Palestine, 1573," Palestine Exploration Fund, Quarterly Statement, (1908), 133-141; (1909), 138-149, 210-218.

McMichael, Steven. [4019] "Francis as Medieval Pilgrim," The Holy Land, 4/1 (Spring, 1984), 3-10.

Malakis, Emile. See Chateaubriand, François Auguste René. [3979]

Mancini, Ignazio. [4020] "The Meaning of Pilgrimage," Holy Land Review, 2/2 (Summer, 1976), 59-64.

Marsy, Louis comte de. [4021] Le Sainct voyage di Hierusalem ou petit tracté du voyage de Hierusalem, de Rome et de Saint Nicolas Bar en Pouille de Jean de Couchermois. Genéve: J.-G. Fick, 1889, 106 pp.

Maundrell, Henry. [4022] A Journey from Aleppo to Jerusalem in 1697, with a new introduction by David Howell. Khayats Oriental Reprints, 3. Beirut: Khayats, 1963, 214 pp.

Maurice, Charles. See de Galbert, Oronce; Maurice, Charles; and Storme, Albert. [4001]

Meisner, H. See Röhricht, Reinhold and Meisner, H. [4051-4053]

Mislin, Jacob. [4023] Les Sainte Lieux: Pèlerinage à Jérusalem en passant par l' Autriche, la Hongrie, la Slavonie, les provinces Danubiennes, Constantinople, l' Archipel, le Liban, la Syrie, Alexandrie, Malte, la Sicile et Marseille, 3 vols. Paris/Lyon: Lecoffre, 3rd edn., 1876, 672 + 831 + 761 pp.

Moulinier, G. See Chateaubriand, François Auguste René. [3980]

Mühlau, Ferdinand. [4024] "Martinus Seusenius' Reise in das heilige Land, 1602/3," Zeitschrift des deutschen Palästina-Vereins, 26 (1903), 1-92.

Nebenzahl, Kenneth. [4024A] "Bernard von Breitenbach and Erhard Reuwich's Civitas Iherusalem," in Maps of the Holy Land: Images of Terra Sancta through Two Millennia. New York: Abbeville Press, 1986, 63-68, pl. 21. [Map/drawng of the city in the late Mamaluk period (ca. 1486); indication of pilgrimage sites.]

Nebenzahl, Kenneth. [4024B] "Christian von Adrichom: Jerusalem," in Maps of the Holy Land: Images of Terra Sancta through Two Millennia. New York: Abbeville Press, 1986, 90-91, pl. 33. [Map/drawng of the city in the early Ottoman period (ca. 1486); indication of pilgrimage sites.]

Nebenzahl, Kenneth. [4024C] [Jerusalem Pilgrimage of William Wey and Gabriele Capodilista (1458)], in Maps of the Holy Land: Images of Terra Sancta through Two Millennia. New York: Abbeville Press, 1986, 49-57, pls. 17-18.

Nebenzahl, Kenneth. [4024D] "Jerusalem and the Pilgrim Route from Jaffa, from the Manuscript of Burchard of Mt. Sion, Made for Philip of Burgundy in 1455," in Maps of the Holy Land: Images of Terra Sancta through Two Millennia. New York: Abbeville Press, 1986, frontispiece. [Drawng of the city in the late Mamaluk period (ca. 1486); views of pilgrimage sites.]

Nebenzahl, Kenneth. [4024E] "Marino Sanuto and Petrus Vesconte: Vesconte's Jerusalem," in Maps of the Holy Land: Images of Terra Sancta through Two

Millennia. New York: Abbeville Press, 1986, 43, fig. 10. [Map/drawng of city in the mid-Mamaluk period (ca. 1320); indication of pilgrimage sites.]

Newett, Margaret. [4025] Canon Pietro Casola's Pilgrimage to Jerusalem in the Year 1494. Manchester: University of Manchester Press, 1907, 427 pp.

Olin, John C. [4026] "The Idea of Pilgrimage in the Experience of Ignatius Loyola," Church History, 48 (1979), 387-397.

Oursel, R. [4027] Pèlerins du moyen âge: Les hommes, les chemins, les sanctuaires. Paris: Fayard, 2nd rev. edn., 1978, 277 pp.

Outrey, A. See Chateaubriand, François Auguste René. [3980]

Partin, Harry B. [4028] "Pilgrimage to Jerusalem: Jewish, Christian, Muslim," Encounter, 46 (1985), 15-35. [Primary emphasis on pilgrimage for Christians.]

Peters, F. E. [4029] "Piety and Polemic: The Crusader Legacy in the Holy City," in Jerusalem: The Holy City in the Eyes of Chroniclers, Visitors, Pilgrims, and Prophets from the Days of Abraham to the Beginnings of Modern Times. Princeton: Princeton University Press, 1985, 427-478. [Primary emphasis on pilgrimage by Western Christians.]

"Die Pilgerfahrt der heiligen Angelaa von Merici nach Jerusalem, 1524," [4030] Das Heilige Land, 37 (1893), 161-170.

Pink, H. L. and Luke, Harry C. [4031] "Narrative of a Journey from Rome to Jerusalem," Palestine Exploration Fund, Quarterly Statement, (1925), 140-151, 193-206; (1926), 23-28, 74-82, 136-143, 196-206; (1927), 18-33.

Prásek, J. V. [4032] "Beschreibung der Stadt Jerusalem und ihrer Umgebung von Martin Kabátnik, 1491-92," Zeitschrift des deutschen Palästina-Vereins, 21 (1898), 47-58.

Prásek, J. V. [4033] "Ein böhmischer Palästinapilger des 15. Jahrhunders," Zeitschrift des deutschen Palästina-Vereins, 19 (1896), 114-119.

Prescott, Hilda Frances Margaret. [4034] Friar Felix at Large: A Fifteenth-Century Pilgrimage to the Holy Land. New Haven: Yale University Press, 1950, 254 pp. Second edition published as Jerusalem Journey: Pilgrimage to the Holy Land in the Fifteenth-Century. London: Eyre and Spottiswoode, 1954, 242 pp. Published in French as Le voyage de Jérusalem au XVe siècle. Paris: Arthaud, 1959, 322 pp.

Rapp, Francis. [4035] "Les pèlerinages dans la vie religieuses de l' occident médiéval aux 14e et 15e siècles," in M. Simon (ed.), Les pèlerinages de l' antiquité biblique et classique à l' occident médiéval. Études d' histoire des religions, 1. Paris: Paul Geuthner, 1973, 117-160.

Rist, Jean. [4036] "Itinéraires: Voyage fait à la Terre Sainte en l' année 1719, par le P. Ladoire," La Terre Sainte, (July-Aug., 1965), 213-219.

Rochcau, Vsevold. [4037] "Les pèlerinages Russes au début du siècle," La Terra Sainte, (March, 1967), 49-58.

Röhricht, Reinhold. [4038] "Antonius de Cremona: Itinerium ad Sepulcrum Domini (1327-1330)," Zeitschrift des deutschen Palästina-Vereins, 13 (1890), 153-174.

Röhricht, Reinhold. [4039] Deutsche Pilgerreisen nach dem heiligen Lande. Gotha: Perthes, 1889, 352 pp.

Röhricht, Reinhold. [4040] Die Deutschen im heiligen Lande. Innsbruck: Verlag der Wagnerschen Universitäts-Buchhandlung, 1894, 169 pp.

Röhricht, Reinhold. [4041] "Die Jerusalemfahrt des Caspar von Mülinen (1506)," Zeitschrift des deutschen Palästina-Vereins, 11 (1888), 184-196.

Röhricht, Reinhold. [4042] "Die Jerusalemfahrt des Christian Perband (1614-1616)," Zeitschrift des deutschen Palästina-Vereins, 19 (1896), 102-104.

Röhricht, Reinhold. [4043] "Die Jerusalemfahrt des Heinrich von Zedlitz (1493)," Zeitschrift des deutschen Palästina-Vereins, 17 (1894), 98-114, 185-200, 277-301.

Röhricht, Reinhold. [4044] "Die Jerusalemfahrt des Herzogs Friedrich von Österreich, nachmaligen Kaiser Friedrich III, von Deutschland (1436)," Zeitschrift für deutsche Philologie, 23 (1891), 26-41.

Röhricht, Reinhold. [4045] "Die Jerusalemfahrt des Herzogs Heinrich des Frommen von Sachsen (1498)," Zeitschrift des deutschen Palästina-Vereins, 24 (1901), 1-25.

Röhricht, Reinhold. [4045A] "Karten und Pläne zur Palästinakunde aus dem 7 bis 16 Jahrhundert," Zeitschrift des deutschen Palästina-Vereins, 14 (1891), 8-11, 87-92, 137-141; 15 (1892),34-39; 18 (1895), 173-182. [Maps by and for pilgrims.]

Röhricht, Reinhold. [4046] "Liber Peregrinationes Fratris Jacobi de Verona," Revue de l' Orient Latin, 3 (1895), 155-302.

Röhricht, Reinhold. [4046A] "Marino Sando sen. als Kartograph Palästinas," Zeitschrift des deutschen Palästina-Vereins, 21 (1898), 84-126. [Map/drawng of city in the mid-Mamaluk period (ca. 1320); indication of pilgrimage sites.]

Röhricht, Reinhold. [4046B] "Die Palästinakarte Bernard von Breitenbach's," Zeitschrift des deutschen Palästina-Vereins, 24 (1901), 129-135. [Map/drawng of the city in the late Mamaluk period (ca. 1486); indication of pilgrimage sites.]

Röhricht, Reinhold. [4047] "Pilgerfahrt des Antonius von Cremona zum Grabe des Herrn, 1327 und 1330," Das Heilige Land, 37 (1893), 99-114.

Röhricht, Reinhold. [4048] "Über das Itinerarium des Johannes Schauenburgh (1645-1648)," Zeitschrift des deutschen Palästina-Vereins, 20 (1897), 54-57.

Röhricht, Reinhold. [4049] "Das Wallfahrt der Herzogin Maria Hippolyta v. Calabrien nach heiligen Lande (1474)," Zeitschrift des deutschen Palästina-Vereins, 14 (1891), 12-16.

Röhricht, Reinhold. [4050] "Zwei Berichte über eine Jerusalemfahrt (1521)," Zeitschrift für deutsche Philologie, 25 (1892), 163-220, 247-501.

Röhricht, Reinhold and Meisner, H. [4051] Deutsche Pilgerreisen nach dem heiligen Lande hrsg. und erläutert. Berlin: Weidmann, 1880, 712 pp.

Röhricht, Reinhold and Meisner, H. [4052] "Die Jerusalemfahrt des Friedrich Eckher von Käpfing und Karl Grimming auf Niederrain (1625)," Zeitschrift des deutschen Palästina-Vereins, 8 (1885), 174-178.

Röhricht, Reinhold and Meisner, H. [4053] "Die Pilgerfahrt des Herzogs Friedrich II von Liegnita und Brieg nach dem heiligen Lande und die Descriptio Templi Domini," Zeitschrift des deutschen Palästina-Vereins, 1 (1878), 101-131, 177-217.

Schefer, Charles. [4054] Le voyage de la cyté de Hierusalem avec la description des lieux, portes, villes, cites et autres passaiges, fait l' an mil quatre cens quatre vingtz. Paris: Leroux, 1882; reprinted, Amsterdam: Philo Press, 1970, 157 pp.

Schepss, G. [4055] "Zu den Eyb'schen Pilgerfahrten," Zeitschrift des deutschen Palästina-Vereins, 14 (1891), 17-29.

Schiller, Ely (ed.). [4056] Jerusalem and the Holy Land in Old Engravings and Illustrations (1483-1800). Jerusalem: Ariel, 1981, 200 pp. [Drawings by Christian pilgrims.]

Schur, Nathan. [4057] Jerusalem in Pilgrims' and Travellers' Accounts: A Thematic Bibliography of Western Christian Itineraries, 1300-1917. Jerusalem: Ariel, 1980, 151 pp.

Sepp, J. N. [4058] Jerusalem und das heilige Lande: Pilgerbuch nach Palästina, Syrien und Aegypten, 2 vols. Schaffhausen: Hurter, 1863, 781 + 866 pp.

Sobosan, J. G. [4059] "Pilgrimage Theology: A Scriptural Basis," The Bible Today, 69 (1973), 1400-1405.

Stewart, Aubrey. [4060] "Felix Fabri (ca. 1480-1483 A. D.), in The Library of the Palestine Pilgrims' Text Society, 7/8-9/10. New York: AMS Press, 1971, 1-641+1-692. [Originally published in 1892-1893.]

Stewart, Aubrey. [4061] "John Poloner's Description of the Holy Land (circa 1421 A. D.)," in The Library of the Palestine Pilgrims' Text Society, 6. New York: AMS Press, 1971, i-vii, 1-52. [Originally published in 1894.]

Stewart, Aubrey. [4062] "Ludolph von Suchem's Description of the Holy Land, and of the Way Thither, written in the Year A. D. 1350," in The Library of the Palestine Pilgrims' Text Society, 12. New York: AMS Press, 1971, i-x, 1-142. [Originally published in 1895.]

Storme, Albert. See de Galbert, Oronce; Maurice, Charles; and Storme, Albert. [4001]

Storme, Albert. [4063] Les Pèlerins célébres de Terre Sainte. Jerusalem: Franciscan Printing Press, 1984, 72 pp.

Storme, Albert. [4064] "Le voyage d' A. Adornes en Terre Sainte (1470-1471)," Studii Biblici Franciscani, Liber Annuus, 31 (1981), 199-216.

Sumption, Jonathan. [4065] Pilgrimage: An Image of Mediaeval Religion. Totowa, NJ: Rowman and Littlefield, 1975, 391 pp.

Turner, Edith. See Turner, Victor and Turner, Edith. [4067]

Turner, Victor. [4066] "The Center Out There: Pilgrim's Goal," History of Religions, 12 (1973), 191-230.

Turner, Victor and Turner, Edith. [4067] Image and Pilgrimage in Christian Culture: Anthropological Perspectives. New York: Columbia University Press, 1978, 281 pp.

Vilnay, Zev. [4068] "Views of the Holy Land in the Writings of Christian Pilgrims," in The Holy Land in Old Prints and Maps. Jerusalem: Rubin Mass, 2nd edn., 1965, 12-30.

Vogt, E. [4069] "Zu Herzog Friedrichs Jerusalemfahrt," Zeitschrift für deutsche Philologie, 23 (1891), 422-424.

Volney, Comte de Constantin François Chasseboeuf. [4070] Voyage en Syrie et en Egypte pendant les années 1783, 1784, et 1785, 2. Paris: 1787, 280-293; reprinted, Paris: Jean Gaulmier, 1959.

Welten, Peter. [4071] "Reisen nach der Ritterschaff Jerusalempilger in der 2. Hälfte des 15. Jahrhunderts," Zeitschrift des deutschen Palästina-Vereins, 93 (1977), 283-293.

Wolfe-Crome, Editha. [4072] Pilger und Forscher im Heiligen Land: Reiseberichte aus Palästina, Syrien, und Mesopotamien vom 11. bis zum 20. Jht., in Briefen und Tagebüchern. Giessen: W. Schmitz, 1977, 584 pp.

For texts and studies of Christian pilgrims of the Byzantine and Crusader periods, see 25/Byzantine Jerusalem and 26/Crusader Jerusalem.

Twenty-Eight

The Christian Churches and Communities of Jerusalem

Abel, Félix-M. [4073] "La sépulture de Sainte Jacques le mineur," *Revue biblique*, 28(1919), 480-499. [Cathedral Church of the Armenians.]

Abu-Manneh, Butrus. [4074] "The Georgians in Jerusalem during the Mamluk Period," in A. Cohen and G. Baer (eds.), *Egypt and Palestine: A Millennium of Association (868-1948)*. New York: St. Martin's Press / Jerusalem: Ben-Zvi Institute, 1984, 102-112.

Ajamian, Shahe. [4075] "Armenian Jerusalem," *Ariel*, 32 (1973), 52-63.

Ajamian, Shahe. [4076] "Armenisches Volk und armenisches Patriarchat von Jerusalem," *Das Heilige Land*, 104 (1972), 20-24.

Ajamian, Shahe. [4077] "Brief Notes on the Armenian People and the Armenian Patriarchate of Jerusalem," *Christian News from Israel*, 18/3-4 (December, 1967), 37-40.

Ajamian, Shahe. [4078] "Sultan 'Abduül-Hamid and the Armenian Patriarchate of Jerusalem," in M. Ma'oz (ed.), *Studies on Palestine during the Ottoman Period*. Jerusalem: Magnes Press, 1975, 341-350.

Alleau, V. Th. [4079] *Le patriarcat de Jérusalem, son origine, ses vicisitudes, sa ruine, son rétablissement, ses oevres*. Monaco: Ordre du Saint-Sépulcre, 1880. [Latin-rite.]

Allison, R. G. [4080] "The Anglican Church in Israel," *Christian News from Israel*, 16/1-2 (June, 1965), 36-39.

Amann, E. [4081] "Jérusalem (Église de)," in A. Vacant and E. Mangenot (eds.), *Dictionnaire de Théologie Catholique*, 8. Paris: Letouzey et Ané, 1924, 997-1010. [Latin-rite.]

Anawati, G. C. [4082] "The Roman Catholic Church and Churches in Communion with Rome," in A. J. Arberry (ed.), *Religion in the Middle East*, 1. Cambridge: Cambridge University Press, 1969, 347-422.

Antreassian, Assadour. [4083] *Jerusalem and the Armenians*. Jerusalem: St. James Press, 2nd edn., 1969, 90 pp.

Arce, Augustín. [4084] "The Custody of the Holy Land," *Christian News from Israel*, 19/1-2 (May, 1968), 31-42. [Latin-rite/Franciscan.]

Arce, Augustín. [4085] "The Custody of the Holy Land," in *Miscelánea de Tierra Santa*, 3. Jerusalem: Franciscan Printing Press, 1974, 141-155.

Arce, Augustín. [4086] Documentos y Textos para la Historia de Tierra Santa y sus Santuarios, 1600-1700. Jerusalem: Franciscan Printing Press, 1970, 407 pp. [Roman Catholic/Franciscan.]

Arce, Augustín. [4087] Expediciones de España a Jerusalén, 1673-1842. Madrid / Jerusalem: Franciscan Printing Press, 1958, 460 pp. [Roman Catholic.]

Arce, Augustín (ed.). [4088] Miscelanea de Tierra Santa, 1-4. Jerusalem: Franciscan Printing Press, 1950-1982, 348 + 437 +490 + 436 pp. [Includes much on the Custody of the Holy Land, the Franciscans, the status quo, etc.]

Arce, Augustín. [4089] "Presencia de España en Jerusalén," Boletin de la Real Academia de la historia, 173 (1976), 469-479. [Roman Catholic.]

Atiya, Aziz S. [4090] "Alexandrine Christianity: The Copts and their Church," in A History of Eastern Christianity. London: Methuen, 1968, 11-166.

Atiya, Aziz S. [4091] "The Armenian Church," in A History of Eastern Christianity. London: Methuen, 1968, 303-356.

Atiya, Aziz S. [4092] "The Nestorian Church," in A History of Eastern Christianity. London: Methuen, 1968, 237-301.

Attwater, Donald. [4093] "The Patriarchate of Jerusalem," in Christian Churches of the East, 2. Milwaukee: Bruce Publishing Co., rev. edn, 1962, 37-44. [Latin-rite.]

Avraham, S. [4094] "Äthioper in Jerusalem," Das Heilige Land, 104 (1972), 33-36.

Awad, S. See Haddad, D.; Awad, S.; and Krueger, E. W. [4170]

Azarya, Victor. [4095] Armenian Quarter of Jerusalem: Life behind Monastery Walls. Berkeley: University of California Press, 1984, 252 pp.

Bagatti, Bellarmino. See Bellorini, T. and Hoade, Eugene. [4102]

Bagatti, Bellarmino. See Hoade, Eugene and Bagatti, Bellarmino. [4179]

Baldi, Donatus. [4096] "Jerusalem: Christian Jerusalem," in New Catholic Encyclopedia, 7. New York: McGraw-Hill, 1967, 881-888.

Baldi, Donatus. [4097] La question des Lieux Saints. Rome: Imprimerie Pontificale de l' Institut Pie IX, 1919; 2nd edn., Jerusalem: Franciscan Printing Press, 1954, 182 pp.

Baldi, Donatus. [4098] The Question of the Holy Places. Jerusalem: Franciscan Printing Press, 1955, 184 pp.

Barkay, Rachel. [4099] "An Axumite Coin from Jerusalem," Israel Numismatic Journal, 5 (1981), 57-59. [Ethiopian Christians, 4th century.]

Baumstark, A. [4100] "Koptische Kunst in Jerusalem," Oriens Christianus, n. s. 5 (1915), 285-292.

Beckingham, Charles F. [4101] "Pantaleào de Aveiro and the Ethiopian Community in Jerusalem," Journal of Semitic Studies, 7 (1962), 325-338.

Bellorini, T. and Hoade, Eugene. [4102] Fra Bernardino Amico: Plans of the Sacred Edifices of the Holy Land, with preface and notes by B. Bagatti. Studium Biblicum Franciscanum, Collectio Major, 10. Jerusalem: Franciscan Printing Press, Jerusalem: Franciscan Printing Press, 1953, 147 pp. + 47 drawings.

Beltritti, J. [4103] "Les Patriarches latins de Jérusalem: S. B. Mgr. Joseph Valerga (1813-1872)," La Terre Sainte, (Jan., 1968), 22-25.

Beltritti, J. [4104] "Les Patriarches latins de Jérusalem: S. B. Mgr. Louis Barlassina (1920-1947)," La Terre Sainte, (Oct., 1968), 225-259; (Nov., 1968), 277-279; (Dec., 1968), 308-312.

Beltritti, J. [4105] "Les Patriarches latins de Jérusalem: S. B. Mgr. Joseph Piavi (1833-1905)," La Terre Sainte, (April, 1968), 103-107.

Beltritti, J. [4106] "Les Patriarches latins de Jérusalem: S. B. Mgr. Philippe Camassei (1848-1921)," La Terre Sainte, (May, 1968), 133-137; (Aug., 1968), 228-231.

Beltritti, J. [4107] "Les Patriarches latins de Jérusalem: S. B. Mgr. Vincent Bracco (1835-1889)," La Terre Sainte, (Feb., 1968), 42-45; (March, 1968), 70-73.

Ben-Ami, Maimon. [4108] "Christian Courts in Israel," Christian News from Israel, 26/3-4 (1978), 128-131.

Ben-Arieh, Yehoshua. [4109] "The Christian Communities; The Christian Quarter; The Armenian Quarter," in Jerusalem in the 19th Century: The Old City. Jerusalem: Yad Izhaq Ben-Zvi / New York: St. Martin's, 1984, 183-264.

Ben-Arieh, Yehoshua. [4110] "Patterns of Christian Activities and Dispersion in Nineteenth Century Jerusalem," Journal of Historical Geography, 2 (1976), 49-69.

Bertram, Anton and Luke, Harry C. [4111] Report of the Commision Appointed by the Government of Palestine to Inquire into the Affairs of the Orthodox Patriarchate of Jerusalem. Oxford: Oxford University Press, 1921, 366 pp.

Bertram, Anton and Young, J. W. A. [4112] The Orthodox Patriarchate: Report of Palestine Commision on Controversies between the Orthodox Patriarchate of Jerusalem and the Arab Orthodox Community. London: Oxford University Press, 1926, 379 pp.

Blyth, Estelle. [4113] "The Greek Easter at Jerusalem," Palestine Exploration Fund, Quarterly Statement, (1920), 69-77, 132-139. [On the Holy Fire.]

Blyth, E. M. E. [4114] "Patriarchate of Jerusalem," The Modern Churchman, n. s. 5 (1962), 224-232. [Greek Orthodox.]

Bouwen, F. [4115] "Relations entre catholiques et orthodoxes à Jérusalem," in D. M. Jaegar (ed.), Christianity in the Holy Land. Studia Oecumenica

Hiersolymitana, 1. Tantur, Jerusalem: Ecumenical Institute for Theological Resaearch, 1981, 213-235.

Bridgeman, Charles T. [4116] The Episcopal Church and the Middle East. New York: Morehouse-Go.ham, 1958, 40 pp.

Bridgeman, Charles T. [4117] Jerusalem at Worship. Jerusalem: Syrian Orphanage Press, 1932, 74 pp.

A British Resident: [4118] "Amongst the Armenians in Jerusalem," Eastern Churches Quarterly, 3 (1939), 297-300. [On the Uniate Catholic Armenians.]

Brlek, M. [4119] "I Francescani a Gerusalemme nel '300," La Terra Santa, 46 (1970), 325-342.

Broadus, John R. [4120] "Church Conflict in Palestine: The Opening of the Holy Places Question during the Period Preceding the Crimean War," Canadian Journal of History, 14 (1979), 395-416.

Brownrigg, Ronald. See Hollis, Christopher and Brownrigg, Ronald. [4180]

Brunot, Amédée. [4121] "Les Lieux Saints," Bible et Terre Sainte, 95 (1967), 24; 96 (1967), 22.

Burrell, David B. [4122] "Tantur: Theology in Jerusalem," America, 148 (Mar. 26, 1983), 229-231. [Roman Catholic/Ecumenical.]

Bushell, Gerard. [4123] "Jerusalem," in Churches of the Holy Land. London: Cassell, 1969, 93-171.

Bushell, Gerard. [4124] "Jerusalem-- The Christian Shrines," Ariel, 23 (1969), 39-42.

Cerulli, Enrico. [4125] Etiopi in Palestina: Storia della comunità Etiopica di Gerusalemme, 2 vols. Collezione scientifica e documentaria, 12. Rome: Libr. d State, 1943-1947, 459 + 439 pp.

Cerulli, Enrico. [4126] "Tre nuovi documenti sugli Etiopi in Palestina nel secolo XV," in Studia Biblica et Orientalia, 3: Oriens Antiquus. Analecta Biblica, 12. Rome: Pontifical Biblical Institue, 1959, 33-47.

Codrington, H. W. [4127] "The Blessing of the Fire in Jerusalem," Eastern Churches Quarterly, 3/2 (1938), 59-62. [Greek Orthodox.]

Cohen, A. [4128] "The Expulsion of the Franciscans from Mt. Sion by the Ottomans," Cathedra: For the History of Eretz-Israel and its Yishuv, 22 (1982), 61-74 (Hebrew).

Colbi, Saul P. [4129] "The Christian Establishment in Jerusalem," in J. L. Kraemer (ed.), Jerusalem: Problems and Prospects. New York: Praeger, 1980, 153-177.

Colbi, Saul P. [4130] Christianity in the Holy Land: Past and Present. Tel Aviv: Am Hassefer, 1969, 272 pp.

Colbi, Saul P. [4131] "The Patriarchs of Jerusalem-- How They are Elected," The Holy Land, 1/2 (Summer, 1981), 62-64. [Latin-rite.]

Collin, Bernardin. [4132] "Documents pour l' histoire des Lieux Saints (1851, 1901-1902)," Studia Orientalia Christiana, 11 (1966), 363-387.

Collin, Bernardin. [4133] Pour une solution au problème des Lieux-Saint. Paris: G.-P. Maison-neuve, 1974, 163 pp.

Collin, Bernardin. [4134] Le problème juridique des Lieux-Saints, 2 vols. Paris: Librairie Sirey, 1956, 208 + 434 pp.

Collin, Bernardin. [4135] Recueil de documents concernant Jérusalem et le Lieux Saints. Jerusalem: Franciscan Printing Press, 1982, 436 pp.

Collin, Bernardin. [4136] Rome, Jérusalem et les Lieux Saints. Preface by René Remond. Paris: Éditions Franciscaines, 1982, 136 pp.

Collin, Bernardin. [4137] "Le Saint-Siège et les Lieux Saints: Les droits du Saint-Siége sur les Lieux Saints," in Mélanges offerts à J. Dauvillier. Toulouse: Université Sciences Sociales, Centre d' Histoire Juridique Méridionale, 1979, 207-221.

Couret, Comte. [4138] Notice historique sur l' Ordre du Saint-Sépulcre de Jérusalem depuis son origine jusqu' à nos jours, 1099-1905. Orleans: Herluisson, 1887; Paris: Au Bureau des Oeuvres d' Orient, 1905, 518 pp.

Cragg, Kenneth. [4139] "The Anglican Church," in A. J. Arberry (ed.), Religion in the Middle East, 1. Cambridge: Cambridge University Press, 1969, 570-595. [Almost exclusively about Jerusalem.]

Cust, L. G. A. [4140] The Status Quo in the Holy Places. London: H. M. S. O., printed for the Government of Palestine, 1929; reprinted, Jerusalem: Ariel, 1980, 70 pp. (English) + 49 pp. (Hebrew). Reprinted in part as appendix 6 to Walter Zander, Israel and the Holy Places of Christendom. London: Weidenfeld and Nicolson, 1971, 195-224. [Includes detailed information on the Status Quo, rights of possession and other privileges of the rival communities in the holy places of Jerusalem and Bethlehem, and the Holy Fire of the Greek Orthodox in the Holy Sepulchre.]

Custody of the Holy Land: [4141] Jerusalem: Custody of the Holy Land. Washington, DC: Commissariat of the Holy Land, 1981, 157 pp. [Roman Catholic/Franciscan.]

Dalmais, I.-H. [4142] "Jérusalem: Source des liturgies," Bible et Terre Sainte, 100 (1968), 6-11.

Dalmais, I.-H. [4143] "La liturgie de l' Anastasis," Bible et Terre Sainte, 140 (1972), 5-6. [Of various churches.]

Danilov, Stavro. [4144] "Dilemmas of Jerusalem's Christians," Middle East Review, 13 3-4 (Spring-Summer, 1981), 41-47.

Dowling, Archdeacon T. E.. [4145] "The Episcopal Succession in Jerusalem, from c. A. D. 30," Palestine Exploration Fund, Quarterly Statement, (1913), 164-177; (1914), 33-40. [Greek Orthodox.]

Dowling, Archdeacon T. E. [4146] "The Georgian Church in Jerusalem," Palestine Exploration Fund, Quarterly Statement, (1911), 181-187.

Dowling, Archdeacon T. E. [4147] "The Greek Fire in the Church of the Resurrection, Jerusalem," Palestine Exploration Fund, Quarterly Statement, (1908), 151-153

Dowling, Archdeacon T. E. [4148] The Orthodox Greek Patriarchate of Jerusalem. London: S. P. C. K. / New York: E. S. Gorham, 3rd edn.,1913, 170 pp.

Dowling, Archdeacon T. E. [4149] "Sixteen Councils of Jerusalem, from c. A. D. 50/1 to A. D. 1672," Palestine Exploration Fund, Quarterly Statement, (1913), 85-90.

Drosos, G. N. [4150] "Les patriarcats orientaux vus par un journaliste hellène: Le patriarcat de Jérusalem," Proche-Orient Chrétien, 13 (1963), 37-41.

Duensing, Hugo. [4151] "Die Abessinier in Jerusalem," Zeitschrift des deutschen Palästina-Vereins, 39 (1916), 98-115.

Düsing, J. A. [4152] "Die byzantinische Kirche in Jerusalem an Ostern 1969: Eine Bestandsaufnahme," Das Heilige Land, 101 (1969), 22-29.

Düsing, J. A. [4153] "Jerusalem und die Christen Russlands," Das Heilige Land, 105 (1973), 17-24.

Durrieu, P. [4154] "Procès-verbale du martyre de quatre Frères Mineurs en 1391," in Archives de l' Orient Latin, 1. Paris: Société de l' Orient Latin / Ernest Leroux, 1881, 539-546.

"The Ecumenical Institute of Tantur," [4155] Christian News from Israel, special issue (June, 1985), 31-33. [Roman Catholic / Ecumenical.]

Every, George. [4156] "Syriac and Arabic in the Church of Jerusalem," Church Quarterly Review, 145 (1948), 230-240.

Every, George. [4157] "Syrian Christians in Jerusalem," Eastern Churches Quarterly, 7/1 (1947), 46-54.

Every, George. [4158] "Syrian Christians in Palestine in the Early Middle Ages," Eastern Churches Quarterly, 6/7 (1946), 363-372.

Fedalto, Giorgio. [4159] "Liste vescovili dei patriarcato di Gerusalemme," Orientalia Christiana Periodica, 49/1 (1983), 5-41.

Fiej, J. M. [4160] "Le pèlerinage des Nestoriens et Jacobites à Jérusalem," Cahiers de Civilization Médiévale, 12 (1969), 113-126.

Fortesque, Adrian. [4161] "Jerusalem: From the End of the Latin Kingdom to the Present Time," in The Catholic Encyclopedia, 8. New York: Appleton, 1910, 364-371. [Primary focus on the Christian communities.]

Gassi, A. [4162] Contributo alla soluzione della questione del Luoghi Santi. Jerusalem: Franciscan Printing Press, 1935, 430 pp.

Germanos, Mgr. [4163] "The Greek Orthodox Patriarchate of Jerusalem," Christian News from Israel, 18/3-4 (December, 1967), 22-26.

Goldman, Jenie. [4164] "The Monastery of the Cross, the Ancient Shrine that Grew from a Tree," Christian News from Israel, 27/1 (1979), 15-17. [Originally Georgian, now Greek Orthodox.]

Graham, Stephen. [4165] "With the Russian Pilgrims to Jerusalem," English Review, 12 (1912), 35-48.

Graham, Stephen. [4166] With the Russian Pilgrims to Jerusalem. London: Thomas Nelson and Sons, n. d. [ca. 1913], 253 pp.

Grumel, V. [4167] "La chronologie des Patriarches grecs de Jérusalem au XIIIe siècle," Revue des Études Byzantines, 20 (1962), 197-201.

Guthe, Hermann. See Zagarelli, A. and Guthe, Hermann. [4309]

Guthe, Hermann. [4168] "Die griechisch-orthodoxe Kirche im heiligen Lande," Zeitschrift des deutschen Palästina-Vereins, 12 (1889), 81-94.

Hachey, Thomas E. [4169] "The Archbishop of Canterbury's Visit to Palestine: An Issue in Anglo-Vatican Relations in 1931," Church History, 41 (1972), 198-207.

Haddad, D.; Awad, S.; and Krueger, E. W. [4170] "Die evang.-luth. arabische Gemeinde in Jerusalem," Im Lande der Bibel, 16 (1970), 2-10.

Hall, I. H. [4171] "On a Nestorian Manuscript from the Last Nestorian Church and Convent in Jerusalem," Journal of the American Oriental Society, 13 (1888), 286-290.

Har-El, Menashe. [4172] "The Christians in Jerusalem and their Holy Sites," in This is Jerusalem. Jerusalem: Canaan Publishing Co., 1977, 293-327.

Hartmann, Richard. [4173] "Arabische Berichte über das Wunder des heiligen Feuers," Palästinajahrbuch, 12 (1916), 76-94. [Greek Orthodox.]

Hatem, Anouar. [4174] "Le saint siège, Jérusalem et les Lieux Saints," Communità Mediterranea, 2 (1969), 349-372.

Heroux, Barthélemy. [4175] "La Casa Nova de Jérusalem," La Terre Sainte, (July-Sept., 1959), 114-119. [Roman Catholic/Franciscan.]

"Heutiger Stand der Russisch-Orthodoxen in Jerusalem," [4176] Das Heilige Land, 105 (1973), 25-31.

Hintlian, Kevork. [4177] History of the Armenians in the Holy Land. Jerusalem: St. James Press, 1977, 68 pp.

Hoade, Eugene. See Bellorini, T. and Hoade, Eugene. [4102]

Hoade, Eugene. [4178] "Jerusalem: The Holy City," in Guide to the Holy Land. Jerusalem: Franciscan Printing Press, 1984, 89-374. [In addition to treatment of the major holy sites, contains information on convents, churches, smaller chapels, etc.]

Hoade, Eugene and Bagatti, Bellarmino. [4179] Fr. Eleazar Horn: Ichnographiae Monumentorum Terrae Sanctae (1724-1744). Second edition of the Latin text with English version by Eugene Hoade and preface and notes by Bellarmino Baggati. Studium Biblicum Franciscanum, Collectio Major, 15. Jerusalem: Franciscan Printing Press, 1962, 271 pp + 63 drawings + 16 pls. [Important source of information on the Christian churches, convents, etc. of Jerusalem in the first half of the eighteenth century. Primary focus, Latin rite/Franciscan.]

Hollis, Christopher and Brownrigg, Ronald. [4180] "Christian Holy Places," in Holy Places: Jewish, Christian and Muslim Monuments in the Holy Land. New York: Praeger, 1969, 75-188.

Hopwood, Derek. [4181] "'The Resurrection of Our Eastern Brethren' (Ignatev); Russia and Orthodox Arab Nationalism in Jerusalem," in M. Ma'oz (ed.), Studies on Palestine during the Ottoman Period. Jerusalem: Magnes Press, 1975, 394-407.

Hopwood, Derek. [4182] The Russian Presence in Syria and Palestine, 1843-1914: Church and Politics in the Near East. Oxford: Clarendon Press, 1969, 232 pp.

Idinopulos, Thomas A. [4183] "Holy Fire in Jerusalem," Christian Century, 99 (1982), 407-409. [Greek Orthodox.]

Idinopulos, Thomas A. [4184] "A New Patriarch for the Holy City," Christian Century, 98 (1981), 373-375. [Greek Orthodox.]

Iliffe, J. H. [4185] "Cemetaries and a 'Monastery' at the Y. M. C. A., Jerusalem," Quarterly of the Department of Antiquities in Palestine, 4 (1934/35), 70-80. [The Georgian church, 5th-7th century.]

"Imperial Firman of February 1852, Concerning the Christian Holy Places," [4186] published as appendix 3 to Walter Zander, Israel and the Holy Places of Christendom. London: Weidenfeld and Nicolson, 1971, 178-180.

Janin, R. [4187] "Les Georgiens à Jérusalem," Echos d' Orient, 16 (1913), 32-38, 211-219.

Jérusalem: Livre de Vie! [4188] Paris: Cerf, 1981, 159 pp.

Johnson, Sherman E. [4189] "Jerusalem Bishopric," Anglican Theological Review, 39 (1957), 105-106.

Kalaydjian, Ara. [4190] "The Correspondence (1725-1740) of the Armenian Patriarch Gregory the Chain-Bearer," in M. Ma'oz (ed.), Studies on Palestine during the Ottoman Period. Jerusalem: Magnes Press, 1975, 562-567.

Karkenz, J. [4191] "Die syrisch-orthodoxe Kirche in Jerusalem und im Heilige Land," Das Heilige Land, 104 (1972), 50-55.

Kernatz, B. [4192] "Die Pröpste auf der Erlöserkirche," Im Lande der Bibel, 17/3 (1971), 9-20. [Lutheran.]

Kitchner, H. H. [4193] "Our Ride from Gaza to Jerusalem with a Description of the Greek Holy Fire," Palestine Exploration Fund, Quarterly Statement, (1917), 66-72.

Klein, L. [4194] "Das Greichisch-Orthodoxe Patriarchat von Jerusalem," Das Heilige Land, 104 (1972), 3-9.

Klein, L. [4195] "Selbstfindung einer Stadt: Zur heutige Lage Jerusalems," Das Heilige Land, 103 (1971), 35-40.

Kloetzli, Godfrey. [4196] "Christian Jerusalem," Holy Land Review, 3/2-3 (Summer-Autumn, 1977), 35-44.

Kloetzli, Godfrey. [4197] "The Equestrian Order of the Holy Sepulchre of Jerusalem," Holy Land Review, 1/3 (Autumn, 1975), 76-82. [Roman Catholic.]

Kloetzli, Godfrey. [4198] "The Franciscans in the Holy Land," Holy Land Review, 1/1 (Sring, 1975), 16-21.

Kreuger, E. W. See Haddad, D.; Awad, S.; and Krueger, E. W. [4170]

Lankin, D. [4199] "Problems of the Status Quo in the Holy Places: High Court Decision on the Coptic-Ethiopic Dispute," Christian News from Israel, 22/1 (1971), 5-8.

"Le 4e centenaire du couvent du Saint-Sauveur," [4200] La Terre Sainte, (Oct.-Dec., 1960), 146-163. [Latin-rite.]

"Les Lieux Saints de la Palestine: Memoire des Latins a la Conférence de la Paix (1919)," [4201] published as appendix 4 to Walter Zander, Israel and the Holy Places of Christendom. London: Weidenfeld and Nicolson, 1971, 181-185.

Luke, Harry C. See Bertram, Anton and Luke, Harry C. [4111]

Luke, Harry C. [4202] "The Christian Communities in the Holy Sepulchre," in Jerusalem, 1920-1922. London: Murray, 1924, 46-56.

Macalister, R. A. Stewart. [4203] "A Tumult in Jerusalem in 1652," Palestine Exploration Fund, Quarterly Statement, (1923), 185-195. [The churches in conflict with one another.]

McNaspy, Clement J. [4204] "An Oasis of Peace in Jerusalem," Liturgical Arts, 39/1 (Nov., 1970), 9-11. [Maison Saint-Isaïe, Roman Catholic.]

McWhirter, Joan. [4205] "The International Christian Embassy in Jerusalem," Christian News from Israel, special issue (June, 1985), 29-31. [Christians in sympathy with Zionism.]

Malik, Charles H. [4206] "The Orthodox Church," in A. J. Arberry (ed.), Religion in the Middle East, 1. Cambridge: Cambridge University Press, 1969, 297-346.

Maloney, G. A. [4207] "Jerusalem, Patriarchate of," in New Catholic Encyclopedia, 7. New York: McGraw-Hill, 1967, 891.

Malsch, Carl. [4208] "Jerusalem-Jordan Lutheran Church," in J. Bodensieck (ed.), The Encyclopedia of the Lutheran Church, 2. Minneapolis: Augsburg, 1965, 1170-1172.

Mamour, Joseph. [4209] "Au Patriarchat Arménien de Jérusalem," Proche-Orient Chrétien, 7 (1957), 65-69.

Mancini, Ignazio. [4210] "La custodia di Terra Santa," Bibbia e Oriente, 2 (1960), 181-183. [Roman Catholic/Franciscan.]

Mancini, Ignazio. [4211] "Le Monastère de Sainte Croix," La Terre Sainte, (May, 1965), 148-152. [Originally Georgian, now Greek Orthodox.]

Manoukian, Serovope. [4212] Album of the Armenian Monastery of Jerusalem. New York: Delphic Press, 1950, 59 pp.

Mantell, A. M. [4213] "Easter Ceremonies of Washing of the Feet," Palestine Exploration Fund, Quarterly Statement, (1882), 158-160. [Greek Orthodox.]

de MasLatrie, L. [4214] "Les patriarches latins de Jérusalem, Revue de l' orient latin, 1 (1893), 16-41. Also in La Terra Santa, 11 (1894), 54-104.

Médebielle, Pierre. [4215] "The Latin Patriarchate of Jerusalem," Christian News from Israel, 18/3-4 (December, 1967), 26-32.

Médebielle, Pierre. [4216] "Le 'Status Quo' des Lieux Saints," La Terre Sainte, (March-April, 1956), 45-52.

Médebielle, Pierre. [4217] "Two Centenaries at the Latin Patriarchate of Jerusalem," Christian News from Israel, 23/3 (1973), 189-191.

Meinardus, Otto. [4218] "The Armenian Jerusalem Proskynitarion at St. James in Jerusalem," Revue des Études Arméniennes, 17 (1983), 457-462.

Meinardus, Otto. [4219] "The Coptic Church," in A. J. Arberry (ed.), Religion in the Middle East, 1. Cambridge: Cambridge University Press, 1969, 423-453, esp. 443-446. [On the Copts and "the question of the holy places."]

Meinardus, Otto. [4220] The Copts in Jerusalem. Cairo: Commission on Oecumenical Affairs of the See of Alexandria, 1960, 98 pp.

Meinardus, Otto. [4221] "Ethiopians in Jerusalem," Zeitschrift für Kirchengeschichte, 76 (1965), 217-232.

Meinardus, Otto. [4222] "A Note on the Nestorians in Jerusalem," Oriens Christianus, 51 (1967), 123-129.

Meinardus, Otto. [4223] "A Stone-Cult in the Armenian Quarter of Jerusalem," Revue des Études Arméniennes, 14 (1980), 367-375.

Meinardus, Otto. [4224] "The Syrian Jacobites in the Holy City," Oriens Suecana, 12 (1963), 60-82.

Meinardus, Otto. [4225] "Zur Ikonographie des Jüngsten Gerichte im der armenischen Kathedrale des Heiligen Jakobus in Jerusalem," Revue des Études Arméniennes, 13, (1978/1979), 235-241.

Melander, H. [4226] "Hakeldama," Zeitschrift des deutschen Palästina-Vereins, 17 (1894), 25-35. [Presently Greek Orthodox.]

"Memorandum of the Greeks submitted to the Peace Conference in Paris, 1919," [4227] published as appendix 5 to Walter Zander, Israel and the Holy Places of Christendom. London: Weidenfeld and Nicolson, 1971, 186-194.

Montoisey, J. D. [4228] Le Vatican et le problème des Lieux Saints. Jerusalem: Franciscan Printing Press, 1984, 170 pp.

Moscow Patriarchate: [4229] "Incidents at the Russian Orthodox Mission in Jerusalem," The Journal of the Moscow Patriarchate, 3 (1980), 7-9.

Musset, Henri. [4230] "Construction de la résidence patriarcal melkite catholique à Jerusalem (Mai, 1844)," Proche-Orient Chrétien, 1 (1951), 326-328. [Greek Catholic.]

Musset, Henri. [4231] "Note historique relative à l' élection du Patriarche grec orthodoxe de Jérusalem," Proche-Orient Chrétien, 6 (1956), 51-68.

Musset, Henri. [4232] "Le Patriarcat de Moscou et l' Orthodoxie dans le Proche-Orient, 2: Dans le Patriarcat de Jérusalem," Proche-Orient Chrétien, 5 (1955), 332-345.

Musset, Henri. [4233] "Relations des Églises orthodoxes du Proch-Orient avec l' Eglise anglicane depuis cinquante ans, 3: Avec le Patriarcat orthodoxe de Jérusalem," Proche-Orient Chrétien, 5 (1955), 240-252.

Narkiss, Bezalel (ed.), in collaboration with Michael E. Stone. [4234] Armenian Art Treasures of Jerusalem. Jerusalem: Massada Press / New Rochelle, NY: Caratzas Brothers, 1979, 174 pp.

Narkiss, Bezalel. [4235] "St. James Cathedral and its Treasures," in B. Narkiss (ed.), in collaboration with M. E. Stone, Armenian Art Treasures of Jerusalem. Jerusalem: Massada Press / New Rochelle, NY: Caratzas Brothers, 1979, 121-144.

Nersoyan, T. [4236] "The Armenian Cathedral of St. James in Jerusalem," Asiatic Review, 37 (1941), 142-153.

Nolet de Brauwere, Yves. [4237] "The Church of the Holy Land Today," Eastern Churches Quarterly, 16 (1964), 117-139. [Latin-rite.]

Nolet de Brauwere, Yves. [4238] "L' Église de Terre Sainte," Irénikon, 36 (1963), 177-203. [Latin-rite.]

"Le patriarchat latin de Jérusalem," [4239] Irénikon, 44 (1971), 123-124.

"Patriarchate of Jerusalem," [4240] Church Quarterly Review, 114 (1932), 296-298. [Greek Orthodox.]

Pedersen, Kirsten. [4241] Ethiopian Institutions in Jerusalem. Jerusalem: Franciscan Printing Press, 1980, 32 pp.

Pedersen, Kirsten. [4242] "The Revitalization of the Ethiopian Church in the Holy Land," in D. M. Jaegar (ed.), Christianity in the Holy Land. Studia Oecumenica Hiersolymitana, 1. Tantur, Jerusalem: Ecumenical Institute for Theological Research, 1981, 197-211.

Perowne, Stewart H. [4243] The Pilgrim's Companion in Jerusalem and Bethlehem. London: Hodder and Stoughton, 1964, 158 pp.

Petrozzi, Maria Teresa. [4244] "On the Roofs of the Holy Sepulchre," Christian News from Israel, 24/1 (1973), 25-29. [Ethiopians.]

Piccirillo, M. (ed.). [4245] La Custodia di Terra Santa e l' Europa. Rome / Jerusalem: Franciscan Printing Press, 1980, 220 pp.

Prawer, Joshua. [4246] "The Armenians in Jerusalem under the Crusades," in M. E. Stone (ed.), Armenian and Biblical Studies. Jerusalem: St. James Press, 1976, 222-236.

Prawer, Joshua. [4247] "The Monastery of the Cross," Ariel, 18 (1967), 59-62. Also in Israel Yearbook, 1968. Tel Aviv: Israel Yearbook Publications, 1968, 269-271. [Originally Georgian, now Greek Orthodox.]

L. R. [4248] "Franciscan Presence in Jerusalem," The Holy Land, 3/2 (Summer, 1983), 35-41.

Rai, P. [4249] "Règlement du patriarcat grec orthodoxe de Jérusalem," Proche-Orient Chrétien, 8 (1958), 227-242.

Ritter, Carl. [4250] "The Georgians," in Comparative Geography of Palestine and the Sinaitic Penninsula, 4. New York: Appleton, 1866, 196-198.

Rochcau, Vsevolod. [4251] "Les pèlerinages Russes au début du siècle," La Terre Sainte, (March, 1967), 49-58.

Rock, Albert. [4252] "The Status Quo of the Holy Places," Holy Land Review, 6/1-4 (Spring-Winter, 1980), 58-64.

Rock, Albert. [4253] Lo Statu Quo nei Luoghi Santi: La questione in generale e due circostanze differenti ed emblematiche riguardanti il Cenaclo e la Cupola del S. Sepolcro. Jerusalem: Franciscan Printing Press, 1977, 64 pp.

Roncaglia, M. [4254] "La questione dei Luoghi Santi: Nuovi documenti," Studia Orientalia Christiana, 1 (1956), 135-138; 2 (1957), 65-69.

Roncaglia, M. [4255] La république de Venise et les Lieux Saints de Jérusalem: Archives de l' Église en Orient. Documents inédits du XVe au XIXe siècles tirés des archives privées du Couvent de S. François de la Vigne. Beirut: Dar el-Kalima, 220 pp.

Rosovsky, Nitza. [4256] "Around the Russian Compound," in Jerusalemwalks. New York: Holt, Rinehart and Winston, 1982, 111-147. [On buildings of the Russian compound as they are today.]

Rubin, R. [4257] "Greek Orthodox Monasteries in the Old City of Jerusalem," in Eretz-Israel: Archaeological, Historical, and Geographical Studies, 17. Jerusalem: Israel Exploration Society, 1984, 109-116 (Hebrew), 5*-6* (English summary).

de Sandoli, Sabino. [4258] Il primo convento Francescano in Gerusalemme (1230-1244). Jerusalem: Franciscan Printing Press, 1983, 32 pp.

Sanjian, Avedis K. [4259] The Armenian Communities in Syria under Ottoman Dominion. Cambridge, MA: Harvard University Press, 1965, 390 pp.

Sanjian, Avedis K. [4260] "The Armenian Communities of Jerusalem," in B. Narkiss (ed.), in collaboration with M. E. Stone, Armenian Art Treasures of Jerusalem. Jerusalem: Massada Press / New Rochelle, NY: Caratzas Brothers, 1979, 11-20.

Sanjian, Avedis K. [4261] "Anastas Vardapet's List of Armenian Monasteries in Seventeenth Century Jerusalem: A Critical Examination," Muséon, 82 (1969), 265-292.

Sayegh, S. [4262] Le Statu Quo des Lieux-Saints: Nature juridique et portée internationale. Jerusalem: Franciscan Printing Press, 1971, 260 pp.

Schick, Conrad. [4263] "Aceldama," Palestine Exploration Fund, Quarterly Statement, (1892), 283-289. [Presently Greek Orthodox.]

Schick, Conrad. [4264] "Church of Mar Jirias of the Greeks," Palestine Exploration Fund, Quarterly Statement, (1896), 217.

Schick, Conrad. [4265] "The Coptic Mar Jirias Church," Palestine Exploration Fund, Quarterly Statement, (1896), 217-218.

Schick, Conrad. [4266] "Mar Metri or the Greek Convent of St. Demetrius at Jerusalem," Palestine Exploration Fund, Quarterly Statement, (1900), 253-257.

Schick, Conrad. [4267] "Old Churches in Jerusalem," Palestine Exploration Fund, Quarterly Statement, (1895), 321-328.

Schick, Conrad. [4268] "Some Old Remains-- Abraham's Convent, etc.," Palestine Exploration Fund, Quarterly Statement, (1896), 218-219.

Schnabl, Karl. [4269] "Die römisch-katholische Kirche in Palästina," Zeitschrift des deutschen Palästina-Vereins, 7 (1884), 263-292.

Schneider, Peter. [4270] "The Christian Communities in Jerusalem in the Context of the Larger Religious Framework of the Holy City," in P. Schneider and G. Wigoder (eds.), Jerusalem Perspectives: A Nineteenth and Twentieth Century Outline of the Holy City. Arundale, West Sussex: London Rainbow Group, 1976, 23-29.

Schur, Nathan. [4271] "The Christians," in Jerusalem in Pilgrims and Travellers' Accounts: A Thematic Bibliography of Western Christian Itineraries, 1300-1917. Jerusalem: Ariel, 1980, 73-83.

Shepstone, Harold J. [4272] "Holy Week in Jerusalem," Palestine Exploration Quarterly, (1944), 218-222.

Sinden, Gilbert. [4273] "Indigenous Leadership and Christian Service: The Episcopal Diocese of Jerusalem, Jordan, Syria and Lebanon (Anglican Church)," Christian News from Israel, special issue (June, 1985), 36-37.

Soetens, C. [4274] Le Congrès eucharistique international de Jérusalem (1893) dans le cadre de la politique du pape Léon XIII. Leuven: Nauwelaerts, 1971, 790 pp.

Sokoloff, I. I. [4275] "The Orthodox Church of Jerusalem," Constructive Quarterly, 6 (1918), 76-98.

Stavrou, T. G. [4276] "Russian Interest in the Levant, 1843-1848: Porfiri Uspenskii and the Establishment of the First Russian Ecclesiastical Mission in Jerusalem," Middle East Journal, 17 (1963), 91-103.

Stendel, Ori. [4277] "The Arabs in Jerusalem, 2: Christians in Jerusalem, 1948-1971," in J. M. Oestrreicher and A. Sinai (eds.), Jerusalem. New York: John Day, 1974, 157-163.

Stendel, Ori. [4278] "Christians in Jerusalem," Christian News from Israel, 22/2 (1971), 52-55.

Stephan, Stephan H. [4279] "A Nestorian Hermitage between Jericho and the Jordan," Quarterly of the Department of Antiquities in Palestine, 4 (1934/35), 81-86, esp 84-86. [Information on the Nestorian community in Jerusalem, 3rd to 17th century.]

Stephan, Stephan H. [4280] "Three Firmans Granted to the Armenian Catholic Community, Jerusalem," Journal of the Palestine Oriental Society, 12 (1933), 238-246.

Stern, Gabriel. [4281] "Chronicles of the Armenian Orthodox Patriarchate of Jerusalem," Christian News from Israel, 21/3 (1970), 6-8.

Stern, Gabriel. [4282] "Profile, From Sheba to Solomon's See: His Grace Abuna Matthew," Christian News from Israel, 24 (1973), 37-40. [On the Ethiopian Church in Jerusalem.]

Stolz, Benedict. [4283] "The Benedictines in the Holy Land," Christian News from Israel, 11/2 (July, 1960), 11-15; 11/3 (October, 1960), 17-21.

Stone, Michael E. See Narkiss, Bezalel (ed.), in collaboration with Michael E. Stone. [4234]

Stone, Michael E. [4284] "Epigraphica armeniaca hierosolymitana," Annual of Armenian Linguistics, 1 (1980), 51-68; 2 (1981), 71-81. [Inscriptions of 6th-12th centuries.]

Stone, Michael E. [4285] "Epigraphica armeniaca hierosolymitana, 3.," Revue des Études Arméniennes, 18 (1984), 559-581. [Inscriptions of 14th-18th centuries.]

Stone, Michael E. [4286] "A Rare Armenian Coin from Jerusalem," Israel Numismatic Review, 4 (1980), 77-78.

Stuhlmueller, Carroll. [4287] "L' Ecole biblique et archéologique de Jérusalem," The Bible Today, 20/1 (1982), 30-35.

Sullivan, Desmond. [4288] "The Franciscanum Studium Biblicum of Jerusalem," The Bible Today, 76 (1975), 247-257.

Texidor, Javier. [4289] "Épitaphes hiérosolymitaaines in syriaque estranghelo," Revue biblique, 68 (1961), 541-545.

Tsimhoni, Daphna. [4290] "The Anglican (Evangelical Episcopal) Community in Jerusalem and the West Bank," Oriente Moderno, 2/1-12 (1983), 251-258.

Tsimhoni, Daphna. [4291] "The Armenians and the Syrians: Ethno-Religious Communities in Jerusalem," Middle East Studies, 20 (1984), 352-369.

Tsimhoni, Daphna. [4292] "The Christian Communities in Jerusalem and the West Bank," Middle East Review, 9 (1976), 41-46.

Tsimhoni, Daphna. [4293] "The Christian Communities in Jerusalem and the West Bank, 1948-1967," in A. Sinai and A. Pollack (eds.), The Hashemite Kingdom of Jordan and the West Bank. New York: American Academic Association for Peace in the Middle East, 1977, 237-244.

Tsimhoni, Daphna. [4294] "Demographic Trends of the Christian Population in Jerusalem and the West Bank, 1948-1978," Middle East Journal, 37 (1983), 54-64.

Tsimhoni, Daphna. [4295] "The Greek Orthodox Patriarchate of Jerusalem during the Formative Years of the British Mandate in Palestine," Asian and African Studies: Journal of the Israel Oriental Society, 12 (1978), 77-121.

Tzaferis, Vassilios. [4296] Museum of the Greek Orthodox Patriarchate in Jerusalem. Jerusalem: Greek Orthodox Patriarchate, 1985, 83 pp. (English) + 25 pp. (Hebrew).

Vincent, Louis-Hugues. [4297] "L'église Saint-Jacques le mineur," Revue biblique, 9 (1900), 451-436, 603. [Cathedral Church of the Armenians.]

de Vries, Guglielmo. [4298] "Il patriarcato di Gerusalemme," in Enciclopedia Cattolico, 6. Vatican City: Libro Cattolico, 1951, 201-205.

Wardi, Chaim. [4299] "Christmas and Epiphany in the Church of Jerusalem," Christian News from Israel, 25/1 (1974), 6-12.

Wardi, Chaim. [4300] "Easter in Jerusalem in Ancient and Modern Times," Christian News from Israel, 23/3 (1973), 152-157.

Wardi, Chaim. [4301] "The Latin Patriarchate of Jerusalem," Journal of the Middle East Society, 11/3-4 (1947), 5-12.

Wardi, Chaim. [4302] "The Monastery of the Cross in Jerusalem," Christian News from Israel, 11/1 (April, 1960), 20-25. [Originally Georgian, now Greek Orthodox.]

Wardi, Chaim. [4303] "The Question of the Holy Places in Ottoman Times," Christian News from Israel, 21/4 (1971), 33-39.

Wardi, Chaim. [4304] "The Question of the Holy Places in Ottoman Times," in M. Ma'oz (ed.), Studies on Palestine during the Ottoman Period. Jerusalem: Magnes Press, 1975, 385-393.

Ware, Kallistos T. [4305] "Patriarch Benedict of Jerusalem," Sobornost, 3/11 (1981), 102. [Greek Orthodox.]

Williams, George. [4306] "Modern Jerusalem and its Inhabitants," in The Holy City: Historical, Topographical, and Antiquarian Notices of Jerusalem, 2. London: John W. Parker, 2nd edn., 1849, 526-600.

Williams, Maynard O. [4307] "Color Records from the Changing Life of the Holy City," National Geographic Magazine, 52/6 (Dec., 1927), 682-707.

Young, J. W. A. See Bertram, Anton and Young, J. W. A. [4112]

Zagarelli, A. [4308] "The Georgian Inscription at Jerusalem," Palestine Exploration Fund, Quarterly Statement, (1883), 112-113.

Zagarelli, A. and Guthe, Hermann. [4309] "Georgische Inschrift aus Jerusalem," Zeitschrift des deutschen Palästina-Vereins, 4 (1881), 222-223. Also in Palestine Exploration Fund, Quarterly Statement, (1883), 112-113.

Zander, Walter. [4310] "Holy Places and Christian Presence in Jerusalem-- a New Emphasis in the Attitude of the Catholic Church," New Middle East, 34 (July, 1971), 18-20.

Zander, Walter. [4311] Israel and the Holy Places of Christendom. London: Weidenfeld and Nicolson, 1971, 248 pp.

Zimmermann, John D. [4312] "Jerusalem Archbishopric," Anglican Theological Review, 44 (1962), 420-423.

For studies on American and British missionary activities of the nineteenth century, the experiment of the Anglican-Prussian bishopric, and the settlement of the German

28/Christian Churches and Communities

Protestants of the Tempelgesellschaft, see 37/Jerusalem during the Nineteenth and Early Twentieth Century.

Twenty-Nine

The Church of the Holy Sepulchre

Abel, Félix-M. See Vincent, Louis-Hugues and Abel, Félix-M. [4501]

Andres, P. [4313] "Historia y arqueologia en el Sto. Sepulcro," Tierra Santa, 40 (March-April, 1965), 274-278.

Aptowitzer, V. [4314] "Les élements juifs dans la légende du Golgotha," Revue des études juives, 79 (1924), 145-162.

Arce, Augustín. [4315] "Hechos sacrilegos en el Sepulcro de Cristo (1757)," Studia Orientalia Christiana, 1 (1956), 106-134. Also published as Studia et Documenta Orientalia, 3. Cairo: Centro de Estudios Orientalis de la Custodia de Terra Santa, 1956, 35 pp.

Arce, Augustín. [4316] "El incendio del Santo Sepulcro (1808) y sus consecuencias," in Miscelánea de Tierra Santa, 2. Jerusalem: Franciscan Printing Press, 1973, 323-398.

Arce, Augustín. [4317] "La restauration de la Basilique du Saint-Sépulcre: Rapport des architectes," La Terre Sainte, (Autumn, 1955), 73-79.

Aroushan. [4318] "Armenian Restoration in the Basilica of the Holy Sepulchre," Christian News from Israel, 26/1 (1976), 15-18.

Baggati, Bellarmino. [4319] "Un acquerello del P. Horn (1727) di un distrutto musaico del S. Sepolcro," Studii Biblici Franciscani, Liber Annuus, 6 (1955/1956), 271-278.

Baggati, Bellarmino. [4320] "Autenticità del S. S. mo Sepolcro," La Terra Santa, 38/12 (Dec., 1962), 299-302.

Baggati, Bellarmino. [4321] "Bonanno of Pisa (1180-1186) and the Holy Sepulchre," The Holy Land, 1/3 (Autumn-Winter, 1981), 93-97.

Baggati, Bellarmino. [4322] "La configurazione semiariana delle costruzioni constantiniane del S. Sepolcro a Gerusalemme," Augustinianum, 24 (1984), 561-571.

Baggati, Bellarmino. [4323] "The Constantinian Sacred Edifices: The Holy Sepulchre," in The Church from the Gentiles in Palestine, History and Archaeology. Studium Biblicum Franciscanum, Collectio Minor, 4. Jerusalem: Franciscan Printing Press, 1971; reprinted, 1984, 163-175.

Baggati, Bellarmino. [4324] "Historical Facts about Golgotha," Holy Land Review, 6/1-4 (Spring-Winter, 1980), 3-6.

29/Church of the Holy Sepulchre

Baggati, Bellarmino. [4325] "Note sull' iconographia di 'Adamo sotto il Calvario,'" Studii Biblici Franciscani, Liber Annuus, 27 (1977), 5-32.

Baggati, Bellarmino. [4326] "Pittura settecentesca inedita del S. Sepolcro," La Terra Santa, 55 (1979), 133-138.

Baggati, Bellarmino. [4327] "La triangolazione del S. Sepolocro di Vienna-Sartorio (1940)," Studii Biblici Franciscani, Liber Annuus, 21 (1971), 149-157.

Baggati, Bellarmino and Testa, Emmanuele. [4328] Il Golgota e la Croce: Rícerche storico-archeologiche. Studium Biblicum Franciscanum, Collectio Minor, 21. Jerusalem: Franciscan Printing Press, 1978; reprinted, 1984, 161 pp.

Bahat, Dan. [4329] "Does the Holy Sepulchre Mark the Burial Place of Jesus?" Biblical Archaeology Review, 12/3 (May/June, 1986), 26-45. Essentially a review of Corbo, Virgilio. [4373]

Bahat, Dan. [4330] Jerusalem: Selected Plans of Historical Sites and Monumental Buildings. Jerusalem: Ariel, 1980, 66-71.

Barag, Dan. [4331] "Glass Pilgrim Vessels from Jerusalem," Journal of Glass Studies, 12 (1970), 33-63; 13 (1971), 45-63.

Barag, Dan and Wilkinson, John. [4332] "The Monza-Bobio Flasks and the Holy Sepulchre," Levant, 6 (1974), 179-187.

Barkay, Gabriel. See Broshi, Magen and Barkey, Gabriel. [4344-4345]

Baumstark, A. [4333] Die modestianischen und die konstantinischen Bauten am Heiligen Grabe zu Jerusalem. Studien zur Geschichte und Kultur des Altertums, 7/3-4. Paderborn: F. Schöningh, 1915, 174 pp.

Ben-Arieh, Yehoshua. [4334] "The Church of the Holy Sepulchre," in Jerusalem in the 19th Century: The Old City. Yad Izhaq Ben-Zvi / New York: St. Martin's, 1984, 202-218.

Bennett, C. M. and Humphreys, C. S. [4335] "The Jerusalem Ship," International Journal of Nautical Archaeology and Underwater Exploration, 3 (1974), 307-310.

Bockel, Pierre. [4336] "Le tombeau du Christ, pierre d' angle et pierre d' achoppement de l' unité chrétienne," Bible et Terre Sainte, 55 (1963), 11-12.

Borg, A. [4337] "Holy Sepulchre Lintel," Journal of the Warburg and Courtauld Institutes, 35 (1972), 389-390.

Borg, A. [4338] "Observations on the Historiated Lintel of the Holy Sepulchre," Journal of the Warburg and Courtauld Institutes, 32 (1969), 25-40.

Bresc-Bautier, G. [4339] "Les imitations du Saint-Sépulcre de Jérusalem (IXe-XVe siècles): Archéologie d' une devotion," Revue d' Histoire de la Spiritualité, 50 (1974), 319-342.

Briend, Jacques. [4340] "L' histoire du Saint-Sépulcre," Bible et Terre Sainte, 140 (1972), 7.

Broshi, Magen. [4341] "Evidence of Earliest Christian Pilgrimage to the Holy Land Comes to Light in Holy Sepulchre Church," Biblical Archaeology Review, 3/4 (Dec., 1977), 42-44. [The Jerusalem ship.]

Broshi, Magen. [4342] "The Jerusalem Ship Reconsidered," International Journal of Nautical Archaeology and Underwater Exploration, 6 (1977), 349-352.

Broshi, Magen. [4343] "Recent Excavations in the Holy Sepulchre Compound," in Israel Yearbook, 1979. Tel Aviv: Israel Yearbook Publications, 1979, 133-135.

Broshi, Magen and Barkay, Gabriel. [4344] "Excavations in the Chapel of St. Vartan in the Holy Sepulchre, Jerusalem," in Eretz-Israel: Archaeological, Historical, and Geographical Studies, 18. Jerusalem: Israel Exploration Society, 1985, 8-20 (Hebrew), 65* (English summary).

Broshi, Magen and Barkay, Gabriel. [4345] "Excavations in the Chapel of St. Vartan in the Holy Sepulchre," Israel Exploration Journal, 35 (1985), 108-128.

Brunot, Amédée. [4346] "Le Calvaire et le Sépulcre, de nos jours aux jours du Christ," Bible et Terre Sainte, 55 (1963), 8-10, 15.

Canard, M. [4347] "La destruction de l' Église de la Résurrection," Byzantion, 35 (1965), 16-43.

Cerny, Edward A. [4348] "Jerusalem: The Basilica of the Holy Sepulchre," Catholic Biblical Quarterly, 3 (1941), 362-365.

Chabot, J. B. [4349] "La ruine du Saint-Sépulcre," Revue Archéologique, 6th ser., 12 (1938), 260-262.

Chen, Doren. [4350] "A Note Pertaining to the Design of the Rotunda Anastasis in Jerusalem," Zeitschrift des deutschen Palästina-Vereins, 95 (1979), 178-181.

Christian Information Center: [4351] "Calvary Hill Uncovered," Holy Land Review, 2/1 (Spring, 1976), 31-32.

Christian Information Center: [4352] "Work of Restoration in the Basilica of Holy Sepulchre," Holy Land Review, 1/4 (Winter, 1975), 127; 2/4 (Winter, 1976), 123.

Clermont-Ganneau, Charles. [4353] L' Authenticité du S. Sépulcre et le tombeau de Josèphe d' Arimathie. Paris: Leroux, 1878, 31 pp.

Clermont-Ganneau, Charles. [4354] "The Church of the Holy Sepulchre," in Archaeological Researches in Palestine during the Years 1873-1874, 1. Translated by Aubrey Stewart. London: Palestine Exploration Fund, 1896, 101-115.

Clermont-Ganneau, Charles. [4355] "The Cufic Inscription in the Basilica of Constantine and the Destruction of the Holy Sepulchre by the Caliph Hâkem," Palestine Exploration Fund, Quarterly Statement, (1901), 246-250.

Clermont-Ganneau, Charles. [4356] "A Fragment of Sculptured Lintel from the Church of the Holy Sepulchre," in Archaeological Researches in Palestine during the Years 1873-1874, 1. Translated by Aubrey Stewart. London: Palestine Exploration Fund, 1896, 112-115.

Clermont-Ganneau, Charles. [4357] "The Holy Sepulchre, 1: Tomb of Joseph of Arimathaea; 2: The Frieze over the South Door," Palestine Exploration Fund, Quarterly Statement, (1877), 76-85.

Clermont-Ganneau, Charles. [4358] "The So-Called Tomb of Joseph of Arimathea," in The Survey of Western Palestine, 5: Jerusalem. Palestine Exploration Fund, 1884, 319-327, with notes by Charles W. Wilson, 327-329, and Claude R. Conder, 329-331.

Clos, E. M. [4359] Kreuz und Grab Jesu: Kritische Untersuchung der Berichte über die Kreuzauffindung. Kempten: Kösel'sche Buchhandlung, 1898, 664 pp. [On the visions of Anne Katharina Emmerich.]

Collas, L.; Coüasnon, Charles; and Voskertchian, D. [4360] "Jérusalem (Saint-Sépulcre)," Revue biblique, 69 (1962), 100-107.

Conant, K. J. and Downey, Glanville. [4361] "Original Buildings at the Holy Sepulchre in Jerusalem," Speculum, 31 (1956), 1-48.

Corbo, Virgilio. See Bahat, Dan. [4329]

Corbo, Virgilio. [4362] La Basilica del S. Sepolcro. Jerusalem: Franciscan Printing Press, 1969, 80 pp.

Corbo, Virgilio. [4363] "La basilica de S. Sepolcro a Gerusalemme: Rassegna archeologica delle strutture degli edifici nel 1969," Studii Biblici Franciscani, Liber Annuus, 19 (1969), 65-144.

Corbo, Virgilio. [4364] "La basilica de S. Sepolcro: Ritrovamenti di edifici constantiniani," La Terra Santa, 47 (1971), 199-205.

Corbo, Virgilio. [4365] "Les découvertes au Saint-Sépulcre," Bible et Terre Sainte, 40 (1961), 14-15.

Corbo, Virgilio. [4366] "Gli edifici della Santa Anastasis a Gerusalemme," Studii Biblici Franciscani, Liber Annuus, 12 (1961/1962), 221-316.

Corbo, Virgilio. [4367] "Fouilles archéologiques à la Grotte de l' Invention de la Sainte-Croix," La Terre Sainte, (June, 1965), 177-182.

Corbo, Virgilio. [4368] "Les Fouilles au St. Sépulcre," La Terre Sainte, (Feb., 1962), 36-41.

Corbo, Virgilio. [4369] "Nuove scoperte archeologiche nella Basilica del S. Sepolcro," Studii Biblici Franciscani, Liber Annuus, 14 (1963/1964), 293-338.

Corbo, Virgilio. [4370] "Problemi sul Santa Sepolcro di Gerusalemme in una recente publicazione," Studii Biblici Franciscani, Liber Annuus, 29 (1979), 279-292. "Recente publicazione" = Coüasnon, Charles. [4378]

Corbo, Virgilio. [4371] "Resultats inesperes des fouilles au Saint-Sépulcre," La Terre Sainte, (June-July, 1961), 164-170.

Corbo, Virgilio. [4372] "La Sainte Anastasis, le résultat des dernières fouilles effectuées dans la basilique du Saint-Sépulcre," Bible et Terre Sainte, 55 (1963), 16-22.

Corbo, Virgilio. [4373] Il Santo Sepolcro di Gerusalemme. Aspetti archeologici dalle origini al periode crociato, 3 vols. Studium Biblicum Franciscanum, Collectio Major, 29. Jerusalem: Franciscan Printing Press, 1981-1982, 235 pp. (with a 16 page summary in English by Stanislao Loffreda) + 68 pls. + 208 photographs.

Corbo, Virgilio. [4374] "Il Santo Sepolcro di Gerusalemme," Antonianum, 58 (1983), 123-127.

Corbo, Virgilio. [4375] "Scavo della cappella dell' Invenzione della S. Croce e nuovi reparti archeologici nella Basilica del S. Sepolcro a Gerusalemme (1965)," Studii Biblici Franciscani, Liber Annuus, 15 (1964/1965), 318-366.

Coüasnon, Charles. See Collas, L.; Coüasnon, Charles; and Voskertchian, D. [4360]

Coüasnon, Charles. [4376] "Analyse des élements du IVe siècle conservés dans la basilique du S. Sépulcre à Jérusalem," in Akten des VII. Internationalen Kongresses für christliche Archäologie, 1. Vatican City: Pontificio Instituto di Archeologia Christiana / Berlin: Deutsches Archäologisches Institut, 1965, 447-463.

Coüasnon, Charles. [4377] "Basilique du Saint-Sépulcre: Découverte de l' abside du Martyrium," La Terre Sainte, (May, 1971), 153-160.

Coüasnon, Charles. [4378] The Church of the Holy Sepulchre in Jerusalem. The Schwiech Lectures, 1972. London: Oxford University Press, 1974, 64 pp. + 28 pls.

Coüasnon, Charles. [4379] "Une église du Golgotha d' apres le texte d' Arculfe," Bible et Terre Sainte, 149 (1973), 16-18.

Coüasnon, Charles. [4380] "Le Golgotha, maquette du sol naturel," Bible et Terre Sainte, 149 (1973), 10-15.

Coüasnon, Charles. [4381] "Restauration de la Basilique du St.-Sépulcre," La Terre Sainte, (Dec., 1964), 308-316.

Coüasnon, Charles. [4382] "La restauration du Saint-Sépulcre," Bible et Terre Sainte, 140 (1972), 8-17.

Coüasnon, Charles. [4383] "Les travaux de restauration au Sainte-Sépulcre," La Terre Sainte, (July-Aug., 1969), 169-178.

Couret, Comte Alphonse. [4384] <u>Les légendes du Saint-Sépulcre</u>. Paris: Petithenry, 1893, 152 pp.

Cust, L. G. A. [4385] "The Church of the Holy Sepulchre," in <u>The Status Quo in the Holy Places</u>. Jerusalem: Ariel, 1980, 13-33. [Originally published in 1929.]

Dalman, Gustaf. [4386] "Golgotha und das Grab Christi," <u>Palästinajahrbuch</u>, 9 (1913), 98-123.

Dalman, Gustaf. [4387] "Die Grabeskirche in Jerusalem," <u>Palästinajahrbuch</u>, 3 (1907), 34-55.

Dalman, Gustaf. [4388] "Die Modelle Grabeskirche und Grabeskapelle in Jerusalem als Quelle ihrer älteren Gestalt," <u>Palästinajahrbuch</u>, 16 (1920), 23-31.

Daoust, Joseph. [4389] "Les ampoules de Monza," <u>Bible et Terre Sainte,</u> 170 (1975), 2-8.

Davies, J. G. [4390] "Eusebius' Description of the Martyrium at Jerusalem," <u>American Journal of Archaeology</u>, 61 (1957), 171-173.

Dickie, Archibald C. [4391] "Masonry Remains around the Church of the Holy Sepulchre," <u>Palestine Exploration Fund, Quarterly Statement,</u> (1908), 298-310.

Dickie, Archibald; Hanauer, James Edward; and Spyridonidis, C. K. [4392] "An Ancient Gate East of the Holy Sepulchre," <u>Palestine Exploration Fund, Quarterly Statement,</u> (1907), 297-302.

Díez, Florentino. [4393] "Cronica arqueologica: Basilica del Santa Sepulcro," <u>Estudios biblicos</u>, 38 (1979/1980), 141-143.

Downey, Glanville. See Conant, K. J. and Downey, Glanville. [4361]

Drake, H. A. [4394] "Coptic Version of the Discovery of the Holy Sepulchre," <u>Greek, Roman, and Byzantine Studies</u>, 20 (1979), 381-392.

Drake, H. A. [4395] "Eusebius on the True Cross," <u>Journal of Ecclesiastical History</u>, 36 (1985), 1-22.

Duncan, Alistair. [4396] <u>The Noble Heritage, Jerusalem and Christianity: A Portrait of the Church of the Resurrection</u>. London: Longman, 1974, 78 pp.

Economopoulos, A. [4397] "Basilica del S. Sepolcro," <u>La Terra Santa</u>, 47 (1971), 107-111.

Elm, Kaspar. [4398] "Fratres et sorores sanctissimi sepulcri: Beiträge zu fraternitas, familia und weiblichen Religiosentum im Umkreis des Kapitels vom Heil Grab," in K. Hauck (ed.), <u>Frühmittelalterliche Studien,</u> 9: <u>Jahrbuch des Instituts für Frühmittelalter-Forschung der Universitats Münster</u>. Berlin: De Gruyter, 1975, 287-333.

Emmerich, Anne Katharina: See Clos, E. M. [4359]

Engemann, Josef. [4399] "Palästinensische Pilgerampullen im F. J. Dölger-Institut in Bonn," in Jahrbuch für Antike und Christentum, 16. Münster: Verlag Aschendorff, 1973, 5-27.

"Entrata ufficiale dei Francescani Pontefici e il S. Sepolcro," [4400] La Terra Santa, 24 (1949), 119-124.

Evans, L. E. Cox. [4401] "The Holy Sepulchre," Palestine Exploration Quarterly, (1968), 112-136.

Every, E. [4402] "Church of the Holy Sepulchre, Past, Present and Future," Ecumenical Review, 4 (1952), 184-190.

Finegan, Jack. [4403] "Plan and Section of the Constantinian Church of the Holy Sepulcher, / Ancient Masonry under the Church of the Holy Sepulcher. / Apse Mosaic in Santa Pudentiana, / Jerusalem on the Madeba Mosaic Map, / Plan of the Church of the Holy Sepulcher according to Arculf, / Bell Tower at the Church of the Holy Sepulcher," in The Archeology of the New Testament: The Life of Jesus and the Beginning of the Early Church. Princeton: Princeton University Press, 1969, 163-172.

Finn, Elisabeth Ann. [4404] "The Church of the Holy Sepulchre in 1862," Palestine Exploration Quarterly, (1938), 162-164.

Fukuzawa, Philip. [4405] "Faith and Memory: The Story of the Church of the Holy Sepulchre," The Bible Today, 18 (1980), 322-328.

Germer-Durand, Joseph. [4406] "La basilique du Saint-Sepulcré," Revue biblique, 5 (1896), 321-334.

Golubovich, Girolama. [4407] "Discovery of an Important Cufic Inscription near the Church of the Holy Sepulchre, Jerusalem," Palestine Exploration Fund, Quarterly Statement, (1897), 302-303.

Govett, R. [4408] "Epiphanius on Golgotha," Palestine Exploration Fund, Quarterly Statement, (1880), 109-110.

Grego, Igino. [4409] "Il Golgota, Monte Santo dei cristiani," Bibbia e Oriente, 23 (1981), 115-124, 221-234.

Guthe, Hermann. [4410] "Zur Topographie der Grabeskirche in Jerusalem," Zeitschrift des deutschen Palästina-Vereins, 14 (1891), 35-40.

Guthe, Hermann and Schick, Conrad. [4411] "Die zweite Mauer Jerusalems und die Bauten Constantins am heiligen Grabe," Zeitschrift des deutschen Palästina-Vereins, 8 (1885), 245-287.

Hamilton, R. W. [4412] "Jerusalem: Patterns of Holiness," in R. Moorey and P. Paar (eds.), Archaeology in the Levant: Essays for Kathleen Kenyon. Warminster, England: Aris and Phillips, 1978, 194-201. [Compares the Temple of Solomon, the Church of the Holy Sepulchre, and the Dome of the Rock in terms of political-religious-mythological statement.]

Hanauer, James Edward. See Dickie, Archibald; Hanauer, James Edward; and Spyridonidis, C. K. [4392]

Harvey, John H. See Harvey, William and Harvey, John H. [4414]

Harvey, William. [4413] Church of the Holy Sepulchre, Jerusalem: Structural Survey, Final Report. With an Introduction by E. T. Richmond. Oxford: Oxford University Press, 1935, xv + 29 pp. + 119 figs. + 5 pls.

Harvey, William and Harvey, John H. [4414] "The Structural Decay of the Church of the Holy Sepulchre," Palestine Exploration Quarterly, (1938), 156-161.

Hoade, Eugene. [4415] "The Holy Sepulchre," in Guide to the Holy Land. Jerusalem: Franciscan Printing Press, 1984, 98-140.

Humphreys, C. S. See Bennett, C. M. and Humphreys, C. S. [4335]

"Inizi dei lavori di restauro al S. Sepolcro," [4416] La Terra Santa, 27 (1961), 226-230.

Jeffrey, George A. [4417] A Brief Description of the Holy Sepulchre Jerusalem and Other Christian Churches in the Holy City, with Some Account of the Medieval Copies of the Holy Sepulchre Surviving in Europe. Cambridge: Cambridge University Press, 1919, 233 pp.

Jeremias, Joachim. [4418] Golgotha. Angelos: Archiv für neuentestamentliche Zeitgeschichte und Kulturkunde, 1. Leipzig: Verlag von Eduard Pfeiffer, 1926, 96 pp.

Jeremias, Joachim. [4419] "Golgatha und das heilige Grab," Im Lande der Bibel, 1 (1955), 15-18.

Join-Lambert, Michel. [4420] "Anastasis et Saint-Sépulcre," Bible et Terre Sainte, 140 (1972), 4-5.

Joseph, Frederick. [4421] "The Holy Sepulchre through the Ages," Holy Land Review, 1/1 (Spring, 1975), 6-14.

Kaswalder, Peter. [4422] "Mary's Chapel Restored: Work in the Holy Sepulchre Basilica," The Holy Land, 5/3 (Fall, 1985), 119-121.

Katsimbinis, Christos. [4423] "The Uncovering of the Eastern Side of the Hill of Calvary and its Base: New Lay-Out of the Area of the Canon's Refectory, by the Greek Orthodox Patriarchate," Studii Biblici Franciscani, Liber Annuus, 27 (1977), 197-208.

Kenaan, Nurith. [4424] "The Sculptured Lintels of the Crusader Church of the Holy Sepulchre in Jerusalem," in B. Z. Kedar (ed.), Jerusalem in the Middle Ages, Selected Papers. Jerusalem: Yad Izhaq Ben-Zvi, 1979, 316-326 (Hebrew), xxiii-xxv (English). English summary also in "From the Hebrew Press: Jerusalem in the Middle Ages, Selected Documents (Yad Izhaq Ben-Zvi, Jerusalem, 1979)," in L. I. Levine (ed.), Jerusalem Cathedra, 2. Jerusalem: Yad Izhaq Ben-Zvi Institute / Detroit: Wayne State University Press, 1982, 325-326.

Krautheimer, R. [4425] "Constantine's Church Foundations," in Akten des VII. Internationalen Kongresses für christliche Archäologie, 1. Vatican City: Pontificio Instituto di Archeologia Christiana / Berlin: Deutsches Archäologisches Institut, 1965, 237-254, with reply by J. B. Ward-Perkins, 254-255.

Le Strange, Guy. [4426] "Notices of the Dome of the Rock and of the Church of the Sepulchre by Arab Historians prior to the First Crusade," Palestine Exploration Fund, Quarterly Statement, (1887), 90-103.

Lethaby, W. R. [4427] "The Temple, the Church of the Ascension, and the Finding of the Cross," Palestine Exploration Fund, Quarterly Statement, (1897), 75-77.

Macpherson, James R. [4428] "The Church of the Resurrection and of the Holy Sepulchre," English Historical Review, 7 (1892), 417-436, 69-684.

Mancini, Ignace. [4429] "Adam sous le Calvaire," La Terre Sainte, (Nov.-Dec., 1965), 274-278.

Mancini, Ignace. [4430] "Conclusion d' un accord sur des travaux de restauration du St. Sépulcre," La Terre Sainte, (July-Sept., 1958), 104-107.

Mancini, Ignace. [4431] "Forse in via di realizzazione i restauri al S. Sepolcro," La Terra Santa, 33 (1957), 233-240.

Manns, Frédéric. [4432] "The Place of the Skull," Holy Land Review, 6/1 (Spring-Winter, 1980), 6-7.

Manns, Frédéric. [4433] "Une prière ancienne du Saint-Sépulcre de Jérusalem," Augustinianum, 20 (1980), 233-241. [Domine Ivimus]

Manns, Frédéric. [4434] "New Eulogiae from the Holy Sepulchre," Holy Land Review, 5/1-2 (Spring-Summer, 1979), 24-26.

Mansurow, B. P. [4435] Die Kirche des Heiligen Grabes zu Jerusalem in ihrer ältesten Gestalt. Trans from the Russian by A. Woehlendorff. Heidelberg: Koester, 1887, 59 pp.

Marijancic, M. [4436] "Il lavori nella Basilica del S. Sepolcro sotto l' amministrazione mandatari," La Terra Santa, 24 (1949), 127-134.

Médebielle, Pierre. [4437] "Vers la restauration du St. Sépulcre," La Terre Sainte, (Nov.-Dec, 1962), 213-221.

Meinardus, Otto. [4438] "A Nautical Graffito outside the Chapel of the Franks," Studii Biblici Franciscani, Liber Annuus, 25 (1975), 85-89.

Meshorer, Yaakov. [4439] "Ancient Gold Ring Depicts the Holy Sepulchre," Biblical Archaeology Review, 12/3 (May/June, 1986), 46-48.

Mommert, Carl. [4440] "The Church of the Holy Sepulchre at Jerusalem on the Mosaic Map at Madeba," Palestine Exploration Fund, Quarterly Statement, (1898), 177-183.

Mommert, Carl. [4441] *Golgotha und das heilige Grab zu Jerusalem*. Leipzig: Haberland, 1900, 280 pp.

Mommert, Carl. [4442] "Die Grabeskirche des Modestus nach Arkulfs Bericht," *Zeitschrift des deutschen Palästina-Vereins*, 20 (1897), 34-53.

Mommert, Carl. [4443] *Die Heilige Grabeskirche zu Jerusalem in ihrem ursprünglichen Zustande*. Leipzig: Haberland, 1898, 256 pp.

Neri, Damiano. [4444] *Il S. Sepolcro riprodotto in Occidente*. Jerusalem: Franciscan Printing Press, 1971, 142 pp.

Ousterhout, Robert. [4445] "The Byzantine Holy Sepulchre," *Byzantine Studies Conference: Abstracts of Papers*, 9 (1983), 61-62. [On the church rebuilt by Constantine IX, Monomachus.]

Ousterhout, Robert. [4446] "Locus sanctus Architecture," *Byzantine Studies Conference: Abstracts of Papers*, 10 (1984), 3-4. [On eulogia of the Holy Sepulchre.]

Parrot, André. [4447] *Golgotha and the Church of the Holy Sepulchre*. *Studies in Biblical Archaeology*, 6. London: SCM, 1957, 127 pp.

Petrozzi, Maria Teresa. [4448] *Dal Calvario al Santo Sepolcro*. Jerusalem: Franciscan Printing Press, 1972, 104 pp.

Petrozzi, Maria Teresa. [4449] "Il Calvario - Il Sepolcro," *La Terra Santa*, 48 (1972), 79-91.

Petrozzi, Maria Teresa. [4450] "On the Roofs of the Holy Sepulchre," *Christian News from Israel*, 24/1 (1973), 25-29.

Piccirillo, Michele. [4451] "La roca del Calvario y el Golgota," *Tierra Santa*, (1979), 93-97.

Piccirillo, Michele. [4452] "The Rock of Calvary and Golgatha," *Holy Land Review*, 5/1-2 (Spring-Summer, 1979), 54-58.

Piganioi, André. [4453] "L' hémispherion et l' Omphalos des Lieux Saints," *Cahiers Archéologiques*, 1 (1962), 7-14.

Prawer, Joshua. [4454] "The Lintels of the Holy Sepulchre," in Y. Yadin (ed.), *Jerusalem Revealed: Archaeology in the Holy City, 1968-1974*. New Haven and London: Yale University Press and the Israel Exploration Society, 1976, 111-113.

Provera, M. [4455] "La Cappella di S. Elena e le vicende della Reliquia della S. Croce," *La Terra Santa*, 54 (1978), 311-317.

Rahmani, L. Y. [4456] "The Eastern Lintels of the Holy Sepulchre," *Israel Exploration Journal*, 26 (1976), 120-129.

"Rapport de la Commission d' Architectes réunis par la Custodie de Terre Sainte pour la Restauration du Saint-Sépulcre," [4457] Proche-Orient Chrétien, 5 (1955), 253-259.

"Rapport de la Commission tripartite experts sur la consolidation de l' édifice du Saint-Sépulcre," [4458] Proche-Orient Chrétien, 5 (1955), 44-47.

Richmond, E. T. See Harvey, William. [4413]

Rock, Albert. [4459] "Basilica del S. Sepolcro: La Cupola Grande," La Terra Santa, 53 (1977), 269-285.

Rock, Albert. [4460] Lo Statu Quo nei Luoghi Santi: La questione in generale e due circostanze differenti ed emblematiche riguardanti il Cenaclo e la Cupola del S. Sepolcro. Jerusalem: Franciscan Printing Press, 1977, 64 pp.

Roncaglia, M. [4461] "Ottavo centenario della consacrazione della Basilica del S. Sepolcro," La Terra Santa, 23 (1948), 16-25.

Rosén-Ayalon, Myriam. [4462] "A Mosaic in the Church of the Holy Sepulchre," in B. Z. Kedar (ed.), Jerusalem in the Middle Ages, Selected Papers. Jerusalem: Yad Izhaq Ben-Zvi, 1979, 338-346 (Hebrew).

Rosén-Ayalon, Myriam. [4463] "Une mosaïque médiévale au Saint-Sépulcre: Contribution à l' histoire de l' art," Revue biblique, 83 (1976), 237-253.

Rosenthal, Gabriella. [4464] "Restoration at the Church of the Holy Sepulchre," Christian News from Israel, 23/3 (1973), 139-143.

Ross, J.-P. B. [4465] "The Evolution of a Church-- Jerusalem's Holy Sepulchre," Biblical Archaeology Review, 2/3 (Sept., 1976), 3-8, 11.

Rubin, Ze'ev. [4466] "The Church of the Holy Sepulchre and the Conflict between the Sees of Jerusalem and Caesarea," in L. I. Levine (ed.), Jerusalem Cathedra, 2. Jerusalem: Yad Izhaq Ben-Zvi Institute / Detroit: Wayne State University Press, 1982, 79-105.

"Le Saint-Sépulcre: L' rapport de l' histoire et de l' archéologie," [4467] Le Monde de la Bible, 33 (1984), 1-52.

St. Clair, George. [4468] "Twin Sacred Mounts at Jerusalem, Palestine Exploration Fund, Quarterly Statement, (1889), 99-102. [On the Church of the Holy Sepulchre as the Christian Holy Mount.]

Salet, F. [4469] "Le Saint-Sépulcre au IVe siècle," Bulletin Monumental (Société Française d' Archéologie), 128 (1970), 319.

Salet, F. [4470] "Linteau du Saint-Sépulcre de Jérusalem," Bulletin Monumental (Société Française d' Archéologie), 128 (1970), 150-151.

Salvoni, F. [4471] "Il Golgota e la caverna di Adamo," Ricerche Bibliche e Religiose, 17 (1982), 52-58.

de Sandoli, Sabino. [4472] Le Calvaire et le Saint-Sépulcre. Jerusalem: Franciscan Printing Press, 1979, 148 pp.

de Sandoli, Sabino. [4473] Il Calvario e il S. Sepolcro. Cenni storici. Jerusalem: Franciscan Printing Press, 1974, 108 pp.

de Sandoli, Sabino. [4474] Calvary and the Holy Sepulchre. Jerusalem: Franciscan Printing Press, 1977, 120 pp.

Il Santo Sepolcro di Gerusalemme: Splendori - Miserie - Speranze. [4475] Bergame: Instituto Italiano d' Arti Grafiche, 1950, 158 pp.

Schick, Conrad. See Guthe, Hermann and Schick, Conrad. [4411]

Schick, Conrad. [4476] "The Byzantine Pavement near the Church of the Holy Sepulchre," Palestine Exploration Fund. Quarterly Statement. (1880), 17-20.

Schick, Conrad. [4477] "The 'Cave' of William the Hermit," Palestine Exploration Fund. Quarterly Statement. (1898), 155-156.

Schick, Conrad. [4478] "The Cufic Inscription from the Basilica of the Holy Sepulchre," Palestine Exploration Fund. Quarterly Statement. (1898), 158.

Schick, Conrad. [4479] "Large Cistern under the New Greek Building South-East of the Chruch of the Holy Sepulchre," Palestine Exploration Fund. Quarterly Statement. (1889), 111-112.

Schick, Conrad. [4480] "Neu aufgedeckte Felsengräber bei der Grabeskirche in Jerusalem," Zeitschrift des deutschen Palästina-Vereins, 8 (1885), 171-173.

Schick, Conrad. [4481] "Notes on the Plans and the Cave East of the Church of the Holy Sepulchre," Palestine Exploration Fund. Quarterly Statement. (1889), 67-68.

Schick, Conrad. [4482] "Old Font in the Church of the Holy Sepulchre," Palestine Exploration Fund. Quarterly Statement. (1898), 155.

Schick, Conrad. [4483] "On the Site of Calvary," Palestine Exploration Fund. Quarterly Statement. (1893), 23-25.

Schick, Conrad. [4484] "Rock Levels in Jerusalem," Palestine Exploration Fund. Quarterly Statement. (1890), 20-21.

Schick, Conrad. [4485] "The Site of the Church of the Holy Sepulchre at Jerusalem," Palestine Exploration Fund. Quarterly Statement. (1898), 145-154.

Schick, Conrad. [4486] "Weitere Ausgrabungen auf dem russischen Platz," Zeitschrift des deutschen Palästina-Vereins, 12 (1889), 10-18.

Schick, Conrad and Wilson, Charles W. [4487] "New Excavations in Jerusalem," Palestine Exploration Fund. Quarterly Statement. (1888), 57-62.

Schur, Nathan. [4488] "Church of the Holy Sepulchre," in Jerusalem in Pilgrims and Travellers' Accounts: A Thematic Bibliography of Western Christian Itineraries, 1300-1917. Jerusalem: Ariel, 1980, 20-24.

Simons, Jan. [4489] "The 'Second Wall' and the Problem of the Holy Sepulchre," in Jerusalem in the Old Testament: Researches and Theories. Leiden: Brill, 1952, 282-343.

Simpson, William. [4490] "Entrance to the Holy Sepulchre," Palestine Exploration Fund, Quarterly Statement, (1891), 159-160.

Simpson, William. [4491] "The Middle of the World, in the Holy Sepulchre," Palestine Exploration Fund, Quarterly Statement, (1888), 260-263.

Smith, Robert Huston. [4492] "The Tomb of Jesus," Biblical Archaeologist, 30 (1967), 74-90.

Spyridonidis, C. K. See Dickie, Archibald; Hanauer, James Edward; and Spyridonidis, C. K. [4392]

Ternant, Paul. [4493] "La signification spirituelle de la Basilique du Saint-Sépulcre," Proche-Orient Chrétien, 2 (1952), 319-332.

Testa, Emmanuele. See Baggati, Bellarmino and Testa, Emmanuele. [4328]

Testa, Emmanuele. [4494] "Il Golgota, port della quite," in E. Testa, I. Mancini, and M. Piccirillo (eds.), Studia HIerosolymitana in onore del P. Bellarmino Bagatti, 1: Studia archeologici. Studium Biblicum Franciscanum, Collectio Major, 22. Jerusalem: Franciscan Printing Press, Jerusalem: Franciscan Printing Press, 1976, 197-244.

Testini, Emmanuele. [4495] "L' Anastasis alla luce della recenti indagini: Nota sulla posizione nell' ambito dell' architettura sacra Constantiniana," Oriens Antiquus, 3 (1964), 263-292.

Tinelli, C. [4496] "Il battistero del S. Sepolcro in Gerusalemme," Studii Biblici Franciscani, Liber Annuus, 23 (1973), 95-104.

Tinelli, C. [4497] "L' identificazione dei proto-capitelli del S. Sepolcro," Studii Biblici Franciscani, Liber Annuus, 22 (1972), 30-47.

Van Bercham, Max. [4498] "An Arabic Inscription from Jerusalem," Palestine Exploration Fund, Quarterly Statement, (1898), 86-93.

Vincent, Louis-Hugues. [4499] "Quelques répresentations antiques du Saint-Sépulcre Constantinien," Revue biblique, 22 (1913), 525-546; 23 (1914), 94-109.

Vincent, Louis-Hugues. [4500] "Un vestige des édifices de Constantin au Saint-Sépulcre," Revue biblique, 16 (1907), 586-607.

Vincent, Louis-Hugues and Abel, Félix-M. [4501] "Le Saint-Sépulcre," in Jérusalem: Recherches de topographie, d' archéologie, et d' histoire, 2: Jérusalem nouvelle, 1. Paris: Gabalda, 1914, 89-300.

de Vogüé, Melchior. [4502] Les Églises de Terre Saint, Fragments d' un voyage en Orient. Paris: Lir. de V. Didron, 1860, 118-232.

Voskertchian, D. See Collas, L.; Coüasnon, Charles; and Voskertchian, D. [4360]

Wallis, Robert. [4503] "Architectural History of the Holy Sepulchre," In George Williams, The Holy City: Historical, Topographical, and Antiquarian Notices of Jerusalem, 2. London: John W. Parker, 2nd edn., 1849, 129-294.

Ward-Perkins, J. B. [4504] "Memoira, Martyr's Tomb and Martyr's Church," in Akten des VII. Internationalen Kongresses für christliche Archäologie, 1. Vatican City: Pontificio Instituto di Archeologia Christiana / Berlin: Deutsches Archäologisches Institut, 1965, 3-24, with reply by W. H. C. Frend, 25, and J. Kollwitz, 26-27.

Watson, Charles M. See Wilson, Charles W. [4515]

Waugh, Evelyne. [4505] "Dans la basilique du Saint-Sépulcre," La Terre Sainte, (Jan.-March, 1959), 13-16.

Weigand, E. [4506] "Zwei neue Hypothesen über die konstantinischen Bauten am heilgen Grabe in Jerusalem," Byzantinische Zeitschrift, 40 (1940), 78-88.

Wilkinson, John. See Barag, Dan and Wilkinson, John. [4332]

Wilkinson, John. [4507] "The Cave of the Anastasis," in Egeria's Travels to the Holy Land. Jerusalem: Ariel, rev. edn., 1981, 242-252. [On the history of the edicules over the cave, based on art history.] Compare Wilkinson, John. [4511]

Wilkinson, John. [4508] "Church of the Holy Sepulchre," Archaeology, 31 (July, 1978), 6-13.

Wilkinson, John. [4509] "Church of the Holy Sepulchre," in Jerusalem as Jesus Knew It. London: Thames and Hudson, 1978, 180-194.

Wilkinson, John. [4510] "Eusebius on the Buildings on Golgotha," in Egeria's Travels to the Holy Land. Jerusalem: Ariel, rev. edn., 1981, 164-171.

Wilkinson, John. [4511] "The Tomb of Christ: An Outline of its Structural History," Levant, 4 (1972), 83-97.

Willoughby, Harold R. [4512] "The Distinctive Sources of Palestinian Iconograpy," Journal of Biblical Literature, 74 (1955), 61-68. [The Church of the Holy Sepulchre on Eulogiae.]

Wilson, Charles W. See Schick, Conrad and Wilson, Charles W. [4487]

Wilson, Charles W. [4513] "Church of the Holy Sepulchre," in Ordnance Survey of Jerusalem. London: Lord's Commissioners of Her Majesty's Treasury, 1865, 48-55.

Wilson, Charles W. [4514] "Golgotha and the Holy Sepulchre," Palestine Exploration Fund, Quarterly Statement, (1902), 66-77, 142-155, 282-297, 376-384; (1903), 51-65, 140-153, 242-249; (1904), 26-41.

Wilson, Charles W. [4515] Golgotha and the Holy Sepulchre. London: Palestine Exploration Fund, 1906, 209 pp. [Based on the series of articles of the same name in the Palestine Exploration Fund, Quarterly Statement, (1902-1904), edited by Charles M. Watson after Wilson's death.]

Wilson, Charles W. [4516] "The Holy Sepulchre: Tomb of Joseph of Arimathea," Palestine Exploration Fund, Quarterly Statement, (1877), 128-132, with note by Claude R. Conder, 132-134.

Wistrand, E. K. H. [4517] Konstantins Kirche am Heiligen Grab in Jerusalem nach den ältesten literarischen Zeugnissen. Acta Universitatis Gotoburgensis. Göteborgs högskolas årsskrift, 58/1. Göteborg: Wettergrin & Kerber, 52 pp.

Worral, Girdler. [4518] "A Note on Golgatha," Palestine Exploration Fund, Quarterly Statement, (1885), 138-139.

Thirty

Rival Sites for Golgotha and the Tomb of Jesus

Barkay, Gabriel. [4519] "The Garden Tomb--Was Jesus Buried Here?" Biblical Archaeology Review, 12/2 (March/April, 1986), 40-53, 56-57. [Negative.]

Benoit, Pierre. [4520] "The Inscription Allegedly Relating to the Garden Tomb," Biblical Archaeology Review, 12/4 (July/August, 1986), 58.

Birch, W. F. [4521] "Golgotha on Mount Zion," Palestine Exploration Fund, Quarterly Statement, (1907), 73-76, 140-147. [contra Church of the Holy Sepulchre.]

Chadwick, Jeffrey. [4522] "In Defense of the Garden Tomb," Biblical Archaeology Review, 12/4 (July/August, 1986), 16-17.

Conder, Claude R. [4523] "The Holy Sepulchre," Palestine Exploration Fund, Quarterly Statement, (1883), 69-78. [Promotes a site north of the Damascus Gate, but not the Garden Tomb.]

Conder, Claude R. [4524] "The Holy Sepulchre and Calvary," in C. Warren and C. R. Conder, The Survey of Western Palestine, 5: Jerusalem. London: Palestine Exploration Fund, 1884, 112-116.

Conder, Claude R. [4525] "Notes on Calvary," Palestine Exploration Fund, Quarterly Statement, (1888), 165-166.

Conder, Claude R. [4526] "Note on the Holy Sepulchre," Palestine Exploration Fund, Quarterly Statement, (1889), 204-205.

Conder, Claude R. [4527] "The Site of Calvary," Palestine Exploration Fund, Quarterly Statement, (1901), 409-412.

Conder, Claude R. [4528] "The Temple and Calvary," in Tent Work in Palestine: A Record of Discovery and Adventure, 1. London: Richard Bentley and Sons, 1879, 346-376.

Crawley-Boevey, A. W. [4529] "The Churches of Constantine," Palestine Exploration Fund, Quarterly Statement, (1907), 215-220. [contra Fergusson.]

Crawley-Boevey, A. W. [4530] "The Damascus Gate or Bab el-Amud," Palestine Exploration Fund, Quarterly Statement, (1912), 196-202. [Main subject of article is the location of the authentic site of Calvary.]

Crawley-Boevey, A. W. [4531] "Golgotha and the Holy Sepulchre," Palestine Exploration Fund, Quarterly Statement, (1906), 269-274.

Crawley-Boevey, A. W. [4532] "Map and Description of Jerusalem by Christian Van Adrichem (1533-1585), Palestine Exploration Fund, Quarterly Statement, (1909), 64-68.

Crawley-Boevey, A. W. [4533] "The New Theory of Calvary," Palestine Exploration Fund, Quarterly Statement, (1912), 21-30.

Crawley-Boevey, A. W. [4534] "The Recovery of the 'Holy Places' in Jerusalem," Palestine Exploration Fund, Quarterly Statement, (1909), 200-205.

Crawley-Boevey, A. W. [4535] "Recent Opinions on the Site of Calvary," Palestine Exploration Fund, Quarterly Statement, (1910), 23-26.

Crawley-Boevey, A. W. [4536] "Sir Charles Wilson's Views on Calvary and the Tomb," Palestine Exploration Fund, Quarterly Statement, (1910), 248-258.

Dobson, C. C. [4537] The Garden Tomb, Jerusalem, and the Resurrection. London: George Pulman and Sons, Ltd., 1958.

Fergusson, James. See Crawley-Boevey, A. W. [4529]

Fergusson, James. See Le Strange, Guy. [4559]

Fergusson, James. See Simpson, William. [4577-4579]

Fergusson, James. [4538] An Essay on the Ancient Topography of Jerusalem, with Restored Plans of the Temple, etc., and Plans, Sections and Details of the Church Built by Constantine the Great, Now Known as the Mosque of Omar. London: J. Weale, 1847, 188 pp. [Dome of the Rock = Constantine's Church of the Holy Sepulchre!]

Fergusson, James. [4539] The Holy Sepulchre and the Temple at Jerusalem. London: John Murray, 1865, 151 pp.

Fergusson, James. [4540] The Temples of the Jews and Other Buildings in the Haram Area at Jerusalem. London: John Murray, 1878, 304 pp.

The Garden Tomb Association: [4541] Jerusalem: The Garden Tomb, Golgotha, and the Garden of the Resurrection. London: Committee of the Garden Tomb (Jerusalem) Association, rev. edn., 1946, 44 pp.

Gell, Francis. [4542] "Excursus on the Resurrection and the Hypothesis that It Took Place from a Tomb Similar in Construction to the Tombs of the Kings, and in that Vicinity," Palestine Exploration Fund, Quarterly Statement, (1901), 413-419. [Promotes the Tombs of the Kings as the authentic site of Jesus' tomb.]

Gell, Francis. [4543] "On the Site of the Holy Sepulchre," Palestine Exploration Fund, Quarterly Statement, (1901), 299-305.

Gordon, Charles. [4544] "Eden and Golgotha," Palestine Exploration Fund, Quarterly Statement, (1885), 78-81. Gordon's mystical topography, often cited as reductio ad absurdum for Gordon's Calvary. Portions of article reproduced in Murphy-O'Connor, Jerome. [4564] and in Wilkinson, John. [4584]

R. F. H. [4545] "Notes on Our Lord's Tomb," Palestine Exploration Fund, Quarterly Statement, (1869/70), 379-381. [Locates authentic site in the Valley of Jehoshaphat.]

Hanauer, James Edward. [4546] "El-Edhemîyeh (Jeremiah's Grotto)," Palestine Exploration Fund, Quarterly Statement, (1903), 86-90. [Apologist for Gordon's Calvary and the Garden Tomb.]

Hanauer, James Edward. [4547] "Model of a Columbarium: An Alleged Model of a Sanctuary from the Garden-Tomb Grounds," Palestine Exploration Fund, Quarterly Statement, (1924), 143-145.

Hanauer, James Edward. [4548] "Notes on the Controversy Regarding the Site of Calvary," Palestine Exploration Fund, Quarterly Statement, (1892), 295-308.

Hanauer, James Edward. [4549] "On the Identification of Calvary," Palestine Exploration Fund, Quarterly Statement, (1892), 199-200.

Hanauer, James Edward. [4550] "Photograph of the Front of 'Gorden's Tomb,'" Palestine Exploration Fund, Quarterly Statement, (1903), 84-86.

Hanauer, James Edward. [4551] "Remarks on the Supposed Shrine of Cybele Found Near the Garden Tomb," Palestine Exploration Fund, Quarterly Statement, (1924), 187-191.

Harper, Henry A. [4552] "The Holy Sepulchre," Palestine Exploration Fund, Quarterly Statement, (1883), 148.

Hill, Gray. [4553] "The Site of Golgotha and the Holy Sepulchre," Palestine Exploration Fund, Quarterly Statement, (1902), 93-94.

Hull, Edward. [4554] "Site of Calvary," Palestine Exploration Fund, Quarterly Statement, (1890), 125.

Hussey, C. [4555] "The Tomb near the Skull Hill, Jerusalem," Palestine Exploration Fund, Quarterly Statement, (1899), 130-131.

Hutchinson, R. F. [4556] "The Tomb of Our Lord," Palestine Exploration Fund, Quarterly Statement, (1893), 79-80. [Locates authentic site near Tomb of the Virgin.]

Isaacs, A. A. [4557] "The Site of Calvary," Palestine Exploration Fund, Quarterly Statement, (1893), 300-301. [Locates authentic site in the Valley of Hinnom.]

Joubert, Christian. [4558] "The Garden Tomb," Christian News from Israel, 25/3 (1975), 126-131.

Le Strange, Guy. [4559] "Notices of the Dome of the Rock and the Church of the Sepulchre by Arab Historians prior to the First Crusade," Palestine Exploration Fund, Quarterly Statement, (1887), 90-103. [contra Fergusson.]

Macalister, R. A. Stewart. [4560] "El-Edhemîyeh (Jeremiah's Grotto)," Palestine Exploration Fund, Quarterly Statement, (1902), 129-132.

Macalister, R. A. Stewart. [4561] "The 'Garden Tomb,'" Palestine Exploration Fund, Quarterly Statement, (1907), 229-234. [Skeptical on all opinions.]

McBirnie, W. S. [4562] The Search for the Authentic Tomb of Jesus. Montrose, CA: Acclaimed Books, 1975. [Apologist for Gordon's Calvary and the Garden Tomb.]

MacColl, Canon. [4563] "The Site of Golgotha and the Holy Sepulchre," Palestine Exploration Fund, Quarterly Statement, (1901), 273-299. [contra Gordon's Calvary and the Garden Tomb.]

Murphy-O'Connor, Jerome. [4564] "Garden Tomb,"in The Holy Land: An Archeological Guide from Earliest Times to 1700. Oxford: Oxford University Press, 1980, 104-106. [contra Gordon's Calvary and the Garden Tomb.]

Murphy-O'Connor, Jerome. [4565] "The Garden Tomb and the Misfortunes of an Inscription," Biblical Archaeology Review, 12/2 (March/April, 1986), 54-55.

Pitcairn, D. Lee. [4566] "A Novel Theory of the Holy Sepulchre," Palestine Exploration Fund, Quarterly Statement, (1912), 211-212.

Robinson, Edward and Smith, Eli. [4567] "Church of the Holy Sepulchre," in Biblical Researches in Palestine and in the Adjacent Religions: A Journal of Travels in the Year 1838, 1. Boston: Crocker and Brewster / London: John Murray, 2nd edn., 1860, 407-418. [contra the traditional site.]

Robinson, Edward and Smith, Eli. [4568] "The Holy Sepulchre," in Later Biblical Researches in Palestine and in the Adjacent Religions: A Journal of Travels in the Year 1852. Boston: Crocker and Brewster / London: John Murray, 1857, 254-263.

Schick, Conrad. [4569] "'Gordon's Tomb,'" Palestine Exploration Fund, Quarterly Statement, (1892), 20-124, with plan. [Descriptive.]

Schick, Conrad. [4570] "Hill of 'Jeremiah's Grotto,' Called by General Gordon 'Skull Hill'", Palestine Exploration Fund, Quarterly Statement, (1901), 402-405.

Schick, Conrad. [4571] "Die neu aufgefundenen Felsengräber neben der Jeremiasgrotte bei Jerusalem," Zeitschrift des deutschen Palästina-Vereins, 9 (1886), 74-78.

Schick, Conrad. [4572] "The Newly Discovered Rock-cut Tombs close to the Jeremiah Grotto near Jerusalem," Palestine Exploration Fund, Quarterly Statement, (18860, 155-157.

Schick, Conrad. [4573] "Notes to Accompany the Plan of Jeremiah's Grotto," Palestine Exploration Fund, Quarterly Statement, (1902), 38-42.

Schick, Conrad. [4574] "On the Site of Calvary," Palestine Exploration Fund, Quarterly Statement, (1893), 23-25. Response to Hanauer, James Edward. [4548]

Schick, Conrad. [4575] "Reflections on the Site of Calvary," Palestine Exploration Fund, Quarterly Statement, (1893), 119-128. [Supports traditional site.]

Schur, Nathan. [4576] "The Garden Tomb ('Gordon's Calvary,' 'Conder's Tomb,')," in Jerusalem in Pilgrims and Travellers' Accounts: A Thematic Bibliography of Western Christian Itineraries, 1300-1917. Jerusalem: Ariel, 1980, 50.

Simpson, William. [4577] "The Holy Places of Jerusalem," Palestine Exploration Fund, Quarterly Statement, (1889), 61-62. [contra Fergusson.]

Simpson, William. [4578] "The Holy Sepulchre and the Dome of the Rock," Palestine Exploration Fund, Quarterly Statement, (1889), 14-17. [contra Fergusson.]

Simpson, William. [4579] "Transference of Sites," Palestine Exploration Fund, Quarterly Statement, (1879), 18-32. [contra Fergusson.]

"The Site of the Holy Sepulchre: Correspondence from the 'Times' on the Site of the Holy Sepulchre," [4580] Palestine Exploration Fund, Quarterly Statement, (1893), 80-91, 167.

Smith, Eli. See Robinson, Edward and Smith, Eli. [4567-4568]

Tenz, J. M. [4581] "Calvary -- 'Place of a Skull,'" Palestine Exploration Fund, Quarterly Statement, (1911), 189-192.

Vincent, Louis-Hugues. [4582] "Garden Tomb, historie d' un mythe," Revue biblique, 34 (1925), 401-431.

Warren, Charles. [4583] The Temple or the Tomb? Giving Further Evidence in Favor of the Authenticity of the Present Site of the Holy Sepulchre. London: Bentley, 1880, 227 pp. [contra Fergusson.]

Wilkinson, John. [4584] "General Gordon on Golgotha, "in Jerusalem as Jesus Knew It: Archaeology as Evidence. London: Thames and Hudson, 1978, 198-200. [reductio ad absurdum.]

Wilson, Charles W. See Crawley-Boevey, A. W. [4536]

Wilson, Charles W. [4585] "Golgotha and the Holy Sepulchre," Palestine Exploration Fund, Quarterly Statement, (1904), 38-41. [That portion of a series of articles on the Church of the Holy Sepulchre which deals with the authenticity of the site contra other positions.]

Worrall, Girdler. [4586] "A Note on Golgotha," Palestine Exploration Fund, Quarterly Statement, (1885), 138-139.

Thirty-One

The Churches of Mt. Sion

Abel, Félix-M. [4587] "Étienne, la chapelle du Sud," in L. Pirot (ed.), Supplément au Dictionnaire de la Bible, 2. Paris: Letouzey et Ané, 1934, 1144-1146.

Abel, Félix-M. [4588] "Petites découvertes au quartier du Cénacle à Jérusalem," Revue biblique, 20 (1911), 119-125.

Alliata, E. See Bagatti, Bellarmino and Alliata, E. [4593]

Avi-Yonah, Michael. [4589] "Mosaic Pavements in Palestine: Jerusalem, Mount Zion," in Art in Ancient Palestine. Collected and prepared for republication by H. Katzenstein and Y. Tsafrir. Jerusalem: Magnes Press, 1981, 316-318. [Originally published in Quarterly of the Department of Antiquities in Palestine, 2 (1932), 169-171.]

Bagatti, Bellarmino. [4590] "Franciscans Restore their Mt. Sion Chapel," The Holy Land, 2/2 (Summer, 1982), 82-85.

Bagatti, Bellarmino. [4591] "Sainte Sion," in Saint Jacques le Mineur: Premier evêque de Jerusalem. Jerusalem: Edition de la Terre Sainte de la Custodie Franciscaine, 1962, 13-21. [On the so-called "Tomb of David" on Mount Sion].

Bagatti, Bellarmino. [4592] "Synagogue and Cenacle of Mount Sion," in The Church from the Circumcision: History and Archaeology of the Judeao-Christians. Studium Biblicum Franciscanum, Collectio Minor, 2. Jerusalem: Franciscan Printing Press, 1971, reprinted, 1984, 116-122.

Bagatti, Bellarmino and Alliata, E. [4593] "Retrovamento archeologico sul Sion," Studii Biblici Franciscani, Liber Annuus, 31(1981), 249-256.

Bahat, Dan. [4594] Jerusalem: Selected Plans of Historical Sites and Monumental Buildings. Jerusalem: Ariel, 1980, 23-36.

Briand, Jean. [4595] "Le Mont Sion Franciscan," La Terre Sainte, (Feb. 1973), 36-44; (Mar. 1973), 85-91; (April, 1973), 121-131.

Briand, Jean. [4596] Sion. Jerusalem: Franciscan Printing Press, 1973, 104 pp.

Briend, Jacques. [4597] "Chronik unserer Abtei Mariä Heimgang auf dem Berg Sion in Jerusalem," Das Heilige Land, 101 (1969), 6-20.

Brunot, Amédée. [4598] "Sion de David et Sion chrétienne," Bible et Terre Sainte, 98 (1968), 20.

31/The Churches of Mt. Sion

Collin, Bernardin. [4599] "Les Frères-Mineurs au Cénacle," La Terre Sainte, (Jan.-March, 1960), 12-18; (April-June, 1960), 67-73.

Collin, Bernardin. [4600] "La Question du Cénacle," Studia Orientalia Christiana, 2 (1957), 1-34.

I. H. D. [4601] "La maison de Marie: Jérusalem ou Ephèse?" Bible et Terre Sainte, 51 (1962), 5.

Decroix, J. [4602] "Le Cénacle," Bible et Terre Sainte, 98 (1968), 8-16.

Dobrena, T. J. [4603] "The Question of the Upper Room," Springfielder, 38 (1973), 97-107. [Promotes Syrian Orthodox church at the Convent of St. Mark as the authentic site.]

Finegan, Jack. [4604] "Plan of the Church on Mount Sion according to Arculf, / The Tomb of David on Mount Sion, / The South Wall of the Tomb of David on Mount Sion, / The Cenacle in Franciscan Restoration of the Fourteenth Century, / The Church of St. Peter in Gallicanto," in The Archeology of the New Testament: The Life of Jesus and the Beginning of the Early Church. Princeton: Princeton University Press, 1969, 147-154.

Franken, Sebastièn. [4605] "Sainte Pierre en Gallicante," La Terre Sainte, (July-Aug.-Sept., 1964), 209-216.

Franken, Sebastièn. [4606] "Sankt Peter zum Hahnenschrei," Das Heilige Land, 95 (1963), 31-41.

Germer-Durand, Joseph. [4607] "La maison de Caïphe et l' église Saint-Pierre à Jérusalem," Revue biblique, 23 (1914), 71-94, 222-246.

Golubovich, Girolamo. [4608] Il Santo Cenacolo: Sua autenticità e sue divine prerogative. Florence: Barbèra, 1938, 156 pp.

Hoade, Eugene. [4609] "Mount Sion," in Guide to the Holy Land. Jerusalem: Franciscan Printing Press, 1984, 298-319.

Kosmala, Hans. [4610] "Der Ort des letzen Mahles Jesu und das heutige Coenaculum," in Studies, Essays, and Reviews, 2. Leiden: Brill, 1978, 48-52.

Lagrange, Marie-Joseph. [4611] "La Dormition de la Sainte Vierge et la maison de Jean-Marc," Revue biblique, 8(1899), 589-600.

Lagrange, Marie-Joseph. [4612] "Épigraphie sémitique: Une inscription trouvée au mont sion et une autre au mont des oliviers," Revue biblique, 2 (1893), 220-222.

Lussier, E. [4613] "The Cenacle," Emmanuel, 67 (1961), 364-366.

Mackowski, Richard M. [4614] "The Upper Room," in Jerusalem, City of Jesus: An Exploration of the Traditions, Writings, and Remains of the Holy City from the Time of Christ. Grand Rapids, MI: Eerdmans, 1980, 139-147.

31/The Churches of Mt. Sion

Mann, Sylvia. [4615] "Mount Zion," Christian News from Israel, 25/4 (1976), 190-198.

Marchet, Xavier. [4616] Le véritable emplacement du palais de Caïphe et l' église Saint-Pierre à Jérusalem. Paris: Gabalda, 1927, 112 pp.

Meistermann, Barnabé. [4617] "Aperçu historique sur le Saint Cénacle," La Terre Sainte (April, 1968), 116-123.

Millás I. Vallicrosa, J. M. [4618] "Origenes de la localizacion de la tumba de David en el Santo Cenáculo," Estudios Eclesiásticos, 34/134-135 (1960), 595-602.

Mommert, Carl. [4619] "Die Dormito und das deutsche Grundstück auf dem traditionellen Zion," Zeitschrift des deutschen Palästina-Vereins, 21(1898), 149-183.

Mommert, Carl. [4620] Die Dormitio und das deutsche Grundstück auf dem traditionellen Zion. Leipzig: Haberland, 1899, 132 pp.

Mommert, Carl. [4621] "Zur Orientirung der arculf'schen Planzeichnung der Zionskirche des VII. Jahrunderts," Zeitschrift des deutschen Palästina-Vereins, 22 (1899), 105-117.

Murphy-O'Connor, Jerome. [4622] "Mt. Sion," in The Holy Land: An Archeological Guide from Earliest Times to 1700. Oxford: Oxford University Press, 1980, 73-77.

North, Robert. [4623] "Mary's Last Home," American Ecclesiastical Review, 123(1950), 242-261.

Petrozzi, Maria Teresa. [4624] "The Holy Place of Mary's Dormition," The Holy Land, 5/3 (Fall, 1985), 134-138.

Pixner, Bargil. [4625] "'Nea Sion:' Topographische und geschichtliche Untersuchung des Sitzes der Urkirche und seiner Bewohner," Das Heilige Land, 111 (1979), 2-13.

Pixner, Bargil. [4626] "Das Essenerquarter in Jerusalem und dessen Einfluss auf die Urkirche," Das Heilige Land, 113/2-3 (1981), 3-14. [Essene Zion becomes Christian Sion.]

Power, E. [4627] "Cénacle," in L. Pirot (ed.), Supplement au Dictionnaire de la Bible,1. Paris: Letouzey et Ané, 1928, 1064-1084.

Power, E. [4628] "The Church of St. Peter at Jerusalem: Its Relation to the House of Caiphas and Sancta Sion," Biblica, 9 (1928), 167-186.

Power, E. [4629] "The House of Caiphas and the Church of St. Peter," Biblica, 10(1929), 275-303, 394-416.

Power, E. [4630] "The House of Caiphas and the Pilgrim of Bordeaux," Biblica, 10(1929), 116-125.

Power, E. [4631] "A New Pre-Crusade Sanctuary of St. Stephen?" Biblica, 10 (1929), 85-93. [In the vicinity of the Cenacle.]

Power, E. [4632] "St. Peter in Gallicantu," Biblica, 12 (1931), 411-446.

Power, E. [4633] "The Upper Church of the Apostles in Jerusalem and the Lateran Sarcophagus no. 174," Biblica, 12(1931), 219-232.

Renoux, Charles. [4634] "L' Église de Sion dans les Homélies sur Job d' Hésychius de Jérusalem," Revue des Études Arméniennes, 18 (1984), 135-146.

Rock, Albert. [4635] Lo Statu Quo nei Luoghi Santi: La questione in generale e due circonstanze differenti ed emblematiche riguardanti il Cenaclo e la Cupola del S. Sepolcro. Jerusalem: Franciscan Printing Press, 1977, 63 pp.

Schick, Conrad. [4636] "Church at Dier ez Zeituny," Palestine Exploration Fund, Quarterly Statement, (1895), 249. [The Armenian Church of the Convent of the Olive Tree.]

Schick, Conrad. [4637] "Excavations by the Augustinian Brethren on Mount Zion," Palestine Exploration Fund, Quarterly Statement, (1894), 15-19. [St. Peter in Gallicantu.]

Schick, Conrad. [4638] "Excavations on the Eastern Brow of Zion," Palestine Exploration Fund, Quarterly Statement, (1890), 12-15. [St. Peter in Gallicantu.]

Schick, Conrad. [4639] "New Discoveries at the House of Caiphas, on the So-called Mt. Zion," Palestine Exploration Fund, Quarterly Statement, (1890), 247-248.

Schick, Conrad. [4640] "Searching for St. Peter's (or Cock-Crow) Church on Zion," Palestine Exploration Fund, Quarterly Statement, (1891), 19-20.

Schneider, Alfons Maria. [4641] "St. Peter in Gallicantu (Das Gefängnis Christi in Palast des Kaiphas)," Oriens Christianus, 27(1930), 175-190.

Sejourne, Paul-M. [4642] "Le Lieu de la dormition de la Très Sainte Vierge," Revue biblique, 8 (1899), 141-144.

Stewart, Aubrey and Wilson, Charles W. [4643] "The Position of Zion in the Fourth and Following Centuries," appendix to "Itinerary from Bordeaux to Jerusalem: The Bordeaux Pilgrim," in The Library of the Palestine Pilgrims' Text Society, 1. New York: AMS Press, 1971, 56-62. [Originally published in 1887.]

Testa, Emmanuele. [4644] "Le céne del Signore," La Terra Santa, (1965), 116-121.

Testa, Emmanuele. [4645] "Lo sviluppo della 'Dormitio Mariae' nella litturatura, nella teologia e nell' archeologia," Marianum, 44 (1982), 316-389.

Testa, Emmanuele. [4646] "La Nuova Sion," Studii Biblici Franciscani, Liber Annuus, 22 (1972), 48-73.

Tobler, Titus. [4647] "The Position of Sion in the Fourth, Fifth, and Sixth Centuries," Palestine Exploration Fund, Quarterly Statement, (1878), 16-17. [Sources, Latin texts.]

Vincent, Louis-Hugues. [4648] "Saint-Pierre-en-Gallicante," Revue biblique, 34 (1925), 586-587; 39 (1930), 226-256.

Watson, Charles M. [4649] "The Traditional Sites on Sion," Palestine Exploration Fund, Quarterly Statement, (1910), 196-220.

Wilkinson, John. [4650] Jerusalem as Jesus Knew It: Archaeology as Evidence. London: Thames and Hudson, 1978, 164-170. [On the early churches on Mt. Sion].

Wilson, Charles W. See Stewart, Aubrey and Wilson, Charles W. [4643]

Wilson, Charles W. [4651] "The Holy Places on Mount Sion and the Basilica of St. Sion," in appendix to A. Stewart and C. W. Wilson, "Of the Holy Places Visited by Antoninus Martyr (circ. 560-570 A.D.)," in The Library of the Palestine Pilgrims' Text Society, 2. New York: AMS Press, 1971, 42-44. [Originally published in 1896, London.]

Thirty-Two

The Churches of Gethsemane, the Mount of Olives, and Bethany

A. Gethsemane

Abel, Félix-M. [4652] "Inscription latin de Gethsémani," Revue biblique, 30(1921), 443-446.

Andrès, Pascal. [4653] "Mort et Sépulture de la Ste Vierge," La Terre Sainte, (Aug.-Sept., 1963), 200-207.

Arce, Augustín. [4654] "Culte islamique au Tombeau de la Vierge," in Atti del Congresso assunzionistico orientale. Jerusalem: Franciscan Printing Press, 1951, 175-194.

Arce, Augustín. [4655] Getsemaní, Jerusalem: Franciscan Printing Press, 1971, 48 pp.

Arce, Augustín. [4656] Getsemaní: Adquisición documentada del Huerto de los Olivos de la Gruta de Getsemaní, de varios olivares. Cuadernos de "Tierra Santa," 6. Jerusalem: Franciscan Printing Press, 1971, 46 pp.

Avi-Yonah, Michael. [4657] "Mosaic Pavements in Palestine: Jerusalem, Gethsemane," in Art in Ancient Palestine. Collected and prepared for republication by H. Katzenstein and Y. Tsafrir. Jerusalem: Magnes Press, 1981, 311. [Originally published in Quarterly of the Department of Antiquities in Palestine, 2 (1932), 164.]

Bagatti, Bellarmino. [4658] "L'apertura della Tomba della Vergine a Getsemani," Studii Biblici Franciscani, Liber Annuus, 23 (1973), 318-321.

Bagatti, Bellarmino. [4659] "Jérusalem: Tombeau de la Vierge," Revue biblique, 80 (1973), 581-582.

Bagatti, Bellarmino. [4660] "Novas descobertas sobre a tumba de Virgen no Getsémani," Revista de Cultura Teológica, 10 (1973), 47-48.

Bagatti, Bellarmino. [4661] "Nuove scoperte alla Tomba della Vergine a Getsemani," Studii Biblici Franciscani, Liber Annuus, 22 (1972), 236-290.

Bagatti, Bellarmino. [4662] "Le origine della 'tomba della Vergine' a Getsemani," Rivista Biblica, 11 (1963), 38-52.

Bagatti, Bellarmino. [4663] "Scoperte archeologiche alla Tomba di Maria a Getsemani," Marianum, 34 (1972), 193-199.

32A/Gethsemane

Bagatti, Bellarmino. [4664] "Tempera dell' antica basilica di Getsemani," Revista di Archeologia Christanna, 15 (1938), 153-162.

Bagatti, Bellarmino. [4665] "Le Tombeau de la Vierge," La Terre Sainte, (May, 1973), 149-157.

Bagatti, Bellarmino. [4666] "La Tombo de la Virgulino," Biblia Revuo, 8 (1972), 161-169.

Bagatti, Bellarmino; Piccirillo, Michele; Prodomo, Alberto. [4667] New Discoveries at the Tomb of the Virgin Mary in Gethsemane. Studium Biblicum Franciscanum, Collectio Minor, 17. Jerusalem: Franciscan Printing Press, 1975, 95 pp. + 35 pls.

Bahat, Dan. [4668] Jerusalem: Selected Plans of Historical Sites and Monumental Buildings. Jerusalem: Ariel, 1980, 107-110.

Barluzzi, A. [4669] "Del modo migliore per far visitare il santuario del Getsemani," La Terra Santa, 24 (1949), 161-165.

Barluzzi, A. [4670] "Il mosaico del l' abside nel Santuario del Getsemani," La Terra Santa, 24 (1949), 135-140.

Brunot, Amédée. [4671] "Gethsémani," Bible et Terre Sainte, 99 (1968), 8-16.

Corbo, Virgilio. [4672] "Dans la vallée de Josaphat: Le culte de Sainte Jacques et le tombeau des Beni Hezir a Jérusalem," Bible et Terre Sainte, 56 (1963), 20-23.

Corbo, Virgilio. [4673] "Gli scavi della grotta del Gethsemani," La Terre Santa, 33 (1957), 161-171.

Corbo, Virgilio. [4674] Ricerche archeologiche al Monte degli Ulivi. Studium Biblicum Franciscanum, Collectio Major,16. Jerusalem: Franciscan Printing Press, 1965, 167 pp. + 118 figs. [In two parts-- the first on the Cave of Gethsemane, the second on the Church of the Ascension.]

Cullmann, Oscar. [4675] "Jardin de prière-- jardin oecumenique sur le Mont des Oliviers," Communio Viatorum, 24/1-2 (1981), 1-5.

Cust, L. G. A. [4676] "The Tomb of the Virgin at Gethsemane," in The Status Quo in the Holy Places. Jerusalem: Ariel, 1980, 34-36. [Originally published in 1929.]

Diez Merino, Luis. [4678] "The Tomb of Mary," The Bible Today, 72 (1974), 1619-1632.

Finegan, Jack. [4679] "The Mount of Olives and the Gethsemane Church, / Plan of the Gethsemane Area, / Plan of the Gethsemane Church," in The Archeology of the New Testament: The Life of Jesus and the Beginning of the Early Church. Princeton: Princeton University Press, 1969, 104-108.

Hammerschmidt, Ernst. [4680] " Die Marienkirche in Gethsemane und das äthiopische Ta'amra Maryam," in Theokratia: Jahrbuch des Institutum Judaicum Delitzschianum, 2 (1970-72). Leiden: Brill, 1973, 3-6.

Hoade, Eugene. [4681] "Church of the Assumption / Gethsemane," in Guide to the Holy Land. Jerusalem: Franciscan Printing Press, 1984, 225-239.

Johns, C. N. [4682] "The Abbey of Saint Mary in the Valley of Jehoshaphat, Jerusalem," Quarterly of the Department of Antiquities in Palestine, 8 (1938), 117-136.

Joseph, Frederick. [4683] "Gethsemane," Holy Land Review, 2/1 (Spring, 1976), 3-12.

Katsimbinis, Christos. [4684] "New Findings at Gethsemane," Studii Biblici Franciscani, Liber Annuus, 26 (1976), 277-280.

Keppler, Paul. [4685] "Gethsemane," Theologische Quartalschrift, 75 (1893), 430-455.

Kopp, Clemens. [4686] "Das Mariengrab in Jerusalem," Theologie und Glaube, 2 (1955), 81-94.

Kopp, Clemens. [4687] Das Mariengrab: Jerusalem? Ephesus? Paderborn: Ferdinand Schönigh, 1955, 46 pp.

Lagrange, Marie-Joseph. [4688] "La basilique de Gethsémani," Revue biblique, 29 (1920), 137.

Manns, Frederic. [4689] "The Virgin's Tomb: Jerusalem or Ephesus?" The Holy Land, 5/3 (Fall, 1985), 115-118.

Meistermann, Barnabé. [4690] Gethsémani: Notices historiques et descriptives. Paris: Picard, 1920. 335 pp.

Orfali, Gaudence. [4691] Gethsémani: Notice sur l' Église de l' Agonie ou de la Prière d' après les fouilles récentes accomplies par la Custodie Françiscaine de Terre Sainte (1909 et 1920). Paris: Picard, 1924, 34 pp.

Piccirillo, Michele. See Bagatti, Bellarmino; Piccirillo, Michele; and Prodomo, Alberto. [4667]

Piccirillo, Michele. [4692] "L' edicola crociata sulla Tomba della Madonna," Studii Biblici Franciscani, Liber Annuus, 22(1972), 291-314.

Prodomo, Alberto. See Bagatti, Bellarmino; Piccirillo, Michele; and Prodomo, Alberto. [4667]

Prodomo, Alberto. [4693] "La tomba della Regina Melisenda al Getsemani," Studii Biblici Franciscani, Liber Annuus, 24 (1974), 202-226.

Spyridonidis, C. K. [4694] "The Church of St. Stephen," Palestine Exploration Fund, Quarterly Statement, (1907), 137-139. [The Greek Orthodox site near the Virgin's Tomb.]

Storme, Albert. [4695] Gethsemane. Jerusalem: Franciscan Printing Press, 2nd ed., 1972, 112 pp. [English; editions also in French, German, Italian, and Spanish.]

Trusen, H. W. [4696] "Geschichte von Gethsemane, " Zeitschrift des deutschen Palästina-Vereins, 33 (1910), 57-97.

Vincent, Louis-Hugues. [4697] "À propos de Gethsémani," Revue biblique, 29 (1920), 169-172.

Vincent, Louis-Hugues. [4698] "L' Églese de Gethsémani," Revue biblique, 28 (1919), 248-252; 29 (1920), 574-576.

Vincent, Louis-Hugues. [4699] "Encore l' inscription de Sainte Étienne à Gethsémani," Revue biblique, 16 (1907), 607-611.

White, L., Jr. [4700] "Forged Letter Concerning the Existance of Latin Monks at St. Mary's Jehosaphat before the First Crusade," Speculum, 9 (1934), 404-407.

Wilkinson, John. [4701] "Gethsemane," in Jerusalem as Jesus Knew It: Archaeology as Evidence. London: Thames and Hudson, 1978, 125-131.

32. B. Mount of Olives

Abel, Félix-M. See Vincent, Louis-Hugues and Abel, Félix-M. [4762]

Abel, Félix-M. [4702] "Mont des Oliviers: Ruine de la grotte de l' Éléona tombeau et mosaïque," Revue biblique, 27 (1918), 555-558.

Avi-Yonah, Michael. [4703] "Mosaic Pavements in Palestine: Jerusalem, Mount of Olives," in Art in Ancient Palestine. Collected and prepared for republication by H. Katzenstein and Y. Tsafrir. Jerusalem: Magnes Press, 1981, 312-316. [Originally published in Quarterly of the Department of Antiquities in Palestine, 2 (1932), 165-169.]

Bagatti, Bellarmino. [4704] "The Constantinian Sacred Edifices: The Church of Eleona," in The Church from the Gentiles in Palestine, History and Archeology. Studium Biblicum Franciscanum, Collectio Minor, 4. Jerusalem: Franciscan Printing Press, 1971; reprinted, 1984, 184-190.

Bagatti, Bellarmino. [4705] "Dominus Flevit: Un Lieu-Saint au flanc du Mont des Oliviers," La Terre Sainte, (April-June, 1957), 61-64.

Bagatti, Bellarmino. [4706] "'Footprints' of the Saviour on the Mount of Olives," The Holy Land, 3/2 (Summer, 1983), 51-52.

Bagatti, Bellarmino. [4707] "Oliviers, mont des," in H. Cazelles and A. Feuillet (eds.), Supplément au Dictionnaire de la Bible, 6. Paris: Letouzey et Ané, 1959, 688-699.

Bagatti, Bellarmino. [4708] "Scavo di un monasterio al 'Dominus Flevit,'" Studii Biblici Franciscani, Liber Annuus, 6 (1955/56), 240-270.

Bahat, Dan. [4709] Jerusalem: Selected Plans of Historical Sites and Monumental Buildings. Jerusalem: Ariel, 1980, 111-114.

Barrois, Georges Augustin. [4710] "Olives, Mount of," in Interpreter's Dictionary of the Bible, 3. New York: Abingdon, 1962, 596-599.

Becq, Jean. [4711] "La montagne de l' orient," Bible et Terre Sainte, 136 (1971), 3-4.

Blenkinsopp, Joseph. [4712] "The Lord's Prayer and the Hill of Olives," Heythrop Journal, 3 (1962), 169-171.

Clark, Elizabeth A. [4713] "Claims on the Bones of Saint Stephen: The Partisans of Melania and Eudocia," Church History, 51/2 (June, 1982), 141-156.

Clermont-Ganneau, Charles. [4714] "The Mount of Olives," in Archaeological Researches in Palestine during the Years 1873-1874, 1. Translated by Aubrey Stewart. London: Palestine Exploration Fund, 1896, 325-380.

Clermont-Ganneau, Charles. [4715] "La Pierre de Bethphagé: Fresques et inscriptions des Croisés récemment découvertes auprès de Jérusalem," Revue archeologique, 18th year; 34 (1877/B), 366-388.

Clermont-Ganneau, Charles. [4716] "The Stone of Bethphage," Palestine Exploration Fund, Quarterly Statement, (1878), 51-60.

Clermont-Ganneau, Charles. [4717] "The Stone of Bethphage," in C. Warren and C. R. Conder, The Survey of Western Palestine, 5: Jerusalem. London: Palestine Exploration Fund, 1884, 331-340.

Clermont-Ganneau, Charles. [4718] "Votive Paten Discovered on the Mount of Olives," Palestine Exploration Fund, Quarterly Statement, (1884), 190-191.

Corbo, Virgilio. [4719] "'Dominus Flevit:' Il nuovo santuario construito sulle pendici dell' Oliveto," La Terra Santa, 33/8-9 (Aug.- Sept., 1957), 246-249.

Corbo, Virgilio. [4720] "Il rinnovato santuario di Betfage," La Terra Santa, 31/11 (Nov., 1955), 338-341.

Corbo, Virgilio. [4721] Ricerche archeologiche al Monte degli Ulivi. Studium Biblicum Franciscanum, Collectio Major,16. Jerusalem: Franciscan Printing Press, 1965, 167 pp. + 118 figs. [In two parts-- the first on the Cave of Gethsemane, the second on the Church of the Ascension.]

Corbo, Virgilio. [4722] "Scavo archeologico a ridosso della basilica dell' Ascensione," Studii Biblici Franciscani, Liber Annuus, 10 (1959/60), 205-248. Also in La Terra Santa, 37/1 (Jan., 1961), 31-32.

Curtis, John B. [4723] "An Investigation of the Mount of Olives in the Judaeo-Christian Tradition," Hebrew Union College Annual, 28 (1957), 137-177.

Cust, L. G. A. [4724] "The Sanctuary of the Ascension," in The Status Quo in the Holy Places. Jerusalem: Ariel, 1980, 33-34. [Originally published in 1929.]

Dalmais, I.-H. [4725] "L' Éléona," Bible et Terre Sainte, 29 (1960), 8-11.

Dalman, Gustaf. [4726] "Der Ölberg zur Himmelfahrtszeit," Palästinajahrbuch, 12 (1916), 58-75.

Desjardins, B. [4727] "Les vestiges du Seigneur au mont des Oliviers: Un courant mystique et iconographie," Bulletin de Littérature Ecclésiastique, 73 (1972), 51-72.

Devos, P. [4727A] "Égérie n' a pas connu d' Église de l' Ascension," Analecta Bollandiana, 87 (1969), 208-212.

Englebert, O. [4728] The Grotto of the Lord's Prayer. Jerusalem: Franciscan Printing Press, 1969, 16 pp.

Finegan, Jack. [4729] "The Franciscan Chapel at Bethphage, / The Crypt of the Eleona Church, / Plan and Section of the Eleona Church, The Church of the Lord's Prayer, / Plan by Arculf of the Church of the Holy Ascension, / Mosque of the Ascension on the Mount of Olives, / Franciscan Chapel at Dominus Flevit," in Archeology of the New Testament: The Life of Jesus and the Beginning of the Early Church. Princeton: Princeton University Press, 1969, 90-91, 95-102.

32B/Mount of Olives

Fransen, Irénée. [4730] "Le mont des Oliviers," Bible et Terre Sainte, 136 (1971), 8-17.

Hoade, Eugene. [4731] "Mount of Olives," in Guide to the Holy Land. Jerusalem: Franciscan Printing Press, 1984, 252-273.

King, James. [4732] "The Stone of Bethphage," Palestine Exploration Fund, Quarterly Statement, (1878), 146-149.

Kretschmar, Georg. [4733] "Festkalendar und Memorialstätten Jerusalems in altkirchlichen Zeit: IV. Der Ölberg als Stätte der Himmelfahrt," Zeitschrift des deutschen Palästina-Vereins, 87 (1971), 183-205.

Kühnel, Bianca. [4734] "Crusader Sculpture at the Ascension Church on the Mount of Olives in Jerusalem," Gesta: International Center of Medieval Art, 16/2 (1977), 41-50.

Kühnel, Bianca. [4735] "The Date of the Crusader Church of the Ascension on the Mount of Olives," in B. Z. Kedar (ed.), Jerusalem in the Middle Ages, Selected Papers. Jerusalem: Yad Izhaq Ben-Zvi, 1979, 327-337 (Hebrew), xxv-xxvi (English summary). English summary also in "From the Hebrew Press: Jerusalem in the Middle Ages, Selected Documents (Yad Izhaq Ben-Zvi, Jerusalem, 1979)," in L. I. Levine (ed.), Jerusalem Cathedra, 2. Jerusalem: Yad Izhaq Ben Zvi Institute / Detroit: Wayne State University Press, 1982, 326-327.

Lagrange, Marie-Joseph. [4736] "Épigraphie sémitique: Une inscription trouvée au mont Sion et une autre au mont des Oliviers," Revue biblique, 2 (1893), 220-222.

La Sor, William S. [4737] "Olives, Mount of," in G. W. Bromiley (ed.), The International Bible Encyclopedia, 3. Grand Rapids: Eerdmans, 1986, 589-591.

La Sor, William S. [4738] "The Sanctity of the Mount of Olives," Christian News from Israel, 13/3-4 (1962), 16-23.

Lemor, Ora. [4739] Byzantine-Arab Era Christian Traditions about Mt. Olivet. Jerusalem: Hebrew University, 1978, 182 pp. (Hebrew).

Lethaby, W. R. [4740] "The Temple, the Church of the Ascension, and the Finding of the Cross," Palestine Exploration Fund, Quarterly Statement, (1897), 75-77.

Mann, Sylvia. [4741] "The Mount of Olives: The Mountain of Everlasting Life," Christian News from Israel, 25/1 (1974), 17-22.

Manns, Frédéric. [4742] "A New Mosaic Pavement on the Mount of Olives," Holy Land Review, 4/2-4 (Summer-Winter, 1978), 92-94.

Masterman, Ernest W. Gurney. [4743] "Mount of Olives," in J. (ed.), Dictionary of Christ and the Gospels, 2. New York: Scribner's, 1906, 206-208.

Murphy- O'Connor, Jerome. [4744] "The Mount of Olives," in The Holy Land: An Archaeological Guide from Earliest Times to 1700. Oxford: Oxford University Press, 1980, 84-97.

Murray, A. S. [4745] "Greek Mosaic Inscription from the Mount of Olives," Palestine Exploration Fund, Quarterly Statement, (1895), 86.

Reiss, Dr. [4746] "Reste eines alten armenischen Klosters auf dem Ölberg und die daselbst aufgefundenen Inschriften," Zeitschrift des deutschen Palästina-Vereins, 8 (1885), 155-161.

René-Burtin, R. P. [4747] "Un texte d' Eutychius relatif a l' Éléona," Revue biblique, 23 (1914), 401-423.

Saller, Sylvester J. [4748] "The Archaeological Setting of the Shrine at Bethphage," Studii Biblici Franciscani, Liber Annuus, 11 (1960/1961), 172-250.

Saller, Sylvester J. and Testa, Emmanuele. [4749] The Archaeological Setting of the Shrine of Bethphage. Studium Biblicum Francescanum, Collectio Minor, 1. Jerusalem: Franciscan Printing Press, 1961, 120 pp.

Schick, Conrad. [4750] "The Church of the Ascension on the Mount of Olives," Palestine Exploration Fund, Quarterly Statement, (1896), 310-327.

Schick, Conrad. [4751] "The Mount of Olives," Palestine Exploration Fund, Quarterly Statement, (1889), 174-184.

Schick, Conrad. [4752] "Recent Discoveries on the Mount of Olives," Palestine Exploration Fund, Quarterly Statement, (1895), 32-37.

Schick, Conrad. [4753] "Some Excavations on the Mount of Olives," Palestine Exploration Fund, Quarterly Statement, (1890), 256-257.

Séjourné, Paul-M. [4754] "Nouvelles mosaïques au mont des Oliviers avec inscription arménienne," Revue biblique, 2 (1893), 241-242.

Storme, Albert. [4755] Le Mont des Oliviers. Jerusalem: Franciscan Printing Press, 1971, 176 pp.

Talik, F. [4756] "Der Ölberg und seine Heiligtümer," Das Heilige Land, 111 (1979), 2-9.

Testa, Emmanuele. See Saller, Sylvester J. and Testa, Emmanuele. [4749]

Vincent, Louis-Hugues. [4757] "L' Église de l' Éléona," Revue biblique, 20 (1911), 219-265.

Vincent, Louis-Hugues. [4758] "L' Éléona, sanctuarie primitif de l' Ascension," Revue biblique, 64 (1957), 48-71.

Vincent, Louis-Hugues. [4759] "Une mosaïque chrétienne au mont des Oliviers," Revue biblique, 17 (1908), 122-125.

Vincent, Louis-Hugues. [4760] "La restauration de l' Éléona," Revue biblique, 29 (1920), 267-269.

Vincent, Louis-Hugues. [4761] "Le Tombeau des prophètes," Revue biblique, 10 (1901), 72-88.

Vincent, Louis-Hugues and Abel, Félix-M. [4762] "Les sanctuaries du mont des Oliviers," in Jérusalem: Recherches de topographie d' archéologie et d' histoire, 2: Jérusalem nouvelle, 1-2. Paris: Gabalda, 1914, 301-419.

Warren, Charles. [4763] "Mount of Olives," in J. Hastings (ed.), Dictionary of the Bible, 3. New York, Scribner's, 1898, 616-620.

Wilkinson, John. [4764] "From Earth to Heaven," in Jerusalem as Jesus Knew It: Archaeology as Evidence. London: Thames and Hudson, 1978, 172-175. [Church of the Ascension.]

32. C. Bethany

Benoit, Pierre and Boismard, M. E. [4765] "Un ancien sanctuaire chrétien à Béthanie," *Revue biblique*, 58 (1951), 200-251.

Boismard, M. E. See Benoit, Pierre and Boismard, M. E. [4765]

Brunot, Amédée. [4766] "Béthanie et ses environs," *Bible et Terre Sainte*, 163 (1974), 7-16.

Clarisse, Fernand. [4767] "Béthanie," *La Terre Sainte*, (April-June, 1960), 56-66.

Finegan, Jack. [4768] "The Village of Bethany, / Plan of the Tomb of Lazarus and Adjacent Buildings, / The Tomb of Lazarus, / Mosaic Pavement of the First Century at Bethany, / The New Church of St. Lazarus at Bethany," in *Archeology of the New Testament: The Life of Jesus and the Beginning of the Early Church*. Princeton: Princeton University Press, 1969, 91-95.

Hoade, Eugene. [4769] "Bethany," in *Guide to the Holy Land*. Jerusalem: Franciscan Printing Press, 1984, 462-472.

Kloetzli, Godfrey. [4770] "Bethany," *Holy Land Review*, 2/4 (Winter, 1976), 99-111.

Saller, Sylvester J. [4771] *Excavations at Bethany, 1949-1953*. *Studium Biblicum Franciscanum, Collectio Major*, 12. Jerusalem: Franciscan Printing Press, 1957, 398 pp. + 134 pls.

Saller, Sylvester J. [4772] "Excavations in the Ancient Town of Bethany," *Studii Biblici Franciscani, Liber Annuus*, 2 (1952), 119-162.

Storme, Albert. [4773] *Bethany*. Jerusalem: Franciscan Printing Press, 1979, 100 pp. [English; editions also in French, German, and Italian.]

Wilkinson, John. [4774] "The Raising of Lazarus," in *Jerusalem as Jesus Knew It: Archaeology as Evidence*. London: Thames and Hudson, 1978, 108-113. [Church around the Tomb of Lazarus.]

Thirty-Three

The Pool of Bethesda and the Church of St. Anne

Avi-Yonah, Michael. [4775] "Mosaic Pavements in Palestine: Jerusalem, St. Anna," in Art in Ancient Palestine. Collected and prepared for republication by H. Katzenstein and Y. Tsafrir. Jerusalem: Magnes Press, 1981, 323. [Originally published in Quarterly of the Department of Antiquities in Palestine, 2 (1932), 176.]

Bagatti, Bellarmino. [4776] "Béthesda, la piscine aux cinq portiques," La Terre Sainte, (April- June, 1959), 66-68.

Bagatti, Bellarmino. [4777] "Il lento disseppellimento della piscina probatica a Gerusalemme," Bibbia e Oriente, 1 (1959), 12-14.

Bahat, Dan. [4778] "À propos de l' église des 'Sept- Douleurs' à Jérusalem," Revue biblique, 85 (1978), 81-83.

Bahat, Dan. [4779] Jerusalem: Selected Plans of Historical Sites and Monumental Buildings. Jerusalem: Ariel, 1980, 73-75.

Baldi, Donato. [4780] "Il santuario dell' Immacolata Concezione a Gerusalemme: Origini, storia, cuto dei Francescani," Antonianum, 29 (1954), 523-542.

Bassi, Alexandre. [4781] L' Antica chiesa Sant' Anna in Gerusalemme. Jerusalem: Franciscan Printing Press, 1863, 157 pp.

Benoit, Pierre. [4782] "Découvertes archéologiques autour de la Piscine de Béthesda," in J. Aviram (ed.), Jerusalem through the Ages. Jerusalem: Israel Exploration Society, 1968, 48-57.

Bissoli, Giovanni. [4783] "S. Cirillo di Gerusalemme: Omelia sul paralitico della piscina Probatica," Studii Biblici Franciscani, Liber Annuus, 31(1981), 177-190.

Clark, K. W. [4784] "Beth-Zatha," in Interpreter's Dictionary of the Bible, 1. New York: Abingdon, 1962, 404.

Conder, Claude R. [4785] "Bethesda," in J. Hastings (ed.), Dictionary of the Bible, 1. New York: Scribner's, 1898, 279.

Conder, Claude R. [4786] "Bezetha," Palestine Exploration Fund, Quarterly Statement, 22 (1890), 122-123.

Conder, Claude R. [4787] "The Piscina Interior," note to "The City of Jerusalem (1220 A.D.)," in The Library of the Palestine Pilgrims' Text Society, 6. New York: AMS Press, 1971, 65-69. [Originally published in 1896.]

Cré, Léon. [4788] "Discovery at the Pool of Bethesda," Palestine Exploration Fund, Quarterly Statement, (1901), 163-165.

Cré, Léon. [4789] "Recerche et découverts du tombeau de St. Joachim et de Ste. Anne sous l' antique Basilique de Sainte-Anne, à Jérusalem," Revue biblique, 2 (1893), 245-274.

Del Verme, M. [4790] "La piscina probatica: Gv. 5, 1-9: Un problema di critica testuale e di esegesi di fronte ai risultati degli ultimi scavi," Bibbia e Oriente, 18 (1976), 109-119.

Díez Fernández, Florentino. [4791] "Crónica arqueológica: Jerusalén," Estudios Bíblicus, 42 (1984), 421-422.

Duprez, A. [4792] Jesus et les Dieux Guerisseurs: À propos de Jean, V. Cahiers de la Revue biblique, 12. Paris: Gabalda, 1970, 184 pp. + 25 pls.

Duprez, A. [4793] "La piscine probatique," Bible et Terre Sainte, 86 (1966), 4-15.

Duprez, A. [4794] "Probatique (Piscine)," in H. Cazelles and A. Fevillet (eds.), Supplément au Dictionnaire de la Bible, 8. Paris: Letouzey et Anè, 1972, 606-621.

Finegan, Jack. [4795] "The Church of St. Anne, / Excavations at the Pool of Bethesda," in The Archeology of the New Testament: The Life of Jesus and the Beginning of the Early Church. Princeton: Princeton University Press, 1969, 142-147.

Hamilton, R. W. [4796] "Note on the Recent Discoveries outside St. Stephen's Gate, Jerusalem," Quarterly of the Department of Antiquities in Palestine, 6 (1937/38), 153-156. [Private tomb of Amos, deacon of the Probatike; Byzantine period.]

Hoade, Eugene. [4797] "St. Anne's / Bethesda," in Guide to the Holy Land. Jerusalem: Franciscan Printing Press, 1984, 205-215.

Jeremias, Joachim. [4798] "The Copper Scroll From Qumran," Expository Times, 71 (1959-60), 227-228. [On reference to the pool of Bethesda in 3Q 15.]

Jeremias, Joachim. [4799] "Die Kupferrolle von Qumran und Bethesda," in Abba: Studien zur neutestamentlichen Theologie und Zeitgeschichte. Göttingen: Vandenhoeck and Ruprecht, 1966, 361-364.

Jeremias, Joachim. [4800] The Rediscovery of Bethesda. New Testament Archaeology Monographs, 1. Louisville, KY: Southern Baptist Theological Seminary, 1966, 38 pp.

Jeremias, Joachim. [4801] Die Wiederentdeckung von Bethesda, Johannes 5, 2. Forschungen zur Religion und Literatur des Alten und Neuen Testaments, 41. Göttingen: Vandenhoeck und Ruprecht, 1949, 26 pp.

Jérusalem, Sainte-Anne / St. Anne's, Jerusalem. [4802] Photographs (hitherto unpublished) by Zodiaque. Jerusalem: Sainte-Anne, 1963, 64 pp.

Klinger, J. [4803] "Bethesda and the Universality of the Logos," St. Vladimir's Theological Quarterly, 27 (1983), 169-185.

Lagrange, Marie-Joseph and Vincent, Louis-Hugues. [4804] "Bésétha," in Floilegium M. de Vogüé. Paris: Imp. Nationale, 1909, 329-348.

Macalister, R. A Stewart. [4805] "The Crypts in St. Anne's Church, Jerusalem," Palestine Exploration Fund, Quarterly Statement, (1905), 144-148.

Masterman, Ernest W. Gurney. [4806] "The Pool of Bethesda," Palestine Exploration Fund, Quarterly Statement, (1921), 91-100.

Mauss, C. [4807] Inventiòn du tombeau de' Sainte Anne à Jérusalem. Paris: Leroux, 1893, 15 pp.

Mauss, C. [4808] La Piscine de Bethesda à Jérusalem. Paris: Leroux, 1889, 83 pp.

Mommert, Carl. [4809] Der Teich Bethesda zu Jerusalem und das Jerusalem des Pilgers von Bordeaux nebst Anhang: Die Grabeskirsche zu Jerusalem auf der Mossaikkarte. Leipzig: E. Haberland, 1907, 88 pp.

Moore, W. W. [4810] "Bethesda," in J. Hastings (ed.), Dictionary of Christ and the Gospels, 1. New York: Scribner's, 1906, 193-195.

Murphy- O'Connor, Jerome. [4811] "St. Anne's," in The Holy Land: An Archaeological Guide from Earliest Times to 1700. Oxford: Oxford University Press, 1980, 22-24.

Pierre, Marie-Joseph and Rousée, Jourdain-Marie. [4812] "Sainte-Marie de la Probatique, état et orientation des recherches," Proche-Orient Chrétien, 31 (1981), 23-42.

Rousée, Jourdain-Marie. See Pierre, Marie-Joseph and Rousée, Jourdain-Marie. [4812]

Rousée, Jourdain-Marie. See de Vaux, Roland and Rousée, Jourdain-Marie. [4823]

Rousée, Jourdain-Marie. [4813] "Jérusalem (Piscine probatique)," Revue biblique, 69 (1962), 107-108.

Rousée, Jourdain-Marie. [4814] "L' Église Sainte-Marie de la Probatique: Chronologie des sanctuaires à Sainte-Anne de Jérusalem d' après les fouilles récentes," in Atti del VI Congresso Internaz. di Arch. Christ. (Ravenna, 1962). Studi di Antichita Christiana, 26. Roma: Pontif. Inst. di Arch. Christ, 1965. 169-176.

Schick, Conrad. [4815] "Further Report on the Pool of Bethesda," Palestine Exploration Fund, Quarterly Statement, (1890), 18-20.

Schick, Conrad. [4816] "The Pool of Bethesda," Palestine Exploration Fund, Quarterly Statement, (1888), 115-134.

Schick, Conrad. [4817] "Der Teich Bethesda in Jerusalem," Zeitschrift des deutschen Palästina-Vereins, 11, (1888), 178-183.

Seidensticker, Philipp. [4818] "Legende und Geschichte um Mariä Geburt: Die Kirche St. Anna in Jerusalem," Das Heilige Land, 86 (1954), 48-51.

Staub, Urs. [4819] "Das Heiligtum der heiligen Anna in Jerusalem," Das Heilige Land, 4/4 (1976), 51-57.

Tamari, D. S. [4820] "Sulla conversione della chiesa di Sant' Anna a Gerusalemme nella Madrasa as-Salahiyya," Rivista degli studi Orientali, 43 (1968), 327-254.

Testa, Emmanuele. [4821] "La piscina probatique, monumento pagano o guidaico?" La Terra Santa, (1964), 311-316.

Van Der Vliet, N. [4822] "Sainte Marie où elle est née" et la Piscine Probatique. Paris: Gabalda, 1938, 211 pp.

de Vaux, Roland and Rousée, Jourdain-Marie. [4823] "Jérusalem," Revue biblique, 64 (1957), 226-228.

Vincent, Louis-Hugues. See Lagrange, Marie-Joseph and Vincent, Louis-Hugues. [4804]

Vincent, Louis-Hugues. [4824] "La crypte de Sainte-Anne à Jérusalem," Revue biblique, 13 (1904), 228-241.

Wieland, David J. [4825] "Bethesda," in International Standard Bible Encyclopedia, 1. Grand Rapids, MI: Eerdmans, 1979, 467-468.

Wieland, David J. [4826] "John V. 2 and the Pool of Bethesda," New Testament Studies, 12 (1965-66), 392-404.

Wilkinson, John. [4827] "At Bethesda," in Jerusalem as Jesus Knew It: Archaeology as Evidence. London: Thames and Hudson, 1978, 95-104.

Wilson, Charles W. [4828] [On questions connected with the Pool of Bethesda] "Appendix 3," in A. Stewart and C. W. Wilson, "Itinerary from Bordeaux to Jerusalem: The Bordeaux Pilgrim," in The Library of the Palestine Pilgrim's Text Society, 1. New York: AMS Press, 1971, 45-55. [Originally published in 1887.]

Thirty-Four

The Praetorium and the Way of the Cross

Abel, Félix-M. See Vincent, Louis-Hugues and Abel, Félix-M. [4915]

Adinolfi, M. [4829] *La Via Crucis a Gerusalemme: Tre modi diversi di rivivere la Passione di Gesù ispirati alla Liturgia e alla Scrittura*. Jerusalem: Franciscan Printing Press, 1974, 112 pp.

Adinolfi, M. [4830] *The Way of the Cross, as Made by the Franciscans in Jerusalem on the Via Dolorosa every Friday at 3 O'Clock*. Jerusalem: Franciscan Printing Press, 1981, 38 pp.

Aline de Sion, Marie. [4831] *La Fortresse Antonia à Jérusalem at la question du Prétoire*. Paris: L' Universite' de Paris, 1955 / Jerusalem: Franciscan Printing Press, 1956, 304 pp. + 76 pls.

von Alten, Baron. [4832] "Die Antonia und ihre Umgebungen," *Zeitschrift des deutschen Palästina-Vereins*, 1 (1878), 61-100.

Andres, Isaias. [4833] "Une moniale orientale: Origines liturgiques de la 'Via Dolorosa'", *La Terre Sainte*, (March, 1968), 86-91.

Así, M. Leonide Guyo. [4834] "Le Prétoire," *Revue Augustinienne*, (1903), 501-513. [Early advocate of praetorium at Hasmonaean palace.]

Avi-Yonah, Michael. [4835] "Mosaic Pavements in Palestine: Jerusalem, Via Dolorosa," in *Art in Ancient Palestine*. Collected and prepared for republication by H. Katzenstein and Y. Tsafrir. Jerusalem: Magnes Press, 1981, 325. [Originally published in *Quarterly of the Department of Antiquities in Palestine*, 2 (1932), 178.]

Baggatti, B. [4836] "Resti romani nell' area della Flagellazione in Gerusalemme," *Studii Biblici Franciscani, Liber Annuus*, 8 (1957/1958), 316-318; 9 (1958/59), 309-352.

Bagatti, Bellarmino. [4837] "La Tradizione della chiesa di Gerusalemme sul pretorio," *Rivista Biblica*, 21 (1973), 429-432. [Article relates to B. Pixner's theory of the praetorium as the Hasmonaean palace.]

Bahat, Dan. [4838] *Jerusalem: Selected Plans of Historical Sites and Monumental Buildings*. Jerusalem: Ariel, 1980, 76-79.

Benoit, Pierre. [4839] "L' Antonia d' Hérode le Grand et le forum oriental d' Aelia Capitolina," *Harvard Theological Review*, 64 (1971), 135-167. Reprinted with some updating in *Exégèse et théologie*, 4 Paris: Cerf, 1982, 311-346.

34/The Praetorium and the Way of the Cross

Benoit, Pierre. [4840] "The Archeological Reconstruction of the Antonia Fortress," in Y. Yadin (ed.), Jerusalem Revealed: Archaeology in the Holy City, 1968-1974. New Haven and London: Yale University Press and the Israel Exploration Society, 1976, 87-89.

Benoit, Pierre. [4841] "De la forteresse Antonia: La reconstitution archéolgique," Australian Journal of Biblical Archeology, 1/6 (1973), 16-22.

Benoit, Pierre. [4842] "Prétoire, Lithostroton et Gabbatha," Revue biblique, 59 (1952), 531-550.

Benoit, Pierre. [4843] "Praetorium, Lithostroton and Gabbatha," in Jesus and the Gospel, 1. New York: Herder and Herder, 1973, 167-188.

Benoit, Pierre. [4844] "Le Prétoire de Pilate à l' époque byzantine, " Revue biblique, 91 (1984), 161-177.

Benoit, Pierre. [4845] "Reconstitution archéologique de l' Antonia," Bible et Terre Sainte, 159 (1974), 2-5.

Blomme, Y. [4846] "Faut-il revenir sur la datation de l' arc de l' Ecce Homo," Revue biblique, 86 (1979), 244-271.

Bondvelle, J. [4847] "Autour du Chemin de Croix," La Vie Spirituelle, 86 (1952), 287-295.

Brandys, Massimiliano. [4848] "Via Crucis," Enciclopedia Cattolica, 12. Città del Vaticano: L' Enciclopedia Cattolica e par Il Libro Cattolico, 1954, 1348-1350.

Brown, B. [4849] "Way of the Cross," in New Catholic Encyclopedia, 14. New York: McGraw-Hill, 1967, 832-835.

Burrows, Millar. [4850] "The Fortress Antonia and the Praetorium," Biblical Archeologist, 1 (1938), 17-19.

Canney, M. A. [4851] "Praetorium," in T. K. Cheyne and J. S. Black (eds.), Encyclopaedia Biblica, 3. New York: Macmillan, 1902, 3822-3823.

Cerny, Edward A. [4852] "Lithostrotos," Catholic Biblical Quarterly, 4 (1942), 159-160.

Clarisse, Fernando. [4853] "Le prétoire de Pilate chez les religieuses de Sion à Jérusalem," La Terre Sainte, (July- September, 1958), 127-132.

Clermont-Ganneau, Charles. [4854] "Excavations at the Scarp of the Rock and in the Caves near the 'Ecce Homo' Arch", in Archaeological Researches in Palestine during the Years 1873-1874, 1. Translated by Aubrey Stewart. London: Palestine Exploration Fund, 1896, 50-77.

Clermont-Ganneau, Charles. [4855] "Rock-Cut Chambers West of the Ecce Homo Church," in C. Warren and C. R. Conder, The Survey of Western Palestine, 5: Jerusalem. London: Palestine Exploration Fund, 1884, 302-307.

Coüasnon, Charles. [4856] "Jérusalem-- Ecce Homo," Revue biblique, 73 (1966), 573-574.

Dalman, Gustaf. [4857] "Die Via dolorosa in Jerusalem," Palästinajahrbuch, 2 (1906), 15-26.

Dressaire, Léopold. [4858] "Recherches topographiques sur la voie douloureuse," Echos d' Orient, 6 (1903), 366-375.

Eckardt, R. [4859] "Das Praetorium des Pilatus," Zeitschrift des deutschen Palästina-Vereins, 34 (1911), 39-48.

Finegan, Jack. [4860] "Plan Showing the Site and Vestiges of the Antonia, / Cistern Belonging to the Antonia, / Plan of the Stone Pavement of the Antonia, / The Ecce Homo Arch," in Archeology of the New Testament: The Life and Jesus and the Beginning of the Early Church. Princeton: Princeton University Press, 1969, 156-163.

Folda, Jaroslav. [4861] "Three Crusader Capitals in Jerusalem," Levant, 10 (1978), 139-155. [Article relates to the "Prison(s) of Christ."]

Folda, Jaroslav. [4862] "A Fourth Capital from the Chapel of the Repose in Jerusalem," Levant, 15 (1983), 194-195.

Gealy, Fred D. [4863] "Praetorium," in Interpreter's Dictionary of the Bible, 3. New York: Abingdon, 1962, 856.

Hanauer, James Edward. [4864] "Recent Discoveries in Jerusalem," Palestine Exploration Fund, Quarterly Statement, (1906), 225-231. [On the Greek Orthodox property along the Via Dolorosa now called the Prison of Christ.]

Hoade, Eugene. [4865] "From the Praetorium to Calvary," in Guide to the Holy Land. Jerusalem: Franciscan Printing Press, 1984, 141-173.

Ita de Sion, Marie. [4866] "The Antonia Fortress," Palestine Exploration Quarterly, (1968), 139-143.

Jaros, Karl. [4867] "Ein neuer Lokalisierungversuch des Praetoriums," Bibel und Liturgie, 53/1 (1980), 13-22. [In support of the Hasmonaean palace identification of B. Pixner.]

Kreyenbühl, J. [4868] "Der Ort Verurteilung Jesu," Zeitschrift für die neutestamentliche Wissenschaft, 3 (1902), 15-22.

Legendre, A. [4869] "Prétoire," in F. Vigouroux (ed.), Dictionnaire de la Bible, 5. Paris: Letouzey et Ané, 1926, 621-640.

Macalister, R. A. Stewart. [4870] "The Mosaic in the Church of Nôtre Dame de Spasm, Jerusalem," Palestine Exploration Fund, Quarterly Statement, (1902), 122-124.

Mackowski, Richard M. [4871] "Herod's Palace and Praetorium," in Jerusalem, City of Jesus: An Exploration of the Traditions, Writings, and Remains of the Holy City from the Time of Christ. Grand Rapids, MI: Eerdmans, 1980, 102-111.

Mallouk, M. Ph. [4872] "Die sechte Station des heiligen Kreuzwegs: Das Haus der heiligen Veronica zu Jerusalem," Das heilige Land, 38 (1894), 33-46.

Marta, Giovanni. [4873] La questione del pretorio di Pilate ed i qui pro quo della "Palestina." Jerusalem: Franciscan Printing Press, 1905, 287 pp.

Masterman, Ernest W. Gurney. [4874] "Praetorium," in International Standard Bible Encyclopaedia, 4. Grand Rapids: Eerdmans, 1939, 2428-2429.

Meisterman, Barnabé. [4875] Le Prétoire de Pilate at la fortresse Antonia. Paris: A. Picard et Fils, 1902, 250 pp.

Miquel Balagué, S. P. [4876] "El Litóstrotos o Pretorio de Pilatos," Cultura Biblica, 14/157 (1957), 390-396.

Mommert, Carl. [4877] Das Praetorium des Pilatus oder der Ort der Verurteilung Jesu. Leipzig: Haberland, 1903, 184 pp.

Moss, R. W. [4878] "Praetorium," in J. Hastings (ed.), Dictionary of Christ and the Gospels, 2. New York: Scribner's, 1906, 389.

Murphy-O'Connor, Jerome. [4879] "Ecce Homo Arch, / Via Dolorosa," in The Holy Land: An Archaeological Guide from Earliest Times to 1700. Oxford: Oxford University Press, 1980, 24-27.

Nebenzahl, Kenneth. [4879A] "Christian von Adrichom: Jerusalem," in Maps of the Holy Land: Images of Terra Sancta through Two Millennia. New York: Abbeville Press, 1986, 90-91, pl. 33. [Map/drawng of the city in the early Ottoman period (ca. 1486); indication of pilgrimage sites including the Via Dolorosa.]

Pixner, Bargil. See Bagatti, Bellarmino. [4837]

Pixner, Bargil. [4880] "Noch einmal das Prätorium, Versuch einer neuen Lösung," Zeitschrift des deutschen Palästina-Vereins, 95 (1979), 56-86. [Praetorium at the Hasmonaean palace.]

Pixner, Bargil. [4881] "The Pit of Jeremiah Rediscovered?" Christian News from Israel, 27/3 (1980), 118-121, 148. [Relates to author's theory on the praetorium.]

Pixner, Bargil. [4882] "Where was the Original Via Dolorosa?" Christian News from Isarel, 27/1(979), 7-10, 51-52.

Potin, Jacques. [4883] "La localisation du Prétroire à l' Antonia," Bible et Terre Sainte, 159 (1974), 6.

Pujol, A. M. [4884] "In loco qui dicitur Lithostrotos," Verbum Domini, 15 (1935), 180-186.

Purves, G. T. [4885] "Praetorium," in J. Hastings (ed.), in Dictionary of the Bible, 4. New York: Scribner's, 1898, 32-33.

Revuelta Sañudo, Manuel. [4886] "La Localización del Pretorio, Estudios Bíblicos, 20 (1962), 261-317.

Revuelta Sañudo, Manuel. [4887] "La polémica del Pretorio de Pilato," Lumen, 10 (1961), 289-321.

Sachsse, Carl. [4888] "Golgotha und das Prätorium des Pilatus," Zeitschrift für die neutestamentliche Wissenschaft, 19 (1920), 29-38.

Saller, Sylvester J. [4889] "Recent Archaeological Work in Palestine: At the Church of Our Lady of the Spasm," Studii Biblici Franciscani, Liber Annuus, 14 (1963 /1964), 281-282.

de Sandoli, Sabino. [4890] "First Franciscan Convent in Jerusalem (1230-1244)," The Holy Land, 4/2 (Summer, 1984), 51-71.

de Saulcy, L. Félicien J. C. [4891] "L' arc de l' Ecce Homo," Revue archéologique, (1861/A), 185-190.

Savignac, M.-R. [4892] "Création d' un sanctuaire et d' une tradition à Jérusalem," Revue biblique, 16 (1907), 113-123. [Urges critical restraint on the identification of caverns (between Ecce Homo arch and Austrian hospital) excavated by Clermont-Ganneau.]

Schick, Conrad. [4893] "An Ancient Church in Tarik Sitti Maryam," Palestine Exploration Fund, Quarterly Statement, (1889), 172-174. [At the Second Station of the Cross.]

Schick, Conrad. [4894] "Deir el' Adas," Palestine Exploration Fund, Quarterly Statement, (1896), 122-128.

Schick, Conrad. [4895] "Herod's House," Palestine Exploration Fund, Quarterly Statement, (1896), 215-217. [Traditional site of Jerusalem residence of Herod Antipas, near Via Dolorosa.]

Schick, Conrad. [4896] "Veronica's House," Palestine Exploration Fund, Quarterly Statement, (1896), 214-215. [Sixth Station of the Cross.]

Schneider, G. [4897] "Praitórion," in H. Balz (ed.), Exegetisches Wörterbuch zum Alten Testament, 3. Stuttgart: Kohlhammer, 1982, 346-348.

Sepp, J. N. [4898] "Der Stein hat-Toim am Eccehomobogen," Zeitschrift des deutschen Palästina-Vereins, 2 (879), 48-51.

Sepp, J. N. [4899] "The Stone Hat-Toim on the Ecce-Homo Arch," Palestine Exploration Fund, Quarterly Statement, (1879), 195-197.

Steve, M.-A. See Vincent, Louis-Hugues and Steve, M.-A. [4916]

Storm, Albert. [4900] La Voie Douloureuse. Jerusalem: Franciscan Printing Press, 1973, 196 pp.

Storme, Albert. [4901] The Way of the Cross: A Historical Sketch. Jerusalem: Franciscan Printing Press, 1973, 196 pp.

Thurston, Herbert. [4902] Étude historique sur le Chemin de la Croix ornée de nombreuses illustrations. Paris: Letouzey et Ané, 1907, 286 pp.

Thurston, Herbert. [4903] "The Praetorium of Pilate and the Pillar of Scourging," Dublin Review, (1906), 120-142.

Thurston, Herbert. [4904] The Stations of the Cross: An Account of their History and Devotional Purpose. London: Burns and Oates / New York: Benziger, 1906, 183 pp.

Van Bebber, M. [4905] "Das Praetorium des Pilatus," Theologoische Quartalschrift, 87 (1905), 179-230.

Vanel, Antoine. [4906] "Où Jésus comparut-il devant Pilate? Arguments pour le palais d' Hérode," Bible et Terre Sainte, 159 (1974), 7-10, 15.

Vanel, Antoine. [4907] "Prétoire," in H. Cazelles and A. Feuillet (eds.), Supplément au Dictionaire de la Bible, 8. Paris: Letouzey et Ané, 1972, 513-554.

Van Elderen, Bastiaan. [4908] "Praetorium," in G. W. Bromiley (ed.), The International Standard Bible Encyclopedia, 3. Grand Rapids: Eerdmans, 1986, 929.

Vincent, Louis-Hugues. [4909] "L' Antonia, palais primitif d' Hérode," Revue biblique, 61 (1954), 87-107.

Vincent, Louis-Hugues. [4910] "L' Antonia et le Prétoire," Revue biblique, 42 (1933), 83-113.

Vincent, Louis-Hugues. [4911] "Autour du Prétoire," Revue biblique, 46 (1937), 563-570.

Vincent, Louis-Hugues. [4912] "La chapelle médiéval 'du repos'" Revue biblique, 29 (1920), 75-90.

Vincent, Louis-Hugues. [4913] "Le lithostrotos évangélique," Revue biblique, 59 (1952), 513-530.

Vincent, Louis-Hugues. [4914] "La voie douloureuse," in Jérusalem: Recherches de topographie, d' archéologie et d' histoire, 2: Jérusalem nouvelle, 3. Paris: Gabalda, 1922, 610-637.

Vincent, Louis-Hugues and Abel, Félix-M. [4915] "Le Prétoire," in Jérusalem: Recherches de topographie, d' archéologie et d' histoire, 2: Jérusalem nouvelle, 3. Paris: Gabalda, 1922, 582-586.

Vincent, Louis-Hugues and Steve, M.-A. [4916] "L' Antonia," in Jérusalem de l' Ancien Testament, 1. Paris: Gabalda, 1954, 193-221.

Wilkinson, John. [4917] "Finding the Way of the Cross," in Jerusalem as Jesus Knew it: Archaeology as Evidence. London: Thames and Hudson, 1978, 144-151.

Thirty-Five

The Church of St. Stephen

Abel, Félix-M. See Vincent, Louis-Hugues and Abel, Félix-M. [4947]

Abel, Félix-M. [4918] "Étienne (Saint), La basilique d' Eudocie, / L' oratoire du Nord (638-1187)," in L. Pirot (ed.), Supplément au Dictionnaire de la Bible, 2. Paris: Letouzey et Ané, 1934, 1139-1144.

Avi-Yonah, Michael. [4919] "Mosaic Pavements in Palestine: Jerusalem, St. Étienne," in Art in Ancient Palestine. Collected and prepared for republication by H. Katzenstein and Y. Tsafrir. Jerusalem: Magnes Press, 1981, 323-324. [Originally published in Quarterly of the Department of Antiquities in Palestine, 2 (1932), 176-177.]

Bagatti, Bellarmino. [4920] "Nuove testimonianze sul luogo della lapidazione de S. Stefano," Antonianum, 49 (1974), 527-532.

Bahat, Dan. [4921] Jerusalem: Selected Plans of Historical Sites and Monumental Buildings. Jerusalem: Ariel, 1980, 98-99.

Conder, Claude R. [4922] "The Asnerie," Palestine Exploration Fund, Quarterly Statement, (1877), 143-144.

Conder, Claude R. and Mantell, A. M. [4923] "Newly Discovered Church," Palestine Exploration Fund, Quarterly Statement, (1882), 116-120.

Finegan, Jack. [4924] "Excavations at the Basilica of St. Stephen, / Inscription of the Deacon Nonnus," in Archeology of the New Testament: The Life of Jesus and the Beginning of the Early Church. Princeton: Princeton University Press, 1969, 174-176.

Frei, A. [4925] "Die neu entdeckte Stephanskirche bei Jerusalem," Zeitschrift des deutschen Palästina-Vereins, 8 (1885), 50-59.

Germer-Durand, Joseph. [4926] "Découvertes des ruines de la Basilique de St. Étienne," Revue Bénédictine, 7 (1890), 232-235.

Hanauer, James Edward. [4927] "The Place of Stoning," Palestine Exploration Fund, Quarterly Statement, 13 (1881), 317-319.

Heidet, L. [4928] Étude critique et topographie: Où se trouve à Jérusalem le lieu de la lapidation de St. Étienne? Jerusalem: Impr. des P.P. Franciscaine, 1887, 57 pp.

Hoade, Eugene. [4929] "Basilica of St. Stephen," in Guide to the Holy Land. Jerusalem: Franciscan Printing Press, 1984, 327-330.

Lagrange, Marie-Joseph. [4930] "À la recherche des sites bibliques," in Conferences de Saint-Etiennes, 2. Paris: Gabalda, 1911, 1-56.

Lagrange, Marie-Joseph. [4931] Saint Étienne et son sanctuaire à Jérusalem. Paris: Picard, 1894, 189 pp.

Lagrange, Marie-Joseph. [4932] "Une tradition biblique à Jérusalem," Revue biblique, 3 (1894), 452-481.

Lewis, T. Hayter. [4933] "Ruins of Church on the Skull Hill, Jerusalem," Palestine Exploration Fund, Quarterly Statement, (1891), 211-218.

Mantell, A. M. See Conder, Claude R. and Mantell, A. M. [4923]

Mantell, A. M. [4934] "Newly Discovered Church," Palestine Exploration Fund, Quarterly Statement, (1882), 116-120.

Merrill, Selah. [4935] "The Newly Discovered Church," Palestine Exploration Fund, Quarterly Statement, (1883), 238-242.

Merrill, Selah. [4936] "New Discoveries in Jerusalem," Palestine Exploration Fund, Quarterly Statement, (1885), 222-228.

Power, E. [4937] "A New Pre-Crusade Sanctuary of St. Stephen?" Biblica, 10(1929), 85-93.

Riess, Dr. [4938] Über die angebliche Aufdeckung der Eudokia-(Stephans-) Kirche," Zeitschrift des deutschen Palästina-Vereins, 8 (1888), 162-170.

Schick, Conrad. [4939] "Discovery of Mosaic Pavement near the (so-called) Church of St. Stephen," Palestine Exploration Fund, Quarterly Statement, (1892), 190-192.

Schick, Conrad. [4940] "Neue Funde im Norden von Jerusalem, beschrieben und aufgezeichnet," Zeitschrift des deutschen Palästina-Vereins, 2 (1879), 102-105.

Schick, Conrad. [4941] "New Discoveries in the North of Jerusalem," Palestine Exploration Fund, Quarterly Statement, (1879), 198-200.

Schick, Conrad. [4942] "Die Stephanskirche der Kaiserin Eudokia bei Jerusalem," Zeitschrift des deutschen Palästina-Vereins, 11 (1888), 249-257, plan.

Séjourné, Paul-M. [4943] "Chronique biblique: Découverte d' un tombeau à Saint-Étienne," Revue biblique, 1 (1892), 258-261.

de Vaux, Baron. [4944] "Mémoire relatif aux fouilles entreprises par les R. P. Dominicains dans leur domaine de Saint-Étienne, près la porte de Damas," Revue archéologique, 3rd series, 12 (1888), 32-60.

Vincent, Louis-Hugues. [4945] "À propos d' une inscription relative à Saint-Étienne," Revue biblique, 16 (1907), 276-277.

Vincent, Louis-Hugues. [4946] "Encore l' inscription de Saint Étienne à Gethsemani," Revue biblique, 16 (1907), 607-611.

Vincent, Louis-Hugues and Abel, Félix-M. [4947] Jérusalem: Recherches de topographie, d' archéologie et d' histoire, 2: Jérusalem nouvelle, 3, 766-804.

Wilson, Charles W. [4948] "The Church of St. Stephen," appendix to "The Pilgrimage of the Russian Abbot Daniel in the Holy Land, 1106-1107 A.D.," in The Library of the Palestine Pilgrims' Text Society, 4. New York: AMS Press, 1971, 83-90. [Originally published in 1895.]

Thirty-Six

Jerusalem as a Muslim City / The City Under the Administration of Muslim Authorities

Aamiry, M. A. [4949] Jerusalem, Arab Origin and Heritage. New York: Longman, 1978, 54 pp.

Abel, Félix-M. [4950] "La Prise de Jérusalem par les Arabes (638)," in Conferences de Saint-Éteinne, École Pratique d' Études Bibliques, 2. Paris: Gabalda, 1911, 105-144.

Abel, Félix-M. [4951] "La conquête de la Palestine par les Arabes," in Histoire de la Palestine, 2. Paris: Lecoffre, 1952, 393-406.

Abu-Manneh, Butrus. [4952] "New Light on the Rise of the Husaini Family of Jerusalem in the Eighteenth Century," A. Cohen (ed.), Jerusalem in the Early Ottoman Period. Jerusalem: Yad Izhaq Ben-Zvi, 1979, 323-342 (Hebrew), xvii-xviii (English summary).

Abul-Hajj, Amal. See Burgoyne, Michael H. and Abul-Hajj, Amal. [4990]

Abul-Hajj, Amal. See Northrup, Linda S. and Abul-Hajj, Amal. [5121]

Abul-Hajj, Amal. See Walls, Archibald G. and Abul-Hajj, Amal. [5198]

Adul, Hajj, Amal. [4953] "Twenty-four Medieval Arabic Inscriptions from Jerusalem," Levant, 11 (1979), 112-137.

el-Aref, Aref. [4954] The Dome of the Rock and Other Muslim Sanctuaries in The Haram of Jerusalem: History and Guide. Jerusalem: Commercial Press, 1951, 158 pp.

el-Aref, Aref. [4955] "The Dome of the Rock and Al-Aqsa Mosque," Ariel, 23 (1969), 34-38. Also in Israel Yearbook, 1970. Tel Aviv: Israel Yearbook Publications, 1970, 233-239.

Ashtour, Eliyahu. [4956] "An Arabic Book on the Merits of Jerusalem," Tarbiz, 30 (1960), 209-214 (Hebrew).

Ashtour, Eliyahu. [4957] "Jerusalem in Muslim Thought," in Encyclopaedia Judaica, 9. Jerusalem: Macmillan, 1971, 1575-1576. Reprinted in Israel Pocket Library: Jerusalem. Jerusalem: Keter, 1973, 321-324.

Ashtour, Eliyahu. [4958] "Muslim and Christian Literature in Praise of Jerusalem," in L. I. Levine (ed.), Jerusalem Cathedra, 1. Jerusalem: Yad Izhaq Ben-Zvi Institute / Detroit: Wayne State University Press, 1981, 187-189.

36/Jerusalem as a Muslim City

Ashtour, Eliyahu. [4959] "Travelers and Travels to Erez-Israel: Muslim Travelers," in Encyclopaedia Judaica, 15. Jerusalem: Macmillan, 1971, 1358-1359.

Ashtour, Eliyahu and Hirschberg, H. Z. [4960] "Jerusalem: Arab Period," in Encyclopaedia Judiaca, 9. Jerusalem: Macmillan , 1971, 1408-1415. Reprinted in Israel Pocket Library: Jerusalem. Jerusalem: Keter, 1973, 48-59.

Ashtour, Eliyahu and Hirschberg, H. Z. [4961] "Jerusalem: Mamluk Period," in Encyclopaedia Judiaca, 9. Jerusalem: Macmillan, 1971, 1423-1426. Reprinted in Israel Pocket Library: Jerusalem. Jerusalem: Keter Books, 1973, pp 69-76.

Avigad, Nahman. [4962] "Muslim and Crusader Remains," in Discovering Jerusalem. Nashville: Thomas Nelson, 1983, 247-257.

el-Azma, Nazeer. [4963] "Some Notes on the Impact of the Story of the Mi`raj on Sufi Literature," Muslim World, 63 (April, 1973), 93-99.

Bagatti, Bellarmo. [4964] "From the Persian Occupation to the Crusades," in The Church from the Gentiles in Palestine, History and Archeology. Studium Biblicum Franciscanum, Collectio Minor, 4. Jerusalem: Franciscan Printing Press, 1971; reprinted, 1984, 126-154.

Bahat, Dan. [4965] "The Ayyubid and Mameluke Period, 1187-1517," in Carta's Historical Atlas of Jerusalem: An Illustrated History. Jerusalem: Carta, 1983, 62-67.

Bahat, Dan. [4966] "The First Moslem Period, 638-1099," in Carta's Historical Atlas of Jerusalem: An Illustrated History. Jerusalem: Carta, 1983, 48-53.

Bahat, Dan. [4967] Jerusalem: Selected Plans of Historical Sites and Monumental Buildings. Jerusalem: Ariel, 1980, passim, esp. 42-61 (Haram area), 86-95 (Mamaluk architecture.).

Bahat, Dan. [4968] "The Turkish Period, 1517-1917," in Carta's Historical Atlas of Jerusalem: An Illustrated History. Jerusalem: Carta, 1983, 68-76.

Ben-Arieh, Yehoshua. [4969] "Ottoman Rule; the Muslim Population; the Temple Mount and the Muslim Quarter," in Jerusalem in the 19th Century: The Old City. Jerusalem: Yad Izhaq Ben-Zvi / New York: St. Martin's, 1984, 103-181.

Ben-Dov, Meir. [4970] "The Area South of the Temple Mount in the Early Islamic Period," in Y. Yadin (ed.), Jerusalem Revealed: Archaeology in the Holy City, 1968-1974. New Haven and London: Yale University Press and the Israel Exploration Society, 1976, 97-101.

Ben-Dov, Meir. [4971] "Building Techniques in the Omayyad Palace near the Temple Mount," in Eretz-Israel: Archaeological, Historical, and Geographical Studies, 11. Jerusalem: Israel Exploration Society, 1973, 75-91 (Hebrew), 24*-25* (English summary).

Ben-Dov, Meir. [4972] "Excavations near the Temple Mount-- The Early Islamic Period," Qadmoniot, 5 (1972), 112-117 (Hebrew).

Ben-Dov, Meir. [4973] "Fatimid Silver Jewelry from the Temple Mount Excavations," Qadmoniot, 16 (1983), 88-91 (Hebrew). [English summary in Old Testament Abstracts, 7 (1984), 224.]

Ben-Dov, Meir. [4974] "The Omayyad Structures near the Temple Mount (Preliminary Report)," in Eretz-Israel: Archaeological, Historical, and Geographical Studies, 10. Jerusalem: Israel Exploration Society, 1971, 35-40 (Hebrew).

Ben-Dov, Meir. [4975] "The Omayyad Structures Near the Temple Mount," in B. Mazar, The Excavations in the Old City of Jerusalem near the Temple Mount. Preliminary Report of the Second and Third Seasons, 1969-1970. Jerusalem: Hebrew University, Institute of Archeology, 1971, 37-44.

Ben-Dov, Meir. [4976] "The Start of the Moslem Age, / The Omayyad Era, / The Days of the Abbasids and Fatimids, / In the Shade of the Crescent Again," in In the Shadow of the Temple: The Discovery of Ancient Jerusalem. Jerusalem: Keter / New York: Harper and Row, 1985, 273-341, 355-373.

Bevan, A. A. [4977] "Mohammed's Ascension to Heaven," in Karl Marti (ed.), Studien zur semitischen Philologie und Relionsgeschichte (Festschrift Julius Wellhausen). Geissen: Alfred Töpelmann, 1914, 49-61.

Bishop, Eric F. F. [4978] "Precincts and the Shrine," Muslim World, 64 (1974), 165-171.

Bjorkman, W. [4979] "Jerusalem in Corpus Inscriptionum Arabicarum," Der Islam: Zeitschrift für Geschichte und Kultur des islamischen Orients, 15 (1926), 96-100.

Borrmans, Maurizio. [4980] "Gerusalemme nella tradizione religiosa musulmans," in M. Borrmans (eds.), Gerusalemme. Brescia: Paideia, 1982, 111-130.

Bosworth, C. E. [4981] "Some Observations on Jerusalem Arabic Inscriptions," Levant, 13 (1981), 266-267.

Braslavi (Braslavsky), J. [4982] "A Guide of Jerusalem from the Cairo Geniza," in Eretz-Israel: Archaeological, Historical, and Geographical Studies, 7. Jerusalem: Israel Exploration Society, 1964, 69-80 (Hebrew), 168-169 (English summary).

Briggs, Martin, S. [4983] Muhammadan Architecture in Egypt and Palestine. Oxford: Clarendon Press, 1924; reprinted, New York: Da Capo Press, 1974, 255 pp.

Brownrigg, Ronald. See Hollis, Christopher and Brownrigg, Ronald. [5065]

Buhl, Frants. [4984] "Al-Kuds," in H. A. R. Gibb and J. H. Kramers (eds.), Shorter Encyclopaedia of Islam. Edited on behalf of the Royal Netherlands Academy. Ithaca: Cornell University Press, 1953, 269-271.

Burgoyne, Michael H. See Kessler, Christel M. and Burgoyne, Michael H. [5079]

Burgoyne, Michael H. [4985] "A Chronological Index to the Muslim Monuments of Jerusalem," in The Architecture of Islamic Jerusalem. Jerusalem: British School of Archeology in Jerusalem, 1976, 3-10.

Burgoyne, Michael H. [4986] "The Continued Survey of the Ribat Kurd/Madrasa Jawhariyya Complex in Tariq al-Hadid, Jerusalem," Levant, 6 (1974), 51-64.

Burgoyne, Michael H. [4987] "A Recently Discovered Marwanid Inscription in Jerusalem," Levant, 14 (1982), 118-121.

Burgoyne, Michael H. [4988] "Some Mameluke Doorways in the Old City of Jerusalem," Levant, 3 (1971), 1-30.

Burgoyne, Michael H. [4989] "Tariq Bab al-Hadid-- A Mamlûk Street in the Old City of Jerusalem," Levant, 5 (1973), 12-35.

Burgoyne, Michael H. and Abul-Hajj, Amal. [4990] "Twenty-four Medieval Arabic Inscriptions from Jerusalem," Levant, 11 (1979), 112-137.

Busnik, Th.A. [4991] "Haran asch Scharif," in Der Tempel von Jerusalem von Salomo bis Middot, 2: Von Ezechiel bis Middot. Leiden: Brill, 1980, 904-1016.

Busse, Heribert. [4992] "Die arabischen Inschriften im und am Felsendom in Jerusalem," Das Heilige Land, 109/1-2 (1977), 8-24.

Busse, Heribert. [4993] "Der Islam und die biblischen Kultstätten," Der Islam: Zeitschrift für Geschichte und Kultur des islamischen Orients, 42 (1966), 113-147.

Busse, Heribert. [4994] "Monotheismus und islamische Christologie in der Bauinschrift des Felsendoms in Jerusalem," Theologische Quartalschrift, 161 (1981), 168-178.

Busse, Heribert. [4995] "'Omar b. al-Hattab in Jerusalem," Jerusalem Studies in Arabic and Islam, 5 (1984), 73-119.

Busse, Heribert. [4996] "The Sanctity of Jerusalem in Islam," Judaism, 17 (1968), 441-468.

Canaan, Taufik. [4997] "Mohammedan Saints and Sanctuaries in Palestine," Journal of the Palestine Oriental Society, 4 (1924), 1-84; 5 (1925), 163-203; 6 (1926), 1-69, 117-157; 7 (1927), 1-88. Reprinted and published in book-form in 1927; reprinted in facsimile edition with illustrations added, Jerusalem: Ariel, n. d., 331 pp.

Canaan, Taufik. [4998] "The Palestinian Arab House: Its Architecture and Folklore," Journal of the Palestine Oriental Society, 12 (1932), 223-247; 13 (1933), 1-83. [Contains glossary of Arabic architectural terms.]

Caskel, Werner. [4999] Der Felsendom und die Wallfafrt nach Jerusalem. Arbeitsgemeinschaft für Forschung des Landes Nordrhein-Westfalen, Geistwissenschaften, 114. Köln und Opladen: Westdeutscher Verlag, 1963, 55 pp.

Chen, Doren. [5000] "The Design of the Dome of the Rock in Jerusalem," Palestine Exploration Quarterly, (1980), 41-50.

Chen, Doren. [5001] "Sir Archibald Creswell's Setting Out of the Plan of the Dome of the Rock Reconsidered," Palestine Exploration Quarterly, (1985), 128-132.

Clermont-Ganneau, Charles. [5002] "Ancient Arabic Inscription Giving the Dimensions of the Haram," Palestine Exploration Fund, Quarterly Statement, (1874), 261-262.

Clermont-Ganneau, Charles. [5003] "The Haram es Sherif and its Neighborhood/ The Kubbat es Sakhra," in Archaeological Researches in Palestine during the Years 1873-1874, 1. Translated by Aubrey Stewart. London: Palestine Exploration Fund, 1896, 127-227.

Clermont-Ganneau, Charles. [5004] "The Haram and the Dome of the Rock/ Excavation Within the Haram/ Inscription in the Haram," in C. Warren and C. R. Conder, The Survey of Western Palestine, 5: Jerusalem. London: Palestine Exploration Fund, 1884, 307-319.

Clermont-Ganneau, Charles. [5005] "Inscription arabe en anciens caractères coufiques décourverte récemment à Jérusalem," Comptes Rendus de l' Académie des Inscriptions et Belles-Lettres, (1898), 630-640.

Clermont-Ganneau, Charles. [5006] "Letter from Jerusalem," Palestine Exploration Fund, Quarterly Statement, (1874), 135-158. [On the Haram esh-Sharif.]

Cohen, Amnon. [5007] "Development Projects in Jerusalem under Early Ottoman Rule," Cathedra: For the History of Eretz-Israel and its Yishuv, 8 (1978), 179-187 (Hebrew).

Cohen, Amnon (ed.). [5008] Jerusalem in the Early Ottoman Period. Jerusalem: Yad Izhaq Ben-Zvi, 1979, 473 pp. (Hebrew) + xx pp. (English summaries).

Cohen, Amnon. [5009] "Local Trade, International Trade and Government Involvement in Jerusalem During the Early Ottoman Period," Asian and African Studies: Journal of the Israel Oriental Society, 12 (1978), 5-12.

Cohen, Amnon. [5010] "On the Realities of the Millet System: Jerusalem in the Sixteenth Century," in B. Braude and B. Lewis (eds.), Christians and Jews in the Ottoman Empire, 2: The Arabic- Speaking Lands. New York/London: Holmes and Meier, 7-18.

Cohen, Amnon. [5011] Palestine in the Eighteenth Century: Patterns of Government and Administration. Jerusalem: Magnes Press / London: Oxford University Press, 1973, 344 pp.

Cohen, Amnon and Lewis, Bernard. [5012] Population and Revenue in the Towns of Palestine in the Sixteenth Century. Princeton: Princeton University Press, 1978. [Jerusalem, 81-104.]

Creswell, K. A. C. See Chen, Doren. [5001]

Creswell, K. A. C. [5013] Early Muslim Architecture, 1: Umayyads, A.D. 622-750, With a Contribution on the Mosaics of the Dome of the Rock and of the Great Mosque at Damascus, by Marguerite Van Berchem. Oxford: Clarendon Press, 1932, 414 pp. [Dome of the Rock, 42-94; contributions by Marguerte Van Berchem, 148-228.]

Creswell, K. A. C. [5014] The Origin and Plan of the Dome of the Rock. British School of Archaeology in Jerusalem, Supplementary Papers, 2. London: Issued by the Council, 1924, 30 pp.

Dajani-Shakeel, Hadia. [5015] "Jihad in Twelfth Century Arabic Poetry: A Moral and Religious Force to Counter the Crusades," Muslim World, 66 (1976), 96-113.

Dalmais, I.-H. [5016] "Le mont des oliviers dans la tradition de l'Islam," Bible et Terre Sainte, 136 (1971), 5.

Daoust, Joseph. [5017] "La via quotitienne à Jérusalem au XVIe siècle," Bible et Terre Sainte, 111 (1969), 22-23.

Diez, E. [5018] "Mosiacs of the Dome of the Rock at Jerusalem," Ars Islam, 1 (1934), 235-238.

Doumani, Beshara B. [5019] "Palestinian Islamic Court Records: A Source for Socioeconomic History," Middle East Studies Association Bulletin, 19 (1985), 155-172.

Drory, Joseph. [5020] "Jerusalem During the Mamluk Period (1250-1517)," in B. Z. Kedar (ed.), Jerusalem in the Middle Ages, Selected Papers. Jerusalem: Yad Izhaq Ben-Zvi, 1979, 148-176 (Hebrew), xvii (English summary). English translation in L. I. Levine (ed.), Jerusalem Cathedra, 2. Jerusalem: Yad Izhaq Ben-Zvi Institute / Detroit: Wayne State University Press, 1982, 190-213.

Drory, Joseph. [5021] "A Map of Mamluk Jerusalem," in B. Z. Kedar (ed.), Jerusalem in the Middle Ages, Selected Papers. Jerusalem: Yad Izhaq Ben-Zvi, 1979, 178-184 (Hebrew).

Duncan, Alistair. [5022] The Noble Sanctuary: Portrait of a Holy Place in Arab Jerusalem. London: Longman, 1972 80 pp.

Duri, Abdel Aziz. [5023] "Bayt al-Maqdis in Islam," Hamdard Islam, 4/1 (Spring, 1981), 23-35. Also in Bulletin of the Christian Institutes of Islamic Studies, 5/3-4 (July-Dec., 1982), 75-91, and in A. Hadidi (ed.), Studies in the History and Archaeology of Jordan, 1. Amman: Department of Antiquities, 1982, 351-355.

Friedman, Yohanan. [5024] "Eretz-Israel and Jerusalem on the Eve of the Ottoman Conquest," in A. Cohen (ed.), Jerusalem in the Early Ottoman Period. Jerusalem: Yad Izhaq Ben-Zvi, 1979, 7-38 (Hebrew), vii (English summary).

Gautier-Van Berchem, Marguerite and Ory, Solange. [5025] La Jérusalem musulmane dans l' oeuvre de Max Van Berchem. Lausanne: Trois Continents, 1978, 121 pp.

Gilbert, Martin. [5026] "Mamluk and Ottoman Jerusalem," in Jerusalem History Atlas. New York: Macmillan, 1977, 29.

Gildemeister, J. [5027] "Die arabischen Nachrichten zur Geschichte der Harambauten, Zeitschrift des deutschen Palästina-Vereins, 13 (1890), 1-24.

Gildemeister, J. [5028] "Beiträge zur Palästinakunde aus arabischen Quellen, 1: Ja'kubi," Zeitschrift des deutschen Palästina-Vereins, 4 (1881), 85-92.

Gildemeister, J. [5029] "Beiträge zur Palästinakunde aus arabischen Quellen, 4: Mukaddasi," Zeitschrift des deutschen Palästina-Vereins, 7 (1884), 143-172 [esp. 158-166], 215-230, 310.

Gildemeister, J. [5030] "Beiträge zur Palästinakunde aus arabischen Quellen, 5: Idrisi," Zeitschrift des deutschen Palästina-Vereins, 8 (1885), 117-145.

Glück, H. [5031] "Ein islamisches Heiligtum auf dem Ölberg: Ein Beitrag zur Geschichte des islamischen Raumbaues," Der Islam: Zeitschrift für Geschichte und Kultur des islamischen Orients, 6 (1915/1916), 328-349.

Goitein, S. D. [5032] "Die Heiligkeit Jerusalems und Palästinas in der muslimischen Frömmigkeit," Emuna, 5 (1970), 196-203.

Goitein, S. D. [5033] "The Historical Background of the Erection of the Dome of the Rock," Journal of American Oriental Society, 70 (1950), 104-108.

Goitein, S. D. [5034] "Jerusalem in the Arab Period (638-1099)," in L. I. Levine (ed.), Jerusalem Cathedra, 2. Jerusalem: Yad Izhaq Ben-Zvi Institute / Detroit: Wayne State University Press, 1982, 168-196.

Goitein, S. D. [5035] "The Sanctity of Jerusalem and Palestine in Early Islam," in Studies in Islamic History and Institutions. Leiden: Brill, 1966, 135-148. [Based on studies which appeared originally in Journal of the American Oriental Society, 70 (1950), 104-108, and Bulletin of the Palestine Exploration Society, 12 (1945/1946), 120-126 (Hebrew).]

Goitein, S. D. and Graber, Oleg. [5036] "al-Kuds," in C. E. Bosworth, E. von Donzel, B. Lewis, and Ch. Pellat (eds.), The Encyclopaedia of Islam, new edn., 5. Leiden: Brill, 1980, 322-344.

Golvin, L. [5037] "Quelques notes sur le suq al-Qattanin et ses annexes à Jérusalem," Bulletin d' Études Orientales, 20 (1967), 101-117.

Gordon, T. [5038] "Some Arab Coins from Ophel and Siloam," Palestine Exploration Fund, Quarterly Statement, (1925), 183-189.

Graber, Oleg. See Goitein, S. D. and Graber, Oleg. [5036]

Graber, Oleg. [5039] "Kubbat al-Sakhra," in C. E. Bosworth, E. von Donzel, B. Lewis, and Ch. Pellat (eds.), The Encyclopaedia of Islam, new edn., 5. Leiden: Brill, 1980, 297-299.

Graber, Oleg. [5040] "New Inscription from the Haram al-Sharif in Jerusalem: A Note on the Medieval Topography of Jerusalem," in C. L. Geddes (ed.),

Studies in Islamic Art and Architecture (K.A.C. Creswell Festschrift). Cairo: American University in Cairo Press, 1965, 72-83.

Grabar, Oleg. [5041] "The Umayyad Dome of the Rock of Jerusalem," Ars Orientalis, 3 (1959), 33-62.

Gray, John. [5042] "Ottoman Obscurity," in A History of Jerusalem. New York: Praeger, 1969, 260-291.

Gray, John. [5043] "The Sword of the Wilderness," in A History of Jerusalem. New York: Praeger, 1969, 210-227.

Gressmann, Hugo. [5044] "Der Felsendom in Jerusalem," Palästinajahrbuch, 4 (1908), 54-66.

Hamarneh, S. K. [5045] "An Unpublished Description of Jerusalem in the Middle Ages as Found in the ar-Rawd al-Mi'tar by 'Abd al-Mun'im al-Himyari," Folia Orientalia, 11 (1969), 145-156.

Hamilton, R. W. [5046] "Jerusalem: Patterns of Holiness," in R. Moorey and P. Parr (eds.), Archaeology in the Levant: Essays for Kathleen Kenyon. Warminster, England: Aris and Phillips, 1978, 194-201.

Hamilton, R. W. [5047] "Some Capitals from Aqsa Mosque," Quarterly of the Department of Antiquities in Palestine, 13 (1947), 103-120.

Hamilton, R. W. [5048] The Structural History of the Aqsa Mosque: A Record of Archaeological Gleanings from the Repairs of 1938-1942. London: Oxford University Press, 1949, 104 pp. + 79pl.

Hanauer, James Edward. [5049] "A Legend of il Hakim," Palestine Exploration Fund, Quarterly Statement, (1894), 210-211.

Har-el, Menashe. [5050] "The Temple Mount and Jerusalem under the Moslems," in This is Jerusalem. Jerusalem: Canaan Publ. Co., 1977, 329-350.

Hartmann, Richard. [5051] Der Felsendom in Jerusalem und seine Geschichte. Strassburg: Heitz und Mündel, 1909.

Hartmann, Richard. [5052] "Die Geschichte des Aksa-Moschee in Jerusalem," Zeitschrift des deutschen Palästina-Vereins, 32 (1909), 185-207.

Hartmann, Richard. [5053] Palästina unter den Arabern, 632-1516. Das Land der Bibel, 4/1. Leipzig: J.C. Hinrichs, 1915, 53 pp.

Hasson, Isaac. [5054] Abu Bakr Muhammad b. Ahmad al-Wasiti: Fada'il al Bayt al-Muqaddas. Max Schloessinger Memorial Series, 3. Jerusalem: Magnes Press, 1979, 29 pp. [introduction] + 124 pp. [Arabic text]. [For summary in English see review by D. S. Richards in Journal of Semitic Studies, 27 (1982), 126.]

Hasson, Isaac. [5055] "Muslim Literature in Praise of Jerusalem," L. I. Levine (ed.), Jerusalem Cathedra, 1. Jerusalem: Yad Izhaq Ben-Zvi Institute / Detroit: Wayne State University Press, 1981, 168-184.

Hasson, R. [5056] "Islamic Glass from Excavations in Jerusalem," Journal of Glass Studies, 25 (1983), 109-113.

Herzfeld, E. [5057] "Die Qubbat al-Sakhra, ein Denkmal frühislamischer Baukunst," Der Islam: Zeitschrift für Geschichte und Kultur des islamischen Orients, 2 (1911), 235-244.

Heyd, Uriel. [5058] "Jerusalem under the Mamluks and the Turks," in J. Aviram (ed.), Jerusalem through the Ages: Proceedings of the 25th Archaeological Convention of the Israel Exploration Society. Jerusalem: Israel Exploration Society, 1968, 193-202 (Hebrew), 65 (English summary).

Heyd, Uriel. [5059] Ottoman Documents on Palestine. Oxford: Clarendon Press, 1960, 163-173.

Hirschberg, H. Z. See Ashtour, Eliyahu and Hirschberg, H. Z. [4960-4961]

Hirschberg, H. Z. [5060] "The Temple Mount in the Arab Period (638-1099) in Jewish and Muslim Traditions, and in Historical Reality," in Jerusalem through the Ages: Proceedings of the 25th Archaeological Convention of the Israel Exploration Society. Jerusalem: Israel Exploration Society, 1968, 109-119 (Hebrew), 62-63 (English summary).

Hirschberg, H. Z.; Pick, W. P.; and Kaniel, J. [5061] "Jerusalem Under Ottoman Rule," in Encyclopaedia Judiaca, 9. Jerusalem: Macmillan, 1971, 1426-1467. Reprinted in Israel Pocket Library: Jerusalem. Jerusalem: Keter, 1973, 77-142.

Hirschberg, J. W. [5062] "Ottoman Rule in Jerusalem in the Light of Firmans and Shari'a Documents," Israel Exploration Journal, 2. (1952), 237-248.

Hirschberg, J. W. [5063] "The Sources of Moslem Traditions Concerning Jerusalem," Rocznik Orientalistyczny, 17 (Krakow, 1952), 314-350.

Hirschberg, J. W. [5064] "The Tombs of David and Solomon in Moslem Traditions," in Eretz-Israel: Archaeological, Historical, and Geographical Studies, 3. Jerusalem: Israel Exploration Society, 1954, 213-220 (Hebrew), XIII (English Summary).

Hollis, Christopher and Brownrigg, Ronald. [5065] "Muslim Holy Places," in Holy Places: Jewish, Christian, and Muslim Monuments in the Holy Land. New York: Praeger, 1969, 191-216.

Hurovitz, J. [5066] "Mi'radj," in H. A. R. Gibb and J. H. Kramers (eds.), Shorter Encyclopaedia of Islam. Edited on behalf of the Royal Netherlands Academy. Ithaca: Cornell University Press, 1953, 381-384.

Iorga, N. [5067] "Un projet relatif à la conquête de Jérusalem, 1609," Revue de l' orient latin, 2 (1894), 183-189.

Jacobson, David M. [5068] "The Golden Section and the Design of the Dome of the Rock," Palestine Exploration Quarterly, (1983), 145-147.

Jeffrey, Arthur. [5069] "Muhammad's Ascension," in Islam: Muhammad and His Religion. New York: Liberal Arts Press, 1958, 35-46.

Jeffrey, Arthur. [5070] "The Story of the Night Journey and the Ascension, by the Imam Najm ad-Din al Ghaiti," in A Reader on Islam. The Hague: Mouton and Co., 1962, 621-639.

Join-Lambert, Michel. [5071] "Moslem Jerusalem," in Jerusalem. London: Elek Books / New York: G.P. Putnam's Sons, 1958, 144-211.

Kahle, Paul. [5072] "Die moslemischen Heiligtümer in und bei Jerusalem," Palästinajahrbuch, 4 (1910), 63-101.

Kahle, Paul. [5073] "Das Wesen der moslemischen Heiligtümer in Palästina," Palästinajahrbuch, 7 (1911), 85-119.

Kaniel, J. See Hirschberg, H. Z.; Pick, W. P.; and Kaniel, J. [5061]

Kark, Ruth and Landman, Shimon. [5074] "Muslim Neighborhoods outside the Jerusalem City Walls during the Ottoman Period," in E. Shaltiel (ed.), Jerusalem in the Modern Period: Yaacov Herzog Memorial Volume. Jerusalem: Yad Izhaq Ben-Zvi and Ministry of Defense, 1981, 174-211 (Hebrew), v (English summary). English version published as "The Establishment of Muslim Neighborhoods in Jerusalem, outside the Old City, during the Late Ottoman Period," Palestine Exploration Quarterly, (1980), 114-135.

Karmi, H. S. [5075] "How Holy is Palestine to the Muslims?" The Isalamic Quarterly, 14 (1970), 63-90.

Kessler, Christel M. [5076] "'Abd al-Malik's Inscription in the Dome of the Rock: A Reconsideration," Journal of the Royal Asiatic Society, (1970), 2-14.

Kessler, Christel M. [5077] "Above the Ceiling of the Outer Ambulatory in the Dome of the Rock in Jerusalem," Journal of the Royal Asiatic Society, (1964), 83-94.

Kessler, Christel M. [5078] "The Tashtimuriyya in Jerusalem in the Light of a Recent Architectural Survey," in Levant, 11 (1979), 138-161.

Kessler, Christel M. and Burgoyne, Michael H. [5079] "The Fountain of Sultan Qaytbay in the Sacred Precinct of Jerusalem," in R. Moorey and P. Parr (eds.), Archaeology in the Levant: Essays for Kathleen Kenyon. Warminster, England: Aris and Phillips, 1978, 250-268.

Kister, Meir. [5080] "A Comment on the Antiquity of Traditions Praising Jerusalem," in L. I. Levine (ed.), Jerusalem Cathedra, 1. Jerusalem: Yad Izhaq Ben-Zvi Institute / Detroit: Wayne State University Press, 1981, 185-186.

Kister, Meir. [5081] "You Shall Only Set Out for Three Mosques: A Study of an Early Tradition," Le Muséon, 82 (1969), 173-196.

Klein, H. Arthur. See Klein, Mina C. and Klein, H. Arthur. [5082]

Klein, Mina C. and Klein, H. Arthur. [5082] "Islam on the Temple Mount (638-763 C.E.), / From Caliphs to Sultans, / Mamelukes and Ottomans on Mount Moriah (1300-1700 C.E.)," in Temple Beyond Time: The Story of the Site of Solomon's Temple at Jerusalem. New York: Van Nostrand Reinhold, 1970, 133-146, 163-233.

Kleinclausz, M. A. [5083] "La Légende du protectorat de Charlemagne sur la Terre Sainte," Syria, 7 (1926), 211-233.

Lagrange, Marie-Joseph. [5084] "Lettre de Jérusalem: Un second milliaire arabe d' Abd-el-Melik," Revue biblique, 3 (1894), 136-138.

Landman, Shimon. See Kark, Ruth and Landman, Shimon. [5074]

Lapidus, Ira M. [5085] Muslim Cities in the Later Middle Ages. Cambridge, MA: Harvard University Press, 1967, 206 pp.

Lazarus-Yafeh, Hava. [5086] "The Sanctity of Jerusalem in Islam," in J. M. Oestrreicher and A. Sinai (eds.), Jerusalem. New York: John Day, 1974, 211-225. Also [with additions and corrections] in Some Religious Aspects of Islam: A Collection of Articles. Studies in the History of Religions, Supplements to Numen, 42. Leiden: Brill, 1981, 58-71.

Lazarus-Yafeh, Hava. [5087] "The Sanctity of Jerusalem in Islamic Tradition," in E. Shaltiel (ed.), Jerusalem in the Modern Period: Yaacov Herzog Memorial Volume. Jerusalem: Yad Izhaq Ben-Zvi and Ministry of Defense, 1981, 117-131 (Hebrew), iii (English summary).

Ledit, Charles J. [5088] "Les Lieux Saints de l'Islam: La Vocation de Jérusalem," La Terre Sainte, (Nov., 1973), 294-306.

Le Strange, Guy. [5089] "Description of the Noble Sanctuary at Jerusalem in 1470 by Kamal (or Shams) ad Din es Suyûti: Extracts Retranslated," Journal of the Royal Asiatic Society, n.s. 19 (1887), 247-305.

Le Strange, Guy. [5090] "Description of Syria Including Palestine by Mukaddasi (circa 985 A.D.)," in The Library of the Palestine Pilgrims' Text Society, 3. New York: AMS Press, 1971, i-xvi, 1-98, with "Appendix Containing Some Further Notes by Colonel Sir C. Wilson, K.C.B.," 99-103. [Originally published in 1896.]

Le Strange, Guy. [5091] "Diary of a Journey through Syria and Palestine by Nâsir-i-Khusrau in 1047 A.D." in The Library of the Palestine Pilgrims' Text Society, 4. New York: AMS Press, 1971, i-xv, 1-72. [Originally published in 1893.]

Le Strange, Guy. [5092] History of Jerusalem under the Moslems. See Le Strange, Guy. Palestine under the Moslems.

Le Strange, Guy. [5093] "Idrisi's Description of Jerusalem in 1154," Palestine Exploration Fund, Quarterly Statement, (1888), 31-35.

Le Strange, Guy. [5094] "Notices of the Dome of the Rock and the Church of the Sepulchre by Arab Historians prior to the First Crusade," Palestine Exploration Fund, Quarterly Statement, (1887), 90-103.

Le Strange, Guy. [5095] Palestine under the Moslems from A. D. 650 to 1500: Translated from the Works of the Medieval Arab Geographers. London: Watt, 1890, 604 pp., esp. 3-57, 138-223. Reprinted, Beirut: Khayats, 1965. [An abridgment exists entitled History of Jerusalem under the Moslems, no ascription of place or date (probably Jerusalem, circa 1980), 344 pp.]

Le Strange, Guy. [5096] "Palestine According to the Arab Geographers and Travellers," Palestine Exploration Fund, Quarterly Statement, (1888), 23-30.

Levi-Yadin, S.; Lipschitz, S. N.; and Waisel, V. [5097] "Ring Analysis of Cedrus libani Beams from the Roof of El-Aqsa Mosque," in in Eretz-Israel: Archaeological, Historical, and Geographical Studies, 17. Jerusalem: Israel Exploration Society, 1984, 92-96. (Hebrew), 4*-5* (English summary).

Lewis, Bernard. See Cohen, Amnon and Lewis, Bernard. [5012]

Lewis, T. Hayter. [5098] "Byzantine Capital Found in the Haram Area," Palestine Exploration Fund, Quarterly Statement, (1887), 59.

Lewis, T. Hayter. [5099] "The Mosque el Aksa, Jerusalem," Palestine Exploration Fund, Quarterly Statement, (1887), 47-49.

Lewis, T. Hayter. [5100] The Holy Places of Jerusalem. London: John Murray, 1888.

Lipschitz, S. N. See Levi-Yadin, S.; Lipschitz, S. N.; and Waisel, V. [5097]

Little, Donald. [5101] "Relations between Jerusalem and Egypt during the Mamluk Period according to Literary and Documentary Sources," in A. Cohen and G. Baer (eds.), Egypt and Palestine: A Millenium of Association (868-1948). New York: St. Martin's Press / Jerusalem: Ben Zvi Institute, 1984, 73-93.

Little, Donald. [5102] "The Significance of the Haram Documents for the Study of Medieval Islamic History," Der Islam: Zeitschrift für Geschichte und Kultur des islamischen Orients, 57 (1980), 189-219.

Macalister, R. A. Stewart. [5103] "A Cistern With Cufic Graffiti near Jerusalem," Palestine Exploration Fund, Quarterly Statement, (1915), 81-85.

Macalister, R. A. Stewart. [5104] "A Note on the 'Holy Stone' in the Dome of the Rock," Palestine Exploration Fund, Quarterly Statement, (1900), 103-104. [This 'holy stone' is not the Sakhra.]

Mandaville, Jon. [5105] "The Jerusalem Shari'a Court Records: A Supplement and Compliment to the Ottoman Archives," in Studies on Palestine during the Ottoman Period. Jerusalem: Magnes Press, 1975, 517-524.

Mantell, A. M. [5106] "Newly Opened Gate in the East Wall of the Haram," Palestine Exploration Fund, Quarterly Statement, (1882), 169-170.

Marmardji, A. S. [5107] "Al-Masjid al-Aqsâ (ou al-Haram ash Sharîf, ou Temple de Salomon, ou Mosquée de 'Umar)," in Textes Géographiques Arabes sur la Palestine. Paris: Gabalda, 1951, 210-260.

Massignon, Louis. [5108] "Documents sur certains waqfs des Lieux Saints de l'Islam," *Revue des études islamiques*, 19 (1951), 73-120.

Matthews, Charles D. [5109] "The 'Kitab ba'itu-n-nufus' of Ibnu-l-Firkah," *Journal of the Palestine Oriental Society*, 14 (1934), 284-293; 15 (1935), 51-87.

Matthews, Charles D. [5110] "Muslim Iconoclast (Ibn Taymiyyeh) on the 'Merits' of Jerusalem and Palestine," *Journal of the American OrientalSociety*, 56 (1936), 1-21.

Matthews, Charles D. [5111] "Palestine, Holy Land of Islam," *Journal of Biblical Literature*, 51 (1932), 171-178.

Matthews, Charles D. [5112] "Palestine--Mohammedan Holy Land," *Muslim World*, 33 (1943), 239-253.

Matthews, Charles D. [5113] *Palestine: Mohammedan Holy Land*. New Haven: Yale University Press, 1949, 176 pp.

Matthews, Charles D. [5114] "The Wailing Wall and al-Buraq: Is the 'Wailing Wall' in Jerusalem the 'Wall of al-Buraq' of Moslem Tradition?" *Muslim World*, 22 (1032), 331-339. [Negative.]

Mayer, Leo A. [5115] "A Medieval Arabic Description of the Haram of Jerusalem," *Quarterly of the Department of Antiqities of Palestine*, 1 (1931/32), 44-51.

Mazar, Benjamin. [5116] "Archaeological Discovery in Jerusalem after A.D. 70: The Early Moslem Period, / Jerusalem in the Mameluke Period, / Four Centuries of Turkish Rule," in *The Mountain of the Lord*. Garden City, NY: Doubleday, 1975, 260-274, 279-293.

Migeon, G. [5117] "Jérusalem musulmane d' après Max van Berchem," *Syria*, 9 (1928), 59-67.

Murböck, J. [5118] In der Omarmosches vor 100 Jahren," *Das Heilige Land*, 91 (1959), 24-26.

Murphy-O'Connor, Jerome. [5119] "Mameluke Buildings," in *The Holy Land: An Archaeological Guide*. Oxford: Oxford University Press, 1980, 27-35. [See also 43-44, 63-65.]

Nori, G. [5120] "La Qubbat al-Sakhra di Gerusalemme: Una testamonianza inedita del 1486," *Rivista storica italiana*, 93 (1981), 55-70.

Northrup, Linda S. and Abul-Hajj, Amal A. [5121] "A Collection of Medieval Arabic Documents in the Islamic Museum at the Haram al-Sharif," *Arabica*, 25 (1978), 282-291.

Nubani, Hamdi. [5122] "Mamilla Cemetary: Historical Tombstones in Arabic," *Annual of the Department of Antiquities of Jordan*, 3 (1956), 8-14.

Offord, Joseph. [5123] "Documents Concerning Jerusalem in the Aphrodito Papyri in the Mohammedan Era," *Palestine Exploration Fund, Quarterly Statement*, (1912), 205-206.

Ollendorf, Franz. [5124] "Two Mamluk Tomb-Chambers in Western Jerusalem," Israel Explorqation Journal, 32 (1982), 245-250.

Ory, Solange. See Gautier-Van Berchem, Marguerite and Ory, Solange. [5025]

Palmer, Edward H. [5125] "History of the Haram es Sherif: Compiled from the Arabic Historians," Palestine Exploration Fund, Quarterly Statement, (1871), 122-132, 164-170.

Partin, Harry B. [5126] "Pilgrimage to Jerusalem: Jewish, Christian, Muslim," Encounter, 46 (1983), 15-35.

Perlmann, Moshe. [5127] "A Seventeenth Century Exhortation Concerning Al-Aqsa," in M. Anbar (ed.), Israel Oriental Studies, 3. Tel Aviv: Tel Aviv University, 1973, 261-292.

Peters, F. E. [5128] "The Holy House: The Muslims Come to Jerusalem, / The Holy War of Islam, / The Face of Medieval Jerusalem, / The End of the Middle Ages," in Jerusalem: The Holy City in the Eyes of Chroniclers, Visitors, Pilgrims, and Prophets from the Days of Abraham to the Beginnings of Modern Times. Princeton: Princeton University Press, 1985, 167-214, 333-426, 479-534.

Pick, W. P. See Hirschberg, H. Z.; Pick, W. P.; and Kaniel, J. [5061]

Richards, D. S. See Hasson, Isaac. [5054]

Richmond, Ernest T. [5129] The Dome of the Rock in Jerusalem: A Description of its Structure and Decoration. Oxford: Clarendon Press, 1924, 111 pp.

von Riess, Richard. [5130] "Zur Baugeschichte des Felsendoms in Jerusalem," Zeitschrift des deutschen Paläsina-Vereins, 11 (1888), 197-211.

Rondot, P. [5131] "Al Aqsa et la signification de Jérusalem pour l' Islam," Études, 331 (1969), 355-365.

Rosén-Ayalon, Myriam. [5132] "An Early Source on the Construction of the Dome of the Chain on the Temple Mount," Cathedra: For the History of Eretz-Israel and its Yishuv, 11 (1979), 184-185 (Hebrew).

Rosén-Ayalon, Myriam. [5133] "Art and Architecture in Ayyubid Jerusalem," in Eretz-Israel: Archaeological, Historical, and Geographical Studies, 18. Jerusalem: Israel Exploration Society, 1985, 65-72 (Hebrew), 67 (English summary).

Rosén-Ayalon, Myriam. [5134] "The Islamic Architecture of Jerusalem," in Y. Yadin (ed.), Jerusalem Revealed: Archaeology in the Holy City, 1968-1974. New Haven and London: Yale University Press and the Israel Exploration Society, 1976, 92-96.

Rosén-Ayalon, Myriam. [5135] "Murals in the Moslem Quarter of Jerusalem," Ariel, 23/3 (1972), 139-145.

Rosén-Ayalon, Myriam. [5136] "Muslim Art in Jerusalem-- Architecture and its Ornamentation," in in B. Z. Kedar (ed.), Jerusalem in the Middle Ages, Selected Papers. Jerusalem: Yad Izhaq Ben-Zvi, 1979, 287-315 (Hebrew), xxii-xxiii (English summary). English summary also in "From the Hebrew Press: Jerusalem in the Middle Ages, Selected Papers (Yad Izhaq Ben-Zvi, Jerusalem, 1979)," in L. I. Levine (ed.), Jerusalem Cathedra, 2. Jerusalem: Yad Izhaq Ben-Zvi Institute / Detroit: Wayne State University Press, 1982, 325.

Rosén-Ayalon, Myriam. [5137] "Popular Moslem Art in Jerusalem," Studio International, 185, (1973), 158-159.

"The Sakhrah: View and Plan," [5138] Palestine Exploration Fund, Quarterly Statement, (1887), 74-75.

Sauvaire, Henry. [5139] Histoire de Jérusalem et d' Hebron depuis Abraham jusqu'à la fin du XVe siècle de J. C.: Fragments de la chronique de Moujfir-ed-Dyn traduits sur le texte arabe. Paris: Ernest Leroux, 1875, 346 pp.

al-Sayeh, Abd al Hamid. [5140] La Position de Jérusalem dans l'Islam. Cairo: Conseil supérieur des affaires islamiques, 1968, 64 pp.

Schedl, Claus. [5141] "Änderung der Gebetrichtung (Qiblah) von Jerusalem nach Mekkah: Exegese von Sure 2, 142-152," in J. B. Bauer and J. Marböck (eds.), Memoria Jerusalem (Festschrift Franz Sauer).

Schedl, Claus. [5142] "Jerusalem, heilige Stadt des Islam?" Theologie der Gegenwart in Auswahl, 25 (1982), 203-212.

Schick, Conrad. [5143] "Arabic Building Terms," Palestine Exploration Fund, Quarterly Statement, (1893), 194-201.

Schick, Conrad. [5144] Beit el Makdas oder der alte Tempelplatz zu Jerusalem: wie es jetzt ist. Jerusalem: Privately printed, 1887; Stuttgart: Steinkopfin Comm., 1887, 175 pp.

Schick, Conrad. [5145] "The Buildings South of the 'Double Gate'", Palestine Exploration Fund, Quarterly Statement, (1892), 19-24.

Schick, Conrad. [5146] "Khan ez-Zeit," Palestine Exploration Fund, Quarterly Statement, (1897), 29-33.

Schick, Conrad. [5147] "The Kubbet Shekfee Sakhra," Palestine Exploration Fund, Quarterly Statement, (1897), 103-105.

Schick, Conrad. [5148] "Newly Found Figure Found in the Haram Wall," Palestine Exploration Fund, Quarterly Statement, (1882), 171.

Schick, Conrad. [5149] "The Shekfee Sakhra (additions)," Palestine Exploration Fund, Quarterly Statement, (1898), 83-84.

Schick, Conrad. [5150] Die Stiftshütte der Tempel in Jerusalem und der Tempelplatz der Jetztzeit. Berlin: Weidmannsche Buchhandlung, 1896, 363 pp.

Schiller, Ely. [5151] Jerusalem and the Holy Land in Old Engravings and Illustrations (1483-1800). Jerusalem: Ariel, 1981, 200 pp.

Schrieke, B. [5152] "Die Himmelfahrt Mohammads," Der Islam: Zeitschrift für Geschichte und Kultur des islamischen Orients, 4 (1916), 1-30.

Schrieke, B. [5153] "Isra'," in H. A. R. Gibb and J. H. Kramers (eds.), Shorter Encyclopaedia of Islam. Edited on behalf of the Royal Netherlands Academy. Ithaca: Cornell University Press, 1953, 183-184.

Schur, Nathan. [5154] "The Moslems," in Jerusalem in Pilgrims and Travellers' Accounts: A Thematic Bibliography of Western Christian Itineraries, 1300-1917. Jerusalem: Ariel, 1980, 87-90.

Sepp, Bernhard. See Sepp, J. N. and Sepp, Bernhard. [5156]

Sepp, J. N. [5155] "Die Felsenkuppel in Jerusalem," Zeitschrift des deutschen Palästina-Vereins, 12 (1889), 167-192.

Sepp, J. N. and Sepp, Bernhard. [5156] Die Felsenkuppel, eine justinianische Sophienkirche und die übrigen Tempel Jerusalem. Munich: Kellerer, 1882, 176 pp.

Seybold, C. F. [5157] "Haram esch-scherif, nicht Haram esch-scherif," Zeitschrift des deutschen Palästina-Vereins, 25 (1902), 106-107.

Sharon, M. [5158] "Arabic Inscriptions from the Excavations at the Western Wall," Israel Exploration Journal, 23 (1973), 214-220.

Sheppard, C. D. [5159] "A Note on the Date of Taq-i-Bustan and its Relevance to Early Christian Art in the Near East," Gesta: International Center of Medieval Art, 20/1 (1981), 9-13.

Simpson, William. [5160] "The Visit of Bonomi, Catherwood, and Arundale to the Haram es Sheriff at Jerusalem in 1833," Palestine Exploration Fund, Quarterly Statement, (1879), 51-53.

Sivan, Emmanuel. [5161] "The Beginnings of the 'Fada'il al-Quds' Literature," Der Islam: Zeitschrift für Geschichte und Kultur des islamichen Orients, 48 (1971), 100-110. Also in J. Blau (ed.), Israel Oriental Studies, 1. Tel Aviv: Tel Aviv University, 1971, 263-271.

Sivan, Emmanuel. [5162] "Le Caractère sacré de Jérusalem dans l'Islam aux XIIe-XIIIe siècles," Studia Islamica, 27 (1967), 147-182.

Sivan, Emmanuel. [5163] L' Islam et la Croisade: Idéologie et propagande dans les réactions musulmanes aux croisades. Paris: Adrien-Maisonneuve, 1968, 222 pp.

Sivan, Emmanuel. [5164] "The Sanctity of Jerusalem in Islam," in Interpretations of Islam: Past and Present. Princeton: Darwin Press, 1985, 75-106.

Sivan, Emmanuel. [5165] "Al-Quds, the Holy," Ariel, 23 (1969), 17-21.

Soucek, P. [5166] "The Temple of Solomon in Islamic Legend and Art," in J. Guttman (ed.), The Temple of Solomon: Archaeological Fact and Medeival Tradition in Christian, Islamic and Jewish Art. Religion and the Arts, 3. Missoula, MT: Scholars Press, 1976, 73-124.

Stendel, Ori. [5167] "The Arabs in Jerusalem: 1. The History of the Arabs in Jerusalem," in J. M. Oestrreicher and A. Sinai (eds.), Jerusalem. New York: John Day, 1974, 148-157.

Stephan, Stephan H. [5168] "Evliya Tshelebi's Travels in Palestine," Quarterly of the Department of Antiquities in Palestine, 8 (1938), 137-156; 9 (1939/41), 81-104. [Sections on Jerusalem.]

Stephan, Stephan H. [5169] Evliya Tshelebi's Travels in Palestine (1648-1650). Jerusalem: Ariel, 1980, 99 pp. (English) + 13 PP (Hebrew). [The complete work of Evliya Tshelebi, reprinted from Quarterly of the Department of Antiquities in Palestine, 4-9 (1935-1942); sections on Jerusalem, 55-94.]

Stephan, Stephan H. [5170] "Two Turkish Inscriptions from the Citadel of Jerusalem," Quarterly of the Department of Antiquities in Palestine, 2 (1933), 132-135.

Stern, H. [5171] "Recherches sur la mosquée al-Aqsa sur ses mosaïques," Ars Orientalis, 5 (1963), 27-47.

Steve, M.-A. See Vincent, Louis-Hugues and Steve, M.-A. [5191-5192]

Stewart, Aubrey. [5172] "Eutychii Annales," in "Extracts from Aristeas, Hecataeus, Origen and Other Early Writers," in The Library of the Palestine Pilgrims' Text Society, 11. New York: AMS Press, 1971, 35-68. [Originally published in 1895.]

Strzygowski, Joseph. [5173] "Felsendom und Aksamoschee: Eine Abwehr," Der Islam: Zeitschrift für Geschichte und Kultur des islamichen Orients, 2 (1911), 79-97.

Tamari, D. S. [5174] "Al-Ashrafiyya: An Imperial Madrasa in Jerusalem," Memoria della Accademia Nazionale dei Lincei, Roma, scienze morali, 19/5 (1976), 535-568.

Tibawi, Abdul Latif. [5175] "The City of Jerusalem," in The Islamic Quarterly, 16 (1972), 3-11.

Tibawi, Abdul Latif. [5176] "Al-Ghazali's Tract on Dogmatic Theology, / Al-Ghazali's Sojourn in Damascus and Jerusalem," The Islamic Quarterly, 9 (1965), 65-77.

Tibawi, Abdul Latif. [5177] The Islamic Pious Foundations in Jerusalem: Origins, History, and Usurption by Israel. London: Islamic Cultural Centre, 1978, 54 pp.

Tibawi, Abdul Latif. [5178] "Jerusalem: Its Place in Islam and Arab History," The Islamic Quarterly, 12 (1968), 185-218. Also in Ibrahim Abu-Lughod (ed.), The Arab-Israeli Confrontation of June 1967: An Arab Perspective. Evanston:

Northwestern University Press, 1970, 10-48. Published as monograph, Beirut: Institute for Palestine Studies, 1969, 45 pp.

Tibawi, Abdul Latif. [5179] "Jerusalem under Islamic Rule," in Jerusalem: The Key to World Peace. London: Islamic Council of Europe, 1980, 141-153.

Tibawi, Abdul Latif. [5180] "Special Report: The Destruction of an Islamic Heritage in Jerusalem," Arab Studies Quarterly, 2 (Spring, 1980), 180-189. [On the destruction of the Magharibah quarter.]

Toledano, Ehud. [5181] "The Sanjaq of Jerusalem in the Sixteenth Century-- Patterns of Rural Settlement and Demographic Trends," in A. Cohen (ed.), Jerusalem in the Early Ottoman Period. Jerusalem: Yad Izhaq Ben-Zvi, 1979, 61-92 (Hebrew), viii-ix (English summary).

Tsafrir, Yoram. [5182] "Muqaddasi's Gates of Jerusalem-- a New Identification Based on Byzantine Sources," Israel Exploration Journal, 27 (1977), 152-161.

Vajda, G. [5183] "La description du Temple de Jérusalem d' après le K. al-masalik wal-mamalik d' Al-Muhallabi: Ses éléments bibliques et rabbiniques," Journal asiatique, 247 (1959), 193-202.

Van Berchem, Marguerite. See Creswell, K. A. C. [5013]

Van Berchem, Marguerite. See Gautier-Van Berchem, Marguerite and Ory, Solange. [5025]

Van Berchem, Marguerite. [5184] "The Mosaics of the Dome of the Rock at Jerusalem and of the Great Mosque at Damascus," in K. A. C. Creswell, Early Muslim Architecture, 1. Oxford: Clarendon Press, 1932, 148-228.

Van Berchem, Max. See Migeon, G. [5117]

Van Berchem, Max. [5185] "An Arabic Inscription from Jerusalem," Palestine Exploration Fund, Quarterly Statement, (1898), 86-93.

Van Berchem, Max. [5186] "Arabische Inschriften aus Jerusalem," Palästinajahrbuch, 16 (1920), 31-32.

Van Berchem, Max. [5187] "Épitaphe arabe de Jerusalem," Revue biblique, 9 (1900), 288-290.

Van Berchem, Max. [5188] Matériaux pour un Corpus Inscriptionum Arabicarum, 2: Syria du Sud, 1. Jérusalem "Ville;" 2. Jérusalem "Haram;" 3. Jérusalem (Planches). Cairo: Imp. d'I.F.A.O. du Caire, 1920, 1922, 1925-27, 464 + 466 + 120 pp.

Van Berchem, Max. [5189] "Note on the Graffiti of the Cistern at Wody el-Joz," Palestine Exploration Fund, Quarterly Statement, (1915), 85-90, 195-198.

Vincent, Louis-Hughes. [5190] "Le Protectorat de Charlemagne sur la Terre Sainte," Revue biblique, 36 (1927), 237-242.

Vincent, Louis-Hughes and Steve, M.-A. [5191] "Adaptation du Temple au Haram et aperçu de son évolution," in Jérusalem de L' Ancien Testament, 2. Paris: Gabalda, 1956, 587-610.

Vincent, Louis-Hughes and Steve, M.-A. [5192] "Le Haram esh Sherif, site du Temple ancien," in Jérusalem de L'Ancien Testament, 2. Paris: Gabalda, 1956, 526-586.

Waisel, V. See Levi-Yadin, S.; Lipschitz, S. N.; and Waisel, V. [5097]

Walker, J. [5193] "Kubbat al-Sakhra," in H. A. R. Gibb and J. H. Kramers (eds.), Shorter Encyclopaedia of Islam. Edited on behalf of the Royal Netherlands Academy. Ithaca: Cornell University Press, 1953, 267-269.

Walls, Archibald G. [5194] "The Mausoleum of the Amir Kilani," Levant, 7 (1975), 39-76.

Walls, Archibald G. [5195] "The Mausoleum of the Amir Kilani: Restored Elevations," Levant, 9 (1977), 168-173.

Walls, Archibald G. [5196] "The Turbat Barakat Khan or Kalidi Library," Levant, 6 (1974), 25-50.

Walls, Archibald G. [5197] "Two Minarets Flanking the Church of the Holy Sepulchre," Levant, 8 (1976), 159-161.

Walls, Archibald G. and Abul-Hajj, Amal. [5198] Arabic Inscriptions in Jerusalem: A Handlist and Maps. London: World of Islam Festival Trust, 1980, 33 pp. + 5 maps.

Wensinck, Arent Jan. [5199] "Kibla," in H. A. R. Gibb and J. H. Kramers (eds.), Shorter Encyclopaedia of Islam. Edited on behalf of the Royal Netherlands Academy. Ithaca: Cornell University Press, 1953, 260-261.

Wensinck, Arent Jan. [5200] "Jerusalem," in A Handbook of Early Mohammadan Tradition. Leiden: Brill, 1960, 177. [Index of Hadith traditions on Jerusalem.]

Werblowsky, R. J. Zwi. [5201] The Meaning of Jerusalem to Jews, Christians and Muslims. Jerusalem: Israel Universities Study Group for Middle Eastern Affairs, 1977; rev. edn., 1978, 16 pp. [Published originally as "Jerusalem, Holy City of Three Religions," in W. Barta (ed.), Jaarbericht Ex Orient Lux, 23 (1975), 423-439.]

Wilkinson, John. [5202] "Architectural Procedures in Byzantine Palestine," Levant, 13 (1981), 156-172. [On the Dome of the Rock.]

Wilson, Charles W. See Le Strange, Guy. [5090]

Wilson, Charles W. [5203] "The 'Buckler' of Hamza," Palestine Exploration Fund, Quarterly Statement, (1903), 175-177.

Wilson, Charles W. [5204] "Haram-ash-Sharif," in Ordnance Survey of Jerusalem. London: Lord's Commissioners of Her Majesty's Treasury, 1865, 23-46.

Wilson, Charles W. [5205] "On the Transference of the Arab Names of Some of the Gates of the Haram ash Sherif between the Eleventh and Fifteenth Centuries," Palestine Exploration Fund, Quarterly Statement, (1888), 141-144.

Wolff, Odilo. [5206] "Der Salomonische Tempelplatz und des heutige Haram zu Jerusalem," Zeitschrift des deutschen Palästina-Vereins, 11 (1888), 60-67., plan.

Wray, G. O. [5207] "Southern Projection from the Masjed al Aksa," Palestine Exploration Fund, Quarterly Statement, (1891), 321-322.

Thirty-Seven

Jerusalem in the Nineteenth and Early Twentieth Centuries

Abir, Mordechai. [5208] "Local Leadership and Early Reforms in Palestine," in M. Ma'oz (ed.), Studies on Palestine During the Ottoman Period. Jerusalem: Magnes Press, 1975, 284-310.

Abu -Jaber, Kamel S. [5209] "The Millet System in the Nineteenth Century Ottoman Empire," Muslim World, 57 (1967), 212-223.

Abu -Manneh, Butrus. [5210] "The Rise of the Sanjak of Jerusalem in the Late 19th Century," in G. Ben-Dor (ed.), The Palestinians and the Middle East Conflict. Ramat Gan, 1978,

Adlerblum, Burton S. [5211] "The Early Days of the Russian Post in Palestine," The Israel Philatelist, 23/ 1-2 (1971), 23.

Adlerblum, Burton S. [5212] "Foreign Consulates in Palestine During the Turkish Period," The Israel Philatelist, 31/11-12 (1980). 2167-2174.

Amiran, David H. K. [5213] "The Development of Jerusalem, 1860-1970," in D. H. K. Amiran, A. Shachar, I. Kimhi (eds.), Urban Geography of Jerusalem: A Companion Volume to the Atlas of Jerusalem. Jerusalem: Massada Press, 1973, 20-52, esp. 20-37.

el-Aref, Aref. [5214] "The Closing Phase of Ottoman Rule in Jerusalem," in M. Ma'oz (ed.), Studies on Palestine during the Ottoman Period. Jerusalem: Magnes Press, 1975, 334-340.

Arundale, Francis. [5215] Illustrations of Jerusalem and Mount Sinai Including the Most Interesting Sites between Grand Cairo and Beirut. London: Colburn, 1837, 116 pp., esp. 40-72, 84-87.

Atkins, Gaius G. [5216] Jerusalem Past and Present: The City of Undying Memories. New York: Fleming H. Revell, 1918, 169 pp.

Baedeker, Karl. [5217] Jerusalem and its Surroundings: Handbook for Travellers. Jerusalem: Carta, 1973, 189 pp. [Reprint of Jerusalem section of 1876 Baedeker Guidebook.]

Baker, Dwight. [5218] "The Origin and Development of the Millet System," Christian News from Israel, 21/2 (1970), 32-34.

Baker, Dwight. [5219] "The Millet System: States Within a State," Christian News from Israel, 21/3 (1970), 20-23.

Baldensperger, Philip J. [5220] "The Immovable East: The General Characteristics of the Different Towns, I: Jerusalem," Palestine Exploration Fund, Quarterly Statement, (1916), 165-172.

Barclay, James T. [5221] "Modern Jerusalem," in The City of the Great King, or Jerusalem as It Was, as It Is, and as It Is To Be. Philadelphia: James Challen and Sons, 1858; reprinted, New York: Arno Press, 1977, 406-603.

Joseph Barclay, Third Anglican Bishop of Jerusalem: A Missionary Biography. [5222] London: S. W. Partridge and Co., 1883, 600 pp.

Bartlett, William H. [5223] Jerusalem Revisited. London: A. Hall, Virtue and Co., 1855, 202 pp. Reprinted with an introduction by Zev Vilnay, Jerusalem: Ariel, 1976.

Bartlett, William H. [5224] Walks about the City and Environs of Jerusalem, Summer 1842. Jerusalem: Canaan Publishing Co., 1974, 255 pp. [Originally published in London, 1844, as Walks in and about the City and Environs of Jerusalem; reprint of the second edition of 1850, with an introduction by Rechavam Zeevy.]

Bausman, Benjamin. [5225] Sinai and Zion, or A Pilgrimage through the Wilderness to the Land of Promise. Philadelphia: S. R. Fisher, 1861, 222-287. Published also in German: Sinai und Zion: Eine Pilgerreise durch die Wüste nach den gelobten Lande. Reading, PA: Daniel Miller, 1875, 3rd edn., 1885, 187-238.

Bedford, W. K. R. and Holbeche, Richard. [5226] "Opthalmic Hospital in Jerusalem," in The Order of the Hospital of St. John of Jerusalem: A History of the English Hospittalers. London: F. E. Robinson, 1902, 149-164.

Ben-Arieh, Yehoshua. [5227] "The Growth of Jerusalem in the Nineteenth Century," Annals of the Association of American Geographers, 65/2 (1975), 252-269.

Ben-Arieh, Yehoshua. [5228] Jerusalem in the 19th Century: The Old City. Jerusalem: Yad Izhaq Ben-Zvi / New York: St. Martin's Press, 1984, 438 pp.

Ben-Arieh, Yehoshua. [5229] "Legislative and Cultural Factors in the Development of Jerusalem, 1800-1914," in Geography in Israel. A Collection of Papers Offered to the 23rd International Geographical Congress, USSR, July-August, 1976. Jerusalem, 1976, 54-105.

Ben-Arieh, Yehoshua. [5230] "Patterns of Christian Activity and Dispersion in Nineteenth Century Jerusalem," Journal of Historical Geography, 2 (1976), 49-69.

Ben-Arieh, Yehoshua. [5231] "The Population of the Large Towns in Palestine during the First Eighty Years of the Nineteenth Century According to Western Sources," in M. Ma'oz (ed.), Studies on Palestine during the Ottoman Period. Jerusalem: Magnes Press, 1975, 49-69. [Jerusalem, 50-53, 68-69.]

Ben-Arieh, Yehoshua. [5232] "The Process of the Jewish Community's Emergence from within Jerusalem's Walls at the End of the Ottoman Period," in A Shinan (ed.), Proceedings of the Sixth World Congress of Jewish Studies, 2. Jerusalem: World Union of Jewish Studies, 1975, 239-315.

Ben-Arieh, Yehoshua. [5233] The Rediscovery of the Holy Land in the Nineteenth Century. Jerusalem: Israel Exploration Society / Detroit: Wayne State University Press, 1979, 266 pp.

Ben-Yehudah, Hemda. [5234] "When the War Came to Palestine: A Dramatic Story of the Long Siege, Sufferings, Persecutions, and Ultimate Relief of the Holy City-- A Glorious Hannucca of Joy and Gladness," in Jerusalem, Its Redemption and Future: The Great Drama of Deliverance Described by Eyewitnesses. New York: The Christian Herald, 1918, 3-61.

Bentwich, Norman. [5235] "The Redemption of Judaea: Sketches on the British Advance to Jerusalem," in Palestine of the Jews, Past, Present, and Future. London: Kegan Paul, Trench, Trubner and Co., 1919, 215-284.

Bezanson, W. E. See Melville, Herman. [5344]

Blumberg, Arnold. [5236] A View from Jerusalem, 1849-1858: The Consular Diary of James and Elisabeth Anne Finn. Rutherford, NJ: Fairleigh Dickinson / Associated University Presses, 1980, 352 pp.

Blyth, Estelle. [5237] When We Lived in Jerusalem. London: John Murray, 1927, 348 pp.

Bonar, Andrew A. [5238] Narrative of a Mission of Inquiry to the Jews from the Church of Scotland in 1839. Edinburgh: William Whyte / Glasgow: W. Collins and D. Bryce, 1845, 555 pp., esp. 126-174, 188-198.

Borrer, Dawson. [5239] A Journey from Naples to Jerusalem. London: J. Modden, 1845, 579 pp., esp. 394-436.

Bovet, Felix. [5240] Egypt, Palestine and Phoenicia: A Visit to Sacred Lands. New York: E. P. Dutton, 1883, 416 pp.

Breen, Andrew E. [5241] A Diary of My Life in the Holy Land. Rochester, NY: John P. Smith, 1905, 637 pp.

Buckingham , James Silk. [5242] Travels in Palestine, through the Countries of Bashan and Gilead, 2 vols. London: Longman, Hurst, Rees, Orme, and Brown, 1821-1822, I, 271-335, 359-402; II, 1-49.

Buckland, Gail. See Vaczek, Louis and Buckland, Gail. [5419]

Burnet, David S. [5243] The Jerusalem Mission under the Direction of the American Christian Missionary Society (1853). New York: Arno, 1977, 319 pp. [Originally published in Cincinnati, 1853.]

Burton, Isabel. [5244] The Inner Life of Syria, Palestine and the Holy Land, from My Private Journal, 2. London: H. S. King and Co., 2nd edn., 1876, 30-192.

Busch, Moritz. [5245] Eine Wallfahrt nach Jerusalem: Bilder ohne Heilgenscheine, 1-2. Leipzig: F. W.Grunow, 3rd edn., 1881, I, 229-265; II, 1-71, 103-128.

Buzzetti, Luciano. [5246] "The Italian Posts in Palestine," The Israel Philatelist, 24, 5/6 (Feb., 1973), 132-141. [Jerusalem office only.]

Carmel, Alex. [5247] Christen als Pioniere im Heiligen Land. Basel: Friedrich Reinhardt Verlag, 1981, 194 pp.

Carmel, Alex. [5248] "The German Settlers in Palestine and their Relations with the Local Arab Population and the Jewish Community, 1868-1918," in M. Ma'oz (ed.), Studies on Palestine during the Nineteenth Century. Jerusalem: Magnes Press, 1975, 442-465.

Carmel, Alex. [5249] "Russian Activity in Palestine during the Late Ottoman Period," in E. Shaltiel (ed.), Jerusalem in the Modern Period: Yaacov Herzog Memorial Volume. Jerusalem: Yad Izhaq Ben-Zvi and Ministry of Defense, 1981, 81-116 (Hebrew), ii-iii (English summary).

Carmel, Alex. [5250] "Wie es zu Conrad Schicks Sendung nach Jerusalem kam," Zeitschrift des deutschen Palästina-Vereins, 99 (1983), 204-218.

Carpenter, Mary. [5251] In Cairo and Jerusalem: An Eastern Notebook. New York: Randolph and Co., 1894, 222 pp.

Carus, Paul. [5252] "City of Jesus and the Via Dolorosa," Open Court, 24 (1910), 164-190.

Carus, Paul. [5253] "The Vicinity of Jerusalem," Open Court, 24 (1910), 335-356.

Chaplin, Thomas. [5254] "Some Jerusalem Notes," Palestine Exploration Fund, Quarterly Statement, (1889), 9-11.

Colbi, Paul S. [5255] "Austrian Presence in the Holy Land," Holy Land Review, 6/1-4 (Spring-Winter, 1980), 54-57.

Colbi, Paul S. [5256] "European and American Consulates in Jerusalem during the Ottoman Period," Holy Land Review, 5/1-2 (Spring-Summer, 1979), 55-63.

Colbi, Paul S. [5257] "Talitha Kumi," The Holy Land, 1/1 (Spring, 1981), 14-15.

Conder, Claude R. [5258] "Jerusalem," in Tent Work in Palestine: A Record of Discovery and Adventure. London: Richard Bentley and Sons, 1879, 307-345.

Conder, Claude R. [5259] "Jews, Russians, and Germans," in Tent Work in Palestine: A Record of Discovery and Adventure. London: Richard Bentley and Sons, 1879, 293-315.

"Constructive Health Work in Jerusalem," [5260] American Journal of Public Health, 8 (1918), 936.

Conway, John S. [5261] "The Jerusalem Bishopric: A 'Union of Foolscap and Blotting-paper,'" Studies in Religion, 7 (1978), 305-315.

Cook's Tourist Handbook for Palestine and Syria. [5262] London: Thomas Cook and Son, 1911, 58-122 (Jerusalem).

Crolly, G. See Roberts, David. [5370]

Curzon, Robert. [5263] Visits to Monasteries in the Levant. Ithaca, NY: Cornell University Press, 1955, 54-178, 196-218. [Originally published in 1849.]

Dalman, Gustaf. [5264] "Das alte und das neue Jerusalem und seine Bedeutung im Weltkreige," Palästinajahrbuch, 11 (1915), 17-38.

Dalman, Gustaf. [5265] "Gegenwärtiger Bestand der judischer Colonien in Palästina, B: Die Umgebung von Jerusalem," Zeitschift des deutschen Palästina-Vereins, 16 (1893), 196-197.

Davis, Helen. [5266] "Jerusalem Model Rediscovered," Biblical Archaeology Review, 13/1 (Jan.-Feb., 1987), 60-62. [Stephan Illes model.]

Davis, L. K. [5267] "The First Americans in Jerusalem," Christian News from Israel, 22 (1971), 127-131.

Davison, Roderic H. [5268] "The Ottoman-Moslem Era: The Search for Sources," in M. Davis (ed.), With Eyes toward Zion: Scholars Colloquium on America-Holy Land Studies. New York: Arno Press, 1977, 88-99.

De Hass, Frank S. [5269] Recent Travels and Explorations in Bible Lands, Consisting of Sketchs Written from Personal Observations. New York: Phillips and Hunt / Cincinati: Walden and Stowe, 1880, 445 pp. Revised and published as Buried Cities Recovered, or Explorations in Bible Lands. Philadelphia: Bradley and Co, 10th edn., 1885, 610 pp., esp. 127-189. [American consul in Jerusalem, 1873-1877.]

Deissmann, A. [5270] "Jerusalem, the Holy City," Constructive Quarterly, 2 (1914), 314-328.

Dixon, William H. [5271] The Holy Land, 2. London: Chapman and Hall, 1865, 1-55, 209-266.

Doerksen, Victor G. [5272] "Eduard Wüst and Jerusalem," Mennonite Quarterly Review, 56 (1982), 169-178.

Dunning, H. W. [5273] "The Holy City, / Around Jerusalem," in To-Day in Palestine. New York: James Pott and Co., 1907, 19-60.

Elath, Eliahu. [5274] "A British Project for the Construction of a Railway between Jaffa and Jerusalem in the Nineteenth Century," in M. Ma'oz (ed.), Studies on Palestine during the Ottoman Period. Jerusalem: Magnes Press, 1975, 415-422.

Ewald, F. C. [5275] Journal of Missionary Labours in the City of Jerusalem during the Years 1842/3/4. London: Wertheim, Aldine Chambers, 1845, 239 pp; 2nd edn., 1846, 276 pp.

Finn, Elisabeth Anne. See Finn, James. [5278]

Finn, Elisabeth Anne. See Webster, Gillian. [5434]

Finn, Elisabeth Anne. [5276] A Home in the Holy Land: A Tale Illustrating Customs and Incidents in Modern Jerusalem. New York: T. Y. Crowell, 1882, 491 pp. [Literature.]

Finn, Elisabeth Anne. [5277] Reminiscences of Mrs. Finn, Member of the Royal Asiatic Society. London and Edinburgh: Marshall, Morgan and Scott, 1929, 256 pp.

Finn, Elisabeth Anne and Finn, James. See Schur, Nathan. [5398]

Finn, Elisabeth Anne and Finn, James. See Blumberg, Arnold. [5236]

Finn, James. [5278] Stirring Times, or Records from Jerusalem Consular Chronicles of 1853 to 1856, 2 vols. Edited and compiled by his widow [Elisabeth Anne Finn]. London: C. Kegan Paul and Co., 1878, 490 + 485 pp.

Frankl, Ludwig A. [5279] Nach Jerusalem, 2. Leipzig: Baumgärtner's Buchhandlung, 1858, 11-301.

Friedberg, Albert. [5280] "Foreign Postal Services in the Holy Land," The Israel Philatelist, 16/8 (1965), 1366-1367.

Friedman, Jack E. [5281] "First Protestant English Accounts of the Holy Land," Christian News from Israel, 25/2 (1975), 82-87.

Fullerton, Kemper. [5282] "Jerusalem-- The World City and the World War," in Jerusalem, Its Redemption and Future: The Great Drama of Deliverance Described by Eyewitnesses. New York: The Christian Herald, 1918, 65-104.

Garfinkel, Martin and Wallach, Josef. [5283] "The Telegraph in the Holy Land," The Isarel Philatelist, 22/5-6 (1971), 104-115.

Gavin, Carney E. S. [5284] The Image of the East: Nineteenth Century Near Eastern Photographs by Bonfils. Chicago: University of Chicago Press, 1982, 115 pp. + 10 microfiche transparencies.

Geikie, Cunningham. [5285] The Holy Land and the Bible, 2. New York: James Pott and Co., 1888, 1-65.

Gerber, Haim. [5286] "The Ottoman Administration of Jerusalem, 1890-1908," Asian and African Studies: Journal of the Israel Oriental Society, 12 (1978), 33-76.

Gidal, Nachum T. [5287] Eternal Jerusalem, 1840-1917. Jerusalem: Steimatzky, 1980, plates, no pagination. [Oversized, art quality reproductions of contemporary photographs with explanatory text.] German edition published as Ewiges Jerusalem, 1850-1910: Einführung und Bildlegenden. Luzern: C. J. Bucher, 1980, 24 pp. + plates.

Gidney, W. T. [5288] History of the London Society for Promoting Christianity amongst the Jews. London: London Society for Promoting Christianity, 1908, 672 pp.

Gilbert, Martin. [5289] Jerusalem: Rebirth of a City. Jerusalem: Domino Press / London: Hogarth Press,1985, 238 pp.

Gilbert, Martin. [5290] [Maps depicting the development of Jerusalem during the period 1830-1914.] in *Jerusalem History Atlas*. New York: Macmillan, 1977, 41 (1830-1850), 42-43 (1842), 44-45 (1850's), 46-47 (1860's), 54-55 (1870's), 57 (1880's), 58-59 (1890's), 60-63 (1900-1914).

Gilbert, Vivian. [5291] *The Romance of the Last Crusade: With Allenby to Jerusalem*. New York and London: D. Appleton, 1923, 235 pp., esp. 136-179.

Goell, Yohai and Katz-Hyman, Martha B. [5292] "Americans in the Holy Land, 1850-1900: A Select Bibliography," in M. Davis (ed.), *With Eyes toward Zion: Scholars Colloquium on America-Holy Land Studies*. New York: Arno Press, 1977, 100-125.

Goodman, Moshe. [5293] "Immortalizing a Historic Moment: The Surrender of Jerusalem, 1917," in L. I. Levine (ed.), *Jerusalem Cathedra*, 3. Jerusalem: Yad Izhaq Ben-Zvi Institute / Detroit: Wayne State University Press, 1983, 280-282.

Goodrich-Freer, A. [5294] *Inner Jerusalem*. London: Constable, 1904, 388 pp.

Gray, John. [5295] "Ottoman Obscurity," in *A History of Jerusalem*. New York: Praeger, 1969, 260-293.

Greaves, R. W. [5296] "The Jerusalem Bishopric, 1841," *English Historical Review*, 64 (1949), 328-352.

Grunwald, Kurt. [5297] "Origins of the Jaffa-Jerusalem Railway," in M. Friedman, B.-Z. Yehoshua, and Y. Tobi (eds.), *Chapters in the History of the Jewish Community in Jerusalem*, 2. Jerusalem: Yad Izhaq Ben-Zvi, 1976, 255-265 (Hebrew), xvii (English summary).

Gutmann, Emmanuel. [5298] "The Beginnings of Local Government in Jerusalem," *Public Administration in Israel and Abroad*, 8 (1967), 52-61.

Halevy, Shoshana. [5299] "Clarifying the Development of Jerusalem outside the Walls," in Y. Ben-Porat, B.-Z. Yehoshua, and A. Kedar (eds.), *Chapters in the History of the Jewish Community in Jerusalem*, 1. Jerusalem: Yad Izhaq Ben-Zvi, 1973, 141-153 (Hebrew).

Halevy, Shoshana. [5300] "The Establishment of the Kollel Ungarn (Neturei Karta) and Batei Ungarn," in E. Shaltiel (ed.), *Jerusalem in the Modern Period: Yaacov Herzog Memorial Volume*. Jerusalem: Yad Izhaq Ben-Zvi and Ministry of Defense, 1981, 227-254 (Hebrew), vii-viii (English summary).

Hamburger, Meir. [5301] "I Worked for the Austrian Post Office in Jerusalem," *The Holy Land Philatelist*, 1/8 (1955), 224-226.

Hanauer, James Edward. [5302] "Notes on the History of Modern Colonization in Palestine," *Palestine Exploration Fund, Quarterly Statement,* (1900), 124-142.

Hanauer, James Edward. [5303] *Walks in and around Jerusalem*. With an introduction by R. A. S. Macalister. London: S.P.C.K., 2nd and rev. edn.,

1926, 430 pp. [Originally published in London, 1910, as Walks about Jerusalem.]

Hannam, Michael. [5304] "Some Nineteenth Century Britons in Jerusalem," Palestine Exploration Quarterly, (1982), 53-65..

Hechler, William H. [5305] The Jerusalem Bishopric: Documents with Translations Chiefly Derived from "Das evangelische Bisthum in Jerusalem." London: Trübner and Co., 1883, 211 pp.

Hoexter, Werner and Lachmann, S. [5306] "Postal History of Palestine and Israel, 1: Palestine under Turkish Rule," The Holy Land Philatelist, 1/3 (1955), 9-10; 1/4 (1955), 112-114; 1/5 (1955), 150-152; 1/6 (1955), 175-177; 1/7 (1955), 196-197; 1/8 (1955), 216-217; 1/9-10 (1955), 242-243; 1/12 (1955), 298-299; 2/13 (1956), 331-333; 2/14 (1956), 356-357; 2/16 (1956), 404-406; 2/18 (1956), 460-461; 2/20 (1956), 507-509 [Jerusalem office]; 2/21-22 (1956), 530-531 [Jerusalem branch offices]; 2/24 (1956), 576-577 [Jaffa-Jerusalem railway]; 3/26-27 (1956/57), 616-618; 3/29 (1957), 666-668 [surroundings of Jerusalem]; 3/30 (1957), 684; 3/33 (1957), 736-737.

Hoexter, Werner and Lachmann, S. [5307] "Postal History of Palestine and Isarel, 2: Foreign Postal Administrations," Holy Land Philatelist, 4/37 (1957), 866-827 [general, French]; 4/38 (1957), 852-853 [French]; 4/40 (1958), 896-898 [French, Jerusalem]; 4/46-47 (1958), 1012-1015 [Austrian]; 4-5/48-49 (1958), 1048-1052 [Austrian].

Hoexter, Werner and Lachmann, S. [5308] "Austrian Postal Services in Jerusalem," The Holy Land Philatelist, 1/1 (1954), 18-21.

Holbeche, Richard. See Bedford, W. K. R. and Holbeche, Richard. [5226]

Hopwood, Derek. [5309] The Russian Presence in Syria and Palestine, 1843-1914: Church and Politics in the Near East. Oxford: Clarendon Press, 1969, 232pp.

Hornus, Jean-Michel. [5310] "L' évêche anglo-prusse à Jérusalem (1841-81): Controverses autour de sa création (1841)," Proche-Orient Chrétien, 13 (1963), 130-149, 234-258; 14 (1964), 184-201, 307-334.

Hornus, Jean-Michel. [5311] "Le missions anglicanes au Proche-Orient avant la création de l' évêche à Jérusalem: Les primiers envoyés-- l' installation à Jérusalem," Proche-Orient Chrétien, 12 (1962), 255-269.

Horsford, Howard C. See Melville, Herman. [5345]

Hyamson, Albert M. [5312] The British Consulate in Jerusalem in Relation to the Jews of Palestine, 1838-1914, 2 vols. London: Jewish Historical Society of London, 1939-41.

"The Jerusalem Year Book," [5313] Palestine Exploration Fund, Quarterly Statement, (1883), 160-162. Report on Luncz, Abraham M. (ed.). [5335]

Johnson, Sarah Barclay. [5314] Hadji in Syria, or Three Years in Jerusalem. Philadelphia: J. Challon and Sons, 1858, 303 pp, esp 53-137, 165-303.

Jowett, William. [5315] Christian Researches in Syria and the Holy Land in 1823 and 1824, in Furtherance of the Objects of the Church Missionary Society. Boston: Crocker and Brewster, 1826, 364 pp., esp. 208-271.

Kaganoff, Nathan M. [5316] "Observations on America-Holy Land Relations in the Period before World War I," in M. Davis (ed.), With Eyes toward Zion: Scholars Colloquium on America-Holy Land Studies. New York: Arno Press, 1977, 79-87.

Kaniel, Yehoshua. [5317] "Organizational and Economic Contentions between Communities in Jerusalem in the Nineteenth Century," in M. Friedman, B.-Z. Yehoshua, and Y. Tobi (eds.), Chapters in the History of the Jewish Community in Jerusalem, 2. Jerusalem: Yad Izhaq Ben-Zvi, 1976, 97-126 (Hebrew), x-xi (English summary).

Kark, Ruth. [5318] "Activities of the Jerusalem Municipality in the Ottoman Period," Cathedra: For the History of Eretz-Israel and its Yishuv, 6 (1977), 74-94 (Hebrew).

Kark, Ruth. [5319] "Population Censuses in Jerusalem in the Later Ottoman Period," Cathedra: For the History of Eretz-Israel and its Yishuv, 6 (1977), 95-107 (Hebrew).

Kark, Ruth. [5320] "The Traditional Middle Eastern City: The Cases of Jerusalem and Jaffa during the Nineteenth Century," Zeitschrift des deutschen Palästina-Vereins, 97 (1981), 93-108.

Kark, Ruth and Landman, Shimon. [5321] "Muslim Neighborhoods outside the Jerusalem City Walls during the Ottoman Period," in E. Shaltiel (ed.), Jerusalem in the Modern Period: Yaacov Herzog Memorial Volume. Jerusalem: Yad Izhaq Ben-Zvi and Ministry of Defense, 1981, 174-211 (Hebrew), v (English summary). English version published as "The Establishment of Muslim Neighborhoods in Jerusalem, outside the Old City, during the Late Ottoman Period," Palestine Exploration Quarterly, (1980), 114-135.

Karmon, Yehudah. [5322] "Changes in the Urban Landscape of Jerusalem in the 19th Century," Cathedra: For the History of Eretz-Israel and its Yishuv, 6 (1977), 38-73 (Hebrew).

Katz-Hyman, Martha B. See Goell, Yohai and Katz-Hyman, Martha B. [5292]

Kenny, Vincent S. [5323] Herman Melville's Clarel: A Spiritual Autobiography. Hamden, CT: Archon Books, 1973, 272 pp. [Literature.]

Kollek, Teddy and Pearlman, Moshe. [5324] "Ottoman Jerusalem," in Jerusalem: A History of Forty Centuries. New York: Random House, 1968, 199-233.

Kroyanker, David and Wahrman, Dror. [5325] Jerusalem Architecture, Periods and Styles: The Jewish Quarters and Public Buildings outside the Old City Walls, 1860-1914. Jerusalem: Domino Press, 1983, 362 pp. [Includes studies of Me'a She'arim, Batei Ungarn, Batei Neitin, Mishkenot Sha'ananim and Yemin Moshe, Sha'arei Hessed, Nahalat Shiva, Mazkeret Moshe and Ohel Moshe, Beit David, Even Israel, Batei Rand, Batei Braude, Knesset Yisrael, Ohel

Shlomo, Sha'arei Yerushalayim, Batei Seidhoff, the Bukharan Quarter, and Zichron Moshe.]

Lachmann, S. See Hoexter, Werner and Lachmann, S. [5306-5308]

Lagrange, Marie-Joseph. [5326] "La prétendue violation de la Mosquée d' Omar," Revue biblique, 20 (1911), 440-442.

Landau, Jacob M. [5327] Abdul-Hamid's Palestine. London: Andre Deutsch, 1979, 144 pp., esp. 35-57.

Landman, Shimon. See Kark, Ruth and Landman, Shimon. [5321]

Lewis, Nahum H. [5328] "The Italian Post Office in Jerusalem," The Israel Philatelist, 18/1-2 (1966), 1720-1721.

Lietzow, Paul. [5329] Jerusalem: Ein Besuch in der heiligen Stadt. Berlin: Behrs Buchhandlung, 1888, 88 pp.

Lindenberg, Paul P. [5330] "The Austrian Post Offices in Palestine," The Israel-Palestine Philatelist, 1/8 (1950), 59-60; 2/1 (1950), 6-7; 14/7 (1963), 890.

Little, Donald P. and Turgay, Üner. [5331] "Documents from the Ottoman Period in the Khalidi Library in Jerusalem," Die Welt des Islams, 20 (1980), 44-72.

Littman, David. [5332] "The Model of Jerusalem as in 1873: A New Look at an Old City," Holy Land, 6/2 (Summer, 1986), 76-81. [Model by Stephan Illes.]

Lohmann, Paul. [5333] "Die Assanierung Jerusalems," Zeitschrift des deutschen Palästina-Vereins, 37 (1914), 271-273.

Loti, Pierre [Pen-name of Viaud, Julien]. [5334] Jérusalem. Paris: Calman Lévy, 1895, 221 pp. English edn., London: T. Werner Laurie Ltd., 1945. [Literature.]

Luncz, Abraham M. (ed.). [5335] Jerusalem Yearbook for the Diffusion of an Accurate Knowledge of Ancient and Modern Palestine, 1. Vienna: Georg Brög, 1882, 194 pp; facsimile edition with forward by Zev Vilnay, Jerusalem: Carta, 1982.

Macalister, R. A. Stewart. See Hanauer, James Edward. [5303]

Macalister, R. A. Stewart. [5336] "Gleanings from the Minute-Books of the Jerusalem Literary Society, 27: The Revolt and Earthquake of Jerusalem in 1834," Palestine Exploration Fund, Quarterly Statement, (1911), 83-89.

Macalister, R.A.Stewart. [5337] "The Revolt of 1834," Palestine Exploration Fund, Quarterly Statement, (1918), 142.

McKeithan, Daniel. See Twain, Mark. [5417]

Ma'oz, Moshe. [5338] "America and the Holy Land during the Ottoman Period," in M. Davis (ed.), With Eyes toward Zion: Scholars Colloquium on America-Holy Land Studies. New York: Arno Press, 1977, 65-78.

Ma'oz, Moshe. [5339] "Jerusalem in the Last Hundred Years of Turkish Ottoman Rule," in Y. Ben-Porat, B.-Z. Yehoshua, and A. Kedar (eds.), Chapters in the History of the Jewish Community in Jerusalem, 1. Jerusalem: Yad Izhaq Ben-Zvi, 1973, 260-272 (Hebrew).

Ma'oz, Moshe. [5340] "Nineteenth Century Jerusalem: Political and Social Developments," in E. Shaltiel (ed.), Jerusalem in the Modern Period: Yaacov Herzog Memorial Volume. Jerusalem: Yad Izhaq Ben-Zvi and Ministry of Defense, 1981, 66-80 (Hebrew), i-ii (English summary).

Ma'oz, Moshe. [5341] Ottoman Reform in Syria and Palestine, 1840-1861: The Impact of the Tanzimat on Politics and Society. Oxford: Clarendon Press, 1968, 266 pp.

Ma'oz, Moshe (ed.). [5342] Studies on Palestine During the Ottoman Period. Jerusalem: Magnes Press, 1975, 582 pp.

Mehnert, Gottfried. [5343] Der englisch-deutsche Zionsfriedhof in Jerusalem und die deutsche evangelische Gemeinde Jerusalem: Ein Beitrag zur ökumenischen Kirchengeschichte Jerusalems. Beihefte zur Zeitschrift für Religions- und Geistesgeschichte, 15. Leiden: Brill, 1971, 52 pp.

Melville, Herman: See Kenny, Vincent S. [5323]

Melville, Herman. [5344] Clarel: A Poem and Pilgrimage. Edited by W. E. Bezanson. New York: Hendricks House, 1960, 652 pp.

Melville, Herman. [5345] Journal of a Visit to Europe and the Levant, October 11, 1856 - May 6, 1857. Edited by Howard C. Horsford. Princeton: Princeton University Press, 1955, 209 pp., esp 125-127, 140-161.

Merrill, Selah. [5346] "Jerusalem: Population, Religion, Poverty," The Old Testament Student, 5 (1885), 97-103. [American consul in Jerusalem, 1882-1885, 1891-1893, 1898-1907.]

Minerbi, Sergio. [5347] "Italian Economic Penetration in Palestine (1908-1919)," M. Ma'oz (ed.), Studies on Palestine during the Ottoman Period. Jerusalem: Magnes Press, 1975, 466-482.

Müller, I. E. [5348] "The Beginning and the End of the Austrian Levant Posts," The Holy Land Philatelist, 4/43 (1958), 962-967. [Originally published in 1930.]

Neider, Charles. See Twain, Mark. [5416]

Neuville, René. [5349] "Heures et malheurs des consuls de France à Jérusalem aux XVIIe, XVILLe et XIXe siècles," Journal of Middle East Sociology, 1 (Spring, 1947), 3-34.

Newton, Benjamin W. [5350] Jerusalem: Its Future History. London: Lucas Collins, 1908, 58 pp.

Nir, Yeshayahu. [5351] The Bible and the Image: The History of Photography in the Holy Land, 1839-1899. Philadelphia: University of Pennsylvania Press, 1985, 294 pp.

Oliphant, Margeret O. [5352] Jerusalem: The Holy City, Its History and Hope. New York and London: Macmillan, 1891, 577 pp.; 2nd edn., 1894, 580 pp.

Paris, M. Le Contre-Amiral Francois Edmond. [5353] Souvenirs de Jérusalem. Paris: Librairie Maritime et Scientifique, 1862, 4 pp. + 14 plates. Edited by E. Schiller and reprinted (in part) in facsimile, Jerusalem: Ariel, 1978, 4 pp. (French) + 5 pp. (English) +14 plates + 16 pp. (Hebrew).

Paulus, Christoph. [5354] "Die Tempelcolonien in Palästina," Zeitschrift des deutschen Palästina-Vereins, 6 (1883), 31-42.

Pearlman, Moshe. See Kollek, Teddy and Pearlman, Moshe. [5324]

Peters, F. E. [5355] "Jerusalem Observed: The Medieval City through Modern Eyes," in Jerusalem: The Holy City in the Eyes of Chroniclers, Visitors, Pilgrims, and Prophets from the Days of Abraham to the Beginnings of Modern Times. Princeton: Princeton University Press, 1985, 535-586.

Pierotti, Ermete. [5356] Jerusalem Explored: Being a Description of the Ancient and Modern City, 2 vols. London: Bell and Daldy, 1864, 339 + 63 pp.

Polay, Abram. [5357] "Forerunner Post Offices in Turkish Palestine," The Israel Philatelist, 13/10 (1962), 742-744.

Polish, David. [5358] "Pre-Zionist Jerusalem," in R. Jospe and S. Z. Fishman (eds.), Go and Study: Essays and Studies in Honor of Alfred Jospe. Washington, DC: B'nai Brith Hillel Foundations, 1980, 327-339.

Pollack, F. W. [5359] "Aus Jerusalem," The Israel Philatelist, 15/5 (19643), 1078.

Pollack, F. W. [5360] "The Italian Post Offices at Jerusalem," The Holy Land Philatelist, 7/73-74 (1961), 1462-1465.

Pollack, F. W. [5361] "The Russian Post Offices in Palestine," The Holy Land Philatelist, 5/50-51 (1959), 1078-1079; 5/54-55 (1959), 1144-1147; 5/56-57 (1959), 1180-183; 5/58-59 (1959), 1206-1208.

Pollack, F. W. [5362] "The Russian Post Offices at Jerusalem," The Holy Land Philatelist, 5/ 56-57 (1959), 1180-1182.

Pollack, F. W. [5363] "Quartier Israelite: The Turkish Post Office in Jerusalem's 'Street of Jews,'" The Holy Land Philatelist, 1/1 (1954), 15-17.

Pollack, F. W. [5364] The Turkish Post in the Holy Land. Holy Land Postal History Handbooks, 1. Tel Aviv: Holy Land Philatelist, n.d., 59 pp. Reprinted, Boston: Barry P. Hoffman and Howard Novitch, n.d., 59 pp., esp. 36-41, 52-55. [Jerusalem].

Porath, Yehoshua. [5365] "The Political Awakening of the Palestinian Arabs and their Leadership towards the End of the Ottoman Period," in M. Ma'oz (ed.), Studies on Palestine during the Ottoman Period. Jerusalem: Magnes Press, 1975, 351-381.

Porter, John L. [5366] Jerusalem, Bethany, and Bethlehem. London: Nelson, 1886, 168 pp, esp. 8-111.

Provera, Mario. [5367] "Gerusalemme nel '800," La Terra Santa, 62 (1986), 152-156.

Reynolds-Ball, Eustace A. [5368] Jerusalem: A Practical Guide to Jerusalem and its Environs. London: A and C. Black, 1901, 14-94, 173-191.

Roberts, David. [5369] The Holy Land. Facsimile edition of the books originally published in 1842 (and reprinted in 1855) under the title The Holy Land, Syria, Idumea, Arabia, and Nubia, vols. 1-3 [with selected pictures from vols 4-6]. Introduction by Ely Schiller. Jerusalem: Ariel, 1979, 332 pp. [Reproduction of the lithographs in black and white].

Roberts, David. [5370] The Holy Land, 1: Jerusalem. Historical descriptions by G. Crolly. Jerusalem: Terra Sancta Arts, Ltd., 1982, 88 pp. with 25 facsimile lithographs in color.

Roberts, David. [5371] Yesterday the Holy Land. Grand Rapids: Zondervan, 1982, 144 pp.

Robinson, Edward and Smith, Eli. [5372] "Jerusalem-- Incidents and First Impressions, / Walks in and around the City," in Biblical Researches in Palestine and the Adjacent Regions: Journal of Travels in the Year 1838, 1. Boston: Crocker and Brewster / London: John Murray, 2nd edn., 1860, 221-250.

Robinson, Edward and Smith, Eli. [5373] "Jerusalem-- Incidents and Observations," in Later Biblical Researches in Palestine and in Adjacent Regions: A Journal of Travels in the Year 1852. Boston: Crocker and Brewster / London: John Murray, 2nd edn., 1857, 161-202.

Rogers, Mary Eliza. [5374] Domestic Life in Palestine. New York: Carlton and Lanaham / Cincinnati: Hitchcock and Walden, n.d., 41-55, 297-359. [Contemporary of Bishop Gobat.]

Roth, E. [5375] Preussens Gloria im Heiligen Land: Die Deutschen und Jerusalem. Munich: Verlag G. Callwey, 1973, 312 pp.

Sandreczki, Ch. [5376] "Facsimile of Notes Supplied by Dr. Sandreczki on the Names of the Streets, Buildings, etc.," in C. W. Wilson, Ordnance Survey of Jerusalem, in 3 parts. London: Lord's Commissioners of Her Majesty's Treasury, 1865. Facsimile reproduction with introduction by Dan Bahat, Jerusalem: Ariel, 1980, 1, no pagination [25 pp. with index to 2 maps].

Sandreczki, Ch. [5377] "Die Namen der Plätze, Strassen, Gassen, usw. jetzigen Jerusalem," Zeitschrift des deutschen Palästina-Vereins, 6 (1883), 43-77.

de Saulcy, L. Félicien J. C. [5378] Voyage en Terre Sainte, 2 vols. Paris: Didier, 1865, 411 + 355 pp., I, 95-144, 344-410; II, 1-127.

Schaff, Philip. [5379] Through Bible Lands: Notes of Travel in Egypt, the Desert, and Palestine. New York: American Tract Society, 1878, 413 pp., esp. 232-277.

Schick, Conrad. See Carmel, Alex. [5250]

Schick, Conrad. See Wilson, Charles W. [5440]

Schick, Conrad. [5380] "Die Baugeschichte der Stadt Jerusalem in kurzen Umrissen von den ältesten Zeiten bis auf die Gegenwart dargestellt, 7: Von Ibrahim Pascha bis heute (1830-1892)," Zeitschift des deutschen Palästina-Vereins, 17 (1894), 264-276.

Schick, Conrad. [5381] "Jerusalem," Palestine Exploration Fund, Quarterly Statement, (1888), 20-22.

Schick, Conrad. [5382] "A Jerusalem Chronicle," Palestine Exploration Fund, Quarterly Statement, (1887), 158-160.

Schick, Conrad. [5383] "Jerusalem Notes," Palestine Exploration Fund, Quarterly Statement, (1894), 261-266.

Schick, Conrad. [5384] "Notes on Changes in Jerusalem Buildings," Palestine Exploration Fund, Quarterly Statement, (1894), 19-21.

Schick, Conrad. [5385] "Notes [on Recent Developments in and around Jerusalem]," Palestine Exploration Fund, Quarterly Statement, (1901), 1-4.

Schick, Conrad. [5386] "The Railway from Jaffa to Jerusalem," Palestine Exploration Fund, Quarterly Statement, (1893), 10-13.

Schick, Conrad. [5387] "Some Innovations at Jerusalem," Palestine Exploration Fund, Quarterly Statement, (1891), 280-281.

Schick, Conrad. [5388] "Preparations Made by the Turkish Authorities for the Visit of the German Emperor and Empress to the Holy Land in the Autumn of 1898," Palestine Exploration Fund, Quarterly Statement, (1899), 116-118.

Schiller, Ely. See Paris, M. Le Contre-Amiral Francois Edmond. [5353]

Schiller, Ely. See Roberts, David. [5369]

Schiller, Ely. See Spyridon, S. N. [5403]

Schiller, Ely. [5389] The First Photographs of Jerusalem: The New City. Jerusalem: Ariel, 1979, 204 pp.

Schiller, Ely. [5390] The First Photographs of Jerusalem: The Old City. Jerusalem: Ariel, 1980, 252 pp.

Schiller, Ely. [5391] The Holy Land in Old Engravings and Illustrations. Jerusalem: Ariel, 1977, 304 pp.

Schiller, Ely. [5392] *Jerusalem in Rare Lithographs and Engravings*. Jerusalem: Ariel, 1981, 170 pp.

Schmidt-Clausen, Kurt. [5393] "Der Beitrag Bunsens zur Gründung des Bistums Jerusalem," *Beihefte der Zeitschrift für Religions- und Geistesgeschichte*, 21 (1980), 45-63.

Schmidt-Clausen, Kurt. [5394] *Vorweggenommene Einheit: Die Gründung des Bistums Jerusalems im Jahre 1841*. *Arbeiten zur Geschichte und Theologie des Luthertums*,15. Berlin: Lutherisches Verlagshaus, 1965, 394 pp.

Schmitz, P. Ernst. [5395] "The Holy Land's Postal Services in 1914," *The Holy Land Philatelist*, 6/73-94 (1961), 1468-1469.

Schölch, Alexander. [5396] "European Penetration and the Economic Development of Palestine, 1856-1882," in R. Owen (ed.), *Studies in the Economic and Social History of Palestine in the Nineteenth and Twentieth Centuries*. London: Macmillan / Carbondale and Edwardsville: Southern Illinois University Press, 1982, 10-87, esp. 27-39, 66-71.

Schölch, Alexander. [5397] "Ein palästinenischer Repräsentant der Tanzimat-Periode: Yusuf Diya'addin al-Halidi (1842-1906)," *Der Islam: Zeitschrift für Geschichte und Kultur des islamischen Orients*, 57 (1980), 311-322.

Schur, Nathan. [5398] "Consul Finn's Last Years in Jerusalem (A Letter by Elizabeth Anne Finn, 1864)," *Cathedra: For the History of Eretz-Israel and its Yishuv*, 30 (1983), 64-90 (Hebrew with reproduction of English source material).

Seetzen, Ulrich J. [5399] *Reisen durch Syrien, Palästina, Phönicien, die transjordanishen Länder, Arabia Petrea, and Unter Aegypten*, 2. Berlin: G. Reimer, 1854-1859, 1-37, 55-64, 197-214, 274-193, 385-400.

Sepp, J. N. [5400] *Jerusalem und das Heilige Land: Pilgerbuch nach Palästina, Syrien, und Aegypten*, 1. Schaffhausen: Hurter, 1863, 59-436, 699-779.

Shamir, Shimon. [5401] "Egyptian Rule (1832-1840) and the Beginning of the Modern Period in the History of Palestine," in A. Cohen and G. Baer (eds.), *Egypt and Palestine: A Millennium of Association (1868-1948)*. New York: St. Martin's Press / Jerusalem: Ben-Zvi Institute, 1984, 214-231.

Silberman, Neil Asher. [5402] *Digging for God and Country: Exploration, Archeology and the Secret Struggle for the Holy Land, 1799-1917*. New York: Alfred Knopf, 1982, 228 pp..

Smith, Eli. See Robinson, Edward and Smith, Eli. [5372-5373]

Spyridon, S. N. [5403] "Annals of Palestine, 1821-1841," *Journal of the Palestine Oriental Society*, 18 (1938), 63-132. Published as monograph, *Extracts from the Annals of Palestine, 1821-1841: Manuscript Monk Neophitos of Cyprus*. Edited by Ely Schiller. Jerusalem: Ariel, 1979, 88 pp. (English) + 39 pp. (Hebrew summary).

Stavrov, T. G. [5404] "Russian Interest in the Levant, 1843-1848: Porfirii Uspenskii and the Establishment of the First Russian Ecclesiastical Mission in Jerusalem," Middle East Journal, 17 (1963), 91-103.

Stoddard, John L. [5405] Jerusalem, Illustrated and Embellished with One Hundred and Twenty-One Reproductions of Photographs. Chicago: Belford, Middlebrook, and Co., 1897, 116 pp.

Tennenbaum, M. [5406] "The British Consulate in Jerusalem (1858-1890)," Cathedra: For the History of Eretz-Israel and its Yishuv, 5 (1977), 83-108 (Hebrew).

Thomson, William M. [5407] The Land and the Book, 1: Southern Palestine and Jerusalem. New York: Harper and Brothers, 1880, 415-567.

Tibawi, Abdul Latif. [5408] British Interests in Palestine, 1800-1901: A Study of Religious and Educational Enterprise. London: Oxford University Press, 1961, 280 pp.

Tibawi, Abdul Latif. [5409] "The Letter Commendatory: Relating to the Anglican Bishopric in Jerusalem," Muslim World, 69 (1979), 1-7.

Tibawi, Abdul Latif. [5410] "Unpublished Letters on Protestant Missions in Palestine," Muslim World, 67 (1977), 258-265.

Tobler, Titus. [5411] Denkblätter aus Jerusalem. Constans: W. Meck, 1856, 761 pp.

Tobler, Titus. [5412] Dritte Wanderung nach Palästina im Jahre 1857. Gotha: Perthes, 1859, 514 pp., esp. 204-370 ["Jerusalem und seine nächste Umgebung"].

Tolkowsky, Edmond. [5413] "Austrian Offices in Palestine," The Israel-Palestine Philatelist, 5/10 (1954), 100-103.

Tolkowsky, Edmond. [5414] "German Post Offices in Palestine," The Israel-Palestine Philatelist, 4/7 (1953), 60-63.

Tristram, H. B. [5415] The Land of Israel: A Journal of Travels in Palestine. London: S. P. C. K., 2nd edn., 1866, 656 pp., esp. 171-193.

Turgay, Uner. See Little, Donald and Turgay, Uner. [5331]

Twain, Mark. [5416] The Complete Travel Books of Mark Twain: The Early Works, The Innocents Abroad and Roughing It. Edited by Charles Neider. Gardern City, NY: Doubleday, 1966, 806 pp.

Twain, Mark. [5417] Travelling with the Innocents Abroad: Mark Twain's Original Reports from Europe and the Holy Land. Edited by Daniel McKeithan. Norman: University of Oklahoma Press, 1958, 342 pp., esp. 264-292 [Jerusalem].

Ussishkin, A. [5418] "Templers (Tempelgesellschaft)," Encyclopaedia Judaica, 15. Jerusalem: Macmillan, 1971, 994-996.

Vaczek, Louis and Buckland, Gail. [5419] Travelers in Ancient Lands : A Portrait of the Middle East, 1839-1919. New York: New York Graphic Society, 1980, 202 pp.

Van de Velde, C. W. M. [5420] Narrative of a Journay through Syria and Palestine in 1851 and 1852, 1. London: W. Blackwood and Sons, 1854, 451-522.

Vereté, Mayir. [5421] "A Plan for the Internationalization of Jerusalem, 1840-1841," Asian and African Studies: Journal of the Israel Oriental Society, 12 (1978), 13-31.

Vereté, Mayir. [5422] "Why was a British Consulate Service Established in Jerusalem?" English Historical Review, 85 (1970), 316-345.

Vester, Bertha Spafford. [5423] Our Jerusalem: An American Family in the Holy City, 1881-1949. New York: Doubleday, 1950, 381 pp.

Viaud, Julien. See Loti, Pierre [Pen-name of Viaud, Julien]. [5334]

Vilnay, Zev. See Bartlett, William H. [5223]

Vilnay, Zev. See Luncz, Abraham M. (ed.). [5335]

Vilnay, Zev. See Wilson, Charles W. [5439]

Vilnay, Zev. [5424] "Jerusalem: The Beginnings of the New City (1860-1917), in Y. Ben-Porat, B.-Z. Yehoshua, and A. Kedar (eds.), Chapters in the History of the Jewish Community in Jerusalem, 1. Jerusalem: Yad Izhaq Ben-Zvi, 1973, 154-177 (Hebrew).

Vilnay, Zev. [5425] "Jerusalem: The 19th Century," Ariel, 23 (1969), 53-59.

Vilnay, Zev. [5426] "Jerusalem in the Modern Era: 1860-1967," in J. M. Oestrreicher and A. Sinai (eds.), Jerusalem. New York: John Day, 1974, 19-30.

de Vogüé, Melchior. [5427] Jerusalem hier et aujourd-hui: Notes de voyage. Paris: Plon-Nourrit, 1912, 109 pp.

Wahrman, Dror. See Kroyanker, David and Wahrman, Dror. [5325]

Walker, Franklin. [5428] Irreverent Pilgrims: Melville, Browne, and Mark Twain in the Holy Land. Seattle: University of Washington Press, 1974, 234 pp.

Wallace, Edwin S. [5429] Jerusalem the Holy: A Brief History of Ancient Jerusalem; with an Account of the Modern City and its Conditions Political, Religious and Social. New York: Fleming H. Revell, 1898, 350 pp. [American consul in Jerusalem, 1893-1898.]

Wallach, Josef. See Garfinkel, Martin and Wallach, Josef. [5283]

Wallach, Josef. [5430] "Ein deutscher Soldat berichtet über Jerusalem im Winter 1916-17," Jahrbuch des Instituts für Deutsche Geschichte, 2 (1973), 337-343.

Wartensleben, A. Graf. [5431] Jerusalem: Gegenwartiges und Vergangenes. Berlin: Mittler, 1886, 228 pp.

Waters, Theodore. [5432] "Palestine after the War: The Jerusalem of To-day, Its Many Nationalities and Religions; Its Picturesqueness, and Its Poverty--Characteristics of the Holy City and its Present Population," in Jerusalem, Its Redemption and Future: The Great Drama of Deliverance Described by Eyewitnesses. New York: The Christian Herald, 1918, 191-227.

Watson, Charles M. [5433] "Relics of the Past," in The Story of Jerusalem. London: J. M. Dent and Sons / New York: E. P. Dutton, 1912, 286-326.

Webster, Gillian. [5434] "Elizabeth Anne Finn," Biblical Archaeologist, 48 (1985), 181-185.

Welch, P. J. [5435] "Anglican Churchmen and the Jerusalem Bishopric," Journal of Ecclesiastical History, 8 (1957), 193-204.

Whiting, John D. [5436] "Jerusalem's Locust Plague," National Geographic, 28/6 (Dec., 1915), 511-550.

Whitley, W. T. [5437] "Friends of the Temple (Tempelfreunde, Templer)," in James Hastings (ed.), Encyclopedia of Religion and Ethics, 6. New York: Scribner's, 1928, 141-142.

Williams, George. [5438] The Holy City: Historical, Topographical, and Antiquarian Notices of Jerusalem, 1-2. London: John W. Parker, 2nd edn., 1849, 496/164 + 618 pp.

Wilson, Charles W. [5439] "Jerusalem," in Picturesque Palestine, Sinai and Egypt, 1. New York and London: D. Appleton and Co.,1980, 1-120. Reprinted as Jerusalem: The Holy City, with an introduction by Zev Vilnay. Jerusalem: Ariel, n.d., 120 pp.

Wilson, Charles W. [5440] "Obituary of Dr. Conrad Schick," Palestine Exploration Fund, Quarterly Statement, (1902), 139-142.

Wilson, John. [5441] The Lands of the Bible Visited and Described in an Extensive Journal Undertaken with Special Reference to the Advancement of Philanthropy,1. Edinburgh: Whyte, 1847, 404-504.

Wolff, Philip. [5442] "Zur neueren Geschichte Jerusalems von1843-1884," Zeitschrift des deutschen Palästina-Vereins, 8 (1885), 1-15.

Wright, James E. [5443] Round about Jerusalem: Letters from the Holy Land. London: Jarrolds, 1918, 247 pp.

Zeevy, Rechavam. See Bartlett, William H. [5224]

See also 22/ Jewish Presence in Jerusalem from Julian II to Modern Times.

Thirty-Eight

Jerusalem Under British Administration

Abel, Félix-M. [5444] "Pour la conservation de Jérusalem," *Revue biblique*, 27 (1918), 550-552.

Abel, Félix-M. [5445] "Le récent treblement de terre en Palestine," *Revue biblique*, 36 (1927), 571-578.

Alsberg, P.-A. [5446] "The Conflict over the Mayoralty of Jerusalem during the Mandate Period," in E. Shaltiel (ed.), *Jerusalem in the Modern Period: Yaacov Herzog Memorial Volume*. Jerusalem: Yad Izhaq Ben-Zvi and Ministry of Defense, 1981, 302-354 (Hebrew), x-xii (English summary).

Amiran, David H. K. [5447] "The Development of Jerusalem, 1860-1970: Growth of the City during the British Mandate," in D. H. K. Amiran, A. Shachar, I. Kimhi (eds.), *Urban Geography of Jerusalem: A Companion Volume to the Atlas of Jerusalem*. Jerusalem: Massada Press, 1973, 37-39.

Andrews, Fannie Fern. [5448] *The Holy Land under Mandate*, 2 vols. New York: Houghton Mifflin, 1931, 361 + 436.

Aroian, Lois A. and Mitchell, Richard P. [5449] "Palestine during the Mandate," in *The Modern Middle East and North Africa*. New York: Macmillan, 1984, 218-249.

Ashbee, Charles Robert. [5450] *Jerusalem, 1918-1920: Being the Records of the Pro-Jerusalem Council during the Period of the British Military Administration*. London: J. Murray for the Council of the Pro-Jerusalem Society, 1921, 87 pp., 79 figs.

Ashbee, Charles Robert. [5451] *A Palestine Notebook, 1918-1923*. Garden City, NY: Doubleday, 1923, 278 pp.

Ashbee, Charles Robert. [5452] "Pro-Jerusalem," *American Magazine of Art*, 12 (1921), 99-102.

Avitsur, Shmuel. [5453] "Jewish Craftsmanship and Industry at the Time of Mandate in Jerusalem," in M. Friedman, B.-Z. Yehoshua, and Y. Tobi (eds.), *Chapters in the History of the Jewish Community in Jerusalem*, 2. Jerusalem: Yad Izhaq Ben-Zvi, 1976, 266-285 (Hebrew), xix (English summary).

Bahat, Dan. [5454] "The British Mandate, 1917-1948," in *Carta's Historical Atlas of Jerusalem : An Illustrated History*. Jerusalem: Carta, 1983, 76-79.

Bell, J. Bowyer. [5455] *Terror out of Zion: Irgun Zvai Leumi, Lehi, and the Palestine Underground, 1929-1949*. New York: St. Martin's Press, 1977, 374 pp.

Bentwich, Helen. See Bentwich, Norman and Bentwich, Helen. [5458]

Bentwich, Norman. [5456] "The Crisis of the Western (Wailing) Wall, 1928-1930," in England in Palestine. London: Kegan Paul, Trench and Trubner, 1932, 170-210.

Bentwich, Norman. [5457] "The Hebrew University at Jerusalem," Palestine Exploration Quarterly, (1942), 113-116.

Bentwich, Norman and Bentwich, Helen. [5458] Mandate Memories, 1918-1948. London: Hogarth Press, 1965, 231 pp.

Bethel, Nicholas. [5459] The Palestine Triangle: The Struggle for the Holy Land, 1935-1948. New York: G. P. Putnam's Sons, 1979, 384 pp.

Biger, Gideon. [5460] "The Development of Jerusalem's Built-Up Area during the First Decade of the British Mandate," in E. Shaltiel (ed.), Jerusalem in the Modern Period: Yaacov Herzog Memorial Volume. Jerusalem: Yad Izhaq Ben-Zvi and Ministry of Defense, 1981, 255-278 (Hebrew), viii-ix (English summary).

Bishop, Eric F. F. [5461] "Jerusalem By-Ways of Memory," The Muslim World, 49 (1959), 124-132; 50 (1960), 19-206; 51 (1961), 265-273; 52 (1962), 97-109, 315-321. [Personal reminiscences of the Mandate period.]

Bovis, H. Eugene. [5462] The Jerusalem Question, 1917-1968. Stanford, CA: Hoover Institute, 1971, 181 pp.

Chesterton, G. K. [5463] The New Jerusalem. London: Hodder and Stoughton, 1920 / New York: Doran, 1921, 307 pp.

Clarke, Thurston. [5464] By Blood and Fire: The Attack on the King David Hotel. New York: G. P. Putnam's Sons, 1981, 304 pp.

Dalman, Gustaf. [5465] Hundert deutsche Fliegerbilder aus Palästina. Gutersloh: C. Bertelsmann, 1925, nos. 1-16, pp. 1-25.

Ervine, St. John Green. [5466] A Journey to Jerusalem. New York: Macmillan, 1937, 366 pp.

ESCO Foundation for Palestine: [5467] Palestine: A Study of Jewish, Arab, and British Policies, 2 vols. New Haven: Yale University Press, 1947, 593 + 1380 pp.

Ferrari, Silvio. [5468] "The Holy See and The Postwar Palestine Issue: The Internationalization of Jerusalem and the Protection of the Holy Places," International Affairs, 60 (1984), 211-283.

Ferrari, Silvio. [5469] "The Vatican, Israel and the Jerusalem Question (1943-1948)," Middle East Journal, 39 (1985), 316-331.

Gilbert, Martin. [5470] [Maps depictng the development of Jerusalem under British administration.] in Jerusalem History Atlas. New York: Macmillan, 1977, 68-69 [under military rule, 1917-1920], 70-71 [water supply and transport, 1918-

1920], 74-75 [under Mandate, 1922-1948], 77 [zoning plan, 1922], 79 [town planning area, 1922], 80-81 [new Jewish suburbs to the north and west of the city, 1921-1938].

Gilbert, Martin. [5471] [Maps depicting Arab and Jewish areas of greater Jerusalem and incidents of strife, 1920-1948.] in Jerusalem History Atlas. New York: Macmillan, 1977, 83-103.

Gilbert, Martin. [5472] "The United Nations Plan for Jerusalem," in Jerusalem History Atlas. New York: Macmillan, 1977, 95.

Graham-Brown, Sarah. [5473] The Palestinians and their Society, 1880-1946. London: Quartet Books, 1980, 184 pp., esp 99-181.

Gray, John. [5474] "A City Divided," in A History of Jerusalem. New York: Praeger, 1969, 294-311. [Mandate period, 294-304.]

Hadawi, Sami. See John, Robert and Hadawi, Sami. [5487]

Hamilton, R. W. [5475] "Le Musée archéologique de Palestine," Mouseion, 12/3-4 (1938), 35-53.

Harris, W. B. [5476] "Modern Jerusalem," English Review, 53 (1931), 429-436.

Harrison, A. St. B. [5477] "New Jerusalem Government House Designed," Architectural Review, 70 (Oct., 1931), 106-107.

Harrison, A. St. B. [5478] "Palestine Archaeological Museum," Architectural Review, 78 (Sept., 1935), 89-96.

Harrison, A. St. B. [5479] "Palestine Archaeological Museum," American Architect and Architecture, 149 (Oct., 1936), 54-63.

Harrison, A. St. B. [5480] "Palestine Archaeological Museum, Jerusalem," Museums Journal, 38 (April, 1938), 1-22; 38 (July, 1938), 212.

Hyamson, Albert M. [5481] "New Jerusalem," Near East and India, 42 (1933), 691-692.

Hyamson, Albert M. [5482] Palestine under the Mandate, 1920-1948. London: Methuen, 1950, 210 pp.

Hyman, Semah C. [5483] "Jerusalem Under Britsh Rule (1917-1948)," in Encyclopaedia Judaica, 9. Jerusalem: Macmillan, 1971, 1469-1483. Also in Israel Pocket Library: Jerusalem. Jerusalem: Keter, 143-167.

Ingrams, Doreen. [5484] Palestine Papers, 1917-1922: Seeds of Conflict. New York: George Braziller, 1972, 198 pp.

International Commission for the Wailing Wall: [5485] The Rights and Claims of Moslems and Jews in Connection with the Wailing Wall at Jerusalem. Beirut: Institute for Palestine Studies, 1968, 93 pp.

"Jerusalem Archaeological Museum," [5486] Art and Archaeology, 32 (July, 1931), 43.

John, Robert and Hadawi, Sami. [5487] The Palestine Diary, 1: 1914-1945. New York: New World Press, 428 pp.

Keith-Roach, Edward. [5488] "The Pageant of Jerusalem," National Geographic Magazine, 52/6 (Dec., 1927), 635-681.

Kendall, Henry. [5489] Jerusalem, the City Plan: Preservation and Development during the British Mandate, 1918-1948. London: His Majesty's Stationery Office, 1948, 123 pp.

Kimche, David. See Kimche, Jon and Kimche, David. [5490]

Kimche, Jon and Kimche, David. [5490] Both Sides of the Hill: Britain and the Palestine War. London: Secher and Warburg, 1960, 287 pp. [Background to the 1948 war.]

Kollek, Teddy and Pearlman, Moshe. [5491] "Jerusalem of the Mandate," in Jerusalem: A History of Forty Centuries. New York: Random House, 1968, 235-247.

Kupperschmidt, Uri M. [5492] "The General Muslim Congress of 1931 in Jerusalem," Asian and African Studies: Journal of the Israel Oriental Society, 12 (1978), 123-162.

Lundstein, Mary Ellen. [5493] "Wall Politics: Zionist and Palestinian Strategies in Jerusalem, 1928," Journal of Palestine Studies, 8/29 (1978), 3-27.

McCormick, T. [5494] "Which Jerusalem?" National Review, 113 (1939), 740-744.

Mansfield, Peter. [5495] "From British Mandate to the Present Day," in Jerusalem: The Key to World Peace. London: Islamic Council of Europe, 1980, 155-172.

Marlowe, John. [5496] The Seat of Pilate: An Account of the Palestine Mandate. London: Cresset Press, 1959, 289 pp.

Mattar, Philip. [5497] "The Role of the Mufti of Jerusalem in the Political Struggle over the Western Wall, 1928-29," Middle Eastern Studies, 19 (1983), 104-118.

Mitchell, Richard P. See Aroian, Lois A. and Mitchell, Richard P. [5449]

Ollendorff, Franz. [5498] "Italian Building in Jerusalem," The Holy Land, 3/1 (Spring,1983), 21-29. [The Italian hospital.]

"Palestine's New Government House," [5499] The Near East and India, 39 (1931), 415.

Parzen, Herbert. [5500] The Hebrew University, 1925-1935. New York: KTAV, 1974, 121pp.

Pearlman, Moshe. See Kollek, Teddy and Pearlman, Moshe. [5491]

Porath, Yehoshua. [5501] "Al-Hajj Amin al-Husayni, Mufti of Jerusalem: His Rise to Power and the Consolidation of His Position," Asian and African Studies: Journal of the Israel Oriental Society, 7 (1971), 121-156.

Prittie, Terrence. [5502] "Jerusalem Under the Mandate," in J. M. Oesterreicher and A. Sinai (eds.), Jerusalem. New York: John Day Co., 1974, 53-60.

"Reconstruction in Jerusalem," [5503] Palestine Exploration Fund, Quarterly Statement, (1919), 79-82.

Romann, M. [5504] "The Economic Development of Jerusalem in Recent Times," in D. H. K. Amiran, A. Shachar, I. Kimhi (eds.), Urban Geography of Jerusalem: A Companion Volume to the Atlas of Jerusalem. Jerusalem: Massada Press, 1973, 91-108, esp. 92-98.

Rubinstein, D. [5505] "The Jerusalem Municipality under the Ottomans, British, and Jordanians," in J. L. Kraemer (ed.), Jerusalem: Problems and Prospects. New York: Praeger, 1980, 72-99.

Sanders, Ronald. [5506] The High Walls of Jerusalem: A History of the Balfour Declaration and the Birth of the British Mandate for Palestine. New York: Holt, Rinehart, and Winston, 1983, 746 pp.

Schiller, Ely. [5507] The First Photographs of Jerusalem: The New City. Jerusalem: Ariel Publishing House, 1979, 204 pp.

Shapiro, S. [5508] "Planning Jerusalem: The First Generation, 1917-1968," in D. H. K. Amiran, A. Shachar, I. Kimhi (eds.), Urban Geography of Jerusalem: A Companion Volume to the Atlas of Jerusalem. Jerusalem: Massada Press, 1973, 139-153, esp. 139-147.

Sykes, Christopher. [5509] Crosroads to Israel, 1917-1948. London: Collins / Cleveland and New York: World Publishing, 1965, 404 pp.

Vincent, Louis-Hugues. [5510] "English Improvements at Jerusalem," Palestine Exploration Fund, Quarterly Statement, (1919), 107-112.

Vincent, Louis-Hugues. [5511] "Nouvelles de Jérusalem," Revue biblique, 28 (1919), 252-254.

Whittemore, Edward. [5512] Jerusalem Poker. New York: Holt, Rinehart and Winston, 1978, 405 pp. [Fiction, the second of a projected "Jerusalem Quartet;" of epic scope but primary setting in Jerusalem of the Mandate period.]

Whittemore, Edward. [5513] Sinai Tapestry. New York: Holt, Rinehart and Winston, 1977, 310 pp. [The first of a projected "Jerusalem Quartet."]

Thirty-Nine

The Divided City, 1948-1967

Amiran, David H. K. [5514] "The Development of Jerusalem, 1860-1970: Divided City," in D. H. K. Amiran, A. Shachar, I. Kimhi (eds.), Urban Geography of Jerusalem: A Companion Volume to the Atlas of Jerusalem. Jerusalem: Massada Press, 1973, 43-47.

Andres, Isaias. [5515] "Profanation de Cimetières à Jérusalem," La Terre Sainte, (March, 1969), 74-77.

de Azcárate, Pablo. [5516] "The Surrender of the Jewish Quarter of Jerusalem," in Mission in Palestine, 1948-1952. Washington, DC: The Middle East Institute, 1966, 64-79. [By the person who negotiated the surrender.]

Bahat, Dan. [5517] "Jerusalem Divided, 1948-1967," in Carta's Historical Atlas of Jerusalem: An Illustrated History. Jerusalem: Carta, 1983, 80-83.

Bailey, Sydney D. [5518] "Nonmilitary Areas in UN Practice," American Journal of International Law, 74 (1980), 499-524. [Jerusalem 1948-1967 included in cases cited.]

Bartos, A. P. See Kiesler, F. J. and Bartos, A. P. [5540]

Bentwich, Norman. [5519] "Hebrew University in Exile: A Visit to Mount Scopus," Commentary, 13 (1952), 469-471.

Bentwich, Norman. [5520] "The Hebrew University of Jerusalem: A Historical Survey," Journal of World History, 10 (1967), 801-817.

Bentwich, Norman. [5521] "Israel's Share of Jerusalem," Contemporary Review, 197 (1960), 328-331.

Benvenisti, Meron. [5522] "Jerusalem: The Divided City (1948-1967)," Encyclopaedia Judaica, 9. Jerusalem: Macmillan, 1971, 1483-1498. Also in Israel Pocket Library: Jerusalem. Jerusalem: Keter, 1973, 168-192.

Benvenisti, Meron. [5523] "Jerusalem Divided," in Jerusalem: The Torn City. Minneapolis: University of Minnesota Press, 1976, 1-77.

Berger, Peter. [5524] "The Internationalization of Jerusalem," Jurist, 10 (1950), 357-387; 491.

Bernadotte, Folke. [5525] To Jerusalem. London: Hodder and Stoughton, 1951, 280 pp. [United Nations mediator for Palestine; assassinated in Jerusalem on 17 September 1948.]

Biran, Avram. [5526] "Israel Museum, Jerusalem," Museum, 20/1 (1967), 5-33.

Bovis, H. Eugene. [5527] The Jerusalem Question, 1917-1968. Stanford, CA: Hoover Institute, 1971, 181 pp.

Brake, Brian. See Scofield, John and Brake, Brian. [5558]

Cabanne, P. [5528] "Symbolism of the Israel Museum at Jerusalem," Connoisseur, 159 (1965), 244-249.

Collins, Larry and La Pierre, Dominique. [5529] O Jerusalem! New York: Simon and Schuster, 1972, 637 pp.

Dupuy, Trever N. [5530] Elusive Victory: The Arab-Israeli Wars, 1947-1974. New York: Harper and Row, 1978, 669 pp.

Efrat, E. [5531] "Hinterland of the New City of Jerusalem and its Economic Significance," Economic Geography, 40 (1964), 254-260.

Fitzgerald, Sir W. [5532] "The Holy Places of Palestine in History and in Politics," International Affairs, 22 (1950), 1-10.

Gad, D. See Mansfield, A and Gad, D. [5544]

Gad, D. and Mansfield, A. [5533] "Israel's Museum," Interiors, 126 (1966), 108-113.

Gilbert, Martin. [5534] "Jerusalem: The Divided City, 1949-1967, / Divided Jerusalem and the Holy Places, 1949-1967," in Jerusalem History Atlas. New York: Macmillan, 1977, 104-107.

Glick, B. [5535] "The Vatican, Latin America, and Jerusalem," International Organization, 11 (1957), 213-219.

González Barros, Luis. [5536] Jerusalén y el futuro histórico jurídico sobre la internacionalizacíon. Madrid: Ediciones Cultura Hispánica, 1958, 422 pp.

Gray, John. [5537] "A City Divided," in A History of Jerusalem. New York: Praeger, 1969, 294-311. [1948-1967, 304-311.]

"International Regime for Jerusalem," [5537A] International Organization, 4 (1950), 293-294, 296-298, 457-460, 466; 5 (1951), 96.

Joseph, Dov. [5538] The Faithful City: The Siege of Jerusalem, 1948. New York: Simon and Schuster, 1960, 350 pp.

Kaufman, Menahem. [5538A] America's Jerusalem Policy, 1947-1948. Jerusalem: Institute of Contemporary Judaism, Hebrew University, 1982, 178 pp.

Kenyon, Kathleen M. [5539] "British School of Archaeology in Jerusalem: New School Building," Palestine Exploration Quarterly, (1957), 97-100.

Kiesler, F. J. and Bartos, A. P. [5540] "Shrine of the Book," Progressive Architecture, 46 (1965), 126-133.

Kimche, David. See Kimche, Jon and Kimche, David. [5541]

Kimche, Jon and Kimche, David. [5541] Both Sides of the Hill: Britain and the Palestine War. London: Secker and Warburg, 1960, 287 pp..

La Pierre, Dominique. See Collins, Larry and La Pierre, Dominique. [5529]

Leymarie, Jean. [5542] Marc Chagall: The Jerusalem Windows. New York: Braziller, 1962, 210 pp., rev. edn., 1967, 111 pp.

Lorch, Netanel. [5543] Israel's War of Independence, 1947-1949. Hartford: Hartmore House, 2nd rev. edn., 1968, 579 pp. Published originally as The Edge of the Sword: Israel's War of Independence, 1947-1949. New York: G. P. Putnam's, 1961.

Mansfield, A. and Gad, D. [5544] "Acropolis in Jerusalem," Progressive Architecture, 46 (1965), 180-187.

Mattar, Ibrahim. [5545] "From Palestinian to Israeli: Jerusalem 1948-1982," Journal of Palestine Studies, 12/48 (1983), 57-63.

Mitchison, N. [5546] "Postscript on Palestine: Around and about Jerusalem," 20th Century, 160 (Aug, 1956), 155-165.

Mohn, Paul. [5547] "Jerusalem and the United Nations," International Concilation, 464 (1950), 421-471.

Orgel, H. Y. [5548] "Internationalizing Jerusalem: An Exchange of Views," America, 97 (April 27, 1957), 114-115.

Orni, Efraim. [5549] "City Planning (1948-1972)," in Encyclopaedia Judaica, 9. Jerusalem: Macmillan, 1971, 1518-1521. also in Israel Pocket Library: Jerusalem. Jerusalem: Keter, 1973, 226-231.

Padon, Gabriel. [5550] "The Divided City: 1948-1967," in J. M. Oesterreicher and A. Sinai (eds.), Jerusalem. New York: John Day Co., 1974, 85-107.

Pa'il, Meir. [5551] "Israel-Zionist Strategy Regarding Jerusalem during the War of Independence, in E. Shaltiel (ed.), Jerusalem in the Modern Period: Yaacov Herzog Memorial Volume. Jerusalem: Yad Izhaq Ben-Zvi and Ministry of Defense, 1981, 355-383 (Hebrew), xii-xiii (English summary).

Parkes, J. W. [5552] "The Religious Future of Jerusalem," Hibbert Journal, 47 (1949), 328-334.

Peretz, D. [5553] "Jerusalem--A Divided City," Journal of International Affairs, 18 (1964), 211-220.

Perowne, Stewart. [5554] The One Remains. London: Hodder and Stoughton, 1954, 192 pp.

Richards, J. M. [5555] "Jerusalem, the Old City," Architectural Review, 104 (1948), 144-148.

Romann, M. [5556] "The Economic Development of Jerusalem in Recent Times," in D. H. K. Amiran, A. Shachar, I. Kimhi (eds.), Urban Geography of

Jerusalem: A Companion Volume to the Atlas of Jerusalem. Jerusalem: Massada Press, 1973, 91-108, esp. 98-105.

Sandberg, W. [5557] "Israel Museum in Jerusalem," Museum, 19/1 (1966), 15-30.

Scofield, John and Brake, Brian. [5558] "Jerusalem, the Divided City," National Geographic, 115/4 (April, 1959), 492-531.

Shapiro, S. [5559] "Planning Jerusalem: The First Generation, 1917-1968," in D. H. K. Amiran, A. Shachar, I. Kimhi (eds.), Urban Geography of Jerusalem: A Companion Volume to the Atlas of Jerusalem. Jerusalem: Massada Press, 1973, 139-153, esp. 147-153.

Sharef, Zeev. [5560] Three Days. Garden City, NY: Doubleday, 1962, 298 pp. [May 12, 13, and 14, 1948.]

Sofer, Naim. [5561] "The Political Status of Jerusalem in the Hashemite Kingdom of Jordan, 1948-1967," Middle Eastern Studies, 12 (1976), 73-94. Also in E. Kedourie and S. G. Haim (eds.), Palestine and Israel in the 19th and 20th Centuries. London: Frank Cass, 1982, 255-276.

Spark, Muriel. [5562] The Mandelbaum Gate. New York: Alfred A. Knopf, 1965; Greenwich, CN: Fawcet Publications, 1967, 287 pp. [Fiction set on both sides of the cease-fire line.]

Syrkin, Marie. [5563] "The Siege of Jerusalem," Midstream, 19/3 (March, 1973), 18-37. Also in in J. M. Oestrreicher and A. Sinai (eds.), Jerusalem. New York: John Day, 1974, 61-84.

Turnowsky, Walter. [5564] Tour Guide to Jerusalem. Jerusalem: Tour, 1956/7, 102 pp.

Vilnay, Zev. [5565] "Visit in New Jerusalem," in The Guide to Israel. Jerusalem: Sivan Press, 1966, 81-130.

Weiss-Rosmarin, Trude. [5566] Jerusalem. New York: Philosophical Library, 1950, 51 pp. [West Jerusalem.]

Yoger, Gedalia (ed.). [5567] Political and Diplomatic Documents, December 1947-May 1948, 2 vols. Jerusalem: Israel State Archives / Central Zionist Archives, 1979.

Forty

Jerusalem From 1967 to the Present

Adams, M. [5568] "New Jerusalem", New Statesman, 82 (July 16, 1971), 74-75.

Ahimeir, Ora and Levin, Michael (eds.). [5568A] Monumental Architecture in Jerusalem. Jerusale: Carta, 1984, 140 pp. (Hebrew). [Primarily contemporary architecture.]

Alexander, Y. [5569] "What Future Jerusalem?" Midstream, 20/3 (March, 1974), 62-67.

Amiran, David H. K. [5570] "The Development of Jerusalem, 1860-1970," in D. H. K. Amiran, A. Shachar, I. Kimhi (eds.), Urban Geography of Jerusalem: A Companion Volume to the Atlas of Jerusalem. Jerusalem: Massada Press, 1973, 20-52, esp. 47-50.

Amiran, David H. K. [5571] "Jerusalem's Urban Development," Middle East Review, 13/3-4 (Spring-Summer, 1981), 53-61.

Aronson, S. [5572] "Accomodating to 3000 Years: A Classical Approach Toward Jerusalem's Historic Center," Landscape Architecture, 68 (1978), 503-509.

Association of Engineers and Architects in Israel: [5573] The Planning of Jerusalem. Tel Aviv: Engineers' Institute, 1974, 43 pp.

Ash, J. [5574] "Jerusalem United," Architectural Review, 145 (1969) 217-218.

Avrahami, A. [5575] "Jerusalem's Not So Golden Plan: Digest of the Interim Master Plan, Planning for Change," Architectural Design, 41 (1971), 209-216.

Bahat, Dan. [5576] "Jerusalem Reunited, Since 1967, / Beautifications and Improvements in the Old City," Carta's Historical Atlas of Jerusalem: An Illustrated History. Jerusalem: Carta, 1983, 84-86.

Baratto, C. [5577] "Gerusalemme: Progetto di rinnovamento e sviluppo di Mamillah," La Terra Santa, 53 (1977), 327-330.

"Basic Law: Jerusalem," [5578] in Israel Yearbook, 1982. Tel Aviv: Israel Yearbook Publications, 1982, 154-158.

"The Battle for Mamilla," [5579] Israel Economist, 35 (April, 1978), 14-15. ["Battle" of architects and city-planners.]

Bayne, Edward A. [5580] Jerusalem, Israeli Capital: Mayor Kollek Faces the Challenge of a City No Longer Divided. American Universities Field Staff Reports Service, Southwest Asia Series, 16/5. New York: American Universities Field Staff, 1967, 31 pp.

Beeson, Trevor. [5581] "Jerusalem's Future," Christian Century, 89 (1972), 1312-1313.

Bellow, Saul. [5582] To Jerusalem and Back: A Personal Account. New York: Viking Press, 1976, 182 pp.

Benvenisti, Meron. [5583] "Dialogue of Action in Jerusalem," The Jerusalem Quarterly, 19 (Spring, 1981), 10-22.

Benevisti, Meron. [5584] Jerusalem: The Torn City. Minneapolis: University of Minnesota Press, 1976, 407 pp.

Benevisti, Meron. [5585] "Some Guidelines for Positive Thinking on Jerusalem," Middle East Review, 13/3-4 (Spring - Summer, 1981), 35-40.

Benziman, Uzi. [5586] "Israeli Policy in East Jerusalem after Reunification," in J. L. Kraemer (ed.), Jerusalem: Problems and Prospects. New York: Praeger, 1980, 100-130.

Bercuson, Daniel J. [5587] "Canada and Jerusalem: An Historical Overview," Middle East Review, 13/3-4 (Spring - Summer, 1981), 48-52.

Berry, Donald L. [5588] "Mutuality in Jerusalem," Religion in Life, 44 (1975), 281-290.

Berry, J. [5589] "The Jerusalem Question: Cutting the Gordion Knot," Parameters: Journal of the U.S. Army War College, 10/2 (June, 1980), 33-43.

Bin Talal, H. R. H. Crown Prince Hassan. [5590] A Study on Jerusalem. New York: Longman, 1983, 62 pp.

Bisharat, George E. [5591] "Palestinian Sovereignity or Internationalization?" Journal of Palestine Studies, 12/48 (1983), 71-81.

Black, Ian. [5592] "Israel and Jerusalem: The Boomerang Effect," Middle East International, 130 (Aug.1, 1980), 9.

Blackwell, J. Kenneth. [5593] "The City of Peace," Middle East Review, 13/3-4 (Spring-Summer, 1981), 5-8.

Blum, Yeduda. [5594] "The Juridical Status of Jerusalem," in J. M. Oesterreicher and A. Sinai (eds.), Jerusalem. New York: John Day Co., 1974, 108-125.

Bodian, Marion. [5595] "Jerusalem and the UNESCO Resolutions," Christian News from Israel, 25/2 (1975), 63-70.

"Bold Hotel Tower for a Jerusalem Hill," [5596] Architectural Record, 162 (Oct. 1977),123-124.

Bonian, Stephen. [5597] "Jerusalem and Fraternity among Her Three Religions," Diakonia, 17 (1982), 265-274.

Bovis, H. Eugene. [5598] The Jerusalem Question, 1917-1968. Stanford, CA: Hoover Institute, 1971, 181 pp.

Brecher, Michael. [5599] "Jerusalem: Israel's Political Decisions, 1947-1977," Middle East Journal, 32 (Winter, 1978), 13-34.

Brecher, Michael. [5600] "The Political Struggle over Jerusalem," in E. Shaltiel (ed.), Jerusalem in the Modern Period: Yaacov Herzog Memorial Volume. Jerusalem: Yad Izhaq Ben-Zvi and Ministry of Defense, 1981, 384-417 (Hebrew), xiv (English summary).

Broome, George. [5601] "The Hottest Issue," American Zionist, 69 (Aug./Sept., 1979), 10-14.

Bush, George. [5602] "U. S. Position on Jerusalem," Department of State Bulletin, 65/1687 (Oct. 25, 1971), 469-470.

Caplan, Gerald and Caplan, Ruth B. [5603] Arab and Jew in Jerusalem: Explorations in Community Mental Health. Cambridge, MA: Harvard University Press, 1980, 300 pp.

Caplan, Ruth B. See Caplan, Gerald and Caplan, Ruth B. [5603]

Caradon, Hugh Foot Mackintosh. [5604] The Future of Jerusalem : A Review of Proposals for the Future of the City. National Security Affairs Monograph Series, 80/1. Washington, D.C.: National Defense University Press, 1980, 37 pp.

Cattan, Henry. [5605] Jerusalem. New York: St. Martin's Press / London: Croom Helm, 1981, 229 pp.

Cattan, Henry. [5606] "Jerusalem and the Palestine Question in International Law," in Jerusalem: The Key to World Peace. London: Islamic Council of Europe, 1980, 211-257.

Cattan, Henry. [5607] The Question of Jerusalem. London: Third World Centre, 1980, 76 pp.

Cattan, Henry. [5608] "The Status of Jerusalem under International Law and United Nations Resolutions," Journal of Palestine Studies, 10/39 (1981), 3-15.

Chiblak, Abbas. [5609] "Jerusalem's Electricity Dispute," Middle East International, 117, (Feb. 1, 1980), 11-12.

"Church's Stance Toward Israel and Jerusalem," [5610] The Holy Land, 1/1 (Spring, 1981), 20-21.

"City of Protest and Prayer: Jerusalem is the Center of the Struggle between Arab and Jew," [5611] Time, (April 12, 1982), 26-37.

Cohen, G. L. [5612] "Jerusalem Reunited," New Statesman, 74 (Aug. 18, 1967), 198-199.

Cohen, Saul B. [5613] "Geopolitical Bases for the Intergration of Jerusalem," Orbis: A Journal of World Affairs, 20 (1976), 287-313.

Cohen, Saul B. [5614] Jerusalem, Bridging the Four Walls: A Geopolitical Perspective. New Yorrk: Herzl Press, 1977, 218 pp.

Cohen, Saul B. [5615] "Jerusalem: A Geopolitical Imperative," Midstream, 21/5 (May, 1975), 18-32.

Cohen, Saul B. [5616] Jerusalem Undivided. New York: Herzl Press, 1980, 70 pp.

Cohen, Saul B. [5617] "Jerusalem's Unity and West Bank Autonomy--Paired Principles," Middle East Review, 13/3-4 (Spring - Summer, 1981), 27-34.

Cohen, Shalom. [5618] "This Year in Jerusalem: Tangled Hopes in the Holy Land," Commonweal, 107/23 (Dec. 19, 1980), 717-721.

"Controversy Continues Over Jerusalem's Growth," [5619] Architectural Record, 157 (March, 1975), 41.

"Council Calls on States to Withdraw Diplomatic Missions from Jerusalem," [5620] United Nations Monthly Chronicle, 17 (Sept./Oct., 1980), 13-18.

"Council Declares Null and Void Measures by Israel to Change Character of Jerusalem," [5621] United Nations Monthly Chronicle, 17 (Aug., 1980), 20-30.

Dakkak, Ibrahim. [5622] "Jerusalem's Via Dolorosa," Journal of Palestine Studies, 11/41 (1981), 136-149.

Dakkak, Ibrahim. [5623] "The Transformation of Jerusalem: Juridical and Physical Changes," in N. H. Aruri (ed.), Occupation: Israel over Palestine. Belmont, MA: Association of Arab-American University Graduates, 1983, 67-96.

Dayan, Moshe. [5624] "My Jerusalem," Saturday Review, 7 (Feb. 16, 1980), 20-21.

"Documents [on Jerusalem]," [5625] Middle East Review, 13/3-4 (Spring-Summer, 1981), 70-76.

"Documents Concerning the Status of Jerusalem," [5626] Journal of Palestine Studies, 1/1 (1972), 171-194.

Draper, G. I. A. D. [5627] "The Legal Status of Jerusalem," Month: A Review of Christian Thought and World Affairs, 14 (March, 1981), 85-91.

Dvir, D. [5628] "The National Park in Jerusalem," in Y. Yadin (ed.), Jerusalem Revealed: Archaeology in the Holy City, 1968-1974. New Haven and London: Yale University Press and the Israel Exploration Society, 1976, 127-129.

Elazar, Daniel J. [5629] "Local Government for Heterogeneous Populations: Some Options for Jerusalem," in J. L. Kraemer (ed.), Jerusalem: Problems and Prospects. New York: Praeger, 1980, 208-228.

Eliot, Alexander. [5630] "What Shall Become of Jerusalem the Golden?" The Atlantic, 242 (Oct., 1978), 57.

Elliot, Elisabeth. [5631] Furnace of the Lord: Reflections on the Redemption of the Holy City. Garden City: Doubleday, 1969, 129 pp.

Eshel, Yohanan. See Klein, Zev and Eshel, Yohanan. [5705]

Eytan, Ovadia. [5632] "Jerusalem-- A Political Issue," in Israel Yearbook, 1980. Tel Aviv: Israel Yearbook Publications, 1980, 145-148.

al-Fahham, Muhammad. [5633] "Restoring Jerusalem," in M. Bisar, et al (eds.), Fifth Congress of the Academy of Islamic Research. Cairo: General Organization for Government Printing Offices, 1971, 35-59.

Falk, Zeev. [5634] "Jerusalem: A View of the Holy City from Christian, Jewish, Islamic and United Nations Sources, Immanuel, 1 (1972), 100-103.

al-Faruqi, Ismail R. [5635] "The Islamic Faith and the Problem of Israel and Jerusalem," in Jerusalem: The Key to World Peace. London: Islamic Council of Europe, 1980, 77-105.

Feinstein, R. [5636] "The Administration of United Jerusalem," Public Administration, 9 (1969), 116-123.

Fitzgerald, Sir W. [5637] "The Holy Places of Palestine in History and in Politics," International Affairs, 26 (1950), 1-10.

Flannery, Edward H. See Pawlikowski, J. T. [5757]

Flannery, Edward H. [5638] "Peace-makers in Jerusalem," America, 126/21 (May 27, 1972), 561-563.

Forster, Arnold. [5639] "Jerusalem United? Health, Education, and Population in Jerusalem," Report from Israel. New York: Anti-Defamation League of B'nai B'rith, n.d. (post-1979), 35-49.

"Il futuro urbanistico di Gerusalemme," [5640] L'Architettura, 19 (1973), 287.

George, James. [5641] "Jerusalem, the Holy City: A Religious Solution for a Political Problem," International Perspectives, (March-April, 1978), 18-24.

Geyer, A. F. [5642] "Christians and the Peace of Jerusalem," Christianity and Crisis, 27 (1967), 160-164.

Gilbert, Martin. [5643] "Jerusalem and the Six Day War, June, 1967," in Jerusalem History Atlas. New York: Macmillan, 1977, 110-111.

Gilbert, Martin. [5644] "The Jerusalem Foundation and the Work Since 1966, / Parks and Gardens, 1966-67," in Jerusalem History Atlas. New York: Macmillan, 1977, 114-117.

Gilbert, Martin. [5645] "Jerusalem since 1967," Jerusalem History Atlas. New York: Macmillan, 1977, 127.

Gilmour, David. [5646] "Jerusalem and the Occupied Territories," in Dispossessed: The Ordeal of the Palestinians, 1917-1980. London: Siggwick and Jackson, 1980, 117-139.

Ginio, Alisa. [5647] "Plans for the Solution of the Jerusalem Problem," in J. L. Kraemer (ed.), Jerusalem: Problems and Prospects. New York: Praeger, 1980, 41-71.

Ginsburg, L. [5648] "Jerusalem Old and New," Journal of the Royal Institute of British Architects, 80 (1973), 611-613.

Glueck, Nelson. [5649] Dateline: Jerusalem, a Diary. Cincinnati: Hebrew Union College Press, 1968, 134 pp. [15 June - 27 August, 1967.]

Goichon, A. M. [5650] Jérusalem: Fin de la ville universelle? Paris: Maison Neuve et Larose, 1976, 380 pp.

Gonen, Rivka. [5651] "Keeping Jerusalem's Past Alive," Biblical Archeology Review, 7/4 (July/Aug., 1981), 16-23.

Goodman, Hirsch. [5653] "Jerusalem as the Capital of Israel," in J. M. Oesterreicher and A. Sinai (eds.), Jerusalem. New York: John Day Co., 1974, 126-134.

Graham-Brown, Sarah. [5654] "Jerusalem: Israelis Dig In," Middle East Economic Digest, 24 (July 18, 1980), 14.

Guiladi, Yael. See Kroyanker, David and Guiladi, Yael. [5720]

Guiladi, Yael. [5655] One Jerusalem. Jerusalem: Keter, 1979, 74 pp.

Gur, Mordechai. [5656] The Battle for Jerusalem. New York: Popular Library, 1974, 380 pp.

Habe, Hans. [5657] Proud Zion. Indianaolis: Bobbs-Merrill, 1973, 287 pp.

Halabi, Rafix. [5658] "Jerusalem," in The West Bank Story. New York: Harcourt, Brace and Jovanovich, 1981, 29-50.

Halprin, Lawrence. [5659] "Jerusalem as Place and Vision," American Institute of Architects Journal, 69 (1980), 32-37.

Halsell, Grace. [5660] Journey to Jerusalem. New York: Macmillan, 1981, 193 pp.

Halsell, Grace. [5661] "Shrine Under Siege (Dome of the Rock)," The Link, 17/3 (Aug.-Sept, 1984), 1-13.

"Harry S. Truman Center," [5662] Progressive Architecture, 52 (Sept., 1971), 140-145.

Harter, W. H. [5663] "Jerusalem," Church and Society, 62 (July-Aug., 1972), 45-50.

Hazan, Ya'akov. [5664] "A Plan for Jerusalem," New Outlook, 19/1 (Jan., 1976), 53.

Heilman, Samuel. [5665] The Gate Behind the Wall: A Pilgrimage to Jerusalem. New York: Summit, 1985, 201 pp.

Hertzberg, Arthur. See Moore, Arthur and Hertzberg, Arthur. [5743]

Hirschfield, Robert Carl. [5666] "Jerusalem, 1970," Catholic World, (Dec., 1970), 134-136.

Hirst, David. [5667] "The New Jerusalem" in The Gun and the Olive Branch: The Roots of Violence in the Middle East. London: Faber and Faber, 1977, 229-242.

Hirst, David. [5668] "Rush to Annexation: Israel in Jerusalem," Journal of Palestine Studies, 3/12 (1974), 3-31.

Hodgkin, E. C. [5669] "O Jerusalem," Atlas, 14 (Aug., 1967), 25-26. [On internationalization.]

Hogg, S. [5670] "Overburdened Magnet: A Survey of Jerusalem," The Economist, 241 (Dec 25, 1971), 35-51.

Hoyt, C. [5671] "Jerusalem Municipal Theater Reflects Local Tradition," Architectural Record, 156 (Nov., 1974), 104-106.

Hudson, Michael C. [5672] "Jerusalem: A City Still Divided," Mideast, 8/4 (!968), 20-25.

Hyman, Benjamin. See Kimhi, Israel and Hyman, Benjamin. [5702-5703]

Idinopulis, Thomas A. [5673] "Christians and Jerusalem," Encounter, 42 (1981), 155-161.

Idinopulis, Thomas A. [5674] "Jerusalem the Blessed: Religion and Politics in the Holy City," Christian Century, 95 (May 10, 1978), 498-503.

Idinopulis, Thomas A. [5675] "Jerusalem the Blessed: The Shrines of Three Faiths," Christian Century, 95 (April 12, 1978), 386-391.

Idinopulis, Thomas A. [5676] "Politics, Theology and Folly in the New Jerusalem Law," Christian Century, 97 (1980), 1005-1007.

Idinopulis, Thomas A. [5677] "Religious Colonialism and Ethnic Awakening in Jerusalem: The Orthodox Hierarchy Remains at the Center of Society and Strife," Worldview, 25/4 (1982), 17-18.

Idinopulis, Thomas A. [5678] "Theopolitics at Jerusalem's Dome of the Rock," Christian Century, 100 (1983), 1018-1021.

Idinopulis, Thomas A. [5679] "UNESCO's War with Israel," Christian Century, 92 (1975), 214-215.

Ingram, O. K. [5680] "Jerusalem and Palestine in Christian Opinion," The Search, 2 (1981), 463-481.

Institute for Palestine Studies: [5681] Israeli Violations of the Religious Status Quo at the Wailing Wall, Jerusalem. Beirut: Institute for Palestine Studies, 1970, 24 pp.

Institute for Palestine Studies: [5682] Jerusalem: A Collection of United Nations Documents. Beirut: The Institute for Palestine Studies, 1970, 105 pp.

Iqbal, Afzal. [5684] "The Conflict on Jerusalem: Causes and Contradictions," in Jerusalem: Key to World Peace. London: Islamic Council of Europe, 1980, 173-186.

Islamic Council of Europe: [5685] Jerusalem: The Key to World Peace. London: Islamic Council of Europe, 1980, 333 pp.

"Jerusalem: Answers to the Riddle of Sovereignity," [5686] New Outlook, 14/5 (June/July, 1971), 35-45.

"Jerusalem: City of Peace and Conflict," [5687] New Outlook, 14/9 (Dec., 1971), 35-44.

"Jerusalem as a Holy City: A Tetralogue," [5688] Christian News from Israel, 25/2 (1975), 71-78.

Jerusalem Foundation: [5689] Proposed Jerusalem Outline Scheme. Jerusalem: Prepared for the Jerusalem Committee by the Jerusalem Foundation, 40 pp. + maps.

"Jerusalem-- the Capital of Israel," [5690] in Israel Yearbook, 1984. Tel Aviv: Israel Yearbook Publications, 1984, 232-236.

"Jerusalem through the Centuries," [5691] in Israel Yearbook, 1982. Tel Aviv: Israel Yearbook Publications, 1982, 159-165. [Primary focus is Jerusalem since 1967.]

Jones, S. Shepard. [5692] "The Status of Jerusalem: Some National and International Aspects," in J. N. Moore (ed.), The Arab-Israel Conflict, 1: Readings. Princeton: Princeton University Press, 1974, 915-928.

Jones, S. Shepard. [5693] "Status of Jerusalem: Some National and International Aspects," Law and Contemporary Problems, 33 (Winter, 1968) 169-182.

Judge, Joseph. [5694] "This Year in Jerusalem," National Geographic, 163/4 (April, 1983), 479-514.

Kerr, Malcolm H. [5696] "The Changing Political Status of Jerusalem," in Ibrahim Abu-Lughod (ed.), The Transformation of Palestine: Essays on the Origin and Development of the Arab-Israeli Conflict. Evanston: Northwestern University Press,1971, 355-377.

al-Khatib, Rouhi. [5697] "Jerusalem: Some Arab Grievances," Church and Society, 62 (July/Aug., 1972), 51-52.

al-Khatib, Rouhi. [5698] The Judaization of Jerusalem. Palestine Essays, 19. Beirut: Palestine Liberation Organization Research Center, 1970, 70 pp.

al-Khatib, Rouhi. [5699] "The Judaization of Jerusalem," in Jerusalem: The Key to World Peace. London: Islamic Council of Europe, 1980, 109-122.

al-Khatib, Rouhi. [5700] "The Status of Jerusalem: The Judaization of Jerusalem," in Y. Alexander and N. N. Kittrie (eds.), Arab and Israeli Perspectives on the Middle East Conflict. New York: AMS Press, 1973, 238-258.

Khouri, Fred J. [5701] "Jerusalem-- City of Peace and Source of Conflict," in The Arab- Israeli Dilemma. Syracuse, N.Y: Syracuse University Press, 1968, 102-122.

Kimhi, Israel and Hyman, Benjamin. [5702] "Demographic and Economic Developments in Jerusalem Since 1967," in J. L. Kraemer (ed.), Jerusalem: Problems and Prospects. New York: Praeger, 1980, 131-152.

Kimhi, Israel and Hyman, Benjamin. [5703] A Socio-Economic History of Jerusalem, 1967-1975. Jerusalem: Jerusalem Committee with the Help of the Jerusalem Foundation, 1978, 72 pp.

Klein, H. Arthur. See Klein, Mina C. and Klein, H. Arthur. [5704]

Klein, Mina C. and Klein, H. Arthur. [5704] "War and Peace, and an Old Wall (mid-1967 and 1968)," in Temple Beyond Time: The Story of the Site of Solomon's Temple at Jerusalem. New York: Von Nostrand Reinhold, 1970, 15-21.

Klein, Zev and Eshel, Yohanan. [5705] Integrating Jerusalem Schools. London / New York: Academic Press, 1980, 175 pp.

Kollek, Teddy. [5706] For Jerusalem: A Life. New York: Random House, 1978, 169 pp.

Kollek, Teddy. [5707] "Jerusalem," Foreign Affairs, 55 (1977), 701-716.

Kollek, Teddy. [5708] "Jerusalem: Present and Future," Foreign Affairs, 59 (1981), 1041-1049.

Kollek, Teddy. [5709] "Jerusalem: Today and Tomorrow," in J. L. Kraemer (ed.), Jerusalem: Problems and Prospects. New York: Praeger, 1980, 1-15.

[Kollek, Teddy.] [5710] "Thoughts of a Famous Mayor," Time, (Nov. 20, 1978), 58.

Kollek, Teddy. [5711] "What it Means to be Mayor of the City of Peace," in J. M. Oesterreicher and A.Sinai (eds.), Jerusalem. New York: John Day, 1974, 184-186.

Kraemer, Joel L. [5712] Jerusalem: Problems and Prospects. New York: Praeger, 1980, 243 pp.

Kraemer, Joel L. [5713] "The Jerusalem Question," in Jerusalem: Problems and Prospects. New York: Praeger, 1980, 16-40.

Kritzeck, James and Ryan, Joseph L. [5714] "Jerusalem and the Holy Places: A Christian Viewpoint," Christian Century, 88 (1971), 1205-1210.

Kroyanker, David. [5715] Developing Jerusalem, 1967-1975: The Planning Process as Reflected by Some Major Projects. Jerusalem: The Jerusalem Institute for Israel Studies for the Jerusalem Committee, 1982, 221 pp.

Kroyanker, David. [5716] Jerusalem Planning and Development, 1978-1979. Jerusalem: The Jerusalem Institute for Israel Studies for the Jerusalem Committee, 1982, 100 pp.

Kroyanker, David. [5717] Jerusalem Planning and Development, 1979-1982. Jerusalem: The Jerusalem Institute for Israel Studies for the Jerusalem Committee, 1982, 188 pp.

Kroyanker, David. [5718] Jerusalem Planning and Development, 1982-85: New Trends. Jerusalem: The Jerusalem Committee, with the Help of the Jerusalem Foundation, in Conjunction with the Jerusalem Institute for Israel Studies, 1985, 155 pp.

Kroyanker, David. [5719] "Preserving Jerusalem, 1967-1980," in E. Shaltiel (ed.), Jerusalem in the Modern Period: Yaacov Herzog Memorial Volume. Jerusalem: Yad Izhaq Ben-Zvi and Ministry of Defense, 1981, 418-454 (Hebrew), xiv-xv (English summary).

Kroyanker, David and Guiladi, Yael. [5720] Jerusalem, 1978: Between Two Decades-- Planning and Development. Jerusalem: The Jerusalem Institute for Israel Studies for the Jerusalem Committee, 1982, 44 pp.

Kutcher, A. [5721] "New Jerusalem," The Architectural Review, 153 (June, 1973), 399-406.

Kutcher, A. [5722] The New Jerusalem: Planning and Politics. London: Thames and Hudson, 1973 / Cambridge, MA: Massachusetts Institute of Technology Press, 1975, 128 pp + 183 plans.

Lapide, Pinchas E. [5723] "Ecumenism in Jerusalem: Despite Serious Obstacles, Interfaith Cooperation is Making Significant Advances in the Holy City," Christian Century, 85 (1968), 839-842.

Laqueur, Shlomit. [5724] "Guiding Jerusalem's Future," Israel Economist, 35 (1979), 26-27.

Laqueur, Shlomit. [5725] "Transforming Jerusalem's 'Seam'", Israel Economist, 35 (Sept./Oct., 1979), 17.

Lauterpacht, Elihu. [5726] Jerusalem and the Holy Places. London: Geerings, 1971.

Lauterpacht, Elihu. [5727] "Jerusalem and the Holy Places," in J. N. Moore (ed.), The Arab-Israeli Conflict, 1: Readings. Princeton: Princeton University Press, 1974, 929-1009.

Lehrman, H. [5728] "UN Tangle Over Jerusalem: Prospects for a Settlement," Commentary, 9 (1950), 105-114.

Levin, Michael. See Ahimeir, Ora and Levin, Michael (eds.). [5568A]

Levine, J. C. [5729] "Old Jerusalem Roadway Plan Approved," Progressive Architecture, 62 (1981), 37.

Lichfield, Nathaniel. [5730] "Jerusalem Planning: A Progress Report," in J. M. Oesterreicher and A. Sinai (eds.), Jerusalem. New York: John Day Co., 1974, 175-183.

Lucy, R. V. [5731] "Canada's Position on Jerusalem," Middle East Focus, (Jan., 1979), 16-17.

Lucy, R. V. [5732] "Jerusalem, The Holy City: The Problem Can Only Be Resolved as a Part of a General Settlement," International Perspectives, (March/April,1978), 24-28.

Lukacs, Yehuda. [5733] Documents on the Israeli-Palestinian Conflict, 1967-1983. New York: Cambridge University Press, 1984, 247 pp.

Macleish, Kenneth and Spiegel, Ted. [5734] "Reunited Jerusalem Faces Its Problems," National Geographic, 134/6 (Dec., 1968), 835-871.

Malachy, Yona. [5735] "New Dimensions for Jewish-Christian Confrontation in United Jerusalem," in in Discussing Jerusalem: From the Proceedings of the Seminar for Visiting Academics Held at the Van-Leer Jerusalem Foundation. Jerusalem: Israel Academic Committee on the Middle East, 1972, 31-38.

Mandel, D. [5736] "Jerusalem's Divisive Unity," New Statesman, 100 (Aug. 29, 1980), 6.

Mansour, Atallah and Stock, Ernest. [5737] "Arab Jerusalem After the Annexation," New Outlook, 14/1 (Jan., 1971), 22-36, 46.

Marcus, Franklin. See Roeder, Larry W.; Marcus, Franklin; Sizer, Harry S. [5773]

Mattar, Ibrahim. [5738] "From Palestinian to Israeli: Jerusalem, 1948-1982," Journal of Palestine Studies, 12/48 (1983), 57-63.

Medzini, M. [5739] "The Jerusalem Dialogues: The International Relations of Jerusalem," The Center Magazine, 18 (Jan./Feb., 1985), 41-50.

Meier, R. [5740] "Planning for Jerusalem," Architectural Forum, 134 (1971), 56-57.

Mezvinsky, Norton. [5741] "The Jewish Faith and the Problem of Israel and Jerusalem," in Jerusalem: The Key to World Peace. London: Islamic Council of Europe, 1980, 21-37.

Mezvinsky, Norton. [5742] "Zionist Claims on Jerusalem," The Search, 2 (1981), 447-462.

Moore, Arthur and Hertzberg, Arthur. [5743] "The Jerusalem Question: Two Views," Christianity and Crisis, 31 (1971), 250-252.

Moore, Donald J. [5744] "Hope in Jerusalem," America, 137 (Oct. 15, 1977), 236-239.

Moore, John N. [5745] "The Status of Jerusalem," in The Arab-Israeli Conflict, 3: Documents. Princeton: Princeton University Press, 1974, 947-1004.

Moskin, J. Robert. [5746] Among Lions: The Battle for Jerusalem, June 5-7, 1967. New York: Arbor House, 1982, 401 pp.

Narkiss, Uzi. [5747] The Liberation of Jerusalem: The Battle of 1967. Totowa, NJ / London: Vallentine, Mitchell, 1983, 285 pp.

Netzer, Ehud. [5748] "Reconstruction of the Jewish Quarter in the Old City," in Y. Yadin. Jerusalem Revealed: Archaeology in the Holy City, 1968-1974. New Haven and London: Yale University Press, 1976, 118-121.

Niv, Amnon. [5749] "Jerusalem's Central Planning Theme: Its Formation and Main Components," in D. Kroyanker, Jerusalem Planning and Development, 1979-1982. Jerusalem: The Jerusalem Institute for Israel Studies for the Jerusalem Committee, 1982, 1-29.

Niv, Amnon. [5750] "New Trends and Tools in Jerusalem City Planning," in D. Kroyanker, Jerusalem Planning and Development, 1982-85: New Trends. Jerusalem: The Jerusalem Committee, with the Help of the Jerusalem Foundation, in Conjunction with the Jerusalem Institute for Israel Studies, 1985, 12-20.

Nuseibeh, Hazem Zaki. [5751] "Jerusalem," in Palestine and the United Nations. New York: Quartet Bokks, 1981, 79-108.

Oesterreicher, John M. [5752] "Jerusalem the Free," in J. M. Oesterreicher and A. Sinai (eds.), Jerusalem. New York: John Day, 1974, 249-260.

Oesterreicher, John M. and Sinai, Anne. [5753] "Appendices" [Documents on the Status of Jerusalem], Jerusalem. New York: John Day Co., 1974, 263-294.

"One Jerusalem: Questions and Answers," [5754] Congress Monthly, 46 (June, 1979), 5-7.

Orni, Efraim. [5755] "City Planning (1948-1972)," in Encyclopaedia Judaica, 9. Jerusalem: Macmillan, 1971, 1518-1521. Also in Israel Pocket Library: Jerusalem. Jerusalem: Keter, 1973, 226-231.

Pallis, Elfi. [5756] "'Co-existance:' The Example of Jerusalem," Middle East International, 126 (June 6, 1980), 9-11.

Pawlikowski, J. T. [5757] "A Summary of 'The Controversy Over Jerusalem: Elements of a Solution,'" Journal of Ecumenical Studies, 9 (1972), 450-452. [Report on a position paper drafted by Edward H. Flannery.]

Peretz, Martin. [5758] "Jerusalem Diarist," New Republic, 180 (May 26, 1979), 47.

Perowne, Stewart H. [5759] "Jerusalem: the Contemporary City," in The New Encyclopaedia Britannica, Macropaedia, 10. Chicago: Encyclopaedia Britannica, Inc., 15th edn., 1974, 140-144.

Pfaff, Richard H. [5760] Jerusalem: Keystone of an Arab-Israeli Settlement. Washington: American Enterprise Institue for Public Research, 1969, 56 pp.

Pfaff, Richard. [5761] "Jerusalem: Keystone of an Arab-Israeli Settlement," in J. N. Moore (ed.), The Arab- Israeli Conflict, 1: Readings. Princeton: Princeton University Press, 1974, 1010-1062.

Pick, W. [5762] "The Six-Day War and after Reunification," Encyclopaedia Judaica, 9. Jerusalem: Macmillan, 1971, 1498-1513. Also in Israel Pocket Library: Jerusalem. Jerusalem: Keter, 1973, 193-214.

Ponger, Anne. [5763] "The Jerusalem Problem," Swiss Review of World Affairs, 29 (May, 1979). 6-7.

"Pope and Patriarch: What to do about Jerusalem," [5764] Economist, 224 (July 22, 1967), 309.

Pressman, R. [5765] "Sultan's Pool Moves into the Limelight," Landscape Architecture, 71 (1981), 63-72.

Prittie, Terence. [5766] "City of Peace?" Middle East Review, 13/3-4 (Spring-Summer, 1981), 20-26.

Prittie, Terence. [5767] Whose Jerusalem? London: Frederick Muller, 1981, 246 pp.

Rabinovich, Abraham. [5768] "Jerusalem," in Encyclopaedia Judaica, 17: Supplement. Jerusalem: Keter, n. d. [1981], 417-421. [The development of the city from 1971-1981.]

Rabinovich, Abraham. [5769] "Planning Jerusalem: In and around the Old City," Christian News from Israel, 26/2 (1977), 58-62.

Reddaway, John. [5770] "Jerusalem and International Organizations," in Jerusalem: The Key to World Peace. London: Islamic Council of Europe, 1980, 189-210.

Reichman, S. [5771] "Transportation in Jerusalem," in D. H. K. Amiran, A. Shachar, I. Kimhi (eds.), Urban Geography of Jerusalem: A Companion Volume to the Atlas of Jerusalem. Jerusalem: Massada Press, 1973, 123-137.

"Residenza del presidente dello stato d' Israele a Gerusalemme," [5772] L'Architettura, 18 (1971), 800-804.

Roeder, Larry W.; Marcus, Franklin; Sizer, Harry S. [5773] "The Palestinian Debate: Palestinian Autonomy and the Jerusalem Question," Worldview, 25/6 (June,1982), 7-9.

Romann, Michael. [5774] "The Economic Development of Jerusalem in Recent Times," in D. H. K. Amiran, A. Shachar, I. Kimhi (eds.), Urban Geography of Jerusalem: A Companion Volume to the Atlas of Jerusalem. Jerusalem: Massada Press, 1973, 91-108. esp. 105-107.

Romann, Michael. [5775] "Jews and Arabs in Jerusalem," The Jerusalem Quarterly, 19 (Spring, 1981), 23-46.

Rotenstreich, Nathan. [5776] "Reflections on Jerusalem: A Philosopher's View," in J. M. Oesterreich and A. Sinai (eds.), Jerusalem. New York: John Day Co., 1974, 244-248.

Rowley, G. [5777] "Divisions in a Holy City," The Geographical Magazine, 56 (1984), 196-202.

Ryan, Joseph L. See Kritzeck, James and Ryan, Joseph L. [5714]

Ryan, Joseph L. [5778] "The Catholic Faith and the Problem of Israel and Jerusalem," in Jerusalem: The Key to World Peace. London: Islamic Council of Europe, 1980, 39-75.

Safadie, Moshe. [5779] [Architect, interview with] Moment, 4 (May 1979), 15-26.

Samuel, Edwin. [5780] "Jerusalem from 1967-1978," Contemporary Review, 236 (May, 1980), 261-265.

Scheidl, Franz J. [5781] Die Internatinalisierung Jerusalems. Wein: Scheidl-Verlag, 1970, 59 pp.

Schleifer, Abdullah. [5782] The Fall of Jerusalem. New York and London: Monthly Review Press, 1972, 247 pp.

Schleifer, Abdullah. [5783] "The Fall of Jerusalem, 1967," Journal of Palestine Studies, 1/1 (1972), 68-86.

Schmelz, Uziel O. [5784] "Notes on the Demography of Jews, Muslims, and Christians in Jerusalem," Middle East Review, 13/3-4 (Spring-Summer, 1981), 62-68.

Schmertz, M. F. [5785] "Three Projects Designed By Moshe Safadie to Help Bind Together Jewish and Arab Jerusalem into One City," Architectural Record, 163 (April, 1978), 103-114.

Schroeter, Leonard W. [5786] "The Status of East Jerusalem," Midstream, 18/7 (Aug./Sept., 1972), 26-35.

Shachar, Arie. [5787] "The Urban Geography of Unified Jerusalem," in J. Aviram, (ed.), Jerusalem Through the Ages. Jerusalem: Israel Exploration Society, 1968, 145-155 (Hebrew), 63-64 (English summary).

Shaliv, A. [5788] "Industrial Jerusalem and its Development," in Israel Yearbook, 1970. Tel Aviv: Israel Yearbook Publications, 1970, 147-148.

Sharabi, Hisham. [5789] "The Problems of Jerusalem and the Suez Canal," in Palestine and Israel: The Lethal Dilemma. New York: Pegasus, 1969, 141-164.

Sharkansky, I. [5790] "Major Teddy Kollek and the Jerusalem Foundation: Governing the Holy City," Public Administration Review, 44 (1984), 299-304.

Sharon. Arieh. [5791] Planning Jerusalem : The Master Plan for the Old City and its Environs. Jerusalem: Weidenfeld and Nicholson, 1972. New York: McGraw-Hill, 1973, 211 pp.

Sharon, Arieh. [5792] "Planning Jerusalem: The Old City and its Environs," Ekistics: The Problems and Science of Human Settlements, 38 (1974), 368-376.

Shipler, David K. [5793] "In Search of Jerusalem," New York Times Magazine, (Dec. 15, 1980), 74-106.

Siegman, Henry. [5794] "The Peace of Jerusalem," Christian Century, 88 (1971), 1203-1205.

Sinai, Anne. See Oesterreicher, John M. and Sinai, Anne. [5753]

Sivan, Gavriel. [5795] "Naming Jerusalem's Streets," Midstream, 22/10 (Dec., 1981), 27-30.

Sizer, Harry S. See Roeder, Larry W.; Marcus, Franklin; Sizer, Harry S. [5773]

Slann, Martin. [5796] "Jewish Ethnicity and the Integration of an Arab Minority in Israel: A Study of the Jerusalem Incorporation," Human Relations, 26/3 (1973), 359-370.

Slann, Martin. [5797] "A Look at Arab-Jewish Cooperation in Jerusalem," New Outlook, 14/3 (April, 1971), 28-33.

Spiegel, Ted. See MacLeish, Kenneth and Spiegel, Ted. [5734]

Stern, Gabriel. [5798] "The Jewish Quarter: Good Neighborhood or Ghetto," New Outlook, 20/1 (Jan./Feb., 1977), 53-56.

Stevens, Richard P. [5799] "The Vatican, the Catholic Church and Jerusalem," Journal of Palestine Studies, 10/39 (1981), 100-110.

Stock, Ernest. See Mansour, Atallah and Stock, Ernest. [5737]

Sykes, C. [5800] "Holy City," Encounter, 30 (Feb., 1968), 39-43.

Syrkin, Marie. [5801] "Jerusalem Belongs to Israel, the Very Heart of the Jewish State," Middle East Review, 13/3-4 (Spring-Summer, 1981), 9-19.

Syrkin, Marie. [5802] "Why Jerusalem Belongs to Israel," New Republic, 183/24 (Dec. 13, 1980), 17-21.

Tekoa, Joseph. [5803] "Life without Discrimination in Jerusalem," in Israel Yearbook, 1972. Tel Aviv: Israel Yearbook Publications, 1972, 51-56.

Tekoa, Joseph. [5804] "The Status of Jerusalem: Barbed Wire Shall Not Return to Jerusalem," in Y. Alexander and N. N. Kittrie (eds.), Arab and Israeli Perspectives on the Middle East Conflict. New York: AMS Press, 1973, 259-277.

Tomer, Yisrael. [5805] "Jewish-Arab Relations in Jerusalem-- Temporary," New Outlook, 20/4 (June/July, 1977), 66-67.

Tsimhoni, Daphne. [5806] "Demographic Trends of the Christian Population of Jerusalem and the West Bank, 1948-1978, Middle East Journal, 37 (1983), 54-64.

Turner, Michael. [5807] "Planning for Tomorrow in Jerusalem," in Discussing Jerusalem: From the Proceedings of the Seminar for Visiting Academics Held at the Van-Leer Jerusalem Foundation. Jerusalem: Israel Academic Committee on the Middle East, 1972, 13-29.

"Unifying a Divided City," [5808] Time, (Nov.20, 1978), 56.

United States Congress, House Committee on Foreign Affairs, Subcommittee on the Near East: [5809] Jerusalem: The Future of the Holy City for Three Monotheisms. Washington, D. C. : United States Government Printing Office, 1971, 226 pp. [92nd Congress/1st session (July 28, 1971).]

"Violence at Al-Aqsa Mosque Brings Heated Debate-- and U.S. Veto," [5810] United Nations Chronicle, 19 (June, 1982), 25-31.

Ward, Richard J. [5811] "The Economics of an Internationalized Jerusalem," International Journal of Middle Eastern Studies, 2 (1971), 311-317. Also in R. Ward, D. Peretz, and E. M. Wilson (eds.), The Palestinian State: A Rational Appraoch. Port Washington, NY: Kennikat Press, 1977, 127-134.

Wasserstein, Bernard. [5812] "Trouble on the Temple Mount," Midstream, 28/7 (Aug./Sept., 1982), 5-9.

Weigert, Gideon. [5814] Israel's Presence in East Jerusalem. Jerusalem: Weigert, 1973, 157 pp.

Weigert, Gideon. [5815] "Jerusalem Planning: A Progress Report," in J. M. Oesterreicher and A. Sinai (eds.), Jerusalem. New York: John Day Co., 1974, 175-183.

Westmacott, Richard N. [5816] Jerusalem: A New Era for a Capital City. London: Anglo-Israel Associattion, 1968, 40 pp.

Wilson, Evan M. [5817] "Internationalization of Jerusalem," Middle East Journal, 23 (Winter, 1969), 1-13.

Wilson, Evan M. [5818] "Jerusalem--Five Years After," America, 127/10 (Oct.7, 1972), 252-254.

Wilson, Evan M. [5819] Jerusalem, Key to Peace. Washington, DC: Middle East Institute, 1969, 176 pp.

Wilson, Evan M. [5820] "The Question of Jerusalem," American-Arab Affairs, 1 (Summer, 1982), 111-119.

Wilson, Evan M. [5821] "The Role of Jerusalem in a Possibe Arab Entity," R. Ward, D. Peretz, and E. M. Wilson (eds.), The Palestinian State: A Rational Approach. Port Washington, NY: Kennikat Press, 1977, 59-78.

World Council of Churches, Central Committee: [5822] "World Council of Churches Statement on Jerusalem," Christian-Jewish Relations: A Documentary Survey, 14/2 (June, 1981), 33-36.

"World Council of Churches Statement on Jerusalem Provokes Strong Reaction," [5823] Ecumenical Review, 33 (1981), 78.

Yehoshua, Avraham B. [5824] "Jerusalem," The Jerusalem Quarterly, 19 (Spring, 1981), 3-9.

Yishai, Yael. [5825] "Israeli Annexation of East Jerusalem and the Golan Heights: Factors and Processes," Middle East Studies, 21 (1985), 45-60.

Zander, Walter. [5826] Israel and the Holy Places of Christendom. London: Weidenfeld and Nicolson, 1971, 248 pp.

Zander, Walter. [5827] "Truce on the Temple Mount," New Outlook, 19/5 (July/Aug., 1976), 14-19.

Index of Authors

Aamiry, M. A. 4949

Aarons, Leroy. 335

Abba, Raymond. 1999-2001

Abecassis, A. 2475

Abel, Félix-M. 569, 588, 915-918, 1823, 2273, 2424, 2763-2764, 2900, 3613-3618, 3807, 4073, 4501, 4587-4588, 4652, 4702, 4762, 4915, 4918, 4947, 4950-4951, 5444-5445

Aberbach, Moses. 2765-2766

Abercrombie, John R. 919

Abir, Mordechai. 5208

Abrahams, Israel. 1699

Abramsky, Samuel. 1536, 2901

Abu-Jaber, Kamel S. 5209

Abu-Manneh, Butrus. 4074, 4952, 5210

Abul-Hajj, Amal. 4953, 4990, 5121, 5198

Ackroyd, Peter R. 2425

Adams, M. 5568

Adan, David. 589

Adinolfi, M. 4829-4830

Adler, Cyrus. 336-337, 3016

Adler, Marcus N. 3017-3018

Adler, Nikolaus. 3951-3953

Adlerblum, Burton S. 5211-5212

Agate, L. D. 3955

Aharoni, Yohanan. 78-79, 1231-1232, 1700, 1824-1826, 2234, 2274-2276, 2767, 2913-2914, 3310

Ahimeir, Ora. 5568A

Ahlström, Gosta W. 1368-1369, 1537-1540, 1701, 2002, 2426

Ahuvia, A. 1541

Ajamian, Shahe. 4075-4078

Albaric, Michel. 3534

Alberti, O. 2277

Albertson, Erik W. 1

Albouy, A. 1827

Albright, William F. 590-591, 788-789, 1233-1236, 1702, 1828-1831

Aleksandrov, G. S. 2902

Alexander, Spain. 3619

Alexander, Y. 5569

Alhassid, Naomi. 106

Aline de Sion, Marie. 4831

Allan, N. 2003

Alleau, V. Th. 4079

Allegretti, S. 920

Allegro, John M. 2678-2679

Alliata, E. 4593

Allison, R. G. 4080

Alon, Gedalyahu. 2768-2769, 2903

Alonso Schökel, Luis. 1511

Alsberg, P.-A. 5446

Alt, Albrecht. 80, 724, 1237-1239, 1294, 1366, 1542-1545, 1703

Index of Authors

von Alten, Baron. 81-83, 2278, 4832

Altmann, Wilhelm. 3956

Amann, E. 4081

Amiot, François. 3498

Amir, Yehoshua. 2279

Amiran, David H. K. 84-85, 5213, 5447, 5514, 5570-5571

Amiran, Ruth. 338-343, 592-593, 790, 921-922, 2280

Amit, Izhak. 2

Amitaï, L. K. [Pseudonym of Lehman Kahn] 2770

Amram, David. 3019

Anawati, G. C. 4082

Anderson, Francis I. 2427

Anderson, G. W. 1546

Andrae, Walter. 1832

Andreasen, Niels-Erik. 1370

Andres, Isaias. 4833, 5515

Andres, Pàscal. 4313, 4653

Andrews, Fannie Fern. 3020, 5448

Andrews, S. J. 1704

Aner, Zeev. 3045

d' Anglure, Baron. 3957

Antreassian, Assadour. 4083

Ap-Thomas, D. R. 344-345

Appelbaum, Shimon. 2281, 2771-2772, 2904-2907

Aptowitzer, V. 4314

Arazi, Simon. 3044

Arce, Augustín. 3021-3024, 3620, 3958-3959, 4084-4089, 4315-4317, 4655-4656

el-Aref, Aref. 4954-4955, 5214

Arensburg, B. 923-924

Ariel, Donald T. 2282

Armerding, Carl E. 1784, 2004

Armstrong, Gregory T. 3621-3623

Arnold, William R. 1705

Aroian, Lois A. 5449

Aronson, S. 5572

Aroushan. 4318

Arranz, Miguel. 2773

Arundale, Francis. 5215

Ash, J. 5574

Ashbee, Charles Robert. 5450-5452

Ashbel, Dov. 86-87

Ashtour, Eliyahu. 3808, 3960, 4956-4961

Asi, M. Leonide Guyo. 4834

Astour, Michael. 1240

Atiya, Aziz S. 3961, 4090-4092

Atiyeh, G. N. 3535

Atkins, Gaius. 5216

Atkinson, Clarissa. 3962

Attwater, Donald. 4093

Aucler, Paul. 2476

Auerbach, Elias. 2005-2006, 2235

Index of Authors

Auerbach, Jacob. 3025

Avi-Yonah, Michael. 3-4, 79, 88, 346-348, 594, 725-727, 791, 1295, 2274-2276, 2283-2289. 2477-2478, 2767, 2774-2775, 2908-2911, 3026, 3310, 3624-3629, 4589, 4657, 4703, 4775, 4835, 4919

Avigad, Nahman. 349-354, 728-729, 753, 877, 925-938, 1126, 1296, 2290-2296, 2912-2914, 3630-3634, 3809, 4962

Aviram, J. 5

Avitsur, Shmuel. 3028, 5453

Avnimelech, M. 89-90

Avraham, S. 4094

Avrahami, A. 5575

Awad, S. 4170

Ayali, M. 2776

Azarya, Victor. 4095

de Azcárate, Pablo. 5516

el-Azma, Nazeer. 4963

Babcock, Emily A. 3810

Bacher, W. 3029

Bachmann, M. 3342

Baedeker, Karl. 5217

Baer, Y. 2777

Bagatti, Bellarmino. 355, 939-945, 2479, 2915, 3536, 3635-3640, 3963, 3965-3968, 4102, 4179, 4319-4328, 4590-4593, 4658-4667, 4704-4708, 4776-4777, 4836-4837, 4920, 4964

Bagnani, Gilbert. 1833

Bahat, Dan. 6, 91, 332, 356-359, 730, 878-879, 946-948, 1297, 2297-2298, 2916-2917, 3031-3032, 3311, 3641, 3811-3817, 4329-4330, 4594, 4668, 4709, 4778-4779, 4838, 4921, 4965-4968, 5454, 5517, 5576

Bailey, Loyd R. 3312

Bailey, Sydney D. 5518

Baillet, Maurice. 2680-2681

Bain, R. Nisbet. 3642

Baker, Dwight. 5218-5219

Baldensperger, Philip J. 595, 5220

Baldi, Donato. 235, 3643, 4096-4098, 4780

Baldwin, Marshall W. 3818

Baltzer, Klaus. 3343

Bammel, Ernst. 2480

Bar-Adon, P. 2913-2914

Bar-Yosef, Ofer. 1241

Barag, Dan. 949, 2918-2921, 4331-4332

Baras, Zvi. 3033, 3819

Baratto, C. 5577

Barclay, James T. 92, 5221

Bardtke, Hans. 1834

Bardy, Gustave. 3452

Barkay, Gabriel. 950-957, 4344-4345, 4519

Barkay, Rachel. 4099

Barluzzi, A. 4669-4670

Index of Authors

Barnai, Ya'acov. 3034

Barnard, L. W. 3344

Barnes, William Emory. 1298, 1835

Barnett, P. W. 2778

Barnett, R. D. 958-959, 1706, 2236, 2481

Barrett, Charles K. 3345

Barrois, Georges Augustin. 93-100, 596-597, 960-961, 1242, 1823, 1836-1837, 2481A, 3346, 4710

Barsottelli, L. 3644

Barthélemy, D. 2682

Bartlett, John R. 2007, 2237

Bartlett, William H. 5223-5224

Barton, George A. 880, 962, 1243, 1837, 2482

Bartos, A. P. 5540

Bartur, R. 3036

Bartura, Avraham. 3037

Bassan, Fernande. 3964

Bashan, Eliezer. 3038-3039

Bassi, Alexandre. 4781

Bauer, Johannes B. 7, 1371

Baumann, Emile. 360

Baumbach, G. 2779

Baumgarten, Joseph M. 2483, 2683

Baumstark, A. 3645-3646, 4100, 4333

Bausman, Benjamin. 5225

Bayer, Bathja. 3196

Bayne, Edward A. 5580

Beaucamp, Evode. 1372

Beaumont, E. F. 881, 888

Becker, F. 164

Beckingham, Charles F. 4101

Becq, Jean. 4711

Bedford, W. K. R. 5226

Be'er, Haim. 361

Beer, M. 2922

Beeson, Trevor. 5581

Beet, J. Agar. 3453

Bell, J. Bowyer. 5455

Belleli, L. 2484

Bellorini, T. 3965-3968, 4102

Bellow, Saul. 5582

Bellows, John. 362

Beltritti, J. 4103-4107

Ben-Ami, Maimon. 3820, 4108

Ben-Ari, M. 879, 948, 3814

Ben-Arieh, Sara. 792-795, 963-964, 1107, 3040-3044

Ben-Arieh, Yehoshua. 101-106, 598, 882, 4109-4110, 4334, 4969, 5227-5233

Ben-Chorin, S. 9

Ben-Dov, Meir. 363-365, 796, 1299, 2299-2303, 2485-2486, 2923, 3045, 3647-3650, 3821, 4970-4976

Ben-Eliezer, Shimon. 3046

Ben-Ori, Z. 1707-1708

Ben-Porat, Yehuda. 3047

Ben-Sasson, Hayim H. 3048

Ben-Shalom, Israel. 2924

Ben-Shammai, M. H. 2780

Ben-Yashar, Menachem. 2684

Ben-Yehudah, Hemda. 5234

Ben-Zvi, Izhaq. 3049-3051

Benayahu, M. 965

Bennett, C. M. 4335

Benoit, Pierre. 797-798, 966, 1126, 2304-2307, 2925, 3969, 4010, 4520, 4765, 4782, 4839-4845

Bentwich, Helen. 5458

Bentwich, Norman. 3052, 5235, 5456-5458, 5519-5521

Bentzen, Aage. 1546, 1709, 2008

Benvenisti, David. 10

Benvenisti, Meron. 3025, 3822, 5522-5523, 5583-5585

Benziman, Uzi. 5586

Benzinger, Immanuel. 284-285, 366, 1710, 1838, 2487

Bercuson, David J. 5587

Berger, Peter. 5524

Bergheim, Samuel. 107

Bergman, Jan. 2009

Bergmeier, Roland. 3347

Berkovits, Eliezer. 3054

Berman, Ariel. 1200

Bernadotte, Folke. 5525

Bernard, John H. 3313, 3651-3653, 3970

Berneim, A. 57

Bernhardt, Karl-Heinz. 1547, 1711

Berry, Donald L. 5588

Berry, George. 1373

Berry, J. 5589

Bertholet, Alfred. 2010-2011, 2186

Berto, P. 2488

Bertram, Anton. 4111-4112

Bertrand, Alexandre. 1839-1840

Besant, Walter. 368-369, 394-395,3823

Besnard, A.-M. 3971

Best, Ernest. 3499

Beswick, S. 108-109, 599-601

Bethel, Nicholas. 5459

Betz, Otto. 2685, 2781, 3500-3501

Beuker, W. A. M. 1374

Bevan, A. A. 4977

Bewer, Julius A. 2187

Bezanson, W. E. 5344

Bic, Milos. 1548

Bickerman, Elias. 2238, 2308-2311, 2490, 3055

Bidot, G. 3972

Bietenhard, H. 2926

Biger, Gideon. 5460

Biguzzi, G. 3348, 3454

Bilde, Per. 2782-2783

Billerbeck, Paul. 2491

Bin Talal, Hassan. 5590

Biran, Avram. 5526

Birch, W. F. 110-131, 601-612, 731-733, 967-978, 2312, 4521

Birnbaum, Solomon. 2988

Bisharat, George E. 5591

Bishko, Herbert. 11

Bishop, Eric F. F. 613, 883, 4978, 5461

Bissoli, Giovanni. 4783

Bitan-Buttenweiser, A. 132

Bjorkman, W. 4979

Black, Ian. 5592

Black, Matthew. 2630, 2784

Blackman, P. 2603

Blackwell, J. Kenneth. 5593

Blanchetière, François. 3056

Blekinsopp, Joseph. 1712-1713, 2239, 4712

Bliss, Frederick J. 370-384, 398, 545, 555, 3654, 3763

Blomme, Y. 4846

Blum, Yehuda Z. 5594

Blumberg, Arnold. 5236

Blyth, Estelle. 3824, 4114, 5237

Boase, T. S. R. 3825

Bobichon, Marius. 3349-3350

Bockel, Pierre. 3351, 3973, 4336

Bocker, Uli. 66A

Bodian, Marion. 5595

Böcher, Otto. 1375, 3455

Böhl, Felix. 1376, 2313

de Boer, P. A. H. 2012

Bogaert, Pierre-Maurice. 2785-2786

Boismard, M. E. 4765

Bonar, Andrew A. 5238

Bondvelle, J. 4847

Bonfil, R. 2314

Bonian, Stephen. 5597

Bonnetain, Nicole. 16.

Bonsirven, Joseph. 2492

Borg, A. 4337-4338

Borg, Marc. 2787

Borger, Hugo. 3537

Bori, Pier C. 3655

Borrer, Dawson. 5239

Borrmans, Maurizio. 12, 4980

Boswell, R. B. 3352

Bosworth, C. E. 4981

Botterweck, G. Johannes. 2079

Boudet, Jacques. 13

Bourke, Joseph. 1549

Bouwen, F. 4115

Index of Authors

Bouyer, L. 3538

Bovet, Felix. 1714, 5240

Bovis, H. Eugene. 5462, 5527, 5598

Bowersock, G. W. 2929

Bowman, John. 2013

Box, G. H. 2014

Brake, Brian. 5558

Brand, J. 2429

Brandenburg, E. 385

Brandon, Samuel G. F. 2788-2794, 3279-3280

Brandys, Massimiliano. 4848

Braslavi (= Braslavsky), Joseph. 614, 3057, 4982

Bratcher, Dennis R. 1377

Brauer, George C., Jr. 2795

Braumann, Georg. 3353

Braun, F.-M. 3354

Braun, Roddy L. 1550-1551, 2430

Braun, Werner. 14, 69

Brecher, Michael. 5599-5600

Bredero, Adriaan H. 3539

Bredy, Michel. 3656

Breen, Andrew E. 5241

Brehier, L. 3974

Brentjes, Burchard. 3826

Brennan, Joseph P. 3540

Bresc-Boutier, G. 4339

Bressan, Gino. 615-616

Bridgeman, Charles T. 4116-4117

Briend, Jacques. 617, 979, 1300, 2315, 2493, 4340, 4595-4597

Bright, John. 1552, 2240, 2431

Briggs, Martin S. 4983

Brlek, M. 4119

Broadus, John R. 4120

Brock, Sebastian P. 3058-3059

Brodie, L. T. 3355

Brooks, E. W. 3657

Brooke, George J. 2686

Broome, George. 5601

Broshi, Magen. 133-135, 358-359, 386-391, 734, 799-800, 884-885, 1301, 2316-2318, 3060, 3658-3660, 4341-4345

Brown, B. 4849

Brown, John P. 1715

Browne, R. A. 3975

Brownlow, Canon. 3661

Brownrigg, Ronald. 3145, 4180, 5065

Bruce, Frederick F. 2796, 3314, 3356, 3502

Brueggemann, Walter. 1378, 1553

Brunet, Gilbert. 618-619, 2241

Brunot, Amédée. 620, 3541, 4121, 4346, 4598, 4671, 4766

Bruston, Ch. 1841

Buchan, Alexander. 136

Buchanan, George W. 3357

Buchtal, H. 3827

Buckingham, James Silk. 5242

Buckland, Gail. 5419

Budde, Karl. 1716-1718, 2015-2016

Büchler, Adolpf. 886, 980, 2494-2499, 2797

Buhl, Frants. 137, 4984

Buis, Pierre. 1379-1380

Bultmann, Rudolf. 3503

Burch, Vacher. 3504

Burgmann, Hans. 2687

Burgoyne, Michael H. 4985-4990, 5079

Burkitt, F. Crawford. 3358

Burnet, David S. 5243

Burney, C. F. 138

Burrell, David B. 4122

Burrows, E. 3281

Burrows, Millar. 139, 621, 735-737, 981, 1302, 2319, 3315, 4850

Burton, Isabel. 5244

Busch, Moritz. 5245

Buse, Ivor. 3359

Bush, George. 5602

Bushell, Gerard. 4123-4124

Busink, Th. A. 1244, 1303, 1842-1843, 2188, 2432, 2500-2502, 4991

Busse, Heribert. 4992-4996

Butin, J.-D. 3360

Butler-Bowden, W. 3976

Buzzetti, Luciano. 5246

Byatt, Anthony. 140, 2320

Cabanne, P. 5528

Caldecott, W. Shaw. 1719

Cagnet, René. 2798

Caird, George B. 3361

Caldecott, A. 3362

Caldecott, W. Shaw. 1719, 2503-2505

Callaway, Joseph. 392

Callaway, Phillip. 2688

Campbell, Anthony F. 1554, 1720

Campbell, Edward J., Jr. 1245

Campbell, Ken M. 3456

Campos, Julio. 3542

Canaan, Taufik. 622, 4997-4998

Canard, M. 4347

Canney, M. A. 4851

Canova, G. 3977

Capa, Cornell. 15

Capelle, B. 3662

Caplan, Gerald. 5603

Caplan, Ruth B. 5603

Caradon, Hugh Foot Mackintosh. 5604

Cardini, Franco. 3543

Index of Authors

Cardman, Francine. 3664

Carlson, Rolf August. 1555

Carmel, Alex. 5247-5250

Carmignac, Jean. 2689

Carmoly, E. 3061

Carpenter, Mary. 5251

Carreira, José Nunes. 1844

Carus, Paul. 5252-5253

Casalegno, A. 3363

Caskel, Werner. 4999

Caspari, Wilhelm. 141, 1381

Cassuto, D. 3062-3063

Cassuto, Umberto. 1247

Cassuto-Salzmann M. 982

Castelar, Emilie. 3978

Castelot, John J. 2017, 3544

Catarivas, Daniel. 16.

Cattan, Henry. 5605-5608

Causse, Antonin. 1382-1384

Cazelles, Henri. 1845, 2242

Celada, B. 2506

Cerny, Edward A. 801, 2321, 4348, 4852

Cerulli, Enrico. 4125-4126

Chabot, J. B. 4349

Chadwick, Jeffrey. 4522

Chaplin, Thomas. 136, 142, 623, 983, 1847, 2507, 5254

Charif, Ruth. 3064

Charles, R. H. 3316, 3457

Chary, T. 2189

Chateaubriand, François Auguste René. 3964, 3979-3981

Chavel, Charles B. 3065

Cheetham, F. P. 3364

Chen, Doren. 2930-2931, 3665-3666, 4350, 5000-5001

Chesterton, G. K. 5463

Cheyne, Thomas K. 144, 1721

Chiblack, Abbas. 5609

Child, Brevard. 1385

Chipiez, Charles. 1848

Chitty, D. J. 3667

Chopineau, J. 2018

Chouraqui, André. 17-18

Christie, W. M. 3066

Chronis, Harry L. 3365

Cignelli, L. 3668

Cipriani, Settimio. 3366

Clarisse, Fernand. 3982, 4767, 4853

Clark, Elizabeth A. 3669, 4713

Clark, K. W. 4784

Clark, Kenneth. 2508, 3317

Clarke, N. P. 802-803

Clarke. Thurston. 5464

Clay, A. T. 1248

Clements, Ronald E. 1386-1389, 2019, 2243

Clermont-Ganneau, Charles. 145-147, 393, 624-627, 984-995, 2322-2323, 2433, 2509-2514, 2624, 2932-2936, 3670-3671, 3828-3835, 4353-4358, 4714-4718, 4854-4855, 5002-5006

Clifford, Richard J. 1390-1391, 1556, 1722

Clifton, Lord Bishop of. 3836

Clos, E. M. 4359

Close, Charles F. 148

Clowney, Edmund P. 3505

Codrington, H. W. 4127

Cody, Aelred. 2020, 3458

Cohen, Amnon. 887, 3067-3074, 4128, 5007-5012

Cohen, Chayim. 1392

Cohen, E. 3983

Cohen, G. L. 5612

Cohen, J. 2515

Cohen, Martin A. 2021

Cohen, Saul B. 5613-5617

Cohen, Shalom. 5618

Cohen, Shaye J. D. 3075

Cohn, Erich W. 149, 628, 3076

Cohn, Robert L. 1393-1394, 3077

Colbi, Paul S. (= Saul P.) 3672, 3984, 4129-4131, 5255-5257

Cole, Dan. 629, 996

Cole, Harris F. G. 1849

Cole, Robert Alan. 3506

Collas, L. 4360

Colli, A. 3545

Collin, Bernardin. 4132-4137, 4599-4600

Collins, Larry. 5529

Collis, Louise. 3985

Colunga, Alberto. 1395

Comay, Joan. 19, 1850, 3078

Comblin, J. 3367, 3459

Compain, M. 3986

Conant, K. J. 3673, 4361

Conder, Claude R. 20, 150-158, 292, 396-400, 504, 578, 630-633, 738, 804, 998-1002, 1304, 2324, 2516-2520, 2799, 2937, 3318, 3674, 3837-3841, 3936-3937, 3987, 4523-4528, 4785-4787, 4922-4923, 5258-5259

Congar, Yves M.-J. 3546

Conrady, Ludwig. 3988

Constantinou, V. H. 2325

Conway, John S. 5261

Conybeare, F. C. 3675

Cook, Stanly A. 144, 2326

Cooke, F. A. 3368

Cooke, Gerald. 1557

Cooke, George A. 2190-2191

Cooper, Alan. 1558

Coppens, Joseph. 1559-1560, 3507

Corbett, Spencer. 2521

Corbo, Virgilio. 1003-1004, 4329, 4362-4375, 4672-4674, 4719-4722

Corney, Richard W. 2022

Cornfeld, Gaalyah. 493, 2327, 2522, 2800, 3079

Corsani, Bruno. 3369

Cothenet, Edouard. 3370

Couard, Ludwig. 1723

Coüasnon, Charles. 4360, 4376-4383, 4856

Couderc, C. 3989

Couret, Comte Alphonse. 3676-3677, 4138, 4384

Couroyer, B. 401

Crace, J. D. 888

Cragg, Kenneth. 3085, 4139

Crawley-Boevey, A. W. 159, 889, 3678, 3989A, 4529-4536

Cré, Léon. 4788-4789

Creswell, K. A. C. 5001, 5013-5014

Crim, Keith. 1561

Crolly, G. 5370

Cross, Frank M. 1005, 1562-1563, 1724-1726, 2023, 2328

Crowfoot, John W. 402-409, 805, 3679

Cruickshank, William. 3319

Cucchi, Francesco. 1396

Cullmann, Oscar. 2690-2691, 3371-3373, 4675

Culpeper, R. Alan. 3374

Curtis, John B. 3080, 4723

Curzon, Robert. 5263

Cust, L. G. A. 21, 4140, 4385, 4676, 4724

I. H. D. 4601

Dagut, M. H. 2692

Dahlberg, Bruce T. 401

Dajani-Shakeel, Hadia. 5015

Dakkak, Ibrahim. 5622-5623

Dalmais, I.-H. 3547, 3680, 4142-4143, 4725, 5016

Dalman, Gustaf. 160-164, 411, 634, 2524-2525, 3081, 3320, 4386-4388, 4726, 4857, 5264-5265, 5465

Dalman, Knut Olaf. 1006

Dalton, G. 635

Dalton, J. N. 890, 2938

Danby, Herbert. 2604, 2606

Daniel, Suzanne. 2024

Daniélou, Jean. 2329, 2526

Danilov, Stavro. 4144

Dannenfeldt, K. H. 3990-3991

Daoust, Joseph. 2801-2802, 3548-3549, 3681-3686, 3842, 3992-3993, 4389, 5017

Dashian, P. J. 3687

Davey, C. J. 1851

David, Abraham. 3082-3084

Davies, D. 1007

Davies, G. Henton. 1397, 1727-1730

Davies, J. G. 3588, 4390

Davies, J. H. 3460

Davies, Philip R. 2693

Davies, T. Witton. 1852, 2527

Davies, William D. 3085-3087, 3282-3284

Davis, Ebenezer. 2938

Davis, Helen. 5266

Davis, L. K. 5267

Davis, Moshe. 3550

Davison, Roderic. 5268

Dawsey, James M. 3375

Dayan, Moshe. 5624

Decroix, J. 1008, 3994, 4602

De Hass, Frank S. 5269

Deissmann, A. 5270

Del Alamo, M. 3461

Delcor, Mathias. 1853, 2025, 2694

da Deliceto, Gerardo. 739

Del Medico, H. E. 2026

Deltombe, F.-L. 3689

Deluz, C. 3995

Del Verme, M. 4790

Demsky, Aaron. 2528

De Munter, L. 22

Derenbourg, Joseph. 2529

Derrett, J. Duncan. 3376-3377

Desjardins, B. 4727

De Souza, B. 3378

De Swaef, A. 22

Dever, William G. 674, 1854, 1939

Devos, P. 4727A

Dhorme, Édouard. 1249, 1731-1732

Diaz y Dias, M. 3735

Dibelius, Martin. 1733

Dickie, Archibald C. 384, 413-414, 1009, 3654, 3690-3691, 4391-4392

Dickson, Gladys. 1010

Dickson, J. 3764

Diebner, B. 3551

Dietrich, Walter. 1564

Diez, E. 5018

Díez Fernandez, Florentino. 4393, 4791

Diez Merino, Luis. 4678

Dinkler, E. 1011

Dinur, B. Z. 3088-3089

Diringer, David. 1012

Di Segni, Riccardo. 2399, 3090

Dixon, William H. 5271

Dobrena, T. J. 4603

Dobson, C. C. 4537

Dodd, Charles H. 3379

Doerksen, Victor G. 5272

Doeve, J. W. 2530, 3380

Donner, Herbert. 1305, 1565, 1855, 2531, 3692

Doran, Robert. 2434

Dorgelès, R. 3091

Dougherty, James. 3552-3553

Douglas, George C. M. 2192-2193

Doumani, Beshara B. 5019

Dowling, Archdeacon T. E. 4145-4149

Downey, Glanville. 3693, 4361

Drake, H. A. 3694-3696, 4394-4395

Draper, G. I. A. D. 5627

Dressaire, Léopold. 23, 4858

Drinkwater, C. H. 3996

Driver, Godfrey. 636

Driver, S. R. 1250

Drory, Joseph. 165, 5020-5021

Drosos, G. N. 4150

Druyan, Nitza. 3092

Dubarle, André-Marie. 3381

Dubois, M. J. 3554-3555

Du Brul, Peter. 3462

Du Buit, M. 2803, 3508, 3556

Duckworth, H. T. F.

Duensing, Hugo. 4151

Dürr, Lorenz. 1566, 1734

Düsing, J. A. 4152-4153

Dumoulin, Anne. 3997

Dunand, Maurice. 2435

Duncalf, Frederic. 3843

Duncan, Alistair. 4396, 5022

Duncan, J. Garrow. 166, 415-420, 474, 806, 1013

Dunkel, P. 421

Dunning, H. W. 5273

Dupuy, Trever N. 5530

Dupont, Jacques. 3382-3383

Dupont-Sommer, A. 2695

Duprez, A. 4792-4794

Duri, Abdel Aziz. 5023

Durrieu, P. 4154

Dus, Jan. 1735-1742

Dussaud, René. 2027, 2532

Dutheil, Michel. 3093

Dvir, D. 5628

Dynes, W. 3557

Eaton, J. H. 1567, 2028

Echegaray, Joaquín González. 2804

Eckardt, R. 4859

Eckart, Otto. 1743

Economopoulos, A. 4397

Edelstein, Gershon. 167-169, 196

Edersheim, Alfred. 2533

Eerdmans, B. D. 1744

Efrat, E. 5531

Efron, Joshua. 2939

Ehrlich, Ernst Ludwig. 1398

Eichrodt, Walther. 2029, 2194-2196

Eisemann, Moshe. 2197

Eisenstein, J. D. 2534-2536

Eisman, Michael. 1306

Eissfeldt, Otto. 1568-1570, 1745-1749, 2030, 2436

Eitan, Avraham. 339-343, 2280

Elath, Eliahu. 5274

Elazar, Daniel J. 5629

Elbogen, I. 2031

Eldar, Yishai. 2696

Elhorst, H. J. 2032

Eliashar, Eliahu. 3094

Eliav, Mordechai. 3095-3100

Eliot, Alexander. 5630

Elitzur, Yoel. 1307

Elliger, Karl. 2198

Elliot, Elisabeth. 5631

Elliott, James K. 3285

Ellis, Frank T. 422, 2330

Ellul, Jacques. 3558

Elm, Kaspar. 4398

Elster, J. 170

Eltester, Walther. 2537

Emerton, J. A. 1251, 2033

Emmanuele da S. Marco. 2331

Engemann, Josef. 4399

Englebert, O. 4728

Englezakis, B. 3844

Engnell, Ivan. 1571

Enlart, Désiré Louis Camile. 3845

Eppstein, Victor. 3384

Erfat, Elisha. 171

Ervine, St. John Green. 5466

Eshel, Yohanan. 5705

Evans, C. A. 3385

Evans, Geoffrey. 172

Evans, L. E. Cox. 4401

Every, George. 4156-4158

Every, E. 4402

Ewald, F. C. 5275

Eytan, Ovadia. 5632

al-Fahham, Muhammad. 5633

Falk, Zev. 2538, 5634

Farhi, David. 3101

Farmer, William R. 2805

Farrar, Frederic W. 2199

al-Faruqi, Ismail R. 5635

Fascher, Erich. 3386, 3559

Fedalto, Giorgio. 4159

Feigin, Samuel. 173, 1014

Feinsilver, Goldie. 335

Index of Authors

Feinstein, R. 5636

Feldman, Jennie. 3697

Feliks, Yehuda. 3102-3103

Ferembach, Denise. 1015

Féret, H.-M. 3560

Fergusson, James. 4529, 4538-4540, 4559, 4577-4579

Fernández, Andreas. 174, 2437

Ferrari, Silvio. 5468-5469

Ferriére, Cinette. 3561

Feuchtwang, D. 2034

Feuillet, André. 3387

Fiej, J. M. 3998, 4160

Figueras, P. 1016

Filson, Floyd V. 333

Finegan, Jack. 807, 1017, 2244, 2332, 2539-2540, 2940, 3321, 3698, 4403, 4604, 4679, 4729, 4768, 4795, 4860, 4924

Finkel, Asher. 2697

Finn, Elisabeth Ann. 637, 808, 891, 4404, 5236, 5276-5278, 5398, 5434

Finn, James. 5278

Fiorenza, Elizabeth Schüssler. 2698, 3509

Fischer, J. 638, 740

Fisher, C. S. 809

Fisher, D. 542

Fisher, Loren R. 1252, 1399

Fishman-Duker, Rivkah. 2941

Fishof, I. 3104

Fishwick, Duncan. 1018

Fitzgerald, Aloysius. 1400-1401

Fitzgerald, Gerald M. 409, 423-424, 2942

Fitzgerald, W. 5532, 5637

Fitzmyer, Joseph A. 2699, 2943, 3463

Flanagan, James W. 1308

Flanagan, Neal M. 3388

Flannery, Edward H. 5638, 5757

Flecker, E. 1019

Fleming, James. 2541

Fletcher, R. A. 3699

Flinders-Petrie, William M. 425, 1020-1021

Flückiger, Felix. 3389

Flusser, David. 2333, 2700, 3390

Foerster, G. 1022

Fohrer, Georg. 1309, 1402-1403, 1572, 2334, 2438

Folda, Jaroslav. 3846-3849, 4862

Forbes, S. R. 175

Ford, J. Massyngberde. 2335, 3105

Forster, Arnold. 5639

Fortesque, Adrian. 4161

Foster, Dave. 24

Foster, William. 3999

Foucherand, L. 53

de Foy, Guy Philppart. 36

Fraenkel, Meir. 176

Fraeyman, M. 3510

de Fraine, Jean. 1573-1575

France, J. 3850

Franco, Ettore. 1404

Frank, Harry T. 3322

Frankel, E. 3106

Franken, Sebastìen. 4605-4606

Frankfort, Henri. 1576

Frankl, Ludwig A. 5279

Fransen, Irénée. 177, 3464, 3562, 3700, 4730

Freedman, David N. 493, 1405, 1563, 2245, 3085

Frei, A. 4925

Freimark, Peter. 160

Frend, W. H. C. 4504

Fretheim, Terence E. 1406, 1750-1751

Frick, Frank S. 178

Friedberg, Albert. 5280

Friedman, Jack E. 5281

Friedman, Menahem. 3108-3109

Friedman, Richard. 1856

Friedman, Yohanan. 5024

Friedrich, Thomas. 1857

Friendly, A. 426

Fritz, Volkmar. 1858

Frizzell, Lawrence E. 3563

Frymer-Kensky, Tivka. 2035

Fuks, Gideon. 2806

Fukuzawa, Philip. 4405

Fulco, William J. 2944

Fullerton, Kemper. 741, 1407, 5282

Furneaux, Rupert. 2807

Fujita, Shozo. 2439

G. M. F. G. 4000

Gabriel, K. R. 179

Gabrieli, Francesco. 3851

Gad, D. 5533, 5544

Gadd, Cyril J. 1577

Gadegaard, Niels H. 1859

Gaechter, Paul. 3465

Gärtner, Bertil. 2701, 3511

Gafni, Isaiah. 1023, 2945

Gafni, Shlomo. 26, 892, 3110

de Galbert, Oronce. 4001

von Gall, August. 1578-1579

Galling, Kurt. 180-181, 427, 1024-1025, 1310, 1580, 1752, 1860-1868, 2200-2201, 2336-2337, 2440-2442, 2542-2543

Gammie, John. 2036

Garber, Paul L. 1831, 1869-1872, 1888

Garcia del Valle, C. 3564

Garciá Martínez, Florentino. 2702-2703

Garfinkel, Martin. 5283

Gari-Jaune, Lorenzo. 3391

Garitte, Gerardo. 3701

Gassi, A. 4162

Gaster, Moses. 2037

Gaster, Theodore H. 2038-2039, 3323

Gaston, Lloyd. 3392-3393, 3512

Gat, Y. 167

Gates, Owen H. 2040

Gath, Joseph 1026

Gatt, Georg. 182-192

Gatti Perer, M. L. 3565

Gautier-Van Berchem, Marguerite. See also Van Berchem, Marguerite. 5025

Gavin, Carney E. S. 5284

Gealy, F. D. 4863

Geffré, C. 3566

Gehman, Henry S. 1920

Geiger, J. 2946

Geike, Cunningham. 5285

Gelin, A. 3567

Gell, Francis. 4542-4543

Gelston, A. 2443

Gelzer, H. 429

George, James. 5641

Georgi, Dieter. 3466

Geraty, Lawrence. 1027

Gerber, Haim. 5286

Germanos, Mgr. 4163

Germer-Durand, Joseph. 193, 1028, 2947-2950, 3702, 4406, 4607, 4926

Gervitz, Stanley. 1873

Gese, Hartmut. 1581, 2202, 2444, 2544

de Geus, C. H. J. 194

Geva, Hillel. 429-430, 742, 810, 1128-1130, 2338, 2951

Geyer, A. F. 5642

Geyer, Paul. 3703

Gibbon, David. 27

Gibbon, H. H. Clifford. 2952, 2990

Giblin, Charles H. 3394

Gibson, Shimon. 167-168, 195-196, 431-432

Gichon, Mordecai. 2808-2809, 2953-2954

Gidal, Nachum T. 5287

Gidney, W. T 5288

Giet, Stanislas. 2810

Gil, Moshe. 3111-3114

Gilbert, M. 1582

Gilbert, Martin. 28, 434, 639-640, 3115-3121, 3852, 4002, 5026, 5289-5291, 5470-5472, 5534, 5643-5645

Gildemeister, J. 1029, 5027-5030

Gilmour, David. 5646

Gingras, G. E. 3704

Ginio, Alisa. 5647

Ginsberg, L. 5648

Glaisher, James. 197

Glasson, T. F. 3395

Glick, B. 5535

Glikson, Yvonne. 4003

Glück, H. 5031

Glueck, Nelson. 5649

Goell, Yohai. 5292

Görg, Manfred. 641, 1408, 1583, 1753-1754, 1874-1878

Goguel, Maurice. 3396

Goichon, A. M. 5650

Goitein, S. D. 3853-3855, 5032-5036

Golan, D. 2339

Gold, Victor R. 3705

Goldenberg, Robert. 2811

Goldman, Bernard. 1409, 3122

Goldman, Jenie. 4164

Goldschmidt-Lehman, Ruth P. 1311, 2545, 3123-3125

Golobowich / Golubovich, Girolamo. 4407, 4608

Golvin, L. 5037

Gonen, Rivka. 435, 1030, 1253, 5651

González Barros, Luis. 5536

Goodall, Terrence. 1584

Goodblatt, David. 2955

Goodenough, Erwin R. 1031, 1585

Gooding, D. W. 1755, 1879-1880

Goodman, Hirsch. 5653

Goodman, Martin. 2812

Goodman, Moshe. 5293

Goodrich-Freer, A. 5294

Gordon, Charles. 4544, 4564, 4584

Gordon, T. 5038

Gottlieb, Hans. 2041

Gourgues, M. 3568

Gousset, M.-Th. 3569-3570

Govett, R. 4408

Gozzo, Serafino. 2813

Graber, Oleg. 5036, 5039-5041

Grabois, Aryeh. 3856-3857

Graetz, H. 2546-2547

Grafman, R. 743, 2548

Graham, Stephen. 4004, 4165-4166

Graham-Brown, Sarah. 5473, 5641

Gray, B. C. 2814, 3286

Gray, George Buchanan. 1410, 2042

Gray, John. 29, 198, 1255, 1586, 1881, 2043, 2340, 2815, 3706, 3858, 5042-5043, 5295, 5474, 5537

Greaves, R. W. 5296

Green, Arthur. 3126

Greenberg, Moshe. 2044, 2203

Greenfield, Jonas C. 2704

Grego, Igino. 4409

Gregg, Andrew J. 642

Grelot, Pierre. 3576

Gressmann, Hugo. 1032, 1756, 5044

Grigsby, Bruce. 3467

Grill, Julius. 199

Grimes, Ronald L. 2045

Grimme, Hubert. 200

Grindea, Miron. 30

Grintz, Yehoshua. M. 1757, 1882

de Groër, Georgette. 4006

Grønbaeck, J. H. 1587

de Groot, J. 1883

Grousset, René. 3859

Grünhut, L. 2549

Grumel, V. 3707, 4167

Grunwald, Kurt. 3127, 5297

Gry, Léon. 2816

Guérin, V. 31

Guiladi, Yael. 5655, 5720

Guillemot, J.-B. 201

Gunneweg, A. H. J. 1588, 2046

Gunther, J. J. 3287

Gunther, John. 2956

Gur, Mordechai. 744, 5656

Gustafsson, Berndt. 1033

Guthe, Hermann. 436-438, 644-645, 811, 1312, 3708, 4168, 4410-4411

Gutmann, Emanuel. 5298

Gutmann, Joseph. 1758, 1884, 2550, 3128-3129, 3571

Guttman, Alexander. 2551

R. F. H. 4545

Haag, Herbert. 745, 1315

Haak, Robert D. 1885

Haas, N. 1034

Habe, Hans. 5657

Hachey, Thomas E. 4169

Hachlili, Rahel. 1886, 2552

Ha'cohen, Mordechai. 3130

Hadawi, Sami. 5487

Haddad, D. 4170

Hadey, Jean. 1411

Hänsler, H. 204

Halabi, Rafik. 5658

Haldar, Alfred. 2047

Halevy, Shoshana. 3132, 5299-5300

Halkin, Abraham S. 3133

Hall, I. H. 4171

Halper, Jeff. 3134

Halpern, Baruch. 1589, 2445

Halprin, L. 5659

Halsell, Grace. 5660-5661

Hamarneh, S. K. 5045

Hamberger, Meir. 5301

Hamdani, Abbas. 3572

Hamerton-Kelly, Robert G. 1412, 2446

Hamilton, Bernard. 3860-3861

Hamilton, Neil Q. 3397

Hamilton, R. W. 202, 439, 646, 812-813, 1035, 1413, 3709, 4412, 4796, 5046-5048, 5475

Hamlin, E. John. 1414

Hamman, Adalbert. 3513-3514

Hamme, Liévin. 203

Hammerschmidt, Ernst. 4680

Hamrick, Emmet W. 814-817

Hanauer, James Edward. 440, 647, 806, 893, 2553-2554, 3135-3136, 3710, 3862-3864, 4392, 4546-4551, 4864, 4927, 5049, 5302-5303

Handy, Robert T. 3573-3575

Hannam, Michael. 5304

Hannay, Thomas. 3398

Hanson, Paul. 2447

Har-El, Menashe. 32, 205-206, 648, 894, 1036, 2341, 3138, 4172, 5050

Haran, Menahem. 1415, 1759-1765, 2048-2054

Hardy, E. R. 2055

von Harff, Arnold. 4005

Harper, Henry A. 4552

Harrelson, Walter. 1590, 2056, 2246

Harris, David. 19

Harris, Rendel. 2957

Harris, W. B. 5476

Harrison, A. St. B. 5477-5480

Harrison, Roland K. 1313

Harter, W. H. 5663

Hartmann, L. 3288

Hartmann, Richard. 1766, 4173, 5051-5053

Harvey, A. E. 3711

Harvey, John H. 4414

Harvey, William. 4413-4414

Hasson, Isaac. 5054-5055

Hasson, R. 5056

Hatch, William H. P. 3399

Hatem, Anouar. 4174

Hauer, Christian. 1314, 2057-2058

Haupt, Paul. 746

Hayes, John H. 1416

Hayim, Abraham. 3139-3140

Hayward, C. T. R. 2817

Hayward, Robert. 2705

Hazan, Ya'akov. 5664

Hechler, William H. 5305

Hecht, Richard D. 2059

Heers, Jacques. 4006

Heidet, L. 4928

Heilman, Samuel. 5665

Heinemann, Joseph. 2555

Helms, S. W. 2958

Henderson, Archibald. 3324

Hengel, Martin. 2819

Hennessy, J. B. 818-819

Hentschke, Richard. 2060

Heroux, Barthélemy. 4175

Herr, Moshe David. 2557, 2959

Hertzberg. 33

Hertzberg, Arthur. 3085, 3141, 5743

Hertzberg, Hans Wilhelm. 1417, 1887, 2061

Herzfeld, E. 5057

Heschel, Abraham J. 3142

Heyd, Uriel. 5058-5059

Heyd, W. 4007

Heydenreich, Ludwig H. 3865

Hiers, Richard. 3400

Hildesheimer, Israel. 2558

Hill, Gray. 4553

Hill, Joyce. 3866

Hill, Rosalind. 3867

Hilliers, Delbert R. 1767

Hintlian, Kevork. 4177

Hirschberg, H. Z. 3143, 3808, 4960-4961, 5060-5061

Hirschberg, J. W. 3144, 5063-5064

Hirschfield, Robert Carl. 5666

Hirst, David. 5667-5668

Hitzig, Ferdinand. 207

Hoade, Eugene. 3965-3968, 4008, 4102, 4178-4179, 4415, 4609, 4681, 4731, 4769, 4797, 4865, 4929

Hoberman, M. 649

Hodgkin, E. C. 5669

Hoenig, Sidney. 2559

Hoexter, Werner. 5306-5308

Hoffmann, Richard A. 3401

Hofius, Otfried. 3468-3469

Hogg, S. 5670

Holbeche, Richard. 5226

Holland, T. A. 1037

Hollis, Christopher. 3145, 4180, 5065

Hollis, Frederick J. 1418, 2560

Holtz, Avraham. 3146-3147

Holtzmann, Oskar. 2561

Holzinger, Heinrich. 2562

Holum, Kenneth G. 3712

Honigmann, E. 3713

Hooke, Samuel H. 1419, 1591, 2062-2064

Hopkins, Ian W. J. 208-209

Hopwood, Derek. 4181-4182, 5309

Horbury, William. 3402-3403

Horgan, Maurya P. 2706

Hornstein, C. A. 1038

Hornus, Jean-Michel. 5310-5311

Horsford, Howard C. 5345

Horsley, Richard A. 2820-2824

Horst, Friedrich. 2065

Horton, Fred L., Jr. 3470

Howell, David. 4022

Howie, Carl G. 2204

Howland, E. G. 1888

Hoyt, C. 5671

Hubbard, R. Pearce S. 210

Hubmann, Franz D. 1420

Hudry-Clergeon, J. 3404

Hudson, Michael C. 5672

Hueso, Vicente Vilar. 1039

Huigens, Petrus. 35

Hull, Edward. 2563, 4554

Humphreys, C. S. 4335

Hunsberger, David R. 211

Hunt, E. D. 3714-3716

Hunt, Ignatius. 1256

Hupfeld, Hermann. 212, 820

Hureau, Jean. 36

Hurley, Frank. 37

Hurley, G. 3717

Hurovitz, J. 5066

Hurowitz, Victor (= Avigdor). 1768

Hurst, Lincoln D. 3471

Hurst, Thomas R. 3718

Hurwitz, Avi. 2205

Husseini, S. A. S. 1035, 2342

Hussey, C. 4555

Hutchinson, R. F. 4556

Hyamson, Albert M. 3149, 5312, 5481-5482

Hyatt, J. Philip. 2247

Hydahl, Niels. 3289

Hyman, Benjamin. 5702-5703

Hyman, Semah C. 4003, 5483

Idinopulos, Thomas A. 4183-4184, 5673-5679

Iliffe, J. H. 2564, 4185

Imbert, J. 2448

Ingram, O. K. 5680

Ingrams, Doreen. 5484

Iorga, N. 5067

Iqbal, Afzal. 5684

Irwin, Patrick. 3151

Irwin, W. H. 1769

Isaac, Benjamin. 2565-2566, 2954, 2960-2962

Issacs, A. A. 4557

Isenberg, Sheldon R. 2567

Ishida, Tomoo. 1529

Israel, Felice. 441

Israel, Gérard. 2825

Israeli, Yael. 443

Issar, Arie. 650

Isserlin, B. S. J. 1889

Ita de Sion, Marie. 2343, 4866

Ivry, Alfred L. 2449

Izrael, Rami. 3152

Jacobi, Paul J. 821

Jacobson, David M. 2568, 5068

Jacoby, Hilla. 39

Jacoby, Max. 39

Jacoby, Zehavia. 3868-3870

Jagodnik, Franklin. 74

James, Edwin Oliver. 1593, 2066-2068

James, Frances. 444

James, Henry. 332

Janin, R. 4187

Japhet, Sara. 2450

Jaros, Karl. 822, 4867

Jefferson, Helen G. 1594, 2069

Jeffrey, Arthur. 5069-5070

Jeffrey, George A. 2963, 4417

Jeremias, Joachim. 213, 1040, 2206, 2344-2345, 2569-2571, 2707-2709, 3290-3291, 3325, 3515-3517, 4418-4419, 4798-4801

Jeremias, Jörg. 1421-1422, 1770

Jeremias, Johannes. 1423

John, Robert. 5487

Johns, C. N. 446-447, 4682

Johnson, Aubrey. R. 1595-1598, 2070-2071

Johnson, Robert F. 1257

Johnson, Sarah Barclay. 5314

Johnson, Sherman E. 4189

Johnsson, William G. 3472-3473

Join-Lambert, Michel. 43-44, 2072, 3576, 3720, 3871, 4420, 5071

Jonas, Rudolf. 2964

Jones, Douglas. 1424, 2073-2074, 2248

Jones, S. Shepard. 5692-5693

de Jonge, M. 2710, 3405-3406, 3474

Jongeling, B. 2711

Joranson, E. 3872

Joseph, Asher. 3240

Joseph, Dov. 5538

Joseph, Frederick. 4421, 4683

Jossua, J. P. 3566

Jotham-Rothschild, Julius. 1041

Joubert, Christian. 4558

Jowett, William. 5315

Judge, Joseph. 2075, 5694

Juel, Donald. 3407

Junker, Hubert. 1425

Kadman, Leo. 2826-2827, 2965-2966

Kadmon, N. 170

Kaeppeli, Thomas. 4010

Käser, Walter. 3408

Kaganoff, Nathan M. 5316

Kahane, P. 1042

Kahle, Paul. 5072-5073

Kahn, Lehman. See Amitaï, L. K.

Kalaydjian, Ara. 4190

Kallai (-Kleinman), Zechariah. 1258, 1316

Kaminker, Sarah F. 45

Kanael, Baruch. 2967

Kane, J. P. 1043-1044

Kaniel, Yehoshua. 3154-3155, 5061, 5317

Kapelrud, Arvid S. 1426, 1771, 2076

Kaplan, Mendel. 534

Kaplan, Zvi. 3156

Kark, Ruth. 5074, 5318-5321

Karkenz, J. 4191

Karmi, H. S. 5075

Karmon, Yehuda. 214-215, 5322

Kasher, A. 2346, 2828

Kasher, Menahem M. 3157

Kaswalder, Peter. 4422

Katsimbinis, Christos. 4423, 4684

Katz-Hyman, Martha B. 5292

Katzburg, Nathaniel. 3158

Katzenstein, H. J. 1045, 2077

Kaufman, Asher. 1890, 2572-2579

Kaufman, Menahem. 5538A

Kaufmann, David. 3159

Kaufmann, Yehzkel. 2078

Kautzsch, Emil. 652

Kedar, Ahron. 3047

Kedar, Benjamin Z. 3160-3161, 3873

Kedar-Kopfstein, Benjamin . 2079

Keel, Othmar. 1427, 1599, 1891, 2080

Keith-Roach, Edward. 5488

Kekelidze, C. S. 3617

Kellermann, Diether. 2081

Kelly, Sidney. 1428

Kenaan, Nurith. 3874-3875, 4424

Kendall, Henry. 5489

Kenik, Helen Ann. 1600

Kennard, J. Spenser. 2829

Kennedy, A. R. S. 1772-1773, 1892, 2580-2581

Kennedy, J. H. 216

Kennett, Robert Hatch. 1774, 2082

Kenny, Vincent S. 5323

Kenyon, Kathleen M. 217-218, 448-459, 823, 1259-1261, 1317-1329, 1893-1895, 2249, 2347-2352, 2830, 2968, 3721, 5539

Keppler, Paul. 4685

Kernatz, B. 4192

Kerr, Malcolm H. 5696

Kessler, Christel M. 5076-5079

Kesten, H. 179

al-Khatib, Rouhi. 5697-5700

Khayyat, Shimon 3162-3163

de Khitrowo, B. 4011

Khouri, Fred J. 5701

Kidner, Derek. 2083

Kiene, Paul. 1775

Kiesler, F. J. 5540

Kimche, David. 5490, 5541

Kimche, Jon. 5490, 5541

Kimhi, Israel. 85, 219, 5703

Kindler, Arie. 2353, 2831, 2969-2971

King, James. 4732

Kingdon, H. Paul. 2833

Kirmis, F. 748

Kislev, Mordechai. 169

Kissane, H. G. 1601

Kister, Meir. 5080-5081

Kitchner, H. H. 4193

Kittel, Rudolf. 1896

von Klaiber, K. 220-221

Klein, H. Arthur. 46, 1330, 1897, 2582, 2834, 3876, 5082, 5704

Klein, Hans. 1602

Klein, L. 4194-4195

Klein, Mina C. 46, 1330, 1897, 2582, 2834, 3876, 5082, 5704

Klein, Zev. 5705

Kleinclausz, M. A. 5083

Klimowsky, Ernst W. 2583

Klingele, Otto Heinrich. 1898

Klinger, J. 4803

Klinzing, Georg. 2712, 3518

Kloetzli, Godfrey. 4196-4198, 4770

Kloner, Amos. 955-957, 1007, 1046-1055

Knierim, Rolph. 2084

Knight, Nicholas. 460

Koch, Klaus. 1776

Köhler, Ludwig. 222, 1603

König, Ed. 2085

Kohler, C. 3741

Kolenkow, Anitra B. 2835

Kollek, Teddy. 15, 47, 5324, 5491, 5706-5711

Kollwitz, J. 4504

Kon, Maximillian. 1056, 2584

Konrad, Robert. 3577

Kopp, Clemens. 3164, 3326-3327, 4686-4687

Kornfeld, Walter. 1899

Kosmala, Hans. 1331, 4610

Kotker, Norman. 48

Kraeling, Carl H. 1057, 2836

Kraemer, Joel L. 5712-5713

Kraemer, Jörg. 3877

Krafft, W. 223

Kraus, Hans-Joachim. 224, 1429, 1604, 2086-2087

Kraus, J. A. 4012

Krauss, Samuel. 225, 1058

Krautheimer, R. 4425

Kremers, H. 3292

Kretschmar, Georg. 3722, 4733

Kreuger, E. W. 4170

Krey, A. C. 3810

Kreyenbühl, J. 4868

Krinetzki, Leo. 1430

Krinsky, C. H. 3165, 3578

Kritzeck, James. 5714

Kroyanker, David. 3166, 5325, 5715-5720

Krueger, E. W. 3878

Kruse, Heinz. 1605-1606, 2088

Kühn, Ernst. 2207

Kühn, Fritz. 3879

Kühnel, Bianca. 4734-4735

Kümmel, August. 226

Kuhn, Heinz-W. 1059-1060

Kupperschmidt, Uri M. 5492

Kurzweil, B. 3167

Kuschke, Arnulf. 1777, 1900-1901

Kutcher, A. 5721-5722

Kutsch, Ernst. 1607, 1778-1779, 2250

Kyle, Melvin G. 1779

Labande, E. R. 4013

Lach, Stanislaw. 1431

Lachmann, S. 5306-5308

Laconi, Mauro. 3293

Läpple, A. 3475

Lagrange, Marie-Joseph. 227, 1061, 2585, 3723, 4611-4612, 4688, 4736, 4804, 4930-4932, 5084, 5326

Lamarche, Paul. 3409

Lamirande, E. 3579

Lancellotti, Angelo. 3401

Landau, Jacob M. 5327

Landay, Jerry M. 49, 461

Lande-Nash, Irene. 50, 2586

Landman, L. 1062

Landman, Shimon. 5074, 5321

Lang, Bernhard. 2009

de Langhe, Robert. 2587

Lankin, D. 4199

Laperrousaz, Ernest-Marie. 228, 462-463, 749-756, 1332, 1902, 2354-2355

Lapide, Pinchas E. 5723

Lapidus, Ira M. 5085

La Pierre, Dominique. 5529

Lapp, Paul. 2356

Laqueur, Shlomit. 5724-5725

Index of Authors

La Sor, William S. 51, 229-231, 757, 2357, 3168, 3328, 4738

Lassus, J. 3724

L'Atrebate, Dominique. 3580

Laubscher, F. 52

Lauterpacht, Elihu. 5726-5727

Lazarus-Yafeh, Hava. 5086-5087

L' Duhaime, Jean. 2251

Leaney, A. R. C. 2837

Le Bas, Edwin E. 2451-2452, 3519

Leclercq, Henri. 3725

Leconte, René. 53, 3726

Ledit, Charles J. 5088

Lee, George A. 232

Leeb, H. 3727

Legasse, Simon. 2588

Legendre, A. 233, 653, 1333, 4869

Lehman, M. 234

Lehmann, Manfed R. 2713

Lehrman, H. 5728

Lemaire, André. 464, 1063, 1608, 1903-1904

Lemaire, Paulin. 235

Lemor, Ora. 4739

Léon-Dufour, Xavier. 3411

Lesétre, Henri. 1780-1781, 1905, 2089, 2589-2590

Leskien, A. 3880

Le Strange, Guy. 236-237, 3881, 4426, 4559, 5089-5096

Lethaby, W. R. 4427, 4740

Levenson, Jon D. 1433-1434, 1609, 2208

Levi Della Vida, Giorgie. 654

Levi-Yadin, S. 5097

Levin, Michael. 5568A

Levine, Baruch. 1435, 1782, 2042, 2090-2092, 2714

Levine, J. C. 5729

Levine, L. I. 2838

Levine, Moshe. 1783

Levinson, N. Peter. 3169

Levy, Abraham. 2209

Lévy, Isaac. 465

Lewin, Thomas. 2839

Lewis, Bernard. 5012

Lewis, Nahum H. 5328

Lewis, T. Hayter. 3653, 3728, 3777, 4933, 5098-5100

Lewittes, M. 2607

Lewy, Julius. 1262

Lewy, Yohanan. 3170

Leymarie, Jean. 5542

Lichfield, Nathaniel. 5730

Licht, Jacob. 2715

Lidzbarski, M. 1064-1065

Lieber, Alfred. 54

Lieberman, Saul. 2591

Lietzow, Paul. 5329

Lifshitz, Baruch. 1066

Lightfoot, Robert H. 3412

Lignée, Hubert. 1436, 3520

Lind, N. F. 3171

Lindblom, Johannes. 1437

Lindenberg, Paul P. 5330

Linder, Amnon. 3172, 3581, 3729

Lindeskog, Gösta. 3413

Lipínski, Edouard. 1610-1614

Lipschitz, S. N. 5097

Little Donald P. 5101-5102, 5331

Littman, David. 5332

Livio, Jean-Bernard. 466, 3329, 4014

Lods, Adolphe. 1615, 1906, 2093

Loewe, L. 3173

Loffreda, Stanislao. 655, 1067-1070, 3330

Lofthouse, William F. 2210

Loftie, W. J. 4015

Loftus, Francis. 2840

Lohmann, Paul. 5333

Lohmeyer, Ernst. 3414-3416

Lohse, Eduard. 2334, 2358, 2592, 3174, 3294

Loisy, Alfred. 2094

Lorch, Netaniel. 5543

Loti, Pierre. (Pen-name of Julien Viaud.) 5334

Lotz, Wilhelm. 1784

Luciani, F. 1071

Lucy, R. V. 5732

Lührmann, Dieter. 3417

Lukacs, Yehuda. 5733

Luke, Harry C. 4016, 4031, 4111, 4202

Luncz, Abraham M. 3175, 5335

Lundquist, John M. 1438-1440

Lundstein, Mary Ellen. 5493

Luria, Ben-Zion. 656-657, 824-825, 1263, 2453-2454, 2972, 3176

Lussier, E. 4613

Lutz, Hans-Martin.

Lux, Ute. 826-828

Maag, Victor. 1616, 2095

Macalster, R. A. Stewart. 467-474, 829, 895, 1072-1083, 2096, 3730-3731, 4017-4018, 4203, 4560-4561, 4805, 4870, 5103-5104, 5303, 5336-5337

McBirnie, W. S. 4562

McCarter, P. Kyle. 658, 1441, 2097

McCarthy, Dennis J. 1616-1617, 2098-2099

McCarthy, M. C. 3732

McClellan, Thomas L. 1334

MacColl, Canon. 4563

McCormick, T. 5494

McCown, Chester C. 475

McCready, Wayne O. 2100, 2716

McCullough, W. Stewart. 1619

Macgregor, R. 659

McGrigor, A. B. 238

Macholz, Georg Christian. 2211

McKane, William. 1785

Mackay, Cameron. 2212-2216, 2455

McKay, John W. 1907

McKeithan, Daniel. 5417

McKelvey, R. J. 1442, 2359, 3521-3523

McKenzie, Leon. 3582

McKenzie, John L. 1443

Mackenzie, R. A. F. 1444

Mackowski, Richard M. 660, 830, 2360-2361, 2593, 2717, 3331, 4614, 4871

MacLeish, Kenneth. 5734

McMichael, Steven. 4019

McNaspy, Clement J. 4204

McNicol, A. J. 2718

McNulty, Ilene B. 831

Macpherson, James R. 3733-3734, 3882, 4428

McQueen, D. H. 3476

MacRae, George W. 2101, 3477-3478, 3524

McWhirter, Joan. 4205

Madaule, Jacques. 55

Madmoni, Zion. 3177

Madsen, Truman. 2456

Mähl, S. 3583

Maertens, Thierry. 1445

Magen, M. 896

Magen, Yizhaq. 2362, 2594-2595, 2719

Maier, Johann. 1786, 2217, 2596, 2720-2721, 2841

Maier, Paul L. 2327, 2522, 2800, 2842

Maigret, Jacques. 1446-1447, 3584-3585

Maisel, J. 75

Maisler, B. (= Mazar, Benjamin). 1084-1085, 1264

Malachy, Yona. 5735

Malakis, Emile. 3979

Malamat, Abraham. 2252-2257

Malik, Charles H. 4206

Mallon, Alexis. 239, 476-479, 661, 832, 1265

Mallouk, M. Ph. 4872

Maloney, G. A. 4207

Malsch, Carl. 4208

Maly, Eugene H. 1620

Mamluk, Gershon. 3178

Mamour, Joseph. 4209

Mancini, Ignazio. 1086, 4020, 4210-4211, 4429-4431

Mandaville, Jon. 5105

Mandel, D. 5736

Mandonnet, P. 3883

Mankin, J. H. 240

Mann, Jacob. 3179-3181

Mann, Sylvia. 56, 4615, 4741

Mann, Thomas W. 1621

Manns, Frédéric. 2597, 4432-4434, 4689, 4742

Manoukian, Serovope. 4212

Mansfield, A. 5544

Mansfield, Peter. 5495

Manson, T. W. 3418

Mansour, Atallah. 5737

Mansurow, B. P. 4435

Mantel, Hugo. 2598, 2973

Mantell, A. M. 897, 1087, 4213, 4923, 4934, 5106

Ma'oz, Moshe. 3182-3183, 5338-5342

Ma'oz, Zvi Uri. 2363

Maraini, Fosco. 57

Maravel, P. 3735

Marböck, Johannes. 7, 1448

Marchet, Xavier. 4616

Marcus, Franklin. 5773

Mare, W. Harold. 480, 3332

Margalit, Sh. 2930-2931

Margoliouth, Moses. 3184

Margovsky, Y. 481

Margueron, Jean. 1908

Marie Ita de Sion. See Ita de Sion, Marie.

Marijancic, M. 4436

Marlowe, John. 5496

Marmardjii, A. S. 241, 5107

Marmorstein, Abraham. 2364

Marmorstein, Emile. 3185

Marsy, Louis comte de. 4021

Marta, Giovanni. 4873

Martin, I. 3332A

Martin, J. P. P. 3884

Martin-Achard, Robert. 1449, 2102, 3586

Martini, Carlo M. 3587

de MasLatrie, L. 4214

Massé, Henri. 3885

Massey, W. T. 662

Massignon, Louis. 5108

Masterman, Ernest W. Gurney. 242-244, 482, 663-664, 833, 3333, 4743, 4806, 4874

Mattar, Ibrahim. 5545, 5738

Mattar, Philip. 5497

Matthews, Charles D. 3186, 5109-5114

Maundrell, Henry. 4022

Maurer, Christian. 665, 2365

Maurice, Charles. 4001

Mauss, C. 4807-4808

May, G. Lacey. 3295

May, Herbert G. 1335, 1450-1451, 1787, 1909, 2076, 2218, 3334

Mayer, Hannes. 1910

Mayer, Hans Eberhard. 3887-3890

Mayer, Leo A. 483, 864, 1088-1089, 3187, 5115

Mazar, Amihay. 594, 666-667, 698, 957, 1090-1091

Mazar, Benjamin. 245, 484-493, 1084-1085, 1092-1093, 1264, 1266-1267, 1336-1345, 1911, 2327, 2366-2376, 2522, 2599-2601, 2800, 2974, 3736, 3891, 5116

Médam. Alain. 58

Médebielle, A. 2103

Médebielle, Pierre. 4215-4217, 4437

Medzini, M. 5739

Meek, Theophile J. 2104-2105

Mees, Michael. 3588

Mehnert, Gottfried. 3589, 5343

Meier, R. 5740

Meimaris, Y. E. 3737

Meinardus, Otto. 4218-4225, 4438

Meisner, H. 4051-4053

Meistermann, Barnabé. 246, 4617, 4690, 4875

Melander, H. 4226

Melville, Herman. 5323, 5344-5345

Mendenhall, George E. 1622

Mendner, Siegfried. 3419

Menes, Abraham. 3188

Merendino, Rosario. 1452

Merhav, Rivka. 1886, 2552

Merrill, A. L. 1453

Merrill, Selah. 494-495, 668-669, 834-836, 898, 1094, 4935-4936, 5346

Mertens, Aurélius. 2843-2844

Meshorer, Ya'akov. 2377-2378, 2845-2846, 2975-2977, 4439

Mettinger, Tryggve N. D. 1454-1456, 1623-1624, 1788

Metzger, Martin. 1456

Metzger, Thérèes. 3189

Metzinger, Adalbert. 2106

Meyer, Hermann M. Z. 247

Meyer, Martin A. 3190

Meyers, Carol L. 1789, 1912-1917, 2602

Meyers, Eric M. 1095-1096

Meyshan, Josef. 2978

Mezvinsky, Norton. 5741-5742

Michaelis, Wilhelm. 3296

Michaud, Henri. 670

Michel, Diethelm. 1625

Michel, O. 3297-3298

Michelant, Henri. 3892

Mickley, Paul. 2379

Migeon, G. 5117

Milani, Celestina. 3738

Mildenberg, Leo. 2979-2982

Milgrom, Jacob. 1457, 1790, 2107-2116, 2722-2725

Milik, J. T. 248-249, 944-945, 1097-1098, 2682, 2709, 2726-2732, 2983, 3739-3740

Millar, F. 2630

Millàs, I. Vallicrosa, J. M. 3191, 4618

Miller, J. Maxwell. 1268

Miller, Patrick D. Jr. 1458, 1791

Minear, Paul. 3589

Minerbi, Sergio. 5347

Miquel, André. 250

Miquel Balagué, S. P. 4876

Mislin, Jacob. 4023

Mitchell, Hinckley G. 758, 899

Mitchell, Richard P. 5449

Mitchison, N. 5546

Moatti, Jacqueline. 16

Moe, Olaf. 3479

Möhlenbrink, Kurt. 1918, 2117

Møller-Christensen, Vilhelm. 1099

Mohrmann, Christine. 3788

Mohn, Paul. 5547

Molin, Georg. 1459, 2219

Molinier, Augustus. 3741, 3786

Momigliano, A. 2886-2847

Mommert, Carl. 251, 671, 1919, 4441-4443, 4619-4621, 4809, 4877

Montefiore, Hugh. 2848, 3420

Montefiòre, Moses. 3173

Montgomery, James A. 1460-1461, 1920, 3192, 3335

Montoisey, J. D. 4228

de Moor, Fl. 2457

Moore, Arthur. 5743

Moore, Donald J. 5744

Moore, Elinor A. 3742

Moore, George F. 2118

Moore, John N. 5745

Moore, W. W. 4810

Mor, Menahem. 3380, 2984

Moraldi, Luigi. 2119-2120

Morales Gomez, G. 3336

Morgenstern, Julian. 1462-1464, 1626, 1792-1794, 2121,

du Mortier, Jean-Bernard. 1627

Moskin, J. Robert. 15, 5746

Moss, R. W. 4878

Motzkin, A. L. 3193

Moule, C. F. D. 3525

Moulinier, G. 3980

Mowinckel, Sigmund. 1628-1633, 1921-1922, 2122-2123, 2733

Mucznik, Sonia. 3749-3750

Mühlau, Ferdinand. 252, 4024

Muehsam, Alice. 2608, 2985

Mueller, James R. 2849

Müller, Hans-Peter. 1465

Müller, I. E. 5348

Müller, W. 3480

Muhly, James D. 1269

Muilenburg, James. 1634

Mulder, H. 2850

Mulder, Martin J. 1923

Mullen, E. Theodore, Jr. 1635

Munro, Dana C. 3893

Muntingh, L. M. 3481

Murböck, J. 5118

Murphy, Richard T. A. 837

Murphy-O'Conner, Jerome. 496, 4564-4565, 4622, 4744, 4811, 4879, 5119

Murray, A. S. 2986, 3743, 4745

Murray, Robert. 2124

Musset, Henri. 4230-4233

Myers, Jacob M. 1924-1925

Myres, J. L. 1926

Nahon, S. A. 3194

Naladian, G. 42

Nantet, Jacques. 59

Narkis, Uzi. 5747

Narkiss, Bezalel. 2609, 3195-3196, 3744, 4234-4235

Nataf, G. 2851

Nau, F. 3197

Naveh, Joseph. 497, 1100-1104

Nebbia, Thomas. 3930

Nebenzahl, Kenneth. 252A, 900A, 3744A, 3893A-3893B, 4024-4024E

Nedava, J. 2852

Negbi, Ora. 498, 1105

Negev, Avraham. 499

Neher, André. 3093

Neider, Charles. 5416

Neri, Damiano. 3591, 4444

Nersoyan, T. 4236

Netzer, Ehud. 794-795, 1106, 2382, 3198-3199, 5748

Neufeld, Edward. 1636

Neumann, W. A. 253

Neusner, Jacob. 2853-2855, 3085, 3200

Neuville, René. 5349

Nevin, J. C. 254, 2856

Newett, Margaret. 4025

Newsom, Carol. 2734

Newton, Benjamin W. 5350

Neyrey, Jerome H. 3421

Nibley, Hugh. 3422

Nicholson, Ernest. 2125-2126

Nickelsburg, George W. E. 2610

Nickolsky, N. M. 2127

Niditch, Susan. 2220

Nielsen, Eduard. 1795

Nikiprowetzki, Valentin. 2383, 2857, 3526-3527

Nir, Yeshayahu. 5351

Niv, Amnon. 5749-5750

Nolet de Brauwere, Yves. 4237-4238

Nolland, John. 2735

von Nordheim, Eckhard. 1637

Nori, G. 5120

Norris, C. T. 838

North, Christopher R. 1638-1639, 2128-2129

North, Francis S. 2130

North, Robert. 839, 4623

Northcote, H. 3482

Northrup, Linda S. 5121

Noth, Martin. 1346, 1466, 1641-1643, 2258-2261, 2384, 2458, 2858

Noy, Dov. 3201

Nubani, Hamdi. 1108, 5122

Nuseibeh, Hazem Zaki. 5751

Obbink, H. Th. 1927

O'Callaghan, R. T. 3745

Oded, Bustenay. 2262

Oesterley, W. O. E. 2131-2132, 2611, 2859, 3337

Oesterreicher, John M. 60, 5752-5753

Offord, Joseph. 1467, 2987-2990, 5123

Olin, John C. 4026

Oliphant, Margeret O. 5352

Ollenburger, Ben C. 1468, 1644

Ollendorf, Franz. 1109, 5124, 5498

Olshausen, Justus. 255

Olyan, Saul. 2133

Oppenheim, A. Leo. 2263-2264

Oppenheimer, Aharon. 2385-2386, 2962, 2991-2992

Oran, Eliézer. 498, 500, 1105, 1110

Orfali, Gaudence. 1111, 4691

Orgel, H. Y. 5548

Orlandi, Tito. 3746

Orlinsky, Harry M. 2265

Orni, Efraim. 5549, 5755

O'Rourke, William J. 2134

Ory, Solange. 5025

Otto, Eckart. 61, 1469

Ottosson, Magnus. 1928

Otzen, Benedikt. 1470

Ouellette, Jean. 1929-1935

Oursel, R. 4027

Ousterhout, Robert. 4445-4446

Outrey, A. 3980

Ovadia, Asher. 3747-3751, 3894-3895

Owsepian, Archdiakonus. 3752

Pace, Giuseppe. 256-257

Padon, Gabriel. 5550

Pa'il, Meir. 5551

Pailloux, X. 1936

Pallis, Elfi. 5756

Palmer, Edward H. 3823, 5125

Palmer, Martin. 1471

Papas, William. 62

Parfitt, Tudor. 3202

Paris, M. Le Contre-Amiral Francois Edmond. 5353

Parkes, J. W. 5552

Parkes, James. 63

Parrot, André. 1937, 2612, 4447

Partin, Harry B. 3203, 4028, 5126

Parunak, H. Van Dyke. 1938

Parzen, Herbert. 5500

Patai, Raphael. 1472, 1645

Paterson, William P. 2135

Paton, Lewis B. 759, 840, 1347

Patrich, Joseph. 672-673

Paul, Shalom M. 674, 1939, 3204-3205

Paulker, Fred. 3254

Paulus, Christoph. 5354

Pawlikowski, J. T. 5757

Pearlman, Moshe. 47, 5324, 5491

Pedersen, Johannes. 2136

Pedersen, Kirsten. 4241-4242

Peli, Pinchas. 3206

Pelletier, André. 2613-2615

Pellett, D. C. 3592

Penna, Angelo. 1348

Peretz, D. 5553

Peretz, Martin. 5758

Perlmann, Moshe. 5127

Perowne, Stewart H. 64, 4243, 5554, 5759

Perrot, Georges. 1848

Peter, Adalbert. 1473

Peterca, Vladimir. 1646

Peters, F. E. 65, 1349, 2387, 2860, 3753, 3896, 4029, 5128, 5355

Peters, John P. 2137

Petersen, Claus. 1474

Petersen, David L. 2459

Petitjean, Albert. 2461-2462

Petrozzi, Maria Teresa. 4244, 4448-4450, 4624

Pfaff, Richard H. 5760-5761

Pfammatter, Josef. 3528

Pfeifer, Claude J. 1475, 2221

Pfeiffer, Charles F. 66, 258

Pfeiffer, Robert H. 1796

Pfennigsdorf, E. 1112

Phillips, Charles R., III. 3207

Piccirillo, Michele. 4245, 4451-4452, 4667, 4692

Pick, W. P. 5061, 5762

Pierotti, Ermete. 259, 5356

Pierre, Marie-Joseph. 4812

Piganioi, André. 4453

Pink, H. L. 4031

Pinkerfeld, Jacob. 3208-3209

Pisano, S. 1582

Pitcairn, D. Lee. 260, 4566

Pixner, Bargil. 2736-2738, 4625-4626, 4837, 4880-4882

Pizzolata, L. F. 3565

Plöger, Otto. 2138

Plooij, D. 3423

Pohl, Alfred. 2222

Polay, Abram. 5337

Poleman, R. 3593

Polish, David. 5358

Polk, Timothy. 2139

Pollack, F. W. 5359-5364

Ponger, Anne. 5763

Pope, H. 261

Popper, William. 3210

Porath, Yehoshua. 5365, 5501

Porten, Bezalel. 2463

Porteous, Norman W. 1476

Porter, John L. 5366

Porter, Joshua R. 1647, 1797-1798, 2140

Potin, Jacques. 4883

de la Potterie, Ignace. 3299-3300

Poulssen, Niek. 1649

Power, E. 4627-4633, 4937

Prásek, J. V. 4033

Prawer, Joshua. 3211-3215, 3594-3596, 3898-3909, 4246-4247, 4454

Prescott, Hilda Frances Margaret. 4034

Pressman, R. 5765

Prete, Benedetto. 3424

Priebatsch, Hans Y. 1271

Prigent, Pierre. 2861-2862, 3483

Prignaud, J. 1350

Pringle, R. Denys. 3910-3911

Prittie, Terence. 5502, 5766-5767

Procksch, Otto. 1351

Prodomo, Alberto. 4667, 4693

Pronobis, C. 1940

Provera, Mario. 3425, 3597, 4455, 5367

Puech, E. 1113-1114

Pujol, A. M. 4884

Purves, G. T. 4885

Quintens, W. 1650

Index of Authors

L. R. 4248

Raanan, Mordecai. 19

Rabe, Virgil W. 1477, 1799

Rabello, Alfredo M. 2616, 2993

Rabinovich, Abraham. 66A, 5768-5769

Rabinowitz, Louis I. 3216

von Rad, Gerhard. 1478-1479, 1651-1653, 1800-1801, 2464

Rahmani, L. Y. 501-502, 1026, 1115-1126, 4456

Rai, P. 4249

Rainey, Anson. 2141-2142

Rajak, T. 2388

Rak, Y. 923-924

Randellini, Lino. 1802

Rapp, Francis. 4035

Rappaport, Uriel. 2380, 2386, 2864, 2984, 2992

Rattray, Susan. 2143

Raynaud, Gaston. 3892

Razhabi, Yehuda. 3217

Reddaway, John. 5770

Reed, William L. 1127

Rehm, Merlin D. 2144

Reich, Ronny. 1128-1130, 3815

Reichman, S. 5771

Reicke, Bo. 1803, 3426

Reid, Stephen B. 1272

Reifenberg, Adolf. 1131, 2865, 2994

Reimpell, W. 1804

Reinach, Salomon. 2617

Reiner, Elchanan. 3219

Reiss, Dr. 4746

René-Burtin, R. P. 4747

Rengstorf, Karl H. 160, 2618, 2866, 3427

Renoux, Charles. 3754, 4634

Renov, Israel. 2619

Rentdorff, R. 2145

Revuelta Sañudo, Manuel. 4886-4887

Reynolds-Ball, Eustace A. 5368

Rhétoré, J. 3755

Rhoads, David M. 2867

Rian, D. 1352

Riant, P. 3912

Richard, Jean. 3913

Richards, D. S. 5054

Richards, J. M. 5555

Richmond, Ernest T. 4413, 5129

Ridderbos, J. 1654

von Riess, Richard. 5130

Riessler, Paul. 760

Riesner, Rainer. 3220

Riley, W. 3484

Riley-Smith, Jonathan. 3914

Ringgren, Helmer. 1655, 2009, 2739

Rist, Jean. 4036

Ritter, Carl. 262, 4250

Roberts, David. 5369-5371

Roberts, J. J. M. 1480-1485, 1656-1658, 1791

Robertson, Edward. 1805

Robins, E. C. 1941

Robinson, A. 1486

Robinson, Edward. 263-264, 4567-4568, 5372-5373

Robinson, H. Wheeler. 2146

Robinson, Ira. 3221

Robinson, Stephen E. 2740

Robinson, Theodore H. 2266

Rochcau, Vsevolod. 4037, 4251

Rock, Albert. 4252-4253, 4459-4460, 4635

Roeder, Larry W. 5773

Röhricht, Reinhold. 252-253, 265-269, 3915-3917, 4038-4053

Rofé, Y. 2620

Rogers, Mary Eliza. 5374

Rohde, Peter P. 67

Rolla, Armando. 503

Romann, Michael. 5504, 5556, 5775

Ron, Zvi. 270

Roncaglia, M. 4254-4255, 4461

Rondot, P. 5131

Rose, André. 3598

Rosen, Baruch. 3756

Rosen, Georg. 271-272

Rosen, H. B. 1273

Rosén-Ayalon, Myriam. 4462-4463, 5132-5137

Rosenau, Helen. 3222-3224, 3599-3600

Rosenau, William. 2223

Rosenberg, Roy A. 1274-1276

Rosenfeld, Alvin H. 3225

Rosenthal, E. S. 1132

Rosenthal, Erwin. I. J. 1659

Rosenthal, Gabriella. 4464

Roshwald, Mordecai. 3226

Rosovsky, Nitza. 68, 3227, 4256

Ross, J.-P. B. 4465

Ross, William. 841

Rost, Leonhard. 1488, 1660-1661, 1806, 2147-2148

Rost, Paul. 2224

Rotenstreich, Nathan. 5776

Rotermund, Ernst. 3918

Roth, Cecil. 2868-2874

Roth, E. 5375

Rothkoff, Aaron. 2621

Rousée, Jourdain-Marie. 4812-4814, 4823

Rousse, Jacques. 3601

Rousseau, O. 3602

Rowley, G. 5777

Rowley, H. H. 2149-2154

Rozemond, Keetje. 3757

Rozen, Micah. 3228

Rozen, Minna. 3229-3230

Rozenthal, Gabriella. 69

Rozin, Mordechai. 3231

Rubenstein, Richard L. 2875

Rubin, R. 4257

Rubin, Ze'ev. 3758-3759, 4466

Rubinstein, D. 5505

Rüger, Hans Peter. 1943

Runciman, Steven. 3760, 3919

Runnalls, Donna. 1662

Rupprecht, Konrad. 1944-1946

Rusche, H. 3603

Russell, Kenneth W. 3232

Rust, H. 273, 1489

Ryan, Joseph L. 5714, 5778

Sa'ad, Y. 1133

Sabourin, Léopold. 3485-3486, 3529

Sachsse, Carl. 4888

Safadie, Moshe. 5779

Safrai, Shmuel. 2389-2393, 2478, 2622-2623, 2876, 2995, 3233-3236

Safran, Alexandre. 3237-3238

St. Clair, George. 274-275, 504, 675, 761-766, 1134-1135, 2624, 4468

da S. Marco, Emmanuele. See Emmanuele da S. Marco.

Salas, Antonio. 3428

Saldarini, Anthony J. 2877

Salet, F. 4469-4470

Saller, Sylvester J. 1136-1140, 1277, 4748-4749, 4771-4772, 4889

Salvoni, F. 4471

Samuel, Edwin. 5780

Sanday, William. 3338

Sandberg, W. 5557

Sanders, J. A. 2741

Sanders, Ronald. 5506

de Sandoli, Sabino. 3920-3922, 4258, 4472-4474, 4890

Sandreczki, Ch. 5376-5377

Sanjian, Avedis K. 4259-4261

Sarna, Nahum. 1663

Sarno, R. A. 3604

Sasson, Victor. 676

de Saulcy, L. Félicien J. C. 276, 1141, 1839, 2878, 4891, 5378

Sauvaire, Henry. 5139

Savage, H. L. 3923

Savignac, M.-R. 1142-1143, 4892

Sawyer, John F. A. 3429

Sayegh, S. 4262

al-Sayeh, Abd al Hamid. 5140

Sayce, Archibald. H. 277-279, 677-678

Saydon, P. 2155

Schäfer, Peter. 1490, 2394, 2996-2998, 3239

Schaff, Philip. 5379

Schaffer, Shaul. 2625, 3240

Schattner, Isaac. 280

Schatz, Werner. 1278

Schedl, Claus. 2267, 5141-5142

Schefer, Charles. 4054

Scheidel, Franz J. 5781

Schein, Bruce E. 842, 1353

Schein, Sylvia. 3241-3242, 3924

Schelke, Karl H. 3301

Scheneker, Adrien. 2156

Schepss, G. 4055

Schick, Conrad. 281-285, 425, 505-515, 573, 679-695, 767-773, 811, 835, 843-850, 901-906, 1144-1164, 1491, 2395-2397, 2626-2628, 2999, 3243, 3339-3340, 3761-3764, 3925-3929, 4263-4268, 4411, 4476-4487, 4569-4575, 4636-4640, 4750-4753, 4815-4817, 4893-4896, 4939-4942, 5143-5150, 5250, 5380-5388, 5440

Schiffman, Lawrence H. 2157

Schiller, Ely. 286, 5151, 5353, 5369, 5389-5392, 5403, 5507

Schleifer, Abdullah. 5782-5783

Schmelz, Uziel O. 287, 3244-3246, 5784

Schmelzer, Menahem. 3247

Schmerer, Constance. 70

Schmertz, M. F. 5785

Schmid, Herbert. 1492-1493, 1948

Schmidt, Hans. 1494, 1664, 1807, 2629

Schmidt, Helmut. 1495

Schmidt, Karl-Ludwig. 1496

Schmidt, Martin Anton. 2158

Schmidt, Werner Hans. 1497, 1665, 1808

Schmidt-Clausen, Kurt. 5393-5394

Schmitt, Götz. 851

Schmitt, John J. 1279, 1498

Schmitt, Rainer. 1809

Schmitz, P. Ernest. 5395

Schnabl, Karl. 4269

Schneider, Alfons Maria. 2571, 3765, 4641

Schneider, Peter. 4270

Schneider, G. 4897

Schnellbächer, Ernest L. 3430

Schölch, Alexander. 5397

von Schönborn, Christoph. 3766

Schoeps, Hans-Joachim. 2879

Schreckenberg, H. 3605

Schreiber, A. 1949

Schreiner, Josef. 1499

Schrenk, Gottlob. 3302

Schrieke, B. 5152-5153

Schroeter, Leonard W. 5786

Schürer, Emil. 2630-2632

Schütz, Roland. 3303

Schult, Hermann. 1950-1951

Schultze, Victor. 1165

Schunck, Klaus-Dietrich. 1280, 1500

Schur, Nathan. 907, 1166, 3248-3249, 4057, 4271, 4488, 4576, 5154, 5398

Schwabe, M. 1167

Schwartz, Daniel R. 2633, 2742

Schwarz, Adolf. 1952, 2634

Schwerin, R. 57

Scippa, Vincenzo. 1354

Scofield, John. 5558

Scott, R. B. Y. 852, 1953

Seeligman, J. A. 2398

Seetzen, Ulrich. 5399

di Segni, Riccardo. 2399, 3090

Seidensticker, Philipp. 3530, 4818

Séjourné, Paul-M. 516, 909, 1168, 4642, 4754, 4934

Sekeles, Eliezer. 1130

Sellin, Ernst. 1810, 2465

Sepp, Bernhard. 5156

Sepp, J. N. 4058, 4898-4899, 5155-5156, 5400

Seybold, C. F. 2466, 5157

Seybold, Klaus. 1666

Shachar, Arie. 85, 288, 5787

Shaheen, Naseeb. 696-697, 774

Shalem, Diane. 71

Shaliv, A. 5788

Shamir, Shimon. 5401

Shamis, Giora. 71

Shanks, Hershel. 517-520, 698, 1169, 1355

Shapiro, S. 5508, 5559

Sharabi, Hisham. 5789

Sharef, Zeev. 5560

Sharkansky, I. 5790

Sharon, Arieh. 5791-5792

Sharon, M. 910, 5158

Sheppard, C. D. 5159

Shepstone, Harold J. 4272

Shiloh, Yigal. 517, 521-534, 699-700, 853

Shipler, David K. 5793

Shohat, A. 3250

Shor, Frank. 3930

Shotwell, Willis. 2400

Shupak, Nili. 1954

Siebeneck, Robert T. 2467

Siegman, Henry. 5794

Silberman, Lou A. 2743

Silberman, Neil Asher. 535-536, 5402

Silk, Dennis. 3251

de Silva, Carla Gomez. 3751

Simcha, Raz. 3064

Siméon, Vailhé. 3768

Simon, Marcel. 1501, 2635, 3431-3432, 3769

Simon, Rita. 3252

Simons, Jan. 289-290, 537-539, 701, 775-776, 855, 1170, 1356, 2636, 4489

Simpson, William. 540, 702, 2637-2639, 4490-4491, 4577-4579, 5160

Simson, P. 3433

Sinai, Anne. 60, 5753

Sinden, Gilbert. 4273

Singer, Suzanne. 2268

Sisti, Adalberto. 2401, 3487

Sivan, Emmanuel. 3931, 5161-5165

Sivan, Gavriel. 5795

Sivan, R. 541

Sizer, Harry S. 5773

Skehan, Patrick W. 1955

Slann, Martin. 5796-5797

Smallwood, E. Mary. 856, 2880-2882

Smith, Eli. 263-264, 4567-4568, 5372-5373

Smith, George Adam. 291-292, 1357

Smith, Jonathan. 3253

Smith, Morton. 2744-2745, 2883

Smith, Patricia. 1171-1172

Smith, Robert H. 1173-1175, 1281, 4492

Smith, W. Robertson. 292, 2159

Snaith, Norman H. 703, 1892, 2160-2164, 2581

Snijders, C. 542

Snijders, L. A. 1956

Soares, Theodore G. 2225

Sobosan, J. G. 4059

Soetens, C. 4274

Sofer, Naim. 5561

Soggin, J. Alberto. 1502, 1667-1670

Sokoloff, I. I. 4275

Sokoloff, M. 1176

Solar, Giora. 541, 2930-2931, 3816-3817

Solomiac, M. 858-859

Soucek, P. 5166

Spark, Muriel. 5562

Sperber, Daniel. 1503, 1957, 2402, 3254

Sperling, S. David. 1504

Spiegel, Ted. 5734

Spiess, F. 293, 860, 2403, 2640-2641

Spijkerman, Auguste. 3000-3001

Sprecafico, Ambrogio. 1505

Spyridon, S. N. 5403

Spyridonidis, C. K. 4392, 4694

Stade, Bernhard. 1958-1959

Staehlin, Wilhelm. 861

Stager, Lawrence. 543

Stamm, Johann Jakob. 1960

Stano, Gaetano. 3434

Starcky, J. 2642

Starobinski-Safran, Esther. 3255

Staub, Urs. 4819

Stauffer, Ethelbert. 1177, 2643

Stavrou, Theofanis G. 4276, 5404

Steck, Odil H. 1506, 2468

Steckoll, Solomon. 911

Stegensek, Augustin. 3770

Stein, Henia. 73

Stein, Murray. 2644

Steinmueller, John E. 2165

Steinschneider, M. 294

Stekelis, M. 1282

Stendahl, Krister. 3085

Stendebach, Franz Josef. 1961

Stendel, Ori. 4277-4278, 5167

Stephan, Stephan H. 4279-4280, 5168-5170

Stephen, F. W. 704

Stern, Ephraim. 1178

Stern, Gabriel. 4281-4282, 5798

Stern, H. 5171

Stern, Menahem. 2286, 2289, 2404, 2645, 2884-2885

Steurnagel. 33

Steve, M.-A. 313, 570, 714, 781, 874, 914, 1219, 1365, 1978, 2228, 2417-2420, 2659-2660, 2895, 3009, 4916, 5191-5192

Stevens, Richard P. 5799

Stevenson, G. H. 2886

Stevenson, Willim B. 2166

Stewart, Aubrey. 3771-3777, 3932-3938, 4060-4062, 4643, 5172

Stinespring, William F. 1507-1508, 1962, 2469, 2646-2649, 3002

Stock, Ernest. 5737

Stoddard, John L. 5405

Stoebe, Hans-Joachim. 705, 1358

Stolz, Benedict. 4283

Stolz, Fritz. 1509-1510

Stone, Michael E. 2610, 2887, 3778-3780, 3939, 4234, 4284-4286

Stookey, L. H. 3506

Storme, Albert. 3781, 3940, 4001, 4063-4064, 4695, 4755, 4773, 4900-4901

Strange, James F. 3782

Strange, John. 1963

Strobel, August. 862

Strugnell, John. 2746-2747

Struz, Andrej. 1511

Stryzgowski, Joseph. 3783, 3941, 5173

Stuhlmueller, Carroll. 296, 4287

Stutchbury, Howard E. 1180

Sukenik, Eleazar L. 863-865, 1056, 1181-1188, 1359, 2405, 3003

Sulley, Henry. 706

Sullivan, Desmond. 4288

Sumption, Jonathan. 4065

Sussman, Vardi. 1189-1190

Swetnam, James. 3488

Sykes, C. 5800

Sykes, Christopher. 5509

Sylva, Dennis D. 3304, 3435

Syme, R. 3004

Syrkin, Marie. 5563, 5801-5802

Szikszai, Stephan. 1671

Szörényi, Andreas. 2167

Tadmor, Hayim. 1258, 1672-1673

Talik, F. 4756

Talmon, Shemaryahu. 1512-1514, 1674

Tamar, D. 3256

Tamari, D. S. 4820, 5174

Tanai, Dan. 3257-3260

de Tarragon, Jean M. 1812

Tasso, Torquato. 3942

Taylor, Vincent. 3436

Taylor, W. R. 2651-2652

Tcherikover, Victor. 2406

Teicher, J. L. 2748

Tekoa, Joseph. 5803-5804

Telfer, W. 3784

Telford, William R. 3437

Tennebaum, M. 5406

Tenz, J. M. 297-300, 1964, 2653, 4581

Ternant, Paul. 4493

Terrien, Samuel. 1515

Testa, Emmanuele. 1191, 1516, 2888-2890, 3438, 3536, 3607, 4328, 4494, 4644-4646, 4749, 4821

Testini, Emmanuele. 4495

Texidor, Javier. 4289

Theissen, Gerd. 3439

Thoma, Clemens. 2891

Thomas, D. Winton. 1360

Thomas, John. 707

Thompson, Leonard. 3489

Thompson, Thomas L. 1283

Thompson, R. J. 2168

Thomsen, Peter. 3785

Thomson, Clive A. 2226

Thomson, H. C. 1965-1966, 2169

Thrupp, Joseph F. 301

Thubron, Colin. 74-75

Thüsing, W. 3490

Thureau-Dangin, M. 1284

Thurston, Herbert. 4902-4904

Tibawi, Abdul Latif. 5175-5180, 5408-5410

Tinelli, C. 4496

Toaff, Elio R. 2892

Tobi, Yosef. 3109, 3261-3262

Tobler, Titus. 302-304, 3786, 3943-3944, 4647, 5411-5412

Todd, E. W. 2170

Toledano, Ehud. 5181

Tolkowsky, Edmund. 5413-5414

Tomer, Yisrael. 5805

Torczyner, Harry (= Tur-Sinai, N. H.). 1813-1814

Torrey, Charles C. 2470

Townsend, John T. 2654

Trifon, Dalia Ben Hayyim. 3005

Tristram, H. B. 305, 5415

Trocmé, Étienne. 3441

Trombley, F. R. 3787

Trummer, Peter. 3305

Trusen, H. W. 4696

Tsafrir, Yoram. 885, 912-913, 2407-2408, 5182

Tsevat, Matitiahu. 1361, 1675-1678

Tsimhoni, Daphna. 4290-4295, 5806

Tufnell, Olga. 545

Tuland, C. G. 777

Tur-Sinai, N. H. See Torczyner, Harry.

Turgay, Üner. 5331

Turner, Edith. 4067

Turner, Harold W. 1517, 3531

Turner, Michael. 5807

Turner, Victor. 4066-4067

Turnowsky, Walter. 5564

Tushingham, A. Douglas. 306-307, 546, 778, 866

Twain, Mark. 5416-5417

Tzaferis, Vassilios. 547-549, 1192-1200, 4296

Ubigli, L. Rosso. 2409

Uhrbach, Ephraim M. 2410, 3263

Uhsadel, Walter. 2894

Ulrichsen, Jarl H. 1679

Urie, D. M. L. 2171

Uris, Jill. 76

Uris, Leon. 76

Ussishkin, A. 5418

Ussishkin, David. 708, 1201-1206, 1362, 1967-1969

Vaczek, Louis. 5419

Vajda, G. 2656, 5183

Van Bebber, M. 4905

Van Berchem, Marguerite. See also Gautier-Van Berchem, Marguerite. 5013, 5025, 5184

Van Berchem, Max. 1207, 4498, 5117, 5185-5189

Van de Velde, C. W. M. 5420

Van den Bussche, Henri. 1680, 3442

Van der Born, A. 1518

Van der Heyden, A. 26, 892, 3110

Van der Kwaak, H. 3443

Van der Meer, F. 3788

Van der Muelen, H. E. Faber. 2657

Van der Ploeg, J. 2749

Van der Vliet, N. 4822

Van der Waal, C. 3444

Van der Woude, Adam S. 2710, 2750-2752, 3474, 3491

Vanel, Antoine. 4906-4907

Van Elderen, Bastiaan. 4908

Van Hoonacker, Albin. 2172-2173

Vanhoye, Albert. 3492-3494

Van Iersel, Bas. 3306

Vanni, Ugo. 3495

Van Selms, A. 308

Van Unnik, W. C. 3307

Vardi, Méir. 3093

Vattioni, Francesco. 1970

de Vaux, Roland. 550, 1519-1521, 1681-1683, 1815-1818, 1971-1972, 2174-2175, 2472, 4823, 4944

Vawter, Bruce. 2076

Veijola, Timo. 1684

Verdier, P. 3006

Vereté, Mayir. 5421-5422

Vermes, G. 2630

Vermes, P. 2630

Vester, Bertha Spafford. 5423

Vetrali, L. 709

Viaud, Julien. 5334

Vilnay, Zev. 309, 3264-3268, 3175, 4068, 5223, 5335, 5424-5426, 5439

Vincent, Louis-Hugues. 310-313, 360, 551-570, 710-714, 779-781, 837, 867-874, 914, 1208-1219, 1285-1287, 1363-1365, 1732, 1973-1978, 2176, 2227-2228, 2411-2420, 2658-2660, 2895, 3007-3009, 3789-3790, 3945, 4297, 4499-4501, 4582, 4648, 4697-4699, 4757-4762, 4804, 4824, 4909-4916, 4945-4947, 5190-5192, 5510-5511

Vogt, Ernst. 315, 1979, 2269-2270, 2661, 4069

de Vogüé, Melchior. 314, 1840, 2662, 5402, 5427

Volney, Constantin François Chasseboeuf. 4070

Volz, Paul. 3946

Voskertchian, D. 4360

de Vries, Guglielmo. 4298

Vriezen, K. J. H. 875-876

Vriezen, Th. C. 1522

Index of Authors

H. B. S. W. 316-319, 1220

Wahrman, Dror. 3166, 5325

Wainright, J. A. 1980

Waisel, V. 5097

Wales, H. G. Quaritch. 1523, 1686

Walker, Franklin. 5428

Walker, J. 5193

Walker, Norman. 2663

Wallace, David H. 2753

Wallace, Edwin S. 5429

Wallach, Josef. 5283, 5430

Wallenstein, M. 3269

Wallis, Gerhard. 1366, 1687

Wallis, Robert. 4503

Walls, Archibald G. 1221-1222, 5194-5198

Walsh, Michael F. 3608

Walter, Nikolaus. 3445

Walther, J. 320

Wanke, Gunther. 1524

Ward, Richard J. 5811

Ward-Perkins, J. B. 4504

Wardi, Chaim. 3609, 4299-4304

Ware, Kallistos T. 4305

Warner, H. J. 715

Warren, Charles. 321-323, 504, 565, 571-578, 586, 1223-1225, 1847, 2664-2665, 4583, 4763

Wartensleben A. Graf. 5431

Wasserstein, Bernard. 5812

Wasserstein, D. 324

Waterman, Leroy. 1981-1983, 1988

Waters, Theodore. 5432

Watson, Charles M. 77, 325-326, 579, 881, 1367, 1984, 2666-2667, 3791-3793, 3947, 4515, 4649, 5433

Watson, W. 3496

Watty, William W. 3446

Watzinger, Carl. 2421

Waugh, Evelyne. 4505

Webster, Gillian. 5434

Weigand, E. 4506

Weigert, Gideon. 5814-5815

Weiler, I. 2896

Weill, Raymond. 327, 580-583

Weinert, Francis D. 3447-3448

Weinfeld, Moshe. 1526, 1688-1690

Weinstein, James M. 1288

Weinstein, Menahem. 3270

Weippert, Manfred. 1289, 1527

Weir, C. J. Mullo. 1290

Weiser, Artur. 1691-1693, 2177

Weiss-Rosmarin, Trude. 5566

Weitz, J. 328

Weitzmann, Kurt. 3794

Welch, Adam C. 2178

Welch, P. J. 5435

Wellhausen, Julius. 2179

Welten, Peter. 1528, 2473, 4071

Wendel, Adolf. 2180

Wenham Gordon J. 2181-2182

Wenning, R. 716

Wenschkewitz, Hans. 3532

Wensinck, Arent Jan. 1529, 5199-5200

Werblowsky, Z. J. (= R. J. Zwi). 42, 3085, 3271-3272, 3610-3611, 5201

Westmacott, Richard N. 5816

Westphal, Gustav. 1530

Whale, J. S. 3085

White, L. , Jr. 4700

Whiting, John D. 5436

Whitley, W. T. 5437

Whittemore, Edward. 5512-5513

Whitty, John Irvine. 717

Widengren, Geo. 1694-1695

Wieland, David J. 329, 4825-4826

Wiener, Harold M. 1819, 1985

Wiesel, Elie. 3273

Wiesenberg, Ernest. 2668

Wildberger, Hans. 1531, 1696

Wilhelm, K. 3274

Wilkinson, John. 330, 718-719, 2422-2423, 3341, 3795-3802, 4332, 4507-4511, 4584, 4650, 4701, 4764, 4774, 4827, 4917, 5202

Willesen, F. 1532

Williams, George. 4306, 5438

Williams, Maynard O. 4307

Williams, Robert. 3948

Williamson, H. G. M. 783

Willoughby, Harold R. 4512

Wills, Lawrence. 2755

Wilms, F.-E. 2754

Wilshire, Leland Edward. 1533

Wilson, Andrew M. 2755

Wilson, Charles W. 331-332, 504, 584-586, 720-722, 782, 2519, 2665, 2669, 3010, 3773-3777, 3938, 3949, 4487, 4513-4516, 4536, 4585, 4643, 4651, 4828, 4948, 5090, 5203-5205, 5439-5440

Wilson, Evan M. 5817-5821

Wilson, John. 5441

Wilson, John A. 1291

Wilson, Robert R. 2183

Wilson-Kastner, Patricia. 3803

Winchester, Dean of. 3612

Windisch, Hans. 2897, 3804

Winkler, G. 3805

Winter, Paul. 3308-3309

Wischnitzer, Rachel. 2670, 3275

Wiseman, Donald J. 2271-2272

Wistrand, E. K. H. 4517

Wolfe-Crome, Editha. 4072

Index of Authors

Wolff, Odilo. 1986-1987, 5206

Wolff, Philip. 5442

Wolverton, W. I. 1534

Worden, T. 1820

Wordsworth, W. A. 723

Worral, Girdler. 4518, 4586

Woudstra, Marten H. 1821

Wray, G. O. 5207

Wright, David P. 2184

Wright, G. Ernest. 333, 1831, 1982, 1988-1991

Wright, James E. 5443

Wright, John Stafford. 2474

Wright, Theodore F. 784-787, 1226

Wright, Thomas. 3806, 3950

Wrightson, T. 2671

Wyatt, Nicolas. 1697

Wylie, C. C. 1992

Yablovitch, Moshe. 3044

Yadin, Yigael. 587, 1227, 1882, 2756-2762, 2913-2914, 3011-3014

Yarden, Leon. 1993

Yehoshua, Avraham B. 5824

Yehoshua, Ben-Zion. 3047, 3109

Yehuda, Shamir. 3276

Yeivin, Samuel. 291, 1228, 1292, 1357, 1698, 1994-1997

Yerkes, R. K. 2185

Yeshaia, Samuel B. 3277

Yishai, Y. 5825

Yoger, Gedalia. 5567

de Young, James C. 3448

Young, Frances M. 3450

Young, J. W. A. 4112

Youngblood, Ronald. 1535

Zagarelli, A. 4308-4309

Zander, Walter. 4310-4311, 5826-5827

Zangemeister, Karl. 3015

Zeevy, Rechavam. 5224

Zehrer, Franz. 3451

Zeilinger, Franz. 3497

Zeitlin, Solomon. 2672-2676, 2898-2899

Zenger, E. 716

Zias, Joseph. 1172, 1229-1230

Zimmer, Robert G. 3533

Zimmerli, Walther. 1293, 2229-2233

Zimmermann, Michael A. 2677

Zimmermann, C. 334

Zimmermann, John D. 4312

Ziv, Shaul. 3278

Zobel, Hans-Jürgen. 1822

Zuidhof, Albert. 1998

Index of Subjects

Abd al-Malik. 507, 5084. See also Jerusalem-- during Early Arab Period.

Abdul Hamid (Sultan). 4078, 5327

Abraham. 1240, 1246-1247, 1251-1252, 1278, 1281, 1285, 1293, 2239

Abyssinians. See Ethiopian Church.

Adomnan (Pilgrim). 3802

Adorno, Anselme (Pilgrim). 4006, 4064

von Adrichem, Christian. See Christian von Adrichem (Cartographer).

Aelia Capitolina. 2000, 2908-2910, 2912, 2915-3920, 2923, 2925, 2930-2938, 2940, 2942, 2947-2952, 2954, 2958, 2961, 2963, 2965-2966, 2968, 2971, 2974, 2986, 2999-3003, 3006-3010, 4839-4845. See also Jerusalem--from A. D. 70 to Constantine.

Akeldama. 1154, 3313, 3317, 3324, 3339, 4226, 4263

Akra. 110-112, 120-121, 124, 128, 130, 182, 186, 191-192, 203, 212, 220-221, 254, 297, 299, 310, 325-326, 331, 820, 2303, 2312, 2325, 2354-2355, 2400, 2407-2408, 2411, 2418

Aksa Mosque. 4955, 5047-5048, 5052, 5089, 5095, 5097, 5099, 5168-5169, 5171, 5173, 5207. See also Arab Geographers and Historians; Haram esh-Sherif.

Altars. 1805, 1828, 1859, 1861-1863, 1883, 1896, 1912, 1927, 1960-1961, 1964, 1984-1985, 2224, 2227, 2524, 2587, 2653, 2666

Amarna Letters. 1231, 1233-1234, 1245, 1249, 1258, 1284, 1289-1290

St. Ambrose. 3579

American Christian Missionary Society. 5243

American Consulate. 3036, 3573-3575, 5256, 5346, 5429

Americans. 3036, 3171, 3573-3575, 5243, 5256, 5267, 5292, 5314-5316, 5338, 5344-5346, 5416-5417, 5423, 5428-5429

Amico, Bernardino (Illustrator). 3965, 4102

Angelaa von Merici (Pilgrim). 4030

Anglican Church. 3151, 4080, 4116, 4139, 4169, 4189, 4233, 4273, 4290, 4312, 5222, 5261, 5275, 5281, 5288, 5296, 5304-5305, 5310-5311, 5343, 5393-5394, 5408-5410, 5435

St. Anne, Church of. 4775, 4778-4781, 4789, 4795, 4797, 4802, 4805, 4807, 4811-4812, 4814, 4818-4820, 4822-4824

St. Anne's Market and Abbey. 3831

Antonia Fortress. See Herodian Buildings; Praetorium, Location of.

Antoninus Martyr. See Piacenza Pilgrim.

Antoninus Placentinus. See Piacenza Pilgrim.

Antonius von Cremona (Pilgrim). 4038, 4047

Apocalypse of St. John. See New Testament: Heavenly City and Sanctuary.

Index of Subjects

Arab Geographers and Historians. 236-237, 241, 912-913, 3851, 2656, 3877, 3881, 3885, 4173, 4426, 4559, 4959, 5027-5030, 5045, 5089-5096, 5107, 5115, 5125, 5139, 5168-5169, 5182-5183

Arab-Israeli War (1948). 5490, 5516, 5525, 5529-5530, 5538, 5541, 5543, 5551, 5560, 5563, 5567

Archaeological Excavations and Studies. 335-587. See also Armenian Quarter, Excavations; City of David, Excavations; Inscriptions and Epigraphy; Jewish Quarter, Excavations; Temple Mount, Excavations on West and South; Tombs and Related Materials; Walls, Gates, and Fortifications; Water Supply.

Architecture. See Art and Architecture.

Arculf (Pilgrim, Illustrator). 3689, 3733, 3796, 4379, 4403, 4442, 4604, 4621, 4729

Aristeas. 2314, 2331

Ark. 1421, 1575, 1701, 1703, 1707, 1709, 1711-1713, 1715-1718, 1720-1721, 1723, 1727-1729, 1733-1736, 1739-1742, 1746-1748, 1750-1752, 1756-1760, 1762, 1766-1767, 1770, 1772, 1774, 1778-1780, 1784-1788, 1791-1793, 1795, 1797, 1800-1802, 1804, 1807, 1809, 1811-1818, 1820-1822, 2473

Armenian Church and Quarter. 3642, 3657, 3687, 3743-3744, 3752, 3763, 3780, 3778-3779, 3898, 3939, 4073, 4075-4078, 4083, 4091, 4095, 4109, 4177, 4190, 4209, 4218, 4223, 4225, 4234-4236, 4246, 4259-4261, 4281, 4284-4286, 4297, 4636, 4746, 4754

Armenian Quarter, Excavations. 356, 358-359, 391, 546

Arnold von Harff (Pilgrim). 4005

Art and Architecture, Church of the Holy Sepulchre Represented in. 3549, 3591, 4331-4332, 4339, 4388-4389, 4403, 4417, 4434, 4439, 4444, 4463, 4491, 4507, 4511-4512

Art and Architecture, Contemporary. 5526-5527, 5528, 5533, 5539, 5540, 5542, 5544, 5557, 5568A, 5576-5577, 5628, 5644, 5648, 5662, 5671, 5715-5722, 5779. See also City Planning.

Art and Architecture, Crusader. 3825-3829, 3832, 3845-3849, 3874-3875, 4337-4338, 4356-4357, 4424, 4454, 4456, 4462-4463, 4470, 4490

Art and Architecture, Islamic. 4967, 4971-4975, 4983, 4985-4990, 4997-4998, 5013, 5025, 5037, 5056, 5065, 5072-5073, 5078-5079, 5082, 5119, 5133-5137, 5143, 5151, 5159, 5166, 5184, 5196-5197, 5202. See also Aksa Mosque; Dome of the Rock; Haram esh-Sherif.

Art and Architecture, Jerusalem Represented in. 900A, 3104, 3196, 3537, 3539, 3541, 3545, 3548-3549, 3565, 3569-3570, 3599, 3506, 4024C. See also Lithographs and Engravings.

Art and Architecture, Temple Represented in. 1884, 2576, 2583, 2608-2609, 2619, 2670, 2780, 2985, 3122, 3128, 3165, 3169, 3189, 3195, 3222-3224, 3275, 3557, 3571, 3578, 3600, 3605

Ascension, Church of. 3688, 4674, 4706, 4721-4722, 4724, 4726-4727A, 4729, 4733-4735, 4740, 4750, 4764

Ashkenazic Community. 3039, 3108, 3154, 3159, 3185. See also Jewish

Neighborhoods outside the Walls; Jewish Quarter.

Atlases, Maps and Cartographic Surveys. 6, 28, 79, 84-85, 91, 101-102, 106, 148, 159, 164-165, 170, 235, 240, 247, 252A, 258, 265-268, 284-286, 295, 303, 306, 309, 312, 332-334, 544, 1297, 1335, 2274-2276, 2916-2917, 3032, 3115-3121, 3310-3311, 3322, 3334, 3641, 3812, 3852, 3865, 3893A-3893B, 3954, 4024A-2024B, 4024E, 4045A, 4046A-4046B, 4068 4532, 4965-4966, 4968, 5021, 5026, 5233, 5290, 5454, 5470-5472, 5517, 5534, 5643-5645. See also Geographical / Topographical Studies; Madeba Mosaic Map.

Austrian Post. 5301, 5307-5308, 5330, 5348, 5413

Ayyubids. See Jerusalem-- during Ayyubid and Mamaluk Period.

Bar Kokhba Revolt. 2901-2907, 2913-2914, 2921, 2924, 2926-2929, 2939, 2941, 2943-2946, 2953, 2955-2957, 2959-2960, 2962, 2967, 2969-2970, 2973, 2975-2985, 2987, 2989, 2991-2994, 2996-2998, 3011-3014. See also Jerusalem-- from A. D. 70 to Constantine.

Batei Braude. 3166, 5325. See Jewish Neighborhoods outside the Walls.

Batei Neitin. 3166, 5325. See Jewish Neighborhoods outside the Walls.

Batei Rand. 3166, 5325. See Jewish Neighborhoods outside the Walls.

Batei Seidhoff. 3166, 5325. See Jewish Neighborhoods outside the Walls.

Batei Ungarn. 3132, 3166, 5300, 5325. See Jewish Neighborhoods outside the Walls.

Bede, The Venerable. 3734

Beit David. 3166, 5325. See Jewish Neighborhoods outside the Walls.

Ben-Zakkai Synagogues. 3046, 3062-3063, 3094, 3194, 3209, 3219, 3257, 3259.

Benjamin of Tudela. 3017-3018, 3021, 3024

Bernard of Clairvaux. 3610

Bernard the Monk (Pilgrim). 380

Bernard von Breitenbach (Cartographer). 170, 252A, 268, 4024A, 4046B

Bernardin Surius (Pilgrim). 3982

Bethany. 1067, 1070, 1137, 1155, 1210, 3314, 3920, 4765-4774, 5366

Bethesda, Pool of. 702, 2707-2709, 4776-4777, 4779, 4782-4788, 4790-4794, 4796-4804, 4806, 4808-4817, 4821-4822, 4823, 4825-4828

Bethphage. 1111, 1136, 1139, 1190, 4715-4717, 4720, 4729, 4732, 4748-4749

Bethso. 108

Bonfils (Photographer). 5284

Bonnano of Pisa. 4321

Bordeaux, Pilgrim of. 3726, 3774, 3799, 4630, 4643, 4809, 4828

von Breitenbach. See Bernard von Breitenbach (Cartographer).

British Consulate. 3149, 5236, 5277-5278, 5312, 5398, 5406, 5408, 5422, 5434

British Mandate. See Jerusalem--under British Administration.

Brygg, Thomas (Pilgrim). 4008

Bukharan Quarter. 3166, 3552. See Jewish Neighborhoods outside the Walls.

Buraq. 3186, 5114

Burchard of Mt. Sion. 3918, 3936, 4024B

Byzantines. See Jerusalem-- during Byzantine Period.

Caiaphas, House of. 387-388, 4607, 4616, 4621, 4628-4630, 4639, 4641

Calvary. See Holy Sepulchre, Church of the; see also Golgotha and Tomb of Jesus, Rival Sites.

Capodilista, Gabriele (Pilgrim). 4024C

Cardo Maximus. 3632, 3660, 3665, 3697, 3710. See also Jerusalem--during Byzantine Period; Madeba Mosaic Map.

Casola, Pietro. See Pietro Casola (Pilgrim).

Caspar von Mülinen (Pilgrim). 4041

Catherwood, Frederick. 102, 5160

Catholic Chrches, Latin Rite. See Roman Catholic Church.

Catholic Chrches, Uniate. 4082, 4118, 4150, 4230

Cenacle. 3191, 3350, 4128, 4253, 4460, 4588, 4590, 4592, 4595-4596, 4599-4600, 4604, 4608-4610, 4613-4615, 4617-4618, 4627, 4635, 4644

Chagall Windows. 5542

Charlemagne. 3974, 5083, 5190

Chateubriand. 3964, 3979-3981

Cherubim. 1454-1455, 1702, 1706, 1731-1732, 1771, 1788, 1796, 1807, 1817, 1970

Christian Churches and Communities. 4073-4312

Christian Perband (Pilgrim). 4042

Christian Quarter. 208, 4096, 4109-4110, 4178, 4196, 4271, 4277, 4292-4294, 5230, 5784, 5806

Christian Thought, Jerusalem in. 3211-3212, 3534-3570, 3572-3577, 3579-3599, 3601-3604, 3607-3612, 4468, 4491. See also New Testament.

Christian von Adrichem (Cartographer). 159, 252A, 3954, 3989A, 4024B, 4532, 4879A

Church of Scotland. 5328

Church Missionary Society. 5315

Citadel. 339-343, 429-430, 446-447, 541, 5170

City of David (including Zion and Ophel). 81, 83, 93, 99, 100, 107, 110-131, 138, 151, 163, 166, 183, 188-192, 220-221, 243-246, 256-257, 260, 278, 289, 298, 300, 316-319, 327, 482. See also Millo.

City of David, Excavations. 360, 370-384, 402-409, 413-420, 423-424, 436-437, 448-459, 467-474, 476-479, 517-534, 537, 543, 550, 552-553, 555-556, 558, 564-567, 572-586

City Planning. 900, 5470, 5489, 5508, 5549, 5559, 5571-5577, 5579, 5619, 5628, 5640, 5644, 5689, 5715-5722, 5725, 5729-5730, 5740, 5748-5750, 5755, 5768-5769, 5785, 5791-5792, 5815

Cleansing of the Temple. 3345-3346, 3354, 3357-3359, 3361-3362, 3368, 3374-3375, 3377, 3380, 3384, 3388, 3397, 3400, 3412, 3416, 3418-3419, 3423, 3439-3940, 3446. See also New Testament: Theological Judgments on the City and Sanctuary.

Climatology. 86-87, 132, 136, 142-143, 179, 197

Constantine. 3724, 3784, 4323, 4425, 4517

Consulates. 4007, 5212, 5256. See also listings by nations.

Coptic Church. 3694, 3746, 3977, 4090, 4100, 4199, 4219-4220, 4265, 4394

Cosmic Mountain. 1390-1391, 1393-1394, 1423, 1482, 1486, 1497, 1513, 1523

Crusaders. See Jerusalem-- during Crusader Period.

Custody of the Holy Land. 3241-3242, 4084-4086, 4088, 4141, 4210. See also Franciscans.

Cyril (Bishop). 3058, 3618, 3799, 4783

Daniel the Abbot (Pilgrim). 3880, 3897, 3949, 4948

Daughter of Zion. 1400, 1507-1508

Davidic Dynasty. See Kingship of YHWH and the Throne of David.

Day of Atonement. 2109, 2111, 2156, 2484

Dead Sea Scrolls. 2678-2762, 3372, 3474, 3501, 3509, 3511.

Deuteronomy and Jerusalem. 1521, 1525, 1527, 2015, 2019, 2032, 2065, 2095, 2125-2126, 2170, 2178, 2181

Divine Kingship. See Kingship of YHWH and the Throne of David.

Dome of the Chain. 5132

Dome of the Rock. 1030, 1243, 1494, 1962, 3826, 3948, 4426, 4954-4955, 4994, 4999-5001, 5003-5004, 5013-5014, 5018, 5022, 5033, 5039, 5041, 5044, 5046, 5051, 5057, 5068, 5076-5077, 5094, 5104, 5118, 5120, 5129-5130, 5138, 5147, 5149, 5155-5156, 5173, 5184, 5193, 5202, 5326. See also Arab Geographers and Historians; Haram esh-Sherif.

Dominus Flevit. 942-945, 939-941, 1039, 1086, 1097, 1138-1140, 4705, 4708, 4719, 4729

Dormition Abbey. 4597, 4601, 4611, 4619-4620, 4623-4624, 4642, 4645, 4652

Economic History. 54, 291, 2292-2293, 2344, 2362, 3027, 3035, 3038, 3070, 3134, 3155, 5009, 5012, 5019, 5317, 5347, 5396, 5453, 5504, 5531, 5556, 5702-5703, 5774, 5788, 5811

Egeria (Pilgrim). 3620, 3651, 3681, 3688, 3704, 3735, 3799-3801, 3803, 4727A

Egyptian Execration Texts. 1232, 1235-1239, 1265, 1283, 1288, 1291-1292

Eleona. See Pater Noster Church.

Emmerich, Anne Katharina (Mystic). 4359

Engravings. See Lithographs and Engravings.

Epiphanius the Monk (Pilgrim). 3765, 3802, 4408

Essenes and Jerusalem. 108, 2678-2762, 4625-4626

Etheria. See Egeria (Pilgrim).

Ethiopian Church. 4094, 4099, 4101, 4125-4126, 4151, 4199, 4221, 4221-4222, 4282, 4440, 4680

Eucharius (Pilgrim). 3773, 3802

Eudokia (Empress, Pilgrim). 3613, 3669, 3672, 3746, 4713, 4918, 4942

Eugenio de San Francisco (Pilgrim). 3958

Eusebius of Caesarea. 3653, 3682, 3695, 3724, 3758, 3759, 3799, 4390, 4395, 4466, 4510

Eutychius. 3656, 3771, 4747, 5172

Even Israel. 3166, 5325. See Jewish Neighborhoods outside the Walls.

Evliya Tshelebi. 5168-5169. See also Arab Geographers and Historians.

Fad'il al-Quds Literature. 4956, 4958, 4963, 5054-5055, 5080, 5109-5113, 5161-5165. See also Islamic Thought, Jerusalem in.

Fatimids. See Jerusalem-- during Early Arab Period.

Felix Fabri (Pilgrim). 4034, 4060

Festivals, Christian. 3662, 3688, 3699, 3722, 3754, 3805, 4152, 4113, 4213, 4272

Festivals, Israelite. 2005, 2032, 2079, 2088, 2101-2102, 2127, 2131, 2137, 2159-2160, 2184

Fetellus (Pilgrim). 3882

Fitzsimons. See Simon Fitzsimons (Pilgrim).

Food Production. 167-169, 194-196, 270

St. Francis. 4019

Franciscans. 4119, 4128, 4154, 4175, 4198, 4100, 4258, 4590, 4595, 4598-4599, 4890. See also Custody of the Holy Land.

François de Ferrus (Pilgrim). 4001

French Consulate. 5349

French Post. 5307

Frescobaldi, Gucci and Sigoli (Pilgrims). 3968

Friedrich Eckher von Käpfing (Pilgrim). 405

Friedrich von Österreich (Pilgrim). 4044

Friedrich II von Liegnita (Pilgrim). 4053

Garden Tomb. See Golgotha and Tomb of Jesus, Rival Sites.

Gates, City. See Walls, Gates, and Fortifications.

Gates, Temple Mount. See Haram esh-Sherif, Gates.

Gehenna. 177, 211, 1460, 3312, 3316, 3323, 3325, 3335. See also Hinnom, Valley of.

General Studies and Historical Overviews. 1-77

Geographical / Topographical Studies. 78-334, 1919, 2363, 2422-2423, 2679, 2695, 2727, 2730-2732, 2738, 3739-3740, 3899, 5213, 5227-5233, 5322, 5376-5377, 5447, 5460, 5514, 5570, 5787. See also Arab Geographers and Historians; Atlases, Maps and Cartographic Surveys.

Geology. 89-90, 280, 460, 5445

Georgian Church. 3617, 4074, 4146, 4164, 4185, 4187, 4211, 4247, 4250, 4302, 4308-4309

German Consulate. 3095-3100

German Post. 5339, 5414

German Settlements. 5247-5248, 5257, 5259, 5272, 5343, 5354, 5375, 5388, 5418, 5437

Gethsemane. 4652-4701

al-Ghazali (Theologian, Mystic). 5176

Gihon. See Water Supply.

Golgotha and Tomb of Jesus. See Holy Sepulchre, Church of the.

Golgotha and Tomb of Jesus, Rival Sites. 4519-4586

Gordon's Calvary. See Golgotha and Tomb of Jesus, Rival Sites.

Government House. 5477, 5499

Greek Holy Fire. 4113, 4127, 4140, 4147, 4173, 4183, 4193

Greek Orthodox Church. 4109, 4111-4115, 4127, 4140, 4147-4149, 4152, 4159, 4163, 4167-4168, 4173, 4183-4184, 4193-4194, 4206, 4213, 4227, 4231, 4233, 4249, 4257, 4275, 4295-4296, 4305, 5677

Hadrian. See Jerusalem-- from A. D. 70 to Constantine.

al-Hakim. 5048

Hall of the Scribes. 181, 2336, 2542

Haram esh-Sherif. 271, 314, 1839, 2628, 2662, 3076, 3143, 3639, 3728, 3941, 4538-4540, 4954, 4967, 4978, 4991, 5002-5004, 5027, 5040, 5050, 5079, 5098, 5106, 5107, 5115, 5125, 5145, 5144, 5148, 5150, 5157, 5160, 5191-5192, 5204, 5206. See also Arab Geographers and Historians.

Haram esh-Sherif, Gates. 886, 895, 897, 911, 2222, 2485, 2521, 2539, 2541, 2561, 2571, 2595, 2600, 3076, 3666, 5106, 5148, 5205

Hasmonaeans. See Jerusalem-- during Second Temple Period: General.

Health Care. 3835, 3842, 3914, 3928, 5226, 5260, 5498, 5603, 5639

Heavenly Jerusalem / Heavenly Temple. 1382, 1405, 1410, 1456, 1496, 1516, 2335, 2389, 2409-2410, 3105, 3233, 3263, 3537, 3545, 3560, 3565, 3569-3570, 3577, 3579, 3592-3594, 3603, 3606. See also Jewish Thought, Jerusalem and Temple in; New Testament: Heavenly City and Sanctuary; Theology / Mythology of the City and Sanctuary (Biblical Period).

Hebrew University. 5457, 5500, 5519-5520

Heinrich des Frommen von Sachsen (Pilgrim). 1498

Heinrich von Zedlitz (Pilgrim). 4043

Herod the Great. See Jerusalem-- during Second Temple Period: General.

Herodian Buildings. 342, 2274, 2278, 2280, 2283, 2288, 2290-2291, 2297, 2300-2301, 2304-2307, 2321, 2332, 2338, 2341-2342, 2343, 2347-2348, 2350, 2357, 2363, 2365-2371, 2382, 2396-2397, 2403, 2412, 2416, 2418-2419, 2421-2423. See also Temple, of Herod.

Hinnom, Valley of. 94, 109, 126-127, 144, 211, 322, 329

Historical Overviews. See General Studies and Historical Overviews.

Holy Places, Problem of. 4088, 4097-4098, 4120, 4128, 4132-4137, 4140, 4162, 4186, 4199, 4201-4203, 4216, 4228, 4252-4254, 4262, 4303-4304, 4310-4311, 4460, 4600, 5532, 5681, 5714, 5726-5727, 5826

Holy Sepulchre, Church of the. 811, 854, 3615, 3623, 3636, 3653, 3694, 3696, 4140, 4143, 4202, 4313-4518, 4523-4524, 4526, 4531, 4552-4553, 4559, 4567-4568, 4578, 4583, 4585, 5094, 5197. See also Art and Architecture, Church of the Holy Sepulchre Represented in.

Horn, Eleazar. 4179, 4319

Hospitals. See Health Care.

House of the Forest of Lebanon. 1848, 1923

al-Husayni, Amin (Mufti). 5497, 5501

Idrisi. 5030, 5093. See also Arab Geographers and Historians.

Ignatius of Loyola. 3978, 4026

Imbomon. See Ascension, Church of.

Inscriptions and Epigraphy, Arabic. 910, 1108-1109, 1207, 4355, 4407, 4468, 4478, 4498, 4953, 4979, 4981, 4987, 4990, 4992, 5002, 5004-5005, 5040, 5076, 5103-5104, 5115, 5122, 5158, 5185-5189, 5198

Inscriptions and Epigraphy: Armenian. 3687, 3743-3744, 3752, 3763, 3778, 3939, 4284-42854746, 4754

Inscriptions and Epigraphy: Georgian. 4185, 4308-4309

Inscriptions and Epigraphy: Greek. 428, 438, 588, 908, 966, 990, 1077, 2281, 2322, 2326, 2364, 2490, 2510, 2513, 2529, 2540, 2564, 2616, 2624, 2651-2652, 2676, 3630-3631, 3702, 3730-3731, 3737, 3767, 4520, 4565, 4699, 4745, 4796, 4924, 4945

Inscriptions and Epigraphy: Hebrew and Aramaic. 248-249, 364, 415, 441, 464, 497, 525, 590, 599, 608, 641, 643-645, 654, 658, 670, 676-678, 703, 723, 886, 895, 919, 925, 929, 930, 935, 952-953, 982, 997, 1005, 1012, 1018, 1027-1028, 1033, 1043-1045, 1064-1066, 1081, 1085, 1088, 1100-1104, 1113-1114, 1131-1132, 1141, 1143, 1165, 1167, 1176, 1181-1182, 1188, 1191-1194, 1202, 1903-1904, 2294, 2328, 2356, 2405, 2414, 2528, 3088-3089, 3187, 4612, 4924, 4736, 4945

Inscriptions and Epigraphy: Latin. 626, 709, 720, 1142, 2909, 2918-2920, 2932, 2934, 2938, 2940, 2949-2950, 2952, 2954, 2958, 2986, 2989-2990, 2999, 3004, 3008, 3015, 3921, 4335, 4341-4345, 4652

Inscriptions and Epigraphy: Syriac. 4289

Inscriptions and Epigraphy: Turkish. 5170

Internationalization, Proposals for. 5421, 5468-5469, 5472, 5524, 5536, 5537A, 5462, 5548, 5591, 5669, 5781, 5817

Islamic Art. See Art and Architecture, Islamic.

Islamic Thought, Jerusalem in. 3143, 3150, 3186, 4949, 4956-4958, 4963, 4977, 4980, 4984, 4993-4994, 4996-4997, 5015-5016, 5023, 5032, 5035-5036, 5046, 5054, 5055, 5063, 5066, 5069-5070, 5075, 5080-5081, 5086-5088, 5107-5114, 5127-5128, 5131, 5140-5142, 5152-5153, 5161-5166, 5175-5178, 5199-5201

Israel Museum. 5526, 5528, 5533, 5557

Italian Post. 5246, 5328, 5360

Jachin and Boaz. 1829, 1835, 1841, 1873, 1877, 1899, 1909, 1914, 1931, 1953-1954, 1994-1995

Jacinthus the Presbyter (Pilgrim). 3802

Jacobi de Verona (Pilgrim). 4046

Jacques de Vitry (Pilgrim). 3933

Jaffa-Jerusalem Railway. 5274, 5297, 5306, 5386

St. James (the Minor), Church of. 1004, 4073, 4218, 4225, 4235-4236, 4297

Jean de Couchermois (Pilgrim). 4021

Jean de Valenciennes (Pilgrim). 3834

Jean le Chrysostomite (Pilgrim). 3844

Jebus, Jebusites. 188, 257, 618, 1138, 1242, 1244, 1250, 1257, 1259-1261, 1263, 1268, 1272, 1298, 1322, 1339, 1367, 1697, 1945-1946

Jehoshaphat, Valley of. See Kidron, Valley (Brook) of.

Jeremiah's Grotto. 1151, 1156, 4546, 4560, 4570-4573, 4596

Jerome. 3597, 3686, 3772, 3802

Jerusalem-- before David. 1231-1293

Jerusalem-- during Biblical Period (to 587 B. C.). 1294-1367

Jerusalem-- during Second Temple Period: General. 2273-2423

Jerusalem-- during Second Temple Period: Jewish Revolt against Rome and Destruction of Jerusalem in A. D. 70. 2763-2899

Jerusalem-- from A. D. 70 to Constantine. 2900-3015, 4839-4845

Jerusalem-- during Byzantine Period. 3029, 3056, 3058-3059, 3136, 3164, 3170, 3197, 3207, 3232, 3613-3806, 4099, 4713

Jerusalem-- during Early Arab Period. 3088-3089, 3111-3114, 3179-3181, 3739, 4950-4951, 4960, 4962, 4964, 4966, 4970-4976, 4982, 4995, 5034, 5049, 5053, 5060, 5067, 5082, 5116, 5123, 5128, 5133

Jerusalem-- during Crusader Period. 3214-3215, 3807-3950, 4246, 4693, 4734-4735, 4962, 5163. See also Art and Architecture, Crusader.

Jerusalem-- during Ayyubid and Mamaluk Period. 165, 3160-3161, 3193, 3256, 4961, 4965, 4967, 4982, 4986, 4988-4989, 5017, 5020-5021, 5024, 5026, 5058, 5078-5079, 5082, 5101-5102, 5116, 5119, 5121, 5128, 5134, 5174, 5194-5196

Jerusalem-- during Ottoman Period (through the 18th century). 3025, 3038, 3048-3051, 3067-3074, 3082-3084, 3119, 3123-3124, 3139-3140, 3159, 3162-3163, 3228-3230, 3248, 3250, 3270, 4952, 5007-5012, 5017, 5019, 5026, 5042, 5058-5059, 5061-5062, 5082, 5105, 5116, 5128, 5181

Jerusalem-- 19th and Early 20th Century. 3034, 3036-3037, 3039, 3040-3044, 3081, 3092, 3095-3101, 3108, 3127, 3131-3132, 3149, 3151, 3154-3155, 3158, 3166, 3177, 3173, 3175, 3177, 3182-3184, 3190, 3202, 3246, 3264, 3269, 4110, 4120, 4181-4182, 4276, 4306, 4969, 5074, 5208-5443

Jerusalem-- under British Administration. 4111-4112, 4295, 4307, 5444-5513

Jerusalem-- 1948-1967. 5514-5567

Jerusalem-- 1967-Present. 5568-5827

Jerusalem Orpheus. 3749-3750, 3756, 3764, 3783, 3789-3790

Jerusalem Ship. 2958, 3658, 4335, 4341-4345

Jesus, Jerusalem during the Time of. See Jerusalem-- during Second Temple Period: General.

Jewish Neighborhoods outside the Walls. 3037, 3040, 3043, 3081, 3131-3132, 3166, 3252, 3261, 3264, 5232, 5265, 5290, 5299-5300, 5322, 5325, 5424, 5460, 5470

Jewish Presence from Julian II to Modern Times. 3016-3278

Jewish Quarter. 208, 3028, 3030-3032, 3041-3042, 3044, 3046, 3053, 3062-3063, 3094, 3106, 3110, 3113, 3118, 3135, 3138, 3148, 3152, 3194, 3198-3199, 3209, 3213, 3218-3219, 3227, 3243, 3257-3260, 3265, 5516, 5748, 5798

Jewish Quarter: Excavations. 335, 349-354, 561, 2292-2293, 2295-2296, 2362, 5363

Jewish Thought, Jerusalem and Temple in: Second Temple Period. 2279, 2313, 2329, 2333-2335, 2346, 2359, 2383, 2394, 2398-2399, 2430, 2434, 2439, 2446, 2454, 2473, 2526, 2536, 2538, 2558, 2567, 2596, 2610, 2678-2762, 3090

Jewish Thought, Jerusalem and Temple in: From A. D. 70 to Modern Times. 2773, 2785-2786, 2803, 2835, 2849, 2853-2855, 2866, 2875, 2877-2879, 2887-2889, 2892, 2922, 2924, 2945, 2972, 3026, 3054-3055, 3060, 3064-3065, 3075, 3077, 3085-3087, 3090, 3093, 3104-3105, 3107, 3126, 3129-3130, 3133, 3141-3143, 3146-3147, 3153, 3156, 3174, 3178, 3192, 3200, 3204-3206, 3211-3212, 3216, 3221, 3225-3226, 3237-3239, 3251, 3253-3255, 3268, 3272, 3276

Johannes von Frankfort (Pilgrim). 3951-3952

John (Bishop). 3614

St. John, Church of. 3135, 3691, 3862, 3927

St. John, Hospital of. 3928. See also Muristan.

John Moschus. 3757

John of La Rochelle (Pilgrim). 3830

John of Würzburg (Pilgrim). 3857, 3938

Josephus. 82, 119, 140, 184-185, 187, 289, 293, 858, 860, 978,

2320, 2327, 2329, 2339, 2526, 2635, 2765, 2782, 2784, 2800

Josiah (King). See Deuteronomy and Jerusalem.

Julian II ("The Apostate"). 3029, 3056, 3058-3059, 3136, 3164, 3170, 3207, 3232

Justinian (Emperor). See Jerusalem--during Byzantine Period; Nea Church.

Juvenal (Bishop). 3616, 3713

Kabatnik, Martin (Pilgrim). 4032

Karaites. 3179-3181

Karl Grimming von Niederrain (Pilgrim). 4052

Kempe. See Margery Kempe (Pilgrim).

Kenesset Yisrael. 3166, 5325. See Jewish Neighborhoods outside the Walls.

Khalidi Library. 5196, 5331

Kibla. 5199. See also Islamic Thought, Jerusalem in.

Kidron, Valley (Brook) of. 95-96, 216, 230, 323

King's Garden. 125, 147

King's Valley. 232

Kingship of YHWH and the Throne of David. 1536-1698

Kiriath-Jearim. 1711

Knights of the Hospital of St. John. 3842, 3914, 5226

Knights Order of the Holy Sepulchre. 4138, 4197

Knights Templar. 3610, 3807

Kollel Ungarn. 3132, 3166, 5300, 5325. See Jewish Neighborhoods outside the Walls.

Last Supper, Room of. See Cenacle.

St. Lazarus, Church of. 4765-4774

St. Lazarus, Hospital (Crusader). 3835

Leonhard Rauwolf (Pilgrim). 3990-3991, 4018

Lithographs and Engravings. 286, 5151, 5223-5224, 5353, 5369-5371, 5391-5392, 5439, 5441

Louis de Rochechouart (Pilgrim). 3989

Ludolph von Suchem (Pilgrim). 4062

Ludwig III (Pilgrim). 3953

Luke/Acts and Jerusalem. 3299-3300, 3342-3343, 3353, 3355, 3369, 3375-3376, 3378, 3385, 3389, 3394, 3408, 3421, 3424, 3428, 3433, 3435-3436, 3444, 3447-3448, 3451. See also New Testament: Theological Judgments on the City and Sanctuary.

Lutheran Church. 4192, 4208. On the Prussian-Anglican Bishopric, see Anglican Church.

Madeba Mosaic Map. 252A, 3626-3628, 3670, 3705, 3708, 3723, 3744A, 3745, 3785, 4403, 4440, 4809

Maimonides. 2489, 2606-2607, 2670, 3275

Mamaluk Architecture. See Art and Architecture, Islamic.

Mamaluks. See Jerusalem-- during Ayyubid and Mamaluk Period.

Maps. See Atlases, Maps and Cartographic Surveys; Madeba Mosaic Map.

Margery Kempe (Pilgrim). 3962, 3976, 3985

Maria Hippolyta von Calabrien (Pilgrim). 4049

Marino Sanuto (Pamphleteer, Cartographer). 252A, 267, 3937, 4024E, 4046A

St. Martin, Church (Crusader). 3135, 3862-3863, 3929

St. Mary, Church of (Justinian). See Nea Church.

St. Mary, Gethsemane Church. See Tomb of Mary.

St. Mary, Site of Death. See Dormition Abbey.

St. Mary of the Latins, Major (Crusader). 3917

St. Mary of the Latins, Minor (Crusader). 3945

Mary Magdalen, Church of (Crusader). 3811

Maximos, Bishop. 3759

Mazkeret Moshe. 3166, 5325. See Jewish Neighborhoods outside the Walls.

Me'a She'arim. 3166, 3252, 5325. See Jewish Neighborhoods outside the Walls.

Melania. 3669, 4713

Melchizedek. 1240, 1243, 1246-1247, 1251-1252, 1256, 1278, 1281, 1293, 1566, 1582, 1601, 2026, 2036, 2061, 2151, 2689, 2699, 2702, 2710, 2726, 2729, 2751, 3491. See also New Testament: Heavenly City and Sanctuary.

Melito (Pilgrim). 3711

Menorah. 1789, 1874, 1886, 1915, 1917, 1957, 1993, 2505, 2537, 2550, 2552, 2584, 2617

Merits of Jerusalem. See Fad'il al-Quds Literature.

Middoth. 2500-2501, 2556, 2558, 2560, 2595, 2603-2605, 2655, 2658-2660

Millet System. 4108, 5010, 5209, 5218-5219

Millicent. 3890, 3920

Millo. 107, 128, 141, 166, 275, 298

Mishkenot Sha'ananim. 3231, 3261, 3166, 5325. See Jewish Neighborhoods outside the Walls.

Model of Jerusalem (A. D. 70), Holy Land Hotel. 2329, 2341

Model of Jerusalem (19th Century), by Stephen Illes. 5266, 5332

Modestus, Bishop. 4333, 4442

Molten Sea. 1833, 1922, 1992, 1998

Monastery of the Cross. 4164, 4211, 4247, 4302

Moriah. 97, 321

Moses Montefiore. 3173

Mother, Zion as. 1498

Muhammad and Jerusalem. See Islamic Thought, Jerusalem in.

Muqaddasi. 912-913, 5029, 5090, 5182. See also Arab Geographers and Historians.

Muristan. 428, 440, 509, 3841, 3878, 3928

Muslim Neighborhoods outside the Walls. 5074, 5321, 5471, 5473

Muslim Quarter. 208, 4967-4969, 4985, 4986-4989, 4998, 5021, 5037, 5078, 5119, 5134-5137, 5143, 5146, 5174, 5177, 5194-5196

Nachmanides. 3065, 3135, 3161, 3258, 3260

Nahalat Shiva. 3166, 5325. See Jewish Neighborhoods outside the Walls.

Names of Jerusalem. 139, 152, 173, 176, 199-200, 225, 229, 233, 242, 273, 307, 311, 1014, 1248, 1287, 1461, 1489, 2223, 3019, 3281, 3291, 3299-3300, 3303-3304, 3309

Navel of the Earth. 1376, 1381, 1504, 1514-1515, 1529, 2313, 3480, 4453, 4491

Nea Church. 3630-3634, 3647-3650, 3762, 3777, 3793

Nehemiah. 715, 727, 731-732, 735-737, 739, 741, 743, 749, 755, 757-758, 760, 762-765, 769, 775, 777, 779-781, 783-786, 972, 1134, 2275, 2375, 2449

Nestorians. 3998, 4092, 4169, 4171, 4174, 4222, 4279

New Jerusalem. 1383-1384, 1396, 1404, 1425, 1449, 1452, 1478, 2221, 2409, 2464, 2680-2682, 2704, 2711, 2715, 2728, 2924, 2926, 3431, 3456, 3576. See also Heavenly Jerusalem / Heavenly Temple; New Testament: Heavenly City and Sanctuary; Temple of Ezekiel's Vision.

New Testament (General). 3279-3309

New Testament: Church as Temple. 3498-3533

New Testament: Heavenly City and Sanctuary. 3452-3497

New Testament: Theological Judgments on the City and Sanctuary. 3342-3451. See also Luke/Acts and Jerusalem; Cleansing of the Temple.

New Testament: Topography of the Gospels and Acts. 3310-3341

Nicanor of Alexandria / Nicanor Gate. 958, 1010, 1073, 2480, 2494, 2496, 2511-2512, 2619, 2643, 2668

Niccolò of Poggibonsi (Pilgrim). 3963, 3966

Numismatics. 2282, 2353, 2377-2378, 2576, 2583, 2608, 2826-2827, 2846, 2870, 2921, 2944, 2969-2971, 2975-2982, 2985, 2994, 3000-3001, 3003, 4099. 4286, 5038

Nuremberg Chronicle. 900A

Ogier VIII (Pilgrim). 3975

Ohel Moshe. 3166, 5325. See Jewish Neighborhoods outside the Walls.

Ohel Shlomo. 3166, 5325. See Jewish Neighborhoods outside the Walls.

Olives, Mt. of. 98, 231, 2638, 3057, 3080, 3168, 4702-4764, 5016, 5031

Omar, Caliph. 4995. See also Jerusalem-- during Early Arab Period.

Omayyads. See Jerusalem-- during Early Arab Period.

Ophel. See City of David.

Ottomans. See Jerusalem-- during Ottoman Period (through the 18th century); Jerusalem-- 19th and Early 20th Century.

Palace of Solomon. 1857, 1875, 1968-1969, 1973. See also House of the Forest of Lebanon.

Paladius of Helenopolis. 3715

Palestine Archaeological Museum. 5475, 5478-5480, 5486

Parker Expedition. 360, 411, 536, 552, 564-567, 574, 576, 5326

Pater Noster Church. 4702, 4704, 4712, 4725, 4728, 4729, 4740, 4747, 4757-4758, 4760

St. Paul (Apostle). 3307, 3314, 3356, 3393, 3425, 3487, 3499, 3507, 3510, 3513, 3528, 3530

Paul VI (Pope). 3973

Paula (Pilgrim). 3686, 3772, 3775, 3802

Perband. See Christian Perband (Pilgrim).

Persian Conquest (A. D. 614). 3654, 3671, 3675, 3577, 3701, 3755, 4604

St. Peter in Gallicantu. 4605-4607, 4616, 4628-4631, 4637-4638, 4640-4641

Peter the Deacon (Pilgrim). 3799

Philippe d' Aubingné (Pilgrim). 3833, 3864

Philo of Alexandria. 2279, 2329, 2346, 2383, 2526

Phocas, John (Pilgrim). 3934

Photius (Pilgrim). 3802

Photography, Early. 332, 4212, 4307, 5284, 5287, 5351, 5389-5390, 5405, 5507, 5465

Piacenza Pilgrim. 3738, 3776, 3802

Pietro Casola (Pilgrim). 4025

Pilgrim Flasks. 4331-4332, 4389, 4399, 4434, 4446, 4512

Pilgrimages, Christian. 3203, 3473, 3613, 3620, 3651, 3652-3653, 3657-3658, 3661, 3668, 3680-3681, 3684, 3686, 3692, 3703-3704, 3711-3712, 3714, 3716, 3718-3719, 3725-3726, 3732-3735, 3738, 3741-3742, 3753, 3760, 3765, 3769, 3771-3777, 3779-3782, 3786, 3796, 3798-3799, 3802-3804, 3806, 3836, 3856-3857, 3866, 3872, 3880, 3882-3883, 3892, 3896, 3912, 3921-3923, 3932-3938, 3940, 3943-3944, 3949-4072, 4160, 4165-4166, 4251

Pilgrimages, Jewish. 1377, 1384, 2072, 2079, 2279, 2390-2393, 2515, 2570, 3017-3018, 3057, 3061, 3076, 3088-3089, 3111, 3115-3117, 3203, 3210, 3235-3236, 3247, 3274

Pilgrimages, Muslim. 3203, 4959, 4999, 5091, 5126, 5168-5169

Polaner, John. (Pilgrim). 4061

Pompey. 2273, 2276, 2692, 2795

Population. 133-135, 140, 213, 283, 287, 296, 718, 2316-2318, 2320, 2345, 2395, 3071, 3244-3245, 3659, 4110, 4294, 5012, 5181, 5231, 5319, 5346, 5784, 5806

Post and Telegraph (Ottoman Period). 5211-5212, 5246, 5280, 5283, 5301, 5306-5308, 5328, 5330, 5337, 5359-5364, 5395, 5413-5414

Praetorium, Location of. 4831-4832, 4834, 4837-4846, 4850-4856, 4859-4860, 4863, 4866-4869, 4871, 4873-4880, 4883-4888, 4897-4899, 4903, 4905-4911, 4913, 4915-4916. See also Way of the Cross.

Priesthood, Israelite. 2000-2001, 2003-2004, 2006-2008, 2013, 2016, 2020-2023, 2026, 2033, 2036, 2040, 2044-2045, 2046, 2048, 2050-2053, 2057-2058, 2061, 2066, 2074-2075, 2077, 2082, 2085, 2092, 2100, 2104-2105, 2113, 2115, 2117, 2121, 2130, 2133, 2138-2140, 2144, 2151, 2154, 2157, 2173-2174, 2182, 2440, 2447, 2498, 2569, 2597-2598, 2630, 2645, 2748

Pro-Jerusalem Council. 5450-5452

Procopius of Caesarea. 3777, 3802

Prophets and Jerusalem. 234, 1369, 1387, 1389, 1411, 1420, 1424-1425, 1437, 1446, 1452, 1470, 1481, 1501, 1519-1520, 1531, 1533, 1543, 1569, 1666, 1675, 1680, 1696, 2002, 2018, 2028, 2041, 2047, 2070-2071, 2122, 2124, 2138, 2146, 2152, 2158, 2183, 2243, 2426, 2437-2438, 2445, 2451-2452, 2454-2455, 2459, 2462, 2464-2468

Prussian-Anglican Bishopric. See Anglican Church.

Psalms, Biblical. 224, 1243 (Ps. 110), 1315, 1371 (Ps. 46: 5), 1372 (Ps. 87), 1374 (Ps. 76), 1380 (Ps. 76), 1428 (Ps. 46), 1430 (Ps. 48), 1445 (Pss. 120-138), 1453 (Ps. 23), 1458 (Ps. 127), 1471 (Ps. 48), 1475, 1483 (Ps. 47), 1491 (Ps 122: 3), 1511 (Ps. 122), 1532 (Ps. 74), 1534, 1538 (Ps. 89), 1548, 1554 (Ps. 78), 1556 (Ps. 78), 1558 (Ps. 24: 7-10), 1559 (Ps 110), 1560, 1561, 1566 (Ps. 110), 1567, 1570 (Ps. 132),1582 (Ps. 110), 1586, 1594 (Ps. 93), 1601 (Ps. 110), 1602 (Ps. 2), 1603, 1606 (Ps. 132, 1610 (Ps. 22: 28-32), 1611 (Ps. 139), 1614, 1619, 1626, 1627 (Ps. 139), 1633, 1634 (Ps. 47), 1647 (Ps. 132), 1650 Ps. 21), 1657 (Ps. 47), 1663 (Ps. 89), 1668, 1670, 1679, 1729, 1751 (Ps. 132), 1767 (Ps. 132), 2055 (Ps. 110), 2069 (Ps. 110), 2088 (Ps. 132), 2122-2123, 2167, 2177, 2251 (Ps. 51: 8); 2495

Quarters. 208. See separate listings for Armenian, Christian, Jewish, and Muslim Quarters.

Ramban Synagogue. See Nachmanides.

Rauwolf. See Leonhard Rauwolf (Pilgrim).

Reunification, International Reaction to. 5587, 5577-5591, 5595, 5602,5604-5608, 5620-5621, 5625-5626, 5692-5693, 5731, 5809, 5822-5823

Reunification, Problems of. See Jerusalem-- 1967-Present.

Reuwich, Erhard (Cartographer). 4024A

Ricaldo de Monte-Croce. 3883

Robert le Diable (Pilgrim). 3684

Roberts, David (Artist). 5369-5371

Rockefeller Museum. See Palestine Archaeological Museum.

Roman Catholic Church. 3241-3242, 4081-4082, 4084-4089, 4093, 4096-4098, 4103-4107, 4109, 4115, 4119, 4128, 4131-4138, 4141, 4154-4155, 4161-4162, 4169, 4174-4175, 4178-4179, 4197-4198, 4200-4201, 4204, 4207, 4210, 4215-4217, 4228, 4237-4239, 4245, 4248, 4252-4255, 4258, 4262, 4269, 4274, 4283, 4287-4288, 4310, 4590, 4595, 4598-4599, 4890. See also Custody of the Holy Land; Catholic Chrches, Uniate; Franciscans.

Romans. See Jerusalem-- during Second Temple Period: General; Jewish Revolt against Rome and Destruction of Jerusalem in A. D. 70; Jerusalem-- from A. D. 70 to Constantine.

Russians and the Russian Orthodox Church. 4004, 4011, 4037, 4153, 4165-4166, 4176, 4181-4182, 4229, 4232, 4251, 4256, 4276, 5249, 5259, 5309, 5404

Russian Post. 5211, 5361-5362

Sacrifices and Offerings. 1999, 2009-2012, 2014, 2017, 2024-2025, 2027, 2030-2031, 2034, 2037-2039, 2042-2043, 2049, 2054, 2059-2060, 2064, 2067, 2068, 2073, 2081, 2083-2084, 2089, 2093-2094, 2096, 2098-2099, 2103, 2106-2108, 2112, 2114-2116, 2118-2120, 2128-2129, 2132, 2134-2135, 2141-2142, 2145-2148, 2150, 2155-2156, 2159, 2161-2166, 2168-2169, 2171-2172, 2174-2176, 2179-2180, 2185, 2226, 2248, 2491-2492, 2497-2498, 2508, 2533, 2535, 2551, 2621, 2623, 2683, 2748, 2753-2754

Saewulf (Pilgrim). 3826

Saladin. 3823, 3885

Sanderson, John (Pilgrim). 3999

Sañdo / Santo / Sanuto. See Marino Sanuto (Pamphleteer, Cartographer).

Schauenburgh, Johannes (Pilgrim). 4048

Scopus, Mt. 155, 3926. See also Tombs.

Sedeq (Pagan Deity). 1275-1276

Seleucids. See Jerusalem-- during Second Temple Period: General.

Sephardic Community. 3062-3063, 3139-3140, 3154, 3194, 3219, 3259, 3262, 3269, 3277. See also Jewish Quarter.

Servant of YHWH, Jerusalem as. 1533

Seusenius, Martinus (Pilgrim). 4024

Sha'arei Hessed. 3166, 5325. See Jewish Neighborhoods outside the Walls.

Sha'arei Yerushalayim. 3166, 5325. See Jewish Neighborhoods outside the Walls.

Shalem (Pagan Deity). 1255, 1276

Shiloh. 170, 1743, 1749, 1765, 2021

Shrine of the Book. 5540

Siloam Pool. 81, 589, 597, 607, 719, 721, 3654, 3690, 3698, 3761, 3797

Silvia of Aquitane. See Egeria (Pilgrim).

Silvia of Aquitane (not Egeria). 3716

Simon Fitzsimons (Pilgrim). 4008, 4017

Sion, Mt. (Western Hill). 321, 355, 389, 390, 422, 557, 2330, 2361, 2696, 2717, 2736-2738, 3144, 3191, 3438, 3607, 4128, 4587-4651

Six Day War. 5643, 5649, 5656, 5746-5747, 5762

Sixty Martyrs. 3717

Solar Cult. 1255, 1262, 1274-1276, 1373, 1418, 1450-1451, 1462-1464, 1626, 1893, 1907, 1938, 2722, 2744-2745

Song of Songs. 228

Sophronius (Bishop). 3766, 3768

Sophronius (Pilgrim, Poet). 3680, 3768, 3802

St. Stephen, Chapel on Mt. Sion. 4587, 4631

St. Stephen, Church near Damascus Gate. 3669, 4918-4948

St. Stephen, Church near St. Stephen's Gate. 4694

Status Quo. See Holy Places, Problem of.

Stone of Foundation. 1376, 1407, 1417, 1419, 1437, 1442, 1494, 1503, 1846-1847, 1855, 1887, 1896, 1948, 2313, 2359, 2507, 2524, 2531, 2629, 5138

Suriano, Francesco (Pilgrim). 3966

Surius. See Bernardin Surius (Pilgrim).

Syrian Orthodox Church (Jacobite). 3884, 3998, 4156-4157, 4191, 4224, 4291

Tabernacle. See Tent Sanctuary.

Talitha Kumi. 5257

Tantur, Ecumenical Institute. 4122, 4155

Tasso. 3942

Tempelgesellschaft. See German Settlements.

Temple, Babylonian Destruction of. 2223, 2234-2272

Temple, Christian Critique of. See New Testament: Theological Judgments on the City and Sanctuary; Luke/Acts and Jerusalem.

Temple, Cultic Activities in. 1999-2185. See also Sacrifices and Offerings; Festivals, Israelite.

Temple, Cultic Personnel of. 1999-2185. See also Priesthood, Israelite; Prophets and Jerusalem.

Temple, Music in. 2444, 2495, 2544, 2547

Temple, Roman Destruction of. See Jerusalem-- during Second Temple Period: Jewish Revolt against Rome and Destruction of Jerusalem in A. D. 70.

Temple and the Divine Presence. 1374, 1386, 1397, 1415, 1422, 1427, 1435, 1436, 1443, 1454-1455, 1465, 1891, 2697

Temple of Ezekiel's Vision. 2085, 2173, 2186-2233, 2455, 3467, 3494

Temple of Herod. 958, 1704, 1756, 2329, 2428, 2475-2677

Temple of Solomon. 1580, 1823-1998, 1706, 1823-1998

Temple of Zerubbabel. 2206, 2309-2310, 2424-2474

Index of Subjects

Temple in Art. See Art and Architecture, Temple Represented in.

Temple Mount, Excavations on West and South. 363, 365, 445, 484-492, 2299-2303, 2366-2376, 4970-4976, 5116

Temple Mount, Gates. See Haram esh-Sherif, Gates.

Tent Sanctuary. 1699, 1703, 1704, 1708, 1710, 1714, 1719, 1722, 1724-1726, 1730, 1737, 1744-1745, 1753-1755, 1761, 1763-1764, 1766, 1768-1769, 1773, 1775-1776, 1779, 1781-1783, 1789-1790, 1792-1797, 1800-1801, 1803, 1806, 1808-1810, 1818-1819, 1825, 1856, 1858, 2113

Theoderich (Pilgrim). 3935, 3944

Theodosius (Pilgrim). 3652, 3802

Theodotos, Synagogue of. 2322, 2326, 2364, 2414

Theology / Mythology of the City and Sanctuary (Biblical Period). 1240, 1368-1535.

St. Thomas of the Germans, Church (Crusader). 3815

Tomb of David (on Mt. Sion). 996, 3021, 3024, 3144, 3191, 3208, 3220, 4591, 4604, 4618, 5064

Tomb of Herod's Family. 1106-1107

Tomb of Jesus. See Holy Sepulchre, Church of the. Compare also Golgotha and Tomb of Jesus, Rival Sites.

Tomb of Joseph of Arimathea. 4353, 4357-4358, 4516

Tomb of Mary. 4653-4654, 4658-4667, 4676, 4678, 4680-4682, 4686-4687, 4689, 4692-4693

Tomb of Simon the Just. 994, 998, 1166

Tombs and Related Materials. 81, 114-116, 551, 765, 850, 915-1230, 1253, 3830, 3832-3834, 3864, 3869, 3941, 4789, 4796, 4805, 5122, 5124, 5194-5195

Tombs of Absalom and Bene Hezir. 478, 992, 1003-1004, 1069, 1141, 1166, 4672

Tombs of the Kings. 918, 1000-1001, 1056, 1112, 1161, 1166, 1220, 4542

Tombs of the Prophets. 980, 990, 993, 1162, 1224, 4561

Tombs of the Sanhedrin. 962, 1041, 1166

Topheth. 125. See also Hinnom, Valley of.

Torkington, Richard (Pilgrim). 4015

Tyropoeon Valley. 157, 202, 308

United Nations. 5472, 5518, 5525, 5547, 5567, 5595, 5606, 5608, 5620-5621, 5625-5626, 5634, 5679, 5682, 5728, 5733, 5751, 5753, 5810. See also Internationalization, Proposals for.

Vatican. 4136-4137, 4174, 4228, 5468-5469, 5535, 5799. See also Holy Places, Problem of; Internationalization, Proposals for.

Vesconte, Petrus (Cartographer). 4024E

Via Dolorosa. See Way of the Cross.

Wailing Wall. See Western Wall (Kotel).

Walls, Gates, and Fortifications (Biblical Period). 172, 724-787

Walls, Gates, and Fortifications (Second Temple Period). 212, 788-876, 2757-2758, 4411, 4489

Walls, Gates, and Fortifications (Medieval). 877-881, 3666, 3814, 5182

Water Supply. 147, 167, 588-716, 1358, 1364, 2025, 2365, 4469, 5103, 5470. See also Bethesda, Pool of; Siloam Pool.

Way of the Cross. 4829-4830, 4833, 4836, 4847-4849, 4857-4858, 4861-4862, 4864-4865, 4870, 4872, 4879, 4879A, 4881-4882, 4889-4896, 4900-4902, 4904, 4912, 4914, 4917. See also Praetorium, Location of.

Western Wall (Kotel). 3016, 3020, 3025, 3045, 3053, 3065-3066, 3078-3079, 3091, 3102-3103, 3110, 3121, 3125, 3150, 3157, 3176, 3186, 3201, 3240, 5456, 5485, 5493, 5497, 5681

Wey, William (Pilgrim). 4024C

William of Tyre. 3810

Willibald (Pilgrim). 3661, 3802

World War I. 5234-5235, 5264, 5282, 5291, 5293, 5430, 5432, 5444

Ya'qubi. 5028. See also Arab Geographers and Historians.

Yemenite Community. 3092, 3134, 3171, 3177, 3217, 3261, 3262. See also Jewish Neighborhoods outside the Walls.

Yemin Moshe. 3166, 5325. See Jewish Neighborhoods outside the Walls.

Zeolots and Sicarii. See Jerusalem--during Second Temple Period: Jewish Revolt against Rome and Destruction of Jerusalem in A. D. 70.

Zichron Moshe. 3166, 5325. See Jewish Neighborhoods outside the Walls.

Zion, Mt. (Biblical). See City of David.

Zion, Mt. (Western Hill). See Sion, Mt. (Western Hill).

Zion Theology. 1371, 1375, 1402-1403, 1416, 1421, 1429, 1459, 1473, 1479-1481, 1484-1485, 1495, 1499, 1510, 1524, 1552, 1656, 1658, 1770. See also Theology / Mythology of the City and Sanctuary (Biblical Period).

Zoheleth, Stone of. 146-147

Zuallardo (Pilgrim). 3987